Western Civilizations

*Their History &
Their Culture*

Brief Third Edition

NORTH POLAR REGION

GLOBAL SATELLITE MOSAIC

The beauty and complexity of Earth's landscapes above and below the oceans is revealed with the Global Satellite Mosaic. The mosaic was prepared for the National Geographic Society by NASA's Jet Propulsion Laboratory using more than 500 satellite images from the National Oceanic and Atmospheric Administration. The cloud-free images show Earth in its natural colors as it would be seen from space. One can easily identify the world's major glaciers, deserts, mountain ranges, and rain forests. For example, follow the green ribbon of lush vegetation along the Nile into the stark, dry Sahara. The mountain ranges seem to rise off the map thanks to digital elevation databases from the Department of Defense. The deepest areas of the ocean realm are colored dark blue in contrast to the light blue areas highlighting continental shelves, submarine ridges, and underwater mountains.

IMAGE PROVIDED BY THE CARTOGRAPHIC APPLICATIONS LAB, JET PROPULSION LABORATORY

BIOSPHERE

Thousands of satellite images were combined to show a picture of biological productivity. In the oceans, red, yellow, and green indicate waters rich in phytoplankton. On land, green areas show high-potential plant productivity; tan areas suffer from productivity limitations due to aridity and temperature.

ILLMAGE PROVIDED BY GODDARD SPACE FLIGHT CENTER, NASA AND ORBIMAGE

THE
SAT

SOUTH POLAR
REGION

ANTARCTICA

Queen Maud Land

Weddell
Sea

WEST   EAST
ANTARCTICA   ANTARCTICA

Marie Byrd Land

Ross
Ice
Shelf

Wilkes Land

NORTH

PACIFIC

OCEAN

TROPIC OF CANCER

ASIA

SIBERIA

Lake
Baikal

ARCTIC CIRCLE

Aral
Sea

Black Sea

EUROPE

HIMALAYA

Plateau of Tibet

PHILIPPINE SEA

INDIA

ARABIAN
PENINSULA

ARABIAN
SEA

BAY
OF
BENGAL

MICRONESIA

RICA

Congo
Basin

INDONESIA

MELANESIA

EQUATOR

Madagascar

NEW GUINEA

INDIAN

OCEAN

AUSTRALIA

TROPIC OF CAPRICORN

New Caledonia

SOUTH
PACIFIC
OCEAN

SOUTHWEST INDIAN RIDGE

SOUTHEAST INDIAN RIDGE

TASMAN
SEA

NEW
ZEALAND

South Island

KERGUELEN
PLATEAU

Wilkes Land

THE NEED FOR SATELLITES

The Global Satellite Mosaic along with the biosphere image (lower left) and
temperature image (lower right) provides an integrated view of our world.
The high elevations of the Himalaya and Tibet show up as a cold area (blue,
temperature image) and as a plant-poor area (tan, biosphere image). Temperature,
rainfall, and landscape are interrelated. The need to understand the forces shaping
environmental change has led to a space race among various countries. In 1997 alone
some 85 rockets launched more than 140 satellites—mostly from China, Europe,
Japan, Russia, and the United States. Some satellites provide vital communication
links propelling economic development; other satellites supply data on patterns
and trends associated with agricultural productivity, pollution monitoring,
weather forecasting, and many other environmental concerns.

WINKEL TRIPEL PROJECTION, CENTRAL MERIDIAN 0°
SCALE 1:38,931,000

TICA

RLD
MAP

**SURFACE
TEMPERATURE**
Reddish colors vividly show
average high temperatures on the
two largest continents, Africa and Asia,
from the Sahara to Central Asia. Latitude,
mountains, and oceans influence land temperatures.

You can reach us on the Internet at nationalgeographic.com.

Joshua Cole

Carol Symes

Judith Coffin

Robert Stacey

Western Civilizations

Their History & Their Culture

BRIEF THIRD EDITION

VOLUME 1

W. W. Norton & Company ▪ NEW YORK ▪ LONDON

W. W. Norton & Company has been independent since its founding in 1923, when William Warder Norton and Mary D. Herter Norton first published lectures delivered at the People's Institute, the adult education division of New York City's Cooper Union. The firm soon expanded its program beyond the Institute, publishing books by celebrated academics from America and abroad. By midcentury, the two major pillars of Norton's publishing program—trade books and college texts—were firmly established. In the 1950s, the Norton family transferred control of the company to its employees, and today—with a staff of four hundred and a comparable number of trade, college, and professional titles published each year—W. W. Norton & Company stands as the largest and oldest publishing house owned wholly by its employees.

Editor: Jon Durbin
Editorial assistants: Jason Spears, Justin Cahill
Project editor: Kathleen Feighery
Copyeditor: Michael Fleming
E-media editor: Steve Hoge
Ancillary editor: Lorraine Klimowich
Photo editor: Junenoire Mitchell
Photo research: Donna Ranieri
Senior production manager, College: Benjamin Reynolds
Design director: Rubina Yeh
Book designer: Judith Abbate / Abbate Design
Composition: TexTech, Inc.—Brattleboro, VT
Cartographer: Mapping Specialists—Madison, WI
Manufacturing: R. R. Donnelley & Sons—Willard, OH

The Library of Congress has cataloged the one-volume edition as follows:

Western civilizations : their history & their culture / Joshua Cole ... [et al.]. — 3rd brief ed.
 p. cm.
Rev. ed. of: Western civilizations : their history & their culture / Judith G. Coffin, Robert C. Stacey. 2nd brief ed. New York
W. W. Norton & Co., c2009.
Includes bibliographical references and index.

1. Civilization, Western—Textbooks. 2. Europe—Civilization—Textbooks. I. Cole, Joshua, 1961– II. Coffin, Judith G., 1952–
Western civilizations.
CB245.W4845 2012
909'.09821—dc23

2011026190

ISBN: 978-0-393-93487-8 (pbk.)
This edition: 978-0-393-93488-5 (pbk.)

W. W. Norton & Company, Inc., 500 Fifth Avenue, New York, N. Y. 10110
wwnorton.com

W. W. Norton & Company Ltd., Castle House, 75/76 Wells Street, London W1T 3QT

6 7 8 9 0

To our families:

Kate Tremel, Lucas and Ruby Cole
Tom, Erin, and Connor Wilson
Willy, Zoe, and Aaron Forbath
Robin, Will, and Anna Stacey

with love and gratitude for their support.
And to all our students, who have also been
our teachers.

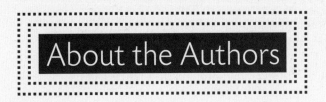

JOSHUA COLE (Ph.D. University of California, Berkeley) is Associate Professor of History at the University of Michigan at Ann Arbor. His publications include work on gender and the history of the population sciences, colonial violence, and the politics of memory in 19th and 20th century France, Germany, and Algeria. His first book was *The Power of Large Numbers: Population, Politics and Gender in Nineteenth-Century France* (Ithaca, NY: Cornell University Press, 2000).

CAROL SYMES (Ph.D. Harvard University) is Associate Professor of history and Director of Undergraduate Studies in the history department at the University of Illinois, Urbana-Champaign, where she has won the top teaching award in the College of Liberal Arts and Sciences. Her main areas of study include medieval Europe, the history of information media and communication technologies, and the history of theatre. Her first book was *A Common Stage: Theater and Public Life in Medieval Arras* (Ithaca: Cornell University Press, 2007).

JUDITH COFFIN (Ph.D. Yale University) is an associate professor at the University of Texas, Austin, where she won University of Texas President's Associates' Award for Teaching Excellence. Previously, she taught at Harvard University and the University of California, Riverside. Her research interests are the social and cultural history of gender, mass culture, slavery, race relations, and colonialism. She is the author of *The Politics of Women's Work: The Paris Garment Trades, 1750–1915*.

ROBERT STACEY (Ph.D. Yale University) is professor of history, Dean of the Humanities, and a member of the Jewish Studies faculty at the University of Washington, Seattle. A long-time teacher of Western civilization and medieval European history, he has received Distinguished Teaching Awards from both the University of Washington and Yale University, where he taught from 1984 to 1988. He has authored and coauthored four books, including a textbook, *The Making of England to 1399*. He holds an M.A. from Oxford University and a Ph.D. from Yale.

Brief Contents

Contents

Chapter 15 ▪ ABSOLUTISM AND EMPIRE, 1660–1789   355

Maps

Documents

The motivating principle for the third brief edition of *Western Civilizations* is a relatively simple idea: that history students will be inspired to engage more effectively with the past if they are given a flexible set of tools to use as they approach their readings. *Western Civilizations* has always been known for its clear and vigorous account of Europe's past, and previous editions have been noteworthy for their selection of primary sources and visual images. As the authors of this new brief edition, we have made a special effort to bring greater unity to the pedagogical elements that accompany each chapter, so that students will be able to work more productively with the textbook in mastering this rich history. This pedagogical structure is designed to empower the students to analyze and interpret the historical evidence on their own, and thus to become participants in the work of history. We have also worked hard to create a coherent narrative, since this is one of the major shortcomings of all brief editions. Here we used our new pedagogical tools as guides, particularly the Story Lines, Chronologies, and Core Objectives, to ensure that the chapter themes and core content remained fully present. Moreover, we cut the narrative by 25 percent, rather than the more traditional 40 percent, which again provides a more coherent reading experience.

Of course, students can only find a textbook useful if they read it, and they can only read it if they purchase it. As the demand for concise, affordable texts grows with each passing year, publishers have responded by offering either bare-bones, brief editions or "value" editions of their textbooks—typically smaller-format, black-and-white editions with far fewer and smaller pictures and maps. Both types are far from being highly valuable teaching tools. Fortunately, W. W. Norton, our publisher, decided to take a different approach. Our new edition is full size and full color, includes innovative pedagogical tools, provides a rich support package, and is priced competitively with the most inexpensive brief books and value editions on the market. We hope that you will see this as the best solution for your course and students when you are considering texts.

Undergraduates today have more choices in introductory history courses than they did only twenty or thirty years ago. As public awareness of the importance of global connections grew in the late twentieth century, many colleges and universities enriched their programs by adding courses in world history as well as introductory surveys in Latin American, African, and Asian history alongside the traditional offerings in the history of the United States and Europe. These developments can only be seen as enormously positive, but they do not in any way diminish the need for a broad-based history of European society and culture such as that represented in *Western Civilizations*. The wide chronological scope of this work offers an unusual opportunity to trace the development of central human themes—population movements, economic development, politics and state-building, changing religious beliefs, and the role of the arts and technology—in a dynamic and complex part of the world whose cultural diversity has been constantly invigorated and renewed by its interactions with peoples living in other places. As in previous editions, we have attempted to balance the coverage of political, social, economic, and cultural phenomena, and the chapters also include extensive coverage of material culture, daily life, gender, sexuality, art, and technology. And following the path laid out by the book's previous authors, Judith Coffin and Robert Stacey, we have insisted that the history of European peoples can be best understood through their interactions with people in other parts of the world. The portrait of European society that emerges from this text is thus both rich and dynamic, attentive to the latest developments in historical scholarship and fully aware of the ways that the teaching of European history has changed in the past decades.

Given the general consensus about the importance of seeing human history in its broadest—and if possible, global—context, Europeanists who teach the histories of ancient, medieval, and modern societies have been mindful of the need to rethink the ways that this history should be taught. For good reasons, few historians at the dawn of the twenty-first century uphold a monolithic vision of a single and enduring "Western civilization" whose inevitable march through history can be traced chapter by chapter through time. This idea, strongly associated with the curriculum of early twentieth-century American colleges and universities, no longer conforms to what we know about the human past. Neither the "West" nor "Europe" can be seen as distinct, unified entities in space or time; the meanings attributed to these geographical expressions have changed in significant ways. Most historians now agree that a linear notion of "civilization" persisting over the centuries was made coherent only by leaving out the intense conflicts, extraordinary ruptures, and dynamic processes of change at the heart of the societies that are the subject of this book. Smoothing out the rough edges of the past does students no favors—even an introductory text such as this one should present the past as it appears to the historians who study it—that is, as an ever-changing panorama of human effort and creation, filled with possibility, but also fraught with discord, uncertainty, accident, and tragedy.

New Pedagogical Features

Our goals as the new authors of this dynamic text are to provide a book that students will read, that reinforces your course objectives, that helps your students master core content, and that provides tools for your students to use in thinking critically about our human past. In order to achieve these primary goals, the traditional strengths of the book have been augmented by several exciting new features. The most revolutionary is the new pedagogical framework that supports each chapter. Many students in introductory survey courses find the sheer quantity of information to be a challenge, and so we have created these new pedagogical features to help them approach their reading in a more systematic way. At the outset of every chapter, a **Before You Read This Chapter** box offers three preliminary windows onto the material to be covered: *Story Lines*, *Chronology*, and *Core Objectives*. The *Story Lines* allow the student to become familiar with the primary narrative threads that tie the chapter's elements together, and the *Chronology* grounds these *Story Lines* in the period under study. The *Core Objectives* provide a checklist to ensure that the student is aware of the primary teaching points in the chapter. The student is then reminded of these teaching points on completing the chapter, in the **After You Read This Chapter** section, which prompts the student to revisit the chapter in three ways. The

first, *Reviewing the Core Objectives*, asks the reader to reconsider core objectives by answering a pointed question about each one. The second, *People, Ideas, and Events in Context*, summarizes some of the particulars that students should retain from their reading, through questions that allow them to relate individual terms to the major objectives and story lines. Finally, questions about long-term *Consequences* allow for more open-ended reflection on the significance of the chapter's material, drawing students' attention to issues that connect the chapter to previous chapters and giving them insight into what comes next. As a package, the pedagogical features at the beginning and end of each chapter work together to empower the student, by breaking down the process of reading and learning into manageable tasks.

A second package of pedagogical features is designed to help students think about history and its underlying issues more critically. For us as teachers, good pedagogy and critical thinking begin with good narrative writing. Each chapter starts with an opening vignette that showcases a particular person or event representative of the era as a whole. Within each chapter, an expanded program of illustrations and maps has been enhanced by the addition of **Guiding Questions** that challenge the reader to explore the historical contexts and significance of the maps and illustrations in a more critical way. The historical value of images, artifacts, and material culture is further emphasized in a new feature, **Interpreting Visual Evidence**. We anticipate that this section will provide discussion leaders with a provocative departure point for conversations about the key issues raised by visual sources, which students often find more approachable than texts. Once this conversation has begun, students will further be able to develop the tools they need to read the primary texts. In this new edition, the selection of primary source texts, **Analyzing Primary Sources**, has been carefully revised and many new questions have been added to frame the readings. The dynamism and diversity of Western civilizations is also illuminated through a look at **Competing Viewpoints** in each chapter, in which specific debates are presented through paired primary source texts. Finally, the bibliographical **For Further Reading** section has been edited and brought up to date and is now located at the end of the book.

REVISED CHAPTER TOURS

There are significant changes to each chapter of the book, as well. In Chapter 1, the challenges of locating and interpreting historical evidence drawn from nontextual sources (archaeological, environmental, anthropological, mythic) is a special focus. Chapter 2 further underscores the degree to which recent archeological discoveries and new historical techniques have revolutionized our understanding of ancient history, and have also corroborated ancient peoples' own understandings of their past. Chapter 3 offers expanded coverage of the diverse polities that emerged in ancient Greece, and of Athens' closely related political, documentary, artistic, and intellectual achievements. Chapter 4's exploration of the Hellenistic world is more wide-ranging than before, and it includes an entirely new discussion of the scientific revolution powered by this first cosmopolitan civilization.

With Chapter 5, the unique values and institutions of the Roman Republic are the focus of a new segment, while the account of the Republic's expansion and transformation under the Principate has been sharpened and clarified. Chapter 6's treatment of early Christianity has been deepened and expanded, and more attention has been paid to the fundamental ways in which this fledgling religion itself transformed as a result of its changing status within the Roman Empire. This chapter also draws on cutting-edge scholarship that has significantly revised our understanding of the so-called "Crisis of the Third Century" and the question of Rome's fragmentation and "fall."

Beginning with this chapter, the chronological structure of Volume 1 has been adjusted in order to make the periodization of the Middle Ages more conceptually manageable and the material easier to teach. Chapter 6 therefore ends with the reign of Theodoric in the West and the consolidation of Christian and pagan cultures in the fifth century. Chapter 7 now begins with the reign of Justinian; and while it still examines Rome's three distinctive successor civilizations, it no longer attempts to encapsulate all of Byzantine and Islamic history down to the fifteenth century. Instead, these interlocking histories and that of northwestern Europe are carried forward to about 950 C.E. in this chapter, and continue to intersect in subsequent chapters. And whereas Chapters 8 and 9 used to cover the period 1000–1300 from two different angles (political, social, and economic *versus* religious and intellectual), the new structure interweaves these forces, with Chapter 8 covering the period 950–1100 and Chapter 9 extending from 1100 to 1300.

Chapters 10–12 all assess the transition from medieval to nearly modern. Chapter 10 looks at Europe in the years 1300 to 1500, the centuries of "Crisis, Unrest, and Opportunity." Chapter 11 explores the simultaneous expansion of Europe through "Commerce, Conquest, and Colonization" between 1300 and 1600. And Chapter 12 examines the "Renaissance Ideals and Realities" that stemmed from, and contributed to, these same events. All three chapters have been revised and expanded for this edition.

Thereafter, Chapter 13 characterizes the sixteenth century as "The Age of Dissent and Division," while Chapter 14 surveys the religious, political, and military struggles that arose in the era of confessional difference, contested sovereignty, and military escalation between 1540 and 1660.

Chapters 15–17 cover the history of early modern Europe between the sixteenth and eighteenth centuries, a time that saw powerful absolutist regimes emerge on the continent; the establishment of wealthy European trading empires in Asia, Africa, and the Americas; and successive periods of intense intellectual and philosophical discussion during the Scientific Revolution and the Enlightenment. Chapter 15 has been reorganized to better relate the emergence of absolutist regimes on the continent with the alternatives to absolutism that developed in England, and to clarify the differences between the colonial empires of France, Britain, and Spain. Chapter 16 emphasizes the many facets of scientific inquiry during the Scientific Revolution and introduces a new section on women scientists. Meanwhile, Chapter 17 adds new emphasis to the ways that Enlightenment figures dealt with cultures and peoples in the parts of the world that Europeans confronted in building their empires.

Chapters 18–19 cover the political and economic revolutions of the late eighteenth and early nineteenth centuries. Chapter 18 covers the French Revolution and the Napoleonic empires in depth, while also drawing attention to the way that these central episodes were rooted in a larger pattern of revolutionary political change that engulfed the Atlantic world. Chapter 19 emphasizes both the economic growth and the technological innovations that were a part of the Industrial Revolution, while also exploring the social and cultural consequences of industrialization for men and women in Europe's new industrial societies. The ***Interpreting Visual Evidence*** box in Chapter 19 allows students to explore the ways that industrialization created new perceptions of the global economy in Europe, changing the way people thought of their place in the world.

Chapters 20–21 explore the successive struggles between conservative reaction and revolutionaries in Europe, as the revolutionary forces of nationalism unleashed by the French Revolution redrew the map of Europe and threatened the dynastic regimes that had ruled for centuries. In all of these chapters, new images have been added to focus students' attention on the many ways that "the people" were represented by liberals, conservatives, and revolutionaries, and the consequences of these contesting representations.

Chapter 22 takes on the history of nineteenth-century colonialism, exploring both its political and economic origins and its consequences for the peoples of Africa and Asia. The chapter gives new emphasis to the significance of colonial conquest for European culture, as colonial power became increasingly associated with national greatness, both in conservative monarchies and in more democratic regimes. Meanwhile, Chapter 23 brings the narrative back to the heart of Europe, covering the long-term consequences of industrialization and the consolidation of a conservative form of nationalism in many European nations even as the electorate was being expanded. The chapter emphasizes the varied nature of the new forms of political dissent, from the feminists who claimed the right to vote to the newly organized socialist movements that proved so enduring in many European countries.

Chapters 24 and 25 bring new vividness to the history of the First World War and the intense conflicts of the interwar period, while Chapter 26 uses the history of the Second World War as a hinge for understanding European and global developments in the second half of the twentieth century. The *Interpreting Visual Evidence* box in Chapter 24 allows for a special focus on the role of propaganda among the belligerent nations in 1914–1918, and the chapter's section on the diplomatic crisis that preceded the First World War has been streamlined to allow students to more easily comprehend the essential issues at the heart of the conflict. In Chapter 25 the *Interpreting Visual Evidence* box continues to explore the theme touched on in earlier chapters, political representations of "the people," this time in the context of fascist spectacles in Germany and Italy in the 1930s. These visual sources help students to understand the vulnerability of Europe's democratic regimes during these years as they faced the dual assault from fascists on the right and Bolsheviks on the left.

Chapters 27–29 bring the volumes to a close in a thorough exploration of the Cold War, decolonization, the collapse of the Soviet Union and the Eastern Bloc in 1989–1991, and the roots of the multifaceted global conflicts that beset the world in the first decade of the twenty-first century. Chapter 27 juxtaposes the Cold War with decolonization, showing how this combination sharply diminished the ability of European nations to control events in the international arena, even as they succeeded in rebuilding their economies at home. Chapter 28 explores the vibrancy of European culture in the crucial period of the 1960s to the early 1990s, bringing new attention to the significance of 1989 as a turning point in European history. Finally, a completely new set of primary documents and questions accompanies Chapter 29, which covers the benefits and tensions of a a newly globalized world. The chapter's conclusion now covers the financial crisis of 2008 and the subsequent election of Barack Obama, as well as recent debates within Islam about Muslims living as minorities in non-Muslim nations.

A Few Words of Thanks

Our first year as members of *Western Civilizations'* authorial team has been a challenging and rewarding one. We are honored to be the partners of two historians whose work we have long admired, and who have been formative influences on us in our careers as students, scholars, and teachers of history. We would also like to thank a number of our colleagues around the country who provided in-depth critiques of large sections of the book: Paul Freedman (Yale University), Sheryl Kroen (University of Florida), Michael Kulikowski (Pennsylvania State University), Harry Liebersohn (University of Illinois, Urbana-Champaign), and Helmut Smith (Vanderbilt University). We are very grateful for the expert assistance and support of the Norton team, especially that of our editor, Jon Durbin. Kate Feighery, our fabulous project editor, has driven the book beautifully through the manuscript process. Jason Spears and Justin Cahill have skillfully dealt with a myriad of issues pertaining to the preparation of the text. Junenoire Mitchell and Donna Ranieri did an excellent job finding many of the exact images we specified. Lorraine Klimowich did an expert job developing the print ancillaries. Ben Reynolds has efficiently marched us through the production process. Steve Hoge has done a great job developing the book's fantastic emedia, particularly the new Author Insight Podcasts and Euro History Tours powered by Google Earth. Michael Fleming and Bob Byrne were terrific in skillfully guiding the manuscript through the copyediting and proofreading stages. Finally, we want to thank Tamara McNeill for spearheading the marketing campaign for the new edition. We are also indebted to the numerous expert readers who commented on various chapters and who thereby strengthened the book as a whole. We are thankful to our families, for their patience and advice, and to our students, whose questions and comments over the years have been essential to the framing of this book. And we extend a special thanks to, and hope to hear from, all the teachers and students we may never meet—their engagement with this book will frame new understandings of our shared past and its bearing on our future.

NEW EDITION REVIEWERS

Donna Allen, Glendale Community College
Marjon Ames, Appalachian State University
Eirlys Barker, Thomas Nelson Community College
Matthew Barlow, John Abbott College
Ken Bartlett, University of Toronto

Volker Benkert, Arizona State University

Dean Bennett, Schenectady City Community College

Patrick Brennan, Gulf Coast Community College

Neil Brooks, Community College of Baltimore County, Essex

James Brophy, University of Delaware

Kevin Caldwell, Blue Ridge Community College

Keith Chu, Bergen Community College

Alex D'erizans, Borough of Manhattan Community College, CUNY

Michael Dusik, College of DuPage

Hilary Earl, Nipissing University

Karin Enloe, Arizona State University

Kirk Ford, Mississippi College

Michael Gattis, Gulf Coast Community College

David M. Gallo, College of Mount Saint Vincent

Jamie Gruring, Arizona State University

Tim Hack, Salem Community College

Bernard Hagerty, University of Pittsburgh

Tony Heideman, Front Range Community College

Paul T. Hietter, Mesa Community College

Paul Hughes, Sussex County Community College

Lacey Hunter, Caldwell College

Kyle Irvin, Jefferson State Community College

Lloyd Johnson, Campbell University

Llana Krug, York College of Pennsylvania

Guy Lalande, St. Francis Xavier University

Chris Laney, Berkshire Community College

Charles Levine, Mesa Community College

Heidi MacDonald, University of Lethbridge

Steven Marks, Clemson University

James Martin, Campbell University

Michael Mckeown, Daytona State University

David Mock, Tallahassee Community College

Dan Puckett, Troy State University

Dan Robinson, Troy State University

Craig Saucier, Southeastern Louisiana University

Aletia Seaborn, Southern Union State College

Nicholas Steneck, Florida Southern College

Victoria Thompson, Arizona State University

Donna Trembinski, St. Francis Xavier University

Pamela West, Jefferson State Community College

Scott White, Scottsdale Community College

Aaron Wilson, Creighton University

Julianna Wilson, Pima Community College

PREVIOUS EDITION REVIEWERS

Eric Ash, Wayne State University

Sacha Auerbach, Virginia Commonwealth University

Ken Bartlett, University of Toronto

Benita Blessing, Ohio University

Chuck Boening, Shelton State Community College

John Bohstedt, University of Tennessee, Knoxville

Dan Brown, Moorpark College

Kevin Caldwell, Blue Ridge Community College

Jodi Campbell, Texas Christian University

Annette Chamberlain, Virginia Western Community College

Jason Coy, College of Charleston

Benjamin Ehlers, University of Georgia

Maryann Farkas, Dawson College

Gloria Fitzgibbon, Wake Forest University

Tina Gaddis, Onondaga Community College

Alex Garman, Eastern New Mexico State University

Norman Goda, Ohio University

Andrew Goldman, Gonzaga University

Robert Grasso, Monmouth University

Sylvia Gray, Portland Community College

Susan Grayzel, University of Mississippi

Timothy Hack, University of Delaware

Hazel Hahn, Seattle University

Derek Hastings, Oakland University

Dawn Hayes, Montclair State University

John Houston, Fordham University

Michael Hughes, Wake Forest University

Bruce Hunt, University of Texas, Austin

Ahmed Ibrahim, Southwest Missouri State University

Kevin James, University of Guelph

Lars Jones, Florida Institute of Technology

John Kearney, Cy Fair Community College

Roman Laba, Hudson Valley Community College

Elizabeth Lehfeldt, Cleveland State University

Thomas Maulucci, State University of New York, Fredonia

Amy McCandless, College of Charleston

John McGrath, Boston University

Nicholas Murray, Adirondack College

Charles Odahl, Boise State University

Bill Olejniczak, College of Charleston

Jeffrey Plaks, University of Central Oklahoma

Peter Pozesky, College of Wooster

Rebecca Schloss, Texas A&M University

James Shedel, Georgetown University

Rebecca Spang, Indiana University, Bloomington

Patrick Speelman, College of Charleston

Robert Taylor, Florida Institute of Technology

Paul Teverow, Missouri Southern State University

James Vanstone, John Abbott College

Kirk Willis, University of Georgia

Ian Worthington, University of Missouri, Columbia

Western Civilizations

Their History &
Their Culture

Brief Third Edition

Before You Read This Chapter

Early Civilizations

CORE OBJECTIVES

- **UNDERSTAND** the challenges involved in studying the distant past.

- **DEFINE** the key characteristics of civilization.

- **IDENTIFY** the factors that shaped the earliest cities.

- **EXPLAIN** how Hammurabi's empire was governed.

- **DESCRIBE** the main differences between Mesopotamian and Egyptian civilizations.

There was a time, the story goes, when all the peoples of the earth shared a common language and could accomplish great things. They developed new technologies, made bricks, and aspired to build a fortified city with a tower reaching to the sky. But their god was troubled by this, so he destroyed their civilization by making it hard for them to understand one another's speech.

We know this as the legend of Babel. It's a story that probably circulated among peoples of the ancient world for thousands of years before it became part of the Hebrew book we call by its Greek name, Genesis, "the beginning." This story lets us glimpse some of the conditions in which the first civilizations arose, and it also reminds us of the ruptures that make studying them hard. We no longer speak the same languages as those ancient peoples, just as we no longer have direct access to their experiences or their beliefs.

Such foundational stories are usually called *myths*, but they are really an early form of history. For the people who told them, these stories helped to make sense of the present by explaining the past. The fate of Babel conveyed a crucial message: human

3

beings are powerful when they share a common goal, and what enables human interaction is civilization. To the peoples of the ancient world, the characteristic benefits of civilization—stability and safety, government, art, literature, science—were always products of city life. The very word "civilization" derives from the Latin word *civis*, "city." Cities, however, became possible only as a result of innovations that began around the end of the last Ice Age, about 13,000 years ago, and that came to fruition in Mesopotamia 8,000 years later. The history of civilization is therefore a short one. Within the study of humanity, which reaches back to the genus *Homo* in Africa, some 1.7 million years ago, it is merely a blip on the radar screen. Even within the history of *Homo sapiens sapiens*, the species to which we belong and which evolved about 50,000 years ago, civilization is a very recent development.

The study of early civilizations is both fascinating and challenging. Historians still do not understand why the first cities should have developed in the region between the Tigris and the Euphrates rivers, in what is now Iraq. Once developed, however, the basic patterns of urban life quickly spread to other parts of the Near East, both by imitation and by conquest. A network of trading connections linked these early cities, but intense competition for resources made alliances among them fragile. Then, around the middle of the second millennium B.C.E. (that is, "Before the Common Era," equivalent to the Christian dating system B.C., "Before Christ"), emerging powers began to shape these fiercely independent cities into empires. How this happened—and how we know that it happened—is the subject of Chapter 1.

BEFORE CIVILIZATION

More than 9,000 years ago, a town began to develop at Çatalhöyük (*sha-tal-HOO-yuk*) in what is now south-central Turkey. Over the next 2,000 years, it grew to cover an area of thirty-three acres, within which some 8,000 inhabitants lived in more than 2,000 separate houses. If this seems small, consider that Çatalhöyük's population density was actually twice that of today's most populous city, Mumbai (India). It was so tightly packed that there were hardly any streets. Instead, each house was built immediately next to its neighbor, and generally on top of a previous house.

The people of Çatalhöyük developed a highly organized and advanced society. They wove wool cloth; they made kiln-fired pottery; they painted elaborate hunting scenes on the plaster-covered walls of their houses; they made weapons and tools from razor-sharp obsidian imported from the nearby Cappadocian mountains. They honored their ancestors with religious rites and buried their dead beneath the floors of their houses. Settled agriculturalists, they grew grains, peas, and lentils and tended herds of domesticated sheep and goats. But they also hunted and gathered fruits and nuts, like their nomadic ancestors, and their society was egalitarian, another feature common to nomadic societies: both men and women did the same kinds of work. But despite their relatively diverse and abundant food supply, their life spans were very short. Men died, on average, at the age of thirty-four. Women, who bore the additional risks of childbirth, died at around age thirty.

The basic features of life in Çatalhöyük are common to all subsequent human civilizations. But how, when, and why did such settlements emerge? And how do we have access to information about this distant past? The era before the appearance of written records, which begin to proliferate around 3100 B.C.E., is of far greater duration than the subsequent eras we are able to document—and no less important. But it requires special ingenuity to identify, collect, and interpret the evidence of the distant past. In fact, historians have just begun to explore the ways that climatology, neuroscience, and evolutionary biology can further illuminate this period, augmenting the older findings of paleontology, archeology, and historical anthropology.

Societies of the Stone Age

Primates with human characteristics originated in Africa 4 to 5 million years ago, and tool-making hominids—species belonging to the genus *Homo*, our distant ancestors—evolved approximately 2 million years ago. Because these early hominids made most of their tools out of stone, they are designated as belonging to the Stone Age. This vast expanse of time is divided into the Paleolithic ("Old Stone") and the Neolithic ("New Stone") Eras, with the break between them falling around 11,000 B.C.E.

Hominids in Africa were kindling and controlling fire as early as 164,000 years ago, using it to make tools. The Neanderthals, a hominid species that flourished about 200,000 years ago, made jewelry, painted on the walls of caves, and buried their dead in distinctive graves with meaningful objects such as horns (blown to make music) and, in one case, flowers. Could these hominids speak? Did they have a language? At present, there is no way that archeology can answer such questions.

CAVE PAINTINGS FROM LASCAUX. These paintings, which date to between 10,000 and 15,000 B.C.E., show several of the different species of animals that were hunted by people of the Ice Age. The largest animal depicted here, a species of long-horned cattle known as the *auroch*, is now extinct.

However, archeology has shown that in the last phase of the Paleolithic Era, around 40,000 B.C.E., the pace of human development began to accelerate dramatically. Human populations in Africa expanded, suggesting that people were better nourished, perhaps as a result of new technologies. In Europe, *Homo sapiens sapiens* began to produce finely crafted and more-effective tools such as fishhooks, arrowheads, and sewing needles made from wood, antler, and bone. The most astonishing evidence of this change was produced by these new tools: cave paintings like those at Lascaux (France), discovered in 1940. These amazing scenes were purposefully painted in recesses where acoustic resonance is greatest, and were probably intended to be experienced as part of multimedia musical ceremonies. This is almost certain evidence for the development of language.

Despite these changes, the basic patterns of human life altered very little. Virtually all human societies consisted of bands of a few dozen people who moved incessantly in search of food. As a result, these groups have left no continuous archeological record. Their lifestyle also had social, economic, and political limitations which help to explain the differences—both positive and negative—between these subsistence societies and those that can be called "civilizations." Early humans had no domestic animals to transport goods, so they could have no significant material possessions aside from basic tools. And because they could not accumulate goods over time, the distinctions of rank and status created by disparities in wealth could not develop. Hierarchical structures were therefore uncommon. When conflicts arose or resources became scarce, the solution was probably to divide and separate. And al-

though scholars once assumed that men did the hunting and women the gathering, it is more likely that all members of a band (except for the very young and very old) engaged in the basic activity of acquiring food.

THE BUILDING BLOCKS OF CIVILIZATION

What changes allowed some hunter-gatherer societies to settle and build civilizations? The historical divide between the Paleolithic ("Old Stone") Age and Neolithic ("New Stone") Age, around 11,000 B.C.E., reflects very evident developments brought about by changes in the climate, which led to the development of managed food production, which in turn fostered settlements that could trade with one another, both locally and over long distances. For the first time, it became possible for individuals and communities to accumulate and store wealth on a large scale. The results were far-reaching. Communities became more stable, and human interactions more complex. Specialization developed, along with distinctions of status and rank. Both the rapidity and the radical implications of these changes have given this era its name: the Neolithic Revolution.

The Neolithic Revolution

The artists who executed the cave paintings at Lascaux were able to survive in harsh climatic conditions. Between 40,000 and 11,000 B.C.E., daytime temperatures in the Mediterranean basin averaged about 60° F (16° C) in the summer and about 30° F (–1° C) in the winter. These are very low compared to today's temperatures in the city of Marseilles, not far from Lascaux, which average about 86° F (30° C) in summer and 52° F (11° C) in winter. Cold-loving reindeer, elk, wild boar, bison, and mountain goats abounded in regions now famous for their beaches and vineyards. But as the glaciers receded northward with the warming climate, these species retreated with them, all the way to Scandinavia. Some humans moved north with the game, but others stayed behind to create a very different world.

Within a few thousand years after the end of the Ice Age, peoples living in the eastern Mediterranean and some other regions of the world accomplished the most

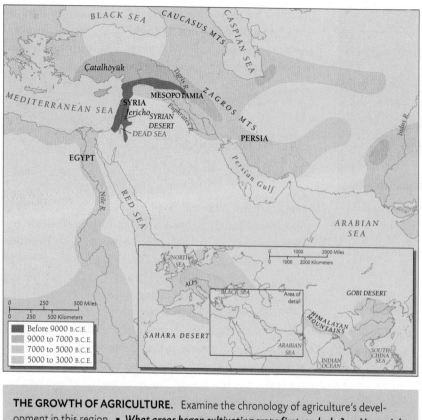

food supply. They therefore had to increase the food-growing capacity of the land and to devise ways of preserving and storing grain between harvests. Some peoples had learned how to preserve wild grain in storage pits as early as 11,500 B.C.E., and eventually they discovered that they could use this seed to produce even more grain the following year. The importance of this latter discovery cannot be overstated: deliberate cultivation could support larger populations and could also compensate for disasters (such as flooding) that might inhibit natural reseeding. Even more important, intensified seeding and storage provided humans with the stable and predictable surpluses needed to support domestic animals. This brought a host of additional benefits, not only guaranteeing a more reliable supply of meat, milk, leather, wool, bone, and horn, but also providing animal power to pull carts and plows and to power mills.

THE GROWTH OF AGRICULTURE. Examine the chronology of agriculture's development in this region. ▪ *What areas began cultivating crops first, and why?* ▪ *How might rivers have played a crucial role in the spread of farming technologies?*

momentous transformation in human history: a switch from food-gathering for subsistence to food production. The warmer, wetter climate allowed wild grains to flourish, geometrically increasing the food supply. People began to domesticate animals and cultivate plants. Stable settlements grew into cities. This process took several thousand years, but it still deserves to be called "revolutionary." In a relatively short time, people altered patterns of existence that were millions of years old.

This revolution produced new challenges and inequalities. Well-nourished women in sedentary communities can bear more children than women in hunter-gatherer groups, and so the women of this era became increasingly sequestered from their male counterparts, who in turn gave up an equal role in child care. The rapid increase in population was countered by the rapid spread of infectious diseases, while dependence on carbohydrates resulted in earlier deaths than were typical among hunter-gatherers.

But eventually, increased fertility and birthrates outweighed these limiting factors, and by about 8000 B.C.E. human populations were beginning to exceed the wild

The Emergence of Towns and Villages

The accelerating changes of the Neolithic Revolution are exemplified by towns like Çatalhöyük and by the simultaneous rise of trade and warfare—sure signs of increased specialization and competition. Hundreds, and probably thousands, of settlements grew up in the Near East between 7500 and 3500 B.C.E. Some of these can even be classified as cities: centers of administration and commerce with a large and diverse population, often protected by walls. Among the earliest of these was Jericho, in the territory lying between modern Israel and Jordan. Jericho emerged as a seasonal, grain-producing settlement, and by 6800 B.C.E. its inhabitants were undertaking a spectacular building program. Many new dwellings were built on stone foundations, and a massive dressed stone wall was constructed around the western edge of the settlement. It included a circular tower whose excavated remains still reach to a height of thirty feet, a powerful expression of its builders' wealth, technical prowess, and political ambitions.

Jericho covered at least eight acres and supported 3,000 people, so it was even more densely settled than

Çatalhöyük. It was sustained by intensive cultivation, made possible by irrigation, of recently domesticated strains of wheat and barley. Jericho's inhabitants also produced some of the earliest-known pottery, which allowed them to store grain, wine, and oils more effectively. Pottery's most important benefits, however, were in cooking. For the first time, it was possible to produce nourishing stews, porridges, and ales. (The capacity to produce beer is a sure sign of civilization.) Pottery production was not only vital to ancient civilizations, it is vital to those who study them. As the techniques for making pottery spread throughout the Near East and Asia, identifiable regional styles also developed. By studying the different varieties, archeologists can construct a reasonably accurate chronology and can also trace the movements of goods and people.

Jericho and Çatalhöyük illustrate the impact that stored agricultural surpluses have on human relations. For the first time, significant differences began to arise in the amount of wealth individuals could stockpile for themselves and their heirs. Dependence on agriculture also made it more difficult for individuals to split off from the community when disputes and inequities arose. The result was the emergence of a much more stratified society, with more opportunities for a few powerful people to become dominant. The new reliance on agriculture also meant a new dependence on the land, the seasons, and the weather, which led to new speculations about the supernatural. Different life forces were believed to require special services and gifts, and the regular practice of ritual and sacrifice ultimately produced a priestly caste of individuals or families who seemed able to communicate with these forces. Such spiritual leadership was allied to more worldly forms of power, including the capacity to lead war bands, to exact tribute from other settlements, to construct defenses, and to resolve disputes.

Trade was another important element in the development of early settlements. Local trading networks were already established around 9000 B.C.E., and by 5000 long-distance routes linked settlements throughout the Near East. Long-distance trade accelerated the exchange of ideas and information throughout the Fertile Crescent, and it further increased social stratification. Because status was enhanced by access to exotic goods from afar, local elites sought to monopolize trade by organizing and controlling the production of commodities within their own communities and by regulating their export. Certain people could now devote at least a portion of their labor to pursuits other than agriculture: making pottery or cloth, manufacturing weapons or tools, building houses and fortifications, or facilitating trade. Thus the elites who fostered and exploited the labor of others eventually became specialized themselves, with the leisure and resources to engage in intellectual, artistic, and political pursuits. The building blocks of civilization had been laid.

URBAN DEVELOPMENT IN MESOPOTAMIA

The Greeks called it Mesopotamia, the "Land between Rivers." It was a land that received only about eight inches (20 cm) of rainfall per year. Its soils are sandy and summer temperatures exceed 110° F (44° C). The two rivers supplying water—the Tigris and Euphrates—are noted for their violence and unpredictability. Both are prone to flooding, and the Tigris was liable to change its course from year to year. It was in this challenging environment that the first urban society, the civilization of Sumer, flourished.

THE WHITE TEMPLE AT URUK, C. 3400 B.C.E. This temple may have been dedicated to the sky god, An, or designed to provide all the region's gods with a mountaintop home in a part of the world known for its level plains.

The Ubaid Culture

The earliest cities of Mesopotamia were founded by the Ubaid peoples, so called because of their settlement at al-Ubaid (now in Iraq), which dates to around 5900 B.C.E. In this era, the headwaters of the Persian Gulf extended at least 100 miles farther inland than they do today, so some Ubaid settlements bordered on fertile marshlands, which enabled them to develop irrigation systems. Although these began as relatively simple channels and collection pools, Ubaid farmers quickly learned to build more sophisticated canals and to line some pools with stone. They also constructed dikes and levees to control the seasonal flooding of the rivers and to direct the excess water into irrigation canals. Despite the hostility of the environment, Ubaid communities were soon producing surpluses sufficient to support specialists in construction, weaving, pottery making, metalwork, and trade: the typical attributes of Neolithic village life.

Yet there is also early evidence of something quite new: central structures that served religious, economic, and administrative functions, something not found in Çatalhöyük. Starting out as shrines, these structures soon became impressive temples built of dried mud brick, like the bricks described in the story of Babel—and unlike the plentiful stone used at Jericho; the scarcity of stone meant that builders in this region had to be more resourceful. Each large settlement had such a temple, from which a priestly class acted as managers of the community's stored wealth and of the complex irrigation systems that would make the civilization of Sumer possible.

Urbanism in Uruk, 4300–2900 B.C.E.

After about 4300 B.C.E., Ubaid settlements developed into larger, more prosperous, and more highly organized communities. The most famous of these sites, Uruk, became the first Sumerian city-state. Its sophistication and scale is exemplified by the White Temple, built between 3500 and 3300 B.C.E. Its massive sloping platform looms nearly forty feet above the surrounding flatlands, and its four corners are oriented toward the cardinal points of the compass. Atop the platform stands the temple proper, dressed in brick and originally painted a brilliant white.

Such temples were eventually constructed in every Sumerian city, reflecting the central role that worship played in civic life. Uruk in particular seems to have owed its rapid growth to its importance as a religious center. By 3100 B.C.E. it encompassed several hundred acres, enclosing a population of 40,000 people within its massive brick walls. The larger villages of Sumer were also growing rapidly, attracting immigrants just as the great cities did. Grain and cloth production grew tenfold. Trade routes expanded dramatically. And to manage this increasingly complex economy, the Sumerians invented the technology on which most historians rely: writing.

CUNEIFORM WRITING. The image on the left shows a Sumerian clay tablet from about 3000 B.C.E. Here, standardized pictures are beginning to represent abstractions: notice the symbol *ninda* (food) near the top. On the right, carvings on limestone from about 2600 B.C.E. reveal the evolution of cuneiform. ▪ *Why would such standardized pictograms have been easier to reproduce quickly?*

The Development of Writing

In 4000 B.C.E., the peoples of the Near East were already using clay tokens to keep inventories. Within a few centuries, they developed a practice of placing tokens inside hollow clay balls and inscribing, on the outside of each ball, the shapes of all the tokens it contained. By 3300 B.C.E., scribes had replaced these balls with flat clay tablets on which they inscribed the symbols representing tokens. These tablets made keeping the tokens themselves unnecessary, and they could also be archived for future reference or sent to other settlements as receipts or requests for goods.

Writing thus evolved as a practical recording technology to support economic pursuits. Because it existed to represent real things, its system of symbols—called pictograms—was also realistic: each pictogram resembled the thing it represented. Over time, however, a pictogram might be used not only to symbolize a physical object but to evoke an idea associated with that object. For example, the symbol for a bowl of food, *ninda*, might be used to express something more abstract, such as "nourishment." Pictograms also came to be associated with particular spoken sounds, or *phonemes*. Thus when a Sumerian scribe needed to employ the sound *ninda*, even as part of another word, he would use the symbol for a bowl of food to represent that phoneme. Later, special marks were added so that a reader could tell whether the writer meant it to represent the object itself, a larger concept, or a sound used in a context that might have nothing to do with food.

By 3100 B.C.E., Sumerian scribes also developed a specialized tool suited to the task of writing, a stylus made of reed. Because this stylus leaves an impression shaped like a wedge (in Latin, *cuneus*), this script is called *cuneiform* (kyoo-NAY-i-form). Cuneiform symbols could now be impressed more quickly into clay. And because the new stylus was not suited to drawing pictograms that accurately represented things, the symbols became even more abstract. Meanwhile, symbols were invented for every possible phonetic combination in the Sumerian language, reducing the number of necessary pictograms from about 1,200 to 600. But whereas the earliest pictograms could have been written and read by anyone, writing and reading now became specialized, powerful skills accessible only to a small and influential minority who were taught in special scribal schools.

THE CULTURE OF SUMER

The great centers of Sumerian civilization shared a common culture and a common language. They also shared a set of beliefs. However, this common religion did not produce peace. The residents of each city considered themselves to be the servants of a particular god, whom they sought to glorify by exalting their own city above others. The result was intense competition that frequently escalated into warfare. There was also an economic dimension to this conflict, since water rights and access to arable land and trade routes were often at stake.

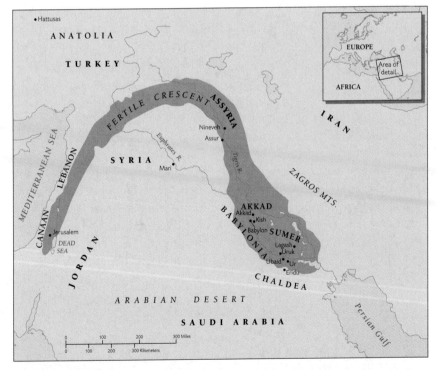

THE FERTILE CRESCENT. Notice the proximity of Sumerian cities to rivers; consider the vital role played by the Tigris and Euphrates in shaping Mesopotamian civilizations. ▪ *How many Sumerian city-states can you count on the map?* ▪ *Why would Sumerian city-states have been clustered so closely together?* ▪ *What challenges and opportunities would this present?*

The Flood: Two Accounts

One of the oldest stories in the world tells of a great flood that decimated the lands and peoples of the earth, an event that can be traced to the warming of the earth's climate at the end of the last Ice Age. Many ancient cultures told versions of this story, and two of these are excerpted below. The first, included in the Epic of Gilgamesh, *was written down during the first half of the third millennium B.C.E., making it at least 1,500 years older than the similar account in the Hebrew Bible. But both are probably the products of much older storytelling traditions. The hero of the Sumerian story is Utnapishtim. The Hebrew story's hero is Noah.*

The Epic of Gilgamesh

Utnapishtim spoke to Gilgamesh, saying: "I will reveal to you, Gilgamesh . . . a secret of the gods. . . . The hearts of the Great Gods moved them to inflict the Flood. Their Father Anu uttered the oath (of secrecy). . . . [But the god] Ea . . . repeated their talk [to me, saying]: 'O man of Shuruppak, son of Ubartutu: Tear down the house and build a boat! . . . Spurn possessions and keep alive living beings! Make all living beings go up into the boat. The boat which you are to build, its dimensions must measure equal to each other: its length must correspond to its width. Roof it over like the Apsu.' I understood and spoke to my lord, Ea: 'My lord, thus is the command which you have uttered. I will heed and will do it.' . . . On the fifth day I laid out her exterior. It was a field in area, its walls were each 10 times 12 cubits in height. . . . I provided it with six decks, thus dividing it into seven (levels). . . . Whatever I had I loaded on it. . . . All the living beings that I had I loaded on it. I had all my kith and kin go up into the boat, all the beasts and animals of the field and the draftsmen I had go up.

"I watched the appearance of the weather—the weather was frightful to behold! I went into the boat and sealed the entry. . . . All day long the South Wind blew . . . , submerging the mountain in water, overwhelming the people like an attack. . . . Six days and seven nights came the wind and flood, the storm flattening the land. When the seventh day arrived . . . [t]he sea calmed, fell still, the whirlwind and flood stopped up. . . . When a seventh day arrived, I sent forth a dove and released it. The dove went off, but came back to me, no perch was visible so it circled back to me. I sent forth a swallow and released it. The swallow went off, but came back to me, no perch was visible so it circled back to me. I sent forth a raven and released it. The raven went off, and saw the waters slither back. It eats, it scratches, it bobs, but does not circle back to me. Then I sent out everything in all directions and sacrificed (a sheep). I offered incense in front of the mountain-ziggurat. . . .

"The gods smelled the savor . . . and collected like flies over a sacrifice. . . . Just then Enlil arrived. He saw the boat and became furious. . . . 'Where did a living being escape? No man was to survive the annihilation!' Ea spoke to Valiant Enlil, saying . . . 'How, how could you bring about a Flood without consideration? Charge the violation to the viola-

Much of the economic production of a city passed through the great temple warehouses, where priests redistributed the city's produce. During the third millennium, these great temples began to control the production of textiles, employing thousands of servile women and children. Temple elites also played a key role in long-distance trade, as both buyers and sellers of goods. So for any city-state to surrender its independence would not only offend the conquered city's god, it would jeopardize its entire economy and the power of its ruling class.

Each Sumerian city had its own aristocracy, the group from which priests were drawn. As much as half tor, charge the offense to the offender, but be compassionate lest (mankind) be cut off, be patient lest they be killed.' Enlil went up inside the boat and, grasp-ing my hand, made me go up. He had my wife go up and kneel by my side. He touched our forehead and, standing be-tween us, he blessed us. . . ."

Source: Maureen Gallery Kovacs, trans., *The Epic of Gilgamesh*, Tablet XI (Stanford, CA: 1985, 1989), pp. 97–103.

The Book of Genesis

The Lord saw that the wicked-ness of humankind was great in the earth and . . . said, "I will blot out from the earth the human be-ings I have created . . . for I am sorry I have made them." But Noah found favor in the sight of the Lord. . . . God saw that the earth was corrupt and . . . said to Noah, "I have determined to make an end to all flesh. . . . Make yourself an ark of cypress wood, make rooms in the ark, and cover it inside and out with pitch. . . . Make a roof for the ark, and put the door of the ark in its side. . . . For my part I am going to bring a flood on the earth, to destroy from under heaven all flesh. . . . But I will establish a covenant with you, and you shall come into the ark, you, your sons, your wife, and your sons' wives with you. And of every living thing you shall bring two of every kind into the ark, to keep them alive with you. . . . Also take with you every kind of food that is eaten." . . . All the foun-tains of the great deep burst forth, and the windows of the heavens were opened. . . . The waters gradually re-ceded from the earth. . . . At the end of forty days, Noah opened a window of the ark . . . and sent out the raven, and it went to and fro until the waters were dried up from the earth. Then he sent out the dove from him, to see if the wa-ters had subsided from the face of the ground, but the dove found no place to set its foot, and it returned. . . . He waited another seven days, and again sent out the dove [which] came back to him . . . and there in its beak was a freshly plucked olive leaf, so Noah knew the wa-ters had subsided from the earth. Then he . . . sent out the dove, and it did not return to him anymore. . . . Noah built an altar to the Lord . . . and offered burnt offerings. And when the Lord smelled the pleasing odor, the Lord said in his heart, "I will never again curse the ground because of humankind . . . nor will I ever again destroy every living crea-ture as I have done." . . . God blessed Noah and his sons.

Source: Genesis 6:5–9:1, *The New Oxford Annotated Bible* (Oxford: 1994).

Questions for Analysis

1. What are the similarities and differ-ences between these two accounts?

2. What do these differences or similari-ties reveal about the two societies that told these stories? Does one seem to derive from the other? Why or why not?

3. How is the geography and climate of Mesopotamia reflected in the Sume-rian version of the story?

the population consisted of free persons who held parcels of land sufficient to sustain themselves, but the rest were dependents of the temple who worked as artisans or as agricultural laborers, and many of these dependents were slaves. Most of these slaves were prisoners of war from other Sumerian city-states whose bondage was limited to three years, after which time a slave had to be released. But non-Sumerians could be held indefinitely, although a few might manage to buy their freedom. In either case, slaves were the property of their owners. They could be beaten, branded, bought, and sold like any other form of merchandise. Perhaps the only positive thing to say about slavery in antiquity is that it was egalitarian: anyone could become a slave. It was not until the beginning of the modern era that slavery became linked to race (see Chapter 11).

The Early Dynastic Period, 2900–2500 B.C.E.

Around 2900 B.C.E., conflicts among the growing Sumerian city-states became more acute. Competition for resources intensified and warfare became more frequent and destructive. A new type of military leadership began to emerge and eventually evolved into a form of kingship. Historians refer to this phase as the Early Dynastic Period because it was dominated by family dynasties, each headed by a war leader whose prestige earned him the title *lugal*: "big man." Unlike the priestly rulers of the Uruk Period, lugals did not see themselves as humble servants of the city's god. Rather, they believed that success in battle had earned them the right to exploit the city's wealth for their own glory.

The most striking expression of this development is the *Epic of Gilgamesh*, a series of stories recited over many generations and eventually written down on cuneiform tablets: the first literary monument in world history. It recounts the exploits of a lugal named Gilgamesh, who probably lived in Uruk sometime around 2700 B.C.E. Gilgamesh earns his legendary reputation through military conquest and personal heroism, particularly in campaigns against uncivilized—that is, nonurban—tribes. But he becomes so powerful that he ignores his own society's code of conduct; he disrespects the priesthood and commits acts of sacrilege. So the people of Uruk pray to the gods for retribution, and the gods fashion a wild man named Enkidu to challenge Gilgamesh.

The confrontation between Gilgamesh and Enkidu reveals the core values of Sumerian society. Gilgamesh is a creature of the city; Enkidu is a creature of the past, a hunter-gatherer. But then Enkidu has a sexual encounter with a beguiling woman and is unable to return to the wilderness: his urban initiation has civilized him and allowed him to befriend the lord of Uruk. Together they have many adventures. But Enkidu is eventually killed by the goddess Inanna, who punishes the friends for mocking her powers. Gilgamesh, distraught with grief, attempts to find a magical plant that will revive his friend. He finds it at the bottom of a deep pool, only to have it stolen from him by a water snake. In the end, he is forced to confront the futility of all human effort. He becomes "The One Who Looked into the Depths," the name by which his story was known to Sumerians. The larger message seems to be that not even civilization can shield humans from the forces of nature and the inevitability of death.

Sumerian Religion

In the Uruk Period, the Sumerians identified their gods with the capricious forces of the natural world. In the Early Dynastic Period, however, they came to imagine their gods as resembling the powerful lugals who now ruled the city-states as kings. Like them, the gods desired to live in the finest palaces and temples, to wear the costliest clothing and jewels, and to consume the tastiest foods. According to this new theology, which clearly reflects changes in Sumerian society, humans exist merely to provide for their gods. This was, indeed, why the gods had created people in the first place. There was thus a reciprocal relationship between humanity and divinity. The gods depended on their human servants to honor and sustain them; and in return, the gods occasionally bestowed gifts and favors.

As the gods' representatives on earth, kings bore special responsibilities and also enjoyed special privileges. Kings were thus set apart from all other men, including priests. But kings were also obliged to honor the gods through offerings, sacrifices, festivals, and massive building projects. Kings who neglected these duties, or who exalted themselves at the expense of the gods, were likely to bring disaster on themselves and their people. And even kings could not evade death.

Science, Technology, and Trade

The Sumerians' worldview was colored by their adversarial relationship with the environment. Precisely because neither their gods nor their environment were trustworthy, Sumerians cultivated a high degree of self-reliance and ingenuity. These qualities made them the most technologically innovative people of the ancient world.

For example, despite the fact that their land had no mineral deposits, the Sumerians became skilled metallurgists. By 6000 B.C.E., a number of cultures throughout the Near East and Europe had learned how to produce weapons and tools using copper. By the Uruk Period (4300–2900 B.C.E.), trade routes were bringing this raw element into Sumer, where it was processed into weapons and tools. Shortly before 3000 B.C.E., people further discovered that

SUMERIAN WAR CHARIOTS. The earliest known representation of the wheel, dating from about 2600 B.C.E., shows how wheels were fashioned from slabs of wood. (For a later Mesopotamian wheel with spokes, see the illustration on page 50.)

copper could be alloyed with arsenic (or later, tin) to produce bronze. Bronze is almost as malleable as copper, and it pours more easily into molds; but when cooled, it maintains its rigidity and shape even better than copper. For almost two thousand years, until about 1200 B.C.E. and the development of techniques for smelting iron, bronze was the strongest metal known to man—the most useful and, in war, the most deadly. Following the Greeks (see Chapter 3), we call this period the Bronze Age.

Alongside writing and the making of bronze, the invention of the wheel was the fundamental technological achievement of the era. The Sumerians were using potter's wheels by the middle of the fourth millennium B.C.E. and could produce high-quality clay vessels in greater quantity than ever before. By around 3200 B.C.E., the Sumerians were also using two- and four-wheeled chariots and carts drawn by donkeys. (Horses were unknown in the Near East until sometime between 2000 and 1700 B.C.E.). Chariots were another new and deadly military technology, giving warriors a tremendous advantage over armies on foot: the earliest depiction of their use, dating from 2600 B.C.E., shows one trampling an enemy. At the same time, wheeled carts dramatically increased the productivity of the Sumerian workforce.

Other inventions derived from the study of mathematics. In order to construct their elaborate irrigation systems, the Sumerians had to develop sophisticated measuring and surveying techniques as well as the art of map making. Agricultural needs may also lie behind the lunar calendar they invented, which consisted of twelve months, six lasting 30 days and six lasting 29 days. Since this produced a year of only 354 days, the Sumerians eventually began to add a month to their calendars every few years in order to predict the recurrence of the seasons with suffi-

cient accuracy. The Sumerian practice of dividing time into multiples of sixty has lasted to the present day, not only in our notion of the 30-day month but also in our division of the hour into sixty minutes, each comprised of sixty seconds. Mathematics also contributed to Sumerian architecture, allowing them to build domes and arches thousands of years before the Romans would adopt and spread these architectural forms throughout the West.

Sumerian technology depended not only on ingenuity but also the spread of information and raw materials through trade. Sumerian pioneers traced routes up and down the rivers and into the hinterlands of Mesopotamia, following the tributaries of the Tigris and Euphrates. They blazed trails across the deserts toward the west, where they interacted with and influenced the Egyptians. By sea, they traded with the peoples of the Persian Gulf and, directly or indirectly, with the civilizations of the Indus Valley (modern Pakistan and India). And, along with merchandise, they carried ideas: stories, art, the use of writing, and the whole cultural complex that arose from their way of life. The elements of civilization, which had fused in their urban crucible, would thus come together in many other places.

THE FIRST EMPIRES

Evidence shows that competition among Sumerian city-states reached a new level around 2500 B.C.E., as ambitious lugals vied to magnify themselves and their kingdoms. Still, it seems that no Sumerian lugal ever attempted to create an empire by imposing centralized rule on the cities he conquered. As a result, Sumer remained a collection of interdependent but mutually hostile states whose rulers were unable to forge any lasting structures of authority. This pattern would ultimately make the people of Sumer vulnerable to a new style of imperial rulership imposed on them from the north, in the person of Sargon the Akkadian.

Sargon and the Akkadian Empire, 2350–2160 B.C.E.

The Akkadians were the predominant people of central Mesopotamia. Their Sumerian neighbors to the south had greatly influenced them, and they had adopted cuneiform script along with many other elements of Sumerian culture. Yet the Akkadians preserved their own Semitic language, part of the linguistic family that includes Hebrew and Arabic. Sumerians tended to regard them as uncivilized, but in the case of the lugal whom the Akkadians called "great king," this probably meant not being bound by the conventions of Sumerian warfare. For Sargon initiated a systematic program of conquest designed to subject all the neighboring regions to his authority. By 2350 B.C.E., he had conquered the cities of Sumer and then moved to establish direct control over all of Mesopotamia.

From his capital at Akkad, Sargon installed Akkadian-speaking governors to rule the cities of Sumer, ordering them to pull down existing fortifications, collect taxes, and impose his will. Sargon thus transformed the independent city-states of Sumer and Akkad into a much larger political unit: the first known empire, a word derived from the Latin *imperium*, "command." This enabled him to manage and exploit the network of trade routes crisscrossing the Near East. So although his political influence was felt only in Mesopotamia, his economic influence stretched from Ethiopia to India. Sargon's capital became the most splendid city in the world, and he exercised unprecedented power for a remarkable fifty-six years. Sargon's imperialism had a marked effect on Sumerian religion. To unite the two halves of his empire, Sargon merged Akkadian and Sumerian divinities. He also tried to lessen the rivalry of Sumerian cities by appointing a single Akkadian high priest or priestess, often a member of his own family, to preside over several temples.

Sargon's successor, his grandson Naram-Sin, extended Akkadian conquests and consolidated trade, helping to stimulate the growth of cities throughout the Near East and binding them more closely together. By 2200 B.C.E., most people in central and southern Mesopotamia would have been able to converse in the language of either the Sumerians or the Akkadians. Indeed, the two civilizations became virtually indistinguishable except for these different languages.

The Dynasty of Ur and the Amorites, 2100–1800 B.C.E.

After Naram-Sin's death, Akkadian rule faltered. Around 2100 B.C.E., however, a new dynasty came to power in Ur under its first king, Ur-Nammu, and his son Shulgi. Ur-Nammu was responsible for the construction of the great ziggurat at Ur, a massive temple complex that originally rose seventy feet above the surrounding plain. Shulgi continued his father's work, subduing the lands up to the

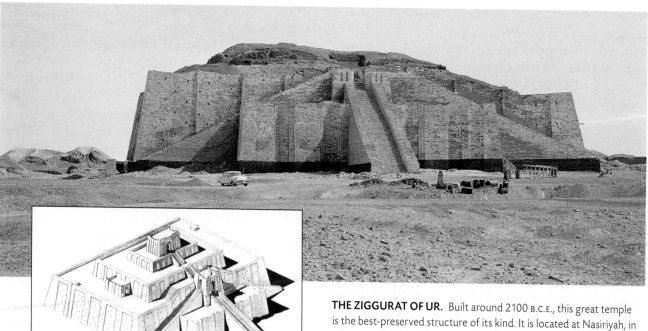

THE ZIGGURAT OF UR. Built around 2100 B.C.E., this great temple is the best-preserved structure of its kind. It is located at Nasiriyah, in what is now Iraq. Archeological investigations (see diagram) reveal that its central shrine, the most sacred part of the temple, was reached by climbing four sets of stairs and passing through a massive portal.

Zagros Mountains northeast of Ur and demanding massive tribute payments from them; one collection site accounted for 350,000 sheep per year, and Shulgi built state-run textile-production facilities to process the wool. He promulgated a code of law, calling for fair weights and measures, the protection of widows and orphans, and limitations on the death penalty for crimes. He also pursued military conquests, the centralization of government, commercial expansion and consolidation, and the patronage of art and literature. Shulgi thus established a pattern of rule that influenced the region for centuries to come.

The Empire of Hammurabi

In 1792 B.C.E., a young Amorite chieftain named Hammurabi (*hah-muh-RAH-bee*) became the ruler of Babylon, an insignificant city in central Mesopotamia. The Amorites, like the Akkadians, were a Semitic people. Until this period they had largely been nomads and warriors, but now they came to control the ancient cities of Mesopotamia.

Hammurabi may have been the first ruler in history to understand that power need not be based on force. He recognized that military intelligence, diplomacy, and strategic planning might accomplish what his small army could not. For Hammurabi used writing itself as a weapon. He did not try to confront his mightier neighbors directly. Rather, through letters and embassies, double-dealing and cunning, he induced his stronger counterparts to fight each other. While other Amorite kings exhausted their resources in costly wars, Hammurabi fanned their mutual hatred and skillfully portrayed himself as a friend and ally to all sides. Meanwhile, he quietly strengthened his kingdom, built up his army, and, when the time was right, fell on his depleted neighbors. By such policies, he transformed his small state into what historians call the Old Babylonian Empire.

Under Hammurabi's rule, Mesopotamia achieved an unprecedented degree of political integration. Ultimately, his empire stretched from the Persian Gulf into Assyria. To help unify these territories, Hammurabi introduced another innovation, promoting the worship of the little-known patron god of Babylon, Marduk, and making him the ruler-god of his entire empire. Although he also paid homage to the ancient gods of Sumer and Akkad, Hammurabi made it clear that all his subjects now owed allegiance to Marduk.

The idea that political power derives from divine approval was nothing new, but Hammurabi's genius was to use Marduk's supremacy over all other gods to legitimate his own claim to rule in Marduk's name, because he was king of Marduk's home city. Hammurabi thus became the first known ruler to launch wars of aggression justified in the name of his primary god. This set a precedent for colonial expansion that would become a characteristic feature of Near Eastern politics, as we will see in Chapter 2, and that lies behind nearly all imperial ventures down to the present day.

Yet Hammurabi did not rely solely on religion to bind his empire together. Building on the precedents of past rulers, he also issued a collection of laws, copies of which were inscribed on stone and set up in public places throughout his realm. The example that survives (see page 17) is an eight-foot-tall *stele* (*STEE-lee*) made of gleaming black basalt, originally erected in a central marketplace. The upper portion shows Hammurabi consulting with the god of justice. The phallic form on which the laws were inscribed would have been immediately recognizable as a potent symbol of Hammurabi's authority, obvious even to those who could not read the laws themselves. (It still makes a strong impression on visitors to the Louvre museum in Paris.)

It is impossible to overemphasize the importance of Hammurabi's decision to become a lawgiver. By collecting and codifying legal precedents, like those of Shulgi, Hammurabi declared himself to be (as he stated in the code's preamble) "the shepherd of the people, the capable king"— not a lugal ruling through fear and caprice. This was setting a new standard of kingship, and expressing a new vision of empire as a union of peoples subject to the same laws.

Law and Society Under Hammurabi

The code of Hammurabi reveals a great deal about the structure and values of Babylonian society. Its 282 pronouncements begin with legislation against false testimony (fraud or lying under oath) and theft; followed by laws regulating business deals; laws regulating the use of public resources, especially water; laws relating to taverns and brothels, many of which appear to have been run by women; laws relating to debt and slavery; many laws dealing with marriage, inheritance, divorce, and widows' rights; and finally laws punishing murder, violent assault, and even medical malpractice. What emerges is a fascinating picture of a complex urban culture that required more formal legislation than the accumulated customs of previous generations.

The division among classes in Babylonian society was marked. As Hammurabi's code indicates, an offense

Analyzing Primary Sources

The Code of Hammurabi

The laws of Hammurabi, published on the authority of this powerful king and set up in central places throughout the Old Babylonian Empire, were influenced both by the needs of an urban society and by older ideas of justice and punishment common among Semitic peoples. In its entirety, the code comprises 282 laws, beginning and ending with statements of Hammurabi's devotion to the gods, his peace-keeping mission, and his sense of his duties as king. The following excerpts are numbered so as to show the order in which these provisions appear on the stele that publicizes them.

hen the god Marduk commanded me to provide just ways for the people of the land in order to attain appropriate behavior, I established truth and justice as the declaration of the land. I enhanced the well-being of the people.

* * *

1. If a man accuses another man and charges him with homicide but cannot bring proof against him, his accuser shall be killed.

2. If a man charges another man with practicing witchcraft but cannot bring proof against him, he who is charged with witchcraft shall go to the divine River Ordeal, he shall indeed submit to the divine River Ordeal; if the divine River Ordeal should overwhelm him,

his accuser shall take full legal possession of his estate; if the divine River Ordeal should clear that man and should he survive, he who made the charge of witchcraft against him shall be killed; he who submitted to the divine River Ordeal shall take full legal possession of his accuser's estate.

If a man comes forward to give false testimony in a case but cannot bring evidence for his accusation, if that case involves a capital offense, that man shall be killed.

* * *

6. If a man steals valuables belonging to the god or to the palace, that man shall be killed, and also he who received the stolen goods from him shall be killed.

7. If a man should purchase silver, gold, a slave, a slave woman, an ox, a sheep, a

donkey, or anything else whatsoever, from a son of a man or from a slave of a man without witnesses or a contract— or if he accepts the goods for safe-keeping—that man is a thief, he shall be killed.

8. If a man steals an ox, a sheep, a donkey, a pig, or a boat—if it belongs either to the god or to the palace, he shall give thirtyfold; if it belongs to a commoner, he shall replace it tenfold; if the thief does not have anything to give, he shall be killed.

* * *

15. If a man should enable a palace slave, a palace slave woman, a commoner's slave, or a commoner's slave woman to leave through the main city-gate, he shall be killed.

* * *

committed against a nobleman carried a far more severe penalty than did the same crime committed against a social equal, or against a dependent or slave; nobles were also punished more severely than were commoners for crimes they committed against other nobles. Hammurabi's code also provides evidence as to the status of women in Babylonian society, and shows that they enjoyed certain important protections under the law, including the right to divorce abusive or indigent husbands. If a husband divorced a wife "without cause," he was obliged to provide financial support for her and their children. However, a wife who went

around the city defaming her spouse was subject to severe punishment, and she would risk death (as would her lover) if she were caught in adultery. The sexual promiscuity of husbands, by contrast, was protected under the law.

Hammurabi died around 1750 B.C.E., but his administrative efforts had created a durable state in Mesopotamia. For another two centuries, the Old Babylonian Empire played a significant role in the Near East, until invaders from the north sacked the capital and occupied it. But even for another thousand years thereafter, Babylon remained the region's most famous city.

53. If a man neglects to reinforce the embankment of the irrigation canal of his field and then a breach opens and allows the water to carry away the common irrigated area, the man in whose embankment the breach opened shall replace the grain whose loss he caused.

* * *

104. If a merchant gives a trading agent grain, wool, oil, or any other commodity for local transactions, the trading agent shall collect a sealed receipt for each payment in silver that he gives to the merchant.

* * *

128. If a man marries a wife but does not draw up a formal contract for her, she is not a wife.

129. If a man's wife should be seized lying with another male, they shall bind them and throw them into the water; if the wife's master allows his wife to live, then the king shall allow his subject (i.e., the other male) to live.

* * *

142. If a woman repudiates her husband, and declares, "You will not have marital relations with me"—her circumstances shall be investigated by the authorities of her city quarter, and if she is circumspect and without fault, but her husband is wayward and disparages her greatly, that woman will not be subject to any penalty; she shall take her dowry and she shall depart for her father's house.

Source: Martha T. Roth, ed., *Law Collections from Ancient Mesopotamia and Asia Minor* (Atlanta, GA: 1995), pp. 76–135 (excerpted).

Questions for Analysis

1. Based on these excerpts, what conclusions can you draw about the values of Old Babylonian society? For example, what types of crimes are punishable by death, and why?

2. In what ways does the code of Hammurabi exhibit the influences of the urban civilization for which these laws were issued? What are some characteristics and consequences of urbanization? What, for example, do we learn about economic developments?

The Code of Hammurabi. The laws of Hammurabi survive on an eight-foot column made of basalt. The top quarter of the column depicts the Babylonian king (standing, at left) being vested with authority by Shamash, the god of justice. Directly below, one can make out the cuneiform inscriptions that are the law code's text. How would the very format of these laws send a powerful message about Hammurabi's kingship?

THE DEVELOPMENT OF CIVILIZATION IN EGYPT

At about the same time that Sumerian civilization was transforming Mesopotamia, another civilization was taking shape in a very different part of the world and in very different ways. Unlike the Sumerians, the Egyptians did not have to wrest survival from a hostile and unpredictable environment. Instead, their land was renewed every year by the flooding of the Nile River. The fertile black soil left behind every summer made theirs the richest agricultural region in the entire Mediterranean world.

The distinctiveness of Egyptian civilization rests on this fundamental ecological fact. It also explains why ancient Egypt was a narrow, elongated kingdom, running along the Nile north from the First Cataract toward the Mediteranean Sea for a distance of more than 600 miles (1,100 km). Outside this narrow band of territory—which ranged from a few hundred yards to no more than 14 miles (23 km)—lay uninhabitable desert. This contrast, between the fertile Black Land along the Nile and the dessicated Red

Land beyond, deeply influenced the Egyptian worldview, in which the Nile itself was the center of the cosmos and the lands beyond were hostile.

Ancient Egyptian civilization enjoyed a remarkable continuity. Its roots date back to (at least) 5000 B.C.E. From about 3000 B.C.E. the defining element of this civilization would be the pervasive influence of a powerful, centralized, bureaucratic state headed by pharaohs who were regarded as living gods. No other civilization in world history has ever been governed so steadily, for so long, as ancient Egypt.

For convenience, historians have traditionally divided ancient Egyptian history into distinctive "kingdoms" and "periods." Following ancient Egyptian chroniclers, modern historians have also tended to portray these Old, Middle, and New Kingdoms as characterized by unity and prosperity, punctuated by chaotic interludes when central authority broke down: the so-called Intermediate Periods. Like all attempts at periodization, these divisions do not capture the complexities of human experience or even the real pace of historical development.

Predynastic Egypt, c. 10,000–3100 B.C.E.

The phrase "Predynastic Egypt" refers to the period before the emergence of the pharaohs and their royal dynasties—an era for which archeological evidence is difficult to find and interpret. The first-known permanent settlement in Egypt, situated at the southwestern edge of the Nile Delta near the modern town of Merimde Beni Salama, dates to approximately 4750 B.C.E. It was a farming community that may have numbered as many as 16,000 residents, and this number suggests that some Egyptian communities were much larger than those of a comparable period in Mesopotamia. Many other Neolithic farming centers have also been discovered in or near the Nile Delta, where a degree of cultural cohesiveness was already developing, fostered by shared interests and trade. In later centuries, this northern area would be known as Lower Egypt, so called because it was downstream.

Although towns in Lower Egypt were numerous, it was in Upper Egypt that the first Egyptian cities developed. By 3200 B.C.E. (when the Sumerian city of Uruk had been thriving for a thousand years), important communities such as Nekhen, This, and Abydos had all developed high degrees of occupational and social specialization. They had encircled themselves with sophisticated fortifications and had begun to build elaborate shrines to honor their gods. Indeed, the establishment of permanent sites of public worship may be key to explaining the growth of these towns into cities. As in Mesopotamia, a city's role as the center of a prominent religious cult attracted travelers and encouraged the growth of industries. And travel in Upper Egypt was relatively easy compared to Mesopotamia. The Nile bound cities together, and almost all Egyptians lived within sight of it.

It was due to the Nile, therefore, that the region south of the delta was able to forge a cultural and eventually a political unity, despite its enormous length. The Nile fed Egypt and was a conduit for people, goods, and ideas. Centralizing rulers could project their power quickly and effectively up and down its course. Within a remarkably short time, just a century or two after the first cities' appearance in Upper Egypt, they had banded together in a confederacy under the leadership of This. The pressure exerted by this confederacy in turn forced the towns of Lower Egypt to adopt their own form of political organization. By 3100 B.C.E., the rivalry between these competing regions had given rise to the two nascent kingdoms of Upper and Lower Egypt.

The Power of the Pharaoh, c. 3100–c. 2686 B.C.E.

With the rise of powerful rulers in these two kingdoms, Egyptian history enters a new phase, one that can be chronicled with unusual precision. The system for numbering the ruling dynasties that emerged in this era—known as the Archaic Period—was actually devised nearly three thousand years later by an historian named Manetho (mahn-EH-thoh), who wrote in the third century B.C.E. By and large, Manetho's work has withstood the scrutiny of modern historians and archeologists, although recent research has added a "Zero Dynasty" of early kings who were instrumental in bringing about the initial unification of Egypt.

Manetho did not record these rulers because he didn't know about them; we know them almost exclusively from archeological evidence. Among them was an Upper Egyptian warlord known to us as King Scorpion, because the image of a scorpion accompanies engravings that assert his authority. Another warlord, King Narmer, appears to have ruled both Upper and Lower Egypt. His exploits, too, come down to us in powerful pictures (see **Interpreting Visual Evidence**). Both of these kings probably came from Abydos in Upper Egypt, where they were buried. Their administrative capital, however, was at Memphis, the capital city of Lower Egypt and an important center for trade with the Sinai Peninsula and the Near East.

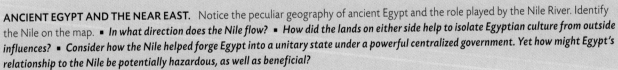

ANCIENT EGYPT AND THE NEAR EAST. Notice the peculiar geography of ancient Egypt and the role played by the Nile River. Identify the Nile on the map. ■ *In what direction does the Nile flow?* ■ *How did the lands on either side help to isolate Egyptian culture from outside influences?* ■ *Consider how the Nile helped forge Egypt into a unitary state under a powerful centralized government. Yet how might Egypt's relationship to the Nile be potentially hazardous, as well as beneficial?*

Following the political unification of Upper and Lower Egypt, the basic features of Egypt's distinctive centralized kingship took shape along lines that would persist for the next 3,000 years. The title used to describe this kingship was *pharaoh*, a word that actually means "great household" and thus refers not to an individual king but to the whole apparatus that sustains his rule. This fact, in turn, helps to explain the extraordinary stability and longevity of Egyptian civilization, which could survive even a dynastic takeover by

Macedonian Greeks in the century before Manetho wrote his chronicle. Indeed, it is comparable to some modern forms of government—none of which has yet lasted so long. As we have seen, kingship in Mesopotamia tended to be a form of personal rule, dependent on the charisma of a particular individual. But in Egypt, the office of the pharaoh was durable enough to survive the deaths of many individual successors, facilitating the peaceful transition of power to new rulers and withstanding the incompetence of many.

The Narmer Palette

he Narmer Palette (c. 3100 B.C.E.) is a double-sided carving made of green silt-stone. Palettes were used to grind pigments for the making of cosmetics, but the large size (63 cm, over 2 feet) of this one is unusual. It was discovered in 1897 by archeologists excavating a temple dedicated to the god Horus at Nekhen, the capital of Upper Egypt. Found nearby were other artifacts, including the so-called Narmer Macehead, thought to depict the marriage of Narmer, king of Upper Egypt, to a princess of Lower Egypt.

On the left, dominating the central panel, Narmer wears the White Crown of Upper Egypt (image A). He wields a mace and seizes the hair of a captive kneeling at his feet. Above the captive's head is a cluster of lotus leaves (a symbol of Lower Egypt) and a falcon representing the god Horus, who may be drawing the captive's life force (*ka*) from his body. The figure behind Narmer is carrying the king's sandals; he is depicted as smaller because he is an inferior. The two men in the lower panel are either running or sprawling on the ground, and the symbols above them indicate the name of a defeated town. On the right, the other side of the palette shows Narmer as the chief figure in a procession (image B). He now wears the Red Crown of Lower

A. Narmer wearing the White Crown of Egypt.

B. Narmer wearing the Red Crown of Egypt.

Egypt and holds a mace and a flail, symbols of conquest. Behind him is the same servant carrying his sandals, and in front of him are a man with long hair and four standard-bearers. There are also ten headless corpses. Below, the entwined necks of two mythical creatures (serpopards, leopards with serpents' heads) are tethered to leashes held by two men. In the lowest section, a bull tramples the body of a man whose city he is destroying.

Questions for Analysis

1. This artifact has been called "the first historical document in the world," but scholars are still debating its meanings.

For example, does it represent something that actually happened, or is it political propaganda? In your view, is this proof that Narmer has united two kingdoms? Why or why not?

2. Do the two sides of the palette tell a coherent story and, if so, on which side does that story begin?

3. What might be significant about the site where the palette was found? Should the palette be interpreted as belonging with the mace found nearby? If so, how might that influence your interpretation of the palette's significance?

This was accomplished, as we shall see, by the efficiency of palace bureaucracy, but it was also a function of the pharaoh's close identification with the divine forces credited with renewing Egypt every year. Like the seasons, the pharaoh died only to be born again, renewed and empowered.

Egyptian rulers thus laid claim to a sacred nature quite different—and much more benign—than that governing Sumeria. And they were more powerful than any Sumerian lugal, who was never more than a mortal who enjoyed (an all too temporary) divine favor.

How the earliest kings of Egypt came to be distinguished as pharaohs and to establish their claims to divinity is still not well understood. We do know, however, that legitimating their rule over all Egypt was difficult. Local civic and religious loyalties remained strong, and for centuries Lower Egyptians would continue to see themselves as distinct from their neighbors to the south. Indeed, it seems probable that the centralization of government in the person of the pharaoh and his association with divinity were related approaches to solving the problem of political unity. And together, these measures had astonishing success. By the end of the Second Dynasty, which coincides with the end of the Archaic Period (2686 B.C.E.), the pharaoh was not just the ruler of Egypt, he *was* Egypt: a personification of the land, the people, and their gods.

The Old Kingdom, C. 2686–2160 B.C.E.

Because so few written sources from the Old Kingdom survive (see below), historians have to rely on funerary texts from the tombs of the elite. These sources are hardly representative, and they have tended to convey the impression that Egyptians were obsessed with death; they also tell us little about the lives of ordinary people. Further complicating the historian's task is the early Egyptians' own belief in the unchanging, cyclical nature of the universe. This makes it difficult for us to reconstruct their history in detail.

However, the surviving inscriptions, papyri, and art of the Third Dynasty (c. 2686–2613 B.C.E.) do tell us a great deal about the workings of the "great household" that undergirded individual rulers' power. This power was vast because the pharaoh was considered to be the intermediary between the land, its people, and their gods, so all the resources of Egypt belonged to him. Long-distance trade was entirely controlled by the pharaoh, as were systems for imposing taxation and conscripting labor. To administer these, the pharaohs installed provincial governors, known to the Greeks as *nomarchs*, many of whom were members of the pharaoh's own family.

Old Kingdom pharaohs kept tight control over the nomarchs and their armies of lesser officials in order to prevent them from establishing local roots in the territories they administered. Writing was therefore critical to internal communication and the management and exploitation of Egypt's vast wealth. This gave rise to a whole class of scribal administrators who enjoyed the power, influence, and status that went along with literacy, a skill few people could command—especially in Egypt, since few could master the

THE ROSETTA STONE. This famous stone, carved in 196 B.C.E., preserves three translations of a single decree in three different forms of writing: hieroglyphs (top), demotic Egyptian (middle), and classical Greek (bottom). ▪ *Why would scholars be able to use the classical Greek text to decipher the hieroglyphic and demotic scripts?*

intricacies of hieroglyphic reading or writing. Even a child just beginning his scribal education was considered worthy of great respect because the training was so difficult. But it carried great rewards. Indeed, the scribal author of a document from the Middle Kingdom called "The Satire of the Trades" exhorted the beginning student to persevere by reminding him how much better off he would be than everyone else.

The Power of Writing

Among the many facets of Egyptian culture that have fascinated generations of scholars is the Egyptian system of pictographic writing. Called *hieroglyphs* (HI-eroh-glifs) or "sacred carvings" by the Greeks, these strange and elaborate symbols remained completely impenetrable (and thus all the more mysterious) until the nineteenth century, when a French scholar named Jean François Champollion deciphered them with the help of history's most famous decoding device, the Rosetta Stone. This *stele* preserves three versions of the same decree issued in 196 B.C.E., written in ancient Greek, demotic (a later Egyptian script), and hieroglyphics—still in use after more than 3,000 years. Because he could read the text in Greek, Champollion was eventually able to translate the demotic and hieroglyphic texts as well. From this beginning, generations of scholars have added to and refined the knowledge of ancient Egyptian language.

The development of hieroglyphic writing in Egypt dates to around 3200 B.C.E., when pictograms begin to appear in Mesopotamia. But the uses of writing for government and administration developed far more quickly in Egypt than in Sumer. And unlike Sumerian cuneiform, Egyptian hieroglyphics never evolved into a system of phonograms. Instead, the Egyptians developed a faster, cursive script for representing hieroglyphics called *hieratic*, which they employed for the everyday business of government and commerce. They also developed a shorthand version that scribes could use for rapid note-taking. Little of this hieratic script remains, however, due to the perishable nature of the medium on which it was usually written, papyrus. Produced by hammering, drying, and processing river reeds, papyrus was much lighter, easier to write on, and more transportable than the clay tablets used by the Sumerians. When sewn together into scrolls, papyrus also made it possible to record and store large quantities of information in very small packages. Production of this versatile writing material remained one of Egypt's most important industries and exports throughout antiquity and into the Middle Ages. Yet even in the arid environment of Egypt, which has preserved so many ancient artifacts, papyrus is fragile and subject to decay. Compared to the huge volume of papryrus documents that would have been produced, therefore, the quantity that survives is small, and this significantly limits our understanding of Old Kingdom Egypt.

The origins of the ancient Egyptian language in which these texts were written has long been a matter of debate, and it can be plausibly linked to both the Semitic languages of the Near East and a number of African language groups. Whatever its origins, the Egyptian language has enjoyed a long history. Eventually, it became the tongue known as Coptic, which is still used today in the liturgy of the Coptic Christian church in Ethiopia.

Imhotep and the Step Pyramid

One of the greatest administrative officials in the history of Egypt exemplifies both the skills and the possibilities for advancement that the consummate scribe could command.

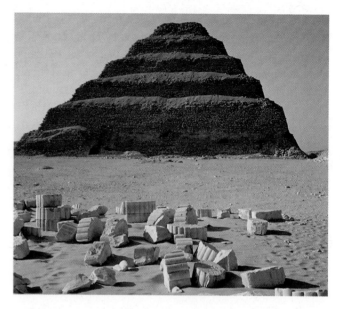

STEP PYRAMID OF KING DJOSER. This monument to the pharoah's power and divinity was designed by the palace official Imhotep around 2650 B.C.E. It served as a prototype for the pyramids constructed at Giza in the following century.

Imhotep (*im-HO-tep*) rose through the ranks of the pharaoh's administration to become a sort of prime minister, the right-hand man to Djoser (*ZOH-ser*), a pharaoh of the Third Dynasty (c. 2686–2613 B.C.E.). Imhotep's learning included medicine, astronomy, theology, and mathematics, but above all he was an architect. Earlier pharaohs had already devoted enormous resources to their burial arrangements at Abydos. It was Imhotep, however, who designed the Step Pyramid, the first building in history constructed entirely of dressed stone. It was not only to be the final resting place of Djoser but an expression of his transcendent power as the pharaoh.

Built west of the administrative capital at Memphis, the Step Pyramid towers over the desert to a height of 200 feet. Surrounding this structure was a huge temple and mortuary complex, perhaps modeled after Djoser's palace. These buildings served two purposes. First and foremost, they would provide Djoser's *ka*, his spirit, with a habitation and sustenance in the afterlife. Second, the design of the buildings, with their labyrinthine passageways, would (it was hoped) thwart tomb robbers, a chronic problem as pharaonic burials became more and more tempting to thieves.

Imhotep set a precedent to which all other Old Kingdom pharaohs would aspire. The pyramids on the plain of Giza, built during the Fourth Dynasty (2613–2494 B.C.E.), are a case in point. The Great Pyramid itself, built for the pharaoh Khufu (*KOO-foo*, called Cheops by the Greeks), was originally 481 feet high and 756 feet along each side of its base, constructed from more than 2.3 million limestone blocks and enclosing a volume of about 91 million cubic feet. In ancient times, the entire pyramid was encased in gleaming white limestone and topped by a gilded capstone, as were the two massive but slightly smaller pyramids built for Khufu's successors. During the Middle Ages, the Muslim rulers of nearby Cairo had their builders strip off the pyramid's casing stones and used them to construct and fortify their new city. (The gold capstones had probably disappeared already.) But in antiquity these pyramids would have glistened brilliantly by day and glowed by night, making them visible for miles in all directions. The Greek historian Herodotus (*heh-RAH-duh-tuhs*), who toured Egypt more than 2,000 years after the pyramids were built, estimated that it must have taken 100,000 laborers 20 years to build the Great Pyramid. This is probably an exaggeration, but it is a measure of the impression these monuments made.

Once thought to have been the work of slaves, the pyramids were in fact raised by tens of thousands of peasant workers, who labored most intensively on the pyramids while their fields were under water during the Nile's annual flood. Still, the investment of human and material resources required to build the great pyramids put grave strains on Egyptian society. Control over the lives of individual Egyptians increased and the number of administrative officials employed by the state grew ever larger. So too did the contrast between the lifestyle of the pharaoh's splendid court at Memphis and that of Egyptian society as a whole.

The End of the Old Kingdom

For reasons that are not entirely clear, the Fifth and Sixth Dynasties of the Old Kingdom (2494–2181 B.C.E.) witnessed the slow erosion of pharaonic power. Although pyramid construction continued, the monuments of this period are less impressive in design, craftsmanship, and size, perhaps mirroring the diminishing prestige of the pharaohs who ordered them built. Instead, the priesthood of Ra at Nekhen, which was the center of worship for the god Horus and the place where Narmer's unification of Egypt was memorialized, began to assert its own authority over that of the pharaoh. Ultimately, it declared that the pharaoh was not an incarnation of Horus or Ra, but merely the god's earthly son. This was a blow to the heart of Egyptian political theology. More practically threatening was the growing power of the pharaoh's nomarchs, whose increased authority in the provinces allowed them to become a hereditary local nobility: precisely what the vigorous kings of earlier dynasties had refused to permit.

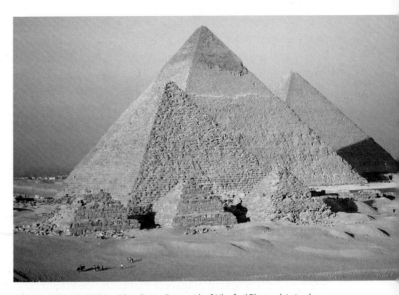

PYRAMIDS AT GIZA. The Great Pyramid of Khufu (Cheops) is in the center, and was completed c. 2560 B.C.E. The pyramids are not only monuments to pharaonic power, they exemplify the enormous wealth and human resources of Egyptian society.

Scholars are uncertain as to how certain priests and local officials were able to take power away from the pharaonic center. It may be that the costly building efforts of the Fourth Dynasty had overstrained the economy, while the continued channeling of resources to the royal capital at Memphis increased shortages and resentments in the provinces. Other evidence points to changing climatic conditions that may have disrupted the regular inundations of the Nile, leading to famine in the countryside. Meanwhile, small states were beginning to form to the south in Nubia. With better organization and equipment, the Nubians may have restricted Egyptian access to precious metal deposits, further crippling the Egyptian economy.

As a result, the pharaoh's power diminished accordingly. Local governors and religious authorities began to emerge as the only effective guarantors of stability and order. By 2160 B.C.E., which marks the beginning of what historians call the First Intermediate Period, Egypt had effectively ceased to exist as a united entity. The central authority of the pharaoh in Memphis collapsed, and a more ancient distribution of power reemerged: a northern center of influence based at Herakleopolis (*her-ah-clay-OH-polis*) was opposed by a southern regime headquartered at Thebes, with families from each region claiming to be the legitimate pharaohs of all Egypt.

Compared to the centralized authority of the Old Kingdom, this looks like chaos. But redistribution of power always leads to some important developments in any society. In Egypt, wealth became much more widely and evenly diffused than it had been, as did access to education, the opportunities for the creation of art, and the possibilities for personal advancement. Resources that the pharaoh's court at Memphis had once monopolized now remained in the provinces, enabling local elites to emerge as both protectors of society and as patrons of local artisans. Many arts and luxuries—including elaborate rites for the dead—had been developed originally at the pharaoh's court, and limited to it. Now, however, they became available to Egyptian society as a whole.

EGYPTIAN SOCIETY AND CULTURE

Given the powerful impression conveyed by their monumental architecture, it may seem surprising that the ancient Egyptians lagged far behind the Sumerians and Akkadians in science and mathematics, as well as in the application of new technologies. Only in the calculation of time did the Egyptians make notable advances, since their close observation of the sun for religious and agricultural reasons led them to develop a solar calendar that was far more accurate than the Mesopotamian lunar calendar. Whereas the Sumerians have bequeathed to us their means of dividing and measuring the day, the Egyptian calendar is the direct ancestor of the Julian Calendar adopted for Rome by Julius Caesar in 45 B.C.E. (see Chapter 5) and later corrected by Pope Gregory XIII in 1582 C.E.: this is the calendar we use today.

The social pyramid of Old Kingdom Egypt was extremely steep. At its apex stood the pharaoh and his extended family, whose prestige and power set them entirely apart from all other Egyptians. Below them was a class of nobles, whose primary role was to serve as priests and officials of the pharaoh's government; scribes were usually recruited and trained from among the sons of these families. All of these Egyptian elites lived in considerable luxury. They owned extensive estates, exotic possessions, and fine furniture. They kept dogs and cats and monkeys as pets, and hunted and fished for sport.

Beneath this tiny minority was everyone else. Most Egyptians lived in crowded conditions in simple mud-brick dwellings. During a period of prosperity, master craftsmen—jewelers, goldsmiths, and the like—could improve their own conditions and those of their families by fulfilling the needs of the wealthy, but they did not constitute anything like a middle class. Other skilled professionals—potters, weavers, masons, bricklayers, brewers, merchants, and schoolteachers— also enjoyed some measure of respect as well as a higher standard of living. The vast majority of Egyptians, however, were laborers who provided the brute force necessary for agriculture and construction. Beneath them were slaves, typically captives from foreign wars rather than native Egyptians.

The Egyptians of this era apparently had no need for written laws beyond what was customary in their communities, or what was proclaimed as law by their pharaoh. Yet despite the enormous demands the pharaohs placed on Egypt's wealth, their rule does not appear to have been perceived as particularly oppressive. Commoners' belief in the pharaoh's divinity made them willing subjects, as did the material benefits of living in a stable, well-governed society. Even slaves had certain legal rights, including the ability to own, sell, and bequeath personal property.

Women in the Old Kingdom

Egyptian women also enjoyed unusual freedoms by the standards of the ancient world. Female commoners were recognized as persons in their own right and were allowed to initiate complaints (including suits for divorce), to defend themselves and act as witnesses, to possess property of their own, and to dispose of it: all without the sanction of a male guardian or representative, as was typically required in other ancient societies—and in most modern ones until the twentieth century. Women were not allowed to undergo formal scribal training, but surviving personal notes exchanged between high-born ladies suggest at least some degree of female literacy.

Women were also barred from holding high office, apart from that of priestess and also, importantly, queen. Queens are often represented as the partners of their royal husbands and were certainly instrumental in ruling alongside them. And occasionally, a woman from the royal family might assume pharaonic authority for a time, as did Queen Khasekhemwy (kah-sehk-KEM-wee, d. 2686 B.C.E.) on behalf of her son Djoser before he came of age. Some may even have ruled in their own right; this was certainly the case under the New Kingdom (see Chapter 2).

Gender divisions were less clearly defined among the peasantry. The limitations of our sources, however, means that we can only glimpse the lives of peasants through the eyes of their social superiors. Whatever their status, it seems that women did not enjoy sexual equality. While most Egyptians practiced monogamy, wealthy men could and did keep a number of lesser wives, concubines, and female slaves; and any Egyptian man, married or not, enjoyed freedoms that were denied to women, who would be subject to severe punishments under the law if they were viewed as guilty of any misconduct.

Egyptian Religion and Worldview

As noted above, the environment of Egypt and the special benefits it conferred on its inhabitants were construed as peculiar divine gifts, renewed each year through the mediation of the pharaoh, who was god on earth. Although the Egyptians told a variety of stories that dealt with the creation of their world, these were not greatly concerned with how humanity came to exist. Rather, what mattered was the means by which all life was created and re-created in an endless cycle of renewal. At the heart of Egyptian religion lay the myth of Osiris and Isis, two of the gods most fundamental to Egyptian belief. Osiris was, in a sense, the first pharaoh: the first god to hold kingship on earth. But his brother, Seth, wanted the throne for himself. So Seth betrayed and killed Osiris, sealing his body in a coffin. Then his loyal sister Isis retrieved the corpse and managed to revive it long enough to conceive her brother's child, the god Horus. Enraged by this, Seth seized Osiris' body and hacked it to pieces, spreading the remains all over Egypt. Still undeterred, Isis sought the help of Anubis, the god of the afterlife. Together, they found, reassembled, and preserved the scattered portions of Osiris' body, thus inventing the practice of mummification. Afterward, Horus, with the help of his mother, managed to defeat Seth. Osiris was avenged and revived as god of the underworld, and the cycle of his death, dismemberment, and resurrection was reflected in the yearly renewal of Egypt itself.

Life and Death in Ancient Egypt

In addition to embodying Egypt's continual regeneration, Osiris exemplified the Egyptian attitude toward death, which was very different from the Sumerians' bleak view. For the Egyptians, death was a rite of passage, a journey to be endured on the way to an afterlife that was more or less like one's earthly existence, only better. To be sure, the journey was full of dangers. After death, the individual body's *ka*, or life force, would have to roam the Duat, the underworld, searching for the House of Judgment. There, Osiris and forty-two other judges would decide the ka's fate. Demons and evil spirits might try to frustrate the ka's quest to reach the House of Judgment, and the journey might take some time. But if successful and judged worthy, the deceased would enjoy immortality as an aspect of Osiris.

Egyptian funerary rites aimed to emulate the example set by Isis and Anubis, who had carefully preserved the parts of Osiris' body and enabled his afterlife. This is why the Egyptians developed their sophisticated techniques of embalming, whereby all of the body's vital organs were removed and then treated with chemicals—except for the heart, which played a key role in the ka's final judgment. A portrait mask was then placed on the mummy before burial, so that the deceased would be recognizable despite being wrapped in hundreds of yards of linen. To sustain the ka on his or her journey, food, clothing, utensils, weapons, and other items of vital importance would be placed in the grave along with the body.

"Coffin texts," or books of the dead, also accompanied the body and were designed to speed the ka's journey. They contained special instructions that would help the ka travel through the underworld and prepare it for the final test. They also described the "negative confession" the ka would make before the court of Osiris, a formal denial of offenses commited in life. The god Anubis would then weigh the deceased's heart against the principle of *ma'at*: truth, order, justice. Because ma'at was often envisioned as a goddess wearing a plumed headdress, a feather from this headdress would be placed in the scales opposite the heart; only if the heart was light (empty of wrongdoing) and in perfect balance with the feather would the ka achieve immortality.

This manner of confronting death has often led to the erroneous assumption that the ancient Egyptians were pessimistic, but in actuality their practices and beliefs were inherently life affirming, bolstered by confidence in the renewal of creation. Binding together this endless cycle was ma'at, the serene order of the universe, and embodying ma'at on earth was the pharaoh. But when that order broke down, so too did their confidence in the pharaoh's power.

The Widening Horizons of the Middle Kingdom (2055 – c. 1650 B.C.E.)

After the disruption of Old Kingdom authority around 2160 B.C.E., warfare between competing pharaonic dynasties would continue for over a century. Then, in 2055 B.C.E., the Theban king Mentuhotep II conquered the northerners and declared himself the ruler of a united Egypt. His reign marks the beginning of Egypt's Middle Kingdom and the reestablishment of a unified government, but this time centered in Thebes rather than Memphis. The architect of this new government was Mentuhotep's chief supporter, Amenemhet (*ah-meh-NEHM-het*), who seized power after the king's death and established himself and his descendants as Egypt's Twelfth Dynasty.

This succession of remarkable pharaohs remained in power for nearly 200 years, and under them the Egyptians began to exploit more thoroughly the potential for trade to the south. They secured their border with Nubia and began to send mounted expeditions to the land they called Punt, probably the coast of Somalia. By the middle of the nineteenth century B.C.E., Nubia was firmly under Egypt's control. Meanwhile, diplomatic relations with the smaller states and principalities of Palestine and Syria led to decisive Egyptian political and economic influence in this region. These lands were not incorporated into Egypt; instead, Amenemhet constructed the Walls of the Prince in Sinai to guard against incursions from the Near East.

These huge fortifications built along Egypt's new frontier demonstrate the great resourcefulness of the Twelfth Dynasty, and their very different ways of allocating resources and expressing ambition. As such, they also display a marked shift in the Egyptian outlook on the world. Gone was the placid serenity epitomized by ma'at and the shared devotion to the pharaoh that had built the pyramids. Egyptians could no longer be dismissive of outsiders or dis-

regard the world beyond their borders. Egypt was not yet an imperial power; the pharaohs of the Middle Kingdom made no attempt to absorb conquests into their kingdom. But unlike their Old Kingdom counterparts, the Egyptians of the Middle Kingdom were not turned in on themselves. Their attitude to the pharaoh also changed. Although they continued to enjoy special position as divine representatives, the pharaohs of the Middle Kingdom represented themselves as what they were expected to be—good shepherds, tenders of their flock. Only by diligently protecting Egypt from a hostile outside world could a pharaoh provide the peace, prosperity, and security desired by his subjects; his alignment with ma'at was now conditional, and it had to be earned.

The literature of the Middle Kingdom expresses the general change in attitude. Among the most popular literary forms were manuals ostensibly written by or for kings, detailing the duties and perils of high office and offering advice for dealing with difficult situations. These include *The Instruction of Ptah-Hotep*, an example of Egyptian "wisdom literature" attributed to a court official of the Old Kingdom, which achieved a wider readership in this new

After You Read
This Chapter

Ⓢ Visit StudySpace for quizzes, additional review materials, and multi-media documents. **wwnorton.com/studyspace**

REVIEWING THE OBJECTIVES

- The study of the distant past is challenging because written sources are rare. What other sources of information do historians use?
- All civilizations require the same basic things and share certain characteristics. What are they?
- The cities of Mesopotamia remained largely independent from one another, yet shared a common culture. Why was this the case?
- Hammurabi's empire created a new precedent for governance in Mesopotamia. How did he achieve this?
- The civilizations of ancient Mesopotamia and Egypt differ in profound ways. What were the major causes of their differences?

era. Ptah-Hotep's teaching is upbeat and practical; by contrast, the examples of this genre produced under the Middle Kingdom are bleakly pragmatic. Reading between the lines, we discern that Egyptians' sense of their own superiority—a product of their isolation and their comparatively benign environment—had been shattered. They saw themselves being drawn into a much wider world, and in the course of the next millennium, they would become more fully a part of it.

CONCLUSION

While the story of Babel records the legendary loss of communication, this chapter shows that people of the distant past can still speak to us. The marks they have left on the landscape, the remains of their daily lives, their written records, and their very bodies make it possible for historians to piece together the evidence and to make sense of it. And every year new sources come to light, meaning that we have to be ready to revise, constantly, our understanding of what happened in the past.

Although this chapter has emphasized the differences between the early civilizations of Mesopotamia and Egypt, it is worth noting some significant similarities. Both developed the fundamental technologies of writing at about the same time, and this facilitated political alliances, long-distance trade, and the transmission of vital information to posterity. During the third millennium, both underwent a process of political consolidation, an elaboration of religious ritual, and a melding of spiritual and political leadership. Both engaged in massive building and irrigation projects, and both commanded material and human resources on an enormous scale. At the same time, each of these civilizations cultivated an inward focus. Although they had some contact with each other, and some transfers of information and technology probably took place, there were few significant political or cultural interactions. For all intents and purposes, they inhabited separate worlds. This relative isolation was about to change, however. The next millennium would see the emergence of large-scale, land-based empires that would transform life in Mesopotamia, Egypt, and the lands that lay between them. These are the developments we examine in Chapter 2.

PEOPLE, IDEAS, AND EVENTS IN CONTEXT

- What fundamental changes associated with the **NEOLITHIC REVOLUTION** made early civilizations possible?
- What new technologies allowed the **SUMERIANS** to master the environment of **MESOPOTAMIA**, and how did these technologies contribute to the development of a new, urbanized society?
- By contrast, why did the Nile River foster a very different civilization and enable the centralized authority of the **PHARAOH**?
- How do the differences between **CUNEIFORM** and **HIEROGLYPHS** reflect the different circumstances in which they were invented and the different uses to which they were put?
- In what ways are the *EPIC OF GILGAMESH* and the *CODE OF HAMMURABI* rich sources of information about the civilizations of Sumer and **BABYLON**?
- How do the **ZIGGURATS** of Mesopotamia and the **PYRAMIDS** of Egypt exemplify different forms of power, different ideas about the gods, and different beliefs about the afterlife?
- Why was the worldview of ancient Egyptians, which was strongly reflected in the concept of **MA'AT** during the **OLD KINGDOM**, altered in significant ways by the time of the **MIDDLE KINGDOM**?

CONSEQUENCES

- How do the surviving sources of any period limit the kinds of questions that we can ask and answer about the distant past? In your view, are there sources for this early era that have been undervalued? For example, if writing had not been developed in Mesopotamia and Egypt, what would we still be able to know about the civilizations of these two regions?
- What features of ancient civilizations do modern civilizations share? What might be the implications of these shared ideas, social structures, and technologies?

Before You Read This Chapter

Peoples, Gods, and Empires, 1700–500 B.C.E.

CORE OBJECTIVES

- **DESCRIBE** the impact of new migrations and settlements on the ancient Near East.

- **DEFINE** the differences between Egypt's New Kingdom and the previous Old and Middle Kingdoms.

- **EXPLAIN** the workings of transnational networks in the late Bronze Age.

- **IDENTIFY** the new empires and kingdoms that emerged in the Iron Age.

- **UNDERSTAND** the historical importance of monotheism.

According to Hesiod, a Greek poet who flourished during the eighth century B.C.E., all of human history falls into five ages. The dawn of time was a golden age, when men lived like gods. Everything was good then, food was plentiful, and work was easy. The next age was silver, when men took gods for granted, killed one another, and lived in dishonor. So the gods destroyed them, sending a mighty flood that spared only the family of Deucalion, who built an ark. Then came the age of bronze, when everything was made of bronze—houses and armor and weapons and tools—and giants fought incessantly from huge strongholds, causing destruction so great that no man's name survives. The time following was short but bright, a heroic age, the time of men who ventured with Theseus and fought beside Achilles and sailed with Odysseus, men whose names will live forever. But Hesiod's own age was iron: a dull age, a time of tedium and strife and bickering and petty feuds.`

Hesiod's periodization captures an understanding of history that had evolved with humanity itself and reflects actual developments. The stories he knew told of a time before cities.

29

They recalled a time when the harmony between gods and men broke down, and the human race was saved by one man's ingenuity: Utnapishtim-Noah-Deucalion. They chronicled the wars of the age we still call Bronze, when the enormous abandoned palaces visible in Hesiod's day were built. And they remembered the race of heroes whose glory was measured by their abiding fame, and who bequeathed a further round of stories. Thanks to new archeological finds, new linguistic discoveries, and new efforts at decoding the historical record, we can both confirm and correct Hesiod's perspective on the past.

In the second millennium B.C.E., the ancient Near East was transformed by the arrival of new peoples and by the emergence of extensive land-based empires built up through systematic military conquest. These migrations and conquests caused upheaval, but they also led to cultural contact and economic integration. By the thirteenth century B.C.E., nations from the southern Balkans in Europe to the western fringes of Iran in the Ancient Near East had been drawn into a wide-ranging web of relationships.

But this extraordinary system proved more fragile than its participants could have imagined. Around 1200 B.C.E., a wave of mysterious invasions led to the destruction of nearly every Bronze Age civilization. As a result, around the turn of the first millennium B.C.E. we enter a new world organized along profoundly different lines. In this new age, iron would slowly replace bronze as the primary component of tools and weapons. New and more brutal empires would come to power, while new ideas about the divine and its relationship to humanity would emerge. Two of the Western world's most enduring religious traditions—Judaism and Zoroastrianism (*zoh-roh-AHS-tree-anism*)—were born, fundamentally altering conceptions of ethics, politics, and the natural world. This Iron Age would prove a fateful historical crossroads, as elements both old and new combined to reconfigure the ancient world.

INDO-EUROPEAN LANGUAGES AND PEOPLES

In 1786, a British judge serving in India made a discovery that transformed the understanding of history. Turning his spare time to the study of Sanskrit, the ancient language of South Asia, Sir William Jones discovered that it shares the same grammar and vocabulary as ancient Greek and Latin—to an extent inexplicable by sheer coincidence. He then examined the early Germanic and Celtic languages of Europe and the Old Persian language of the Near East, and found that they also exhibit marked similarities. He concluded that all of these languages must have evolved from a common source. Within another generation, the ancient language whose existence Jones had hypothesized, and the later languages derived from it, would be labeled Indo-European, reflecting their wide distribution from India to Ireland. The Biblical story of mankind's shared language, the story of Babel, turns out to be partly true.

Since then, scholars have greatly enlarged our understanding of Indo-European languages and their speakers. Yet much remains controversial. It is certain that Indo-European linguistic forms begin to appear in the Near East and eastern Mediterranean shortly after 2000 B.C.E. Around this same time, a group of Indo-European speakers also moved into the Aegean basin, where the resulting language became an early form of Greek. Other Indo-European speakers went east; some may have reached western China.

These were not the only new peoples moving into the Near East. As we noted in Chapter 1, Semitic-speaking peoples were also making their mark, beginning with the Akkadians and the Amorites, from whose ranks Hammurabi came. The Assyrians, the Phoenicians, and the Canaanites would also become prominent. These newcomers did not wipe out existing cultures; rather, they built on established patterns of urban life and organization. But their collective impact was enormous.

New Settlers in Anatolia

By 1900 B.C.E., the nomadic Assyrians had become caravan merchants whose extensive trade networks stretched across Anatolia and Mesopotamia. They relied on the protection of local rulers and, in turn, they made these rulers rich. They also served as advisers and officials, and married into important urban families. In the process, they carried Mesopotamian civilization and its trappings into far-flung regions.

In their wake, new population groups were attracted to Anatolia, northern Syria, and Mesopotamia. The most formidable of these were the Hittites, an Indo-European-speaking people who arrived around 2000 B.C.E. In contrast to the Assyrians, the Hittites were conquerors and colonists who imposed themselves and their language on the peoples they vanquished. By 1700 B.C.E., they had integrated many city-states into a larger kingdom.

The Hittites' warrior aristocracy fielded the most fearsome army of the Bronze Age. They were quick to adopt the latest technologies, including the chariot and (eventually) the use of iron for weaponry. But the Hittites also adopted the more peaceful practices of those they conquered, using cuneiform to record their own language and laws. And they sought to control trade routes, particularly the overland trade in copper and arsenic, the raw materials for making bronze. By 1595 B.C.E., they had captured Babylon.

A century later, the Kassites, another new people, moved into that devastated city. For the next 500 years, they presided over a largely prosperous Babylonian realm. The Hittites, however, continued to destabilize the region, until they were themselves checked by the arrival of a people known as the Mitannians, whose initial advantage was their use of horses, hitherto unknown outside the steppes of Asia. Their light, horse-drawn chariots became terrifying death-machines, transporting archers rapidly around the battlefield. The Mitannians also pioneered cavalry tactics. Eventually, however, their opponents borrowed these same technologies, and the Hittites once again achieved the advantage and turned their attention to Egypt.

THE NEW KINGDOM OF EGYPT

As we have seen, Egypt's Middle Kingdom had been formed by the many internal changes of the First Intermediate Period, chiefly the redistribution of wealth and power. Now it was further transformed by external forces, through the dynamic movement of new peoples. Some of these came to Egypt as immigrants; others were hired as mercenaries. And for a while, a strategy of accommodation preserved Egypt from large-scale armed attack and fostered commercial exchange with neighboring regions. But around 1700 B.C.E., Egypt was invaded for the first time since the unification of the Upper and Lower Kingdoms. These invaders' origins and identity remain mysterious; the Egyptians called them simply Hyksos (HIHK-sohs), "rulers of foreign lands." The Hyksos began to project their authority over most of Lower Egypt.

With this conquest, the central authority of the pharaoh once again dissolved and Egypt entered what scholars call the Second Intermediate Period (c. 1650–1550 B.C.E.). Significantly, however, the Hyksos took over the machinery of pharaonic government in Lower Egypt and took steps to legitimize their rule. In Upper Egypt, by contrast, Hyksos power was weak. Here, a native pharaonic regime maintained a tenuous independence at the traditional capital of Thebes.

Although the Hyksos established Lower Egypt as the most significant power in the Near East, their conquest also weakened the dominion of Upper Egypt over the Nubians, who eventually founded an independent kingdom called Kush. This Nubian kingdom posed a much greater threat to the native dynasty at Thebes than to the Hyksos in Lower Egypt—but it also provided additional incentive to southern pharaohs determined to oust the Hyksos. By the end of the sixteenth century B.C.E., the pharaoh Ahmose had driven them out, establishing the Eighteenth Dynasty and the New Kingdom of Egypt.

The Pharaohs of the Eighteenth Dynasty

Under the Eighteenth Dynasty, Egyptian civilization reached the height of its magnificence and power. Although many Egyptian traditions were renewed and strengthened, the dynamism of the New Kingdom—particularly its new focus on imperial expansion—changed the very fabric of Egyptian life, which had never before looked beyond the narrow world of the Nile Valley. Among the striking developments that took place during this period was the rise of a new aristocracy whose wealth was acquired through warfare and the winning of lands (with slaves to work them) which they received from the pharaoh as rewards for service. The Eighteenth Dynasty itself was forged in battle. Ahmose, the man who expelled the Hyksos, had been reared by the warrior queen Ahhotep. His eventual successor, Thutmose I (r. 1504–1492 B.C.E.), was the son of an unknown warrior who married Ahmose's daughter.

Under Thutmose's leadership, the Egyptians subdued the Nubians to the south, seizing control of their gold mines. They also penetrated beyond their northeastern frontier, driving deep into Palestine and Syria. By the time of his death, Thutmose could claim to rule the land from beyond the Nile's Fourth Cataract to the banks of the Euphrates. Never had Egypt so clearly declared its imperial ambitions. Nor was this success fleeting. The Egyptians would sustain a strong military presence in the Near East for the next 400 years.

The Legacy of Hatshepsut

The early death of Thutmose's son and successor could have resulted in a crisis for the Eighteenth Dynasty. Instead, it led to one of the most remarkable reigns in Egypt's history,

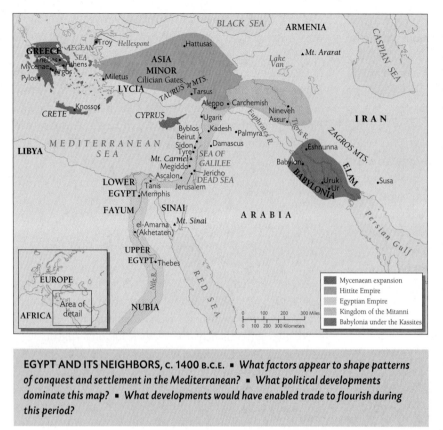

EGYPT AND ITS NEIGHBORS, C. 1400 B.C.E. ▪ *What factors appear to shape patterns of conquest and settlement in the Mediterranean?* ▪ *What political developments dominate this map?* ▪ *What developments would have enabled trade to flourish during this period?*

and extended trade. The arts also flourished, setting standards that would be emulated for a thousand years. Indeed, Hatshepsut was one of the most ambitious builders in Egyptian history, which is saying something. Her own mortuary temple was probably the first tomb constructed in the Valley of the Kings, the New Kingdom's answer to the pyramids.

Yet after Hatshepsut's death in 1458 B.C.E. her legacy was called into question. At some point late in her nephew's reign, attempts were made to remove her name from inscriptions and to destroy her images (see ***Interpreting Visual Evidence*** on page 34). Scholars used to assume that Thutmose himself was responsible for this, because he resented his stepmother/aunt's power over him. But more recent research has suggested that the culprit was his son, Amenhotep II (r. 1427–1400 B.C.E.), who was thereby blocking the claims of royal rivals, possibly Hatshepsut's daughter, Neferure.

for Thutmose II (r. 1492–1479 B.C.E.) passed the power of pharaoh to his sister, wife, and co-ruler Hatshepsut *(haht-SHEHP-soot*, r. 1479–1458 B.C.E.). Such brother-sister unions were common in the Egyptian royal family, although they do not appear to have been the routine way to produce royal children: pharaohs customarily kept a harem of subsidiary wives and concubines for this purpose. However, Thutmose II and Hatshepsut did conceive at least one child together, Neferure; in fact, she may have been their designated heir. For 21 years, Hatshepsut ruled as pharaoh in her own right, while her daughter took on the usual duties of queen.

Like her great-grandmother, Ahhotep, Hatshepsut was a warrior. Moroever, she was routinely protrayed on monuments and in statuary with the masculine figure and ceremonial beard characteristic of pharaohs. She did not pretend to be a man: inscriptions almost always indicate her gender, and she herself claimed to be the most beautiful woman in the world. But it was important to Egyptians that she use the conventional iconography of power to locate herself firmly within a long history of male dynastic rule.

Hatshepsut's statecraft proved crucial to the continuing success of Egypt. With her stepson/nephew, Thutmose III, she launched several successful military campaigns

The Power of the Priesthood

The great conquests of the Eighteenth Dynasty brought mind-boggling riches to Egypt. Much of this wealth went to the glorification of the pharaoh in the form of grand temples, tombs, and other monuments, including the thousands of steles that provide us with so much information about this era. Another significant portion of the plunder went to the military aristocracy that made such conquests possible. But the lion's share went to the gods as offerings of thanks. As the temples became wealthy and powerful, so too did their priests. But no temple complex was so well endowed as that of Amon at Thebes.

Thebes was not only the capital of New Kingdom Egypt, it was also the place most sacred to Amon (or Amun), the god of creation, who played an important role in the dynasty's self-image. Amon had come into prominence when the political center of gravity shifted to Thebes during the Middle Kingdom, and his cult had steadily increased in status and popularity. By 1550 B.C.E. he had become identified as another manifestation of the sun god Ra, and was believed to be the divine force behind the Eighteenth Dynasty's triumph over the Hyksos. This accounts for the favor shown to his priests at Thebes, who became a formidable political force. Eventually, they surpassed even the military aristocracy in importance and influence.

The Reign of Akhenaten (1352–1336 B.C.E.)

All of these factors are important when we consider the reign of Amenhotep IV, who inherited the vast, well-governed kingdom assembled by his predecessors. This young pharaoh showed an early inclination toward the worship of the sun, but not as an aspect of Amon. Instead, Amenhotep (whose dynastic name means "Amon Is Pleased") exalted Ra as a discrete divinity and laid aside the traditional iconography of this god as a falcon (or a falcon-headed man), replacing it with the symbol *Aten*, the hieroglyph representing the sun's rays. He then went farther, changing his own name to Akhenaten (*AH-keh-NAH-ton*), "He Who Is Profitable to the Aten," and building a new capital to honor the god. Located halfway between Memphis and Thebes, it was called Akhetaten ("The Horizon of the Aten").

Although the priesthood of Amon exalted Amon-Ra, it also recognized all the other gods of Egypt. Akhenaten's theology, by contrast, was closer to monotheism. And unlike traditional Egyptian deities, the Aten could not be imagined as taking on human or animal form. Akhenaten also celebrated his new religion by representing himself in a very unconventional way. In a complete departure from the divine virility of his ancestors—which even his ancestor Hatshepsut had emulated—Akhenaten had himself pictured as a family man enjoying the company of his wife, Nefertiti, and their children. This emphasis on his own humanity might have been an extension of his theology, which honored the life force within every being. But it was also dangerous to the ideology of royal power. The pharaoh was not supposed to be a man with quirky personality. He was supposed to be a god on earth.

Akhenaten's spiritual revolution therefore had enormous political implications. Not surprisingly, the priesthood of Amon also put up strenuous resistance. To make matters worse, Akhenaten did not balance his theological enthusiasm with attention to Egypt's interests abroad. This cost him the support of his nobility and may even have led to his deposition. He was ultimately succeeded by one of his younger sons, Tutankhaten ("Living Image of Aten"), a child of nine whose name was quickly changed to reflect the restoration of the god Amon and his priesthood. He became Tutankhamun (r. 1333–1324 B.C.E.), the boy king whose sumptuous tomb was discovered in

AKHENATEN, HIS WIFE NEFERTITI, AND THEIR CHILDREN. The Aten is depicted here as a sun disk, raining down power on the royal family. ▪ *What messages might this image have conveyed to contemporary Egyptians?* ▪ *How does this depiction of the pharaoh differ from earlier precedents?*

1922. After his early death, he was succeeded by a general called Horemheb, who reigned as the last pharaoh of the Eighteenth Dynasty. When he died, he passed his office to another general. This was Ramses, the founder of the Nineteenth Dynasty, who would restore Egypt to glory in the Near East.

TRANSNATIONAL NETWORKS OF THE LATE BRONZE AGE

Bronze Age history must be understood within the context of what we might call international relations. Yet it is more accurate to call the political and economic networks of this period *transnational*, because this web of alliances and relationships transcended any idea of national identity.

Transnational Diplomacy

The Late Bronze Age was an age of superpowers. The great pharaohs of the Eighteenth Dynasty had transformed Egypt into a conquering state, and the Hittites had created an empire out of the disparate city-states and kingdoms of Anatolia. The Assyrians controlled Near Eastern trade, and

Interpreting Visual Evidence

Remembering Hatshepsut

The pharaohs of Egypt's New Kingdom carefully controlled their public images. The visual language they used was highly symbolic, an iconography (vocabulary of images) intended to make each successive pharaoh look as much like his royal predecessors as possible: god-like, steadfast, virile, authoritative—even when the pharaoh was a woman, Hatshepsut (r. 1479–1458 B.C.E., images A and B). So many statues and portraits of her survive that nearly every major museum in the world has at least one (the Metropolitan Museum of Art in New York has a whole room set aside for them). But many of these images show signs of having been defaced during the reign of her successor, Thutmose III, who was also her nephew and stepson. Until very recently, scholars assumed that Hatshepsut must have usurped his powers, and that this was his revenge. Yet the evidence clearly shows that Hatshepsut was Egypt's legitimate ruler. Why, then, would Thutmose III or his heirs have tried to efface her memory?

The two unblemished steles shown here depict Hatshepsut and Thutmose III. In the stele on the left (image C), Hatshepsut is placed in the center of the frame, wearing a royal helmet; she is offering wine to the god Amun. Behind her stands Thutmose III, wearing the crown of Upper Egypt. In the stele on the right (image D), Thutmose III wears the warrior's crown, while Hatshepsut wears the double crown of Upper and Lower Egypt and wields a mace.

A. Defaced head of Hatshepsut.

B. Undefaced statue of Hatshepsut.

the Kassite kingdom of Babylonia remained a significant force in economic and military relationships. In addition to these imperial entities, numerous smaller states also flourished and extended their influence.

Although warfare remained the fundamental mode of interaction, a balance of power among the larger empires gradually helped to stabilize the region. By the fourteenth century B.C.E., a wide-ranging correspondence was binding leaders together and promoting a set of mutual goals and understandings. Surviving letters show that the most powerful rulers address one another as "brother," while lesser princes and chieftains show their deference to the pharaoh, the Hittite king, and other sovereigns by using the term "father." Rulers of this period also exchanged lavish gifts and entered into marriage alliances with each other. Professional envoys journeyed back and forth, conveying gifts and handling politically sensitive missions. Some of these emissaries were also merchants, sent to explore the possibility of trading opportunities as well as to cement alliances.

Questions for Analysis

1. Bearing in mind that few Egyptians could read the hieroglyphs accompanying these images, how might they have "read" the relationship between these two royal relatives? Does this evidence support the hypothesis that Thutmose was slighted by Hatshepsut?

2. What can these images tell us about gender roles? What else would we need to know before making a judgment about masculine and feminine characteristics in ancient Egypt?

3. Given that Hatshepsut was Egypt's legitimate pharaoh, what might have motivated either Thutmose III or his son Amenhotep II to deface her image many years after her death?

C. Stele of Hatshepsut and Thutmose.

D. Stele of Thutmos and Hatshepsut, from the Red Chapel at Karnak.

Transnational Trade

Indeed, it was trade that allowed smaller communities to become integral parts of this transnational network. Seaside centers such as Ugarit and Byblos became centers for the exchange of dazzling commodities. A single vessel's cargo might contain scores of distinct items originating anywhere from the interior of Africa to the Baltic Sea, as demonstrated by the contents of a merchant ship discovered at Uluburun off the Turkish coast in 1982. The region was also supplied with goods brought in overland, via contacts reaching into India and the Far East.

Trade was not only the basis for a new economy, but the conduit for art, ideas, and technology. In the past, such influences spread slowly and unevenly; now, the societies of the late Bronze Age could keep abreast of all the latest developments. This trend was particularly marked in large coastal towns. At Ugarit, on the coast of modern-day Syria, the swirl of commerce and the multiplicity of languages spoken by traders even propelled the development of a simpler form of writing than the cuneiform still current throughout most of the Near East. The Ugaritic alphabet consisted of about thirty symbols representing the sounds of consonants. (Vowels had to be inferred.) This system was far more easily mastered and more flexible than cuneiform, and it would become the model for the development of all modern alphabets.

The search for markets, resources, and trade routes also promoted greater understanding among cultures. After a great battle between Egyptians and Hittites near Kadesh (c. 1275 B.C.E.), the pharaoh Ramses II realized that more was to be gained through peaceful relations with his northern neighbors than through warfare. The treaty he established with the Hittites fostered stability and allowed further economic exchanges to flourish. But greater integration also meant greater mutual dependence. If one economy suffered, the effects of that decline were sure to be felt elsewhere. And the farther this transnational system spread, the more vulnerable it became. Many of the new markets depended on emerging societies in regions far less stable, where civilization was also new.

AEGEAN CIVILIZATION: MINOAN CRETE, MYCENAEAN GREECE

Greek poets like Hesiod described a heroic age when great men mingled with gods and powerful kingdoms contended for wealth and glory. For a long time, modern scholars dismissed these stories as fables. Tales of Theseus and the Minotaur, the Trojan War, and the wanderings of Odysseus were regarded as reflecting no historical reality. Greek history was assumed to begin in 776 B.C.E., when the first recorded Olympic Games occurred. Greece in the Bronze Age was considered a primitive backwater that played no significant role in the Mediterranean world or in the later, glorious history of classical Greece.

But in the late nineteenth century, an amateur archeologist named Heinrich Schliemann became convinced that these myths were really historical accounts. Using the epic poems of Homer as his guide, he found the site of Ilium (Troy) near the coast of northwest Anatolia. He also identified a number of once-powerful citadels on the Greek mainland, including the home of the legendary king Agamemnon at Mycenae (*MY-seh-nee*). Soon afterward, the British archeologist Sir Arthur Evans took credit for discovering the remains of a great palace at Knossos on the island of Crete that predated any of the major citadels on the Greek mainland. He dubbed this magnificent culture—which no modern person had known to exist—"Minoan," after King Minos, the powerful ruler whom the ancient Greeks described as dominating the Aegean, and the man for whom the engineer Daedalus had designed the Labyrinth. Although some of their conclusions have proven false, the discoveries of Schliemann and Evans forced scholars to revise, entirely, the history of Western civilizations. It is now clear that Bronze Age Greece—or, as it is often termed, Mycenaean Greece—was an important and integrated part of the Mediterranean world during the second millennium B.C.E.

The Minoan Thalassocracy

In the fifth century B.C.E., the Athenian historian Thucydides wrote that King Minos of Crete had ruled a *thalassocracy*, an empire of the sea. We now know that he was correct, that a very wealthy civilization began to flourish on the island of Crete around 2500 B.C.E. Thereafter, for about a millennium, the Minoans controlled shipping around the central Mediterranean and the Aegean, and may have exacted tribute from many smaller islands. At its height between 1900 and 1500 B.C.E., Minoan civilization was the contemporary of Egypt's Middle Kingdom and the Hittite kingdom. And unlike them, it was virtually unassailable by outside forces, protected by the surrounding sea.

Thanks to its strategic position, Crete was not only a safe haven but also a nexus of vibrant economic exchange. Like its counterparts in the Near East, it acted as a magnet for the collection of resources which were then redistributed by its rulers and their emissaries. Knossos was also a production center for textiles, pottery, and metalwork. Minoan merchants traded these with Egypt, southwest Anatolia, and Cyprus for a range of exotic goods. Artistic influences also traveled along these routes; among much else, Minoan-style paintings from this period appear regularly in the Nile Delta and the Levant.

Traces of the bright colors and graceful lines of these paintings are still evident on the ruined walls of the palace at Knossos. Endowed with indoor plumbing, among other luxuries, it covered several acres and comprised hundreds of rooms joined by an intricate network of winding hallways that inspired the famous story of the Labyrinth. The Minoans probably worshiped a god in the form of a bull or bull-man, and they appear to have devised an elaborate ritual sport known as bull-leaping, similar to bull-fighting but

MINOAN FRESCO, C. 1500 B.C.E. A stylized representation of bull-leaping, painted into the plaster of a wall at Knossos. ▪ *Is this likely to represent real practices?* ▪ *Why or why not?*

involving an element of athletic dance. There is also some evidence that they practiced human sacrifice (possibly facilitated by the dangers of bull-dancing) as a religious rite.

Despite all these fascinating remains, Minoan culture remains mysterious because its language has yet to be decoded. Its script is called Linear A, to distinguish it from Linear B, used in Mycenaean Greece, a script that *has* been deciphered. Although Linear A and Linear B represent different languages, the formal relationship between them reflects the fact that Minoan commercial activity engaged the mainland of Greece. The presence of a wide variety of Minoan objects on the Greek mainland corroborates this.

Yet the dynamics of the relationship between Minoans and Mycenaeans remains debatable. Before 1600 B.C.E., the Minoans were clearly much more sophisticated and may have dominated their Greek neighbors. One story told of Theseus describes how the hero was sent to Crete as a hostage, intending to free Athens from the heavy tribute imposed by King Minos. Given what we have already learned about the close relationship between myth and history, it is probable that this story preserves ancient memory, just as

the story of Daedalus is an attempt to explain the technological marvels of the palace at Knossos.

Mycenaean Greece

When Linear B was deciphered in the early 1950s, the texts written in this script spurred scholars to reconsider the history of ancient Greece. Since then, new research shows that the Indo-Europeans whose language became Greek entered the region in several waves after the turn of the second millennium, dominating and displacing the indigenous inhabitants. By 1500 B.C.E., huge citadels dotted the Greek landscape, ruled by warriors whose epitaphs boast of their martial prowess and who were buried with their weapons. The power of these rulers was based on their leadership and their ability to reward followers with plunder. The most successful of them gained control of strategic sites from which they could exploit major trade routes, engaging in both trade and piracy.

LINEAR B TABLET FROM KNOSSOS. Unlike cuneiform, whose characters are formed using the wedge-shaped tip of a reed, the scripts of Linear A and B used a sharp stylus that incised fine lines in clay or soft stone.

Over time, and perhaps under the influence of Minoan culture, the Mycenaean citadels developed into much more complex societies. They served as both centers of government and warehouses for storage. By the thirteenth century B.C.E., some rulers had carved out territorial kingdoms with as many as 100,000 inhabitants, dwarfing the city-states of the later classical age; Hesiod would imagine their citadels to have been built by giants. These palace centers were adapted from Near Eastern models and their massive size was not ideally suited to the Greek landscape. In war also, Mycenaean imitation of Near Eastern examples had its limits. For example, Mycenaean kings cherished the chariots used by their contemporaries on the plains of Anatolia, yet such chariots were highly impractical on rocky terrain.

Despite these and other differences from their Mediterranean neighbors, the Mycenaean Greeks played an important role in Bronze Age networks. By about 1400 B.C.E., they had subjugated Crete, taking over Knossos and using it as a Mycenaean center. In western Anatolia, not far from Troy, at least one Mycenaean king exercised enough influence for a Hittite ruler to address him as "my brother." This evidence suggests that the Mycenaeans earned prestige as warriors and mercenaries, as the Greeks' heroic poems attest.

The basic political and commercial unit of the Mycenaean world—a powerful king and war leader, a warrior aristocracy, a palace bureaucracy, a complex economy, large territorial kingdoms—differs markedly from the Greek city-state of the classical age (Chapter 3). However, we can trace some features of this later civilization back to the Mycenaeans, including the Greek language. Linear B tablets speak of a social group with considerable economic and political rights, the *damos*; this may be the precursor of the *demos*, the urban population that sought political empowerment in many Greek cities. The tablets also preserve the names of several gods familiar from the later period, such as Zeus, Poseidon, and Dionysos. And later Greeks believed themselves to be descended from these legendary forebears, whom they credited with superhuman achievements. Although they knew little about their Mycenaean ancestors in fact, the impact of what they imagined about them was considerable.

The Sea Peoples and the End of the Bronze Age

The civilization of Mycenaean Greece seems to have collapsed around the end of the thirteenth century B.C.E. What triggered this cannot be determined with any certainty, but the consequences of the collapse are clear. Because Mycenaean Greece was an integrated part of a transnational network, the effects of its demise were felt throughout the Near East. Thereafter, a wave of devastation swept from north to south, caused by a group of people so thoroughly destructive that they obliterated everything in their path. We might know nothing about them were it not for a narrow victory by the pharaoh Ramses III around 1176 B.C.E.

In the stele set up to commemorate his triumph, Ramses III referred to these invaders as "Sea Peoples" and named several groups as part of a coalition. Some were familiar to the Egyptians, and it seems that many were from the Aegean. Most notable were the Philistines who, after their defeat, withdrew to populate the coast of the region named after them: Palestine.

Because the Sea Peoples' arc of annihilation started in the north, it may have been one of the factors contributing to the collapse of Mycenaean Greece. Disruption of northern commercial networks would have devastated the Mycenaean kingdoms, which could not support their enormous populations without trade. Suddenly faced with an apocalyptic combination of overpopulation, famine, and violence, bands of desperate refugees would have fled the Aegean basin. Meanwhile, the damage to commerce devastated the economy of the Hittites, whose ancient kingdom rapidly disintegrated. Along the Mediterranean coast we find other clues. The king of Ugarit wrote a letter to a "brother" king on the

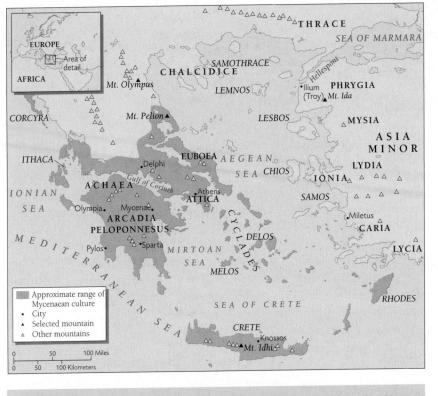

MYCENAEAN GREECE. ▪ *What are the main geographical features of Greece?* ▪ *How might this dry, mountainous country surrounded by the sea determine the nature of Greek civilization and economic interests?* ▪ *Why was Mycenaean culture able to spread so widely?*

island of Cyprus, begging for immediate aid because he had sent all his own warriors to help the Hittites. Poignantly, however, we have his letter only because the clay tablet on which it was written baked hard in the fire that destroyed his palace. The letter was never sent.

In the end, the Sea Peoples destroyed the civilizations that had flourished in the Near East and Mediterranean for over two thousand years. The devastation was not total; not all cities disappeared, and trade did not cease entirely. But the Hittite Empire was gone, leaving behind it many weak, short-lived principalities. The great cosmopolitan cities of the eastern Mediterranean lay in ruins, and new groups—sometimes contingents of Sea Peoples like the Philistines—populated the coast. The citadels of Mycenaean Greece were depopulated by as much as 90 percent over the next century, and Greece entered into a period of cultural and economic isolation that would last for 250 years.

The victorious Egyptians survived, but with their major trading partners diminished or dead their civilization suffered. The Assyrians, the original architects of the networks that had undergirded the transnational system,

had to fight for their very existence. In Babylon, the peaceful and prosperous rule of the Kassites withered. In the vacuum left behind, new political configurations took shape and a new metallurgical technology began to supplant the use of bronze. Out of the ashes arose the culture of the Iron Age.

THE STATES OF THE EARLY IRON AGE

With the destruction of transnational networks, the geopolitical map of the Near East changed significantly. In Anatolia, a patchwork of small kingdoms grew up within the territories once controlled by the Hittites. Similar developments took place in the Levant, the eastern Mediterranean coastline that today comprises Israel, Lebanon, and parts of Syria. For centuries, this region had been controlled either by the Egyptians or the Hittites. With the collapse of these empires, new states began to emerge here, too. They were small, but they had a huge impact on the history of Western civilizations.

The Phoenicians

The most influential civilization of this period was that of a people whom the Greeks called Phoenicians. They are also known as Canaanites, and were speakers of a Semitic language closely related to Hebrew. During the Late Bronze Age, most Phoenician cities had been controlled by Egypt. But the erosion of Egyptian imperial power after 1200 B.C.E. gave these cities the opportunity to forge a new independence and to capitalize on their commercial advantages. One Phoenician city, Gubla, was a clearing house for papyrus, the highly prized Egyptian writing material. This explains why the Greek name for this city, Byblos, became the basis for the Greek word *biblion*, meaning "book." (The Bible is so called from the plural *biblia*, "the books.") Another valuable commodity came to be the name by which the Phoenicians themselves were known: a rare purple dye derived from the shells of snails culled from seabeds off the

Analyzing Primary Sources

The Diplomacy of the Mycenaeans and the Hittites

Around 1260 B.C.E., the powerful Hittite king Hattusilis III sent the following letter to a "King of Ahhiyawa," identifiable as a leader of the Mycenaean Greeks, who often called themselves Akhaiwoi, Achaeans. This fascinating document exemplifies the tangle of close ties that bound powerful men together within the transnational system of the Late Bronze Age, as well as the problems and misunderstandings that could arise from the misbehavior of men under their command. The events referenced here all occur in western Anatolia (Turkey), a region controlled partly by the Hittites and partly by the Greeks, the same region in which Troy (Ilium) was located. (See the map on page 39.)

 have to complain of the insolent and treacherous conduct of one Tawagalawas [*tah-wah-GAH-la-wahs*]. We came into contact in the land of Lycia, and he offered to become a vassal of the Hittite Empire. I agreed, and sent an officer of most exalted rank to conduct him to my presence. He had the audacity to complain that the officer's rank was not exalted enough; he insulted my ambassador in public, and demanded that he be declared vassal-king there and then, without the formality of an interview. Very well: I order him, if he desires to become a vassal of mine, to make sure that no troops of his are found in Iyalanda when I arrive there. And what do I find when I arrive in Iyalanda?—the troops of Tawagalawas, fighting on the side of my enemies. I defeat them, take many prisoners . . . scrupulously leaving the fortress of Atriya intact out of respect for my treaty with you. Now a Hittite subject, Piyamaradus [*pie-yah-ma-RA-dus*] by name, steals my 7,000 prisoners, and makes off to your city of Miletus. I command him to return to me: he disobeys. I write to you: you send a surly message unaccompanied by gift or greeting, to say that you have ordered your representative in Miletus, a certain Atpas, to deliver up Piyamaradus. Nothing happens, so I go fetch him. I enter your city of Miletus, for I have something to say to Piyamaradus, and it would be well that your subjects there should hear me say it. But my visit is not a success. I ask for Tawagalawas: he is not at home. I should like to see Piyamaradus: he has gone to sea. You refer me to your representative Atpas: I find that both he and his brother are married to daughters of Piyamaradus; they are not likely to give me satisfaction or to give you an unbiased account of these transactions. . . . Are you aware, and is it with your blessing, that Piyamaradus is going round saying that he intends to leave his wife and family, and incidentally my 7,000 prisoners, under your protection while he makes continual inroads on my dominion? . . . Do not let him use Achaea [in Greece] as a base for operations against me. You and I are friends. There has been no quarrel between us since we came to terms in the matter of Ilios [the territory of Troy]: the trouble there was my fault, and I promise it will not happen again. As for my military occupation of Miletus, please regard it as a friendly visit. . . . [As for the problems between us], I suggest that the fault may not lie with ourselves but with our messengers; let us bring them to trial, cut off their heads, mutilate their bodies, and live henceforth in perfect friendship.

Source: Adapted from Denys Page, *History and the Homeric Iliad* (Berkeley, CA: 1959), pp. 11–12.

Questions for Analysis

1. Reconstruct the relationship between Hattusilis III and the Achaean king, based on the references to people and places in this letter. What picture emerges of their interactions, and of the connections between the Hittite Empire and Mycenaean Greece?

2. Why is Hattusilis so concerned about the disrespect shown to him by the Achaeans? Reading between the lines, what do you think he wanted to accomplish by sending this letter?

3. Based on this letter, what can you deduce about the standards of behavior expected of civilized participants in the transnational system of the Late Bronze Age? Within this code of conduct, what sanctions or penalties could be imposed on individuals or their nations?

Levantine coast. So as far as the Greeks were concerned, those who suppled this dye were *phoinikeoi*, "purple people." The Phoenicians also became expert metalworkers, ivory carvers, and shipbuilders.

Phoenician Colonies and Cultural Influence

The Phoenicians were also aggressive colonists. By the end of the tenth century B.C.E., they had planted settlements from one end of the Mediterranean to the other and had begun to venture out into the Atlantic Ocean.

The widespread colonial and mercantile efforts of the Phoenicians meant that they impacted cultures across the Mediterranean. Among their early overseas trading partners were the Greeks, and the Phoenicians may have played an important role in reintroducing urban life to Greece after the collapse of the Mycenaean citadels. While each city of the Phoenician mainland had its own hereditary royal government, in the Phoenicians' overseas colonies, a new type of political system emerged in which power was shared among a handful of elite families. This aristocratic form of government would become a model for many other Western societies, including those of Greece and Rome.

Without question, however, the most important contribution of the Phoenicians was their alphabet. As we noted earlier, a thirty-character alphabet had evolved at Ugarit by the end of the Bronze Age. Around 1100 B.C.E., the Phoenicians refined this writing system to twenty-two characters. This simpler system further facilitated trade and accounting, and the Phoenicians may have wanted to encourage similar practices among their partners, to safeguard their own interests. The Greeks certainly remained aware of their debt to the Phoenicians: their legends ascribe

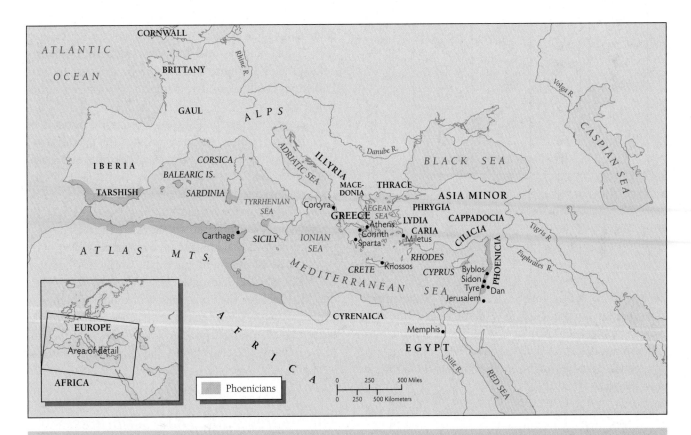

PHOENICIAN COLONIZATION. Compare this map to the more detailed one of Palestine on page 44. ▪ *What part of the Mediterranean serves as the homeland for the Phoenician city-states, and where did Phoenicians establish colonies?* ▪ *Why would overseas colonization be of such crucial importance to Phoenician city-states?* ▪ *What does their westward colonization imply about the Phoenicians' aims and about the different opportunities available in the West, as compared with the East?*

Phoenician	Hebrew	Classical Greek	Modern Alphabetic
⊀	א	A	A
⟨	ב	B	B
⋀	ג	Γ	G
◁	ד	Δ	D
⟩	ה	E	E
Y	ו	Y	V
I	ז	Z	Z
⊟	ח	H	H
⊗	ט	Θ	TH
⟋	י	I	Y
⋎	כ	K	K
⟨	ל	Λ	L
⋎	מ	M	M
⟨	נ	N	N
⟊	ס	Ξ	S
O	ע	O	O
⟋	פ	Π	P
⟊	צ		TZ
φ	ק		Q
⟨	ר	P	R
W	שׁ	Σ	S
X	ת	T	T

THE EVOLUTION OF THE ALPHABET. This table shows how the shapes of letters changed as the Phoenician alphabet was adapted by the Hebrews, the Greeks, and eventually the Romans (from whom our modern alphabet derives).

the invention of the alphabet to Cadmus, a Phoenician who settled in Greece. Their debt is also clear in the close relationship between the names of letters in Greek (alpha, beta, gamma, delta . . .) and Phoenician letter names (aleph, bayt, gimel, dalet . . .), and from the obvious similarities in letter shapes.

The Philistines

Southward along the Levantine coast from Phoenicia lay the land of the Philistines, descendants of the Sea Peoples defeated by Ramses III. Their bad reputation is the result

of their dominance over their neighbors, the herdsmen known as the Hebrews, who used writing as an effective weapon. The Philistines are accordingly the great villains of the Hebrew scriptures, and the word *philistine* has accordingly come to mean a boorish, uncultured person. Unfortunately, the Philistines do not appear to have made use of the same powerful technology to record their own outlook on the world, and almost everything we know about them comes from the work of archeologists, or has to be sifted through the bad press of their detractors. We know little about their language, but their material culture, behavior, and organization exhibit close affinities with Mycenaean Greece.

Philistine power was based on five great strongholds, the so-called Pentapolis (Greek for "five cities"): Gaza, Ashkelon, and Ashdod on the coast, and the inland cities of Ekron and Gath. Again, these citadels are strikingly similar to the fortified palaces of Mycenaean civilization, and they appear to have served many of the same functions. From these strongholds, the Philistines dominated the surrounding countryside by organizing agricultural production and controlling trade routes. An independent lord ruled over each citadel, and no doubt tensions and rivalries existed among them. But much like the heroes of Greek epic, the Philistines could set aside differences when facing a common enemy.

Because we see the Philistines primarily through the eyes of their Hebrew enemies, we must be careful about drawing conclusions about them from the stories of Goliath's brutality or Delilah's sexual treachery. Yet the Hebrews had good reason to fear the Philistines, whose pressure on the Hebrew hill country was constant and who threatened the Hebrews' holy sanctuary at Shiloh, where the sacred Ark of the Covenant was said to contain the original tablets of the law given to Moses on Mount Sinai. In Hebrew tradition, the tribes of Israel had once carried the Ark before them into battle against the Philistines, only to lose it in the fray and to witness thereafter the destruction of Shiloh. The Philistines then established garrisons throughout the land of the Hebrews, exacted tribute, and denied them access to weapons.

The Hebrews and Their Scriptures

The central feature of Hebrew culture, their conception of and relationship to their god, will be discussed at greater length toward the end of this chapter. In this section, we focus our attention on the development of Hebrew society—

while acknowledging that religion is always related to politics, as well as to economic conditions and the concerns of everyday life. Indeed the Hebrews, like all ancient peoples, could not have distinguished among these phenomena.

In reconstructing the early history of the Hebrews, we are indebted to an unusual textual source: a series of scriptures (literally "writings") that comprise mythology, laws and ritual practices, genealogical records, books of prophecy, proverbs, poetry, and royal chronicles. These are collectively known as the Hebrew Bible or (among Christians) as the Old Testament. The books of the Bible were assembled over many centuries, mostly by unknown authors, copyists, and editors. Like other sources, they have to be treated as artifacts produced by particular historical circumstances, which also governed the way that certain texts were preserved and put together.

The first five books of the Hebrew Bible are traditionally attributed to Moses, but most of the materials in these books were borrowed from other Near Eastern cultures, including the stories of creation and the flood, which parallel those of Sumer (as we saw in Chapter 1). The story of Moses' childhood draws on a legend told about the Akkadian king Sargon the Great. And the story of the exodus from Egypt is fraught with problems. Although the later Book of Joshua claims that the Hebrews who returned from Egypt conquered and expelled the native Canaanites, archeological and linguistic evidence suggests that the Hebrews were essentially Canaanites themselves. They may have merged with scattered refugees from Egypt in the aftermath of the Sea Peoples' invasions, but for the most part they had been continuously resident in Canaan for centuries. In other words, the first five books of the Bible constitute a retrospective history whose purpose was to justify Hebrew traditions and claims to territory.

Among the other writings included in the Hebrew Bible are a group of texts which record events of the more recent past, those of the period we are considering now. These books are more straightforwardly verifiable, even if many details are difficult to confirm. According to the Book of Judges, the Hebrews were wandering herdsmen who had just begun to establish permanent settlements around the time of the Philistines' arrival in the Levant. They had organized themselves into twelve tribes—extended clan units whose families owed one another mutual aid and protection in times of war, but who frequently fought over cattle and grazing rights. Each tribe was ruled by a patriarch known as a judge, who exercised the typical functions of authority in a clan-based society: war leadership, high priesthood, and dispute settlement. By the middle of the twelfth century B.C.E., these tribes occupied two major territories, with those settled in the south calling themselves the tribes of Judah, and those in the north the tribes of Israel.

The Struggle for Hebrew Identity

The Hebrew tribes of this period had little experience of organized activity. This made them highly vulnerable, especially when the Philistines conquered the Levantine coast around 1050 B.C.E. To counter the Philistine threat effectively, they needed a leader. Accordingly, around 1025 B.C.E., an influential tribal judge called Samuel selected a king to lead the Hebrew resistance against the Philistines. His name was Saul. However, Saul proved to be an ineffective war-leader. So Samuel withdrew his support from Saul and threw it behind a young warrior in Saul's entourage, Saul's son-in-law David. Waging his own independent military campaigns, David achieved one triumph after another over the Philistines—that is, according to those chroniclers of the Bible who wrote their accounts under David's patronage.

These same books reveal that David was a man on the make; and when Saul finally drove him from his court, he became an outlaw on the fringes of Hebrew society and then a mercenary in Philistine service. It was as a Philistine mercenary that David fought against Saul in the climactic battle in which Saul was killed. Soon thereafter, David himself became king, first over the tribes of Judah, his home territory, and later over Saul's territory of Israel as well.

The Consolidation of the Hebrew Kingdom

After David's victory around 1000 B.C.E., he took advantage of the opportunity afforded by Egypt's decline to expand his control southward, eventually confining the Philistines to an inconsequential strip of coastal land. By the time of his death in 973 B.C.E., David's kingdom stretched from the middle Euphrates in the north to the Gulf of Aqaba in the south, and from the Mediterranean coast eastward into the Syrian deserts.

As David's power and prestige grew, he was able to impose on his subjects a highly unpopular system of taxation and forced labor. His goal was to build a glorious capital at Jerusalem, a Canaanite settlement that he designated as the central city of his realm. It was a shrewd choice. As a newly

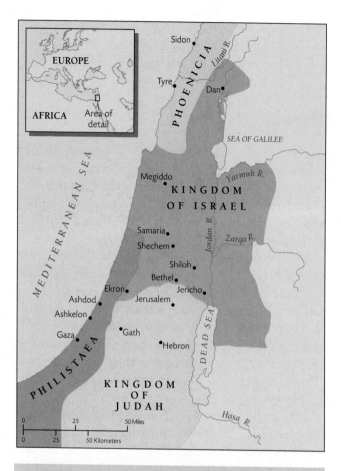

THE HEBREW KINGDOM, c. 900 B.C.E. Notice the scale of the map and consider the comparatively small size of the Hebrews' world. ▪ *What advantages did the Philistines and Phoenicians possess, geographically and otherwise?* ▪ *Why did they present such a challenge to the Hebrews?* ▪ *What political and religious consequences might have resulted from the division of the kingdom after the death of King Solomon, given the location of Jerusalem?*

The Reign of King Solomon (r. 973–937 B.C.E.)

Continuing his father's policies, but on a much grander scale, David's son Solomon built a great temple complex at Jerusalem to house the Ark. Such visible support of Yahweh's cult was approved by the historians whose works are included in the Bible, and who portray Solomon's reign as a golden age. However, Solomon was a ruthless and often brutal ruler whose promotion of Yahweh coincided with a program of despotism. To finance his expensive tastes and programs, Solomon instituted oppressive taxation and imposed customs duties on the lucrative caravan trade that passed through his country. With the help of the Phoenician king of Tyre, Solomon constructed a commercial fleet whose ships plied the waters of the Red Sea and beyond, trading—among other commodities—the gold and copper mined by Solomon's slaves.

Solomon also maintained a large standing army of conscripts from his own people. To undertake his ambitious building projects, Solomon required many of his subjects to perform forced labor four months out of every year. This level of oppression was too much for many Israelites, and the north seethed with rebellion against the royal capital. Within a decade or so of Solomon's death, in fact, the fragile monarchy split in two. The dynasty descended from David continued to rule the southern kingdom of Judah with its capital at Jerusalem, but the ten northern tribes banded together as the kingdom of Israel, with their capital at Shechem. In the meantime, the changing political situation of the Near East made the Hebrew kingdoms increasingly vulnerable.

conquered city, Jerusalem had no previous affiliation with any of Israel's twelve tribes and so stood outside the ancient rivalries that divided them. Geographically too, Jerusalem was a strategic choice, lying between the southern tribes of Judah (David's people) and the northern tribes of Israel. David also took steps to exalt the city by making Jerusalem the resting place of the sacred Ark and reorganizing the priesthood of the Hebrew god, Yahweh. By these measures, he sought to forge a new collective identity centered on his own family and its connections to Yahweh. To this end, he also encouraged the writing of histories and prophecies that would affirm this identity and his central role in forging it.

THE REVIVAL OF THE ASSYRIAN EMPIRE

The Assyrians had long played an important role in spreading trade and promoting urban settlements. But like the other great powers of the Near East, their civilization had been devastated by the Sea Peoples. For several centuries afterward they struggled for survival. Then, in the ninth century B.C.E., a brilliant but brutal ruler laid the foundations of what historians call the Neo-Assyrian Empire. Under the leadership of Assurnasirpal II (*ah-sur-NAH-sur-PAHL*, r. 883–859 B.C.E.), these "new" Assyrians began to conduct aggressive military campaigns against their neighbors. Those whom they defeated either had to pay tribute or face the full onslaught of the Assyrian war machine, which under Assurnasirpal acquired a deserved reputation for savagery.

Despite their military successes, Assurnasirpal and his successors inspired stiff resistance. The northern kingdom of Israel formed an alliance with other small states to halt Assyrian expansion. This coalition ultimately forced the Assyrians to settle for smaller victories against the Armenians to the northwest and the Medes to the northeast. Thereafter, a cycle of violent oppression and rebellion continued until the reign of a military commander who took the name Sargon II (r. 722–705 B.C.E.). He claimed to be the direct successor of Sargon of Akkad, the first great king in Mesopotamian history, nearly 1,500 years earlier (Chapter 1).

Like the Hebrews, Sargon and his heirs skillfully deployed history as a political tool. And eventually, they extended the frontiers of the Neo-Assyrian Empire from western Iran to the shores of the Mediterranean. Briefly, they even subjugated parts of Egypt. Sargon himself put an end to the kingdom of Israel in 722 B.C.E., enslaving and deporting most of the population, and he terrified the southern kingdom of Judah into remaining a quiet vassal. By the seventh century B.C.E., Assyria was the unrivaled power of the ancient Near East.

ASSYRIAN ATROCITIES. Judean captives whose city has fallen to the Assyrian king Sennacherib (704–681 B.C.E.) are shown being impaled on stakes. This triumphal carving comes from the walls of Sennacherib's palace at Nineveh. ▪ *What would be the purpose of advertising these captives' fates?*

Neo-Assyrian Government and Administration

The Neo-Assyrian Empire was built on the ability of its army to oppress both enemies and subjects alike. At its head was a hereditary monarch regarded as the earthly representative of the Assyrians' patron god, Assur. Supporting the empire's centralized authority was an extensive bureaucracy of governors, high priests, and military commanders—professions by no means mutually exclusive. These administrators exercised local authority on behalf of the king. They maintained lines of transport and communication and they oversaw construction of an extensive network of roads across the Near East. The Assyrians also deployed a system of spies and messengers to report on the activities of subjects and provincial governors.

Not surprising for a people so mindful of historical precedent, the Assyrians modeled their laws on the code of Hammurabi, though many of their penalties were more severe. Assyrian law was also rigidly patriarchal, which entailed substantial revision of Hammurabi's code: now only husbands had the power of divorce, and they were legally permitted to inflict a variety of penalties on their wives, ranging from corporal punishment to mutilation and death.

The Assyrian Military-Religious Ethos

The Assyrians' religious, political, and military ideology took shape during the long centuries when they fought for survival. Its two fundamental tenets were the waging of holy war and the exaction of tribute through terror.

Rather than defeating their foes once and imposing formal obligations, the Assyrians raided even their vanquished foes each year. This strategy kept the Assyrian military machine primed for battle, but it did little to inspire loyalty among subject peoples. Assyrian battle tactics were notoriously savage—even by the standards of ancient warfare, which regarded the mutilation of prisoners, systematic rape, and mass deportations as commonplace. Moreover, the Assyrian army was not a seasonal army of part-time conscripts or peasants, but a massive standing force of more than 100,000 soldiers. And because the Assyrians mastered iron-smelting techniques on a large scale, they could equip their fighting men with high-quality steel weapons that overwhelmed opponents still reliant on bronze.

The organization of this army also contributed to its success. At its core were heavily armed and armored shock troops, the main force for crushing enemy infantry in the field and for routing the inhabitants of an enemy city once inside. To harass enemy infantry, the Assyrians deployed light skirmishers with slings and javelins, combined archery and chariotry, and also developed the first true cavalry force in the West. They even trained a highly skilled corps of combat engineers to undermine city walls and to build catapults, siege engines, battering rams, and battle towers.

The Assyrians were convinced that their god demanded the constant expansion of his worship through military conquest. Ritual humiliation of a defeated city's gods was therefore a regular feature of Assyrian conquests. Statues of conquered gods would be carried off to the Assyrian capital, where they would remain as hostages. Meanwhile, an image of Assur himself—usually represented as a sun disk with the head and shoulders of an archer—would be installed in the defeated city, and the conquered people would be required to worship him. Although subject peoples did not have to abandon their previous gods altogether, they were made to feel their gods' inferiority. The Assyrians were therefore strict henotheists, meaning that they acknowledged the existence of other gods but believed that one god should be the supreme deity of all peoples.

The Legacy of Assyrian Power

The successors of Sargon II continued Assyrian military policies while devoting great energy to promoting an Assyrian cultural legacy. Sargon's immediate successor Sennacherib (sen-AH-sher-ib, r. 704–681 B.C.E.) rebuilt the ancient Assyrian city of Nineveh, fortifying it with a double wall for a circuit of nine miles. He constructed an enormous palace there, and he ordered the construction of a massive irrigation system, including an aqueduct that carried fresh water to the city from thirty miles away. His son rebuilt the conquered city of Babylon along similar lines. His grandson Assurbanipal (ah-sur-BAHN-uh-pahl, r. 669–627 B.C.E.) was perhaps the greatest of all the Assyrian kings. For a time, he ruled the entire delta region of northern Egypt. He also enacted a series of internal reforms, seeking ways to govern his empire more peacefully.

By Assyrian standards, Assurbanipal was an enlightened ruler, and one to whom all students of history owe a tremendous debt. Like his grandfather Sargon II, he had a strong sense of the rich traditions of Mesopotamian history and laid claim to them. But he did this much more systematically: he ordered the construction of a magnificent library at Nineveh, where all the cultural monuments of Mesopotamian literature were to be copied and preserved. This library also served as an archive for the correspondence and official acts of the king. Fortunately, this trove of documentation has survived. Our knowledge of history, not to mention all modern editions of the *Epic of Gilgamesh*, derive from the library at Nineveh.

When Assurbanipal died in 627 B.C.E., the Assyrian Empire appeared to be at its zenith. Its kings had adorned their capitals with magnificent artwork, and the hanging gardens of Babylon were already famous: these were artificial slopes whose cascading flowers and trees were fed by irrigation systems that pumped water uphill, an amazing marriage of engineering and horticulture. The end of Assyria is therefore all the more dramatic for its suddenness. Within fifteen years of Assurbanipal's reign, Nineveh lay in ruins. An alliance had formed between the Indo-European Medes of Iran and the Chaldeans, a Semitic people who controlled the southern half of Babylonia. By 605 B.C.E., the Chaldeans occupied Babylon itself and had become the predominant imperial power in Mesopotamia and the Levant. In 586 B.C.E. they captured Jerusalem, destroyed the Temple, and deported the population of Judea to Babylon. Meanwhile, the Medes retired to the Iranian Plateau to extend their dominion there.

THE RISE OF THE PERSIANS

The Persian Empire emerged as the successor state to the Assyrians, after the region was ruled for a few decades by the Chaldeans and Medes. On these foundations, the Persians would construct the largest empire known to humanity up until that time.

The Persian Empire of Cyrus the Great

The Persians emerge from obscurity rather suddenly, under an extraordinary prince named Cyrus who succeeded to the rule of a single Persian tribe in 559 B.C.E. Shortly thereafter, Cyrus made himself ruler of all the Persians and then, around 549 B.C.E., threw off the lordship of the Medes and began to claim dominion over lands stretching from the Persian Gulf to the Halys River in Asia Minor.

This brought the Persians into close contact with the kingdom of Lydia. The Lydians had attained great prosperity as producers of gold and silver and as intermediaries for overland commerce between Mesopotamia and the Aegean. Most important, they were the first people in the ancient Near East to use precious-metal coinage as a medium of exchange for goods and services. When Cyrus came to power, their king was Croesus (*CREE-suhs*), a man whose reputation as the possessor of untold riches survives in the expression "rich as Croesus." Distrusting his new neighbor, Croesus decided to launch a preemptive strike against the Persians to preserve his own kingdom from conquest. According to the Greek historian Herodotus, he took the precaution of asking the oracle of Apollo at Delphi whether this strategy was a good one, and was told that he would destroy a great nation if he pursued it. The oracle's pronouncement was both ambiguous and true: but the nation Croesus destroyed was his own. Cyrus defeated his forces in 546 B.C.E.

Cyrus then invaded Mesopotamia in 539 B.C.E., striking so quickly that he took Babylon without a fight. Once in Babylon, the entire Chaldean Empire was his, and his imperial policies proved very different from those of his predecessors in that region. Cyrus freed the Hebrews who had been held captive in Babylon since 586 B.C.E. and sent them back to Jerusalem, helping them to rebuild their temple and allowing them to set up a semi-independent vassal state. Cyrus also allowed other conquered peoples considerable self-determination, especially with respect to cultural and religious practices, a marked reversal of Assyrian and Chaldean policies. Two hundred years later, a young Macedonian king, Alexander, would emulate many of his exploits and build an empire sustained by many of the same strategies (see Chapter 4).

The Consolidation of Persia

When Cyrus died in battle in 530 B.C.E., Persian expansion continued, and his son conquered Egypt in 525 B.C.E. But although Cambyses was a warrior king like his father, he left the Persian Empire a poorly organized collection of rapid conquests. After a short period of civil war, the aristocratic inner circle that had served both Cyrus and his son settled on a collateral member of the royal family as the new king. This was Darius, whose long reign of 35 years (r. 521–486 B.C.E.) consolidated his predecessors' military gains by improving the administration of the Persian state. Darius divided the empire into provinces, each of which was administered by an official called a *satrap*. Satraps enjoyed extensive powers and considerable political latitude, yet they owed absolute loyalty to the central government, as did vassal states such as the technically autonomous Hebrew kingdom.

Adhering to the tolerant policy of Cyrus, Darius allowed the various peoples of the empire to retain most of their local institutions while enforcing a standardized currency and a system of weights and measures. Beyond this, he had little interest in imposing onerous

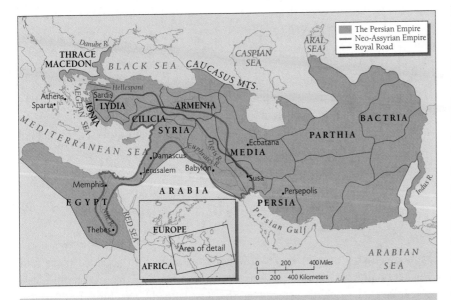

THE PERSIAN EMPIRE UNDER DARIUS I, 521–486 B.C.E. Consider the location of the Persian heartland and the four administrative centers of Persepolis, Susa, Ecbatana, and Sardis. ■ *What older kingdoms and empires did the Persian Empire contain?* ■ *Why is the Royal Road especially noted on this map?* ■ *How did Darius I successfully rule such a large and complex empire?*

Two Perspectives on Imperial Rule

These two inscriptions exemplify two very different attitudes toward imperial power and two very different methods of achieving it. The first glorifies the victories of the Assyrian king Esarhaddon in Syria, and is one of the most important records of his reign (r. 681–669 B.C.E.). The second commemorates the taking of Babylon by the Persian king Cyrus the Great (r. 559–530 B.C.E.), whose empire came to encompass and surpass that of the Assyrians.

The Stele of King Esarhaddon at Senjirli, c. 680 B.C.E.

To Assur, father of the gods, lover of my priesthood, Anu mighty and preeminent, who called me by name, Ba'al, the exalted lord, establisher of my dynasty, Ea, the wise, all-knowing . . . Ishtar, lady of battle and combat, who goes at my side . . . all of them who determine my destiny, who grant to the king, their favorite, power and might . . . [I am] the king, the offering of whose sacrifices the great gods love . . . [he] who has brought all the lands in submission at his feet, who has imposed tribute and tax upon them; conqueror of his foes, destroyer of his enemies, the king, who as to his walk is a storm, and as to his deeds, a raging wolf; . . . The onset of his battle is powerful, he is a consuming flame, a fire that does not sink: son of Sennacherib, king of the universe, king of Assyria, grandson of Sargon, king of the universe, king of Assyria, viceroy of Babylon, king of Sumer and Akkad. . . . I am powerful, I am all-powerful, I am a hero, I am gigantic, I am colossal, I am honored, I am magnified, I am without an equal among all kings, the chosen one of Assur . . . the great lord [who], in order to show to the peoples the immensity of my mighty deeds, made powerful my kingship over the four regions of the world and made my name great.

. . . Of Tirhakah, king of Egypt and Kush, the accursed . . . without cessation I slew multitudes of his men, and him I smote five times with the point of my javelin, with wounds, no recovery. Memphis, his royal city, in half a day . . . I besieged, I captured, I destroyed, I devastated, I burned with fire. . . . The root of Kush I tore up out of Egypt and not one therein escaped to submit to me.

Source: Daniel David Luckenbill, ed., *Ancient Records of Assyria and Babylonia*, Vol. 2 (Chicago: 1926–27), pp. 224–27.

Inscription Honoring Cyrus, c. 539 B.C.E.

He [the god Marduk] scanned and looked (through) all the countries, searching for a righteous ruler who would lead him. (Then) he pronounced the name of Cyrus, king of Anshan [Persia], declared him to be the leader of the world. . . . And he (Cyrus) did always endeavor to treat according to justice the black-headed

taxes, martial law, or hegemonic religious practices. After centuries of Assyrian and Chaldean tyranny, the light hand of Persian rule was welcomed throughout the Near East.

Darius was also a great builder. He erected a new royal residence and ceremonial capital which the Greeks called Persepolis ("Persia City"). He ordered a canal dug from the Nile to the Red Sea to facilitate trade with the Egyptian interior, and directed the installation of irrigation systems on the Persian plateau and the fringe of the Syrian desert to increase agricultural production. Darius also expanded the existing Assyrian road system to enhance trade and communications throughout his huge realm. The most famous artery was the Royal Road, stretching 1,600 miles from Susa, near the Persian Gulf, to Sardis (the old Lydian capital) near the Aegean. Government couriers along this road constituted the first postal system, carrying messages and goods in relay stages from one post to another. Each post was a day's horseback ride from the next, where a fresh horse and rider would be ready to carry the dispatches brought by the postman before him. An extensive imperial [people] whom he (Marduk) made him conquer. Marduk, the great lord, a protector of his people/worshipers, beheld with pleasure his good deeds and his upright mind, (and therefore) ordered him to march against his city Babylon. He made him set out on the road to Babylon, going at his side like a real friend. His widespread troops—their number, like the water of a river, could not be established—strolled along, their weapons packed away. Without any battle, he made them enter his town Babylon, sparing Babylon any calamity. He delivered into his hands Nabonidus, the king who did not worship him. All the inhabitants of Babylon as well as of the entire country of Sumer and Akkad, princes and governors (included), bowed to him and kissed his feet, jubilant that he (had received) the kingship, and with shining faces. Happily they greeted him as a master through whose help they had come (again) to life from death (and) had all been spared damage and disaster, and they worshiped his name.

I am Cyrus, king of the world, great king, legitimate king, king of Babylon, king of Sumer and Akkad, king of the four rims (of the earth), son of Cambyses, great king, king of Anshan, grandson of Cyrus, great king, king of Anshan, descendent of Teipes, great king, king of Anshan, of a family (which) always (exercised) kingship; whose rule Bel and Nebo love, whom they want as king to please their hearts.

When I entered Babylon as a friend and (when) I established the seat of the government in the palace of the ruler under jubilation and rejoicing. . . . My numerous troops walked around Babylon in peace, I did not allow anybody to terrorize (any place) of the (country of Sumer) and Akkad. I strove for peace in Babylon and in all his (other) sacred cities. . . . I abolished the . . . [yoke] which was against their (social) standing, I brought relief to their dilapidated housing, putting (thus) an end to their (main) complaints. . . . All the kings of the entire world from the Upper to the Lower Sea, those who are seated in throne rooms, (those who) live in other (types of buildings as well as) all the kings of the West living in tents, brought their heavy tributes and kissed my feet in Babylon.

Source: Excerpted from James B. Pritchard, ed. *Ancient Near Eastern Texts Relating to the Old Testament*, 3rd ed. (Princeton, NJ: 1969), pp. 315–16.

Questions for Analysis

1. Both of these inscriptions constitute propaganda, but of different kinds. How do they differ? What audience(s) are they addressing? What function(s) does each inscription serve?

2. Each of these rulers claims to have a close relationship with the divine. How do those relationships differ, and what do those differences reveal about their attitudes to kingship and its sources of power?

3. Both of these kings boast of their royal lineage and their connections to past rulers. How different or similar are these perspectives? What do they reveal about these kings' awareness of history?

spy network also used this postal system, famed throughout Persia as "the eyes and ears of the king."

Clearly, Darius was a gifted administrator. But as a military strategist he made an enormous mistake when he attempted to extend Persian rule into Greece. Cyrus's conquest of Lydia had made the Persian king the overlord of some long-established Greek-speaking cities on the western coast of Asia Minor, a region called Ionia. But these cities resisted even the easy terms of Persian rule, desiring instead to model themselves on the self-governing city-states across the Aegean. Consequently, between 499 and 494 B.C.E., the Greeks of Asia waged a war for independence and briefly gained the support of troops from Athens. Darius quelled this uprising, and then decided to send a force to punish Athens and serve notice of Persian dominion over all Greek states. But at the battle of Marathon in 490 B.C.E., the Athenians dealt Darius the only major setback of his reign. And when his son and successor, Xerxes (ZEHRK-zees), attempted to avenge this humiliation in 480 B.C.E., a resistance led by both Athens

A CYLINDRICAL SEAL OF DARIUS THE GREAT (522–486 B.C.E.).
Seals were used in place of signatures to authenticate documents and correspondence. The cylindrical matrix (right) was rolled in soft wax to create an impression. This finely wrought example shows the king in a chariot, hunting lions with a bow. A winged representation of the god Ahura-Mazda rises above the scene.

and Sparta forced him to retreat and abandon his plans a year later. (We will discuss these events at greater length in Chapter 3.)

The Persians were thus compelled to recognize that they had reached the limits of their expansion. Thereafter, they concentrated on their Asian possessions and used money and diplomacy to keep the Greeks in check. This was not difficult, because the Greeks' hasty union in the face of Persian hegemony was short-lived, and they were too embroiled in wars with one another to pose any real threat to Persia.

The richness of their culture and the general tolerance they exhibited served the Persians well in maintaining their enormous empire. Unlike the Assyrians or Chaldeans, the Persians could count on the loyalty and even the affection of their subjects. In fact, their imperial model—the accommodation of local institutions and practices, consistent administration through a trained bureaucracy, and rapid communications between center and periphery—would be the one adopted by the great and lasting empires of the near and distant future.

The Legacy of Zoroastrianism

Persia's political and cultural achievements were paralleled by a spiritual one, Zoroastrianism. This important religion was one of the three major universal faiths known to the world before Christianity and Islam, along with Buddhism and Judaism (see below). Its founder was Zarathustra, known to the Greeks as Zoroaster, a Persian who probably lived shortly before 600 B.C.E. Zarathustra sought to reform the traditional customs of the Persian tribes by eradicating polytheism, animal sacrifice, and magic. That is, he wanted to redefine religion as an ethical practice common to all, rather than as a set of rituals and superstitions that caused divisions among people.

Zoroastrianism teaches that there is one supreme god in the universe, whom Zarathustra called Ahura-Mazda, "Wise Lord." Ahura-Mazda is the essence of light, truth, and righteousness; there is nothing wrathful or wicked about him, and his goodness extends to everyone, not just to one people or tribe. How, then, can there be evil and suffering in the world? Because, Zarathustra posited, there is a counter deity, Ahriman, who rules the forces of darkness. Yet he also posited that Ahura-Mazda must be vastly stronger than Ahriman.

Later teachers and priests of Zoroastrianism, the magi, placed greater emphasis on the dualism of these divine forces. They insisted that Ahura-Mazda and Ahriman are evenly matched, engaged in a desperate and eternal struggle for supremacy. Accordingly, light will not triumph over darkness until the Last Day, when the forces of Ahura-Mazda vanquish those of Ahriman forever. This vision of the universe would prove enormously influential, later informing the developing theologies of Christianity and Islam—not to mention the plots of much modern science fiction, fantasy literature, and film.

The devotion of the Persian imperial dynasty to Zarathustra's teachings made Zoroastrianism important to the conduct of Persian government, and also helps to explain the moderation of Persian rule. Unlike the Assyrians, the Chaldeans, or even the Egyptians, Persian kings saw themselves as presiding over an assemblage of different nations whose customs and beliefs they were prepared to tolerate. Whereas Mesopotamian potentates characteristically called themselves "true king," Persian rulers took the title "king of kings" or "great king," implying that they recognized the legitimacy of other kings who ruled under their canopy.

Unlike other ancient religions, then, Zoroastrianism did not exalt the power of a godlike ruler or support any particular regime. It was a personal religion, making private, spiritual demands as opposed to public, ritual ones. Its Wise Lord supported neither tribes nor states, but only individuals who serve the cause of truth and justice. According to its tenets, individuals possess free will and can choose to sin or not to sin; they are not compelled by an array of conflicting gods to act in particular ways. Zoroastrianism thus urges its adherents to choose good over evil, to be truthful, to love and help one another to the best of their powers, to aid the poor, and to practice generous hospitality. Those who do so will be rewarded in an afterlife, when the dead are resurrected on Judgment Day and consigned either to a realm of joy or to the flames of despair. In the scriptures of the Zoroastrian faith, known as the Avesta (compiled, like the Bible, over the course of many centuries), the rewards for righteousness are great, but not immediate. They are spiritual, not material.

THE DEVELOPMENT OF HEBREW MONOTHEISM

Of all the important trends that we have traced in our study of the Iron Age Near East, perhaps none is of greater significance to the civilizations of the West than monotheism: the belief in a single god, the creator and ruler of all things. This development is traditionally associated with the Hebrews, but even the Hebrews were not always monotheists. Those who argued for the exclusive worship of Yahweh were a minority within Hebrew society, albeit a vocal and assertive one. How the Hebrews came to regard Yahweh as the only divine being in the universe, and to root their identity in such an exclusive religious outlook, is therefore a phenomenon that can only be understood within its historical context.

From Monolatry to Monotheism

For those who later advocated the exclusive worship of Yahweh, the early history of the Hebrews was full of embarrassments. Even the Hebrew scriptures reveal their propensity for the worship of many gods. Yahweh himself, in commanding that his people "have no other gods before me," acknowledged the existence of those gods. The older, polytheistic Hebrew religion honored nature spirits such as Azazel and the Canaanite deity El, whose name is an important element in many Hebrew place-names (for example, Bethel) and soon became a synonym for "God." The temple built by Solomon at Jerusalem even included altars to Ba'al and his wife Asherah, a fertility goddess. Later Hebrew kings continued such practices, overriding the protests of religious purists devoted to Yahweh.

By the beginning of the first millennium, however, the Hebrews living under the rule of David began to practice monolatry, meaning that they worshiped one god exclusively without denying the existence of others. Although the legendary prophet Moses is often credited as the first promoter of Yahweh's cult, sometime around the middle

THE GODDESS ASHERAH. The Canaanite fertility goddess, Asherah, was the wife of the god Ba'al (or his father, El), but she also figures in some inscriptions as the wife of the Hebrew god Yahweh. One Hebrew king even placed an image of her in the temple of Yahweh at Jerusalem. ■ *Why would this be viewed as controversial?*

of the second millennium B.C.E., the ascendancy of Yahweh took place much later under the influence of the Levites, a tribe who claimed unique priestly authority and sought to enhance their own power and prestige by discrediting other gods.

The success of their campaign rested on the Levites' access to writing. The written word was especially potent in the ancient world because the skills necessary for its mastery were rare. In an age of constant threats to Hebrew religious and political sovereignty, the literacy of the Levites helped to preserve and promote Yahweh's worship. So did the political supremacy of the House of David, which bolstered its own legitimacy by allying itself with the Levites. The result was a centralized cult situated in the new royal capital of Jerusalem, which linked the political and the

RECONSTRUCTION OF THE ISHTAR GATE. This is a reconstruction of one of the fifty-foot-high entrance gates built into the walls of Babylon by King Nebuchadnezzar around 575 B.C.E. About half of this reconstruction is original.

religious identity of the Hebrews to the worship of Yahweh as the supreme god.

Nevertheless, the worship of other gods actually increased in the eighth and seventh centuries B.C.E., perhaps in reaction to the austere morality demanded and imposed by the Yahwists. Thus religious figures like Jeremiah (c. 637–587 B.C.E.) railed against "foreign" cults and warned of the disastrous consequences that would arise if Yahweh's people did not remain faithful to him. Moreover, Yahweh remained a somewhat conventional god, even in the eyes of his promoters. He was conceived as possessing a physical body and was often capricious and irascible. Further, he was not omnipotent; his power was largely confined to the territory occupied by the Hebrews.

Still, some of the Hebrews' most important contributions to subsequent Western religions crystallized by the middle of the eighth century B.C.E. One was their theology of Yahweh's transcendence: the teaching that God is not part of nature but exists outside of it. God can therefore be understood in purely intellectual or abstract terms, as entirely separate from the operations of the natural world. Complementing this principle was the belief that Yahweh had appointed humans to be the rulers of nature by divine mandate. When Yahweh orders Adam and Eve to "replenish the earth and subdue it, and have dominion over . . . every living thing," his injunction stands in striking contrast to other accounts of creation in which humans are made to serve the gods. Finally, Hebrew religious thought was moving in this period toward the articulation of universal ethics—a universal theory of justice and righteousness. According to the Babylonian flood story, for example, a

particularly petulant god destroys humanity because their noise deprives him of sleep. In Genesis, Yahweh sends a flood in punishment for human wickedness but saves Noah and his family because "Noah was a just man."

The Hebrews honored Yahweh during this period by subscribing to certain moral precepts and taboos. The Ten Commandments in the exact form as they now appear in Exodus 20:3–17 may not have existed, but they certainly reflect earlier ethical injunctions against murder, adultery, lying, and greed. In addition, the Hebrews observed an array of ritual practices unusual in the ancient world, such as infant circumcision, adherence to strict dietary laws, and refraining from labor on the seventh day of the week.

Yet the moral standards imposed by Yahweh on the Hebrew community were not binding when the Hebrews dealt with outsiders. Lending at interest, for example, was not acceptable among Hebrews, but was quite acceptable between a Hebrew and a non-Hebrew. Such distinctions applied also to more serious issues, such as the killing of civilians in battle. When the Hebrews conquered territories in Canaan, they took "all the spoil of the cities, and every man they smote with the sword . . . until they had destroyed them." Far from having any doubts about such a brutal policy, the Hebrews believed that Yahweh had inspired the Canaanites to resist so that the Hebrews could slaughter them: "For it was the Lord's doing to harden their hearts that they should come against Israel in battle, in order that they should be utterly destroyed, and should receive no mercy but be exterminated" (Joshua 11:20).

With the political fragmentation of the Hebrew kingdoms after Solomon's death, important regional distinctions arose within Yahweh's cult. As we noted above, the rulers of the northern kingdom discouraged their citizens from participating in ritual activities at Jerusalem, thereby earning the disapproval of the Jerusalem-based Yahwists who shaped the biblical tradition. The erosion of a cohesive Hebrew identity was further accelerated by the Assyrians, who under Sargon II absorbed the northern kingdom as a province and enslaved nearly 28,000 Hebrews. The southern kingdom of Judah survived, but political collaboration with the Assyrians meant acceptance of the god Assur.

This was the whetstone on which the Yahwist prophets sharpened their demands for an exclusive monotheism that went beyond monolatry. Hebrew prophets were practical political leaders as well as religious figures, and most of them understood that military resistance to the Assyrians was futile. So if the Hebrews were to survive as a people, they had to emphasize the one thing that separated them from everyone else in the known world: the worship of Yahweh and the denial of all other gods. The prophets' insistence that Yahweh alone should be exalted was thus an aggressive reaction to the equally aggressive promotion of Assur by the Assyrians.

The foremost Hebrew prophets of this era were Amos and Hosea, who preached in the kingdom of Israel before it fell to the Assyrians in 722 B.C.E.; Isaiah and Jeremiah, who prophesied in Judah before its fall in 586 B.C.E.; and Ezekiel and the "second Isaiah" (the Book of Isaiah had at least two different authors), who continued to preach "by the waters of Babylon" during the exile there. Despite some differences in emphasis, these prophets' messages consistently emphasize three core doctrines.

1. **Yahweh is the ruler of the universe.** He even makes use of peoples other than the Hebrews to accomplish his purposes. The gods of other nations are false gods. There has never been and never will be more than this one god.
2. **Yahweh is exclusively a god of righteousness.** He wills only the good, and evil in the world comes from humanity, not from him.
3. **Because Yahweh is righteous, he demands ethical behavior from his people.** Over and above ritual and sacrifice, he requires that his followers "seek justice, relieve the oppressed, protect the fatherless, and plead for the widow."

Judaism Takes Shape

Through their insistence on monotheism as the cornerstone of Hebrew identity, the Yahwists made it possible for the Hebrews to survive under Assyrian domination. And as the Assyrian threat receded in the late seventh century B.C.E., so the Yahwists triumphed religiously and politically. The king of Judah during the waning years of the Assyrian Empire, Josiah (r. 621–609 B.C.E.), was a committed monotheist whose court employed prominent prophets, including Jeremiah. With Assyrian power crumbling, Josiah found himself in a position to pursue significant reforms. He presided over the redrafting and revision of the "Law of Moses" to bring it into line with current policies, and it was during his reign that the Book of Deuteronomy was "discovered" and hailed as Moses' "Second Law." Deuteronomy is the most stridently monotheistic book of the Hebrew Bible, and it lent weight to this new political program.

But within a generation of King Josiah's death, the Chaldeans under Nebuchadnezzar conquered Jerusalem, destroyed the Temple, and carried thousands of Hebrews off to Babylon in 587/586 B.C.E. This Babylonian Captivity brought many challenges, paramount among them the maintenance of the Hebrews' identity. The leading voices in defining that identity continued to be the patriotic Yahwists, the same people who would later spearhead the return to Palestine after Cyrus captured Babylon and liberated the Hebrews two generations later. Among the Yahwists, the prophet Ezekiel stressed that salvation could be found only through religious purity, which meant ignoring all foreign gods and acknowledging only Yahweh. Kingdoms and states and empires came to nothing in the long run, Ezekiel said. What mattered for those living in exile was the creature God had made in his image—man—and the relationship between God and his creation.

The period of captivity was therefore decisive in forging a universal religion that transcended politics. Just as Yahweh existed outside creation, so the people who worshiped him could exist outside of a Hebrew kingdom. In Babylon, the worship of Yahweh therefore became something different: it became Judaism, a religion that was not tied to any particular political system or territory, for after 586 B.C.E. there was neither a Hebrew ruling class nor a Hebrew state. Outside of Judah, Judaism flourished. This was an unparalleled achievement in the ancient world: the survival of a religion that had no political power to back it and no holy place to ground it.

After 538 B.C.E., when Cyrus permitted the Hebrews of Babylon to return to their lands and to rebuild the Temple, Jerusalem became once again the central holy place of Hebrew religious life. But the new developments that had fashioned Judaism during captivity would prove lasting, despite the religious conflicts that soon erupted. These conflicts led to ever more specific assertions about the nature of Judaism, and to religious teachings that focused on ethical conduct as an obligation owed by all human beings toward their creator, independent of place or political identity. The observance of ritual requirements and religious taboos would continue, but not as the essence of religious life; rather, they would be symbolic of the special relationship binding Yahweh to the Hebrews. Eventually, the transcendental monotheism that emerged from these historical processes would become common to the worldview of all Western civilizations.

CONCLUSION

The centuries between 1700 and 500 B.C.E. were an epoch of empires. While the two great powers of the second millennium were New Kingdom Egypt and the Hittite Empire in Anatolia, a host of lesser empires also coalesced during this period, including Minoan Crete, Mycenaean Greece, and the trading empire of the Assyrians. All were sustained by a sophisticated network of trade and diplomacy. But between 1200 and 1000 B.C.E. the devastation wrought by the Sea Peoples brought this integrated civilization to an end. These invasions cleared the way for many new, small states, including those of the Phoenicians, the Philistines, the Lydians, and the Hebrews. Many crucial cultural and economic developments were fostered by these small states, including alphabetic writing, coinage, mercantile colonization, and monotheism. But the dominant states of the Iron Age continued to be the great land empires centered in western Asia: first the Neo-Assyrians, then briefly the Chaldeans, and finally the Persians.

The empires of the early Iron Age were quite different from those that had dominated the Near East a thousand years before. These new empires were much more highly unified. They had capital cities, centrally managed systems of communication, sophisticated administrative structures, and ideologies that justified their aggressive imperialism as a religious obligation imposed on them by a single, all-powerful god. They commanded armies of unprecedented size, and they demanded from their subjects a degree of

After You Read This Chapter

Ⓢ Visit StudySpace for quizzes, additional review materials, and multi-media documents. **wwnorton.com/studyspace**

REVIEWING THE OBJECTIVES

- The settlement of Indo-European peoples in the Near East had marked effects on the older civilizations there. What were some major consequences?

- Egypt's New Kingdom differed profoundly from the Old and Middle Kingdoms that preceded it. Why was this the case?

- The civilizations of the late Bronze Age were bound together by transnational networks. What were the strengths and fragilities of these relationships?

- What kingdoms and empires emerged in the Near East after the devastation caused by the Sea Peoples?

- Monotheism was a significant historical development of the first millennium B.C.E. Why is it so important?

obedience impossible for any previous Bronze Age emperor to imagine or enforce. Their rulers declared themselves the chosen instruments of their god's divine will.

At the same time, we can trace the emergence of more personalized religions. Zoroastrian dualism and Hebrew monotheism added an important new emphasis on ethical conduct, and both pioneered the development of authoritative written scriptures that advanced religious teachings. Zoroastrianism, despite its radical re-imagining of the cosmos, proved fully compatible with imperialism and became the driving spiritual force behind the Persian Empire.

Judaism, by contrast, was forged in the struggle to resist the imperialism of the Assyrians and Chaldeans. Both systems of belief would exercise enormous influence on future civilizations. In particular, they would provide the models on which Christianity and Islam would ultimately erect their own traditions, just as the models of imperial governance forged in this period would become the template for future empires. In Chapter 3, we will look at the ways in which the city-states of ancient Greece both built on and departed from these models.

PEOPLE, IDEAS, AND EVENTS IN CONTEXT

- How did the Hittite Empire integrate the cultures of **INDO-EUROPEAN PEOPLES** with the older civilizations of this region?
- What do the reigns of **HATSHEPSUT** and **AKHENATEN** tell us about the continuities and limitations of pharaonic power?
- What factors produced the transnational networks of the Late **BRONZE AGE**?
- How did the civilizations of **MINOAN CRETE** and **MYCENAEAN GREECE** differ from one another, and from the neighboring civilizations of the Near East?
- In what ways do the **PHOENICIANS**, the **PHILISTINES**, and the **HEBREWS** exemplify three different approaches to state-building at the beginning of the first millennium B.C.E.?
- What was new about the **NEO-ASSYRIAN EMPIRE**? How do its methods of conquest and its military-religious ethos compare to the **PERSIAN EMPIRE** that followed it?
- How and why did monotheism develop in the Hebrew kingdoms? In what ways might **JUDAISM** have been influenced by **ZOROASTRIANISM**?

CONSEQUENCES

- In the religions of Akhenaten, the Persians, and the Hebrews we see a rejection of polytheism. What cultural factors may have contributed to this? What would you consider to be the long-term effects of monotheism as a motivating force in history?
- What patterns of success or failure appear to be emerging when we consider the empires that flourished in the Iron Age, particularly those of the Assyrians and the Persians? Are similar patterns visible in other periods of history, including our own?

Before
You
Read
This
Chapter

The Civilization of Greece, 1000–400 B.C.E.

I n the fifth century B.C.E., a Greek-speaking subject of the Persian Empire began to write a book. He had been to Egypt and along the African coast, to the Greek colonies of Italy, the cities of Persia, the wilds of Thrace and Macedonia, and all over the Aegean. He had collected stories about peoples and places even farther afield: Ethiopia, India, the Black Sea. We have already met this intrepid traveler, Herodotus (c. 484–c. 425 B.C.E.), who marveled at the pyramids of Giza (Chapter 1) and who told how the king of Lydia lost his power to the Persians (Chapter 2). His reason for compiling this information was timely: he wanted to write a history of recent events. As he put it, "Herodotus of Halicarnassus here sets forth the results of his research, with the aim of preserving the remembrance of what men have done, and of preventing the great and wonderful deeds of both Greeks and barbarians from losing their glory; and in particular to examine the causes that made them fight one another."

Herodotus' fascination with the Persians, Phoenicians, and Egyptians underscores the extent to which all Greek-speakers regarded themselves as different from other peoples. In fact, they had responded very differently to the Bronze Age collapse.

THE ACROPOLIS OF ATHENS AND THE PARTHENON. Many Greek cities were built upon mountain strongholds, but the most famous of these is the Acropolis of Athens. First settled in the Neolithic Period, during the Bronze Age it became a fortified palace— allegedly that of the hero Theseus—and then a precinct sacred to the goddess Athena, for whom the city was named. The Parthenon, its most important surviving structure, was built on the site of an older temple after the Athenian victory over the Persians at Marathon in 490 B.C.E., and then rebuilt after the Persians sacked Athens ten years later. Most of the damage it sustained thereafter occurred during modern wars. ■ *Why was this site the focal point of so much activity?* ■ *What do these successive events tell us about the relationship between place and identity?*

off from trade and communication. The use of writing declined to such an extent that knowledge of Linear B disappeared. Archeological evidence suggests a world in stasis, isolated from the centers of civilization that were re-emerging in the Near East.

The material realities of life in this era profoundly shaped the civilization that emerged from it. This civilization would emphasize political equality and modest display, principles that formed the basis of early democracies. At the same time, the hardships of daily life, which contrasted sharply with stories of a heroic and opulent past, made the Greeks suspicious of their gods. They came to rely far more on the power of individual human beings than on divine intervention in human affairs. They also developed an awareness that excessive pride in one's own accomplishments could be dangerous. While the gods favored those who showed initiative and daring, they would punish the *hubris* of those who failed to acknowledge their own limitations.

While they struggled to cooperate politically, they were able to unite around a common language and culture, and their shared values were distinct from those of the people they called *barbarians*: peoples whose speech, to Greek ears, sounded like gibberish ("bar-bar-bar"). They cherished individual liberty, participatory government, artistic innovation, scientific investigation, and the creative powers of the human mind. Although the practical implementation of these ideals would prove problematic—and continues to be so—our own civilization would be unimaginable without the political experiments and cultural achievements of ancient Greece.

FROM CHAOS TO POLIS

By the end of the twelfth century B.C.E., Mycenaean civilization had vanished. Except at Athens, the great citadels that had crowned the heights of mainland kingdoms were destroyed. Settlements shrank in size and moved inland, away from vulnerable coastlines, thus cutting themselves

Homer and the Heroic Tradition

Around the year 1000 B.C.E., the chaotic conditions that had contributed to the isolation of Greece were alleviated by a period of relative peace. The standard of living improved, artisans developed their crafts, and increased contact among individual settlements fostered trade. Greek pottery, in particular, became a sophisticated and sought-after commodity, which Greek merchants could exchange for luxury goods from abroad.

As trade became an increasingly important feature of the new economy, the personal fortunes of those who engaged in trade increased accordingly, leading to a new kind of social stratification based on wealth. The men who controlled that wealth were aware that their status was not founded on warfare or noble birth, as had been the case in the past. Instead, they began to justify their preeminence as a reflection of their own superior qualities as "best men" (*aristoi*). Wealth was one sign of this superiority, but it was not sufficient in itself as a claim to aristocracy, which literally means "the rule of the best." Those who aspired to this status were therefore expected to emulate, as far as possible, the heroes of old, whose stories lived in the prodigious memories and agile voices of the singers of tales.

These singers, the guardians of a rich oral history that had never been written down, were part poets in their own right and part *rhapsodes*, "weavers of songs." The most famous is Homer, the poet credited with having woven together the mesh of stories that we know as the *Iliad* and the *Odyssey*, which crystallized around 800 B.C.E. The epics ascribed to Homer are vast encyclopedias of lore set at the end of the Bronze Age, the time his contemporary Hesiod called "the Age of Heroes" (Chapter 2): the age of Achilles and his Trojan rival, Hector; the age of Odysseus.

But these stories were not fixed in that time. Over centuries of retelling, the social and political relationships portrayed in the poems changed to reflect the assumptions and agendas of later ages. Treating these epics as historical sources, therefore, requires the historian to peel back layers of meaning. For example, Homer depicts a world in which competition and status are of paramount importance to the warrior elite, just as they were of vital concern to the aristocrats of his own day. Through the exchange of expensive gifts and hospitality, men aspiring to positions of power sought to create strong ties of guest friendship (*xenía, zeh-NEE-ah*) with one another, and thus to construct networks of influence that would support their economic, social, and political ambitions. This suggests that aristocrats in the Greek world conceived of themselves as having more in common with each other than they did with the local societies they dominated, something that is also reflected in the essential similarity of Trojans and Greeks in the *Iliad*.

However, the shared sense of a common culture among aristocratic households did not lessen the competition among them. Indeed, it led to competition over the epic past, as fledgling aristocratic clans vied to claim descent from one or another legendary hero. A hero cult might begin when an important family claimed an impressive Mycenaean tomb as that of their own famous ancestor, someone named in the *Iliad* said to have come from that place. They would then develop a pious tradition of devotion that would extend to their followers and dependents; eventually, an entire community might come to identify itself with the famous local hero. The heroic ideal thus became a deeply ingrained feature of Greek society, as did the stories that the epics preserved and propagated.

The Rise of the Polis

In the ninth century B.C.E., contacts between Greeks and Phoenicians intensified. Most crucially, the Greeks adopted the Phoenician alphabet, which replaced the long-disused Linear B. The Phoenicians also pointed the way to the revival of another lost art among the Greeks: seafaring. After the devastation of the late Bronze Age, Greek vessels hugged the shoreline and traveled only short distances. By the tenth century, however, Greeks were copying Phoenician designs for merchant vessels, which allowed them to set out on trading ventures of their own. As commercial activity increased, significant numbers of Greeks began to move to the shores of the mainland, to outlying islands, and to the coast of Anatolia.

These economic and cultural developments were accompanied by dramatic growth in the Greek population, which placed heavy demands on the resources of a mountainous country with limited agricultural land. Soon, some degree of economic, political, and social cooperation among the inhabitants of rival communities became necessary. But the values that had developed during centuries of isolation did not make such cooperation easy. Each local community treasured its autonomy and independence, celebrated its own rituals, and honored its own heroes. On what basis could such communities unite?

The Greek solution to this challenge was the *polis*, the root from which we derive the words *politics* and *political*. Yet the Greeks considered the polis to be a social collectivity, first and foremost—not a place. For this reason, our sources speak of groups of people—"the Athenians," "the Spartans"—rather than individual cities (Athens, Sparta). *Poleis* (the plural of *polis*) came to be considered so essential to Greek identity that Aristotle would later define man as "a political animal," someone who participates in the life of the polis and who cannot survive outside it.

In practice, poleis combined both formal institutions and informal structures that could differ widely. Most poleis were organized around a social center known as the *agora*, where markets and important meetings were held. Surrounding the whole urban settlement, the *asty*, was the *khora*, "land." The khora of a large polis might support several other towns or smaller poleis, as well as numerous villages. The Greeks described this early process of community building as the "bringing together of dwellings" (*synoikismos*, synoecism).

Polis formation could also come about through the conquest of one settlement by another and/or through the gradual alliance of neighboring communities. Some poleis took shape around fortified hilltops, such as the Athenian acropolis. Other communities may have borrowed a Near Eastern (and particularly Phoenician) practice of orienting the urban center around a temple precinct. In many Greek cities, however, temple building may have been a consequence of polis formation rather than a cause, as elites competed with one another to exalt their poleis and glorify themselves.

THE CULTURE OF ARCHAIC GREECE, 800–500 B.C.E.

Scholars date the Archaic Period of Greek history to the emergence of the polis and the return of writing, which the Greeks would put to a wide variety of uses. The Athenians, in particular, used writing to establish their cultural dominance over other Greek poleis, controlling the inscription of the Homeric canon, promoting the work of contemporary poets, and fostering the writing of prose histories, which allowed them to pass on to posterity a narrative of history in which they played the central role. It is therefore important to bear in mind that much of what we know about this early period derives from the work of later authors who wrote from this Athenian perspective: these include the Ionian-born Herodotus, who spent much of his later life in Athens; the historians Thucydides (c. 460–c. 395 B.C.E.) and Xenophon (430–354); and the philosophers Plato (c. 428–348) and his pupil Aristotle (384–322).

Colonization and Panhellenism

In the eighth and seventh centuries B.C.E., small-scale Greek trading ventures and settlements had developed into a full-fledged colonial enterprise that followed the example of the Phoenicians. Many larger poleis competed with one another to establish colonies, with Athens and Corinth being particularly successful in such ventures.

Although each of these colonies was an independent foundation, it sustained familial and affective ties to its mother polis; so it was often called upon to support the polis and could become entangled in the political and military affairs of the mainland. At the same time, these individual Greek colonies celebrated their shared language and heritage, which was exported to far-flung reaches of the known world, creating a Panhellenic ("all-Greek") culture that eventually stretched from the Black Sea to the Mediterranean coastline of modern France and Spain.

Greek colonization permanently altered the cultural geography of the Mediterranean world. The western shores of Anatolia would remain a stronghold of Greek culture for the next two thousand years. So many Greeks settled in southern Italy that later Romans called the region Magna Graecia, "Greater Greece"; Greek-speaking enclaves would survive there into the twentieth century of our era. By the fourth century B.C.E., more Greeks lived in Magna Graecia than in Greece itself.

Motives for colonization varied. Some poleis, such as Corinth, were blessed by their strategic location on the land bridge between Attica and the Peloponnesus (*pel-oh-poh-NEE-suss*; the large peninsula of mainland Greece), but cursed by the poverty of their land. Trade therefore became the lifeblood of this polis and of the ruling aristocracy who bankrolled the ambitious planting of colonies. Other poleis, confronted by the pressures of growing populations and political unrest, sponsored new colonies as outlets for undesirable elements or unwanted multitudes. These colonial projects parallel, in many ways, those of modern nation-states.

Colonial expansion also intensified Greek contacts with other cultures. Phoenician pottery brought new artistic motifs, while Egypt profoundly influenced early Greek sculptural representations of the human form (see **Interpreting Visual Evidence**). However, intensified contact with other cultures simultaneously sharpened Greeks' awareness of their own identity as Hellenes (the Greeks' name for themselves). Such self-conscious Hellenism did not lead to greater political cooperation, but it did encourage the establishment of Panhellenic festivals, such as the Olympic Games, and of holy sites.

The most important of these was the temple of Apollo at Delphi, home to the oracle of the sun god. Suppliants who sought to have their questions answered would offer gifts to the shrine and then wait while the god spoke through his priestess, whose mysterious answers would be translated into enigmatic Greek verse by an attending priest. The resulting advice was essentially a riddle that called for further interpretation on the part of the recipient—who often misconstrued it: as we noted in Chapter 2, Croesus of Lydia thought that he was following the advice of the oracle when he attacked the Persians, but the great nation he destroyed turned out to be his own.

At the Olympic Games, Greeks honored the king of the gods, Zeus, near the giant temple dedicated to him at Olympia. The Greeks took great pride in these athletic competitions, and only Hellenes were permitted to participate in them. Like colonization, these games did little to alleviate rivalry among the poleis; in fact, they often increased it. But they further strengthened the Greeks' awareness of their common culture, an awareness that could be harnessed when they faced a common threat.

Hoplite Warfare

In the centuries immediately following the calamities of the late Bronze Age, the defense of surviving Greek communities rested with the few elite warriors who had the resources to invest in armor, chariots, and weaponry. This monopoly on military prowess gave the aristocracy tremendous political and social leverage. As a result, aristocrats dominated political offices and priesthoods in the poleis, as well as economic life.

But during the Archaic Period, a revolution in military tactics brought aristocratic military dominance to an end. Increasingly, the effective defense of a polis required that it be able to call on a standing militia. Accordingly, able-bodied citizens began to equip themselves for battle and to train alongside one another. These citizen-soldiers became known as *hoplites*, from the large round shield (*hoplon*) carried by each. In battle, hoplites stood shoulder to shoulder in a close formation called a *phalanx*, several columns across and several rows deep, with each hoplite carrying his shield on the left arm to protect the unshielded right side of the man next to him. In his right hand, each hoplite carried a spear or sword, so that an approaching phalanx presented a nearly impenetrable wall of armor and weaponry to its opponents. If a man in the front rank fell, the one behind him stepped up to take his place; as a result, the weight of the entire phalanx was literally behind the front line, with each soldier leaning with his shield into the man in front of him.

This tight formation required only one shared skill: the ability to stay together. As long as the phalanx remained intact, it was nearly unbeatable. But like the polis itself, it could fall apart if its men did not share a common goal. The hoplite revolution was therefore bound up with a parallel revolution in politics. As a polis came increasingly to draw upon the resources of more and more citizens, it was forced to offer them a larger part in the exercise of political power. By the seventh century B.C.E., these citizen-soldiers formed a hoplite class that could demand a say in decision-making and thereby challenge the hegemony of old elites.

Aristocracy, Tyranny, and Democracy

For the better part of the seventh and sixth centuries B.C.E., aristocrats continued to dominate the Greek poleis. Struggles for influence among competing families were

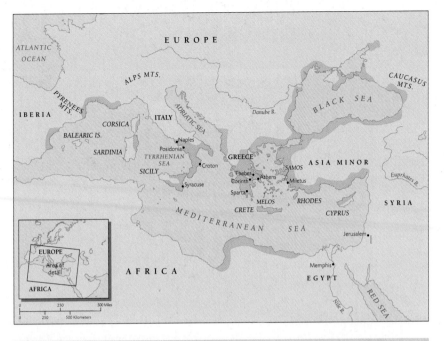

GREEK COLONIZATION, C. 550 B.C.E. Compare this map with that on page 41.
■ *How do you account for the differences in Greek and Phoenician patterns of colonization?* ■ *Were Greek colonies likely to compete with Phoenician colonies?* ■ *Where were such conflicts most likely to erupt?*

commonplace, and these differences affected polis government at every level, not least because aristocrats were the only members of society who could afford to hold unpaid and time-consuming political offices.

The aristocrats of this period pursued not only wealth, power, and fame; they also cultivated a distinctive lifestyle. Participating in politics and holding office was part of this lifestyle. So too was the *symposium*, a "drinking party" at which elite men would enjoy wine, poetry and poetic competition, performances by trained dancers and acrobats, and the company of *hetaeras* (courtesans) who provided witty conversation, music, and the promise of sex. Respectable women were excluded from such meetings, as they were from nearly all other aspects of social and political life (see below). So too were non-aristocratic men. The symposium was thus an arena for the display of aristocratic masculinity.

The glorification of male sexuality was another important aspect of this homosocial aristocratic culture. Typically, a man in his late twenties to late thirties, who had just begun to make his career in political life, would take as his lover and protégé an aristocratic youth in his early to mid-teens. The two would form an intimate bond in which sexual intercourse played an important role. This benefited

Interpreting Visual Evidence

The Ideal of Male Beauty

The Greek word *kouros* ("young man" or "youth") is now applied to a whole series of life-sized statues from the Archaic Period. The one shown here comes from Anavyssos in Attica, and was made between 540 and 515 B.C.E. (It is now in the National Archeological Museum of Athens.) Although scholars used to believe that such statues were meant to represent the god Apollo, further research has shown that most were made to commemorate the dead, especially young warriors who had fallen in battle. This one appears to be walking forward, smiling, but his eyes are closed. The accompanying inscription reads: "Stop and show your pity here for Kroisos, now dead, who once fighting in the foremost ranks of battle was destroyed by raging Ares."

Questions for Analysis

1. What aspects of the body does the kouros emphasize? If this is intended to be a model of Greek manhood, what values would it convey to contemporary youths?

2. Is this a representation of the young man as he was when living, or in death? How do your conclusions about the ideal of male beauty change if this is a glorification of death?

3. Compare this image to the values expressed in the verses by Tyrtaeus of Sparta on "The Beautiful and the Good" (page 65). How do these two perspectives complement one another?

both partners and their familes, and allowed the younger partner to learn the workings of politics while making valuable social connections. Many later philosophers, including Plato, argued that true love could exist only between such lovers, because only within such a relationship could a man find a partner worthy of his affections.

A whole complex of values, ideas, practices, and assumptions thus shaped aristocratic identity. As a result, it was impossible for those outside this elite world to participate fully in the public life of the polis. By the middle of the Archaic Period, moreover, the circle of the aristocratic elite tightened even further, as smaller and smaller groups came to dominate higher offices. Many aristocrats found themselves on the outside of their own culture, looking in.

For these men, one remedy lay close at hand: an alliance with the rising class of hoplites. And occasionally, a single aristocrat with the backing of the hoplites would succeed in setting up an alternative form of government, a *tyranny*. The word *tyrannos* had been borrowed from the Lydians, and it signified someone who ruled outside the traditional framework of the polis.

A tyrant in Archaic Greece was not necessarily an abusive ruler. Indeed, tyranny often led the way to wider political enfranchisement because anyone who sought the support of the hoplite class would have to appease that class by extending further rights of political participation, while all the time striving to keep the reins of power in his own hands. But this was an inherently unstable state of affairs,

HOPLITE INFANTRY ADVANCING INTO COMBAT. This Corinthian vase, dating from around 650 B.C.E., displays the earliest-known depiction of hoplites fighting in a phalanx formation.

because the continuance of tyranny became an obstacle to even greater power for the hoplite class. For this reason, tyrannies rarely lasted for more than two generations and could serve as a stepping-stone from aristocracy to a more broadly participatory form of government: democracy.

It is important to stress that our notion of democracy is quite different from that of the Greeks. In fact, Aristotle denegrated this form of government as "mob rule," because it gave too much power to the *demos*, a word meaning "neighborhood" or "affinity group." He saw it as a system too easily controlled by a particular faction. Our ideal of democracy is closer to what Aristotle would have called a polity, governance by the polis as a whole.

The Power of Poetry

The aristocracy of the Archaic Period were deeply invested in the heroic ideal enshrined in the Homeric epics. But they also strove to express their unique culture in newer poetic forms. The most characteristic of these is the lyric, a series of rhythmic verses sung to the music of the lyre. Because these songs would have been composed orally, even improvised, relatively few survive. But those that do are valuable historical sources. Because they were the focus of entertainment at gatherings, they are often politically charged, sexually explicit, or daringly subversive of accepted norms. For

example, the poet Archilochus of Paros (c. 680–640 B.C.E.) flouts the conventions of epic poetry by mocking his own failures on the battlefield: "Some barbarian waves my shield, since I had to abandon it / . . . but I escaped, so it scarcely matters / . . . I can get another just as good." So much for the heroic ideal of returning either with one's shield, or on it! In another lyric, Archilochus castigates his faithless (female) lover and his even more faithless (male) lover with whom she has run off.

Given the male domination of Greek culture, it is paradoxical that the most famous lyric poet of this age was not a man. Rather, it was Sappho (*SAF-foh*, c. 620–550 B.C.E.), who lived in the polis of Mytilene on the island of Lesbos. Revered by her contemporaries as the Tenth Muse, Sappho composed songs for a wide array of occasions and a range of moods: songs of courtship and marriage, longing and desire, loss, old age, and death. Often, they are passionately dedicated to women: both the women whom Sappho loved and the historical women who occupy the margins of masculine epic. Frequently, they take some image or incident from that inherited tradition and give it a distinctive spin. In one song, Sappho compares herself to Agamemnon, who was only able to return from Troy after he prayed to Hera, a goddess worshiped at Lesbos; Sappho now prays that her beloved will arrive safely with the goddess's help. In another, she imagines a scene not included in the *Iliad*, the joyous wedding of the Trojan Hector and his bride,

Andromache. The intimacy of lyric thus reveals something that few sources from antiquity are able to convey: the feelings and desires of individuals who were often at odds with the dominant culture of their time.

PORTRAITS OF THREE POLEIS

The poleis of the Archaic Period developed in very different ways. To illustrate this diversity, we will examine three particularly well-documented examples: Athens, Sparta, and the Ionian city of Miletus. None of these, however, can be considered typical. There were approximately one thousand poleis in Greece, and about most of them we know almost nothing. But at least we can survey some of the features that, with variations, made each polis unique—and yet comparable, in some ways, to its neighbors.

Athens

The Athenians liked to boast that their city had been a great metropolis since the Bronze Age: a claim integral to their identity and their sense of self-importance within the larger Greek world. But although Attica had long been a populous and prosperous region, Athens itself was of no great significance during the Mycenaean Era. When Athenians first came together to form a polis, theirs was a distinctly agricultural economy. Whatever profits aristocrats acquired through trade, they reinvested in land on the Attic Peninsula. Indeed, Athenian elites came to regard commerce as a disreputable means of earning a living, a mentality that persisted even when the city's excellent harbors made Athens famous as a mercantile polis.

In the Archaic Period, aristocratic dominance over this polis rested on the monopolization of elected offices and control of the city's council, the Areopagus (ah-ree-OP-ah-guhs). By the early seventh century B.C.E., an even smaller group of aristocratic officials wielded executive authority in Athens: the archons or "first men." Ultimately, nine archons presided over the entire governance of the polis. Although each served for only one year, all became lifetime members of the Areopagus. And because the Areopagus appointed the archons, it could therefore control its own future membership.

As power was consolidated by this small group, deep economic and social divisions developed. A significant proportion of the population fell into slavery through debt, while struggles among aristocratic families destabilized the government and fomented cycles of revenge killings.

Finally, this situation inspired Athens' first attempt to promulgate a set of written laws. In 621 B.C.E., an aristocrat named Drakon sought to control civic violence through harsh punishments: hence our use of the term "draconian" to describe any severe penalty, policy, or regime. This attempt failed, but ultimately led both aristocrats and hoplites to an agreement. In 594 B.C.E., they elected one man, the poet Solon, as the sole archon for one year, and they gave him sweeping powers. Solon was an aristocrat, but he had made his fortune as a merchant and did not hold that vocation in contempt; this meant that he was not allied with any single interest.

Solon's political and economic reforms laid the foundations for the later development of Athenian democracy. He forbade the practice of debt slavery and set up a fund to buy back Athenian slaves who had been sold abroad. He encouraged the cultivation of olives and grapes, thus spurring cash-crop farming and urban industries such as oil and wine production, and the manufacture of pottery storage jars and decorative drinking cups. He also broadened rights of political participation and set up courts in which a range of citizens served as jurors and to which any Athenian might appeal. He based eligibility for political office on property qualifications, not birth, thus making it possible for someone not born into the aristocracy to gain access to power. Moreover, he convened an Athenian assembly, the *ekklesia* (eh-KLAY-see-a), and gave it the right to elect archons. Now all free-born Athenian men over the age of eighteen could participate in government.

Yet Solon's reforms were not widely accepted. The aristocracy thought them too radical; the people of the demos, not radical enough. In the resulting generation of turmoil, an aristocrat named Peisistratos (pi-SIS-trah-tohs) succeeded in establishing himself as tyrant in 546 B.C.E. Somewhat ironically, Peisistratos then proceeded to institute Solon's reforms. But the apparent mildness of his rule was undergirded by the quiet, persistent intimidation of Athenians by his fellow foreign mercenaries and the ruthlessness with which he crushed any dissent. Still, by enforcing Solon's laws, he strengthened the political role of the demos and remained a popular ruler until his death. His sons, however, were less able to control the various factions that threatened their rule: one was assassinated and the other ousted with the help of the Spartans in 510 B.C.E.

But the following period of Spartan-sponsored oligarchy ("rule of the few") was brief. Two generations of increasing access to power had left the Athenian demos with a taste for self-government. For the first time in recorded history, a group of commoners can be credited with the overthrow of a regime. They rallied behind Cleisthenes (CLIE-sthen-ees), an aristocrat who had championed the

Analyzing Primary Sources

"The Beautiful and The Good"

The poet known as Tyrtaeus of Sparta flourished during the middle of the sixth century B.C.E. He may originally have come from Athens, but whatever his origins he expressed ideas of honor, beauty, and virtue that were universal among the hoplite warriors of the new poleis. The key terms he uses in the following verses cannot be adequately translated into English, since these short Greek adjectives are freighted with ancient meanings: kalos *(beautiful, honorable),* agathos *(good, brave, manly). They stand in opposition to the term* aischros *(shameful, ugly, mean).*

alos it is for an *agathos* warrior to die, fallen among the foremost fighters, in battle for his native land; but to leave his polis and rich fields and beg— that is most painful of all, as he wanders with his dear mother and aged father, his small children and his wedded wife. Detested he will be in the eyes of all those to whom he comes, constrained by need and hateful poverty. He shames his birth and belies his glorious appearance; dishonor and misery are his companions.

If no account is taken of a warrior who is a wanderer, if there is no respect for him or his family in the future, then let us fight with all our hearts for this land and die for our children, no longer hesitating to risk our lives. Young men, stand firm beside each other and fight.

Do not begin shameful flight or fear. Rather, create a mighty, valorous spirit in your breasts, and show no love for your lives when you are fighting. Do not flee, abandoning the older men, whose knees are no longer nimble.

For *aischros* it is for an older warrior to fall among the foremost fighters and lie out ahead of the young men—a man whose hair is already white and his beard grey—as he breathes out his valorous spirit in the dust, holding his bloody guts in his own hands, his body laid bare. *Aischros* is this to the eyes, and a cause of resentment to look upon.

But to the young men all is seemly, while the glorious flower of lovely youth is theirs. To men the young man is admirable to look upon, and to women lovable while he lives and *kalos* when he lies among the foremost fighters. So let a man take a firm stance and stand fast, with both feet planted upon the ground, biting his lip with his teeth.

Source: Excerpted and modified from *The Greek Polis*, eds. W. H. Adkins and Peter White (Chicago: 1986), pp. 23–24.

Questions for Analysis

1. How does Tyrtaeus characterize defeat? How does this poem exemplify the values and tactics of hoplite warfare?

2. Why is so much emphasis placed on physical beauty and youth? What other qualities are associated with the word *kalos*? Why is old age potentially *aischros*?

3. How does this ideal of male beauty compare with that made visible in the kouros of Anavyssos (page 62)?

---

cause of the demos after the fall of the Peisistratids. Once voted in as archon in 508/7 B.C.E., Cleisthenes took steps to limit aristocratic power. By reorganizing the Athenian population into ten voting districts, he suppressed traditional aristocratic loyalties. He also introduced the practice of ostracism, whereby Athenians could decide each year whether they wanted to banish someone for a decade and, if so, whom. With this power, Cleisthenes hoped that the demos could prevent the return of a tyrant and quell factional strife.

By 500 B.C.E., these struggles had given Athens a far more populist government than any other Greek polis, and had strengthened its political institutions. In the mean-time, Athens had become the principal exporter of olive oil, wine, and pottery in the Greek world. It was poised to assume the role it would claim for itself during the fifth century B.C.E. as the exemplar of Greek culture and the proponent of democracy.

Sparta

Located in the southern part of the Peloponnesus, Sparta took shape when four villages (and ultimately a fifth) combined to form a single polis. Perhaps as a relic of this unification process, Sparta retained a dual monarchy throughout its history, with two royal families and two lines of succession: a situation that often led to political in-fighting among their respective supporters.

According to local tradition, Spartan hegemony in the surrounding region of Laconia began with the conquest of Messenia, one of the mainland's few agriculturally viable territories. Around 720 B.C.E., the Spartans subjugated and enslaved the indigenous people there, the *helots*, who were forced to work under Spartan lordship. Around 650 B.C.E., however, the helots revolted, briefly threatening Sparta with annihilation. Eventually, Sparta triumphed; but the shock of this rebellion brought about a permanent transformation.

Determined to prevent another uprising, Sparta became the most militarized polis in Greece. By 600 B.C.E. everything was oriented to the maintenance of its hoplite army, a force so superior that Spartans confidently left their city unfortified. At a time when Athenian society was becoming more democratic and when citizens spent more time legislating than fighting, Spartan society was becoming increasingly devoted to an older aristocratic ideal of perpetual warfare.

The Spartan system made every male citizen a professional soldier of the phalanx. At birth, every Spartiate child was examined by officials who determined whether it was healthy enough to raise; if not, the infant was abandoned in the mountains. This was a custom observed elsewhere in the ancient world, but only in Sparta was it institutionalized. If deemed worthy of upbringing, the child was placed at age seven in the polis-run educational system. Boys and girls trained together until age twelve, participating in exercise, gymnastics, and other physical drills and competitions. Boys then went to live in barracks, where their military training would commence in earnest. Girls continued their training until they became the mates of eligible Spartiate males. No such thing as "marriage" was possible under the Spartiate system, or even desirable, for it would merely create a new set of loyalties and interests that would compete with the Spartan state.

Barracks life was designed to accustom youths to physical hardship. At age eighteen, the young man who survived this training would try for membership in a brotherhood whose sworn comrades lived and fought together. Failure to gain acceptance would mean that the young man would lose his rights as a citizen. If accepted, however, he remained with his brotherhood until he was thirty years of age. He was also expected to mate with a Spartiate woman, but occasions for this were few, a fact that partially accounts for the low birth-rate among Spartan citizens. After age thirty, a Spartiate male could opt to live with his family, but he was still required to remain on active military duty until he was sixty.

All Spartiate males over the age of thirty were members of the citizens' assembly, the *apella*, which voted on matters proposed to it by the two kings and twenty-eight elders. This *gerousia* (gher-oo-SEE-ah, "council of elders") was the main policymaking body of the polis and also its primary court. Its members were elected for life, but had to be over the age of sixty before they could stand for office. Meanwhile, five *ephors* (overseers), elected annually, supervised the educational system and acted as guardians of Spartan tradition. In the latter role, ephors could even depose an errant king from command of the army while on campaign. The ephors also supervised the Spartan secret service, the *krypteia*. Agents spied on citizens, but their main job was to infiltrate the helot population and identify potential troublemakers.

Spartan policy hinged on the precarious relationship between the Spartiates and the helots, who outnumbered the Spartiates ten to one. Helots accompanied the Spartiates on campaign as shield bearers, spear bearers, and baggage handlers. At home, however, the helots were a constant security concern. Every year the Spartans ritually declared war on them as a reminder that they would not tolerate dissent. Moreover, the threat of unrest meant that the polis was notoriously reluctant to send its army abroad.

Helot slavery therefore made the Spartan system possible, but Sparta's reliance on a hostile population of slaves was also a serious limitation. This system also limited Spartans' contact with the outside world in other respects. Spartiates were forbidden to engage in commerce, because wealth might distract them from the pursuit of martial glory. Nor did Spartiates farm their own lands, as Athenians did. economic activity fell either to the helots or to the free residents of other Peloponnesian cities, who were known as *perioikoi* (pair-ee-OY-koy), "those dwelling round about." The perioikoi enjoyed certain rights and protections within Spartan society, but unlike the residents of Attica, the perioikoi exercised no political rights.

The Spartans also self-consciously rejected innovation, styling themselves as the protectors of the "traditional customs" of Greece. In this role, Sparta tried to prevent the establishment of tyrannies in neighboring states and tried to overthrow them when they arose: hence their willing intervention in the affairs of Athens under the Peisistratids. Indeed, Sparta's stern defense of tradition made it an object of admiration throughout the Greek world, even though few Greeks had any desire to live as the Spartans did.

The fatal flaw in the Spartan system was demographic. There were many ways to fall from the status of Spartiate,

Songs of Sappho

Although Sappho of Lesbos (c. 620–550 B.C.E.) was a prolific poet and skilled musician, we know very little about her life and only a few examples of her extraordinary verse survive. Of the nine books collected in the third century B.C.E., we now have just one complete lyric and a series of fragments, some consisting of only two or three words, often preserved because they were quoted admiringly by other authors. Astonishingly, though, a papyrus scroll containing a previously unknown part of a poem was identified as recently as 2004.

Fragment 16

Some say thronging cavalry, some say
    foot soldiers,
others call a fleet the most beautiful of
sights the dark earth offers, but I say it's
    whatever you love best.

And it's easy to make this understood by
everyone, for she who surpassed all
    human
kind in beauty, Helen, abandoning her
    husband—that best of
men—went sailing off to the shores of
    Troy and
never spent a thought on her child or
    loving
parents: when the goddess seduced her
    wits and left her to wander,
she forgot them all, she could not
    remember
anything but longing, and lightly straying
aside, lost her way. But that reminds me
    now: Anactória,

she's not here, and I'd rather see her lovely
step, her sparkling glance and her face
    than gaze on
all the troops in Lydia in their chariots
    and glittering armor.

Source: Translated by Jim Powell, *The Poetry of Sappho* (New York: 2007), pp. 6–7.

The New Fragment (2004)

Live for the gifts the fragrant-breasted
    Muses
send, for the clear, the singing, lyre, my
    children.
Old age freezes my body, once so lithe,
rinses the darkness from my hair, now
    white.
My heart's heavy, my knees no longer
    keep me
up through the dance they used to
    prance like fawns in.
Oh, I grumble about it, but for what?
Nothing can stop a person's growing old.

They say that Tithonus was swept away
in Dawn's passionate, rose-flushed arms
    to live
forever, but he lost his looks, his youth,
failing husband of an immortal bride.

Source: Translated by Lachlan Mackinnon, *Times Literary Supplement*, July 15, 2005.

Questions for Analysis

1. How does Sappho use stories from the older tradition she has inherited to address her own concerns? How does the perspective of the female poet transform masculine ideas about heroism, beauty, warfare, aging?

2. What are the challenges of working with such fragmentary sources as these? If these were the only pieces of evidence to survive from Archaic Greece, what conclusions could you draw about the society and its values?

---

but the only way to become one was by birth—and the Spartan birthrate simply could not keep pace with the demand for trained warriors. As a result, the number of full Spartiates declined from perhaps as many as 10,000 in the seventh century to only about 1,000 by the middle of the fourth century B.C.E. Another flaw is historical: because the Spartans placed little value on written records, almost everything we know about them (including the summary offered here) must be gleaned from archeological investigations or the propaganda of their enemies, notably the Athenians.

Miletus and the Ionian Revolution in Thought

Across the Aegean from the Greek mainland lay the Greek cities of Ionia on the central part of the Anatolian coast. Here, Miletus was the foremost commercial and cultural power. Long a part of the Greek world (see *Analyzing Primary Sources* in Chapter 2, page 40), it had also been shaped by Mesopotamian and Egyptian influences, and Milesian intellectuals were well aware of Near Eastern

literature and learning. Some even echoed the vaunting rhetoric of Persian imperial decrees ("thus speaks Darius the Great King. . . .") to make their own, quite different observations ("thus speaks Hecataeus of Miletus: the sayings of the Greeks are many and foolish").

The relationship between the Ionians of the coast and the interior kingdom of Lydia was close but difficult. It was through the Ionians that the Lydian invention of coinage was introduced to the Greek world, where it revolutionized trade, made wealth portable for the first time, and introduced a host of new philosophical and ethical problems. The Ionians, in turn, played a crucial role in Hellenizing Asia Minor while at the same time insisting on their independence. The major cities of Ionia ultimately banded together to form the Ionian League, a political and religious confederation of poleis pledged to support each other. This was the first such organization in the Greek world.

The Milesians founded many colonies, especially in and around the Black Sea. They were also active in Egypt. These colonial efforts, combined with its advantageous position for trade, brought Miletus extraordinary wealth. At the same time, it became a center for what the Greeks called *philosophia*, "the love of wisdom." Beginning in the sixth century B.C.E., a series of intellectuals now known as the pre-Socratics (because they came before Socrates) raised new and vital questions about the relationship between the natural world (the *kosmos*), the gods, and men. Often, their explanations moved the direct influence of the gods to the margins or removed it altogether, something that other Greeks regarded as blasphemous. For example, Milesian philosophers sought physical explanations for the movements of the heavens, and did not presume that heavenly bodies were divine. By making human observations the starting point for their knowledge, they began to formulate scientific explanations for the working of the universe.

Stimulated by the cultural diversity of their city, Milesian philosophers also began to rethink humans' place in the cosmos. When Hecataeus (*heck-ah-TAY-us*) remarked that "the sayings of the Greeks are many and foolish," he was deriding his contemporaries' unquestioning acceptance of a narrow worldview. He set out to expand their horizons by traveling extensively and studying the customs and beliefs of other cultures. Xenophanes (*zee-NOFF-uh-nees*) further posited that all human knowledge is relative and conditioned by experience: he observed that the Thracians (a people living north of Greece) believed that the gods had blue eyes and red hair as the Thracians themselves did, whereas Ethiopians portrayed the gods as dark skinned and curly haired, as they themselves were. He concluded that human beings make gods in their own image, not the other way around. If oxen could pray, Xenophanes declared, they would pray to gods who looked like oxen.

Such theories would become a distinctive strand in later Greek philosophy, yet they would continue to be regarded as disturbing and dangerous—dangerous enough to warrant the execution of Socrates in Athens a hundred years later (see below). By that time, the Persian conquest of Lydia had made Miletus and its sister cities subject to that great empire. Ultimately, those poleis' resistance to Persian rule would trigger the greatest clash the Greek world had yet known.

THE CHALLENGE OF THE PERSIAN WARS

The two major wars fought between the Greeks and the Persians were construed as defining events by those who witnessed and looked back on them. From the first, the contest was unequal. Persia was the largest and most efficient state the world had ever seen, capable of mustering over a million armed men. The Greeks, by contrast, remained a collection of disparate communities, fiercely competitive and suspicious of one another. An exceptionally large polis, such as Athens or Sparta, might put 10,000 hoplites in the field; but the vast majority of Greek states could only provide a few hundred each. So the threat of Persian conquest loomed large on the Greek horizon.

The Ionian Revolt (499–494 B.C.E.)

For the first time in the history of Western civilizations, we can follow the unfolding of events through the narrative of a contemporary historian: Herodotus, the first person who self-consciously set out to write an account of his own times in careful, unambiguous prose, rather than in the form of heroic poetry or the boastful language of victorious inscriptions. And luckily for us, Herodotus was uniquely qualified to probe the long-term and more immediate causes of the Persian Wars. Raised in the Ionian polis of Halicarnassus, he regarded both the Greeks and the Persians as great peoples. Yet, as a Greek himself—albeit one born within the Persian dominion—he was not impartial. Indeed, his surviving account reflects the intellectual currents of Athens, where he spent the better part of his career, as well as many Athenian prejudices. This is something we must be bear in mind when reading his work.

Herodotus was careful to show that the war between the Persians and Greeks had ancient roots, but his narrative also shows that the catalyst was a political conflict in Miletus. In 501 B.C.E., the city was governed by Aristagoras, a tyrant who owed his power to the backing of the Persian emperor, Darius. But apparently Aristagoras came to believe that his days as the emperor's favorite were numbered. So he turned abruptly from puppet to patriot, rousing the Milesians and the rest of Ionia to revolt against Persian rule. As a safeguard, he also sought military support from sympathetic poleis on the Greek mainland. The Spartans refused to send their army abroad, but Athens and Eretria, on the island of Euboea, agreed to send twenty-five ships and crews. This small force managed to capture the old Lydian capital of Sardis (by then a Persian administrative center) and burn it to the ground. Then the Athenians and Eretrians went home, leaving the Ionians to their own devices. In 494 B.C.E., the rebellious poleis were finally overwhelmed by the vastly superior might of Persia.

Darius realized, however, that so long as his Greek subjects in Asia Minor could cast a hopeful eye to their neighbors across the Aegean, they would forge alliances. He therefore decided to launch a preemptive strike against Athens and Eretria, to teach these upstart poleis a lesson. In the summer of 490 B.C.E., a punitive expedition of 20,000 soldiers crossed the Aegean. Their forces sacked and burned Eretria to the ground, sending its population into captivity in Persia. They then crossed the narrow strait to Attica, landing on the plain of Marathon, approximately 26 miles from Athens.

Marathon and Its Aftermath

In this emergency, the Athenians sought help from the only polis that could conceivably help them forestall annihilation: Sparta. But the Spartans responded that they were unable to assist—they were celebrating a religious festival. Only the small, nearby polis of Plataea offered the Athenians aid. Heavily outnumbered and without effective cavalry to counter that of the Persians, the Athenian hoplites took a position between two hills blocking the main road to the

A MODERN REPLICA OF AN ATHENIAN TRIREME. These versatile warships were much more powerful than the old fifty-oared pentakonters that had been in use for centuries. As the name suggests, a trireme featured three banks of oars on each side, 170 oars in total. These were manned by citizen rowers seated on benches at three different levels in the vessel's hold. In battle, rowers could help power a ship forward, turn it, and keep it on course in a chase, even when sailing into the wind. In favorable winds, sails could be used to add speed. ▪ *How does this new military technology build on some of the same strategies as hoplite warfare?*

polis. After a standoff of several days, the Athenian general Miltiades (*mil-TIE-uh-dees*) received word that the Persians were watering their horses, and that the Persian infantry was vulnerable. Miltiades led a charge that smashed the Persian force and resulted in crippling losses. Almost unbelievably, the Athenians had defeated the world's major imperial power, and they had done it without Spartan help. It was a vindication of hoplite tactics and a tremendous boost to Athenian confidence.

Yet the Athenian politician Themistocles (*theh-MIS-toh-klees*) warned that the Persians would retaliate with an even larger force. So when the Athenians discovered a rich vein of silver ore in the Attic countryside a few years later, they used the windfall to finance a fleet of 200 triremes, state-of-the-art warships.

Xerxes' Invasion

Darius the Great was succeeded by his son Xerxes (*ZERK-sees*), who almost immediately began preparing a massive invasion of Greece to avenge his father's shame. Supported by a fleet of 600 ships, this grand army set out in 480 B.C.E.,

THE PERSIAN WARS WITH GREECE. Imagine that you are the Persian emperor Xerxes, planning the conquest of Greece in 480 B.C.E.
■ *What are the two possible routes that you could take to attack Greece?* ■ *What geographical considerations would dictate your military strategy?* ■ *Bearing in mind that Xerxes' attempt failed, what would you have done differently?*

crossing the narrow strait separating Europe from Asia. But unlike his father, who had dispatched talented generals to lead the earlier attack on Athens, Xerxes led this campaign himself.

Many Greek poleis capitulated immediately. But Athens, Sparta, Corinth, and some thirty others hastily formed a Hellenic League: an unprecedented alliance in the face of an unprecedented threat. In August of 480, a major Persian offensive was held at bay when the outnumbered Greek allies, under the military leadership of Sparta, confronted Xerxes at the mountain pass of Thermopylae (*ther-MO-pih-lie*). For three days, they valiantly held off

the Persian multitude. Meanwhile, a Greek fleet led by Athens engaged a Persian flotilla. The Spartans' defense of Thermopylae ultimately failed, but their sacrifice of some 300 warriors allowed the new Athenian warships to inflict heavy losses on the Persians.

However, these engagements left Athens without any men to defend their city. Themistocles therefore persuaded the entire population to abandon Athens for the island of Salamis. From there, the Athenians watched the Persians torch their city. Time, however, was on their side. Xerxes' massive army depended on his damaged fleet for supplies, and the Persians' military tactics—which included a heavy

GREEK FORCES DEFEAT PERSIANS. This detail from a bowl commemorating the defeat of Xerxes' army depicts an Athenian hoplite poised to strike a death-blow to his Persian opponent. The artist has carefully delineated the differences between the enemies' dress and weaponry. To the Greeks, the Persian preference for trousers over short tunics seemed particularly barbaric and effeminate.

reliance on cavalry and chariots—were not adapted for the rocky terrain of Greece.

In late September, the numerically superior Persian fleet sailed into the straits of Salamis. So confident was Xerxes that he had a throne placed above the bay, where he would have a good view of his victory. Instead, he watched as the Athenian triremes demolished the Persian fleet. This was the turning point of the war. When the allied Greek army met the Persians on favorable terrain the next spring—an open plain near Plataea—the Greeks prevailed. Against all odds, the small, fractious poleis had defeated the mightiest army of the known world.

THE GOLDEN AGE OF CLASSICAL GREECE

In the half century after the Persian Wars, Athens enjoyed a meteoric rise in power and prestige, becoming the premier naval power of the eastern Mediterranean. Athens also emerged as leader of the Delian League, a group of poleis whose representatives met on the sacred island of Delos

and pledged to continue the war against Persia. The fifth century B.C.E. also witnessed the greatest achievements in Athenian culture and politics.

Periclean Athens

The reforms of the decades before the Persian Wars continued to encourage further experiments in democracy, including the selection of major officeholders by lot. Only one key position was now filled by traditional voting: the office of *strategos*, or general. This office became the career goal of Athens' most ambitious figures.

Meanwhile, new voices were demanding a greater role in government. Most prominent were the *thetes* (THAY-tees), the lowest class of free men that provided the triremes' rowers, the backbone of the all-important Athenian fleet. Like the hoplites of the Archaic Period, who had achieved citizenship because they were indispensible to the defense of the poleis, thetes wanted higher status and equal representation. The man who emerged to champion their cause was Pericles (PEHR-eh-klees), an aristocrat from one of Athens' most prestigious families.

Pericles also advocated a foreign policy that was oriented away from cooperation with Sparta. In 462–461 B.C.E. he was elected strategos and immediately used his position to push through reforms that gave every Athenian citizen the right to propose and amend legislation, not just to vote yes or no in the citizens' assembly. And by paying an average day's wage for attendance, he made it easier for poorer citizens to participate in the assembly and in courts of justice. Through such measures, the thetes and other free men of modest means became a dominant force in politics—and loyal to the man who had made that dominance possible.

Athenian Literature and Drama

Pericles also glorified Athens with an ambitious scheme of public building and lavish festivals honoring the gods. The most important of these was the Dionysia, a great spring feast devoted to the god Dionysius, which became a forum for the presentation of drama. From the beginning, therefore, Greek theater was closely connected to the political and religious life of the state that sponsored it. Indeed, the very format of classical tragedy replicates the tensions of democracy, showcasing the conflict among opposing perspectives. This format was perfected under the great tragedian Aeschylus (EYE-skihl-uhs, 525–456 B.C.E.) and his

THE THEATER AT EPIDAUROS. Greek dramas were invariably presented in the open air, usually at dawn. Since these were civic spectacles, theaters had to be large enough to accommodate all citizens. Most, like this one at Epidauros (right), took advantage of the natural slope of a hill. The plan for the theater is shown above (left). The acting area would have been backed by a high wall, the *skene*, which housed stage machinery and enhanced the acoustics. A trained actor standing in the circular *orchestra* would have been audible even to those seated in the top tier. ▪ *How would the size and setting of such a theater enhance the political character of the plays performed within it?*

younger contemporary, Sophocles (496–406 B.C.E.). Their dramas made use of two and eventually three professional actors (each of whom could play numerous roles) and a chorus of Athenian citizens, which represented collective opinion and could comment on the action.

Tragedies were almost always set in the distant or mythical past, yet were intended to address the cutting-edge issues of their day. Indeed, the very earliest of all surviving tragedies, Aeschylus' *The Persians*, represents events of the playwright's own lifetime; and we know for certain that he fought at Marathon, because he had this fact proudly recorded on his tomb. Performed for the first time in 472, it tells the story of the great Athenian victory at Salamis, but through the eyes of the defeated Xerxes, who thus becomes its tragic hero.

But even when its subject matter was derived from the epics of Homer, the fundamental themes of tragedy—the conflicting demands of personal desire and public duty, the unforeseen consequences of human actions, the brutalizing effects of power—addressed problems of immediate concern to Athenians. For example, *Oedipus at Colonus*, one of Sophocles' later tragedies, used a story of the mythical king of Thebes to comment bitterly on Athens' disastrous war with Sparta (see below). Similarly, the *Trojan Women* of Euripides (485–406 B.C.E.), presented in 415, marks the tragic turning point in the Athenians' march toward defeat in this war. By looking back at the capture, rape, and enslavement of Troy's defeated women, Athenians were forced to look ahead to the consequences of their own imperial policies.

Comedy was even more obviously a genre of political commentary, and could deal openly with the absurdities and atrocities of current events. Indeed comedy—then as now—could be effectively deployed to deal with issues that were too hot to handle in any other form: sexual scandals, political corruption, moral hypocrisy, intellectual pretension, popular fads. Aristophanes (*EHR-ih-STOFF-ah-nees*, c. 446–386 B.C.E.), the greatest of the Athenian comic playwrights, lampooned everything from the philosophy of Socrates to the tragedies of his contemporary Euripides, and was an especially outspoken critic of Athenian war-mongers and their imperialist aims. He was repeatedly dragged into court to defend himself against the demagogues he attacked, but the power and popularity of comic theater was such that politicians never dared to shut it down for long.

Periclean Athens was also fertile ground for the development of new literary forms. Even though the Greeks were becoming more dependent on writing for legal and commercial transactions, intellectuals had long been used to expressing themselves through poetry, which was always intended to be sung and enjoyed in performance, not to be read. Now, though, the rise of functional literacy in Athens encouraged the emergence of prose as a distinct literary form. Herodotus found a ready market for his histories in Athens. His younger contemporary Thucydides (*thu-SID-ih-dees*) followed suit, using his time in exile to write a masterful—and scathingly critical—history of the war between his polis and Sparta.

Between them, these two historians developed a new approach to the study of the past, emphasizing the need to collect and interpret multiple sources and focusing on human agency as the driving force of history (rather than divine intervention). Both conceived the historian's role as distinct from that of a storyteller. The word *historia* would continue to mean both "story" and "history" in Greek, but for Herodotus and Thucydides the historian's task was to investigate and critically reflect on the events of his own time, as well as to illuminate those of the past. These methods and goals would increasingly come to inform other prose genres, including the philosophical writings of Plato and Aristotle (see Chapter 4).

Art and Architecture

The artists of fifth-century B.C.E. Athens revealed the same range of talents in the visual arts as poets did in their dramas. Perhaps the most striking development was the new attention paid to the crafting of naturalistic figures, both clothed and nude. Nothing like it had ever been seen before, although it is a trend already discernible in the figure of the *kouros* examined above (page 62). What hastened the acceptance of naturalism is a matter of intense debate,

APOLLO OF TENEA, APOLLO OF PIOMBINO, AND THE CRITIAN BOY. These three statues, dating from about 560, 500, and 480 B.C.E., respectively, display the development of Greek statuary art. The first rather stiff and symmetrical statue (left) is imitative of Egyptian sculpture. Roughly half a century later, the second representation (middle) of Apollo begins to display motion, not unlike the kouros on page 62. The last figure (right), showing a boy standing in a relaxed posture with his weight resting on one leg, displays even greater naturalism.

but scholars have long wanted to link this innovation to the triumphant victories over the Persians. Greeks tended to regard the Persian male's modesty of dress, preference for trousers, fondness for jewelry, and luxurious long hair as proofs of effeminacy (see the vase painting on page 71), whereas Greek men took pride in exercising, sculpting their physiques, and participating in athletic contests in the nude. A Greek might have said that only barbarians covered their shameful bodies in constricting clothes; free men celebrate their individuality in the care of the body and its representation.

The Athenians also made exceptional contributions to architecture in this period. All Greek temples sought to create an impression of harmony, but the Parthenon of Athens, built between 447 and 438 B.C.E., is generally considered the finest example of this (see page 58). Construction of this expensive and structurally ambitious building was urged on the Athenians by Pericles as a tribute to their patron goddess, Athena Parthenos ("Athena the Virgin"), and as a symbol of their own power, confidence, and genius.

Women and Men in the Daily Life of Athens

Toward the end of his famous funeral oration, which Thucydides included in his history, Pericles addresses only a few brief remarks to the women of Athens who mourn their fallen fathers, husbands, and sons in the first year of the disastrous war with Sparta (430 B.C.E.). He urges them to do three things: rear more children for the support of Athens, show no more weakness than is "natural to their sex," and attract no attention to themselves. His remarks reveal widely held attitudes toward women in classical Greece, especially in Athens.

The growth of democracy did not lead to greater equality between the sexes; in fact, it had the opposite result. In Mycenaean Greece, women had been viewed as possessing extraordinary funds of courage and wisdom. They were prized for their shrewd advice on political and military matters, and they played an active role in the world. Sometimes they ruled kingdoms in their own right. But as aristocratic ideals gave way to more democratic ones, Greek women increasingly spent their lives in the shadows.

The importance of the hoplite infantry and its spirit of shared purpose encouraged men to train together and to develop close relationships. At the same time, that spirit of equality discouraged displays of wealth, especially by women. Instead, the rearing of children to supply the infantry became the female imperative. Public spaces were restricted to male activities, while domestic, private spaces were reserved for female endeavors such as child care and weaving. Respectable women lived in seclusion, rarely (if ever) venturing forth from their homes.

In Athens, girls could be married at age fourteen—to husbands more than twice their age. A girl's father arranged her marriage and provided a dowry that her husband could use for her support. Legally, wives became the property of their husbands. And shortly after a wife entered her new home, a regular schedule of childbirth would begin. The average young wife would bear between four and six children before she died, usually around the age of thirty-five. Her place might then be taken by another, younger woman. Available evidence even suggests that husbands were not encouraged to form emotional attachments to their wives, although some obviously did. In a revealing passage, Herodotus reports of a certain Lydian king that he "fell in love with his own wife, a fancy that had strange consequences." By contrast, an Athenian orator remarked that "we have prostitutes for pleasure, concubines for daily physical attendance, and wives to bear us legitimate children and be our faithful housekeepers."

Because respectable women seldom went out of doors, since it was thought immodest for them to be seen by men outside their immediate families, slaves did whatever shopping or marketing the household required. Even at home, women were expected to withdraw into private rooms if visitors arrived. But they were not supposed to sit around idly, and their main occupation was spinning and weaving. This was true of all women, from royalty to slaves. And since women's work was basically menial, men looked down on them for it, even though their own livelihoods and comfort depended on it.

In addition to depending on the faithful labor and fertility of its "free" women, Athenians were as reliant on slaves as Spartans were on helots. Without slavery, none of the Athenian accomplishments in politics, philosophy, or art would have been possible. The Athenian ideal of dividing and rotating governmental duties among all free men depended on slaves who worked in fields, businesses, and homes. In fact, the Athenian democratic system began to function fully only with the expansion of Athenian commerce around 500 B.C.E., which enabled the Athenians to buy slaves in larger numbers. Freedom and slavery were thus inescapably, and paradoxically, linked in this democracy—much as they would be many centuries later in the United States.

Although widespread, Athenian slavery was modest in scale. Slaves did not ordinarily work in teams or in factories; the only exceptions were the state-owned silver mines, where large numbers of slaves toiled in miserable conditions. Most slaves were owned in small numbers by a wide range of Athenian families, including the relatively poor. As domestic servants and farm laborers, slaves might even be considered trusted members of the household, although their masters were legally empowered to beat them or abuse them; concubines were often drawn from among this class of slaves. Yet slaves could never be entirely dehumanized, as they were in modern slaveholding societies: the misfortune of becoming a slave through debt was a reality of Athens' recent past, and the real possibility of being enslaved in war would become a widespread consequence of Athens' overreaching ambitions.

"THE GREATEST WAR IN HISTORY" AND ITS CONSEQUENCES

And ultimately, Athens' foreign policy and imperial ambitions undermined its civic and cultural achievements. Since the 470s, Athens had begun crushing those allies who attempted to break from its control. By the early 440s, its only rival for supremacy in the Greek world was Sparta. Rather than attempting to maintain a balance of power, however, Pericles determined on a more aggressive policy. In order to ensure that military resources would be directed toward any Spartan opposition, he concluded a formal peace with Persia. Yet the sole purpose of the Delian League had been the defense of Greece against Persian aggression, so Athens now had no justification for compelling its members to maintain their allegiance. Many remained loyal nonetheless, enjoying the economic benefits of warm relations with Athens. Others, however, did not, and Athens found itself increasingly having to force its allies back into line, often installing Athenian garrisons and planting Athenian colonists—who retained their Athenian citizenship—to ensure future loyalty.

In the context of recent history and longstanding Greek values, such behavior was disturbing. The Persian wars had been fought to preserve Greek independence. Now Athens itself was becoming an oppressive, imperial power. Foremost among its accusers were the Corinthians, whose own economic standing was threatened by Athenian dominance. The Corinthians were close allies of the Spartans, who were in turn the dominant power in what historians call the Peloponnesian League. (The Greeks called it simply the "Spartans and their allies.") When war finally erupted between Athens and Sparta, Thucydides—himself an Athenian—ascribed it to the growing power of Athens and the anxiety this inspired in other poleis. No modern historian has improved on Thucydides' thesis. Yet for the Athenians and their leaders, there could be no question of relinquishing their empire, or the dream of dominating the Mediterranean world. For Sparta and its allies, meanwhile, the prospect of relinquishing their independence was equally unthinkable. Two very different ideas of Greek superiority were about to fight to the death.

The Peloponnesian War Begins

When the Athenians and Spartans found themselves at war with one another in 431 B.C.E., both sides believed a conclusion would come quickly—a delusion common to many of history's pivotal contests. Instead, the war dragged on for twenty-seven years. Thucydides, writing about it in exile, recalled that he knew from the time of its outbreak that it was going to be "the greatest war in history," amounting to the first world war, because by the time it was over it would involve the entire Mediterranean. He also meant that it was the worst, so devastating to both sides that it destroyed the proud heritage of freedom the Greeks had treasured. By the time Athens was forced to concede defeat, all the poleis were weakened to such an extent that they would never again be able to withstand outside threats.

From the beginning, Athens knew that it could not defeat Sparta on land; and neither Sparta nor its allies had a fleet capable of facing the Athenians at sea. Pericles therefore developed a bold strategy: he would pull the entire population of Attica within the walls of Athens and not attempt to defend the countryside against Sparta. For sustenance, Athens would rely on supplies shipped in by its fleet, which would also be deployed to ravage the coasts of the Peloponnesus.

The Spartans duly plundered the farms and pastures of Attica, frustrated that the Athenians would not engage them in battle. Meanwhile, the Athenians inflicted significant destruction on Spartan territory in a series of raids and by successfully encouraging rebellion among the helots. Time appeared to be on Athens' side. But in 429 B.C.E. the crowded conditions of the besieged city gave rise to a typhus epidemic that killed over a third of the population, including the aged Pericles.

Pericles' death revealed that he had been the only man capable of managing the political forces he had unleashed. His successors were mostly demagogues, ambitious men who played to the worst instincts of the demos. The most successful of these was Cleon, who refused a Spartan offer of peace in 425 B.C.E. and continued the war until his own death in battle four years later. It was under Cleon that Thucydides was given the impossible task of liberating a city under Spartan control; his failure in 423 led to his exile.

THE PELOPONNESIAN WAR. This map shows the patchwork of colonies and alliances that bound together the supporters of Sparta and Athens at the outbreak of the Peloponnesian War in 431 B.C.E. ▪ *Which side had the geographical advantage?* ▪ *Which neutral powers might have been able to tip the balance by entering the war on one side or the other?* ▪ *What strategic and military choices did geography impose on the two combatants and their allies?*

After the death of Cleon, a truce with Sparta was negotiated by an able Athenian leader named Nicias (*NICK-ee-ahs*). But Athenians continued to pursue a "dirty war" by preying on poleis that it feared might support the Spartans. This led to atrocities like the destruction of the entire city of Melos, an island colonized by the Spartans that had maintained its neutrality since the beginning of the war. When the inhabitants of Melos refused to compromise this position by accepting Athenian rule, Athens had the entire male population slaughtered and every woman and child sold into slavery.

Thereafter, Athens' policy of preemptive warfare proved destructive to itself. In 415 B.C.E., a charismatic young aristocrat named Alcibiades (*al-ki-BY-uh-dees*) convinced the

Athenians to attack the powerful Greek city of Syracuse in Sicily, which was allegedly harrying Athenian allies in the western Mediterranean. The expedition ended disastrously, with the death or enslavement of thousands of Athenian warriors.

News of the Syracusan disaster shattered the Athenians. Many political leaders were driven from the polis as scapegoats, and in 411 B.C.E. a hastily convened assembly of citizens voted the democracy out of existence, replacing it with an oligarchy of 400 men, many of whom had been present at this vote. The remains of the Athenian fleet, then stationed in Samos on the Ionian coast, responded by declaring a democratic government in exile under the leadership of none other than Alcibiades. The oligarchy proved to be brief, and democracy was restored to Athens by 409. But a pattern of self-destruction had been established, making it difficult for anyone in Athens or outside it to believe in the possibility of restored greatness.

THE FAILURE OF ATHENIAN DEMOCRACY

The Spartans too despaired of bringing the war to an end. Even in its weakened condition, the Athenian fleet was still invincible. Finally, Sparta turned to the Persians, who were glad to avenge themselves on Athens and agreed to supply the gold and expertise necessary to train an effective Spartan navy. Meanwhile, Athenians were turning against each other and making the Spartans' task easier. In 406 B.C.E., a rare Athenian naval victory ended in a sudden storm that prevented Athenian commanders from rescuing the sailors whose ships had been wrecked. A firestorm of protest was fanned by demagogues who insisted on making an example of those generals brave enough to return to Athens. One of these was Pericles' son Pericles, who died a victim of his father's policies. Through such measures, the Athenians killed or exiled the last of their able commanders.

The poorly led Athenian fleet was destroyed in 404 B.C.E. Without ships, the Athenians could neither feed themselves nor defend their city. The Spartans sailed the Aegean unopposed, installing pro-Spartan oligarchies. Finally, they besieged Athens, which surrendered. Corinth and Thebes, remembering the ruthless treatment of Melos, called for Athens' destruction. The Spartans refused, but imposed harsh terms: the dismantling of Athens' defensive walls, the scrapping of its fleet, and the acceptance of an oligarchy under Spartan supervision. These so-called Thirty Tyrants confiscated private property and murdered their political opponents. Their excesses drove committed democrats to plan a desperate coup, a bloodbath averted only through the intervention of the Spartan king.

By the end of 401 B.C.E., Athens had restored a semblance of democratic governance, but it was never more than a shadow of its former self. Meanwhile, Sparta succeeded Athens as the arbiter of the Greek world. But this was a thankless job, made worse by the losses the Spartans had suffered during the war and by the fact that they were even more aggressive in their control than the Athenians had been. In fact, the Spartans found themselves in a position they had avoided throughout their history, because their far-flung interests now sapped their manpower and

undermined their control over the helots. They also faced a reinvigorated Persian Empire, which increased its naval presence in the Aegean.

These were the circumstances in which the Athenian philosopher Socrates (469–399 B.C.E.) attempted to reform his city's ethical and political traditions. To understand something of his accomplishments, and to assess the reasons for his tragic death, we must trace briefly the history of philosophical speculation in the half century before his birth.

The Pythagoreans and the Sophists

After the Persian conquest of Ionia, many Milesian philosophers fled to southern Italy. Philosophical speculation thus continued in the Greek "far west." A major figure here was Pythagoras (*pith-AG-or-us*), who founded a philosophical community. Pythagoras and his followers regarded the speculative life as the highest good, and believed that one must be purified of fleshly desires in order to achieve this. Just as the essence of life lay in the mind, they believed that the essence of the universe was to be found not in the natural world but in the study of abstractions. The Pythagoreans established the key properties of odd and even numbers and also proved an old Babylonian hypothesis in geometry,

SOCRATES. According to Plato, Socrates looked like a goatman but spoke like a god.

Competing Viewpoints

Two Views of Socrates

Socrates as a Sophist

Most people regard Socrates as the sage thinker who challenged the prevailing prejudices of his day. During his own time, however, he was not so universally admired. In Aristophanes' comedy The Clouds, *the protagonist, Strepsiades (strep-SIGH-uh-dees), goes to Socrates and his "Thought Shop" to ask that Socrates make him and his son, Pheidippides (phi-DIP-pid-ees), orators capable of winning lawsuits and growing rich. Aristophanes implies throughout that Socrates is a charlatan who teaches word games and tricks for hire.*

STREPSIADES: See that he [Pheidippides] learns your two Arguments, whatever you call them—oh yes, Right and Wrong—the one that takes a bad case and defeats Right with it. If he can't manage both, then at least Wrong—that will do—but that he must have.

SOCRATES: Well, I'll go and send the Arguments here in person, and they'll teach him themselves.

STREPSIADES: Don't forget, he's got to be able to argue against any kind of justified claim at all.

RIGHT: This way. Let the audience see you. . . .

WRONG: Sure, go wherever you like. The more of an audience we have, the more soundly I'll trounce you.

RIGHT: What sort of trick will you use?

WRONG: Oh, just a few new ideas.

RIGHT: Yes, they're in fashion now, aren't they, [*to the audience*] thanks to you idiots. . . . [*to Pheiddipides*] You don't want to be the sort of chap who's always in the agora telling stories about other people's sex lives, or in the courts arguing about some petty, filthy little dispute. . . .

WRONG: People here at the Thought Shop call me Wrong, because I was the one who invented ways of proving anything wrong, laws, prosecutors, anything. Isn't that worth millions—to have a really bad case and yet win? . . . Suppose you fall in love with a married woman—have a bit of fun—and get caught in the act. As you are now, without a tongue in your head, you're done for. But if you come and learn from me, then you can do whatever you like and get away with it . . . and supposing you do get caught with someone's wife, you can say to him. . . . "What have I done wrong? Look at Zeus; wasn't he always a slave of his sexual passions? And do you expect a mere mortal like me to do any better than a god?" . . .

STREPSIADES [*to Socrates*]: I wonder if you'd accept a token of my appreciation? But my son, has he learned that Argument we were listening to a moment ago?

SOCRATES: Yes, he has.

STREPSIADES: Holy Fraud, how wonderful!

SOCRATES: Yes, you'll now be able to win any case at all.

Source: Aristophanes, *The Clouds*, trans. Alan H. Sommerstein (New York: 1973), pp. 148–50, 154, 159–60 (slightly revised).

Socrates and the Laws of Athens

According to his pupil Plato, Socrates spent the last days of his life in conversation with his friends and followers, some of whom urged him to escape from captivity and live in exile. In the dialogue Crito, *a young aristocrat of that name argues that the very laws that have condemned Socrates are unjust, and that by choosing to obey them Socrates is giving them a legitimacy they do not deserve. Halfway through the debate, Socrates turns the tables on him.*

SOCRATES: I should like you to consider whether we are still satisfied on this point: that the really important thing is not to live, but to live well.

CRITO: Why, yes.

SOCRATES: And that to live well means the same thing as to live honorably, or rightly?

CRITO: Yes.

SOCRATES: Then in light of this agreement we must consider whether or not it is right for me to try to get away without an official pardon. If it turns out to be right, we must make the attempt; if not, we must let it drop. . . .

CRITO: I agree with what you say, Socrates. . . .

SOCRATES: Well, here is my next point, or rather question. Ought one to fulfill all one's agreements, provided they are right, or break them?

CRITO: One ought to fulfill them.

SOCRATES: Then consider the logical consequence. If we leave this place without first persuading the polis to let us go . . . are we or are we not abiding by our just agreements?

CRITO: I can't answer your question, Socrates. I am not clear in my mind.

SOCRATES: Look at it this way. Suppose that while we were preparing to run away (or however one should describe it), the Laws of Athens were to come and confront us with this question: "Now, Socrates, what are you proposing to do? Can you deny that by this act which you are contemplating you intend, so far as you have the power, to destroy us, the Laws, and the whole polis as well? Do you imagine that a city can continue to exist and not be turned upside down, if the legal judgments which are pronounced in it have no force but are nullified and destroyed by private persons?"—How shall we answer this question, Crito, and others of the same kind? . . . Shall we say, "Yes, I do intend to destroy the Laws, because the polis has wronged me by passing a faulty judgment at my trial"? Is this to be our answer, or what?

CRITO: What you have just said, by all means, Socrates.

SOCRATES: Then supposing the Laws say, "Was there provision for this in the agreement between you and us, Socrates? Or did you pledge to abide by whatever judgments the polis pronounced? . . . [I]f you cannot persuade your country you must do whatever it orders, and patiently submit to any punishment it imposes, whether it be flogging or imprisonment. And if it leads you out to war, you must comply, and it is right that you should do so; you must not give way or retreat or abandon your position. Both in war and in the law courts you must do whatever your city and your country commands."

Source: Plato, *Crito*, excerpted (with modifications) from *The Last Days of Socrates*, trans. Hugh Tredennick (New York: 1969), pp. 87–91.

Questions for Analysis

1. Socrates actually refused to teach the art of "making the weaker argument defeat the stronger." But in *The Clouds*, Aristophanes shows him teaching how "to win any case at all." Why were the powers of persuasion considered potentially dangerous in democratic Athens? Why might Aristophanes choose to represent Socrates in this way?

2. How do the arguments of Plato's Socrates compare to those of Aristophanes' character?

3. How does Socrates' sense of honor and his duty toward the polis compare to that of Tyrtaeus of Sparta (page 65)?

known today as the Pythagorean theorem. Even though they shunned the material world, they still exhibited the characteristic Greek quest for regularity and predictability in that world.

Meanwhile, philosophy as it developed in mainland Greece was more attuned to questions of ethics and politics. The increasing power of individual citizens begged the question of how a man should conduct himself, in public and private life, so as to embrace "the beautiful and the good"—or at least to advance himself by the use of his wits. To answer this latter need were a new group of teachers known as Sophists, a term meaning "wise men." Unlike the Milesian philosophers or the Pythagoreans, however, the Sophists made their living from selling their knowledge. Their teachings are best exemplified by Protagoras (*pro-TAB-or-us*), an older contemporary of Socrates. His famous dictum, "man is the measure of all things," means that goodness, truth, and justice are relative concepts, adaptable to the needs and interests of human beings. They are not moral absolutes, established by the gods. Indeed, Protagoras declared that no one could know whether the gods existed or, if they did, what they wanted. He thus concluded that there could be no absolute standards of right and wrong. Empirical facts, established by the perception of the senses, were the only source of knowledge. And because each man experienced the world in a different way, there could be only particular truths valid for the individual knower.

Such teachings struck many Athenians as dangerous. Sophists like Protagoras made everyday life a subject for philosophical discussion, but their relativism could too easily degenerate into a conviction that the wise man (or the wise polis) is the one best able to manipulate others. Both individually and collectively, this conviction could rationalize monstrous acts of brutality—like those committed by Athens in the case of Melos. Indeed, the lessons of the Peloponnesian War went a long way toward demonstrating the disastrous consequences of this self-serving logic: if justice is merely relative, then neither personal morality nor society can survive. This conviction led to the growth of a new philosophical movement grounded on the theory that absolute standards do exist, and that human beings can determine what these are, through the exercise of reason. The initiator of this trend was Socrates.

The Life and Thought of Socrates

Socrates was not a professional teacher, like the Sophists. He may have trained as a stonemason, and he certainly had some sort of livelihood that enabled him to maintain his status as a citizen and hoplite. Having fought in three campaigns as part of the Athenian infantry during the war with Sparta, he was both an ardent patriot and a sincere critic of Athenian policy. His method of instruction was conversation: through dialogue with passers-by, he submitted every presumed truth to examination in order to establish a firm foundation for further inquiry. Everything we know about Socrates' teachings comes from the writings of younger men who considered themselves his pupils, and who participated in these conversations. The most important of these followers was Plato.

According to Plato, Socrates sought to show that all supposed certainties are merely unexamined prejudices inherited from others. Socrates always said that he himself knew nothing, because this was a more secure place from which to begin the learning process. He sought to base his speculations on sound definitions of key concepts—justice, virtue, beauty, love—which he and his pupils could arrive at only by investigating their own assumptions. And he focused his attention on practical ethics rather than the study of the physical world (like the Milesians did) or abstractions (like the Pythagoreans). He urged his listeners to reflect on the principles of proper conduct, both for their own sakes and for that of society as a whole. One should consider the meaning and consequences of one's actions at all times, he taught, and be prepared to take responsibility for them. According to one of his most memorable sayings, "the unexamined life is not worth living."

It is bitterly ironic that such a man, the product of Athenian democracy, should have been put to death by democratic processes. Shortly after the end of the Peloponnesian War in 399 B.C.E., when Athens was reeling from the shock of defeat and from violent internal upheavals, a democratic faction decided that Socrates was a threat to the state. A democratic court agreed, condemning him to death for denying the gods, disloyalty to the polis, and "corrupting the youth." Although his friends made arrangements for him to flee the city and thus evade punishment, Socrates insisted on abiding by the laws, proving himself true to his own principles and setting an example for future citizens. He died calmly by the prescribed method, self-administered poison.

According to Socrates, the goal of philosophy is to help human beings understand and apply standards of absolute good, rather than to master a series of mental tricks that facilitate personal gain at the expense of others. The

After You Read This Chapter

Visit StudySpace for quizzes, additional review materials, and multi-media documents. **wwnorton.com/studyspace**

REVIEWING THE OBJECTIVES

- The Greek polis was a unique form of government. What factors led to its emergence?
- Hoplite warfare had a direct effect on the shaping of early democracy. Why?
- Poleis could develop in very different ways. What are some of the reasons for this?
- In what ways did Athenian culture, philosophy, and art reflect democratic ideals?
- The Persian and Peloponnesian Wars affected Greek civilization in profound ways. Describe some of the consequences of Athens' victory in the former and its defeat in the latter.

circumstances of his death, however, show that it is difficult to translate this philosophy into principles that can be widely accepted. This would be the task of Plato, who would lay the groundwork for all subsequent Western philosophy (see Chapter 4).

CONCLUSION

There are many striking similarities between the civilization of ancient Greece and our own—and many stark differences. Perhaps the most salient example of both is the concept of democracy, which in ancient Greece was defined as rule by a class of propertied male citizens supported by slavery. In theory and in practice, this amounted to only a small percentage of the population in Athens, whereas in Sparta the vast majority were subject to the rule of an even smaller class of Spartiates. At the same time, the growth of Athenian democracy meant, increasingly, the exploitation of other poleis and the spread of imperialism, a ruinous policy of preemptive warfare, and increased intolerance and paranoia. (Socrates was not the only man put to death for expressing his opinions.) Finally, the status of women in this "golden age" was lower than it had been in earlier periods of Greek history, and women had fewer personal rights than in any of the ancient societies we have studied so far.

The profound significance of Greek experiments with new forms of governance, and new ideas about the world, is undeniable. This can be seen with particular clarity if we compare the Greek poleis with the empires and kingdoms of Mesopotamia and ancient Egypt. The typical political regime of the ancient Near Eastern world was, as we have seen, that of a monarch supported by a powerful priesthood. In this context, cultural achievements were mainly instruments to enhance the prestige of rulers, and economic life was controlled by palaces and temples. By contrast, the core values of the Greeks were the primacy of the human male and the principles of competition, individual achievement, responsibility, and human freedom. (The very word for freedom—*eleutheria*—cannot be translated into any ancient Near Eastern language, not even Hebrew.) In his history, Herodotus records a conversation between a Greek (in this case a Spartan) and a Persian, who expresses surprise that the Greeks should raise spears against the supposedly benign rule of his emperor. The Spartan retorts, "You understand how to be a slave, but you know nothing of freedom. Had you tasted it, you would advise us to fight not only with spears but with axes." The story of how the Greeks came to turn those spears on one another within a few generations of their united victory is worthy of one of their own tragedies.

Another way of appreciating the enduring importance of Greek civilization is to recall the essential vocabulary we have inherited from it: not only the word *democracy* but *politics*, *philosophy*, *theater*, *history*. The very notion of humanity comes to us from the Greeks. For them, the fullest development of one's potential should be the aim of existence: every free man is the sculptor of his own monument. This work of growing from childishness to personhood is what the Greeks called *paideia* (*pie-DAY-ah*); the Romans called it *humanitas*. How this and other ideas came to be disseminated beyond Greece, to be adopted by the peoples and places of a much wider world, is the subject of Chapter 4.

PEOPLE, IDEAS, AND EVENTS IN CONTEXT

- How did the epics of **HOMER** transmit the values of the Bronze Age to the **ARISTOCRACY** of the new Greek **POLEIS**?
- How did the spread of **GREEK CULTURE** transform the Mediterranean, even as the adoption of **HOPLITE** military tactics transformed Greek politics?
- Compare and contrast the historical circumstances that led to the development of **ATHENS, SPARTA,** and **MILETUS.** What were the main differences among them?
- What were the different motives for the invasions of **DARIUS** and **XERXES**? By what methods did the Greek poleis manage to emerge victorious from the **PERSIAN WARS**?
- What were the triumphs and limitations of **DEMOCRACY** in **PERICLEAN ATHENS**?
- How did the **PELOPONNESIAN WAR** transform Athens and affect the balance of power in the Mediterranean?

CONSEQUENCES

- The trial and execution of Socrates can be seen as a referendum on the relationship between the individual and the state. What does this incident reveal about the limitations of personal power and individual rights? To what degree was this incident a product of Athenian losses during the Peloponnesian War? To what extent does it reflect long-term trends in the Greek world?
- We like to think that we can trace our democratic ideals and institutions back to Athens, but does this mean that the failings of Athenian democracy also mirror those of our own? What parallels can you draw between ancient Athens and today's United States? What are some key differences?

Before
You
Read
This
Chapter

The Greek World Expands, 400–150 B.C.E.

When the young Alexander of Macedonia set out for Persia in 334 B.C.E, he brought along two favorite books. The first was a copy of the *Iliad*, which his teacher Aristotle had given him. The second was the *Anabasis*, "The Inland Expedition," by an Athenian called Xenophon (ZEN-oh-fon, 430–354 B.C.E). Both choices are significant. The *Iliad* recounts the story of a much earlier Greek assault on Asia, and its protagonist is the hero Achilles—a figure with whom Alexander identified: consummate warrior, favorite of the gods, a man who inspired passionate loyalty. It is also full of information useful to someone planning a long campaign in foreign lands against a formidable enemy, with a fractious army drawn from all parts of Greece and little prospect of bringing them home safely or soon. The *Anabasis* was an even more practical choice. Its author had been one of 10,000 Greek mercenaries hired by a Persian prince to overthrow his older brother, the Great King. The attempted coup failed, but Xenophon's book made the prince, Cyrus, another role model for Alexander. It also told, in detail, how Persians fought, how they lived, how they were governed, and what the terrain of their vast empire was like. Moreover, it showed what a dedicated army of hoplites could accomplish on Persian soil. This book would be Alexander's bible for the next ten years.

By the time of Alexander the Great's early death, a united Greek and Macedonian army had extended Greek culture and Greek governance from Egypt to the frontiers of India. This personal empire, the empire of Alexander, could not last. But the cultural empire built upon it did. This Hellenistic ("Greek-like") civilization joined disparate lands and peoples, forming the basis of the Roman Empire and mirroring the cosmopolitan world of our own time. How this happened is the subject of Chapter 4.

THE DOWNFALL OF THE GREEK POLIS

The Peloponnesian War had left Sparta the dominant power in the Greek world. But by 395, a significant number of poleis were aligned against Sparta in the so-called Corinthian War (395–387 B.C.E.). To quell this rebellion, the Spartans turned once again to Persia, as they had done in the final stages of the Peloponnesian War. This pattern of violence, temporarily halted by the intervention of Persia, would be repeated time and again over the next fifty years.

The Struggle for Hegemony

After the Corinthian War, the Spartans punished the most dangerous of their rivals, Thebes, by occupying the city for four years. But when the Thebans regained their autonomy they elected as their leader a fierce patriot who was also a military genius, Epaminondas (*eh-pa-min-OHN-das*, c. 410–362 B.C.E.). In imitation of the Spartan system, he formed an elite hoplite unit known as the Theban Sacred Band, made up of 150 couples: sworn lovers who pledged to fight to the death for their polis and for each other's honor.

When the Theban and Spartan armies met at Leuctra in 371 B.C.E., the Sacred Band helped carry the Thebans to victory. Epaminondas then marched through the Spartan territory of Messenia and freed the helots. Spartan power—and the unique social system that had supported it—was thereby brought to an end. But as Theban power grew, so did the animosity of the other Greek poleis. In 362, when Epaminondas fell in battle, Athens attempted—and failed—to fill the vacuum by establishing a naval confederacy. Greece thus remained a constellation of petty warring states.

Social and Economic Crises

Meanwhile, the poleis were also riven by internal turmoil. Incessant warfare and political struggles profoundly affected their economic and social infrastructures. Many people were driven from their homes or reduced to slavery. Country towns had been ravaged, as had farmlands throughout Greece. Prices rose while standards of living declined. Taxes increased.

Unemployment was also widespread, and many men turned to mercenary service. Cyrus, brother of the Persian emperor Artaxerxes II, even hired a Greek mercenary force of 10,000 men in an attempt to seize the throne in 401 B.C.E. But when Cyrus was killed in battle, the army—marooned in a hostile country—had to fight its way out under elected leaders. One of these was Xenophon, a former pupil of Socrates, and it was his account of this expedition that would become Alexander the Great's guidebook.

RE-IMAGINING THE POLIS: THE ARTISTIC AND INTELLECTUAL RESPONSE

399 B.C.E., the year of Socrates' execution, marks the end of an era—that of the polis. This basic engine of Greek life had continued to drive innovation and cultural production even during the Peloponnesian War. But now, the failure of democracy had a profound impact on the arts, philosophy, and especially political thought.

The Arts of the Fourth Century

As we observed in Chapter 3, the painters and sculptors of the fifth century B.C.E. were already working to achieve a heightened appearance of realism in their works. This experimentation continued in the fourth century, especially in the relatively new art of portraiture. Artists also grew bolder in their use of tricky techniques, like the casting of full-size statues in bronze. This was a medium in which the era's most famous sculptor, Praxiteles, excelled. Praxiteles was bold, too, in his choice of subjects, and is widely regarded as the first artist to create full-size female nudes (see **Interpreting Visual Evidence**).

In contrast to the visual arts, the forms and functions of drama changed considerably. Tragedy and comedy were no longer mounted as part of publicly funded festivals, but were instead financed by private individuals who could exercise greater control over the content of performances.

Xenophon Describes an Ideal Leader

In his history of "The Inland Expedition" undertaken by the Ten Thousand, Xenophon (430–354 B.C.E.) mourns the death of Cyrus the Younger, whom he believes would have made a better Great King of Persia than the brother he challenged, Artaxerxes II. The following description of the prince's character and leadership became very famous in its time, often circulating as a separate booklet. It is likely to have influenced the young Alexander.

Thus then died Cyrus, a man who, of all the Persians since Cyrus the elder [the Great], was the most princely and the most worthy of rule, as is agreed by all who appear to have had personal knowledge of him. In the first place, while he was yet a boy, and when he was receiving his education with his brother and other youths, he was thought to surpass them all in everything. For all the sons of the Persian nobles are educated at the gates of the king, where they may learn many a lesson of virtuous conduct, but can see or hear nothing disgraceful. Here the boys see some honored by the king, and others disgraced, and hear of them, so that in their very childhood they learn to govern and to obey.

Here Cyrus, first of all, showed himself most remarkable for modesty among those of his own age, and for paying more ready obedience to his elders than even those who were inferior to him in station; and next, he was noted for his fondness for horses, and for managing them in a superior manner. They found him, too, very desirous of learning, and most assiduous in practicing, the warlike exercises of archery and hurling the javelin. When it suited his age, he grew extremely fond of the chase and of braving dangers in encounters with wild beasts. On one occasion he did not shrink from a she-bear that attacked him, but, in grappling with her, was dragged from off his horse, and received some wounds, the scars of which were visible on his body, but at last killed her. The person who first came to his assistance he made a happy man in the eyes of many.

When he was sent down by his father, as satrap of Lydia and Great Phrygia and Cappadocia, and was also appointed commander of all the troops whose duty it is to muster in the plain of Castolus, he soon showed that if he made a league or compact with anyone, or gave a promise, he deemed it of the utmost importance not to break his word. Accordingly the states that were committed to his charge, as well as individuals, had the greatest confidence in him; and if anyone had been his enemy, he felt secure that if Cyrus entered into a treaty with him, he should suffer no infraction of the stipulations. When, therefore, he waged war against Tissaphernes, all the cities, of their own accord, chose to adhere to Cyrus in preference to Tissaphernes, except the Milesians; but they feared him, because he would not abandon the cause of the exiles; for he both showed by his deeds and declared in words that he would never desert them, since he had once become a friend to them, not even though they should grow still fewer in number, and be in a worse condition than they were.

Whenever anyone did him a kindness or an injury, he showed himself anxious to go beyond him in those respects; and some used to mention a wish of his that he desired to live long enough to outdo both those who had done him good, and those who had done him ill, in the requital that he should make. Accordingly to him alone of the men of our days were so great a number of people desirous of committing the disposal of their property, their cities, and their own persons.

Source: Excerpted from Xenophon, *Anabasis*, ed. M. I. Finley in *The Portable Greek Historians* (New York: 1959), pp. 383–84.

Questions for Analysis

1. According to Xenophon, what are the attributes of a great leader? How would Alexander have applied these to his own situation?

2. What seems to be Xenophon's attitude toward the Persians? How might his portrayal of them have been influenced by his travels among them? How might it have been colored by his attitude toward his own countrymen?

3. In what ways does Cyrus the Younger appear to have followed the example of his ancestor, Cyrus the Great (Chapter 2, page 47)?

As a result, fourth-century playwrights did not have the freedom to use drama as a vehicle for political and social critique, as earlier dramatists had done. Instead, the "New Comedy" of this era relied more and more on mistaken identities, tangled familial relationships, and breaches of etiquette. Similar trends toward escapism are also apparent in a new literary genre: the prose novel. These pleasant fictions targeted an increasingly literate audience, including (as with many modern romance novels) an audience of women.

Philosophy after Socrates: The Schools of Plato and Aristotle

The intellectual and political legacy of Socrates was carried forward by Plato (429–349 B.C.E.), who as a young man witnessed the trial and death of his mentor. Plato strove to vindicate Socrates by constructing a philosophical system based on his precepts. He did this by founding an informal school called the Academy and by writing a series of dialogues that feature Socrates as the central character.

The longest and most famous of these dialogues is now known by its Latin title, the *Republic*. In it, Plato argues that social harmony and order are more important than individual liberty or equality. He imagines an ideal polis governed by a superior group of "guardians" chosen in their youth for natural attributes of intelligence and character. Those found to be the wisest would ultimately become "philosopher-kings." This imaginary system is clearly a response to the failures of Athenian democracy. But whether Plato himself believed in it is open to question. For such a system presumes that properly educated rulers will never be corrupted by power, a proposition that has yet to be sustained in practice.

The practical application of philosophy would be the preoccupation of Plato's own student, Aristotle (384–322 B.C.E.). The son of a physician, Aristotle learned from

PLATO AND ARISTOTLE. Although many artistic representations of Plato and Aristotle were made in antiquity, the image that best captures the essential difference between their philosophies is this one, the focal point of a fresco by the Renaissance painter Raphael Sanzio (1483–1520 C.E., to be discussed further in Chapter 12). Plato is the older central figure to the viewer's left, who points with his right hand to the heavens; Aristotle is the younger man beside him, gesturing with an open palm to the earth. ▪ *How does this double portrait reflect these philosophers' teachings and perspectives?*

Reconstructing an Ideal of Female Beauty

The lost statue known as the Aphrodite of Knidos was considered the most beautiful in the ancient world, but we can only study it by looking at later copies. It was the work of the fourth century's most renowned sculptor, Praxiteles (*prak-SIT-el-eez*), who was reputed to have modeled it after the Athenian courtesan known as Phryne, a renowned beauty who inspired several contemporary artists and many apocryphal stories. The most reliable of these concerns the riches she accrued: apparently she became so wealthy that she offered to finance the rebuilding of Thebes in 336—on the condition that the slogan "destroyed by Alexander, restored by Phryne the Courtesan" be prominently displayed on the new walls. (Her offer was rejected.)

Praxiteles' original statue is thought to have been the first monumental female nude fashioned in antiquity. According to one authority, he had initially received a commission from the island of Kos, for which he made both clothed and naked versions of Aphrodite. Apparently, the scandalized citizens approved only the draped version and refused to pay for the nude. It was purchased instead by the city of Knidos on Cyprus, where it was displayed in an open-air temple so that it could be seen from all sides. It quickly became a tourist attraction and was widely copied and emulated. Two of the more faithful replicas, made by artists working in Rome, are pictured here.

Questions for Analysis

1. As we have seen, the male nude was a favorite subject of Greek artists from the Archaic Period onward. Based on your knowledge of contemporary Greek culture and society, why was it only in the fourth century B.C.E. that a life-size female nude could be publicly displayed? Are there any precedents for statues like this?

2. Compare and contrast the ideal of female beauty suggested by the Knidian Aphrodite with the male ideals discussed in Chapter 3. What can you conclude about the relationship between these ideals and the different expectations of male and female behavior in Greek society? Why, for example, would ancient sources insist that the model for the original statue was a courtesan?

3. Among the Romans, a statue like the Knidian Aphrodite was called a *Venus pudica*, a "modest Venus" (image A). Yet the citizens of Kos were allegedly shocked by its indecency, while old photographs of the copy in the Vatican Museum (image B) show that it was displayed until 1932 with additional draperies made of tin. How do you account for these very different standards of decency? To what degree do they suggest that concepts of "beauty" or "modesty" are historically constructed?

A. Roman copy of the Aphrodite of Knidos.

B. Second century C.E. copy of the Aphrodite of Knidos.

his father the importance of observing natural phenomena. His own philosophical system was geared toward understanding the workings of the world through empirical knowledge—that is, information gained through sensory experience. In contrast to Plato, who taught that everything we see and touch is an untrustworthy reflection of some intangible ideal, Aristotle advocated the rigorous investigation of real phenomena. His method of instruction was also different. Unlike Socrates and Plato, whose dialogues were witty and often playful, Aristotle delivered lectures on which his students took detailed notes, and which eventually became the basis of treatises on politics, ethics, logic, metaphysics, and poetics.

Aristotle taught that the highest good consists in the harmonious functioning of the individual human mind and body. Good conduct is therefore rational conduct, and consists in acting moderately. And whereas Plato conceived of politics as a means to an end which could never be achieved in this life, Aristotle thought of politics as an end in itself: the collective exercise of moderation.

Aristotle also took it for granted that some people—like barbarians—are not fully human, and so are intended by nature to be slaves. He also believed that women are not endowed with a full measure of humanity. So when Aristotle asserted that "man is by nature a political animal" (or, to be more faithful to the Greek, "a creature of the polis"), he meant only Greek males of privileged status. Nor did he believe that the best form of government is a democracy. Like Plato, he saw that as a "debased" form of government.

Men of Thought, Men of Action

Despite these philosophical breakthroughs, Plato and Aristotle offered few prescriptions for reforming their own societies. But there were other intellectuals who were considering more radical alternatives. The Athenian Xenophon, a veteran of the Ten Thousand and another product of the Socratic tradition, spent much of his adult life in Sparta, and it is thanks to his admiring account that we know anything about the Spartiate system described in Chapter 3. He intended his description to be a rebuke to democratic Athens and a model for a different kind of ideal society.

The Athenian orator Isocrates (436–338 B.C.E.) was another direct contemporary of Plato. But rather than imagining an ideal polis, he proposed instead that the Greeks stage a massive invasion of Persia. This assault, he prophesied, should be led by a man of vision and ability who could unite the Greek world behind his cause. Isocrates spent most of his life casting about to find such a leader.

Finally, he began to think that the man for the job was someone most Greeks considered no Greek at all: the king of Macedonia, Philip II.

THE RISE OF MACEDONIA

Until the fourth century, Macedonia (or Macedon) had been a weak kingdom, regarded by most Greeks as a throwback to the "dark ages" before the emergence of enlightened poleis. As recently as the 360s, it had nearly succumbed to the even smaller kingdoms and predatory tribes that surrounded it. No one knows whether the ancient Macedonians were Greek-speaking during this period, but the royal family and nobility would at least have spoken Greek as a second language. Still, they were definitely outsiders. So when a young and energetic king consolidated the southern Balkans under his rule, many Greeks saw it as an alarming development.

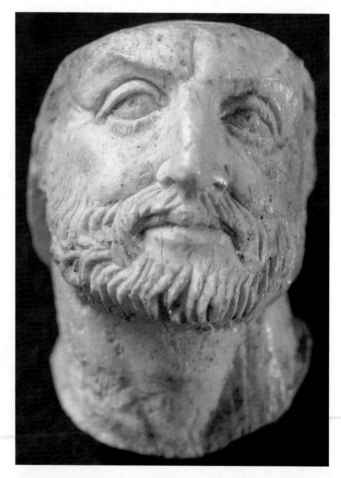

PHILIP II OF MACEDONIA. This tiny ivory head was discovered in a royal tomb at Vergina and is almost certainly a bust of the king himself. Contemporary sources report that Philip the Great had his right eye blinded by a catapult bolt, a deformity visible here—and testimony to the unflinching realism of Greek portraiture in the fourth century B.C.E.

MACEDONIAN PHALANX. Philip of Macedonia's hoplite infantry—the model for Alexander's—was armed with two-handed pikes of graduated lengths, from 13 to 21 feet, and was massed in squares sixteen rows deep and wide. Members of the phalanx were trained to wheel quickly in step formation and to double the width of their front rank as needed, by filing off in rows of eight. The reach of their spears, called *sarissas*, extended the phalanx's fighting range.

The Reign of Philip II (359–336 B.C.E.)

Philip II of Macedonia was not supposed to be its ruler. Born in 382, he was the third and youngest son of King Amyntas III, and was considered so dispensable that he was sent to Thebes as hostage when he was fourteen. This turns out to have been the making of him: he become the protégé of the brilliant Epaminondas and may even have trained in the Theban Sacred Band. By the time he returned to the Macedonian capital of Pella, he had received a more thorough education than any Macedonian before him. He was also ambitious. So when both of his older brothers died in battle, Philip was not content with the role of regent for an infant nephew. By 356, he was reigning as king, the same year that his queen, Olympias, bore him an heir. The boy was given the dynastic name Alexandros, "leader of men."

The first problem of Philip's reign was the fragility of Macedonia's northern borders. Through a combination of warfare and diplomacy, he subdued the tribes of the southern Balkans and incorporated their territory into his kingdom. His success had much to do with his reorganization of Macedonian warriors into a hoplite infantry along Theban lines, as well as access to mineral resources that he used to pay and equip a standing professional army. Philip also organized an elite cavalry squad—the Companions—who fought with and beside the king, perhaps in emulation of the Sacred Band. These young men were drawn exclusively from the nobility, and Philip thereby gained valuable young hostages to ensure the good conduct of fractious men. Their sons were now being brought up alongside Alexander and sharing his lessons with Aristotle, who had arrived at the Macedonian court in 343 B.C.E.

Isocrates saw in Philip a potential savior of Greece, but many Athenians believed that his ultimate aim was to conquer them. In actuality, he was probably trying to forge an alliance with Athens, whose fleet could facilitate an invasion of Persia by sea; in return, Philip promised to support Athens' old claim to hegemony over Greece.

But the Athenians refused to cooperate. This miscalculation ultimately led to war, which sent the Athenians scrambling to ally with Thebes. At the battle of Chaeronea in 338 B.C.E., an army led jointly by Philip and Alexander (aged 18) won a narrow victory, decimating the Athenian forces and destroying the Theban Sacred Band. In the aftermath, Philip called delegates from around mainland Greece to Corinth, where he established a new league whose main purpose was to provide forces for the planned invasion of Persia and maintain peace among the rival poleis.

But Philip never realized his dream of Persian conquest. Two years later, in 336 B.C.E., he was assassinated during a festival at Pella. The kingship now fell to Alexander. Among the Greeks, he would be known as Alexander, the Sacker of Cities. To the Romans, he was Alexander the Great.

THE CONQUESTS OF ALEXANDER, 336–323 B.C.E.

By the time of Alexander's early death at the age of 32, a monumental legend had already built up around him. This makes it all the more ironic that no contemporary account of his life and achievements survives. The great library assembled in his capital of Alexandria in Egypt—the repository of all Greek learning and literature—was destroyed centuries later, and with it a great portion of assembled knowledge. So when we try to reconstruct the history of Alexander, we are depending on the writings of men who lived and worked under the Roman Empire, notably Plutarch (46–120 C.E.) and Arrian (c. 86–160 C.E.), both of whom were separated from their subject by a distance of four hundred years. Luckily, they were basing their histories on sources derived from two first-hand accounts, one written by Alexander's general (and purported half-brother) Ptolemy (c. 367–c. 284 B.C.E.), who founded a new dynasty of Egyptian pharaohs, and another by Æschines Socraticus (c. 387–322 B.C.E.), an Athenian statesman.

It is a salutary reminder of how fragile the historical record of antiquity is, that the sources for the life of the era's most famous man are so hard to come by.

The Conquest of Persia

When Alexander succeeded his father in 336 B.C.E, he had to put down the revolts that erupted immediately after Philip's death—notably at Thebes, which he punished by destroying its famous walls. Two years later, he was crossing the Hellespont to challenge the Great King of Persia, Darius III.

Darius was a minor member of the royal family who had been placed on the throne after a palace coup, at the relatively old age of 45—in the same year that Alexander himself became king at 20. Darius and his advisors failed to take the Macedonian threat seriously, despite the Persians' past history of defeat at the hands of Greek armies. Perhaps they assumed that the enormous forces they could rally in defense of their empire would easily overwhelm a comparatively small army of 42,000; perhaps they misunderstood Alexander's aims.

In any event, Alexander soon achieved a series of extraordinary victories, beginning in northwest Anatolia, near the site of the epic field of Troy, and continuing down the Ionian coastline. A year later, in 333 B.C.E. Darius was persuaded to engage Alexander personally. But the chosen site, on the banks of a river near Issus, favored Alexander's fast-moving infantry, not the heavy cavalry and chariots of the

Persians. No warrior himself, Darius disgraced himself by fleeing the battlefield, abandoning not only his army but his entire household, which included his wife and his mother. (They were captured by Alexander and treated with great respect.) Darius spent the remainder of his life running from Alexander's advancing forces, until his decisive defeat at Gaugamela (near Mosul in modern Iraq) in 331, when he was killed by a local chieftain who hoped to win Alexander's favor. Instead, Alexander—acting as the new Great King—had the chieftain executed for treason. The next spring, Alexander destroyed the royal capital of Persepolis, lest it serve as a rallying point for Persian resistance.

Meanwhile, in the two years that had passed since Darius' humiliation at Issus, Alexander had completed his conquest of Asia Minor. One by one, the cities of Syria and Palestine surrendered. Following the example of Cyrus the Great, Alexander had developed a policy of offering amnesty to cities that submitted peacefully—but dealing mercilessly with those that resisted. The fortified city of Gaza, the last Persian stronghold on the Egyptian border, provides an example: when the fortress was finally taken, Alexander's troops slew all the adult males and enslaved the women and children. According to a later Roman historian, Alexander also dragged the body of the commander around the city's walls behind his chariot, imitating Achilles' legendary treatment of Hector.

Alexander in Egypt

After this, Alexander marched into Egypt unopposed. In fact, he was welcomed as a liberator: Egypt had been governed as a Persian satrapy since 525 B.C.E. Now Alexander himself was hailed as pharaoh and given the double crown of Upper and Lower Egypt, becoming the latest in a succession of rulers reaching back three thousand years to the time of King Narmer (Chapter 1). The "barbarian" chieftain of a backwater kingdom had become pharaoh of the oldest civilization on earth and heir to its immense riches and extraordinary history.

While the Persians had long been the Greeks' traditional enemies, the Egyptians had always been too far away to pose a threat; indeed, they were an object of awe. This may help to explain Alexander's response to the oracle of Ammon, the name the Greeks gave to the Egyptian sun god Amun-Ra, whom they identified with Zeus. At the oracle's desert oasis of Siwa, Alexander was reportedly told that he was "son of Ammon" and a god himself. Ever mindful of historical precedent, Alexander seems to have decided at this point that Egypt should be the capital of his new empire: it was in Egypt that he would build his shining new

ALEXANDER'S WORLD. This view of the world, modeled on maps made in antiquity, represents what intellectuals of Alexander's own time knew about geography. ▪ *Comparing it to the map of Alexander's campaigns on page 91, how do you think this worldview affected the planning of his route?* ▪ *Based on available knowledge, why would he have traveled down the Indus river (near the marking India) and traveled overland to Susa?* ▪ *What similarities and differences do you find generally, comparing this ancient map with the other maps that appear in this book?*

THE CAMPAIGNS OF ALEXANDER. The conquests of Alexander the Great brought Greek culture to the vast expanse of the former Persian Empire, as far east as the Indus River. Trace Alexander's route with your finger. ▪ *Where did he start and end?* ▪ *What was the farthest point east that he traveled on his conquests?* ▪ *Why might Alexander have chosen to found so many cities named after him, and what can you conclude about the purposes of these cities, based on their locations?*

city of Alexandria. In the end, he just had time to lay out a plan for the streets. When he finally returned, he was in his sarcophagus.

Alexander's Final Campaigns

Over the ensuing five years, Alexander campaigned in the far reaches of the Persian Empire, in the mountainous regions that had been only loosely yoked with the more settled lands of Mesopotamia. This is the region encompassed today by Afghanistan, and a terrain famous for defeating every attempt at conquest. Here, Alexander and his army experienced the hardest fighting of their long campaign. Indeed, they never succeeded in getting more than a tenuous hold on the territory, despite Alexander's marriage to Roxane, daughter of a local chieftain. Thereafter, Alexander moved down through what is now Pakistan to the Indus Valley, meeting stiff resistance from its warlords

but eventually defeating their leader, Porus, at the Battle of Hydaspes in 326 B.C.E.

This was to be the last major battle of his career, and the one in which his famous warhorse, Bucephalus, was killed. And it was here that Alexander's exhausted army refused to go on, thousands of miles and eight years from home. He was forced to turn back, and rather than attempting to recross the mountains, he pressed southward to the shores of the Arabian Sea—what was then the end of the world. The ensuing march through the Gedrosian Desert, combined with a decade of continuous fighting, weakened him and his army considerably.

When Alexander reached the royal palace of Susa he took steps that indicate how he would have tried to combine his Greco-Macedonian Empire with that of Persia, had he lived. He announced that he would begin training Persian youths to fight alongside Greeks and Macedonians in hoplite formation. He arranged a mass marriage between hundreds of his officers and a corresponding number of Persian

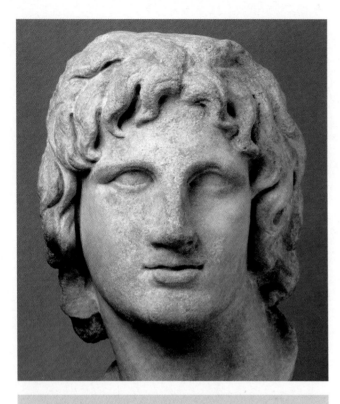

MARBLE HEAD OF ALEXANDER. Alexander the Great is reported to have been very striking in appearance, although sources vary in their assessment. This portrait bust was made in 180 B.C.E., about 150 years after his death. ∎ *Given the trends in sculpture during that period (see page 102), is this likely to have been an accurate portrait?*

on further conquests, perhaps in Arabia, perhaps toward "Greater Greece"—Italy and Sicily. But in late May of 323 B.C.E., he began to show signs of what may have been malarial fever. Some ancient sources even suggest that he was poisoned; his closest companion, Hephaistion, had died the year before at Ecbatana, leaving Alexander without his most vigilant bodyguard. In any case, Alexander ignored the advice of his doctors. His condition worsened, and he died on June 10 or 11, 323 B.C.E., in the palace built by the Chaldean king Nebuchadnezzar in Babylon, the ancient capital of Hammurabi. He was not yet thirty-three years old.

THE HELLENISTIC KINGDOMS

According to one account—by a later Roman historian—Alexander's officers gathered around his bed as he lay dying and asked to whom he wished to leave his empire. He had replied, "To the strongest." According to other sources, he was actually incapable of speech. According to still other sources, he silently gave his signet ring to a Macedonian called Perdiccas, the leader of his cavalry.

It was certainly Perdiccas who attempted to arrange a settlement among all the possible claimants for power, albeit unsuccessfully. It was eventually decided that the infant Alexander IV, his son by Roxane, should rule jointly with Alexander's half-brother, Philip, the son of Philip II by one of his lesser wives. But this solution was never put into effect, because both the child and his uncle were soon murdered, as was Perdiccas. Meanwhile, the satrapies that had been allotted to various leaders of Alexander's armies became the bases from which these men attempted to seize control.

The turmoil lasted for two generations. By about 275 B.C.E., however, three separate axes of military and political power had emerged, each headed by a Greco-Macedonian ruling class but with a distinctive character. Indeed, a striking feature of this period is the renewal of ancient political patterns within the common culture that continued to unite Alexander's fragmented empire. This is why the world created by his conquests is called Hellenistic, "Greek-like."

noblewomen. Most controversially, he showed respect for his Persian subjects by adopting Persian dress—considered by Greeks to be effeminate and barbaric—and by encouraging those around him to perform the ritual of *proskynesis* (*pros-kin-EE-sis*). This was a gesture of bodily submission performed by those of lesser social standing when they met their superiors, and by all Persians—even those of royal rank—to honor the Great King. The person paying homage would bow deeply, in some cases prostrating himself entirely. To the Greeks, this practice suggested that the Persians worshiped their king as a god. To Alexander and his close advisors, it was more likely intended to level cultural differences. In any case, it was not a success, and it fueled a mutiny among the Macedonians, which Alexander himself had to quell.

Alexander's Death

Apart from these attempts to create cohesion, Alexander took no realistic steps to create an administration for his vast empire. He seems to have fixed his sights more clearly

Ptolemaic Egypt

By far the most stable of these three Hellenistic states was Egypt, thanks in large part to the canny governance of Alexander's former general Ptolemy (*TOHL-eh-mee*), who was possibly an illegitimate son of Philip II. Ptolemy decided to

Analyzing Primary Sources

Alexander Puts Down a Mutiny

The following account comes from the history of Alexander's campaigns by the Greek-speaking Roman historian Arrian (c. 86–160 C.E.), who lived in the Roman province of Bythinia in northern Anatolia. This is the closest thing we have to a primary source, since histories written by Alexander's own contemporaries have not survived. The following passage describes Alexander's response to a mutiny among his troops after his return from India in 324 B.C.E.

My countrymen, you are sick for home—so be it! I shall make no attempt to check your longing to return. Go wherever you will; I shall not hinder you. But if go you must, there is one thing I would have you understand—what I have done for you, and in what coin you have repaid me. . . .

"[M]arching out from a country too poor to maintain you decently, [I] laid open for you at a blow, and in spite of Persia's naval supremacy, the gates of the Hellespont. My cavalry crushed the satraps of Darius, and I added all Ionia and Aeolia, the two Phrygias and Lydia to your empire. . . . I took them and gave them to you for your profit and enjoyment. The wealth of Egypt and Cyrene, which I shed no blood to win, now flows in your hands; Palestine and the plains of Syria and Mesopotamia are now your property; Babylon and Bactria and Susa are yours; you are the masters of the gold of Lydia, the treasures of Persia, the wealth of India—yes, and the seas beyond India, too. You are my captains, my generals, my governors of provinces.

"From all this that I have labored to win for you, what is left for me myself except the purple and the crown? I keep nothing for my own. . . . Perhaps you will say that, in my position as your com-mander, I had none of the labors and distress which you had to endure to win me what I have won. . . . Come now—if you are wounded, strip and show your wounds, and I will show mine. There is no part of my body but my back which does not have a scar; not a weapon a man may grasp or fling, the mark of which I do not carry on me . . . and all for your sakes: for your glory and your gain. Over every land and sea, across river, mountain, and plain, I led you to the world's end, a vic-torious army. I marry as you marry, and many of you will have children related by blood to my own. . . . But you all wish to leave me. Go then! And when you reach home, tell them that Alexander your king, who vanquished the Persians and Medes and Bactrians . . . tell them, I say, that you deserted him and left him to the mercy of barbarian men, whom you yourselves conquered. . . ."

On the Macedonians, the immedi-ate effect of Alexander's speech was profound. . . . But when they were told [three days later that] . . . command was being given to Persian officers, foreign troops drafted into Macedonian units, a Persian corps of Guards called by a Macedonian name, Persian infantry units given the coveted title of Com-panions, . . . every man of them hurried to the palace . . . and [they] swore they would not stir from the spot until Alex-ander took pity on them.

Source: Arrian, *The Campaigns of Alexander*, trans. Aubrey de Selincourt (New York: 1958), pp. 360–65 (slightly modified).

Questions for Analysis

1. What qualities of leadership does Al-exander display in this speech? How do these qualities compare to those of Cyrus the Younger, in Xenophon's description of him (page 85)?

2. Given the circumstances that precipi-tated this mutiny, why does Alexander use the term *barbarians* to describe the Persians and other conquered peo-ples? What does he hope to convey by using this word, and then by reorganiz-ing his forces to replace Macedonians with Persians?

3. Histories written well into the nine-teenth century of our era feature speeches that were allegedly spoken by historical characters on momen-tous occasions. How closely do you think Arrian's reconstruction of this speech reflects historical reality? How might you go about arguing that it is, in fact, an accurate reflection of what Alexander actually said?

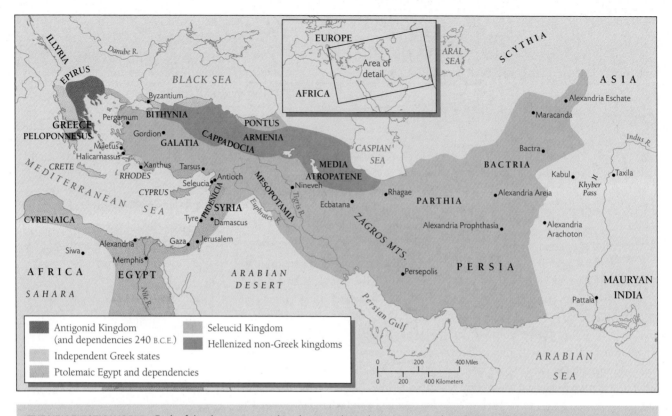

THE HELLENISTIC WORLD. Each of the three successor kingdoms to Alexander's empire was based in one of the three major civilizations we have studied so far: Egyptian, Mesopotamian, and Greek. ▪ *Based on the map above, what were the names of the three main successor states and where were they located?* ▪ *What might the division of Alexander's empire along such lines suggest about the lasting cultural differences among these regions?* ▪ *What might it suggest about the likelihood of forging a united empire, had he lived?*

withdraw from the contest over the larger empire and asked only to be given Egypt as his satrapy. Clearly, he recognized Egypt's virtual invulnerability to attack. He also seems to have appreciated, as had Alexander, its historical cachet. And he may already have been planning to make Egypt an independent monarchy and a shrine to Alexander's memory. It was thanks to Ptolemy, in fact, that Alexander's embalmed body was brought to Egypt in 323 B.C.E. It was supposed to have gone to the royal burial ground in Macedonia, but Ptolemy hijacked the funeral cortege and brought it to Memphis. Later, his son Ptolemy II moved the sarcophagus to a tomb in Alexandria, where it became a pilgrimage site and an object of veneration.

The Ptolemies ruled for 300 years, until Egypt became a Roman province in 30 B.C.E. (see Chapter 5). This dynasty, the thirty-second since the fourth millennium B.C.E., would be the last. The male heirs of the line all took the name Ptolemy (hence the term "Ptolemaic Egypt"). Many of their sisters were called Cleopatra, the name of Alexander's own sister and a dynastic name among Macedonian royal women. Beginning in the reign of Ptolemy II Philadelphus ("sibling-lover"), the Ptolemies even began to follow ancient Egyptian custom by marrying their sisters. And in many

other ways, they showed reverence for the culture of their kingdom while bringing it within the ambit of the wider Hellenistic world.

They achieved this, in part, by ruling from the new city of Alexandria on the Mediterranean coast. In Alexandria, they acted as Macedonian kings toward their Greek and Macedonian citizens; outside of Alexandria, they played the role of pharaohs, surrounding themselves with the trappings and symbols of Egypt's heritage. But until the last Ptolemaic ruler, Cleopatra VII (69–30 B.C.E.), none of them bothered to learn the Egyptian language—although, as the Rosetta Stone attests (Chapter 1), they surrounded themselves with able administrators who could communicate effectively with their multilingual and multicultural subjects.

For the Ptolemies, as for the ancient pharaohs, all of Egypt was land to be exploited for the benefit of the royal house. Supporting this tradition was the Macedonian idea that conquered land was plunder, to be used for personal enrichment and glorification. Accordingly, the Ptolemies exploited the wealth of the Egyptian countryside to the fullest. Most of this wealth ended up in Alexandria, which became the brilliant hub of the Hellenistic world. But there was little interest in improving the lives of the Egyptian

TWO PORTRAITS OF PTOLEMY I OF EGYPT. The Ptolemaic rulers of Egypt represented themselves as pharaohs to their Egyptian subjects (as in this bust) and as Greeks to their Macedonian and Greek subjects (as on this gold coin). ▪ *Why would it have been important to project these two very different images?*

peasantry, whose bread-winning labors made their rulers rich. So although the third century was a prosperous and relatively peaceful one in Egypt, future pharoahs would face regular and dangerous revolts.

Nevertheless, Ptolemaic Egypt was the most succesful of the Hellenistic kingdoms. It was also the most influential, because of its key role in preserving and transmitting the accumulated heritage of the civilizations that had preceded it: Egyptian, Mesopotamian, and Greek. The Ptolemies used much of their wealth to patronize science and the arts, and they established a great Museum ("home of the Muses") and library which attracted the greatest minds of the Hellenistic world. Many breakthroughs in astronomy, mechanical engineering, and physics occurred in Alexandria. In particular, the study of medicine advanced greatly: freed from the taboos of their homeland, Greek researchers were permitted to perform autopsies, making it possible for anatomy to become a scientific discipline in its own right. It was also in Alexandria that the texts of Greek poetry, drama, history, and philosophy were copied and preserved in the forms in which we know them, and here that the Hebrew scriptures were translated into Greek for a wider audience. Any history of western civilizations would be impossible without these initiatives.

Seleucid Asia

The vast possessions that Alexander had accumulated in Asia—both within the Persian Empire and outside of it—eventually fell to another Macedonian, Seleucus (*seh-LOO-kus*). Seleucus had navigated the turmoil after Alexander's death successfully and exploited the connections he made

through his Persian wife. At his death in 281 B.C.E., his half-Persian son Antiochus inherited an expansive realm whose capital was the city named after him, Antioch.

Throughout its history, the dynasty founded by Seleucus (known as the Seleucids) struggled with the problem of holding the disparate parts of this realm together. Seleucus himself solved part of this problem by ceding much of the Indus Valley to the great warrior-king Chandragupta in exchange for a squad of war elephants. By the middle of the third century B.C.E., the Seleucids had also lost control of Bactria, where a series of Indo-Greek states were emerging with a uniquely complex culture of their own. The Seleucid heartland now became northern Syria, parts of Anatolia, Mesopotamia, and the western half of Persia: still a great, wealthy kingdom, but far less than what Alexander had left.

Like the Ptolemies, the Seleucids presented two faces to their subjects, one looking to ancient Mesopotamian tradition, another looking to Greece. In his proclamations, Antiochus used terms reminiscent of Sargon, Hammurabi, and Cyrus: "I am Antiochus, Great King, legitimate king . . . king of Babylon, king of all countries." But on his coins, he wore his hair short in the fashion of the Greeks and styled himself *basileus*, the Greek word for "king." Although the Seleucids' bureaucracy was less organized than that of the Ptolemies, even haphazard tax collection could reap huge rewards in an empire of 30 million inhabitants. They had more than enough cash to defend their borders through the third century, a period of regular warfare with Egypt. It was not until the second century, when Antiochus III lost a costly war with the Romans, that he had to plunder temples and private wealth to pay off the indemnity imposed on him.

Antigonid Macedon and Greece

The Macedonian homeland did not possess the vast wealth of the new kingdoms carved from Alexander's conquests. It also remained highly unstable from the time of Alexander's death until 276 B.C.E., when a general named Antigonus finally established his own dynasty (known as the Antigonids). Thereafter, Macedonia drew its strength from its considerable natural resources and from its influence over Aegean trade, as well as its status as overlord of Greece. Moreover, the Macedonians continued to field the most effective army in the Hellenistic world.

Antigonus himself was influenced by a philosophical outlook called Stoicism (discussed later in this chapter) and viewed kingship as a form of noble servitude, to be endured rather than enjoyed. This perspective, combined with his modest resources, convinced him not to compete with the Seleucids and Ptolemies for dominance. Instead, Antigonid policy was to keep these other two powers at war with one another and away from the Macedonian sphere of influence. Antigonus and his successors thus pursued a strategy more reminiscent of Philip II than of his son. They secured the northern frontiers, maintained a strong, standing army, and kept the fractious Greeks at heel.

The Greeks, however, were restive under the Antigonids, and two emergent powers served as rallying points for those who resented "barbarian" rule. These two forces, the Aetolian League and the Achaean League, were a departure in Greek political organization. Unlike the defensive alliances of the classical period, each represented a real political unification, with some centralization of governance. Citizens of the leagues' member poleis participated in councils of state that dealt with foreign policy and military affairs. New members were admitted on an equal footing with existing members, and all citizens of the various poleis enjoyed joint citizenship throughout the league. The same laws, weights and measures, coinage, and judicial procedures also applied throughout each federation. So effective was this mode of cooperation that James Madison, John Jay, and Alexander Hamilton employed it as one of their models for federalism in the United States.

FROM POLIS TO COSMOPOLIS

So what became of the polis, that building-block of classical Greece? As we have seen, the changes of the fourth century B.C.E. were already disrupting patterns of social and political life. Alexander's conquests hastened this process of transformation, and they also opened up a wider world—a world that came to admire all things Greek. By 300 B.C.E., a common Hellenistic culture was transcending political and geographical boundaries. It was fueled by the hundreds of thousands of adventurers who joined the Greek *diaspora* ("dispersion"), and whose emigration reduced the population of the Greek mainland by as much as fifty percent in the century after 325 B.C.E.

This exciting, urbane world was made up of interconnected cities whose scale dwarfed anything imaginable in Periclean Athens. In the fifth century B.C.E., direct participation in government had meant that every male citizen had some share in his society, its institutions, its gods, its army, and its cultural life. In the huge and cosmopolitan Hellenistic city, by contrast, all these ways of defining oneself were no longer relevant. The individual male's intimate connection with the state was broken, as was his

nexus of social relationships. An average Greek in one of the Hellenistic kingdoms might have only his immediate family to rely on, if that. Very often, he was alone. What resulted was a traumatic disjunction between the traditional values and assumptions of Greek life and these new realities—and a host of entirely new opportunities.

Commerce and Urbanization

The Hellenistic world was prosperous. Alexander's conquests had opened up a vast trading area stretching from Egypt to the Persian Gulf, dominated by Greek-speaking rulers and well-established merchant communities. These conquests also stimulated the economy by putting into circulation hoards of Persian gold and silver coins, jewelry, and other commodities acquired through plunder. Industries benefited too, because autocratic rulers found manufacturing to be a further means of increasing their revenues.

Every facility was provided by the Ptolemies and the Seleucids for the encouragement of commerce. Harbors were improved, warships were sent out to police the seas, roads and canals were built. The Ptolemies even employed geographers to discover new routes to distant lands. As a result of such methods, Egypt developed a flourishing commerce in the widest variety of products obtainable. Into the port of Alexandria came spices from Arabia, gold from Ethiopia and India, tin from Britain, elephants and ivory from Nubia, silver from Spain, fine carpets from Asia Minor, and even silk from China.

The rapid growth of cities had both political and economic ramifications. Greek rulers imported Greek officials and especially Greek soldiers to maintain their control over non-Greek populations, making many new settlements necessary. Alexander himself had founded some 70 cities as outposts of domination; in the next two centuries, his successors founded about 200 more. Urbanization also increased due to the expansion of commerce and industry, but the most significant factors were the Greek diaspora and the migration of workers from rural areas. Population growth in some centers was explosive. At Antioch, the population quadrupled during a single century. Seleucia on the Tigris grew from nothing to a metropolis of several hundred thousand in less than two centuries. Alexandria in Egypt had half a million inhabitants; only imperial Rome would have surpassed it in size, and it would not be until the eighteenth century of our era that European cities like London and Paris were as large. Alexandria was not only populous, it was magnificent and spacious—which Rome never was. Its wide streets were paved and laid out in an orderly grid. It had splendid public buildings and parks, the great

Museum, and the famous library containing half a million books. It was the storehouse and showcase of Greek culture.

Not everyone enjoyed prosperity. Agriculture remained the major occupation, and small farmers in particular suffered severely from exploitative taxation. Although industrial production increased, it continued to be based on manual labor by individual artisans, most of whom lived in poverty. Among the teeming populations of Hellenistic cities, unemployment was a constant concern. Even those who prospered in the new economy were subject to drastic fluctuations in their fortunes, owing to the precarious nature of mercantile endeavors. Merchants were also vulnerable to the boom-and-bust syndrome: an investor, thinking he could make a fortune during an upward price spiral, might go into debt to take advantage of the trend, only to find that supply exceeded demand, leaving him nothing with which to pay his creditors. The economic landscape of the Hellenistic world was therefore one of contrasting extremes. In many ways, this was also the case with respect to its culture.

HELLENISTIC WORLDVIEWS

Life in the Hellenistic boomtowns produced new worldviews and new philosophies that differed significantly from those of Plato and Aristotle. Another major departure was the separation of philosophy from scientific inquiry, which now became its own field of study. Despite these differences, however, scientists, philosophers, and religious teachers were all motivated by the same thing: the need to make human existence meaningful in a new age that lacked traditional civic structures and social values.

Two Paths to Tranquility: Stoicism and Epicureanism

The two strains of philosophy that dominated the Hellenistic world both originated in Athens around 300 B.C.E.: Stoicism and Epicureanism. Their teachings had several features in common. Both were concerned with the well-being of the individual, not with the welfare of society as a whole. Both were firmly rooted in the material world; even the soul was considered to be part of the mortal body. Both responded to the new cosmopolitan age by promoting universal values: they taught that people are the same the world over, and recognized no distinctions between Greeks and the peoples hitherto known as "barbarians."

But in other ways the two systems were radically different. The Stoics who followed Zeno of Citium (c. 335–

c. 263 B.C.E.)—they took their name from the *stoa* ("colonnade") in which he regularly taught—believed that the cosmos is an ordered whole in which all contradictions are resolved for ultimate good. Evil is only relative; the particular misfortunes that befall human beings are merely incidents that will lead to the final perfection of the universe. Everything that happens is therefore predetermined. People are free only in the sense that they can accept fate or rebel against it. By freely submitting to the workings of the universe, and by acknowledging that whatever happens must be for the best, one can attain true happiness: tranquility of mind.

The Stoics' theory of ethics and social responsibility grew out of this personal philosophy. Believing that the highest good is serenity of mind, they emphasized self-discipline and the fulfillment of one's duties. They taught tolerance and forgiveness, and they also urged participation in public affairs as a special responsibility for those with able minds. They condemned slavery and violence, although they took no real actions against these evils because they saw them as inevitable—and because extreme social change might be worse.

With some some later modifications, Stoic philosophy became the driving force behind the values of the Roman Republic and of early Christianity, and can be considered one of the most important products of the Hellenistic world. Even those who do not embrace its tenets or its perspective may recognize that they have been influenced by it.

The teachings of Epicurus (341–270 B.C.E.) were based on the atomic theory of an earlier Greek philosopher called Democritus, who lived in the latter part of the fifth century B.C.E. According to his central thesis, the universe is made up entirely of atoms, and every individual object or organism is therefore the product of a combination of atoms. Studying Democritus' writings, Epicurus reached a conclusion exactly opposite to that of the Stoics: he interpreted the atomic theory to mean that there is no ultimate purpose in the workings of the universe. So the highest good cannot come of submitting oneself stoically to the endurance of hardship, because suffering is not part of a larger plan: it is merely the chance by-product of random atomic actions. The highest good, then, must be pleasure: the moderate satisfaction of bodily appetites, the intellectual pleasure of contemplating excellence and remembering past enjoyments, and serenity in the face of death. Indeed, an individual who understands that the soul itself is material, that the universe operates at random, and that no gods intervene in human affairs will have no fear of death or any other supernatural phenomena.

The Epicureans thus came by a very different route to the same general conclusion as the Stoics: nothing is better than tranquility of mind. In contrast to the Stoics, however,

Debating the Education and Role of Women

The drastic political, social, and economic changes of the fourth century led philosophers to re-imagine the traditional structures of the polis, and to debate the proper role of women within these structures. Meanwhile, the cosmopolitan culture of the expanding Hellenistic world made it increasingly difficult to limit women's access to public spaces. The following excerpts represent two philosophical responses to these problems. The first comes from Plato's treatise on "Polis-matters" (Politeía), known to us as The Republic, *the longest of his philosophical dialogues and the most influential work of political thought in history. Its conceptual narrator and protagonist is Socrates, who engages in a series of debates with his pupils. The second excerpt is taken from a philosophical treatise attributed to a female follower of Pythagoras (see Chapter 3), but it was really written around 200 B.C.E. in Hellenistic Italy, and by a man.*

Plato, *The Republic*, c. 380 B.C.E.

SOCRATES: For men born and educated like our citizens, the only way, in my opinion, of arriving at a right conclusion about the possession and use of women and children is to follow the path on which we originally started, when we said that the men were to be the guardians and watchdogs of the herd.

GLAUCON: True.

SOCRATES: Let us further suppose the birth and education of our women to be subject to similar or nearly similar regulations; then we shall see whether the result accords with our design.

GLAUCON: What do you mean?

SOCRATES: . . . The education which was assigned to the men was music and gymnastic[s].

GLAUCON: Yes.

SOCRATES: Then women must be taught music and gymnastic[s] and also the art of war, which they must practice like the men?

GLAUCON: That is the inference, I suppose.

SOCRATES: I should rather expect . . . that several of our proposals, if they are carried out, being unusual, may appear ridiculous.

GLAUCON: No doubt of it.

SOCRATES: Yes, and the most ridiculous thing of all will be the sight of women naked in the palaestra, exercising with the men, especially when they are no longer young; they certainly will not be a vision of beauty, any more than the enthusiastic old men who in spite of wrinkles and ugliness continue to frequent the gymnasia. . . . [Yet] not long ago, as we shall remind them, the Hellenes were of the opinion, which is still generally received among the barbarians, that the sight of a naked man was ridiculous and improper; and when first the Cretans and then the Lacedaemonians [Spartans] introduced the custom, the wits of that day might equally have ridiculed the innovation.

GLAUCON: No doubt . . .

SOCRATES: First, then, whether the question is to be put in jest or in earnest, let us come to an understanding about the nature of woman: Is she capable of sharing either wholly or partially in the actions of men, or not at all? And is the art of war one of those arts in which she can or cannot share? That will be the best way of commencing the enquiry, and will probably lead to the fairest conclusion. . . .

GLAUCON: I suppose so. . . .

SOCRATES: And if . . . the male and female sex appear to differ in their fitness for any art or pursuit, we should say that such pursuit or art ought to be assigned to one or the other of them; but if the difference consists only in women bearing and men begetting children, this does not amount to a proof that a woman differs from a man in respect of the sort of education she should receive; and we shall therefore continue to maintain that our guardians and their wives ought to have the same pursuits.

GLAUCON: Very true.

SOCRATES: Next, we shall ask . . . how, in reference to any of the pursuits or arts of civic life, the nature of a woman differs from that of a man? . . .

GLAUCON: By all means.

SOCRATES: . . . [W]hen you spoke of a nature gifted or not gifted in any respect, did you mean to say that one man will acquire a thing easily, another with difficulty; a little learning will lead the one to discover a great deal; whereas the other, after much study and application, no sooner learns than he forgets? Or again, did you mean, that the one has a body which is a good servant to his mind, while the body of the other is a hindrance to him? Would not these be the sort of differences which distinguish the man gifted by nature from the one who is ungifted?

GLAUCON: No one will deny that.

SOCRATES: And can you mention any pursuit of mankind in which the male sex has not all these gifts and qualities in a higher degree than the female? Need I waste time in speaking of the art of weaving, and the management of pancakes and preserves, in which womankind does really appear to be great, and in which for her to be beaten by a man is of all things the most absurd?

GLAUCON: You are quite right . . . in maintaining the general inferiority of the female sex: although many women are in many things superior to many men, yet on the whole what you say is true.

Source: Excerpted from Plato, *The Republic*, Book V, trans. Benjamin Jowett (New York: 1982), pp. 170–76.

Treatise Attributed to Phintys, Third/Second Century B.C.E.

Now some people think that it is not appropriate for a woman to be a philosopher, just as a woman should not be a cavalry officer or a politician. . . . I agree that men should be generals and city officials and politicians, and women should keep house and stay inside and receive and take care of their husbands. But I believe that courage, justice, and intelligence are qualities that men and women have in common. . . . Courage and intelligence are more appropriately male qualities because of the strength of men's bodies and the power of their minds. Chastity is more appropriately female.

Accordingly, a woman must learn about chastity and realize what she must do quantitatively and qualitatively to be able to obtain this womanly virtue. I believe that there are five qualifications: (1) the sanctity of her marriage bed, (2) the cleanliness of her body, (3) the manner in which she chooses to leave her house, (4) her refusal to participate in secret cults . . . , (5) her readiness and moderation in sacrificing to the gods.

Of these, the most important quality for chastity is to be pure in respect of the marriage bed, and for her not to have affairs with men from other households. If she breaks the law in this way she wrongs the gods of her family and provides her family and home not with its own offspring but with bastards. . . . She should

also consider the following: that there is no means of atoning for this sin; no way she can approach the shrines or the altars of the gods as a pure woman. . . . The greatest glory a freeborn woman can have—her foremost honor—is the witness her own children will give to her chastity toward her husband, the stamp of the likeness they bear to the father whose seed produced them. . . .

As far as adornment of her body is concerned . . . [h]er clothes should not be transparent or ornate. She should not put on silken material, but moderate, white-colored clothes. In this way, she will avoid being overdressed or luxurious or made-up, and not give other women cause to be uncomfortably envious. . . . She should not apply imported or artificial coloring to her face—with her own natural coloring, by washing only with water, she can ornament herself with modesty. . . .

Women of importance leave the house to sacrifice to the leading divinity of the community on behalf of their husbands and their households. They do not leave home at night nor in the evening, but at midday, to attend a religious festival or to make some purchase, accompanied by a single female servant or decorously escorted by two servants at most. . . . They keep away from secret cults . . . particularly because these forms of worship encourage drunkenness and ecstasy. The mistress of the house and head of the household should be chaste and untouched in all respects.

Source: From Mary R. Lefkowitz and Maureen B. Fant, eds., *Women's Life in Greece & Rome: A Source Book in Translation*, 2nd ed. (Baltimore, MD: 1992), pp. 163–64.

Questions for Analysis

1. Follow the steps of the argument made by Socrates. How does he go about proving that women and men are different, and should have different roles in society? Are there flaws in this argument? What are they?

2. How does the author of the treatise seem to define "chastity," and why does "she" (actually he) say that it corresponds to more masculine qualities of courage and intelligence? Why would this author have wanted to attribute these reflections to female members of the community founded by the philosopher Pythagoras (c. 570–c. 495), three centuries earlier? How might this treatise be responding to the changes brought about by the expansion of the Greek world in the fourth and third centuries B.C.E?

3. What are main points on which these two perspectives agree? How might ideas like those expressed here have influenced contemporary ideas of female beauty and modesty (see *Interpreting Visual Evidence*, page 87)?

they did not insist on virtue as an end in itself, or on the fulfillment of one's duties. For an Epicurean, the only duty a person has is to the self, and the only reason to act virtuously is to increase one's own happiness. Similarly, Epicureans denied that there is any such thing as justice; laws and political institutions are "just" only insofar as they contribute to the welfare of the individual. Yes, certain rules have been found necessary for the maintenance of order, but these rules should be obeyed solely because that is to one's advantage. The state is, at best, a mere convenience, and the wise man should take no active part in politics. Instead, he should withdraw to study philosophy and enjoy the fellowship of a few congenial friends. Modern libertarian and anarchic movements share many characteristics with Epicureanism.

Extreme Doubt: Skepticism

The most pessimistic philosophy generated by the Hellenistic era was propounded by the Skeptics, whose name means "those on the lookout" or "the spies." Skepticism reached the zenith of its popularity in the second century under the influence of Carneades (car-ne-AH-dehs, c. 214–129 B.C.E.), a man born in the Greek city of Cyrene, in North Africa, who spent his youth in Athens. His chief teaching (filtered through Aristotle) was that all knowledge is based on sense perception and is therefore limited and relative. From this, the Skeptics concluded that no one can prove anything. Moreover, because our senses can deceive us, we cannot even be certain about the truth we think we have gained by observation of the world. All we can say is that things *appear* to be such and such; we do not *know* that they really *are* that way. It follows, furthermore, that we can have no definite knowledge of the supernatural, of the meaning of life, or of right and wrong.

The only sensible course for the Skeptic is therefore to suspend judgment. If we abandon the fruitless quest for truth and cease to worry about good conduct and the existence of evil, we can at least attain a certain peace of mind, the highest satisfaction that an uncertain life affords. Needless to say, the Skeptics were even less concerned than the Epicureans with political and social problems, from which they felt wholly alienated. Their ideal was one of escape from an incomprehensible world. In some key respects they anticipated modern existentialism and nihilism.

Varieties of Religion

Like Epicureanism and Skepticism, Hellenistic religion tended to offer vehicles of escape from political commitments. When we think back to how close was the link between Greek selfhood and politics down to the middle of the fourth century B.C.E.—"man is a creature of the polis"—we can begin to appreciate what a radical change had occurred in just a few generations. In all the societies we have studied so far, religion was wholly interconnected with politics. Divine worship centered on the gods who protected a community and furthered its interests. Hence, the most serious of the charges brought against Socrates was that he had "denied the gods of the polis" and thus committed treason. Religious crimes were political crimes, and piety was the same as patriotism.

Although this sense of a vital connection between a place and its gods persisted to a certain extent during the Hellenistic period, civic-oriented worship was compromised by rootless multiculturalism. In its place, some elite members of society gravitated toward one of the philosophies discussed above. Ordinary people, though, were more likely to embrace religious cults that offered emotional gratification or the diversion of colorful rituals, as well as some assurance of an afterlife.

Cults that stressed extreme methods of atonement, mystical union with the divine, or contact with supernatural forces accordingly attracted many followers. Among these so-called mystery religions was the cult of Dionysus, which celebrated the cyclical death and resurrection of that Greek god. The Egyptian cult of Isis (Chapter 1) also revolved around rituals of death and rebirth. So too did Zoroastrianism (Chapter 2), which became increasingly dualistic: its magi now taught that the material world was entirely evil and urged believers to adopt ascetic practices that would purify their souls and prepare them for ethereal joy in the afterlife.

Like the peoples who worshiped them, the gods of the Hellenistic world were often immigrants from other lands. Temples to Greek gods and goddesses were dedicated throughout the Near East and Egypt; conversely, temples to Near Eastern divinities were constructed in the cities of the Greek homeland. In Alexandria, scholars of religion collected Egyptian and Near Eastern mythologies, which were recorded and reformulated for Greek-speaking audiences.

Even among the Jews of Palestine, who resisted assimilation and the adoption of foreign customs, Hellenistic culture put down deep roots. This was especially true among elite Jews living outside Palestine, who outnumbered the Palestinian population by a considerable margin. To meet the needs of these Greek-speaking Jews, and to satisfy the curiosity of Gentiles interested in Jewish beliefs, scholars working in Alexandria produced a Greek version of the Hebrew scriptures. It is known as the Septuagint (sep-TOO-ah-gint), from the Greek word meaning "the seventy": legend has it that seventy scribes, each working independently, produced individual translations from Hebrew to Greek that were identical in every respect. This meant that the Septuagint could be regarded as no less a product of divine inspiration than the original books that made up the Hebrew Bible, and could be treated as an authoritative text in its own right. For Jews concerned about their social and cultural standing vis-à-vis their Greek neighbors, the Septuagint was proof of their Hellenistic values—although, ironically, some of the very portions of scripture that were now written in Greek disapproved strongly of those values.

THE SCIENTIFIC REVOLUTION OF ANTIQUITY

The Hellenistic period was the most brilliant age in the history of science before the seventeenth century of our era. There are three major reasons for this. First, there was the stimulus to intellectual inquiry caused by the fusion of Mesopotamian and Egyptian science with the philosophical methods of the Greeks. Second, as in the more famous scientific revolution, the use of a common language (in the seventeenth century it was Latin) and the ease of communication facilitated by affordable travel made the circulation of knowledge and sharing of ideas easier (in the seventeenth century, communication was increased by the printing press). Finally, as in the seventeenth century, the competition among patrons of science was intense: every autocrat wanted to be thought enlightened and to be associated with new discoveries. Even purely theoretical advances were so much admired that a Hellenistic prince who had bankrolled such a breakthrough would share the glory of it. It was especially profitable to subsidize research that led to the development of new technologies, because they might have military applications.

The arts were also transformed by the economic and political conditions of the Hellenistic world. Artists working in various media strove to demonstrate their mastery of difficult techniques and so to attract the notice of potential patrons. New markets for art also changed *what* was being made, how, and for whom. In all of the civilizations we have studied so far, artists

worked directly for royal or civic patrons. In the Hellenistic world, art became commodified. Sometimes a work would be made expressly for a particular patron, but many works of art were fashioned for the open market. They were also designed to suit the tastes and lifestyles of those merchant classes who had disposable income and wanted to increase their social standing through conspicuous consumption. This was as true of literature as of sculpture or the decorative arts: we know the names of over a thousand Hellenistic authors. Indeed, the number of texts and *objets d'art* that exist from this period is huge when compared to earlier eras.

Measuring and Mapping: Astronomy, Geography, and Mathematics

Hellenistic scientists took a major interest in measurements and mapmaking, whether of the heavens (astronomy), the earth (geography), or the forms occuring in nature (geometry). The most renowned—and most wronged—of the Hellenistic astronomers was Aristarchus of Samos (310–230 B.C.E.), whose major discovery anticipated that of Copernicus by 1,700 years: he deduced that the earth and other planets revolve around the sun. Unfortunately,

THE CITADEL OF PERGAMON. An artist's reconstruction of Pergamon in the second century B.C.E., based on the work of nineteenth-century German archeologists. High atop the hill is the massive altar of Zeus (now in the Pergamon Museum in Berlin) and below it slope the tiers of the theater. Other features include fortifications, terraces, and artificial landscaping for public gardens. ■ *How does this complex of buildings compare to that of another citadel, the Acropolis of Athens (see Chapter 3, page 58)?*

however, this view was not accepted by many of his contemporaries or successors because it conflicted with the teachings of Aristotle, which in turn reflected the Greek conviction that humanity, and therefore the earth, must be at the center of the universe. The sad fate of his discovery was sealed in the second century C.E., when the Alexandrian scholar Claudius Ptolemaeus (known as Ptolemy) unequivocally argued that Aristotle was correct, and that all heavenly bodies revolve around the earth. This misinformative view would not be overturned until the much later scientific revolution occurred (see Chapter 16).

Closely allied with astronomy were geography and mathematics. The most influential Hellenistic mathematician was Euclid, whose *Elements of Geometry* (c. 300 B.C.E.) remained the basic textbook of that subject until the twentieth century of our era. In the field of geography—and in a host of other pursuits, too—the most original thinker was Eratosthenes of Alexandria (air-ah-TOS-then-ees, c. 276–c. 196 B.C.E.). Not only did he accurately calculate the circumference of the earth (within a tiny margin of error, less than 200 miles), he was the first to suggest the possibility of reaching eastern Asia by sailing west. In addition, he founded the science of chronology by attempting to establish the dates of major events reaching back to the siege of Troy. Students of history are forever in his debt.

Medicine and Mechanics: The Sciences of Physiology and Physics

Before the third century B.C.E., physics had been a branch of philosophy. Now it became a separate, experimental science thanks to the genius of one man, Archimedes of Syracuse (c. 287–212 B.C.E.). It was he who discovered the law of floating bodies, or specific gravity, now known as "Archimedes' principle." According to legend, the idea came to him when he was in his bath, and the stunning insight so excited him that he lept from the water and dashed out naked into the street, shouting *Eureka!* ("I have found it!"). Archimedes also established the principles of the lever, the pulley, and the screw, and he invented both a compound pulley and a propeller. All of these discoveries had numerous practical uses in the construction of buildings, ships, and military machinery.

Other extraordinary advances were made in the field of medicine. Especially significant was the work of Herophilus of Chalcedon (c. 335–c. 280 B.C.E.), the greatest anatomist of antiquity and probably the first to practice human dissection. Herophilus' achievements included a detailed description of the brain, which allowed him to prove that it was the engine of human intellect (Aristotle thought that it was

the heart), as well as the discovery that the arteries contain blood alone (not a mixture of blood and air, as Aristotle had taught), and that their function is to carry blood from the heart to all parts of the body. His colleague Erasistratus (air-ah-sis-STRAH-tus) made allied discoveries, establishing that the heart was a pump and not an organ of emotion. Erasistratus also rejected the widely held theory of the physician Hippocrates (c. 460–c. 370), who had posited that the body consists of four "humors" which need to be kept in balance through bloodletting and other invasive practices. Unfortunately, this discovery went the way of the heliocentric universe posited by Aristarchus: another encyclopedist of the second century C.E., Galen, preferred the erroneous theory of Hippocrates. The practice of bloodletting thus persisted into the nineteenth century of our era.

Urban Architecture and Sculpture

Hellenistic architecture drew on Greek models, but it was also influenced by tastes more characteristic of Egypt and Persia. The best surviving example comes from Pergamon, a city on the coast of Anatolia that became the capital of a new kingdom wrested from the control of the Seleucids in

DYING GAUL. The original (now lost) statue on which this Roman copy was based was sculpted in Pergamon around 220 B.C.E. The sculptor clearly wished to exhibit skill in depicting an unusual subject: the Gauls were a Celtic people about whom very little was known in this era. ▪ *How does this sympathetic representation of a "barbarian" express the new values of Hellenistic philosophy?*

the second century B.C.E. It boasted an enormous altar dedicated to Zeus that crowned the heights of the city, below which an open-air theater was built into the steep slope of the hill. In Ephesus, not far away, the streets were not only paved, they were paved with marble.

But the most influential of all Hellenistic arts was sculpture, which placed even more emphasis on realism than the fourth-century sculptures discussed earlier in this chapter. And because awkward human postures offered the greatest technical challenges, sculptors often preferred to show people stretching themselves or balancing on one leg or performing other unusual feats. It is clear that the goal was to create something unique in both conception and craftsmanship—something a collector could show off as the only one of its type. It is not surprising, therefore, that complexity came to be admired for its own sake, and extreme naturalism sometimes teetered on the brink of absurdity. Yet to our eyes, such works appear familiar because of the influence they exerted on later sculptors like

Michelangelo (see Chapter 12) and Auguste Rodin. Three of the most famous examples are pictured here, each exhibiting different aesthetic qualities and artistic techniques: the *Dying Gaul*, made in Pergamon around 220 B.C.E.; the *Winged Victory of Samothrace*, dating from around 200 B.C.E.; and the *Laocoön* group, from the first century B.C.E.

Literary Fantasy and Historical Reality

In the sixth century B.C.E. it was the lyric, in the fifth century it was tragedy, and in the fourth century it was the novel; but in the Hellenistic era, the new literary genre was pastoral verse. These poems tapped into a strong vein of nostalgia for rural pastimes and simple pleasures, a make-believe world of shepherds and wood nymphs. The most important pastoral poet of the age was Theocritus, who flourished around 270 B.C.E. in the big-city environment of Alexandria. In the midst of urban bustle and within sight

THE WINGED VICTORY OF SAMOTHRACE (left). This marble sculpture of the goddess Nike (Victory) may originally have been displayed on the prow of a monumental ship. It formed part of a temple complex on the island of Samothrace in the northern Aegean, and dates to around the year 200 B.C.E. It is now in the Louvre Museum, Paris. **LAOCOÖN AND HIS SONS (right).** In sharp contrast to the serene and confident *Winged Victory* is this famous sculpture group from the first century B.C.E. According to legend, Laocoön warned the Trojans not to accept the wooden horse sent by the Greeks and was accordingly punished by the sea-god Poseidon, who sent two serpents to kill him and his sons. The intense physicality of this work was an important influence on Michelangelo, a millennium and a half later.

of overcrowded slums, he celebrated the charms of country life and lazy summer afternoons. He thereby founded an enduring tradition that would be taken up by poets from the Roman Virgil to the Englishman (and classical scholar) A. E. Houseman, which has provided a wealth of themes for the visual arts. Even composers like Beethoven and Debussy owe a debt to Theocritus.

By contrast, Hellenistic prose literature was dominated by historians who modeled their work on earlier pioneers, especially Thucydides. By far the most important was Polybius (c. 203–120 B.C.E.), a well-born Greek whose father was a prominent politician in the Achaean League. Polybius himself was trained as a cavalry officer at a time when the Achaean League was trying to position itself favorably in ongoing wars between the rising republic of Rome and the various kingdoms of northern Greece. In 168 B.C.E., the Romans became suspicious of the Achaeans' declared neutrality and demanded that a thousand noble hostages be sent to Rome as a guarantee of the League's good behavior. Polybius was one of those hostages, and he spent the next seventeen years living in Rome, where he became a fervent admirer of its unique form of government (see Chapter 5).

The result was a series of histories that glorified the achievements of Rome and its political system. Polybius also attempted to account for the patterns that he discerned in the history of Greece since the Peloponnesian War. He argued that historical developments follow regular cycles, and that nations pass inevitably through stages of growth and decay. Hence, it should be possible to predict exactly where a given state is heading if one knows what has happened to it in the past. Yet Polybius also argued that the special character of Rome's constitution would allow it to break the cycle, because it combined all of the different forms of government that Aristotle had outlined in his *Politics*. This view of history galvanized the framers of the United States Constitution, directly influencing their conception of our own political institutions.

CONCLUSION

Judged from the perspective of classical Greece, Hellenistic civilization seems strange. The autocratic governments of the age that followed Alexander's conquests would probably appear repugnant to a staunch proponent of Athenian democracy, and the Hellenistic love of extravagance can contrast strikingly with the tastes of the fifth century B.C.E.

After You Read This Chapter

Visit StudySpace for quizzes, additional review materials, and multi-media documents. **wwnorton.com/studyspace**

REVIEWING THE OBJECTIVES

- Macedonia's successful conquest of the Greek poleis can be attributed to several factors. What are they?
- Alexander the Great's imperial policies were influenced by his own upbringing, the different cultures he encountered, and some key historical precedents. Give at least one example of each type of influence.
- Explain how the three Hellenistic kingdoms reflect the differences among the three main civilizations we have studied so far.
- Why is the Hellenistic world described as "cosmopolitan"? How did this urban culture differ from that of the Greek poleis?
- The philosophies of Plato and Aristotle both derive from the teachings of Socrates, but they diverge in some important ways. What are those main differences?

Yet Hellenistic civilization had its own achievements that the classical age could not match. Most Hellenistic cities offered a greater range of public facilities than any Greek cities of the previous period, and the numerous advances in science and technology are astonishing when compared to anything that came before, or even after.

But the most important contribution of the Hellenistic era to subsequent historical developments was its role as intermediary between the nascent empire of Rome and the older civilizations of Mesopotamia, Egypt, and Greece. The economic and political infrastuctures that were put in place after Alexander's conquests would form the framework of Roman imperial government. The Romans would also take advantage of the common language and cultural expectations that bound the far reaches of the Greek-speaking world together. Their own Latin language would never supplant Greek as the preeminent language of scholarship and administration in the eastern portions of their empire.

The Hellenistic era must also be recognized as the bridge that connects us to the earlier ages of antiquity: most of what is contained in the first four chapters of this book is known to us because older texts and artifacts were copied and collected by the scholars of Alexandria and other Hellenistic cities. And it was Hellenistic art and architecture, Hellenistic city planning and civic culture, that the Romans strove to emulate—not those of Periclean Athens. The same can be said of drama and poetry.

For us, two further aspects of Hellenistic culture deserve special mention: its cosmopolitanism and its modernity. The word *cosmopolitan* means "universal city," and it was the Hellenistic period that came closest to turning this ideal of globalization into reality. Around 250 B.C.E. a Greek tourist could have traveled from Sicily to the borders of India—the two ends of the earth—and never have found himself among people who did not speak his language or share his basic outlook. Nor would this tourist have identified himself in ethnic or nationalist terms, or felt any exclusive loyalty to a city-state or kingdom. He would have considered himself a citizen of the world. He would also have considered himself a modern man, not bound by the old prejudices and superstitions of the past. It is for these reasons that Hellenistic civilization seems so closely related to our own. It was a world of stark contrasts and infinite possibilities, where economic instability, extremism, and authoritarian regimes existed side by side with unprecedented prosperity, rational inquiry, and extraodinary freedoms. In Chapter 5, we will see how this world adapted itself to the dominion of a single Italian city.

PEOPLE, IDEAS, EVENTS IN CONTEXT

- In what ways were the military strategies of **PHILIP II OF MACEDON** variations on older forms of hoplite warfare? How did the rise of mercenary armies and of **THEBES** further change military strategies in the fourth century?
- How did the philosophies of **PLATO** and **ARISTOTLE** respond to the crisis of the polis?
- To what degree did the conquests of **ALEXANDER THE GREAT** unite Mesopotamia, Egypt, and Greece?
- Why and how did the three **HELLENISTIC KINGDOMS** emerge? How were the **AETOLIAN AND ACHAEAN LEAGUES** new models for governance and cooperation in Greece?
- In what ways were **STOICISM, EPICUREANISM,** and other new philosophies a response to **COSMOPOLITANISM** and the breakdown of traditional societies and values?
- What were the driving forces behind the **SCIENTIFIC REVOLUTION OF ANTIQUITY**? What were its main achievements?
- What are some essential characteristics of **HELLENISTIC ART**? In what ways did it differ from that of the fifth century B.C.E. (Chapter 3)?

CONSEQUENCES

- "The history of the world is but the biography of great men"—so the Scottish historian Thomas Carlyle (1795–1881) summarized the impact of figures like Alexander the Great. How would you construct an argument in support of this proposition, using what you've learned in this chapter? How would you refute it?
- In what ways do Alexander's actions demonstrate his own knowledge of history, as well as a capacity to apply that knowledge to his own circumstances? Can you identify leaders of our own day who have mobilized their understanding of history in similar ways?
- In your view, which civilization more resembles our own: classical Athens or the Hellenistic world? Why? What characteristics make an era seem "modern"?

STORY LINES

- Romans were proud of their unique history, especially the legend that they had overthrown their kings. They clung to this story even when individual men came to wield kingly powers.

- Roman identity, religion, and politics were intimately bound up in the worship of ancestors, especially male ancestors. As a result, fathers (living and dead) wielded extraordinary power in early Rome.

- Roman women enjoyed more freedoms than the women of ancient Greece, but they were still subject to the authority of their male relatives.

- The Roman army had unprecedented strength and importance in this civilization, but the army's relationship to Roman politics and society changed drastically as Rome's empire grew.

- Paradoxically, the Romans celebrated their farming heritage even as they built a highly urbanized society. At the same time, they regarded Greek culture as both superior and dangerous.

Before You Read This Chapter

CHRONOLOGY

753 B.C.E.	Legendary founding of Rome
c. 509 B.C.E.	Roman Republic established
c. 450 B.C.E.	Law of the Twelve Tables
287 B.C.E.	"Struggle of the Orders" ends
264–146 B.C.E.	Punic Wars
134–104 B.C.E.	Slave revolts in Sicily
133–122 B.C.E.	Reforms of the Gracchi
107–86 B.C.E.	Consulship of Marius
82–79 B.C.E.	Dictatorship of Sulla
73–71 B.C.E.	Rebellion of Spartacus
52–48 B.C.E.	Struggle of Pompey and Caesar
48–44 B.C.E.	Dictatorship of Casear
44–30 B.C.E.	Rivalry of Octavian and Antony
27 B.C.E.–14 C.E.	Principate of the Emperor Augustus
27–180 C.E.	Flowering of the *Pax Romana*
79 C.E.	Eruption of Mount Vesuvius destroys (and preserves) Pompeii
117 C.E.	Roman Empire reaches its greatest extent under Trajan

The Civilization of Ancient Rome

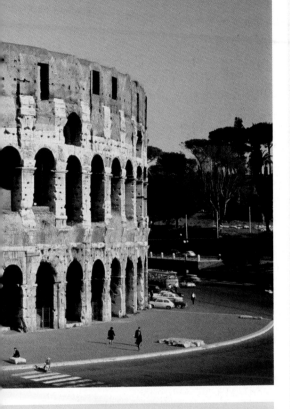

CORE OBJECTIVES

- **IDENTIFY** the factors that influenced the formation of the Roman Republic.

- **UNDERSTAND** the basic elements of Roman identity.

- **DEFINE** the classes of people who struggled for power in Rome.

- **DESCRIBE** the impact of territorial expansion on Roman society.

- **TRACE** the events leading up to the establishment of the Principate.

C ould anyone be so indifferent or slow-witted as not to care how, and under what system of government, the Romans managed to bring nearly the whole inhabited world under their rule? Can anything be more important than understanding this?" So the Greek soldier Polybius (c. 203–120 B.C.E.) addresses Greek readers in a history celebrating the achievements of the Roman Republic. Polybius had witnessed some of these firsthand: on the battlefield, in Rome itself as a hostage and guest, and on a visit to newly conquered Carthage. What better testament could there be to the success of a small Italian city than the admiration of a cultivated Greek aristocrat who, having been subjected to Roman authority, wholeheartedly embraced it? None, unless we cite the equally enthusiastic endorsement of the same Jews who had rebelled against Greek influence in 164 B.C.E. They, too, could not say enough in praise of the Romans, and they willingly placed themselves under Roman protection.

Those whom they wish to help and to make kings, they make kings, and those whom they wish they depose; and they have been greatly exalted. Yet for all

107

that, not one of them has put on a crown or worn purple as a mark of pride, but they have built for themselves a senate chamber and every day three hundred and twenty senators constantly deliberate concerning the people, to govern them well. (1 Maccabees 8:12–15)

The only people who could say more in praise of Rome were the Romans themselves. To them, the enormous success of their empire meant that they were divinely chosen to colonize the world. This was the message conveyed by the poet Virgil (70–19 B.C.E.), commissioned by the Emperor Augustus to tell the story of Rome's rise to glory in a manner imitating the epics of Homer. In one key passage, the father of Aeneas, Virgil's epic hero, "foretells" the future and addresses posterity: "Remember, Roman, you whose power rules / all peoples, that these are your arts: plant peace, / make law, spare subjects, and put down the proud" (*Aeneid*, Book VI, lines 851–3).

While the Greeks struggled against the Persians and against each other, a new civilization emerged beyond the northern fringes of the Greek world, on the banks of the river Tiber in central Italy. By 300 B.C.E. Rome was the dominant power on the Italian peninsula. Two centuries later, it had conquered Greece itself. For the next three centuries after that—an unprecedented period of sustained expansion—its power steadily increased. In the first century of our era, it ruled the Hellenistic world as well as a vast region that Greek culture had never touched: northwestern Europe. Eventually, Rome's empire united the entire Mediterranean and most of Asia Minor, while at the same time embracing provinces that are now parts of France, Spain, Portugal, Britain, Belgium, Germany, Switzerland, and the Balkans. Rome thus built a historical arch that enabled Europe to share in a rich heritage reaching back to ancient Mesopotamia and Egypt. Without Rome, European culture as we know it would not exist, and neither would the political and legal institutions that formed the United States. To echo Polybius: "Can anything be more important than understanding this?"

THE TIME OF THE KINGS

Romans looked back uneasily on their early history, for this was the time when they were ruled by kings. It may have been necessary in those days: Romans had never been peaceful settlers, and their land did not yield an easy living. Although Italy had much more fertile land than Greece, its extensive coastline boasts only a few good harbors, and most of these are on the western side, away from the commercial hubs of Greece and the Near East. Nor does the length of this coastline offer secure natural defenses. So the Romans were a warlike people from the first, continually forced to defend their own conquests against other invaders.

Early Influences

When the Romans arrived in Italy, the dominant inhabitants of the peninsula were the Etruscans, a people who remain mysterious despite the rich archeological record they left behind. This is because their language (not a branch of Indo-European) has never been fully deciphered, even though the Etruscans used an alphabet borrowed from the Greeks. By the sixth century B.C.E., the Etruscans had established a confederation of independent city-states in north-central Italy. They were skilled metalworkers, artists, and architects, from whom the Romans later took their knowledge of the arch and the vault, among much else, including the bloody sport of gladiatorial combat.

The two most important foundation myths told by the Romans were also derived from Etruscan tradition: the story of Aeneas' escape from Troy, which became the basis of Virgil's *Aeneid*, and also the story of the infant twins Romulus and Remus, abandoned at birth and then raised by a maternal wolf, afterward founding a fledgling city. Both legends would be mined by Rome's historians for their metaphorical significance, and further details would be added to increase their relevance for a changing audience. For example, the story of Aeneas' seduction and abandonment of Dido, queen of Carthage, reflected Rome's defeat of that powerful North African civilization.

In marked contrast to Greek society, Etruscan women enjoyed a very high status and played important roles in public life. Etruscan wives even ate meals with their husbands, another departure from both Greek and Roman custom. After death, devoted couples were buried together in the same mortuary vaults, and their tombstones and sarcophagi often emphasize mutual affection. Some of these practices certainly affected the Romans, whose women were less sequestered than their Greek counterparts. Yet Rome's women did not enjoy the same freedoms as Etruscan women until very late in Roman history, and by then such freedoms were condemned as signs of decadence (see below).

The Romans also borrowed ideas from the Greek settlers who had begun to colonize southern Italy and Sicily during the eighth century B.C.E. From them, Romans derived their alphabet, many of their religious beliefs, and much of their art. But the Romans downplayed Greek influence in their founding mythology, preferring to emphasize their alleged descent from the Trojans and also from an

AN ETRUSCAN COUPLE. This sarcophagus lid dates from middle of the fourth century B.C.E. and depicts a deceased couple as they lie together naked, emphasizing by their embrace the closeness of their marital bond.

Italic people called the Sabines, from whom (according to legend) Romulus and his men had forcibly abducted their wives. This was a practice Romans would continue, as the legions who planted new colonies intermarried with indigenous populations from the Persian Gulf to the lowlands of Scotland.

The Founding of Rome

The real founders of Rome were a tribe called the Latins, descendents of Indo-European-speaking peoples who crossed the Alps into Italy and settled on the banks of the Tiber by the tenth century B.C.E. This location was advantageous. Trading ships (but not large war fleets) could navigate the

river as far as the city, yet no farther; Rome could thus serve as a commercial port and was not threatened by attack from the sea. Rome also sat astride the first good ford across the Tiber, making it a major crossroads. There were also strategic advantages to the seven hills among which Rome was nestled. Eventually, its central markeplace—the *forum* or "open space"—would become the beating heart of the world's most populous and powerful city, with approximately a million people crowded into an area of five square miles.

At an early date, the Romans negotiated a series of agreements with their neighbors which were collectively known as the Latin Right: a trading pact called the *commercium*, provisions for intermarriage called the *connubium*, and the *migratio*, which allowed a Latin resident of one settlement to emigrate to another and, after a year's residence, to have the full rights of a citizen there. These privileges contrast strongly with the mutual suspicion that divided the cities of Sumer or Greece. Indeed, the Romans' later willingness to extend the Latin Right far beyond Latium was a key factor in the success of their empire.

According to their own legends, the Romans' early government mirrored the structure of Roman households, with a patriarchal king whose power was checked only by a council of elders, the Senate (from the Latin *senex*, "old man"). Seven kings, including Romulus, are said to have ruled in succession. The last, Tarquinus Superbus (Tarquin the Arrogant), is reputed to have been an Etruscan who paved the way for Rome's imperial expansion by dominating the agriculturally wealthy district of Campania to the south. But his power came at the price of Roman freedom and dignity, as was made clear when Tarquin's son raped a virtuous Roman wife, Lucretia, around 510 B.C.E. When she commited suicide to avoid dishonor, the Romans—led by Lucretia's kinsman, Lucius Junius Brutus—rose up in rebellion, overthrowing not only the Etruscan dynasty but rejecting the very idea of monarchy as a legitimate form of government. Henceforth, any claim to royal authority in Rome was considered anathema, and the very word "king" (*rex*) was a term of insult. The Brutus who would be instrumental in the assassination of Julius Caesar nearly five centuries later was a descendant of that same Brutus who had driven out the Tarquin kings—something he and his contemporaries never forgot.

THE TRIUMPH OF THE EARLY REPUBLIC

The story of Lucretia was both a patriotic myth and a potent statement of Roman attitudes toward female chastity and family honor. And it signalled a radical change in Roman governance. This change was so radical, in fact, that it did not match any of Aristotle's political categories (see Chapter 4), but instead combined elements of them all. The Romans themselves didn't know what to call their political system: they spoke of it merely as *res publica*, "the public thing."

The early Republic was marked by almost constant warfare aimed at stitching together a patchwork of valuable territories that could support Rome's growing population. Gradually, Romans came to control the valuable port of Ostia at the mouth of the Tiber, about twenty miles from their city. They also pushed northward into Etruscan territory, and southward to Naples, another good port. By 300 B.C.E., Rome had absorbed or allied itself with all of central Italy and began to look even farther south, to the wealthy Greek colonies of Sicily. Their rapid success is remarkable when compared to the patterns familiar to us from our study of classical Greece. What was the secret of it? For one thing, the Romans did not impose heavy burdens of taxation and tribute on the settlements they conquered. More often, they demanded that they contribute only soldiers to the Roman army. Rome also extended the Latin Right to many of these conquered territories, giving them a further stake in its political and military expansion.

Rome thus gained for itself nearly inexhaustible reserves of fighting men. By the middle of the third century B.C.E, its army may have numbered as many as 300,000—a huge force even by modern standards. As we have seen, the Greeks had eventually turned to paid soldiering out of economic necessity, but they fought in smaller numbers; Xenophon's army was 10,000 and Alexander's 100,000. The Great King of Persia could claim to muster a million men, but these were private or tribal armies commanded by his satraps, not a standing army loyal to him.

The Romans also devoted themselves to the discipline of warfare in ways the Greeks (except for the Spartans) and the Persians did not. Although they originally used the phalanx formation, they quickly replaced it with smaller, more flexible divisions that could adjust to the hilly conditions of central Italy. While the major unit of the Roman army was always the legion (5,000 men), the combat unit was the *maniple* ("handful"), a group of 120 infantrymen who trained together and who often performed specialized tasks or used special weaponry. The Greek Polybius could not say enough in praise of this system, which made the army adaptable to climate, terrain, and new military techniques.

The Republic's early history reinforced not only the military character of the Roman nation but its commitment to agriculture as the only proper peacetime employment for a Roman. The acquisition of new lands made it possible for citizens to maintain themselves as farmers. As a result, Romans developed an interest in commerce fairly late when compared with the Greeks or Phoenicians. And they would continue—even at the height of their empire—to valorize rural life over that of the city.

The paragon of Roman heroism in this era was Lucius Quinctius Cincinnatus (519–c. 430 B.C.E.), a stouthearted citizen-farmer who reluctantly accepted political office when Rome was threatened by attack. According to legend, he was found plowing his fields when a delegation of senators arrived to bring him to Rome, where he found that he had been named *dictator* ["decider"]. This was a position of power to which the Romans elected one man during times of crisis that required decisive leadership. As legend has it, Cincinnatus dutifully performed this role, led Rome in wars with hostile neighbors—and then went back to his plow. If Lucretia was the Roman ideal of female fortitude, Cincinnatus was the paradigm of manly virtue. George Washington was frequently compared to him, to his own satisfaction.

The Constitution of the Early Republic

During this period of expansion, Rome's political system evolved accordingly. Initially, the overthrow of the monarchy had resulted in only moderate changes; instead of a king, the Republic was headed by two elected officers called *consuls*. Although the consuls of the infant republic were supposedly chosen by all citizens, they were inevitably members of aristocratic families, known in Rome as *patricians* because they traced descent from a famous ancestor or "father" (*pater*). During his term of office, which lasted for one year, each consul exercised essentially the same power as a king: dealing justice, making law, and commanding the army. The only limit on power was the right of each consul to veto the actions of the other, which often led to stalemate or violent conflict. In times of grave emergency, such as that resulting in Cincinnatus' election, a dictator might be appointed for a term not longer than six months.

By the early fifth century, within a generation after the establishment of the Republic, patrician dominance of the government began to be challenged by the *plebs* ("people"). This was the first stage in a centuries-long contest known as the Struggle of the Orders. The plebeian classes made up nearly 98 percent of the Roman population. Some had grown wealthy through trade, but most were smallholding farmers, artisans, or the urban poor. Their causes for grievance were numerous. Although they were forced to serve in the army, they were nevertheless excluded from holding office. They were also the victims of discriminatory decisions in judicial trials, which were judged by patricians. They did not even know what their legal rights were, because Rome had as yet no established laws: there were only unwritten customs whose meaning was interpreted by the patricians to their own advantage. The plebians were also, like the poorer citizens of Greek poleis, threatened with debt slavery.

These wrongs prompted a rebellion in the early fifth century B.C.E., when plebeians refused to join in the defense of Rome and instead seceded from the city, camping out on the Aventine hill (see the map of Rome on page 128). This general strike of military labor forced the patricians to allow the people to elect of their own officers, who were known as *tribunes* (tribal leaders). The job of each tribune was to protect his constituents from patrician injustice. Moreover, the plebeians guaranteed the safety of these officers by vowing to kill any person who hindered the exercise of their powers.

The plebs' victory led to the codification of the Law of the Twelve Tables, issued around 450 B.C.E. and inscribed on wooden tablets (hence "tables"). Although it was really a perpetuation of ancient custom, the fact that the law was now *defined* made it a significant improvement. Plebeians were made eligible to hold elected offices and they gradually gained access to the Senate. A further victory came in 287 B.C.E., when they succeeded in passing a law that made decisions enacted in their own assembly binding on the Roman government—whether the Senate approved them or not. It was at this time that the phrase *Senatus Populusque Romanum* came into regular use, abbreviated *SPQR* and designating any decree or decision made by "the Roman Senate and People." Visitors to Rome will still find *SPQR* emblazoned on everything from public buildings to the manhole covers of Rome's sewers.

These reforms had several important consequences. Successful plebeians could now work their way into the upper reaches of Roman society, which loosened the hold of patrician families. At the same time, laws prevented senators from engaging directly in commerce. This restriction had the effect of creating a new social order, that of the equestrians ("horsemen" or knights): men whose wealth made it possible for them to own and equip warhorses, and thus to provide Rome's cavalry. But the equestrians and the senators were never wholly distinct. Often, some members of a wealthy family would underwrite the political careers of their brothers and cousins. Those families who managed to win election by such means, generation after generation, became increasingly influential. Meanwhile, patricians who chose politics over wealth became impoverished and resentful. By the first century B.C.E., many were

tempted to pursue their political agendas by styling themselves champions of the people (see below).

Later Roman patriots would regard this as a golden age of shared government, but Rome was never a democracy. A republic differs from a monarchy only because power is exercised by officers whose offices are not (at least in theory) hereditary. It is essentially a system for reserving power to an oligarchy or privileged group. The constitution that emerged in these key centuries therefore broadened and stabilized oligarchy by the balance it struck between competing institutions: the assembly, the Senate, and executive officeholders. Thanks to this distribution of powers, no single individual or clique could become overwhelmingly strong; but neither could direct expressions of the popular will affect Roman policy.

For the Greek historian Polybius, this was an ideal system, combining elements of the monarchy (executive officeholders, the consuls), the aristocracy (the Senate), and the polity (the people's assembly and the tribunes). For the framers of the United States Constitution, it was a model for the three branches of a new government designed to *prevent* the vast majority of Americans from participating directly in politics, while allowing some citizens (white men with sufficient property) a say in choosing their representatives. Polybius prophesied that such a system would break the political cycle that had destroyed the Greek poleis—that it could last forever. He was wrong.

THE ESSENCE OF ROMAN IDENTITY

Romans accepted new things reluctantly but then preserved them fiercely. The prevailing force was the *mos maiorum*, "the custom of the ancestors" or even—to use a word derived from the Latin *mos*—"morality." This unwritten code was essential to Roman identity. It accounts for the remarkable coherence of Roman culture, religion, and law, all of which rested on ancestor worship. The Latin word *pietas* ("piety") meant reverence for family traditions and for one's fathers—living and dead. What made the legendary Aeneas "pious Aeneas" was his devotion to his father, Anchises, whom he carried to safety while Troy burned. Metaphorically, this meant that Aeneas was the carrier of tradition, a man willing to shoulder the burdens of his ancestors and carry them forever.

This helps to explain why the Romans, in the ensuing centuries of their world domination, continued to identify so strongly with their homeland and its customs: to a Roman, "going native" in a foreign place was a terrible betrayal of the *mos maiorum*. It also explains the maxim of *patria potestas* ("fatherly power") upheld by the Twelve Tables. A Roman father, no matter what his social class, had absolute authority within his household. If he was too poor to raise a child, he could expose it (leaving it to perish or to charity) or sell it into slavery. If his wife or child dishonored him, he could kill with impunity. We begin to understand why Lucretia killed herself: otherwise, her father would have killed her with his own hands.

These values set the Romans apart. The Greeks, for example, never condoned anything like *patria potestas*. When fathers kill their children in Greek mythology, they are inevitably killed in revenge by another family member or by the gods. And while pride in one's ancestry is a very human attribute, the Romans' contemporaries were awed by their extreme devotion to these principles.

While Roman religion resembled that of the Greeks in some respects, the Roman equation of religion with family meant that all gods were essentially family gods of the Roman state. The Republic was like a giant, timeless household run by "elders" (senators) and "father figures" (patricians), some of whom traced their ancestry back to these gods: the mother of Aeneas was Venus. Like a Roman household, then, the Roman state could flourish only if the ancestral gods lent their continuing and active support. Committees of priests therefore functioned as branches of the government; and in stark contrast to other ancient societies, these priests were not full-time professionals who formed a special caste, but prominent men who rotated in and out of office while serving as leaders of the Senate. Their dual roles made Roman religion even more integral to political life than it had been in Greece (Chapter 3), similar in some ways to the integration of religion and politics in ancient Mesopotamia (Chapter 1).

The all-important devotion to ancestors is further reflected in Roman naming practices, another custom that separated them from other cultures. Most free men in antiquity were known by a given name and their father's name only: Alexander was "son of Philip." A free-born Roman, by contrast, had at least two names. The name that mattered was the name of his earliest ancestor. Gaius Julius Caesar, to take a famous example, would have entered public life as Julius, a member of the family of the Julii, who claimed ancestry from Iulus, the son of Aeneas. His forename, Gaius (*GUY-us*), was the most common name in Rome, the equivalent of "Joe" or "John," and he would never be addressed by this name in public, except perhaps by very intimate friends. His third name, Caesar, was a nickname he acquired in the course of his career: "hairy head." And because it was the most distinctive of his names, it became the name by which he was universally known. The same

A ROMAN PATRICIAN OF THE FIRST CENTURY B.C.E. This man, who wears the toga of an aristocrat, displays his piety by holding the busts of his ancestors. Busts, like the funerary masks described by Polybius (see page 113), commemorated the dead and served as the focus for family worship in household shrines. ▪ *How does the Roman attitude toward age and death differ from that of the Greeks (see the image on page 102)?* ▪ *What do these differences suggest about the broader values of these two societies?*

Analyzing Primary Sources

Polybius Describes the Romans' Worship of Their Ancestors

The Law of the Twelve Tables forbade excessive display at funerals, especially displays of wealth and grief on the part of women. Instead, funerals were supposed to be occasions for the display of family piety. In the following passage, the Greek historian Polybius—who had spent a formative fourteen years of his life in Rome—describes Roman burial customs and these rites' relationship to the strength of republican ideals.

quote just one example to illustrate the pains taken by the Roman state to produce men who will endure anything to win a reputation for valor in their country. Whenever one of their celebrated men dies . . . his body is carried with every kind of honor into the Forum . . . sometimes in an upright position so as to be conspicuous, or else, more rarely, recumbent. The whole mass of the people stand round to watch, and his son, if he has one of adult age who can be present, or if not some other relative, then . . . delivers an address which recounts the virtues and successes achieved by the dead man during his lifetime. By these means the whole populace . . . are involved in the ceremony, so that when the facts of the dead man's career are recalled . . . their sympathies are so deeply engaged that the loss seems . . . to be a public one which affects the whole people. Then, after the burial of the body and the performance of the customary rites, they place the image of the dead man in the most conspicuous position in the house, where it is enclosed in a wooden shrine. This image consists of a mask which is fashioned with extraordinary fidelity . . . to represent the features of these dead men. On occasions when public sacrifices are offered, these masks are displayed and decorated with great care. And when any distinguished member of the family dies, the masks are taken to the funeral, and are worn by men who are considered to bear the closest resemblance to the original, both in height and their general appearance and bearing. . . .

It would be hard to imagine a more impressive scene for a young man who aspires to win fame and practice virtue. For who could remain unmoved at the sight of the images of all these men who have won renown in their time, now gathered together as if alive and breathing? What spectacle could be more glorious than this?

Source: Polybius, *The Rise of the Roman Empire*, trans. Ian Scott-Kilvert (New York: 1979), pp. 346–47.

Questions for Analysis

1. Why does Polybius place so high a premium on the Romans' conduct of funerals? How can such rites be related to republican ideals?

2. Compare this analysis of Roman funerary rites to the image of a Roman patrician and his ancestors on page 112. How do they complement one another?

---

goes for Marcus Tullius Cicero (Cicero means "chickpea"). The illustrious Cincinnatus was actually "Curly."

What's in a name? Everything, if you were a Roman man. And nothing, at least nothing of personal significance, if you were a Roman woman. Lucretia's name was not her own, but her father's—or forefathers': the feminine version of Lucretius. If she had a sister, they would both be called Lucretia, differentiated only as Major and Minor ("big/elder" and "little/younger") Lucretia. If there were two more girls, they would be Tertia and Quarta ("Third" and "Fourth") Lucretia, and so on. The only people in Rome who had personal names were slaves (who were named by their masters, like pets) or very low-born Romans and immigrants who had no lineage that mattered.

FROM REPUBLIC TO EMPIRE

For more than two centuries after the founding of the Republic, warfare and agriculture remained the chief occupations of most Romans. The fact that Rome had no standard

system of coinage until 289 B.C.E suggests strongly that commerce was an insignificant component of its economy. Apparently, Romans didn't need portable wealth; when they weren't fighting, they wanted to be home on the farm, not gadding about the world. If they had money, they put it into real estate: land or slaves.

All of this changed rapidly when Romans began to look beyond Italy. In 265 B.C.E., they controlled most of the peninsula. A year later, they were already embroiled in a war overseas. For a home-loving people with ample resources, this seems paradoxical. Indeed, historians still argue about the motives for Roman expansion. Did Rome constantly extend its rule as a matter of policy, to feed a collective appetite for warfare and plunder? Or was it an accidental empire, built up in a series of reactions to changing pressures and threats—real and imagined? No definitive answer is possible, but it is in this crucial period that the Roman Republic began to transform Western civilizations, and to transform itself into the Roman Empire.

The Punic Wars, 264–146 B.C.E.

In 265 B.C.E., Roman territory extended to the tip of Italy's "boot," but there it ended. Just off its coast, the large islands of Corsica and Sardinia and the western half of Sicily were part of another state, much older and far wealthier. This was the great maritime empire of Carthage, which stretched along the northern coast of Africa from modern-day Tunisia through the Straits of Gibraltar and into modern Spain. Carthage itself had been founded around 800 B.C.E. as a Phoenician colony (see Chapter 2). It had the largest and most effective navy of its day, and it commanded the vast resources of commercial networks that reached as far north as Britain and deep into Egypt and the Near East. In every respect but one it was far superior to Rome. Yet that one factor was decisive: Carthage had no standing army. It relied on mercenaries bankrolled by the enormous profits of its merchants.

The epic struggle between Rome and Carthage lasted well over a century. It crystallized in three periods of concentrated warfare known as the Punic Wars (because the Romans called their enemies Poeni, "Phoenicians"). The first of these wars began in 264 B.C.E. Twenty-three years of bitter fighting were protracted because the Carthaginians only needed to suffer one defeat in a land battle before resolving to engage the Romans solely at sea. There, they had the advantage—until the Romans built their own navy. Eventually, in 241 B.C.E., Carthage was forced to cede all of her Sicilian lands to Rome and to pay a large indemnity.

Thereafter, the Romans were determined not to let Carthage revive its maritime power. So when Carthage attempted to expand its presence in Spain, Rome interpreted this as a threat and declared a new war that lasted for sixteen years: the Second Punic War. This time, Rome was thrown entirely off its guard by the brilliant exploits of the Carthaginian commander Hannibal (247–183 B.C.E.), who very nearly defeated the Romans at their own game. Daringly, Hannibal raised an army in Spain and equipped it with dozens of war elephants and siege engines. He then led this entire force across the Pyrenees into Gaul (now southern France), and then over the Alps into Italy. There, he harried Roman forces in their home territories for nearly sixteen years, from 218 to 202 B.C.E.

Hannibal was challenged more by the difficulty of supplying his army than by the Romans themselves. He also seems to have counted on winning the support of the Italian provinces that Rome had conquered, but Rome's generous treatment of its Latin allies kept them loyal. As a result, Rome could call on vast resources while Hannibal had only his exhausted army and no reserves forthcoming. Nevertheless, he won several amazing victories in Italy before retreating—technically undefeated—in 203. He also won the admiration of the Romans themselves, whose own histories frankly acknowledge his genius.

This phase of warfare ended only when a Roman general, Publius Cornelius Scipio [SKIP-ee-oh], took a leaf out of Hannibal's book. After campaigning successfully in Spain, he crossed into Africa and met Hannibal at Zama, near Carthage, in 201 B.C.E. His victory ended the Second Punic War and won him a new name, "Africanus," in honor of his conquest.

Carthage was now compelled to abandon all of its possessions except the city itself and its immediate hinterlands, and to pay an indemnity three times greater than the already crippling reparations demanded after the First Punic War. Yet Roman suspicion remained obsessive, and by the middle of the second century, some warmongers were urging a preemptive strike. Among the most vocal was an elderly patrician called Marcus Porcius Cato, who ended every speech he gave—no matter what the topic—with the words: "And furthermore, I strongly advise that Carthage be destroyed." This won him the nickname Cato the Censor, from the Latin verb "to advise."

In 149 B.C.E., the Senate seized on a minor pretext to demand that the Carthaginians abandon their city and settle at least ten miles from the sea. Of course, this absurd mandate amounted to a death sentence for a city dependent on maritime commerce, and it was refused—as the Romans knew it would be. The result was the Third Punic War and the siege of Carthage, which ended in 146 B.C.E. Those who survived the ensuing massacre were sold into slavery, and their once-magnificent city was razed to the ground.

The legend that the Romans sowed the land with salt (to make it infertile) is a myth, but a vivid way of describing the successful eradication of an entire civilization. It would stand as a warning to Rome's other potential enemies.

Roman Control of the Hellenistic World

Rome's victories over Carthage led to the creation of new colonial provinces in Sicily, North Africa, and Hispania (Spain). This not only brought Rome great new wealth, it was also the beginning of the westward expansion that became Rome's defining influence on the history of Western civilizations.

At the same time, Rome's expansion brought it into conflict with eastern Mediterranean powers. During the Second Punic War, for example, Philip V of Macedonia had entered into an alliance with Carthage. Rome sent an army to stop him, and later foiled the plans of the Achaean League (see Chapter 4). This was when Polybius was sent to Rome as a hostage, and became a guest-friend in the family of Scipio Africanus, later witnessing the destruction of Carthage. Rome also thwarted similar efforts by the Seleucid monarch Antiochus III. In neither of these cases did Rome set out to conquer the eastern Mediterranean. By 146 B.C.E., however, both Greece and Macedonia had become Roman provinces, Seleucid Asia had lost most of its territories, and Ptolemaic Egypt had largely become a pawn of Roman interests.

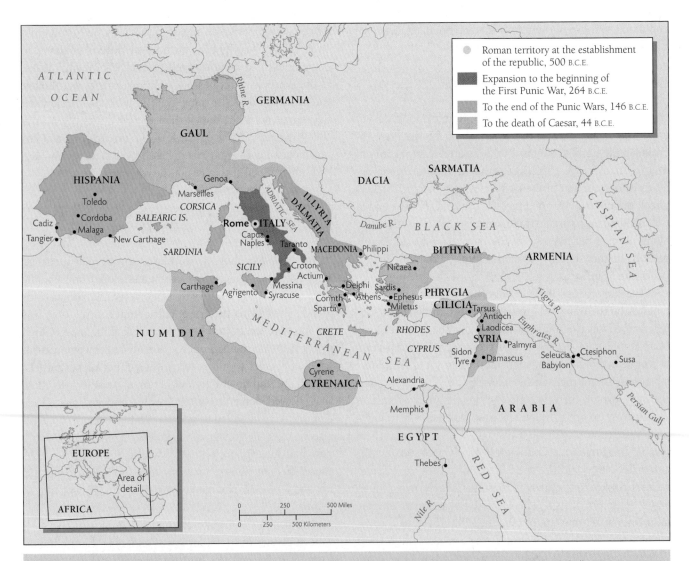

THE EXPANSION OF ROME, 264–44 B.C.E. The rapid increase of Rome's territories opened up new opportunities and challenges.
▪ *Looking at the phases of expansion on this map, in what directions did Roman dominion move?* ▪ *Why was this the case?* ▪ *What particular problems might have been created by the eventual extension of Roman rule into Gaul, well beyond the "Roman lake" of the Mediterranean?*

THE CONSEQUENCES OF IMPERIALISM

Rome's inadvertent conquest of Greece and Asia Minor transformed the Republic. New wealth poured in, increasing the inequalities within Roman society and challenging traditional values. Small farmers left the land and swelled the impoverished urban population, unable to compete with huge plantations worked by gangs of slaves. Slaves also played an increasing role in Roman cities as artisans, merchants, and household servants.

Roman rule over the Hellenistic world had a particularly pervasive impact—so much so that many Romans considered themselves to have been "conquered" by Greece. Hitherto self-assured and self-satisfied, they now felt their own language and customs to be uncouth and barbaric compared to those of their cultivated colonial subjects.

Economic Change and Social Upheaval

Like all peoples of the ancient world, Romans took slavery for granted. But they were not prepared for the huge increase in the number of slaves that resulted from these conquests. In 146 B.C.E., 55,000 Carthaginians were enslaved after the destruction of their city; not long before, 150,000 Greek prisoners of war had met the same fate. By the end of the second century B.C.E., there were a million slaves in Italy alone. Rome's became one of the most slave-based economies in history, rivaling ancient Egypt or the antebellum American South.

The majority of Roman slaves worked as agricultural laborers on the vast (and growing) estates known as *latifundia*, created when Roman aristocrats absorbed the holdings of citizen-farmers who were now required to serve for years at a time on foreign campaigns and often found it impossible to maintain their farms. Consequently, they moved to the city—where there was no way for free men to sustain themselves, except through trade or violence. With abundant, cheap slaves to do all the rough work, moreover, there was no incentive for technological innovation. Meanwhile, expensive slaves did the specialized jobs: they were secretaries, bookkeepers, personal assistants, playwrights, musicians, sculptors, artists. There was little reason to employ paid labor at all, or even to train oneself in these arts, as the Greeks had. By the first century B.C.E., as a result, a third of Rome's one million inhabitants were receiving free grain from the state, partly to keep them alive and partly to keep them quiet. The poet Juvenal would later satirize the plebs as needing only "bread and circuses."

The ready availability of slaves made Roman slavery a far more impersonal and brutal institution than it had been in other ancient civilizations. The standard policy of slave owners was to get as much work out of their human possessions as possible, until they died of exhaustion or were "freed" in old age to fend for themselves. The same irascible Cato the Censor who had demanded the destruction of Carthage even wrote a "how-to" book on this subject. Of course, there were exceptions. Some domestic slaves were treated as trusted family members, and slave secretaries vital to the business of Roman governance and literature could even win fame or earn enough to buy their freedoms. Some slave artisans were permitted to run their own businesses, keeping some of the profits.

But the general lot of slaves was horrendous. Some businessmen owned slaves whom they trained as gladiators, to be mauled by wild animals or by other gladiators for the amusement of a paying public. The luxurious lifestyles of the wealthy also meant that dozens of slaves in every household were trapped in a cycle of menial tasks, as doorkeepers, litter-bearers, couriers, valets, wet-nurses, and child-minders. In some great households, designated slaves had no other duties than to rub down the master after his bath or to keep track of the mistress's social engagements. It was a life that debased both slave and owner, and undermined the values of the republic.

New Money, New Values

In the early Republic, as we have seen, Roman men had nearly absolute powers over their individual households. During the second century B.C.E., however, two innovations greatly altered this pattern of patriarchal control. One was the introduction of new laws that allowed married women to control their own property; if a married woman died, her possessions would revert to her father or her father's heirs if she had no children of her own. Another was a law that allowed women to initiate divorce proceedings. These changes were intended to safeguard family wealth, but they also resulted in greater independence for women. A wife now had much more authority within the household because she contributed to its upkeep. If her husband did not show respect, she could leave him and deprive him of income.

Ironically, the growth of Rome's slave system also gave women greater freedom, for slaves took over the traditional work of child rearing, household maintenance, and the endless tasks of spinning and weaving. Women from well-to-do families now began to engage in a range of social, intellectual, and artistic activities. Indeed, women were

among the chief consumers of the new Hellenistic fashions, commodities, and ideas available in Rome.

In earlier centuries, Romans had taken pride in the simplicity of their lives. Now, however, elite Romans began to indulge in creature comforts and to cultivate Hellenistic habits. Bilingualism became increasingly common, and Greek literature became the standard against which Roman authors measured themselves. For Latin was not yet a literary language. It was fine for politics or farming, but if one wanted to express lofty or beautiful thoughts one did so in Greek, which was far more flexible and sophisticated. Well-educated Greek slaves were therefore at a premium, to lend social cachet, to write letters, and to tutor Roman children.

But many Romans regarded these foreign influences with disgust. For them, the good old ways of paternal authority and stern discipline were giving way to effeminacy and soft living. Increasingly, hard-line conservatives passed laws to restore "family values" and regulate the conspicuous consumption of luxuries, especially by women. These measures were ineffectual. Rome was being irreversibly transformed into a complex metropolitan empire reliant on foreign slaves, foreign grain, and foreign luxuries, in which a vast gulf was widening between rich and poor, and where traditional behavioral constraints were giving way to new freedoms for both men and women.

Spirituality and Philosophy in the Late Republic

The religious practices of Rome changed markedly in this era. The most pronounced innovation was the spread of Eastern mystery cults, which satisfied a need for more emotionally intense spiritual experiences—especially for women, who were largely excluded from the rites of the patriarchal state religion. From Egypt came the cults of Isis and Osiris, while from Asia came the worship of the Great Mother, all emphasizing the power of female sexuality and reproduction. Despite the attractions of these new cults, Romans continued to honor their traditional gods alongside these new, exotic deities. Roman polytheism could absorb them all, so long as the ancestor gods of the household and the city were paid due reverence.

The Hellenistic philosophies of Epicureanism and Stoicism both found strong adherents in Rome (Chapter 4), but more congenial to Roman values was Stoicism. Its most influential proponent was Cicero (106–43 B.C.E.), famous in his day as an orator, statesman, and staunch defender of republican virtues. Cicero based his ethical teachings on the Stoic premise that tranquility of mind is the highest good: the

ideal man is rational, indifferent to sorrow and pain. Yet Cicero diverged from the Stoics in his approval of the active, political life. He became an advocate for the revival of Roman tradition through service to the state. His elegant prose style also advanced the use of Latin as a language of eloquence and became the standard model for literary composition. Students learning Latin today still begin with Cicero.

"RESTORING THE REPUBLIC": THE STRUGGLE FOR POWER

Politically, the century after the Third Punic War was one of turbulence. Bloody competitions among rival dictators and insurrections were common occurrences. Slave uprisings added to the general disorder. The most threatening revolt of all was led by Spartacus, a Thracian captive who was being trained as a gladiator. He and a band of 200 fellow slaves escaped from a gladiatorial training camp at Capua [KAH-poo-ah] (near Naples), heavily armed, to the slopes of Mount Vesuvius, where their cause attracted a huge host of other fugitives. From 73 to 71 B.C.E. this desperate army defeated Roman forces of as many as 10,000 men before Spartacus himself was killed. The Senate, terrified of the precedent, ordered 6,000 of the captured slaves to be crucified along the length of the road from Capua to Rome—about 150 miles—as a warning to future insurgents. Crucifixion was a form of punishment reserved for slaves and non-Roman rebels, and it meant a slow, terrible, and public death from gradual suffocation and exposure.

The Reforming Efforts of the Gracchi

These waves of rebellion were mirrored by urban unrest in various forms, and the poorer classes were finding new champions among some progressive patricians. In 133 B.C.E., a grandson of Scipio Africanus, Tiberius Gracchus [GRAH-cus], was elected a tribune of the people. He proposed to alleviate social and economic stress by instituting major reforms, chiefly the redistribution of property. As we have noted, small farmers had been losing their lands to those whose new wealth allowed them to amass giant estates, the latifundia. To counter this, Tiberius Gracchus invoked old laws that had, under the early republic, limited the amount of land that could be held by a single person. His motives were not entirely populist. There was now a grave manpower shortage in the Roman army, which had been forced to expand its presence in the far reaches of the

world and had left Rome itself prey to uprisings like that of Spartacus. Since a man had to meet certain property qualifications to serve in the Roman army, the available pool of citizen soldiers was contracting. So Tiberius Gracchus aimed to refresh the reserves by creating new citizens.

With the support of his brother Gaius, Tiberius Gracchus proposed a law that would restrict estates to a maximum of 300 acres per citizen, plus 150 acres for each child in his family, with the excess land to be divided among poor settlers. Not surprisingly, most senators stood to lose from this legislation, and so engineered its veto by Gracchus's fellow tribunes. Gracchus retaliated, arguing that tribunes who opposed the people's interests were betraying their offices, and he announced plans to stand for reelection. A conservative faction in the Senate then alleged that Gracchus had his sights set on a dictatorship, and with this excuse they attacked and murdered him and his supporters on the day of the elections.

Ten years later, Gaius Gracchus renewed his older brother's struggle after being elected to the same office. Although a version of Tiberius's land reforms had finally been enacted, Gaius believed that the campaign had to go further. In 123 B.C.E. he enacted several laws for the benefit of the poor. He also imposed controls on provincial governors suspected of exploiting their subjects for personal gain. Most controversially, Gaius proposed to extend full Roman citizenship to all the allied states of Italy, a move that would have kept the army well supplied with new soldiers, but which would alter the political landscape of Rome to the detriment of the existing elite. Accordingly, the Senate proclaimed Gaius Gracchus an outlaw. In the ensuing conflict, Gaius and about 3,000 of his followers became the victims of a purge.

Rivalry among Rome's Generals

Although the reforms of the Gracchi were ultimately unsuccesful, they exposed the weakness of the Senate and increased the power of the plebs, whose favor was now courted by a succession of ambitious men. Most were professional soldiers who controlled one or more legions of the Roman army and who traded on military victories abroad to win the confidence of the people. The first of these was Gaius Marius, who had fought a successful campaign against King Jugurtha of Numidia, a small kingdom in North Africa. In 107 B.C.E. Marius's popularity catapulted him to the consulship, despite the protests of the Senate's aristocracy, and he would be elected to that office six more times.

Marius set a powerful precedent by demonstrating how easily an army command could be an alternative path to political power. He also changed the course of Rome's history by reorganizing and expanding the army. Desperate for more men to fight in Africa and in Gaul, Marius abolished the property qualification that had hitherto limited military service; the potential pool of soldiers now included the urban poor and landless peasants. As a result, a career as a Roman legionnaire became an end in itself, and a soldier's loyalty was directed toward his commander—whose success would win rewards for his men—rather than to an abstract ideal of patriotism. This change also meant that factional fighting could lead to full-blown civil war, as legions loyal to one general were pitted against those of another.

This happened in Marius's own lifetime. The aristocratic general Lucius Cornelius Sulla [SUH-la] had fought with distinction in the so-called Social War of 91–88 B.C.E., a conflict between Rome and her Italian allies that resulted in the extension of Roman citizenship throughout the peninsula. Therafter, Sulla seemed the likely person to lead Rome's army to war in Asia Minor. Marius, however, forced the Senate to deny Sulla's claim. Sulla's response was to rally the five victorious legions that had just fought under his command and, with a Roman army at his back, to march on Rome.

Strong taboos had long prevented any armed force from entering the city limits, but Sulla argued that his actions were in keeping with the mos maiorum, which Marius and the Senate had betrayed. He was then given the coveted command in Asia Minor, after which Marius again seized control of the city. When Marius died soon afterward, a conservative backlash led the aristocracy to appoint Sulla to the office of dictator—and not for the traditional six months. Instead, Sulla's term had no limits, and he used this time to exterminate his opponents. He packed the Senate with men loyal to himself and curtailed the authority of the peoples' tribunes. Then, after three years of rule, he retired to a life of luxury on his country estate.

Caesar's Triumph—and His Downfall

The effect of Sulla's dictatorship was to empower the aristocracy and weaken the power of the plebs. Soon, however, new leaders emerged to espouse the people's cause, once again using the army as their tool of influence. The most prominent of these military men were Gnaeus Pompeius Magnus (106–48 B.C.E.) and Gaius Julius Caesar (100–44 B.C.E.). Initially, they cooperated in a plot to "restore the republic" by forming an alliance with a third general, Marcus Junius Crassus, the man credited with finally defeating Spartacus. This alliance was known as a triumvirate, meaning "rule of three men," but it soon dissolved into open rivalry. Pompey (as generations of English-speaking historians have called him) had won fame as the conqueror of Syria and Palestine, while Caesar had campaigned in Gaul, adding the territories of modern France,

Belgium, and western Germany to the Roman Empire, and extending its northern border the length of the Rhine.

It had become accepted that the best general should be the leader of Rome, and the example of Sulla had made it possible for that leader to be a dictator for life, a king in all but name. But it was Pompey, not Caesar, who was actually in Rome and in a position to influence the Senate directly. So in the face of tremendous popular protest and even some opposition from the aristocracy, Pompey had himself elected sole consul. Essentially, this meant that he could act as dictator. Using this authority, he declared that Caesar, who was still stationed in Gaul, was an enemy of the republic, and that his ambition was to make himself king.

The result was a pervasive and deadly civil war. In 49 B.C.E., Caesar crossed the Rubicon River, the northern boundary of Rome's Italian territories, thereby signalling his intention to take Rome by force. Pompey fled to the east in the hope of gathering an army large enough to confront Ceasar's legions. Caesar pursued him, and in 48 B.C.E. the two Roman armies met at Pharsalus in Greece. Pompey was defeated and fled to Alexandria, where he was murdered by a Roman officer attached to the court of Ptolemy XIII (62/61–47? B.C.E.). Ptolemy was then about fourteen years old and engaged in a civil war of his own—with his elder sister and co-ruler, Cleopatra VII (69–30 B.C.E.). Caesar threw his support on the side of the twenty-one-year old queen. The two must have become lovers soon after their

first meeting, because their son Caesarion ("Little Ceasar") was born nine months later.

After that, Caesar returned to Rome in triumph—literally. A *triumph* was a spectacular honor awarded to a victorious Roman general by the Senate, and was the only legal occasion on which (unarmed) soldiers were allowed to parade in the streets of Rome. Triumphs had been celebrated since the earliest days of the republic and featured columns of prisoners and spoils of war, chained captives (often enemy kings) led in humiliation to their public executions, floats commemorating the achievements of the triumphant man, and thousands of cheering Romans who received extra rations of grain and gathered up coins thrown by the handful. Through it all, Caesar would have ridden in a chariot with a golden wreath held above his head, while a slave stood behind him, murmuring in his ear the words *Memento mori*: "Remember: you will die." A triumph was so glorious and—under the republic—so rarely granted that those thus honored might forget their own mortality.

Caesar's power seemed absolute. In 46 B.C.E. he was named dictator for ten years; two years later, this was changed to a lifetime appointment. In addition, he assumed nearly every other title that could augment his power. He even governed the reckoning of time: in imitation of the Egyptian calendar, he revised the Roman calendar so as to make a 365-day year with an extra day added every fourth year. This Julian calendar (as adjusted by Pope Gregory XIII

CLEOPATRA VII AS EGYPTIAN PHARAOH AND HELLENISTIC RULER. Like her ancestor, Ptolemy I, Cleopatra represented herself as both enlightened Greek monarch and as Pharaoh. It was perhaps due to her example that Julius Caesar was the first Roman leader to issue coins impressed with his own image. ▪ *How does Cleopatra's self-representation compare to that of Hatshepsut (see Chapter 2) or Ptolemy (Chapter 4)?*

in 1582) is still observed, and the seventh month is still named after Julius.

Caesar also took important steps toward eliminating the distinction between Italians and provincials within the empire by conferring citizenship on the residents of Hispania (Spain) and the newly annexed provinces in Gaul. By settling many of his army veterans in these lands, moreover, he furthered colonization. By incorporating Gaul into the Roman world he brought in a much-needed source of food and natural resources and created a new outlet for the spread of Roman influence.

In the eyes of many contemporaries, however, Caesar's achievements were further signs that he intended to make himself king: a hateful thought to those who still glorified the early days of the republic. Indeed, it was around a descendant of Lucretia's avenger, Brutus, that a faction of the Senate crystallized into conspiracy. On the Ides of March in 44 B.C.E.—the midpoint of the month, according to his own calendar—Caesar was attacked on the floor of the Senate's chamber and stabbed to death by a group of men. His body would later be autopsied, the first such examination in recorded history. It was found that he had received 23 wounds.

THE PRINCIPATE AND THE *PAX ROMANA*, 27 B.C.E.–180 C.E.

In his will, Caesar had adopted his grandnephew Gaius Octavius (or Octavian, 63 B.C.E.–14 C.E.), then a young man of eighteen. On learning of Caesar's death, Octavian hastened to claim his inheritance and to avenge his slain "father," whose name he took: he was now Gaius Julius Caesar the younger. But he soon found that he had rivals among those supporters of Caesar who had not been implicated in the plot to kill him, most notably Marcus Antonius (or Mark Antony, 83–30 B.C.E.), who had served under Caesar in Gaul and was determined to make himself governor of that whole province.

Octavian engineered his own election to the office of consul (though he was far too young for this honor) and used his powers to have Caesar's assassins declared outlaws. He then pursued Antony to Gaul, at the head of an army. Antony's forces were overwhelmed, and in 43 B.C.E. he and Octavian reconciled and formed an alliance, bringing in a third man, a senator called Marcus Aemilius Lepidus, to make up a second triumvirate. They then set about crushing the faction responsible for Caesar's murder.

Their methods were brutal: prominent conspirators were hunted down and their property confiscated. The most

OCTAVIAN. Caesar's adopted heir was later granted the title "Augustus" by the Senate, and was also known as *princeps*, "first man." Eventually, he would be worshiped as a god in Rome's provinces, and idealized statues like this one would be erected in temples and public places throughout the empire.

notable of these victims was Cicero. Meanwhile, the masterminds behind the assasination, Brutus and Gaius Cassius, fled Rome and raised an army of legions from Greece and Asia Minor. But they were defeated by the united forces of Antony and Octavian on a battlefield near the Macedonian town of Philippi (founded by Alexander's father) in 42 B.C.E. Both Brutus and Cassius committed suicide.

Analyzing Primary Sources

Antony and Cleopatra

In his Parallel Lives, *the Greek intellectual Plutarch (c. 46–120 C.E.) paired the biographies of famous Greeks with those of famous Romans, always to the disadvantage of the latter; for example, Julius Caesar suffers in comparison to Alexander the Great, as Romulus does when set up against Theseus. The following excerpt is from Plutarch's* Life of Mark Antony, *in which the Hellenistic ruler of Egypt, Cleopatra, plays a starring role.*

Caesar and Pompey knew Cleopatra when she was] still a girl, and ignorant of the world, but it was a different matter in the case of Antony, because she was ready to meet him when she had reached the time of life when women are most beautiful and have full understanding. So she prepared for him many gifts and money and adornment, of a magnitude appropriate to her great wealth and prosperous kingdom, but she put most of her hopes in her own magical arts and charms. . . . For (as they say), it was not because her beauty in itself was so striking that it stunned the onlooker, but the inescapable impression produced by daily contact with her: the attractiveness in the persuasiveness of her talk, and the character that surrounded her conversation was stimulating. It was a pleasure to hear the sound of her voice, and she tuned her tongue like a many-stringed instrument expertly to whatever language she chose, and only used interpreters to talk to a few

foreigners. . . . She is said to have learned the languages of many peoples, although her predecessors on the throne did not bother to learn Egyptian, and some had even forgotten how to speak the Macedonian dialect.

She took such a hold over Antony that, while his wife Fulvia was carrying on the war in Rome against Octavian on his behalf, and the Parthian army . . . was about to invade Syria, Antony was carried off by Cleopatra to Alexandria, and amused himself there with the pastimes of a boy . . . Whether Antony was in a serious or a playful mood, she could always produce some new pleasure or charm, and she kept watch on him by night and day and never let him out of her sight. She played dice with him and hunted with him and watched him exercising with his weapons and she roamed around and wandered about with him at night when he stood at people's doors and windows and made fun of people inside, dressed in a slave-woman's outfit; for he also attempted to dress up like a slave. He returned from these

expeditions having been mocked in return, and often beaten, although most people suspected who he was. But the Alexandrians got pleasure from his irreverence . . . enjoying his humor and saying that he showed his tragic face to the Romans and his comic one to them.

Source: Plutarch, *Life of Marcus Antonius,* cc. 25–29, excerpted in *Women's Life in Greece & Rome: A Sourcebook in Translation,* eds. Mary R. Lefkowitz and Maureen B. Fant (Baltimore, MD: 1992), pp. 147–49.

Questions for Analysis

1. How do Cleopatra's behavior and accomplishments, in Plutarch's description of her, compare to those of Roman women?

2. Given what you have learned about the values of the Roman Republic, how would a Roman reader respond to this description of Antony's behavior under the influence of the Egyptian queen? What do you think were Plutarch's motives in portraying him in this light?

With the opposition destroyed, tensions mounted between Antony and Octavian. Antony went to the East and made an alliance with Cleopatra. Octavian, meanwhile, reestablished himself in Rome, where he skillfully portrayed Antony as having been seduced and emasculated by the Egyptian queen. For ten years, Antony played the king in Egypt, fathering three of Cleopatra's children and making big plans for annex-

ing Rome's eastern provinces. Eventually, Octavian had him declared a traitor while the Senate declared war on Cleopatra.

In 31 B.C.E. Octavian's superior forces defeated those of Antony and Cleopatra in the naval battle of Actium, off the coast of Greece. Soon afterward, both Antony and Cleopatra committed suicide. Their children were taken back to Rome, and although their lives were spared they

Two Views of Augustus's Rule

Augustus Speaks for Himself

The emperor Augustus was a master propagandist with an unrivaled capacity for presenting his own actions in the best possible light. This list of his own deeds was written by Augustus himself and was displayed on two bronze pillars set up in the Roman forum.

Below is a copy of the accomplishments of the deified Augustus by which he brought the whole world under the empire of the Roman people, and of the moneys expended by him on the state and the Roman people. . . .

1. At the age of nineteen, on my own initiative and at my own expense, I raised an army by means of which I liberated the republic, which was oppressed by the tyranny of a faction.

2. Those who assassinated my father I drove into exile, avenging their crime by due process of law.

3. I waged many wars throughout the whole world by land and by sea, both civil and foreign. . . .

5. The dictatorship offered to me . . . by the people and by the Senate . . . I refused to accept. . . . The consulship, too, which was offered to me . . . as an annual office for life, I refused to accept.

6. [T]hough the Roman Senate and people together agreed that I should be elected sole guardian of the laws and morals with supreme authority, I refused to accept any office offered me which was contrary to the traditions of our ancestors.

7. I have been ranking senator for forty years. . . . I have been *pontifex maximus*, augur, member of the college of fifteen for performing sacrifices, member of the college of seven for conducting religious banquets, member of the Arval Brotherhood, one of the *Titii sodales*, and a *fetial* [all priestly offices].

9. The Senate decreed that vows for my health should be offered up every fifth year by the consuls and priests. . . . [T]he whole citizen body, with one accord, . . . prayed continuously for my health at all the shrines.

17. Four times I came to the assistance of the treasury with my own money . . . providing bonuses for soldiers who had completed twenty or more years of service.

20. I repaired the Capitol and the theater of Pompey with enormous expenditures on both works, without having my name inscribed on them. I repaired . . . the aqueducts which were falling into ruin in many places . . . I repaired eighty-two temples. . . . I reconstructed the Flaminian Way. . . .

34. [H]aving attained supreme power by universal consent, I transferred the state from my own power to the control of the Roman Senate and people. . . . After that time I excelled all in authority, but I possessed no more power than the others who were my colleagues in each magistracy.

35. At the time I wrote this document I was in my seventy-sixth year.

Source: "Res Gestae Divi Augusti," in *Roman Civilization, Sourcebook II: The Empire,* eds. Naphtali Lewis and Meyer Reinhold (New York: 1966), pp. 9–19.

---

were paraded through the streets as captives. This marked the end of Egypt's independence: Cleopatra had been its last pharaoh. After more than three thousand years of self-rule, Egypt was now another province in Rome's empire. Octavian's power was consolidated.

The Principate of Augustus

The victory at Actium ushered in a new period of Roman history. The new Gaius Julius Caesar was now the only man left standing, with no rivals for power. For the first time in

The Historian Tacitus Evaluates Augustus's Reign

Writing in the first decades of the second century C.E., *the senatorial historian Tacitus (c. 56–117) began his chronicle of imperial rule, the* Annals, *with the death of Augustus a century earlier.*

Intelligent people praised or criticized Augustus in varying terms. One opinion was as follows. Filial duty and a national emergency, in which there was no place for law-abiding conduct, had driven him to civil war—and this can be neither initiated nor maintained by decent methods. He had made many concessions to Antony and to Lepidus for the sake of vengeance on his father's murderers. When Lepidus grew old and lazy, and Antony's self-indulgence got the better of him, the only possible cure for the distracted country had been government by one man. However, Augustus had put the State in order not by making himself king or dictator but by creating the Principate. The empire's frontiers were on the ocean, or on distant rivers. Armies, provinces, fleets, the whole system was interrelated. Roman citizens were protected by the law. Provincials were decently treated. Rome itself had been lavishly beautified. Force had been sparingly used—merely to preserve peace for the majority.

The opposite view went like this. Filial duty and national crisis had been merely pretexts. In actual fact, the motive of Octavian, the future Augustus, was lust for power. Inspired by that, he had mobilized ex-army settlers by gifts of money, raised an army—while he was only a half-grown boy without any official status—won over a consul's brigade by bribery, pretended to support Sextus Pompeius [the son of Pompey], and by senatorial decree usurped the status and rank of a praetor. Soon both consuls . . . had met their deaths—by enemy action; or perhaps in the one case by the deliberate poisoning of his wound, and in the other at the hand of his own troops, instigated by Octavian. In any case, it was he who took over both their armies. Then he had forced the reluctant Senate to make him consul. But the forces given him to deal with Antony he used against the State. His judicial murders and land distributions were distasteful even to those who carried them out. True, Cassius and Brutus died because he had inherited a feud against them; nevertheless, personal enmities ought to be sacrificed to the public interest. Next he had cheated Sextus Pompeius by a spurious peace treaty, Lepidus by spurious friendship. Then Antony, enticed by treaties and his marriage with Octavian's sister, had paid the penalty of that delusive relationship with his life. After that, there had certainly been peace, but it was a bloodstained peace. . . . And gossip did not spare his personal affairs—how he had abducted [Livia] the wife of Tiberius Claudius Nero, and asked the priests the farcical question whether it was in order for her to marry while pregnant. Then there was the debauchery of his friend Publius Vedius Pollio. But Livia was a real catastrophe, to the nation as a mother and to the house of the Caesars as a stepmother.

Source: Tacitus, *Annals* i.9–10. Based on *Tacitus: The Annals of Imperial Rome*, trans. Michael Grant (New York: 1989), pp. 37–39.

Questions for Analysis

1. How does Augustus organize his list, and why? What does he leave out and what does he choose to emphasize?

2. Tacitus presents two contrasting views of Augustus's motives. Which does he himself seem to believe? How does his account complement or undermine that of Augustus himself?

3. Could you write a new account of Augustus's life making use of both sources? How would you strike a balance between them? What would your own conclusion be?

nearly a century, Rome was not embroiled in civil war. But it was no longer a republic, even though Octavian maintained the fiction that he was governing as a mere citizen. For four years he ruled as sole consul, until he accepted the titles of *imperator* (emperor) and *augustus*. Although these honorifics had been in use under the republic—*imperator* meant "victorious general" and *augustus* meant "worthy of honor"—they now became attached to the person of the sole ruler. Rome had long been an empire, but it was only now that it had a single emperor. To avoid confusion,

historians therefore refer to this phase of Rome's history as the Principate, from the title Augustus himself preferred: *princeps*, or "first man."

Because Augustus was determined not to be regarded as a tyrant or (worse) a king, he left most of Rome's republican institutions in place—but emptied them of their power. In theory, the emperor served at the will of "the Roman Senate and People." In practice, though, he controlled the army, which meant that he also controlled the workings of government. Fortunately, Augustus was an able ruler. He introduced a range of public services, including a police force and fire brigade; he reorganized the army; and he allowed cities and provinces more substantial rights of self-government than they had enjoyed before. He instituted a new system of coinage throughout the empire, and he abolished the old, corrupt system of taxation, whereby tax collectors were compensated by being allowed to keep a portion of what they collected. Instead, Augustus appointed his own representatives, paid them regular salaries, and kept them under strict supervision. He also conducted a census of the empire's population, and it was during one of these "enrollments" that the birth of Jesus is said to have taken place, according to the gospel of Luke (see Chapter 6). Augustus also established new colonies in the provinces, encouraging the emigration of Rome's urban and rural poor, thereby removing a major source of social tension and promoting the integration of the Roman heartland with its far-flung hinterland.

Although his rule had definitively ended the republic, Augustus represented himself as a stern defender of the *mos maiorum* and traditional Roman virtues. He rebuilt many of the city's ancient temples and prohibited the worship of foreign gods. In an attempt to increase the birthrate of Rome's citizens, he penalized men who failed to marry, required widows to remarry within two years of their husbands' deaths, and rewarded women who gave birth to more than two children. He also introduced laws punishing adultery and making divorces more difficult to obtain. To hammer the message home, Augustan propaganda portrayed the imperial family as a model of domestic virtue and propriety, despite the emperor's own notorious extramarital affairs and the well-known fact that the sexual promiscuity of his daughter Julia finally forced Augustus to have her exiled.

More land was gained for Rome in the lifetime of Augustus than in that of any other ruler. His generals advanced into central Europe, conquering the modern-day territories of Switzerland, Austria, and Bulgaria. Only in Germania did Roman troops meet defeat, when three legions were slaughtered in 9 C.E., a setback that convinced Augustus to hold the Roman borders at the Rhine and Danube rivers. Subsequently, though, the Emperor Claudius would begin the conquest of Britain in 43 C.E., while the Emperor Trajan (91–117 C.E.) would push beyond the Danube to add Dacia (now Romania) to the empire. Trajan also conquered territories in the heartland of Mesopotamia, but in so doing aroused the enmity of the Parthians, who now ruled in Persia. His successor, Hadrian (117–138 C.E.), accordingly halted Rome's expansion and embarked on a defensive policy epitomized by the construction of Hadrian's Wall in northern Britain. The empire had now reached its greatest extent; in the third century, as we shall see (Chapter 6), the tide would turn and these limits would recede.

When Octavian died in 14 C.E. he was not only Caesar, Imperator, and Augustus; he was *pontifex maximus* (high priest) and "father of the fatherland" (*pater patriae*). He was even deified by the Senate. These titles would be passed on to his successors, as would the system of government he had devised. And even those who mourned the passing of the republic and loathed these displays of imperial *hubris* had to admit that the system worked. Rome enjoyed nearly two centuries of peace, prosperity, and stability because of it. For the true test of any political institution is its capacity to survive incompetent officeholders. Aside from one brief period of civil war in 68 C.E., the transition of power between emperors was generally peaceful and the growing imperial bureaucracy could manage affairs competently even when individual emperors proved vicious and ineffectual, as did Caligula (37–41 C.E.). Nevertheless, the fact that

HADRIAN'S WALL. Stretching 73.5 miles across northern England, this fortification (begun in 122 C.E.) marked the frontier of Britain as established by the emperor Hadrian. (A later wall, built farther north by Antoninus Pius in 142, was quickly abandoned.) Long stretches of the wall still exist, as do many of the forts built along it. The tree in this photograph stands on the site of a "mile castle," one of the smaller watchtowers built at intervals of a Roman mile and garrisoned by sentries.

Rome had become an autocratic state became harder and harder to conceal.

The height of the Augustan system is generally considered to be the era between 96 and 180 C.E., often known as the reign of the "Five Good Emperors": Nerva (96–98 C.E.), Trajan (98–117 C.E.), Hadrian (117–138 C.E.), Antoninus Pius (138–161 C.E.), and Marcus Aurelius (161–180 C.E.). All were capable politicians, and since none but the last had a son that survived him, each adopted a worthy successor—a policy that avoided the messy family dysfunctions that absorbed Augustus and his immediate heirs. They also benefited from the fact that Rome had few external enemies left. The Mediterranean was under the control of a single power for the first time in history. On land, Roman officials ruled from Britain to Persia. Now was the *Pax Romana*, the time of Roman Peace.

SPOILS FROM JERUSALEM. A bas-relief inside the triumphal Arch of Titus in the Roman forum shows plundered treasures from the Temple at Jerusalem, including the Menorah, being carried in triumph through Rome.

MAKING THE WORLD ROMAN

Occasionally, the Roman Peace was broken. In Britannia, Roman legions had to put down a rebellion led by the Celtic warrior queen Boudica ([*BOO-di-kah*] d. 60/61 C.E.), a war that ended in a massacre of the island's inhabitants. Another rebellion was violently quashed in Judea, the most restive of all Roman provinces, leading to the destruction of the Temple at Jerusalem in 70 C.E. In 135 C.E., a second rebellion completed the destruction of the city. Although Jerusalem was later refounded by Hadrian as Aelia Capitolina, a colony for veterans of Rome's army, Jews were forbidden to settle there.

Such rebellions were not the norm, however. Although the Roman Empire had been gradually achieved by conquest, it was not maintained by force. Instead, Rome controlled its territories by offering incentives to assimilation. Local elites were encouraged to adopt Roman modes of behavior and dress in order to gain entrance to political office. Local gods became Roman gods and were adopted into the Roman pantheon. Cities were constructed on a set model of urban planning, and the amenities of urban life were introduced: baths, temples, amphitheaters, aqueducts, and paved roads (see **Interpreting Visual Evidence** on page 128). Rights of citizenship were extended, and able provincials could rise far in the imperial government. Some, like the emperors Trajan and Hadrian—both raised

in Hispania—came to control it. Meanwhile, tens of thousands of army veterans were settled in the provinces, marrying local women and putting down local roots. It was common for soldiers born in Syria to end their days peacefully in northern Gaul. In Camulodunum (now Colchester, England), the gravestone of a legionnaire called Longinus sketches a typical career: born in Serdica (modern Sofia, in Bulgaria) to a local man named Szdapezematygus, he rose through the ranks to become sergeant of the First Thracian Cavalry under the emperor Claudius and one of the first Roman colonists of Britannia.

Even the outer fringes of the empire need to be understood as part of Rome's orbit. Although historians speak of the empire's "borders" for the sake of convenience, these were in fact permeable zones of intensive interaction. Roman influence reached far beyond these zones, into the heartland of Germania and lands farther to the east. By the middle of the third century C.E., when some frontier garrisons were withdrawn to take part in civil wars within the empire, many of these peoples moved southward, too, sometimes as plunderers but more often as aspiring Romans (see Chapter 6).

The Entertainments of Empire

The cultural and intellectual developments of the late Republic came to fruition during the Principate, and are richly reflected in its literature. For the first time, Latin began to replace Greek as a language of learning and poetry— much of it, not surprisingly, propagandistic: its purpose was to advertise and justify Rome's achievements. The poetry of Publius Virgilius Maro (Virgil, 70–19 B.C.E.) is typical, and

we have already noted his strategic use of "prophecy" in the story of Aeneas (see page 108). Other major poets of the Augustan age were Quintus Horatius Flaccus (Horace, 65–8 B.C.E.) and Publius Ovidius Naso (Ovid, 43 B.C.E.–17 C.E.): the former a master of the lovely short lyric and the latter our major source for Greek mythology, which he retold in a long poem called the *Metamorphoses* ("Transformations").

After Augustus's death, Roman authors had more license and became important cultural critics. The tales of Petronius and Apuleius describe the more bizarre and sometimes sordid aspects of Roman life, and the satirist Juvenal (60?–140 C.E.) wrote with savage wit about the moral degeneracy he saw in his contemporaries. A similar attitude toward Roman society characterizes the writings of Tacitus (55?–117? C.E.), an aristocratic historian who describes the events and people of his age largely for the purpose of passing judgment on them. His *Annals* offer a subtle but devastating portrait of the political system constructed

by Augustus and ruled by his heirs; his *Germania* contrasts the manly virtues of northern barbarians with the effeminate vices of the decadent Romans.

To many people today, the most fascinating (and repellant) aspect of Roman culture during the Principate was its spectacular cruelty. Gladiatorial contests were not new, but they were now presented in ampitheaters built to hold tens of thousands. Everyone, even emperors, attended these events, and they became increasingly bloody and brutal as people demanded more and more innovative violence. Individual gladiators fought to the death with swords or the exotic weapons of their homelands. Teams of gladiators fought pitched battles, often simulating historic Roman victories. Occasionally, a wealthy entrepreneur would fill an arena with water and stage a naval battle. Hundreds of men would die in these organized slaughters. On other occasions, hundreds of half-starved animals imported from Africa, India, or the forests of Germania would tear one another—

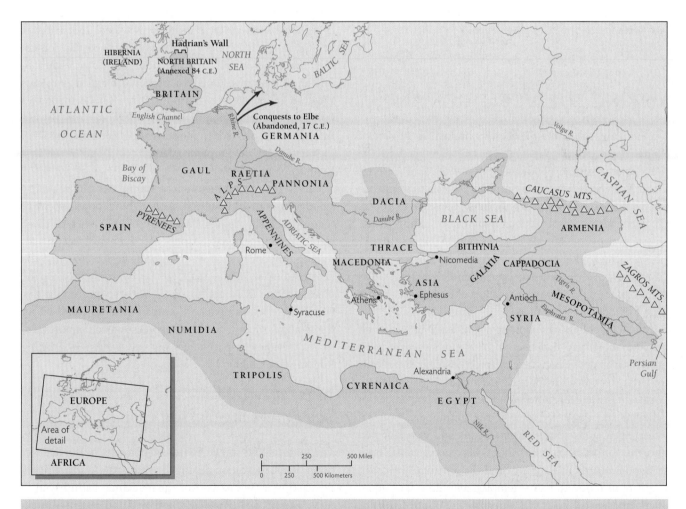

THE ROMAN EMPIRE AT ITS GREATEST EXTENT, 97–117 C.E. ▪ *How much farther north and west does the empire now reach compared to its earlier extent (see map on page 115)?* ▪ *How did geography influence the process of expansion?* ▪ *How did it dictate its limits?* ▪ *For example, what role do major river systems seem to play?*

or their human victims—apart. When a fighter went down with a disabling wound, the crowd would be asked to decide whether to spare his life or to kill him. If the arena floor became too slippery with blood, a fresh layer of sand would be spread over the gore so that the performance could continue.

Roman Art, Architecture, and Engineering

Like Latin literature, Roman art assumed its distinctive character during the Principate. Before this time, most artworks displayed in Roman homes were imported from the Hellenistic east. As demand for such works increased, hundreds of copies were made by Roman artisans. In many cases, these copies proved more durable than their originals: in Chapter 4, for example, we were able to examine the lost Aphrodite of Knidos, courtesy of Roman sculptors.

Encouraged by the patronage of Augustus and his successors, artists began to experiment with more distinctively Roman styles and subjects. The relief sculpture of this period is particularly notable for its delicacy and naturalism, and sculptors also became adept at portraiture. Painting, however, was the Romans' most original and most intimate art. Romans loved intense colors, and those who could afford it surrounded themselves with brilliant wall paintings and mosaics made of tiny fragments of glass and stone, which were often set into the floors of houses or which formed the centerpieces of gardens. Lavish mosaics have been found in the remains of Roman villas in all the

ROMAN AQUEDUCT IN SOUTHERN GAUL (FRANCE). Aqueducts conveyed water from mountains and lakes to the larger cities of the Roman Empire. The massive arches shown here were originally part of a 31-mile-long complex that supplied water to the city of Nemausus (Nîmes). It is now known as the Pont du Gard (Bridge of the Gardon), reflecting the use to which it was put after the aqueduct ceased to function, some eight centuries after its construction in the first century C.E. Many Roman aqueducts remained operational into the modern era: the one at Segovia, Spain was still in use at the end of the twentieth century. ▪ *What does the magnitude and longevity of such projects tell us about Roman power and technology?*

territories of the empire, and similar design features indicate that many were mosaic "kits" that could be ordered from a manufacturer, who would ship out all the necessary components, along with a team of workmen to assemble them.

Augustus liked to boast that he had found Rome a city of clay and left it a city of marble. But in reality, marble was too precious to be used in common construction. Instead, marble panels or ornaments were added to the facings of buildings that were otherwise made of concrete. For the Roman had discovered how to make a mixture of quicklime, volcanic ash, and pumice, and it was this—along with superior engineering skills—that allowed them to build massive structures like the Colosseum, which could accommodate 50,000 spectators at gladiatorial combats.

Roman engineers also excelled in the building of roads and bridges, many of which were constructed by Rome's armies as they moved into new territories. Like the Persian Royal Road of the sixth century B.C.E. or the German Autobahn of the 1930s and the interstate highways of the United States begun in the 1950s, roads have always been, first and foremost, a device for moving armies and then, secondarily, for moving goods and people. Many of these Roman roads still survive, or form the basis for modern European highways. In Britain, for example, the only major thoroughfares before the building of high-speed motorways were based on Roman roads, to which the motorways now run parallel.

THE COLOSSEUM. Constructed between 75 and 80 C.E., this was the first ampitheater in Rome purposely built to showcase gladiatorial combats. Prior to this, gladiators would often fight in improvised arenas in the Forum or in other public places. ▪ *How does this fact change your perception of Roman history?*

Interpreting Visual Evidence

Roman Urban Planning

Prior to Roman imperial expansion, most cities in the ancient world were not planned cities—with the exception of the new settlements established by Alexander the Great, notably Alexandria in Egypt. Rome itself was not carefully planned, but grew up over many centuries, expanding outward and up the slopes of its seven hills from the nucleus of the Forum. By the time of Augustus, it was a haphazard jumble of buildings and narrow streets. Outside of Rome, however, the efficiency of Roman government was in large part due to the uniformity of imperial urban planning. As their colonial reach expanded, Romans sought to ensure that travelers moving within their vast domain would encounter the same amenities in every major city. They also wanted to convey, through the organization of the urban landscape, the ubiquity of Roman authority and majesty.

A. Imperial Rome

B. Roman settlement in Aelia Capitolina (Jerusalem) after 135 C.E.

The inhabitants of Roman cities also enjoyed the benefits of a public water supply. By the early decades of the second century C.E., eleven aqueducts brought water into Rome from the nearby hills for drinking and bathing and for flushing a well-designed sewage system. These amenities were common in cities throughout the empire, and the homes of the wealthy even had indoor plumbing and central heating. Water was also funneled into the homes of the rich for private gardens, fountains, and pools. The emperor Nero (54–68 C.E.) built a famous Golden House with special pipes that sprinkled his guests with perfume, baths supplied with medicinal waters, and a pond "like a sea." "At last," said Nero on moving day, "I can live like a human being."

The Reach of Roman Law

Roman architecture and engineering are impressive, but the most durable and useful of this civilization's legacies was its legal system. Over the course of several centuries,

Questions for Analysis

1. Looking closely at the map of Rome (map A), how have topographical features—like the river Tiber and the seven hills—determined the shape and layout of the city? What are the major buildings and public areas? What were the functions of these spaces, and what do they reveal about Roman society and values?

2. Compare the plan of Rome to those of Roman London (map C) and Jerusalem (map B). What features do all three have in common, and why? What features are unique to each place, and what might this reveal about the different regions of the empire and the needs of the different cities' inhabitants?

3. Given that all Roman cities share certain features, what message(s) were Roman authorities trying to convey to inhabitants and travelers through urban planning? Why, for example, would they have insisted on rebuilding Jerusalem as a Roman city—Aelia Capitolina—after the rebellion of 135 C.E.?

C. London under the Romans, c. 200 C.E.

the primitive code of the Twelve Tables was largely replaced by a series of new laws that reflect the changing needs of Rome's diverse and ever-growing population.

The most sweeping legal changes occurred during the Principate. This was partly because the reach of Roman law had to match the reach of the empire. But the major reason for the rapid development of Roman legal thinking during these years was the fact that Augustus and his successors appointed a small number of eminent jurists to deliver opinions on the issues raised by cases under trial in the courts. The five most prominent of these experts flourished in the second century C.E.: Gaius (only this most common of his names is known), Domitius Ulpianus (Ulpian), Modestinus, Aemelianus Papinianus (Papinian), and Paulus. Taken together, their legal opinions constitute the first philosophy of law and the foundation for all subsequent jurisprudence, a word derived from the Latin phrase meaning "legal wisdom."

As it was developed by the jurists, Roman law comprised three great branches: civil law, the law of nations, and natural law. Civil law was the law of Rome and its citizens, both written and unwritten. It included the statutes of the Senate, the decrees of the emperor, the edicts of magistrates, and ancient customs that had the force of law (like the *mos maiorum*). The law of nations was not specific to Rome but extended to all people of the world regardless of their origins and ethnicity: it is the precursor of international law. This law authorized slavery; protected the private ownership of property; and defined the mechanisms of purchase and sale, partnership, and contract. It supplemented civil law and applied especially to those inhabitants of the empire who were not citizens, as well as to foreigners.

The most interesting (and in many ways the most important) branch of Roman law was natural law, a product not of judicial practice but of legal philosophy. Roman Stoics, following in the footsteps of Cicero, posited that nature itself is rationally ordered, and that careful study will reveal the laws by which the natural world operates, including the nature of justice. They affirmed that all men are by nature equal, and that they are entitled to certain basic rights that governments have no authority to transgress. Accordingly, no person or institution has the authority to infringe on this law, repeal it, or ignore it. This law supersedes any state or ruler; a ruler who transgresses it is a tyrant.

Although the practical law applied in local Roman courts often bore little resemblance to the law of nature, the development of a concept of abstract justice as a fundamental principle was one of the noblest achievements of Roman civilization. It has given us the doctrine of human rights, even if it has not resulted in ending abuses of those rights.

CONCLUSION

The resemblances between Rome's history and that of Great Britain and the United States have often been noted. Like the British Empire, the Roman Empire was founded on conquest and overseas colonization intended to benefit both the homeland and its colonial subjects, who were seen as the beneficiaries of a "civilizing mission." Like America's, the Roman economy evolved from agrarianism to a complex system of domestic and foreign markets, problems of unemployment, gross disparities of wealth, and vulnerability to financial crisis. And like both the British and the American

After You Read This Chapter

Visit StudySpace for quizzes, additional review materials, and multi-media documents. **wwnorton.com/studyspace**

REVIEWING THE OBJECTIVES

- The founding of the Roman Republic was both a cherished myth and a series of events. What factors contributed to this unique system of government?
- The shared identity and values of the Roman people differed in many ways from those of other ancient civilizations. What were some of these major differences?
- Rome's population was divided among classes of people who often struggled with one another for power. Identify these classes and their points of contention.
- The expansion of Rome's empire had a profound impact on Roman society. Why?
- The establishment of the Principate ushered in a new era in the history of Rome. What events led to this?

empires, the Roman Empire justified itself by celebrating the peace its conquests allegedly brought to the world.

Ultimately, however, such parallels break down when we remember that Rome's civilization differed profoundly from any society of the modern world. It was not an industrialized society. Its government never pretended to be representative of all its citizens. Roman class divisions are not directly comparable to ours. The Roman economy rested on slavery to a degree unmatched in any modern state. As a result, technological advances were not encouraged, social stratification was extreme, and gender relations were profoundly unequal. Religious practice and political life were inseparable.

Nevertheless, the civilization of ancient Rome continues to structure our everyday lives in ways so profound that they often go unnoticed. Our days are mapped onto the Roman calendar. The constitution of the United States is largely modeled on that of the Republic, and Roman architecture survives in the design of our public buildings. Roman law forms the basis of most European legal codes, and American judges still cite Gaius and Ulpian. Virtually all modern sculpture is inspired by Roman sculpture, and Roman au-

thors continue to set the standards for prose composition in many Western countries. Indeed, most European languages are either derived from Latin—Romance languages are so called because they are "Roman-like"—or have borrowed Latin grammatical structures or vocabulary. As we shall see in the following chapters, the organization of the modern Roman Catholic Church can be traced back to the structure of the Roman state: even today, the pope bears the title of Rome's high priest, *pontifex maximus*.

But perhaps the most important of all Rome's contributions was its role as mediator between Europe and the civilizations of the ancient Near East and Mediterranean. Had Rome's empire not come to encompass much of Europe, there would be no such thing as the concept of Western civilization and no shared ideas and heritage to link us to those distant places and times. Although we shall pursue the history of Rome's fragmentation and witness the emergence of three different civilizations in the territories once united by its empire, we shall see that they all shared a common cultural inheritance. In this sense, the Roman Empire did not collapse. But it was transformed, and the factors driving that transformation will be the subject of Chapter 6.

PEOPLE, IDEAS, AND EVENTS IN CONTEXT

- In what ways were the early Romans influenced by their **ETRUSCAN** neighbors and by their location in central **ITALY**?
- What were the components of the **REPUBLIC'S CONSTITUTION**? What was the relationship between **ROMAN CITIZENSHIP** and the **ROMAN ARMY** in this era?
- How do the stories of **AENEAS**, **LUCRETIA**, and **CINCINNATUS** reflect core Roman values? How did those values, summarized in the phrase *MOS MAIORUM*, set the Romans apart from the other civilizations we have studied?
- Why did the Romans come into conflict with **CARTHAGE**? How did the **PUNIC WARS** and Rome's other conquests change the balance of power in the Mediterranean?
- How did **IMPERIALISM** and contact with **HELLENISTIC CULTURE** affect the core values of Roman society, its economy, and its political system? What role did **SLAVERY** play in this civilization?
- What were the major crises of the late republic, and what were the means by which ambitious men achieved power? How did **JULIUS CAESAR** emerge triumphant, and why was he assassinated?
- In what ways did the **PRINCIPATE** differ from the **REPUBLIC**? What were the new powers of the **EMPEROR**, and how did **AUGUSTUS** exemplify these?
- How did the Romans consolidate their **EMPIRE** during the *PAX ROMANA*? By what means did they spread Roman culture?

CONSEQUENCES

- Polybius believed that the Roman Republic would last forever, because it fused together aspects of monarchy, aristocracy, and polity. What were the chief factors that led to its demise in the first century B.C.E.? Could these have been avoided—and if so, how?
- In what ways does the Roman Empire share the characteristics of earlier empires, especially that of Alexander? In what ways does it differ from them?
- The Roman Empire could be said to resemble our own civilization in different ways. What features does today's United States share with the Republic? With the Principate? What lessons can we draw from this?

STORY LINES

- In a little over three centuries, Christianity grew from obscure beginnings in a small Roman province to become the official religion of the empire.

- Meanwhile, it was becoming clear during the first three centuries of the common era that the Roman Empire was too large and diverse to be governed by a single centralized authority. Significant political, military, and economic changes therefore occurred during the third century of our era.

- In the fourth century, the founding of a new capital at Constantinople shifted the focus of imperial administration to the East. At the same time, mass migrations of frontier peoples created new polities within the western half of Rome's empire.

- Christianity's new association with political power changed the religion in profound ways, as Christian intellectuals adapted Rome's traditional culture to meet Christian needs.

CHRONOLOGY

Before You Read This Chapter

The Transformation of Rome

CORE OBJECTIVES

- **IDENTIFY** the historical factors that shaped early Christianity.

- **DESCRIBE** the crises that faced Roman imperial administration during the third century.

- **TRACE** the ways that Christianity changed after it became a legal religion.

- **EXPLAIN** how the mass migrations of the fourth century affected the empire.

- **UNDERSTAND** the difference between the traditional Roman and Christian worldviews.

I n the year 203 C.E., a young woman called Vivia Perpetua was brought before the Roman governor at Carthage. She was twenty-two years old, well educated, from a respectable family. At the time of her arrest she had an infant child who was still nursing. She also had two brothers (one of whom was arrested with her) and a father who doted on her. She must, one presumes, have had a husband, but he is conspicuously absent from the firsthand account of her experiences. Perpetua herself says nothing about him, though she says a great deal about her father's grief and the efforts he made to intercede on her behalf. Not only did he beg the judge for mercy, he begged his daughter to confess so that her life could be spared. He admitted to having loved her more than her brothers and blamed himself for the liberal education he had given her. Clearly, he had failed as a Roman father. For Perpetua's crime was terrible. It was not only treason against the Roman state but an act of gross impiety toward her family and her ancestors. Worse, it was punishable by a death so debasing that it was reserved for slaves, barbarian prisoners, and hardened criminals. No respectable Roman matron would allow herself to be stripped

133

naked before a holiday crowd and mauled by wild beasts in the arena of her own city. Yet that was the death Perpetua died. Perpetua was a Christian.

Early Christianity posed a challenge to the Roman Empire and its core values at almost every level. To be a Christian was to be, by definition, an enemy of Rome, because Christians refused to worship the emperor as the embodiment of Rome's gods; denying his divinity meant denying his authority. Moreover, the Christ whom Christians worshiped had himself been declared a criminal, a political insurgent, and had been duly tried and put to death by the Roman state. How, then, did a Roman emperor become a Christian just a few centuries after Christ's death—and just a century or so after Perpetua's? What changes did both Rome and Christianity have to undergo in order for this to happen?

The Rome in which Perpetua was raised stretched from central Asia to the British Isles, from the Rhine to her own province of North Africa. But as we shall see, the governance of this enormous state and its diverse population was straining the bureaucracy that had been built on the foundations of the old Republic. By the end of the third century, it was increasingly obvious that Rome's western and eastern provinces could not be controlled by a single centralized authority. In the fourth century, Rome itself ceased to be the capital and hub of the empire; it now shared prestige with the new city of Constantinople, named by the Christian emperor who founded it. At the same time, Rome's settled provinces were coming under increased pressure from groups of people who had long lived beyond its borders, but who were now moving from the periphery to the center. These peoples, too, would challenge what it meant to be Roman, and would contribute to the transformation of the Roman world.

THE CHALLENGE OF CHRISTIANITY

All faiths have histories. Like the Hebrew monotheism that undergirds Judaism or the central tenets of Zoroastriansm (Chapter 2), Christianity was (and is) the product of historical processes. It began with the teachings of Jesus, who lived and worked among his fellow Jews in rural Judea and Galilee around the year 30 C.E. It took root, however, in the Hellenistic world we studied in Chapter 4: the cosmopolitan, Greek-speaking cities around the eastern Mediterranean, which had now been absorbed into the Roman Empire.

The Career of Jesus

Yeshua bar Yosef (Joshua, son of Joseph), known to the Greeks as Jesus, is one of the few figures of the ancient world—certainly one of the few commoners—about whose life we know a great deal. The earliest writings that mention Jesus specifically are the letters of his follower, Paul of Tarsus, a Hellenized Jew and Roman citizen who was active during the 50s and 60s C.E. These are closely followed by many different narratives of Jesus's life and teachings, most written between 70 and 100 C.E. Four such accounts were eventually included in the New Testament, a collection of Christian writings appended to the Greek text of the Hebrew Bible around the third century C.E. In their original Greek, these accounts were called *evangelia* ("good messages"); we know them as *gospels*, an Old English word that means the same thing.

Jesus was born around the year 4 B.C.E., a generation or so after Augustus came to power in Rome. (He was not born precisely in the first year of the Common Era as we now reckon it. When the monk Dionysius Exiguus first calculated time "in the year of Our Lord" during the sixth century, he made some mistakes.) When Jesus was around thirty years old, he was endorsed by a Jewish preacher of moral reform, John the Baptist, whom some considered to be a prophet. Thereafter, Jesus began preaching and displaying unusual healing powers. He accumulated a number of disciples, some of whom had political ambitions.

Around the year 30 C.E., Jesus staged an entry into Jerusalem during Passover, a major religious holiday. This move was interpreted as a bid for political power by both the Roman colonial government and the high-ranking Jews of the Temple. Three gospel accounts say that Jesus also drew attention to himself by physically attacking merchants and moneychangers associated with the Temple. The city's religious leaders therefore arrested him and turned him over to the Roman governor, Pontius Pilate, for sentencing.

Pilate's main concern was to preserve peace during a volatile religious festival. He knew that his authority depended on maintaining good relations with local Jewish elites and with Herod, who ruled the province of Galilee as a client king of the empire. Because Jesus was a resident of Galilee, not a citizen of Roman Judea, Pilate sent Jesus to Herod for sentencing. But Herod sent him back to Pilate, politely indicating that dealing with Jesus fell under Roman jurisdiction. So Pilate chose to make an example of Jesus by condemning him to death by crucifixion, the standard criminal penalty for those judged guilty of sedition. It had been rumored that Jesus planned to lead a rebellion, and something similar had happened in the second century B.C.E., when the Maccabbees overthrew Seleucid rule. Indeed, Roman occupation of this region had only begun in 67 B.C.E. and was still resented by many Jews. Pilate would have been mindful of all this.

That might have been the end of the story. But soon after Jesus's execution, his followers began to assert that he had risen from the dead before being taken up into Heaven. Moreover, they said that Jesus had promised to return again at the end of time. Meanwhile, he had promised spiritual support to his followers. His entire career now had to be rethought and reinterpreted. The evidence of this reinterpretation has come down to us in the letters of Paul and in the gospel narratives.

Jesus and Second Temple Judaism

In 1947, an extraordinary cache of scrolls was discovered in a cave near Qumran, on the shores of the Dead Sea. Over the course of the next decade, eleven more caves were found to house similar texts, all dating from the first century C.E. Written in Hebrew, Greek, and Aramaic at various times between 100 B.C.E and 70 C.E., the Dead Sea Scrolls have revolutionized our understanding of Judaism in the lifetime of Jesus, a period known as Second Temple Judaism. What these documents show, overwhelmingly, is the diversity of religious practice in this period, and the intense competition among groups of believers.

When Jesus was born, Roman rule was still inspiring extreme responses among Jews. Many were content to live under Rome's protection—especially the urban elite, who reaped the rewards of participation in the Roman economy. But those disadvantaged by Roman rule hoped for a messiah, a leader who would establish a new Jewish kingdom. The most extreme of these were the Zealots, whose activities eventually led to two disastrous revolts. The first, between 66 and 70 C.E., ended in the Romans' destruction of the Temple that had been rebuilt when Cyrus the Great released the Jews from captivity in Babylon (Chapter 2). The second, in 132–35 C.E., caused the destruction of Jerusalem itself and prompted the Romans to expel the entire Jewish population. Whereas the first exile of the Jews had ended after fifty years, this new diaspora would not be reversed until the controversial establishment of the modern state of Israel in 1948. For over 500 years, Jerusalem even ceased to exist; on its ruins the Romans built the colony of Aelia Capitolina (Chapter 5). It was only in 638, when the Islamic Caliphate established Arab rule in the region and restored Jerusalem as a holy site, that Jews were allowed to settle there (see Chapter 7).

This political context is essential to understanding the circumstances of Jesus's death and the many different interpretations of his words and actions. The Dead Sea Scrolls reveal that significant divisions had arisen among Jewish communities, and that Jesus would have participated in several key debates. The hereditary Temple priesthood was controlled by a group known as the Sadducees, who collaborated closely with Rome; the high priest of the Temple was even appointed by the Roman Senate. The Sadducees' chief rivals were the Pharisees, preachers of religious doctrine who were heirs to the prophetic tradition of the First Temple period. In contrast to the Sadducees, who claimed the right to control the interpretation of the Torah (the five books attributed to Moses) the Pharisees argued that Yahweh had given Moses a Torah as well as a written one, a tradition which they now claimed as their special inheritance.

The Pharisees were accordingly quite flexible in the practical application of religious law. They also believed in a life after death, a day of judgment, and the damnation or reward of individual souls. They actively sought out converts through preaching, and looked forward to the imminent arrival of the messiah whom God (through the prophets) had long promised. In all these respects they differed significantly from the Sadducees, who interpreted the Torah more strictly, who considered Judaism closed to anyone who had not been born a Jew, and who had a vested interest in maintaining the political *status quo*. Even more radical than the Pharisees was a faction known as the Essenes, a quasi-monastic group that hoped for spiritual deliverance through repentance, asceticism, and sectarian separation from their fellow Jews.

Although some scholars see Essene influence behind the career of Jesus, his contemporaries probably saw him as some sort of Pharisee. Jesus's emphasis on the ethical requirements of the law rather than its literal interpretation is reflected in many of his teachings. Jesus's apparent belief in life after death and the imminent coming of "the kingdom of God" also fits within a Pharisaic framework, as does his willingness to reach out to people beyond the Jewish community. Yet he seems to have carried these principles considerably further than did the Pharisees.

For most Jews at this time, Judaism consisted of going up to the Temple on holy days; paying the annual Temple tax; reciting the morning and evening prayers; and observing certain fundamental laws, such as circumcision (for men), ritual purity (especially for women), and prohibitions on the consumption of certain foods. Jesus de-emphasized such observances, and it may have seemed to some that he wished to abolish them. But what made him most controversial was his followers' claim that he was the messiah sent to deliver Israel from its enemies.

After Jesus's death, such claims grew more assertive, yet they never persuaded more than a small minority of Jews.

But when Jesus's followers began to preach to non-Jewish audiences, they found many willing listeners. They began to represent Jesus in terms that made sense to the Greek-speaking communities of the Hellenistic world. Jesus, his followers now proclaimed, was not merely a messiah for the Jews. He was the "anointed one" (in Greek, *Christos*), who had suffered and died for the sins of all humanity. He had risen from the dead and ascended into Heaven, and he would return to judge all the world's inhabitants at the end of time.

Christianity in the Hellenistic World

The key figure to develop this new understanding of Jesus's divinity was his younger contemporary, Paul of Tarsus (c. 10–c. 67 C.E.). Named Saul when he was born in the capital city of the Roman province of Cilicia (now south-central Turkey), he was the son of a Pharisee and staunchly sympathetic to that cause. The *Acts of the Apostles*, the continuation of Luke's gospel and a major source for Saul's early life, says that he was dedicated to stamping out the cult that had grown up around the crucified Jesus. But at some point in his mid-twenties—a few years after Jesus's death—he underwent a dramatic conversion experience, changed his name to Paul, and devoted the rest of his life to spreading the new faith to Greek-speaking, mainly non-Jewish communities.

Unlike Peter and the other early disciples, Paul had never met Jesus. Instead, he claimed to have received a direct revelation of his teachings. This led to a number of major disputes. For example, Peter and his companions believed that followers of Jesus had to be Jews or converts to Judaism. Paul declared that Jewish religious law was now irrelevant: Jesus had made a new covenant possible between God and humanity, and the old covenant between God and the Jews no longer applied. This position was vehemently opposed by the Jewish Christians of Jerusalem, a group led by Jesus's brother, James. But after a series of difficult debates that took place around 49 C.E., Paul's position triumphed. Although some early Christians would continue to obey Jewish law, most of the converts who swelled the movement were Gentiles. Paul began to call this new community of believers an *ekklesia*, the Greek word for a legislative assembly. The Latinized form of this word is translated as "church."

These earliest converts to Christianity were attracted for a variety of reasons. Some were Hellenized Jews like Paul himself. Some were non-Jews known as "God-fearers," who gathered around Greek-speaking Jewish communities. God-fearers did not follow all the precepts of Jewish law, but they admired the Jews for their loyalty to ancestral tradition and their high ethical standards. Christianity was also attractive to ordinary cosmopolitan Greeks. Some saw Jesus as living by Stoic principles or as the embodiment of Ahura-Mazda, the good god of Zoroastrianism. Others were already devotees of mystery religions, like the very old cult of the Egyptian goddess Isis or the newer worship of the warrior-god Mithras, popular among Rome's soldiers. Both of these religions also revolved around stories of sacrifice, death, and regeneration. Indeed, it was largely for the benefit of these converts that Christians began to practice elaborate initiation ceremonies such as baptism, a ritual purification common to many ancient religions and exemplified among Jews in the ministry of John the Baptist.

At the same time, there were significant differences between Christianity and these other religions. Most mystery cults stressed the rebirth of the *individual* through spiritual transformation, but Christianity emphasized the importance of community. By the middle of the second century, the Christian church at Rome even had a recognizable structure, headed by a bishop (in Greek, *episcopos* or "overseer") and lesser officeholders, including priests, deacons, confessors, and exorcists. Women were extremely prominent in these churches, not only as benefactors but as officeholders. This was unusual: in other ancient religions, women could be priests only in cults open solely to women; they never took precedence over men. Many cults denied them access entirely. The fact that Christianity drew its adherents from a broad range of social classes also distinguished it from other cults, which were accessible mainly to those with money and leisure. In time, these unusual features were distorted by Christianity's detractors, who alleged that Christians were political insurgents like the Jesus they worshiped, that they engaged in illicit acts during their "love feasts," and even that they practiced human sacrifice and cannibalism.

As both Christianity and Judaism redefined themselves during the second and third centuries, they grew further apart. Judaism was adapting to the destruction of the Temple and the mass exile of Jews from Jerusalem and surrounding provinces. By and large, the scholars who reshaped it during these difficult years ignored Christianity. It simply did not matter to them. Christians, however, could not ignore Judaism. Their religion rested on the belief that Jesus was the savior promised by God to Israel in the Hebrew Bible. The fact that so few Jews accepted this claim threatened to undermine the credibility of the Christian message.

More Christians could have responded as did Marcion, a second-century Christian scholar who declared that the entire Hebrew Bible could be ignored. Most Christians, however, refused to abandon their religion's Jewish foundation. For them, the heroes of Jewish scripture prefigured Jesus, while the major events of Hebrew history could be read, allegorically, as Christian paradigms. Christ was the

PAUL'S MISSIONARY JOURNEYS. Quite apart from its theological importance, Paul's career offers fascinating glimpses into the life of a Roman citizen from one of the empire's eastern provinces. ▪ **What were the main phases of Paul's travels in the eastern Mediterranean?** ▪ **How were his itineraries probably shaped by geography and by various modes of transport?** ▪ **What conclusions about his mission can you draw from the extent of his travels and his major destinations?**

new Adam, reversing man's original sin. Christ, like Abel, had died at the hands of a brother and his blood continued to cry out from the ground. Christ was the new Noah, saving creation from its sins. Christ was prefigured in Isaac, in Joseph, in Moses. All the words of the Hebrew prophets point to Jesus, as do the Psalms and the Proverbs.

In short, Christian theologians argued that the Christian church is the true Israel, and that when the Jews rejected Jesus, God rejected the Jews and made Christians his new chosen people. The Hebrew Bible was henceforth the Old Testament, vital to understanding Christianity but superceded by the New Testament. At the end of time, the Jews would see the error of their ways and convert. Until then, their own impiety had caused their exile from the Holy Land and would continue to bring suffering down on their descendants.

Christianity and the Roman State

So long as Christianity remained a minority religion within the Roman Empire, such attitudes had no effect on the position of Jews under Roman rule. Judaism remained a legally recognized religion and many Jews were further protected by their Roman citizenship. Because of this, Paul could not be summarily put to death (as the noncitizen Jesus had been) when brought up on charges of treason. Instead, the *Acts of the Apostles* follows his progress through the Roman judicial system, until he was finally brought to trial at Rome and executed (by beheading) under Nero. Even the Jews of the diaspora were allowed to maintain the special status they had always had under Roman rule and were not required, as other subject peoples were, to offer sacrifices to the emperor as a god.

Analyzing Primary Sources

The Prosecution of a Roman Citizen

The Acts of the Apostles *was written by the same author as Luke's gospel, and was intended as a continuation of that book. It recounts the adventures and ministry of Jesus's original disciples and also follows the career of Paul, a Hellenized Jew who became apostle to Gentiles throughout the Roman world. It offers fascinating glimpses into the workings of the Roman legal system because Paul, as a Roman citizen, had special rights under Roman law (as Jesus had not). In this passage, Paul has been accused of treason against the emperor by a group of Pharisees and has been sent to Felix, the governor of Judea. These events took place between 57 and 59 C.E.*

o the soldiers, according to their instructions, took Paul and brought him by night to Antipatris. The next day, they let the horsemen go on with him, while they returned to the barracks. When they came to Caesarea and delivered the letter to the governor, they presented Paul also before him. On reading the letter, he asked what province he belonged to, and when he learned that he was from Cilicia he said, "I will give you a hearing when your accusers arrive." Then he ordered that he be kept under guard in Herod's headquarters.

Five days later the high priest Ananias came down with some elders and an attorney, a certain Tertullus, and they reported their case against Paul to the governor. When Paul had been summoned, Tertullus began to accuse him, saying: "Your Excellency, because of you we have long enjoyed peace, and reforms have been made for this people because of your foresight. We welcome this in every way and everywhere with utmost gratitude. But, to detain you no further, I beg you to hear us briefly with your customary graciousness. We have, in fact, found this man a pestilent fellow, an agitator among all the Jews throughout the world, and a ringleader of the sect of the Nazarenes. He even tried to profane the temple, and so we seized him. By examining him yourself you will be able to learn from him concerning everything of which we accuse him." The Jews also joined in the charge by asserting that all this was true.

When the governor motioned to him to speak, Paul replied: "I cheerfully make my defense, knowing that for many years you have been a judge over this nation. As you can find out, it is not more than twelve days since I went up to worship in Jerusalem. They did not find me disputing with anyone in the temple or stirring up a crowd either in synagogues or throughout the city. Neither can they prove to you the charge that they now bring against me. But this I admit to you, that according to the Way, which they call a sect, I worship the God of our ancestors, believing everything laid down according to the law or written in the prophets. I have hope in God—a hope that they themselves also accept—that there will be a resurrection of both the righteous and the unrighteous. Therefore I do my best always to have a clear conscience toward God and all people. . . ."

But Felix, who was rather well informed about the Way [i.e. Paul's approach to Jesus], adjourned the hearing with the comment, "When Lysias the tribune comes down, I will decide your case." Then he ordered the centurion to keep him in custody, but to let him have some liberty and not to prevent any of his friends from taking care of his needs.

When some days Felix later came with his wife Drusilla, who was Jewish, he sent for Paul and heard him speak concerning faith in Christ Jesus. And as he discussed justice and self-control and future judgment, Felix was alarmed and said, "Go away for the present; when I have an opportunity I will summon you." At the same time he hoped that money would be given him by Paul. So he sent for him often and conversed with him. But when two years had elapsed, Felix was succeeded by Porcius Festus; and desiring to do the Jews a favor, Felix left Paul in prison.

Source: *Acts of the Apostles* 23:31–24:27, in *The New Oxford Annotated Bible*, New Revised Standard Version, eds. Bruce M. Metzger and Roland E. Murphy (New York: 1994).

Questions for Analysis

1. Based on this account, what legal procedures are in place for dealing with any Roman citizen accused of a crime?

2. What seems to be the relationship between the Jewish elite of Judea and the Roman governor? What is the role of their spokesman, Tertullus?

3. What is the nature of the accusation against Paul, and how does he defend himself?

A CHRISTIAN LOVE FEAST. This fresco, an image from the catacombs of Rome, shows Christians celebrating a feast. The inscription above reads, "I join with you in love." ▪ *How might a Roman viewer interpret this scene?* ▪ *How might this interpretation differ from that of a Christian?*

Christianity, by contrast, raised suspicions on many levels: it encouraged women and slaves to hold office and therefore to rise above their proper stations; it revolved around the worship of a criminal condemned by the Roman state; its secret meetings could be breeding grounds for illegal activities. Nevertheless, the official attitude of the Roman state toward Christians was largely one of indifference. There were not enough of them to matter, and few of them had any political power. During the first and second centuries C.E., therefore, Christians were tolerated by Roman officials, except when local magistrates chose to make an example of someone who flagrantly flouted authority.

THE CHALLENGE OF IMPERIAL EXPANSION

The emergence of Christianity coincided with the Roman Empire's most dramatic period of growth and with a growing variety of challenges. For a long time, emperors and administrators had clung to the methods of governance put in place under Augustus, which were based on a single centralized authority. The reality, however, was that Rome's empire was no longer centered on Rome, or even on Italy. It embraced ecosystems, ethnicities, economies, and political systems of vastly different kinds. More and more people could claim to be Roman citizens, and more and more people wanted a share of Rome's power. This placed enormous stress on the imperial administration, as the centrifugal forces of Rome's own making constantly pulled

resources into her far-flung provinces. The fact that the empire had no defensible borders was another problem. Hadrian had attempted to establish one after 122, by building a wall between Roman settlements in southern Britannia and the badlands of northern tribes (Chapter 5); but this act was more symbolic than defensive.

For much of the second century, these stresses were masked by the peaceful transfer of power among the aforementioned "Five Good Emperors": Nerva, Trajan, Hadrian, Antoninus Pius, and Marcus Aurelius (Chapter 5). Because none of these first four rulers had a surviving male heir, and so a custom developed whereby each adopted a young man of a good family and trained his successor in the craft of government. But this sensible practice changed with the death of Marcus Aurelius in 180 C.E.

Although he was the closest Roman equivalent to Plato's ideal of the philosopher-king, Marcus was not wise enough to recognize that his own son, Commodus, lacked the capacity to rule effectively. After his father's death, Commodus alienated the army by withdrawing from costly wars along the Danube. This move was also unpopular with the Senate, as were Commodus's violent tendencies and his scorn for the traditional norms of aristocratic conduct, including his appearance as a gladiator in the Colosseum. In 192, a conspiracy was hatched inside his own palace, where he was strangled by his wrestling coach.

The Empire of the Severan Dynasty

Because Commodus had no obvious successor, the armies stationed in various provinces of the empire raised their own candidates. Civil war ensued, as it had during the crises of the late republic and in 68 C.E., when three men had struggled for imperial power. In this case, there were five major contenders. The eventual victor was a North African general called Septimius Severus (r. 193–211 C.E.).

Under Severus and his successors, the administration of Rome's empire changed to a greater extent than it had since the time of Augustus. In many respects, these changes were long overdue. Even the "Five Good Emperors" had been somewhat insulated from the realities of colonial rule. Many of them were able commanders, but they were not professional soldiers as Severus was. Another major difference was that fact that Severus had been born and raised in the North African town of Leptis Magna (now in Libya) and identified strongly with his father's Punic ancestors. Unlike Trajan and Hadrian, who had also grown up in the provinces, Severus did not regard Rome as the center of the universe, and the time he spent in the imperial capital as a

The Development of an Imperial Policy toward Christians

It was not until the third century that the Roman imperial government began to initiate full-scale investigations into the activities of Christians. Instead, the official position was akin to a policy of "don't ask, don't tell." Local administrators handled only occasional cases, and they were often unsure as to whether the behavior of Christians was illegal. The following letter was sent to the Emperor Trajan by Gaius Plinius Caecilius Secundus (Pliny the Younger), the governor of Bithynia-Pontus (Asia Minor), around 112 C.E. Pliny was anxious to follow proper procedures in dealing with the new sect and wanted advice about this. His letter indicates what Romans did and didn't know about early Christian beliefs and practices.

From Pliny to Trajan

It is my regular custom, my lord, to refer to you all questions which cause me doubt, for who can better guide my hesitant steps or instruct my ignorance? I have never attended hearings concerning Christians, so I am unaware what is usually punished or investigated, and to what extent. . . . In the meantime, this is the procedure I have followed in the cases of those brought before me as Christians. I asked them whether they were Christians. If they admitted it, I asked them a second and a third time, threatening them with execution. Those who remained obdurate I ordered to be executed, for I was in no doubt . . . that their obstinacy and inflexible stubbornness should at any rate be punished. Others similarly lunatic were Roman citizens, so I registered them to be sent back to Rome.

Later in the course of the hearings, as usually happens, the charge rippled outwards, and more examples appeared. An anonymous document was published containing the names of many. Those who denied that they were or had been Christians and called upon the gods after me, and with incense and wine made obeisance to your statue . . . and who moreover cursed Christ . . . I ordered to be acquitted.

Others, who were named by an informer, stated that they were Christians and then denied it. They said that they had been, but had abandoned their

young man seems to have convinced him that little could be accomplished there.

In fact, Severus represents the degree to which the Roman Empire had succeeded in making the world Roman—succeeded so well that Rome itself was becoming irrelevant. One could be as much a Roman in Britannia or Africa as in central Italy. Severus's second wife, Julia Domna, exemplifies this trend in a different way. Descended from the Aramaic aristocracy who ruled the Roman client kingdom of Emesa (Syria), her father was the high priest of its sun-god Ba'al. She was highly educated and proved an effective governer during her husband's almost perpetual absence on campaign.

Severus largely ignored the politics of the Senate and slighted what remained of its powers. He preferred to rule through the army, which he reorganized and expanded. Two of his reforms had long-term consequences. The first was a drastic raise in army pay, perhaps as much as 100 percent, which had the effect of securing the soldiers' absolute loyalty and diminishing their need to augment their wages through plunder. The other was a relaxation of the long-standing rule forbidding soldiers to marry while still in service. This encouraged men to put down roots in local communities, but it also made them reluctant to move when their legion was called up. On the one hand, this domesticated the army (hitherto a highly mobile fighting machine) and may have made it less effective. On the other, it gave the army a stake in the peaceful governance of Rome's colonies and further contributed to the decentralization of power.

Severus died at Eboracum (York, England) in 211, after conducting a series of successful negotiations with Pictish tribes north of Hadrian's Wall. He is reported to have said to his sons, "Get along together, you two, keep the soldiers

allegiance some years previously.... They maintained, however, that all that their guilt or error involved was that they were accustomed to assemble at dawn on a fixed day, to sing a hymn antiphonally to Christ as God, and to bind themselves by an oath ... to avoid acts of theft, brigandage, and adultery.... When these rites were completed, it was their custom to depart, and then reassemble again to take food, which was, however, common and harmless. They had ceased, they said, to do this following my edict, by which in accordance with your instructions I had outlawed the existence of secret brotherhoods. So I thought it all the more necessary to ascertain the truth from two maidservants [i.e., slaves], who were called deaconesses, even by employing torture. I found nothing other than a debased and boundless superstition....

From Trajan to Pliny

You have followed the appropriate procedures, my Secundus.... [N]o general rule can be laid down which would establish a definite routine. Christians are not to be sought out. If brought before you and found guilty, they must be punished, but in such a way that a person who denies that he is a Christian, and demonstrates this by his action ... may obtain pardon for his repentance, even if his previous record is suspect. Documents published anonymously must play no role in any accusation, for they give the worst example, and are foreign to our age.

Source: Exerpted from *Pliny the Younger: The Complete Letters*, trans. P. G. Walsh (Oxford: 2006), pp. 278–79 (X.96–97).

Questions for Analysis

1. How does Pliny's treatment of Christians differ according to their social class? How does it differ from Felix's treatment of Paul (above)?

2. Why would Trajan insist that anonymous accusations, like those discussed by Pliny, should not be used as evidence? Why is this "foreign to our age"?

3. What do you conclude from this exchange about the relationship between religion and politics under the Roman Empire?

rich, and don't bother about anyone else." His elder son, Caracalla, didn't heed the first of these injunctions for long: by the end of the year, he had assassinated his brother. The second of his father's orders he did obey, by extending the rights of Roman citizenship to everyone in the empire, including the entire army. This was beneficial in some respects, but it may also have cheapened Roman citizenship, which was no longer a prize to be won through service or the adoption of Roman values and manners. His father's final piece of advice helped to shorten Caracalla's reign significantly, since it exacerbated his already pronounced tendency to alienate everyone who disagreed with him. He was assassinated in 217.

Caracalla's true successor was his mother's sister, Julia Maesa, who ruled through his heir and cousin, her adolescent grandson. This youth was known as Heliogabalus (or Elagabalus, r. 218–22) because of his devotion to the Syrian sun-god Ba'al. But when Heliogabalus caused controversy by attempting to replace Jupiter, Rome's patron god, with a Latinized version of this Eastern deity, Sol Invictus ("Invincible Sun"), his own grandmother engineered his assassination. Another of her grandsons, Alexander Severus (r. 222–35 c.e.), took his place. Alexander, in turn, was ruled by his mother, Julia Mamea—the third in a succession of strong women behind the Severan dynasty—who even traveled with her son on military campaigns. This eventually proved fatal. The new prominence of the army made Rome's legions engines of political advancement even more so than under the dictators of the late Republic. In 235 Alexander and his mother were murdered in Germania when the army of the region turned against them. The Pax Romana was over.

The End of the Roman Peace

From 235 to 284 C.E. there were no fewer than twenty-six "barracks emperors": military commanders who, backed by a few loyal legions, struggled with one another. This period is sometimes called the "Third-Century Crisis" and interpreted as the time when the Roman Empire was nearly destroyed. It is more accurately interpreted as a time when the consequences of Roman imperialism made themselves acutely felt. Those aspects of the empire that were strong survived. Those that had always been fragile gave way.

In particular, the disruptions of the mid-third century exposed weaknesses in economic and administrative infrastructures. Inflation, caused by the devaluation of currency under Severus, nearly drained Roman coinage of its value. Meanwhile, aspiring emperors levied exorbitant taxes on civilians in their provinces, as warfare among rival claimants and their armies destroyed crops and interrupted trade, causing food shortages. Poverty and famine led to a new form of slavery in Italy, as free artisans, local businessmen, and small farmers were forced to labor on the estates of large landholders in exchange for protection and food.

In 251, a terrible plague, probably smallpox, swept through the empire's territories and recurred in some areas for almost two decades. A similar plague had ravaged Rome a century earlier, but its effects had been mitigated by sound governance. Now, with an estimated 5,000 people dying every day in the crowded city, people sought local scapegoats. Christians were among those targeted. Beginning in the short reign of Decius (r. 249–51), all Roman citizens were required to swear a public oath affirming their loyalty to Rome, which meant worshipping Rome's gods. Large numbers of Christians were implicated when this edict was put into effect. The enlightened policies of earlier emperors were abandoned.

The Reorganized Empire of Diocletian

As it happens, the most zealous persecutor of Christians was also responsible for reining in these destructive forces. Diocletian (r. 284–305) was a cavalry officer from the Roman province of Dalmatia (modern Croatia) who had risen through the ranks. He could have been another "barracks emperor." Instead, he embraced the reality of Rome as a multicultural entity that could not be governed from one place by one person with one centralized bureaucracy. He appointed a fellow officer, Maximian, as co-emperor, putting him in charge of the western half of the empire and retaining the wealthier eastern half for himself. In 293, he delegated new authority to two junior emperors or "caesars," Galerius and Constantius. The result was a tetrarchy, a "rule of four," with each man governing a quarter of the empire, further subdivided into administrative units called *dioceses*. This system not only responded to the challenges of imperial administration, it was designed to secure a peaceful transfer of power, since the two young "caesars" were being groomed to take the place of the two senior "augusti."

Diocletian recognized that disputes over succession had been a fatal flaw of the Augustan system. Also unlike Augustus, who had cloaked the reality of power in the trappings of the Republic, Diocletian presented himself as an undisguised autocrat. His title was not *princeps* ("first man"), but *dominus* ("lord"). In fact, his style of imperial rule borrowed more from the Persian model than it did from the Roman. Gone were the days of republican simplicity and the scorn of kingly pomp. Diocletian wore a diadem and a purple gown of silk interwoven with gold, and he introduced Persian-style ceremonies at his court. Those lucky enough to gain an audience with him had to prostrate themselves, while a privileged few could kiss his robe. Too much familiarity with their soldiers had bred contempt for the "barracks emperors;" as a soldier-turned-emperor himself, Diocletian was able to avoid this mistake.

Although Diocletian retained close personal control over the army, he took steps to separate military from civilian chains of command: never again would Roman armies make and unmake emperors. To control the devastatingly high rates of inflation that were undermining the economy, Diocletian

THE TETRARCHY: DIOCLETIAN AND HIS COLLEAGUES. This grouping, carved from a valuable purple stone called porphyry, shows the two augusti, Diocletian and Maximian, embracing their younger ceasars, Galerius and Constantius. ▪ *Why do you think that these rulers are portrayed with identical facial features and military regalia?* ▪ *What message does this convey?*

stabilized the currency and attempted to fix prices and wages. He reformed the tax system. He even moved the administrative capital of the empire away from Italy to Nicomedia, in the Roman province of Bithynia (modern Turkey). Rome remained the symbolic capital of the empire, not least because the Senate continued to meet there. But Diocletian had little need for the Senate's advice. The real power lay elsewhere.

THE CONVERSION OF CHRISTIANITY

By the beginning of the fourth century, the number of Christians living within the jurisdiction of Rome was statistically insignificant, probably no more than 5 percent of the total population in the West and possibly 10 percent of the Greek-speaking East. Still, Christians were making an impact, and one of Diocletian's methods for promoting unity within the empire was to take a proactive stance against any group perceived as subversive. Those who could not show proof of their loyalty to Rome's gods were stripped of their rights as citizens. Christians who had been serving in the army or in government offices were dismissed. So were Manicheans, followers of the Persian prophet Mani (c. 216–276), whose teachings paralleled Zoroastrianism. Indeed, Christianity and Manichaeism must have seemed very similar to outsiders, and both were implicated in a full-scale purge of religious dissidents in 303. This was the Great Persecution, a time when many became martyrs—a Greek word meaning "witnesses"—to their faith.

Christianity and Neoplatonism

Ironically, the very crises that prompted Diocletian's Great Persecution were contributing to a growing interest in Christianity. Its message of social justice and equality before God was attractive to those suffering from the breakdown of political, economic, and social structures. It also appealed to followers of a new and influential philosophical system called Neoplatonism ("New Platonism"), which drew upon the more mystical aspects of Plato's thought. Its founder was Plotinus (204–270 C.E.), a Hellenistic philosopher from Egypt.

Plotinus taught that everything has its source in a single supreme being. The material world is part of this creation, but it is merely the residue of the divine, from which all spirituality has been drained. Human beings are thus composed of matter (bodies) and emanations of the divine (souls). This means that the individual soul is separated from its divine source by the fact of its embodiment.

The highest goal of life is therefore to attain spiritual reunion with God through acts of self-denial that will help to liberate the soul from its earthly bondage. Asceticism (from the Greek word meaning "exercise" or "training") was therefore a major focus: Plotinus believed that the body could be tamed by fasting and other forms of self-denial, and thus made a more fitting vessel for the soul.

Neoplatonism became so popular in Rome that it almost supplanted Stoicism. Neoplatonism also struck a blow at traditional Roman precepts, including the worship of ancestors and the devotion to the empire's gods. It was thus a natural ally of Christianity, and many important Christian theologians would be influenced by it, while many educated Romans found their way to Christianity because of it. This was not, however, the path by which Christianity's first imperial convert reached it.

Constantine's Vision

In 305 Diocletian built a palace near his hometown of Split and retired there to raise cabbages—the first time a Roman ruler had voluntarily removed himself from power since Sulla had resigned his dictatorship, nearly four hundred years earlier (Chapter 5). Diocletian obliged his fellow augustus Maximian to retire at the same time, and the two caesars Galerius and Constantius moved up the ladder of succession. But the transfer of power was not as orderly as Diocletian had intended. One of the candidates to fill the now vacant post of ceasar was Constantius's son, Constantine, who was being trained at Galerius's court. But when he was mysteriously passed over, Constantine left Nicomedia and joined his father in Gaul. From there, father and son went to Britannia and campaigned on the northern borders until 306, when Constantius died and named Constantine as his successor. This infuriated Galerius, but with Constantine in control of a large army he was forced to concede.

Meanwhile, war broke out among several other claimants to imperial authority, reducing Diocletian's tetrarchy to chaos. Constantine remained aloof from this struggle, waged mostly in Italy, and concentrated on securing his quarter of the empire. Beginning around 310, he also began to promote himself as a devotee of the sun-god Sol Invictus, whose cult had been revived and was associated not only with the Roman gods of light and war, Apollo and Mars, but also with Mithras, the cult popular with soldiers. It was increasingly popular in Rome as well, where the feast long dedicated to the sky-god Saturn, the Saturnalia, was now being celebrated as the rebirth of the sun after the winter solstice, on December 25.

From the worship of the "Invincible Sun" to the worship of Christ was, at least for Constantine, a small step

(see **Interpreting Visual Evidence** on page 145). In 312, Constantine decided to march on Italy, which was now in the hands of a man called Maxentius, who had declared himself emperor and was trying to build up a coalition of supporters. Among them was the Christian community of Rome. It may have been this that gave Constantine the idea of currying favor in the same way, or it may have been divine inspiration that led him to emblazon Christian symbols on his banners and on the shields of his soldiers the night before a major battle north of Rome, at the Milvian Bridge over the Tiber. According to later legend, Constantine had seen a vision of two intertwined letters inscribed on the sky, the first two letters in the name of Christ, and was told that "In this sign, you will conquer." He did.

In gratitude for his victory, Constantine showered benefits on the Christian clergy of Rome and patronized the construction of churches throughout the empire. He also forced Licinius, the augustus of the East, to join him in promoting religious tolerance when they met at Milan in 313. Their Edict of Milan guaranteed freedom of worship to all Rome's citizens, Christian and non-Christian. But it soon became apparent that Christianity was the pathway for anyone with political ambitions. Almost overnight, Christians ceased to be members of an illegal cult and became affiliates of a prestigious religion. The entire basis of Christianity's appeal had changed.

From Illegal Sect to Imperial Institution

In his letters, Paul of Tarsus had addressed small Christian assemblies that he called churches. But it is doubtful that Paul could have imagined a day when representatives of an official Church could meet openly, or a time when his letters to separate churches would be gathered together in a single book.

Early Christianity had grown organically; it had not been designed as a religious system. It had no absolute teachings, apart from the words of Jesus reported in the gospels—which do not always agree on those teachings. And not all Christian communities had access to the same scriptures. Some churches had a few of Paul's letters, some had none. Some had bishops, priests, deacons, and other officeholders; some had only a handful of believers. Some counted women as their leaders; others disapproved of women in authority. Some had come under the influence of Neoplatonism or Manichaeism; others considered Neoplatonism and Manichaeism to be perversions.

In every respect, then, the Christianity that emerged after Constantine's conversion had to reinvent itself. Members of this new official Church needed to agree on a shared set of beliefs. They needed a shared set of scriptures. They needed a chain of command. All of these fundamentals had to be hammered out in a painful process that never quite managed to forge a common understanding. For the varieties of Christianity had been too separate for too long, and were products of the same diversity that made the Roman Empire hard to govern. Indeed,

DIOCLETIAN'S DIVISION OF THE EMPIRE, C. 304 C.E. ▪ *What areas did each of the four divisions of the empire cover?* ▪ *What seems to be the strategy behind the location of the four major capitals, both within their respective quarters and in relation to one another?* ▪ *What is the status of Rome itself, according to this map?*

Interpreting Visual Evidence

The Power of the Invincible Sun

Roman emperors often linked their power with those of Rome's traditional gods, and they were also worshipped as gods in their own right. Look carefully at the following images and consider the visual language of power that came to be associated with Sol Invictus, "the Invincible Sun," and eventually with Jesus Christ.

Questions for Analysis

1. How did Constantine use the iconography of Sol Invictus (image A)? What messages did this convey?

2. How might Constantine's use of this imagery have been interpreted by Christians? How might it have been interpreted by followers of Rome's other religions? Do you think it was designed to be ambiguous?

3. The mosaic shown at right was found beneath St. Peter's Basilica (image B). Is it likely that this is a representation of Jesus as Sol Invictus? How would you explain the later association of this pagan deity with the Christian God?

A. This gold medallion was issued by Constantine in 313, a year after his victory at the Battle of the Milvian Bridge. The legend calls him "Invincible Constantine."

B. This mosaic comes from a necropolis (cemetery) found beneath St. Peter's Basilica in Rome. Its precise dating is in dispute, but it was made sometime between the mid-third and mid-fourth century.

the degree to which Christians of the fourth century were able to agree on so many things is remarkable, given these challenges.

The Hierarchy of the Church

When it came to organization, Rome's imperial administration provided practical models. Because the empire's basic unit of governance was the city, the city became the basic unit of ecclesiastical administration, too. Each major city now had a bishop who oversaw all the churches and rural areas of his diocese. Bishops of the empire's largest cities were called *metropolitans*, and those who ruled the most

prestigious Christian communities were called *patriarchs*. These patriarchal cities also jockeyed for preeminence: among the main contenders were Rome, Alexandria, and Constantinople, the new city founded by Constantine on the Hellespont between Europe and Asia. Which of these Roman cities should be the capital of the Roman Church?

The patriarch of Rome's claim rested on several foundations. Rome had long been venerated as the place where both Peter and Paul were martyred. And according to one of the gospels (Matthew 16:18–19), Jesus had designated Peter as his representative on earth. Peter's successors, the subsequent bishops of Rome, thus claimed to exercise the same powers. But so far as Rome's eastern bishops were concerned, the patriarch of Constantinople should exercise

control over the entire Church. In time, this difference of opinion would lead to a very real division within Christianity, one that has never been resolved.

Orthodoxy, Heresy, and Imperial Authority

While followers of Jesus had disagreed about his teachings since the time of his death, these disagreements were of little political consequence so long as Christianity remained an illegal movement. Under Constantine, however, doctrinal disputes had the potential to ignite riots and to undermine the credibility of the emperor. It was imperative, therefore, that these disputes be resolved.

The most divisive theological issue concerned the nature of God. Jesus had taught his followers that he was the Son of God, and that after his death he would leave behind him a comforting Spirit that would also be an emanation of God. Accordingly, many Christians believed that God encompassed a Trinity of equal persons: Father, Son, and Holy Spirit. But some Christians, influenced by Neoplatonism, rejected the idea that Jesus could be equal with God. Instead, they maintained that Jesus was part of God's creation and therefore not equal to God. This latter school of thought was called Arianism, after the Christian teacher Arius. (It should not be confused with Aryanism, a modern racial concept.) After protracted struggles, Arianism was condemned as a heresy, a word that comes from the Greek verb meaning "to choose for oneself" and which became the Church's term for false beliefs punished with damnation.

This new emphasis on orthodoxy (Greek for "correct teaching") was another major consequence of Christianity's conversion. Before Christianity became a legal religion, doctrinal disputes could only be addressed informally, by small local councils that had no power to enforce their decisions. In the fourth century, however, doctrinal disputes had real political consequences. At the same time, Christian intellectuals had to demonstrate that their beliefs could withstand intense scrutiny, and that they were in fact superior to pagan philosophy.

As a result of these trends, the Roman state became increasingly enmeshed in the governance of the Church. In 325 C.E., in recognition of this, Constantine summoned Christian representatives to the first ecumenical ("worldwide") meeting of the Christian community, the Council of Nicea, where Arianism was condemned and discrepancies over the canon of the Christian Bible were largely resolved. His successors carried this intervention much further, claiming to preside over Church councils as Christ's representatives on earth.

Essentially, these imperial interventions were an extension of Augustan policies, which had made the emperor *pontifex maximus*, Rome's high priest. It began to look as though this tradition would continue, and that secular and spritual authority would be combined in the person of the emperor.

New Attitudes toward Women and the Body

Even though they had long been deacons and may even have performed priestly duties, women were now firmly and completely excluded from any position of power within the Church. This was an enormous change. Jesus had included many women among his close followers, and one of the early gospels (now rejected from the biblical canon) was ascribed to Mary Magdalene. Paul had relied on women to organize and preside over churches, and had declared in one letter (Galatians 3:28) that there should be no distinctions of gender, rank, or ethnicity among Christians. Women like Perpetua were prominent among the martyrs, and were often regarded as prophets.

What acounts for this drastic reversal? Three factors can be clearly identified. When Christianity was absorbed into the staunch patriarchy of Rome, it could no longer promote the authority of women. The Church now replicated the structures of governance that had been the province of men since the founding of the Republic. It thus had the capacity to censor writings that represented women as the companions of Jesus and as founders of the religion based on his teachings. These efforts were so successful that it was not until the Dead Sea Scrolls were discovered that the gospel attributed to Mary Magdalene (among other writings) was known to exist.

The second factor was the growing identification of Christianity with Roman cults that emphasized masculinity, particularly the worship of Sol Invictus and the soldier-god Mithras. This was a deliberate strategy. It is easier to convert people to a new religion if that religion embraces elements of other religions. In common with these two cults, Christianity emphasized the heroic suffering and death of a male god and his eventual victory over death itself. Christ was increasingly identified with Sol Invictus and his birthday came to be celebrated on December 25, which marked the passing of the winter solstice.

The third factor contributing to women's exclusion from power was the new emphasis on asceticism. As we noted above, Neoplatonism taught that the goal of life was to liberate the soul from the tyranny of bodily desires. None of this was emphasized in the teachings of Christ. Quite the contrary: Christ celebrated the body, and had encouraged feasting,

touching, bathing, and marriage. His followers insisted that he had been bodily resurrected, and that the bodies of all the faithful would be resurrected, too. Although early Christians had to be willing to sacrifice their lives for their faith, if need be, they were not required to renounce pleasures.

After Christianity became legal, however, there were few opportunities to "bear witness" through martyrdom. Instead, some Christians began to practice asceticism as an alternative path to sanctity. This meant renunciation of the flesh, especially sex and eating: activities both associated with women, who were in charge of any household's food supply and who were (obviously) sexual partners. A new spiritual movement called monasticism also took hold, providing an alternative lifestyle for men who wanted to reject the world entirely; the word for this movement and its followers comes from the Greek word *monos*, "alone." Early monks lived as hermits and practiced extraordinary feats of self-denial and self-abasement. Some penned themselves in small cages, while others hung heavy weights around their necks. A monk named Simeon "the Stylite" lived on top of a high pillar for thirty-seven years while crowds gathered below to marvel.

SAINT SIMEON THE STYLITE. This gold plaque dating from the sixth century depicts the exertions of the ascetic saint who defied the devil (shown as a huge snake) by abusing his own body. Admirers wishing to speak to the saint could climb the ladder shown on the left. ■ *What do you make of the relationship between the luxurious medium of this image (gold) and the austere message it conveys?*

This extreme denial of the body was a departure not only from previous Christian practices but from the practices of nearly all civilizations up to this point. All ancient religions celebrated sexuality as a delight, as well as a necessity. Moreover, marriage was so important a marker of social respectability in the ancient world that unmarried men were objects of deep suspicion. Furthermore, Romans had regarded citizens' bodies as being at the service of the state: men as soldiers and fathers, women as mothers and wives. Now, however, some Christians were asserting that to serve God fully meant no longer serving the state—or posterity—by bearing children.

This was a revolutionary shift. Celibacy for both men and women began to be preached as the highest spiritual standard. Marriage remained acceptable for average people, the laity, but was often represented as a second-best option. Moreover, because pseudo-scientific theories stemming back to Aristotle posited that women were inherently more lustful than men, the denigration of sexuality had a disproportionately negative effect on attitudes toward women.

Christians and Pagans

The urban focus of Christianity is reflected in the Latin word referring to a non-Christian: *paganus*, meaning someone who lives in the countryside. The implication is that only a rustic would cling to the old Roman religion and so spoil his chances of advancement. For as Christians came to occupy positions of power, men with political ambitions were increasingly forced to convert—or at least to conform.

Constantine had retained both pagan and Christian officials in his court, but his successors were less inclined to tolerate competing faiths. (The sole exception was Julian "the Apostate" [r. 360–63], Constantine's nephew, who attempted to revive traditional Roman piety.) By 391, the emperor Theodosius (r. 379–95) had prohibited pagan worship. Within three generations, Christianity had gone from being a persecuted faith to a persecuting religion. Theodosius even removed the altar to the goddess Victory from the Senate house, prompting pagan loyalists to prophecy the end of the empire. Fifteen years later, Rome fell to a barbarian army.

SHIFTING CENTERS AND MOVING FRONTIERS

In 324, Constantine broke ground for the capital city he named after himself. It was built on the site of a settlement called Byzantium, chosen for its strategic location at the

mouth of the Black Sea and the crossroads between Europe and Asia. It would remain the political and economic center of the Roman Empire until 1453, when it was conquered by the Ottoman Turks and became the capital of a new empire (see Chapters 11 and 12).

East and West

The founding of Constantinople epitomizes the shift in Rome's center of gravity from west to east. It also signalled Constantine's intention to abandon the institution of the tetrarchy. Instead, imperial succession became hereditary—the very form of dynastic monarchy that Romans had rejected 800 years earlier. Even more ominously, Constantine divided the empire among his three sons. Civil war ensued, made more bitter because each son represented a different faction within the Church. As a result, the empire became ever more fragmented. The last ruler who could claim to govern a united Rome was the same Theodosius who outlawed its venerable religion. Then he, too, divided the empire between his sons.

As we have seen, there had always been linguistic and cultural differences between the Greek- and Latin-speaking peoples under Roman rule. Now these differences were heightened. The Greek East was becoming more prosperous and more central to imperial policy; the Latin West was becoming poorer and more peripheral. Rome itself, which had been demoted to provincial status under Diocletian, now lost even its symbolic position: the Italian city of Ravenna on the Adriatic coast became the new stopping-place for emperors and ambassadors traveling to the administrative centers of Milan and Trier. Thereafter, only two of Constantine's successors ever visited Rome, and none of them lived there.

Internal and External Pressures

The shifting center of the empire and the widening gap between East and West were not the only fault lines emerging in this period. There were also secessionist movements among residents of Britannia, Gaul, Hispania, and Germania. The residents of Egypt were particularly affected by high levels of taxation, which targeted their rich agricultural lands. Meanwhile, North Africans and other citizens living in the empire's interior regions were increasingly ignored by authorities. Italians especially resented their status as provincial subjects of Constantinople. The fourth-century empire was slowly dissolving into its constituent parts.

It was also coming under renewed pressure from its borders. Since the third century, the growing power of a new Persian dynasty, the Sassanids, had shifted Roman military weight to the eastern frontier, reducing the number of troops stationed elsewhere. Partly as a result of this, the western empire suffered a devastating series of raids along the porous frontier of Germania. Relations between Romans and their non-Roman neighbors had been generally peaceful. But now, starting in the early fifth century, a new wave of settlers moved into the empire's oldest provinces, permanently altering their histories and cultures.

From the Periphery to the Center

The tribes that lived along the empire's northern frontiers were barbarians in the pure sense of that (Greek) term: they did not speak either of the empire's civilized languages and they did not live in cities. But in no sense were they a savage people. They were settled agriculturalists and sophisticated metalworkers who had enjoyed trading relationships with the Roman world for centuries. In some frontier areas, entire tribes had become Roman *foederati*: allied troops who reinforced Roman garrisons or even took their places when legions were withdrawn. By the end of the fourth century, many of these tribes had even adopted the form of Christianity preached by disciples of Arius. Although this made them heretics from the perspective of the institutional Church, it also tied them more closely to Roman civilization.

What altered this relatively peaceful coexistence? Our study of many previous civilizations has prepared us to answer this question: the arrival of new peoples, and the subsequent struggle for land and resources. During the mid-fourth century, a group of nomadic herdsmen known as the Huns began to migrate westward from central Asia, into the region north and east of the Black Sea. Around 370, their arrival forced a number of other groups, notably the Goths, to migrate south and west—and in a hurry. Within a few years, they had reached the Roman frontier along the Danube River. Although the Goths had been clients of the Roman state for several centuries, they were now refugees, and too numerous and too desperate to repel by force. The Romans therefore permitted them to cross the Danube and settle within the empire. In return for food and other supplies, they were to guard the region against other migrant groups.

Local officials, however, failed to uphold their end of the bargain. Instead, they forced the starving Goths to sell themselves and their children into slavery in return for food. So in 378, the Goths revolted and the Roman army sent to suppress them was defeated at Adrianople. Peace was restored by accommodating the Goths' demands for goods and farmland and by enrolling them in the Roman army under their own military leaders.

A Senator Defends the Traditional Religion of Rome

In 382 the emperor Theodosius ordered the removal of the ancient altar dedicated to the goddess of Victory from the Senate chamber in Rome, as part of his efforts to make Christianity the dominant religion in the empire. This controversial move sparked heated debate and strong protests from Rome's senatorial elites. The following statement of their case was made by Quintus Aurelius Symmachus (c. 345–402), at that time prefect of the city of Rome.

 o what is it more suitable that we defend the institutions of our ancestors, and the rights and destiny of our country . . . than to the glory of these times, which is all the greater when you understand that you may not do anything contrary to the custom of your ancestors? We demand then the restoration of that condition of religious affairs which was so long advantageous to the state. . . .

For who is so friendly with the barbarians as not to require an Altar of Victory? . . . But even if the avoidance of such an omen were not sufficient, it would at least have been seemly to abstain from injuring the ornaments of the Senate House. Allow us, we beseech you, as old men to leave to posterity what we received as boys. The love of custom is great. . . . Where shall we swear to obey your laws and commands? By what religious sanction shall the false mind be terrified, so as not to lie in bearing witness? All things are indeed filled with God, and no place is safe for the perjured, but to be urged in the very presence of religious forms has great power in producing a fear of sinning. That altar preserves the concord of all, that altar appeals to the good faith of each, and nothing gives more authority to our decrees than that the whole of our order issues every decree as it were under the sanction of an oath. . . .

Let us now suppose that Rome is present and addresses you in these words: "Excellent princes, fathers of your country, respect my years to which pious rites have brought me. Let me use the ancestral ceremonies, for I do not repent of them. Let me live after my own fashion, for I am free. This worship subdued the world to my laws, these sacred rites repelled Hannibal from the walls, and the Senones [Gauls] from the capitol. Have I been reserved for this, that in my old age I should be blamed? I will consider what it is thought should be set in order, but tardy and discreditable is the reformation of old age."

We ask, then, for peace for the gods of our fathers and of our country. It is just that all worship should be considered as one. We look on the same stars, the sky is common, the same world surrounds us. What difference does it make by what pains each seeks the truth? We cannot attain to so great a secret by one road; but this discussion is rather for persons at ease, we offer now prayers, not conflict.

Source: Excerpted from *A Select Library of the Nicene and Post-Nicene Fathers*, 2nd Series, Vol. X, (New York: 1896), pp. 411–14.

Questions for Analysis

1. How does Symmachus's defense exemplify the traditional values of the Roman Republic?

2. How does Symmachus justify the coexistence of Christianity and Rome's state religion? How would a Christian refute his position?

3. Less than a decade after the altar's removal, Theodosius outlawed all religions but Christianity. Based on your reading of this letter, how would that edict have affected Romans like Symmachus?

But when Theodosius divided the empire between his two young sons, their military advisors constantly undermined one another. This provided an opening for Alaric, a young leader of the Goths. Targeting the wealthier East, he led his army into Greece, looting or capturing many ancient cities, including Athens. In a desperate attempt to halt these incursions, Alaric was offered a Roman military command and encouraged to move into Italy. Meanwhile, the Huns had arrived in the region corresponding to modern-day Hungary, forcing several other peoples westward toward the Rhine. In 406, a people known as the Vandals invaded Gaul but were repulsed by Alaric and his Goths.

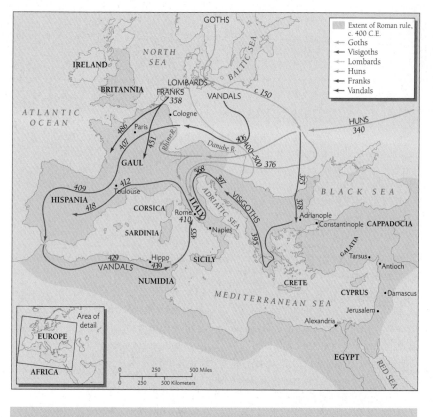

THE MIGRATIONS OF ROME'S FRONTIER PEOPLES. ▪ *What do the routes followed by these different peoples suggest about their identities and motives?* ▪ *Why did so many converge on Rome, even though the city was no longer the capital of the Roman Empire?* ▪ *Why did the Romans refer to these peoples as "barbarians"?*

Alaric seems to have wanted to win a permanent place for himself in the imperial hierarchy. Yet he did not understand how to use violence as a means toward that end, as many aspiring emperors had before him. In 410, after a protracted siege, his army even sacked the city of Rome. By now, though, Rome had little to offer in the way of spoils. So many of the Goths moved on, eventually settling in southern Gaul and Hispania, where they established what came to be known as the Visigothic ("West Gothic") kingdom. Others, known as the Ostrogoths ("East Goths") remained in Italy. The Vandals, meanwhile, crossed the Strait of Gibraltar to settle in North Africa. Other tribes, including the Franks and the Burgundians, followed the Vandals across the Rhine into Gaul and established kingdoms of their own.

A generation later, the Huns—whose migrations had set all of these gears in motion—themselves invaded Roman territory under the leadership of their warlord, Attila. Britannia, meanwhile, had been abandoned when its remaining legions were hastily withdrawn in 410. Eventually, its mixed population of Romans and Celts were overcome by invaders from northwestern Germania and Scandinavia: Angles, Saxons, and Jutes. These conquering tribes were so efficient that they dominated all but the westernmost and northern portions of the island within a few generations. Many Celts accordingly settled in the regions where Celtic languages are still spoken today, including Wales and Scotland. The rest of Britain became Angle-land: England (see Chapter 7).

The last Roman emperor in the West was an ineffectual usurper derisively known as Romulus Augustulus ("Little Augustus"), who was deposed in 476 by a mixed band of barbarians and disgruntled Romans. Viewed from the perspective of Constantinople, this event was decisive; the only way Rome's imperial agenda could be carried forward in the West was through a strong barbarian ruler. Luckily, the emperor Zeno (r. 474–91) knew just the man: Theodoric, the son of an Ostrogothic king who had been sent to Constantinople as a hostage and raised in the civilized surroundings of the imperial court. After a decade of fierce fighting, Theodoric and his imperially equipped Gothic army managed to establish an Ostrogothic kingdom based in Ravenna, which he ruled (with imperial support from Constantinople) until his death in 526.

The Impact of the Fifth-Century Migrations

The migrations of the fifth century exposed the fragility of the empire's northern boundaries and penetrated to its core western provinces. Yet the groups that moved through these territories were never more than war-bands. So why couldn't long-established imperial cities sustain themselves?

By the beginning of the fifth century, many Roman legions in the West had been withdrawn to protect the richer East. Those that remained tended to be integrated into local populations, making it difficult to move troops even in an emergency. And even if the citizens of Rome's western provinces had been able to maintain a fighting force on the frontier, there was little reason to think that such expenditure was necessary. Many of their barbarian neighbors were so Romanized that cultural differences are difficult to trace.

THEODORIC THE OSTROGOTH. This coin shows the king in Roman dress but with the long hair characteristic of a barbarian chieftain. The inscription reads *Rex Theodericvs pivs princis*, "King Theodoric, pious prince." ▪ *How does this image compare to that of Constantine (see page 145)?*

In the East, by contrast, a thriving economy made it easier to equip and maintain a strong fighting force. Moreover, potential invaders could be bought off or bribed to direct their attention elsewhere—as Alaric had been. For all these reasons, the eastern empire prospered while the western empire floundered.

After the fifth-century migrations, these differences were exacerbated. Ten years after the Goths sacked Rome, the area was capable of producing only 15 percent of the revenues it had generated in 407. And as barbarian newcomers began to set up their own kingdoms in the West, these areas ceased to pay any taxes at all to imperial authorities.

The consequences of these structural changes were far-reaching. Although regional and local systems of exchange continued after 500, long-distance trade in bulk goods could be sustained only in the East. As markets disappeared in the West, skilled artisans had to find other ways to make a living, or had to emigrate. Standards of living there declined, and so did the overall population. It is likely that the population of western Europe did not return to its fourth-century levels for a thousand years, until just before the Black Death (see Chapter 10).

Other aspects of Roman life in the West changed, too, but more gradually. Roman bureaucracies often survived, although the proceeds from taxes now went to the new barbarian rulers or Christian bishops. Roman agricultural patterns, too, continued in most areas, while Roman aristocrats continued to dominate civic life and Roman cities continued to dominate their surrounding regions. Nor did the influx of new peoples bring an end to Roman culture or to the influence of Roman values. As King Theodoric was fond of remarking: "An able Goth wishes to be like a Roman; but only a poor Roman would want to be like a Goth."

THE SHAPING OF A NEW WORLDVIEW

Throughout these upheavals, Christian intellectuals were formulating a new outlook on the world that would remain dominant until the sixteenth century. As the empire succumbed to attack, it seemed clearer than ever that a new age was beginning. Christ had promised to come again at the end of time, when all human souls would be judged. How, then, should Christians prepare for that imminent event?

The men who forged answers to this question were contemporaries who knew and influenced one another, though they did not always agree. They are now regarded as saints and "fathers" of the Church: Jerome (c. 340–420), who came from the northeastern edge of Italy; Ambrose (c. 340–397), who grew up in Trier (Germany) and was eventually named bishop of Milan; and Augustine (354–430), born and raised in North Africa, where he became a bishop in later life.

Jerome: Translating the Christian Message

Jerome's signal contribution was his translation of the Bible from Hebrew and Greek into Latin. Known as the Vulgate or "common" version, Jerome's translation is vigorous, colloquial, and clear; its powerful prose and poetry would influence Latin authors for a thousand years. Jerome was also an influential commentator on the Bible's interpretation, encouraging readings that emphasized a passage's symbolic or allegorical significance, as well as its literal or historical meaning.

Jerome was among the first to argue that pagan learning could and should be adapted to Christian aims. Yet Jerome himself never succeeded in subordinating his love of classical authors to his love for God. He liked to tell a story about a dream he'd experienced, in which he arrived at the gates of Heaven and was asked by God if he were a Christian. When he replied that he was, God retorted, "You're not a Christian; you're a Ciceronian." Perhaps in an effort to compensate for this, Jerome became a rigorous ascetic and promoter of monasticism. He also held a narrow view of women's roles that exercised a strong influence on later Christian teachers.

Ambrose and the Authority of the Church

While Jerome was primarily a scholar, Ambrose was a man of the world who helped to define the relationship between the sacred authority of the Church and the secular authority of rulers. As patriarch of the administrative capital at Milan, for example, he fearlessly rebuked the pious emperor Theodosius for massacring innocent civilians in one of his periodic purges of pagan communities: until he did penance for his sins, Ambrose refused to admit him into his church. On matters of faith, Ambrose declared, "The emperor is within the Church, not above the Church."

Like Jerome, Ambrose was an admirer of Cicero—but because of Cicero's Stoicism, not his prose. He wrote an ethics handbook, *On the Duties of Ministers*, that drew heavily on Cicero's treatise *On Duties*, written nearly four centuries earlier for the senatorial elite of the Roman Republic. Unlike Cicero, however, Ambrose argued that the motive and goal of human conduct should be reverence for God, not social or political advancement. Ambrose also argued that God assists all Christians by sharing with them the power of divine grace, but extends more grace to some Christians than to others. This view would be refined and amplified by his disciple, Augustine.

The Salvation of Saint Augustine

Apart from Jesus, Augustine is often considered the greatest of all Christianity's founders. His theology is essential to the doctrine of the medieval Church and thus to modern Catholicism, and it also had a profound effect on Martin Luther and the development of Protestant Christianities (see Chapter 13). Many Christian philosophers describe themselves as neo-Augustinians.

Augustine's Christianity was the result of a long process of self-discovery which he described in a remarkable book: the *Confessions*, a series of autobiographical reflections addressed to God. For Augustine was not, as Jerome and Ambrose were, a confident Christian from the cradle. His father was a pagan, and although his mother was a Christian he scorned her influence and refused baptism. Full of ambition, he left North Africa for Italy when he was still a young man, winning early fame as a teacher and charismatic orator. All the while, he gravitated from one philosophical system to another without finding intellectual or spiritual satisfaction. He regarded Christianity as a religion for fools, and only his increasing doubts and the appeal of Ambrose's teachings drove him to enquire further. After a spiritual epiph-

any, Augustine decided at the age of thirty-three to embrace Christianity. His skills as a preacher and commentator led to his rapid advancement in the Church hierarchy, and he returned to North Africa as the bishop of Hippo Regis in 395.

Although he led an extremely active life—when he died in 430, he was defending Hippo against the Vandals—Augustine found time to write more than a hundred profound and powerful treatises analyzing the problems of Christian belief. All of these grapple with a basic question: if humanity is the creation of an omnipotent God whose nature is entirely good, why are human beings so profoundly wicked? He adduced himself as a supreme example. In the *Confessions*, he remembers that he and a few other boys once stole some pears from a neighbor's garden, simply for the sake of doing something bad. He also recounted his many sexual adventures as a young man, when rather than asking God's help in suppressing his desires he had prayed, "O God, give me chastity—but not right now!" In short, he argued that the human inclination toward evil is innate. But how, if we are the creatures of a good God?

Augustine traced the origin of evil back to the Garden of Eden, where God had given Adam and Eve the freedom to follow either his will or their own. All the evils that plague the world are thus the result of the human propensity to place our own desires ahead of God's. This fact alone would justify God's condemnation of all mankind. But because God is merciful, he chose instead to save some human beings through the sacrifice of his son, Jesus.

Why only some? Because human beings are inherently sinful, Augustine reasoned, they cannot achieve salvation on their own; they need to be led to accept Jesus by an act of God's grace. (Hence the power of Augustine's own transformative experience, which led him to embrace Christianity *against his own will*, but in accordance with God's.) By granting grace to some and not to others, God predestines a portion of the human race to salvation and sentences the rest to be damned. If this seems unfair, Augustine would answer that strict fairness would condemn everyone to Hell. Moreover, he would say that the basis for God's choice is a mystery far beyond the realm of human comprehension.

Defending the City of God

Augustine's audience consisted of converted Christians and intelligent skeptics, like he himself had been. And after the sack of Rome in 410, he knew that some Romans blamed Christianity for it. In response, Augustine wrote one of his most famous works, *On the City of God*, a new interpretation of human history. He argued that mankind has always been divided into two opposing societies: those who live for the

world and those who seek eternal life. The former belong to the City of Man and their rewards are the riches, fame, and power they may win on earth—all of which are tainted by sin. Only those predestined to salvation, members of the City of God, will be saved on Judgment Day.

Augustine knew that many biblical texts are obscure and that a certain amount of education is needed to understand them. In consequence, he approved of some Christians acquiring a classical education, so long as they directed their learning toward its proper end. Along with Jerome, Augustine thus formulated the rationale for Christianity's preservation of the pagan past.

CLASSICAL LEARNING AND THE CHRISTIAN LIFE

Jerome, Ambrose, and Augustine were members of the first generation to grow up in a world where Christianity was legal, even normal. For three centuries there had been no such thing as a Roman Christian: this was a contradiction in terms. Now, many Romans *were* Christians. How could these identities be reconciled? As we have seen, none of these influential teachers wanted to discard the heritage of the past. But for all of them it posed serious challenges. Since the time of Socrates, philosophy had been characterized by its capacity to absorb and blend many competing ideas. Christian intellectuals wanted to be regarded as philosophers, but they also wanted to replace the doctrines of pagan philosophy with the doctrine of Christ. To do this, they needed to make classical learning applicable to a Christian way of life.

Preserving and Recycling the Classics

Reinterpreting pagan culture for a Christian audience involved careful selection, something made easier by the fact that a gradual winnowing of Greek texts had already occurred in Alexandria centuries before and had continued in Rome. Those Roman authors whose works were most immediately useful to Christians, like Cicero and Virgil, enjoyed continued celebrity. So did the major classics of Latin poetry, as well as the histories that recorded the errors of Rome's pagan past. But texts that could not be readily adapted were subjected to careful editing. One of the men who undertook this task was Anicius Manlius Severinus Boethius (*boh-EE-thee-us*, c. 480–524), an aristocrat attached to the court of Theodoric. His goal was to preserve the best aspects of ancient learning in a series of handbooks

and anthologies that packaged and explained classical texts in ways appropriate for Christian readers.

Boethius devoted special attention to logic, translating several of Aristotle's treatises from Greek into Latin. Because Roman philosophers had never been much interested in logic, Boethius thus forged a crucial link between classical Greek thought and the new intellectual culture of Christianity. This is also evident in *The Consolation of Philosophy*, which he wrote in prison after Theodoric condemned him to death for treason. (The justice of the charge is unclear.) In this treatise, Boethius concludes that happiness is not found in earthly rewards such as riches or fame but in the "highest good," which is God. Yet he comes to this realization not through any reference to Christian revelation but through a series of imaginary conversations with "Lady Philosophy," the embodiment of wisdom. For the next millennium, Boethius's *Consolation* was one of the most read and imitated books in the West: the ultimate example of classical philosophy's absorption into the Christian worldview.

Monastic Education

The vital work of preserving selected classics was increasingly done by monks, whose way of life had undergone some significant changes during the fourth century. Leaders of

CASSIODORUS. This frontispiece from a Bible depicts Cassiodorus as a copyist and keeper of books. Monasteries were instrumental in changing the form of the book from the ancient scroll to the modern codex. Because their parchment pages were heavy, codices were customarily stored in cupboards, lying flat, as we see them here.

the monastic movement recognized that few men were capable of ascetic feats, and some disapproved of such showmanship. Rather, they advocated a more moderate approach and emphasized the benefits of communal life. In the East, the most important figure in this new monasticism was Basil of Caesarea (c. 330–379). Basil's guidelines prohibited monks from engaging in prolonged fasts or extreme self-discipline. Instead, he encouraged useful work and silent meditation.

In the West, the most influential proponent of the monastic movement was a contemporary of Boethius, Benedict of Nursia (c. 480–c. 547), the son of a Roman nobleman. Benedict founded a monastery at Monte Cassino, southeast of Rome, where he urged his followers to adopt "a simple rule for beginners." Benedict's *Rule* is notable for its brevity and practicality. It established a carefully defined cycle of daily prayers, lessons, and communal worship. It laid down guidelines for what monks should eat and how the work of the monastery should be performed. Physical labor was encouraged, but there was also time for private study and contemplation. In all such matters, Benedict left much to the discretion of the monastery's abbot (from the Syriac word *abba*, "father").

Cassiodorus and the Classical Canon

Benedict believed that monks must study the Bible in order to participate fully in a life of worship. This meant they had to be educated along the lines prescribed by Augustine.

And because many monks entered religious life as children, the monastery would need to provide schooling. Through this somewhat roundabout path, classical learning entered the monastic curriculum.

The man largely responsible for this was Flavius Magnus Aurelius Cassiodorus Senator (c. 490–c. 583), a younger contemporary of Benedict. Like Boethius, Cassiodorus was attached to Theodoric's court, and was for many years the secretary in charge of the king's correspondence. He also wrote a *History of the Goths*, which depicted Theodoric's people as part of Rome's history. After Theodoric's death, Cassiodorus founded an important monastery at Vivarium in southern Italy. There he composed his most influential work, the *Institutes*. The *Institutes* is essentially a syllabus, a list of readings arranged so that a monk could begin with simpler, straightfoward works of pagan literature before moving on to more difficult works and finally to the demanding study of theology. Cassiodorus thereby defined a classical canon that formed the basis of Christian education in the West for a thousand years.

In order to ensure that monks had access to the necessary readings, Cassiodorus encouraged the copying of books. Monasteries thus became engines for the collection, preservation, and transmission of knowledge. Nearly all the Greek and Latin texts on which we rely for our study of Western civilizations survive because they were copied in monasteries. Monks also developed an important new information technology: the codex. For millennia, the book

After You Read This Chapter

Visit StudySpace for quizzes, additional review materials, and multi-media documents. **wwnorton.com/studyspace**

had been a scroll, a clumsy format that made searching for a particular passage difficult and confined the reader to one passage at a time. By contrast, the codex facilitates indexing (from the Latin word for "finger"), because a reader can flip back and forth among various pages and keep a finger in one place while looking at another. Codices also store information more safely and efficiently, because they compress many hundreds of pages within protective bindings. They are less wasteful, too, because texts can be copied on both sides of a page. They even make finding a given book easier, since titles can be written on the codex's spine. It's arguable, in fact, that the invention of the codex was more revolutionary than the invention of printing a thousand years later. Your copy of *Western Civilizations* is a codex—unless you are reading an e-book!

CONCLUSION

Since the English historian Edward Gibbon published the first volume of *The Decline and Fall of the Roman Empire* in 1776—a year when Britain's own empire suffered a setback—more has been written about "the fall of Rome" than the passing of any other civilization. Gibbon himself blamed Christianity, depicting it as a debilitating disease that sapped the empire's strength. Others have accused the barbarian peoples whose movements put pressure on Rome's frontiers. But even in the time of Augustus, Roman moralists had declared that Rome was already in decline. Indeed, any self-respecting republican would say that Rome fell when Augustus came to power.

More recent scholarship has stressed that this period should really be understood as one of transformation. No civilization is static and unchanging; civilizations, like human beings, are living organisms. Moreover, any evidence of Rome's decline can also be read as evidence of its adaptability. The imperial policies of Septimius Severus and Diocletian responded to the realities of Rome's size and diversity. The settlement of frontier peoples in Rome's western provinces gave rise to hybrid polities that found new uses for Roman buildings, political offices, and laws. Through Christianity, the language, adminstrative structures, and culture of ancient Rome were preserved and extended. The flexibility of the Roman political system made this possible, because it was inclusive to a degree no modern empire has ever matched.

This transformation changed what it meant to be Roman, to the extent that historians now call this period "late antiquity" to distinguish it from the classical world that preceded it. By the seventh century, indeed, so much had changed that the contours of three distinctive civilizations can be discerned, each one exhibiting different aspects of Roman influence and crystallizing around different regions of the former empire. We will explore each of these civilizations in Chapter 7.

PEOPLE, IDEAS, AND EVENTS IN CONTEXT

- What were the main differences between **JESUS** and other Jewish leaders of his day?
- How did **PAUL OF TARSUS** reach out to peoples of the **HELLENISTIC WORLD**? How did his teachings influence the development of early Christianity?
- In what ways did **DIOCLETIAN**'s division of the empire and his institution of the **TETRARCHY** respond to longstanding problems?
- How and why was Christianity changed under **CONSTANTINE**? What effects did this have on attitudes toward women and their role in the Church?
- How did the relocation of the imperial capital to **CONSTANTINOPLE** contribute to the growing divide between the **GREEK EAST** and the **LATIN WEST**? How did the mass migrations of frontier peoples further transform the West?
- What were the key contributions of **JEROME**, **AMBROSE**, and **AUGUSTINE** to the development of a specifically Christian outlook toward the end of the fourth century?
- How did **BOETHIUS**, **BENEDICT**, and **CASSIODORUS** reshape classical culture in the fifth century?

CONSEQUENCES

- In your opinion, which phenomenon had a more profound impact on Rome: the overextension of imperial power or the mass migration of peoples from Rome's frontier? Why?
- Few historians would now agree with the judgment of Edward Gibbon, who posited that Christianity destroyed the Roman Empire. But to what extent did Christianity alter the traditional values and infrastructure of the Roman state? Were these alterations inevitable?

Before
You
Read
This
Chapter

Rome's Three Heirs, 500–950

CORE OBJECTIVES

- **EXPLAIN** why Justinian's efforts to reunite the Roman Empire proved destructive.

- **IDENTIFY** the distinctive features of Byzantine culture.

- **UNDERSTAND** the reasons for Islam's rapid expansion.

- **DEFINE** the relationship between monasticism and secular power in early medieval Europe.

- **DESCRIBE** the importance of the Carolingian Empire.

A round the year 600, Anglo-Saxon tribes on the island of Britain were approached by missionaries sent from Rome. These Latin-speaking Christians faced an enormous challenge: they had to find a way to translate the central ideas of their faith into languages and concepts that made sense in a new cultural context. They also needed to look for ways to meld Roman practices with Anglo-Saxon ones, building churches on sacred sites and gradually turning the worship of pagan gods into the rituals of Christianity. An account of these negotiations comes down to us in *The History of the English Church and People*, written by a monk named Bede (c. 672–735) several generations later. Bede describes how Celtic and Anglo-Saxon peoples came to adopt Latin as a language of learning and worship. At the same time, he shows how Roman ideals were changed and adapted to meet new needs.

This is but one of the ways in which the legacy of Rome was transmitted and transformed during the pivotal period known as the Middle Ages. This term is an unfortunate one. In fact, "The Middle Ages" is a modern invention: in the seventeenth century, intellectuals began to argue that an intermediate, "medieval period" (*medium ævum*) separated their own "modern age" from the empire of ancient Rome, which many European states were trying to emulate by establishing empires of their own. But in fact, it is arguable that the period between 500 and 1500 was the beginning of that "modern age." In this era, the foundations of modern political institutions were laid. In this era, the relationships among Judaism, Christianity, and Islam were first articulated. In this era, three new civilizations became heirs of the Western civilizations formerly encompassed by the Roman Empire: the New Rome of Byzantium, the new empire of Islam, and the western European territories that looked increasingly to the Roman Church for leadership. Each civilization preserved and modified different aspects of their shared inheritance, and our world is still being shaped by the interactions among them.

JUSTINIAN'S IMPERIAL AMBITIONS

As we observed in Chapter 6, the eastern and western portions of Rome's empire were divided along linguistic, cultural, and economic lines. By the end of the fourth century, this division also became political. The Ostrogothic conquest of Italy under Theodoric (r. 493–526)—which was supported by the imperial government—briefly placed Constantinople in a position to influence affairs in the old Roman heartland. But in 535 this Ostrogothic kingdom was overthrown in an attempt reunify the Roman Empire.

The man responsible for this was Justinian (r. 527–65), the most ambitious emperor since Constantine. Although his efforts to reconstruct the empire ultimately failed, they had a lasting influence on the entire Mediterranean world.

The Codification of Roman Law

Justinian's most positive and lasting accomplishment was his codification of Roman law. This was a necessary project, and long overdue: since the time of the third-century jurists (Chapter 5), the number of statutes and legal decisions had multiplied, while social and political conditions had changed so radically that many legal principles could no longer be applied. To carry out this work, Justinian appointed a team of lawyers under the supervision of a jurist called Tribonian. Within two years, this commission published the Code, a systematic compilation of imperial statutes which was later supplemented by the Novels (*Novellae*, "new laws").The commission also completed the Digest, a summary of the writings of Rome's great legal authorities. Its final product was the Institutes, a textbook of legal principles. Together, these four volumes constitute the *Corpus Juris Civilis*, or the "body of civil law." Eventually it would influence the legal systems of many European nations.

The *Corpus* also had a profound impact on political philosophy. Starting from the maxim that "what pleases the prince has the force of law," it granted unlimited powers to the emperor and was therefore adopted by early modern rulers as a foundation for absolutism (see Chapter 15). But the *Corpus* also provided support for constitutional forms of government, because it maintained that a sovereign's powers are delegated to him by the people, and that what is mandated by the people can also be taken away by them. Equally important is the fundamental principle that the state is a corporate body, not the extension of an

THE MEDITERRANEAN WORLD UNDER JUSTINIAN, 527–65. Compare this map with the one on page 144. (Here, the green shading represents those regions controlled by Justinian.) ▪ *What was the geographical extent of Justinian's empire?* ▪ *Which areas of the former Roman Empire did Justinian not attempt to reconquer?* ▪ *What may have been the strategy behind this decision?*

individual's private property. The modern conception of the state as a public entity derives from the legal maxims of the *Corpus*.

Justinian's Attempted Reconquest

Justinian's initial efforts to reunite the Roman Empire seemed successful. In 533, his general Belisarius conquered the Vandal kingdom of northwest Africa, thereby facilitating campaigns in Ostrogothic Italy and Visigothic Spain. By 536, he appeared poised to occupy Rome's old homeland. But these early victories were illusory. When Justinian died in 565, the human and financial costs of these campaigns had drastically strained imperial resources. The Roman army in Italy was overextended, and Justinian's need to levy soldiers had led to oppressive taxes which undermined support for his imperial project.

Justinian's campaigns also distracted attention from dangers closer to Constantinople: in particular, the developing strength of Persia under the Sassanid dynasty. His successors were eventually forced to withdraw their troops from Italy and North Africa. This left both regions dangerously exposed to further invasions and still failed to protect the eastern frontier.

Justinian's Impact on the West

Justinian's wars proved more devastating to Italy than the previous incursions of barbarian peoples. Around Rome, the vital supply lines of the aqueducts were cut and the elaborate system of conduits, drainage ditches, and reservoirs was destroyed. In 568 a new people, the Lombards, took advantage of the chaos to conquer the northern third of the peninsula. Thereafter, Italy would be divided between Lombard territories in the north and imperial territories in the southeast, with Rome and its region precariously sandwiched between them. The controlling forces within these territories would change over time, but this tripartite division remained the essential political configuration of Italy until the nineteenth century. It divides Italian politics to this day.

Meanwhile Constantinople's control over North Africa lasted only a few generations longer. Weakened by religious conflict and heavy taxation, this area fell easily to invading Muslims in the seventh century, along with Egypt and the rest of Roman Africa (see below). Meanwhile, tensions between Arian Visigoths and their Latin subjects in Hispania continued even after after the Visigothic king officially submitted to the Roman church in 587. This mutual hostility would subsist until the Visigothic kingdom, too, was largely absorbed by Islam. By the end of the eighth century, Christian rulers controlled only the northernmost parts of the Iberian peninsula, and Al-Andalus (Muslim Spain) became part of a new Islamic world.

THE ROMAN EMPIRE OF BYZANTIUM

With the failure of Justinian's imperial project, the history of the Eastern Roman Empire can be said to enter a new phase. Indeed, many historians regard it as a new empire,

JUSTINIAN AND THEODORA. These sixth-century mosaics from the Church of San Vitale, in the imperial capital of Ravenna, show the emperor and empress processing toward the main altar of the church carrying the holy vessels used for the consecration of bread and wine. ▪ *What do these images convey about the sacred and secular powers of both figures?*

the Byzantine Empire, from the name of the ancient port where Constantinople was situated. Byzantium thus became *one* of Rome's three heirs, not the sole heir of Roman authority, as Justinian had claimed. But according to its inhabitants, it never ceased to be Rome, and they were never anything but Romans.

As a result of Justinian's policies, however, this Rome was struggling for survival. By 610, the Greek-speaking dynasty that began with Heraclius (r. 610–41) was unable to extend its influence farther west than the Adriatic. Meanwhile, the Persians had conquered almost all of the empire's eastern and southern territories in Syria and Palestine. They had even plundered Jerusalem. With an enormous effort, Heraclius rallied his remaining military powers and routed the Persians, recapturing Jerusalem in 627.

But these gains were short-lived. Arab armies, inspired by the new religion of Islam, soon occupied the newly reconquered Byzantine territories and claimed Jerusalem as a holy site for Muslims. They also absorbed the entire Persian Empire and rapidly made their way westward to North Africa. They then took to the sea, and in 677 attempted a naval conquest of Constantinople. Repulsed, they made another attempt in 717. This new threat was countered by the emperor Leo III (r. 717–41). Deploying keen strategy and a secret incendiary mixture now known as "Greek fire" (of course, the Byzantines called it "Roman fire"), Leo's forces were able to defeat the Arabs. Over the next few decades, moreover, Byzantium reconquered most of Asia Minor, which remained the imperial heartland for the next 300 years.

Sources of Stability

In many ways, the internal politics of the Byzantine Empire were as tumultuous as the history of its changing neighborhood. Because all power was concentrated in the imperial court at Constantinople, opposition usually took the form of intrigue, treason, and violence. Indeed, Byzantine politics is now so famous for its cloak-and-dagger complexity that the word *byzantine* denotes devious or elaborate systems of courtship and bureaucracy. Yet many able rulers in Byzantium wielded their powers very effectively, while a centralized government continued to function even in times of upheaval. No polity in western Europe had anything like it until a much later period.

Strong, self-perpetuating political institutions thus constituted a major source of stability in Byzantium and offer an explanation for the extraordinary longevity of the empire's core provinces: nearly a thousand years. The imperial bureaucracy in Constantinople regulated prices and wages, maintained systems of licensing, and controlled exports and trade. Its highly educated officials also supervised many aspects of social and cultural life, overseeing schools, the organization of the Orthodox Church, and the observance of religious rites and holidays. Established bureaucracies also regulated the army and navy, the courts, and the diplomatic service.

Another source of stability was Byzantium's well-managed economy, which was far superior to that of western Europe. Commerce and cities continued to flourish as they had done in late antiquity. Constantinople became a central emporium for Far Eastern luxury goods and western raw materials. The empire also nurtured and protected its own industries, most notably the manufacture and weaving of silk; and it was renowned for its stable gold and silver coinage, which undergirded the entire economy. Nor was Constantinople the only great urban center of Byzantium. The Hellenistic capital Antioch and the bustling cities of Thessalonica and Trebizond each dwarfed any western European city. Constantinople may have had a population of close to a million when Paris was still a village and Rome may have had only a few thousand people living among the ruins.

Orthodoxy, Iconoclasm, and Identity

Law, strong governance, and a thriving economy: viewed from our perspective, these seem to be the basis of Byzantine civilization. Yet the inhabitants of Byzantium seem to have cared more about religion. In old Rome, the *mos maiorum* had undergirded Roman pride and superiority (Chapter 5); in New Rome, Orthodox Christianity occupied the same fundamental place. Intense preoccupation with questions of religious doctrine could thus be a catalyst for political and social dissension, but it was also essential to Byzantine identity and endowed the empire's inhabitants with a sense of shared purpose.

The most contentious issue resulted in a violent clash over the meaning and use of religious images, known as the Iconoclast ("image-breaking") Controversy. Christians had long been accustomed to expressing their devotion to Christ and the saints through the making and veneration of images. At the same time, however, there was an awareness that any representation of a holy person came close to being a form of idolatry, something that Jewish tradition strongly condemned. Although Christians insisted that images were only *aids* to worship, not *objects* of worship, the line between the two was always fine.

In Byzantium, where the veneration of icons was an especially potent part of daily devotion, any suggestion that such images should be suppressed or destroyed was bound to be divisive. Yet iconoclasts argued that honoring images was blasphemous, and that Christ's divinity could not be represented artistically. Traditionalists, known as iconodules, responded that images themselves were never objects of worship; rather, icons were windows through which a glimpse of Heaven might be granted to human beings.

The Iconoclast movement was initiated by the same Emperor Leo III who had saved Constantinople from invasion by Muslims, and it is even possible that the iconoclasm so central to Islamic belief played an influential role in his thinking: in other words, it may have been his attempt to answer one of Islam's greatest criticisms of Christianity. The emperor may also have intended to reassert control over the Orthodox Church and thus to combat the growing strength of monasteries, which were major producers of

icons, as well as books. So when the monasteries rallied to the cause of images, Leo's successors took this opportunity to confiscate much of their wealth.

The Iconoclast Controversy was resolved toward the end of the eighth century, and in favor of the iconodules, the promoters of religious imagery. But it had some long-lasting effects. One was that much of the art produced or preserved in Byzantium was destroyed by imperial edict. A second consequence was the opening of another religious and political breach between the Greek East and the Latin West. Prior to Emperor Leo's iconoclastic initiatives, the patriarch of Rome—known familiarly as "papa" in Latin slang—had often been a close ally of Byzantium's rulers. But iconoclasm called into question not only the veneration of images but the cult of the saints, and by extension the claims of papal primacy that were based on the Roman patriarch's claim to be Saint Peter's successor.

The ultimate defeat of iconoclasm also crystallized some characteristics of Byzantine identity. One was a renewed emphasis on the Orthodox faith of the empire as the key to political unity and military success. This emphasis on tradition helped orthodoxy gain new adherents in the ninth and tenth centuries, but it also reinforced the hegemony of Constantinople's own Christian traditions, marginalizing those of Syria and Armenia. Fear of heresy tended to inhibit freedom of thought, too. Although the Byzantine emperors eventually founded a university in Constantinople, its students and faculty were never permitted to express dissenting opinions or to engage in any significant degree of intellectual speculation—in marked contrast to the freewheeling intellectual atmosphere cultivated by the universities of western Europe (see Chapters 8 and 9).

Tradition and Innovation

Although religion was central to the identity of Romans in Byzantium, so was their direct link with the Hellenistic past. Byzantine schools based their instruction on classical Greek literature to a degree that might seem surprising given the more tentative attitude toward classical learning in western Europe (Chapter 6). Educated people around the Byzantine court who quoted only a single line of Homer could expect their listeners to recognize the entire passage from which it came. In the English-speaking world, only the King James Bible has ever achieved the same degree of cultural saturation.

Byzantine scholars also studied the philosophy of Plato and the historical prose of Thucydides intensively. By contrast, Aristotle's works were less well known. Meanwhile,

Debating the Power of Icons

> The Iconoclast Controversy of the eighth century divided Byzantine society and was a factor in the growing division between the Latin Church of Rome and the Eastern Orthodox Church. The excerpts below are representative of the two main arguments voiced at the time. The first is from a treatise by John of Damascus (c. 675–749), a Christian in the service of the Muslim Umayyad caliphs. The second is an official report issuing from the synod convened by the emperor Constantine V (r. 741–75) in 754. Constantine was carrying forward the iconoclastic policies of his father, Leo III.

John of Damascus on Holy Images

Now adversaries say: God's commands to Moses the law-giver were, "Thou shalt adore the Lord thy God, and thou shalt worship him alone, and thou shalt not make to thyself a graven thing that is in heaven above, or in the earth beneath." . . .

These injunctions were given to the Jews on account of their proneness to idolatry. Now we, on the contrary, are no longer in leading strings. . . . We have passed the stage of infancy, and reached the perfection of manhood . . . and we know what may be imaged and what may not. . . . An image is a likeness of the original with a certain difference, for it is not an exact reproduction of the original. Thus, the Son is the living, substantial, unchangeable Image of the invisible God, bearing in Himself the whole Father, being in all things equal to Him, differing only in being begotten by the Father. . . . That which is divine is immutable; there is no change in Him, nor shadow of change. . . . God has noted and settled all that He would do, the unchanging future events before they came to pass. In the same way, a man who wished to build a house, would first make and think out a plan. Again, visible things are images of invisible and intangible things, on which they throw a faint light. Holy Scripture clothes in figure God and the angels. . . . If, therefore, Holy Scripture, providing for our need, ever putting before us what is intangible, clothes it in flesh, does it not make an image of what is thus invested with our nature, and brought to the level of our desires, yet invisible? . . . For the invisible things of God since the creation of the world are made visible through images. We see images in creation which remind us faintly of God, as when, for instance, we speak of the holy and adorable Trinity, imaged by the sun, or light, or burning rays, or by a running fountain, or a full river, or by the mind, speech, or the spirit within us, or by a rose tree, or a sprouting flower, or a sweet fragrance. . . .

Source: Excerpted from *St. John Damascene on Holy Images*, trans. Mary H. Allies (London: 1898), pp. 6–12.

the living philosophical traditions of the pagan past were deemed dangerous to orthodox belief. Even Justinian, who had presided over the codification of ancient Roman (and thus pagan) law, registered his distrust of philosophy by shutting down the Athenian Academy founded by Plato. Eventually, the emperor Alexius Comnenus (d. 1118) would ban the teaching of Aristotelian logic. The traditions of Greek scientific inquiry and the advances of Hellenistic science were also neglected. Tradition was more highly prized than originality, as was preservation over innovation. The benefit of this, for posterity, is that Byzantium rescued Greek and Hellenistic writings for later ages. The vast majority of ancient Greek texts known today survive because they were copied by Byzantine scribes.

Also in contrast to the West, as we shall see, Byzantine classicism and learning were the products of an educational system that extended to the laity and was open to women as well as to men. This commitment to the formal education of women was especially unusual. Although most girls from aristocratic or prosperous families were educated at home by private tutors, they nevertheless mingled freely with their male counterparts at court or on social occasions, and many

Canons of the Synod of 754

It is the unanimous doctrine of all the holy Fathers and of the six Ecumenical Synods, that no one may imagine any kind of separation or mingling in opposition to the unsearchable, unspeakable, and incomprehensible union of the two natures in the one hypostasis or person. What avails, then, the folly of the painter, who from sinful love of gain depicts that which should not be depicted—that is, with his polluted hands he tries to fashion that which should only be believed in the heart and confessed with the mouth? He makes an image and calls it Christ. The name *Christ* signifies *God and man.* Consequently it is an image of God and man, and consequently he has in his foolish mind, in his representation of the created flesh, depicted the Godhead which cannot be represented, and thus mingled what should not be mingled. Thus he is guilty of a double blasphemy—the one in making an image of the Godhead, and the other by mingling the Godhead and manhood . . .

like the Monophysites, or he represents the body of Christ as not made divine and separate and as a person apart, like the Nestorians.

The only admissible figure of the humanity of Christ, however, is bread and wine in the holy Supper. This and no other form, this and no other type, has he chosen to represent his incarnation. Bread he ordered to be brought, but not a representation of the human form, so that idolatry might not arise. And as the body of Christ is made divine, so also this figure of the body of Christ, the bread, is made divine by the descent of the Holy Spirit; it becomes the divine body of Christ by the mediation of the priest who, separating the oblation from that which is common, sanctifies it. . . .

Source: Excerpted from *The Seven Ecumenical Councils of the Undivided Church*, trans. H. R. Percival, in *Nicene and Post-Nicene Fathers*, 2d Series, ed. P. Schaff and H. Wace (repr. Grand Rapids, MI: 1955), pp. 543–44.

Questions for Analysis

1. To what other phenomena does John of Damascus compare the making of images? How do these comparisons help him to make his argument in favor of them?

2. To what phenomena do the theologians of the synod compare the making of images? Why do they declare the bread and wine of the Eucharist to be the only legitimate representations of Christ?

3. What is the significance of the fact that John of Damascus did not fall under the jurisdiction of the emperor of Byzantium, but that of the Muslim Umayyad caliph? What conclusions can you draw about the relative religious freedoms in these two realms?

learned women were praised for being able to discourse on Plato or Pythagoras. There were also female physicians in the Byzantine Empire, another extraordinary departure both from ancient tradition and from the practices of western Europe until the latter part of the nineteenth century.

Byzantine achievements in the realms of architecture and art are also remarkable. The finest example of both may be the church of Hagia Sophia (Greek for "Holy Wisdom") in Constantinople, constructed at enormous cost under the patronage of Justinian. Its purpose was not to express pride in human accomplishment, but rather to symbolize the mysteries of the holy knowledge imparted by Christ to the soul of the believer. For this reason, the architects paid little attention to the external appearance of the building. The interior, however, was decorated with richly colored mosaics, gold leaf, colored marble columns, and bits of tinted glass set on edge to refract rays of sunlight like sparkling gems. Light appeared to be generated from within. The magnificent dome over its central square represented an unprecedented engineering feat, and was upheld by four great arches springing from pillars at the four corners of the square. Its effect is heightened by the many windows placed around the dome's rim, which convey the impression that it floats in midair.

Many aspects of Byzantine arts and learning exerted strong influence on the craftsmen and scholars of western Europe through New Rome's continued economic and cultural contact with portions of Italy. The basilica of San Marco in Venice (c. 1063) reflects this influence, as do medieval mosaics in such cities as Ravenna and Palermo. Greek-speaking monasteries in southeastern Italy also maintained close ties with their counterparts in the eastern empire, and many were allowed to practice the rituals of the Orthodox Church. But much of the heritage of Western civilizations that was cultivated in Byzantium was largely inaccessible elsewhere in Europe, as the knowledge of Greek became increasingly rare.

MUHAMMAD AND THE TEACHINGS OF ISLAM

In many ways, the civilization that formed around the religion of Islam mirrors the Roman Empire in its global reach and longevity. Islam (Arabic for "submission") also resembles the early Republic of Rome in that it demands from its followers not just adherence to common forms of worship but also to certain social and cultural norms. But whereas the Roman Empire undergirded Christianity and helped to advance it, the Islamic faith was itself the engine of imperial expansion. Indeed, Islam is unique among the major religions in the way that it *created* empires rather than relying on them.

The Revelations of Muhammad

Islam had its beginnings in Arabia, a desert land considered so forbidding that neither the Romans nor the Persians sought to conquer it. Arabian society was tribal, and did not revolve around urban settlements. But like the Hittites in the second millennium B.C.E. (Chapter 2), the Arabs' mobility, ingenuity, and pioneering spirit made them excellent explorers and long-distance traders. In the second half of the sixth century, they quickly established themselves as guides, couriers, and guardians of transit routes between Africa and Asia.

As part of this process, towns began to emerge. The most prominent of these was Mecca, a sacred site that lay at the crossroads of major caravan routes. Mecca was home to the Kaaba, a shrine housing the Black Stone worshiped by

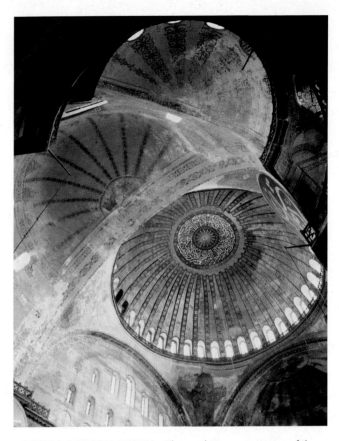

INTERIOR OF HAGIA SOPHIA. The revolutionary structure of the church, shown here, made it appear as if the enormous dome floated on light and air.

many Arabian tribes. The tribe that controlled this shrine, the Quraish (*kur-AYSH*), thus came to control the economic and spiritual life of the whole region.

Muhammad, the founder of Islam, was a member of this tribe. He was born in Mecca about 570. Until middle age he probably lived as a prosperous trader, little different from his fellow townsmen. At this time, the Arabs worshipped many gods. Yet like the ancient Hebrews they also acknowledged one god as more powerful. For the Hebrews, God was Yahweh; for the Arabs, Allah. But whereas the Hebrews' embrace of monotheism was a long and gradual process, Muhammad's dedication to Allah alone was a sudden spiritual epiphany experienced around 610.

At first, Muhammad was not very successful in gaining converts to this new faith, perhaps because tribal leaders feared that his teachings would diminish the importance of the Kaaba, and thus of Mecca. So Muhammad and a few loyal friends moved north to the settlement of Yathrib in 622. This migration—in Arabic, the Hijrah (*HIJ-ruh*)—marks the beginning of Muhammad's wider influence. Just as Christians date all events according to the birth of Jesus, so Muslims begin their dating system with the Hijrah.

Analyzing Primary Sources

A Sura from the Qu'ran

> The Qu'ran preserves the teachings of Muhammad in a series of suras, or chapters. Composed in verse forms that draw on much older traditions of Arabic poetry, they are meant to be sung or chanted. Indeed, the word Qu'ran means "recitations," referring both to Muhammad's method of revealing divine truths and to the Muslim practice of memorizing and repeating portions of this sacred scripture.

Sura 81: The Overturning

In the Name of God the Compassionate
the Caring

When the sun is overturned
When the stars fall away
When the mountains are moved
When the ten-month pregnant
   camels are abandoned
When the beasts of the wild
   are herded together   5
When the seas are boiled over
When the souls are coupled
When the girl-child buried alive
is asked what she did to deserve
   murder
When the pages are folded out   10
When the sky is flayed open
When Jahím [the Day of Reckoning]
   is set ablaze

When the garden is brought near
Then a soul will know what it
   has prepared
I swear by the stars that slide,   15
stars streaming, stars that sweep
   along the sky
By the night as it slips away
By the morning when the fragrant
   air breathes
This is the word of a messenger
   ennobled,
empowered, ordained before
   the lord of the throne,   20
holding sway there, keeping trust
Your friend [Muhammad] has
   not gone mad
He saw him on the horizon clear
He does not hoard for himself
   the unseen
This is not the word of a satan
   struck with stones   25

Where are you going?
This is a reminder to all beings
For those who wish to walk straight
Your only will is the will of God lord
   of all beings

Source: From *Approaching the Qu'ran: The Early Revelations*, trans. Michael Sells (Ashland, OR: 1999), pp. 48–50.

Questions for Analysis

1. What impressions of Arab culture emerge from this *sura*? What does the litany of unlikely or mystical events reveal about the values of Muhammad's contemporaries?

2. How does Muhammad speak of himself and his role in society?

Muhammad changed the name of Yathrib to Medina ("City of the Prophet") and established himself as its ruler. Yet he did not abandon his desire to exercise political and prophetic authority among his own people, the Quraish. Accordingly, he and his followers began raiding Quraish caravans traveling beyond Mecca. The Quraish could not continue to operate an extensive commercial enterprise in the face of such threats, and by 630 they submitted themselves to Muhammad's authority. Muhammad, for his part, ensured that the Kaaba was established as Islam's holy shrine, a status it maintains today. And because Mecca had long been a pilgrimage site and gathering place for tribes throughout Arabia, many people were exposed to Muhammad's teachings. At the time of his death in 632, Islam had become an established faith.

Muhammad and the Qu'ran

As its name indicates, the faith of Islam calls for absolute submission to Allah, the same God worshiped by Jews and Christians. The Muslim saying "there is no god but Allah" is more accurately translated as "there is no divinity but God." For Muslims, the history and prophecies of the Hebrews are therefore important components of their religion, as are the teachings of Jesus, who is venerated as a great prophet. But they consider Muhammad to be the last and greatest prophet, and the closest to God.

Muhammad's teachings are preserved in the sacred scripture of Islam, the Qu'ran (*kuhr-AHN*), an Arabic word meaning "recitations." This is because Muhammad recited his revelations to his listeners, and these were eventually gathered together and transcribed, a process that continued after Muhammad's death. Unlike the Christian gospels, which offer different perspectives on Jesus' ministry and which were recorded a generation or two after his crucifixion, the Qu'ran is considered a direct link with Muhammad. It is also unlike most books of the Bible because it takes the form of poetry, drawing on ancient genres of Arabic song.

Like Christianity, Islam teaches that a day of judgment is coming—and soon. On this day, the righteous will be granted eternal life in a paradise of delights, but wrongdoers will be damned to a realm of eternal fire. Every person is therefore offered a fundamental choice: to begin a new life of divine service or to follow their own path. If they choose to follow God, they will be blessed; if they do not, God will turn away from them. Thus the only sure means of achieving salvation is observance of the Five Pillars of the faith: submission to God's will as described in the teachings of Muhammad, frequent prayer, ritual fasting, the giving of alms, and an annual pilgrimage to Mecca (the Hajj).

Unlike Christianity, Islam is a religion without sacraments or priests. It more closely resembles Judaism as it developed after the Diaspora, when Jews no longer had access to the Temple but instead gathered around a master teacher (*rabbi*). Similarly, Muslims often rely on a community leader (*imam*) or scholar qualified to comment on matters of faith, who may also act as a judge in disputes. Like Judaism, Islam emphasizes the inextricable connection between religious observance and daily life, between spirituality and politics. There is no opposition of sacred and secular authority, as in Christianity. But in marked contrast to Judaism, Islam is a religion that aspires to unite the world in a shared faith. This means that Muslims, like Christians, consider it their duty to engage in the work of conversion. This further means that there will inevitably be competition between the followers of Christianity and Islam, as both try to carry out this mission.

THE WIDENING ISLAMIC WORLD

As we have frequently observed, the death of any charismatic leader precipitates a series of crises. Muhammad and Alexander the Great represent different types of leadership, but both created communities whose very survival seemed to depend on that leadership. Neither designated his own successor, and both left behind a number of close followers who disagreed as to the proper uses of the power they had inherited.

Arab Conquests

Muhammad's closest followers were his father-in-law, Abu-Bakr (*ah-BOO-BAK-uhr*), and an early convert named Umar. After Muhammad's death, Abu-Bakr took the title *caliph*, a word meaning "deputy" or "representative." In this capacity, he began a campaign to subdue various tribes unwilling to accept his authority as Muhammad's successor. In the course of this, Abu-Bakr's forces began to move northward beyond the borders of Arabia, where they met only minimal resistance from Byzantine and Persian armies.

When Abu-Bakr died two year later, he was succeeded as caliph by Umar, who continued to direct his growing warrior bands against Byzantium and Persia. In 636 they routed a Byzantine army in Syria and then occupied the cities of Antioch, Damascus, and Jerusalem. In 637 they took the Persian capital of Ctesiphon. By 651, the Muslim conquest of the entire Persian Empire was complete.

Islamic forces now turned westward, capturing Byzantine Egypt and extending their control throughout the rest of North Africa. Attempts to capture Constantinople were not successful, as we noted earlier, but in 711 Muslims crossed from North Africa into Visigothic Spain and quickly absorbed most of that territory, too. Within less than a century, they had conquered the ancient Near East and much of the Roman Mediterranean.

How can we explain this prodigious achievement? On a basic level, what motivated the Arabs had motivated the Sumerians, the Neo-Assyrians, the Greeks, the Macedonians, and the Romans: the search for richer territory and new wealth. There is little evidence that Arab Muslims attempted to convert subject peoples to the faith of Islam at this time. Instead, they aimed to establish themselves as a superior ruling class. Yet religious enthusiasm certainly played a crucial role in forging a shared identity among tribes hitherto at war with one another. This identity and sense of superiority must have been further strengthenend by the absence of any serious opposition. Indeed, many of the local populations living within the Persian and Byzantine empires were restive and exhausted by the demands of these far-reaching imperial bureaucracies. To them, conquest brought deliverance. The Arabs did not demand that Jews or Christians convert to Islam, and because they exacted fewer taxes, they were often preferred to the old rulers. For all these reasons, Islam quickly spread over the territory between Egypt and Iran, and has been rooted there ever since.

The Shi'ite–Sunni Schism

As Arab conquests widened the reach of Islam, disputes continued to divide the Muslims of Mecca. When the caliph Umar died in 644, he was replaced by a member of the Umayyad (oo-MY-yad) family, a wealthy clan that had originally resisted Muhammad's authority. Opponents of this new caliph, Uthman, rallied instead around Muhammad's cousin and son-in-law, Ali, whose family ties to Muhammad made him seem a more appropriate choice. When Uthman wasmurdered in 656, Ali's supporters declared him the new caliph. But Uthman's powerful family refused to accept this. Ali was murdered and another member of the Umayyad family replaced him. From 661 to 750, this Umayyad dynasty ruled the Islamic world, establishing its capital at Damascus in Syria.

Ali's followers, however, did not accept defeat. They formed a separate group known as the Shi'ites (from shi'a, the Arabic word for "faction"). The Shi'ites insisted that only descendants of Ali and his wife, Muhammad's daughter Fatimah, could legitimately rule the Muslim community. Moreover, the Shi'ites did not accept the customary religious practices (sunna) that had developed under the first two caliphs who succeeded Muhammad. Hence those Muslims who supported the Umayyad family and who did regard these customs as binding were called Sunnis. This division between Shi'ites and Sunnis has lasted until the present day. Often persecuted by the Sunni majority as heretics, Shi'ites consider themselves the only true exponents of Islam. Today, Shi'ites predominate in Iran and are the largest single Muslim group in Iraq, yet they constitute only one-tenth of the world's Muslims.

The Umayyad and Abbasid Dynasties

The political triumph of the Umayyads in 661 created a strong state centered on Damascus, formerly an administrative center of the Roman Empire. And in many ways, the Umayyad caliphate functioned as a Roman successor state; it even continued to employ Greek-speaking bureaucrats trained in the techniques of Byzantine governance. But the failure of its attacks on Constantinople checked Umayyad power, which was also being challenged by a rival dynasty, the Abbasids. In 750, the Abbasids led a successful rebellion with the help of the Persians, forcing the Umayyads to retreat to their territories in Al-Andalus (Spain).

In contrast with the Umayyads, the Abbasid caliphate stressed Persian elements over Roman ones. Symbolic of this change was its relocation from Damascus to Baghdad, the old Persian capital. The Abbasid caliphs also modeled their behavior on that of Persian princes, presiding over an extravagantly luxurious court. This is the world described in the 1001 Nights whose dominating presence is Harun al-Rashid, the caliph who ruled from 786 to 809. His reign marked the height of Abbasid power.

Meanwhile, the Umayyad dynasty continued to claim that it was the only legitimate sucessor of Muhammad. Relations between the Umayyads of Al-Andalus and Abbasids of Persia were therefore very cold; but because their realms were far apart, the hostility between them rarely erupted into war. Instead, the two courts competed for preeminence through literary and cultural patronage, much as the Hellenistic kingdoms had done (Chapter 4). Philosophers, artists, and especially poets flocked to both. The 1001 Nights was one

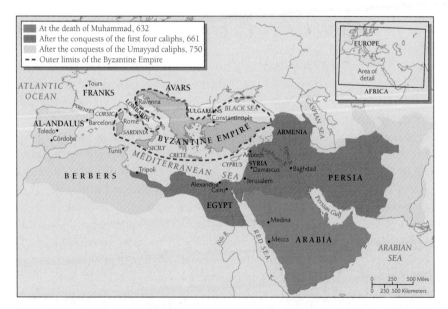

THE EXPANSION OF ISLAM TO 750. This map shows the spread of Islam from the time of Muhammad to the middle of the eighth century. ▪ *What was the geographical extent of Islam in 750?* ▪ *What role did the Byzantine Empire play in the expansion of Islam?* ▪ *What conclusions can you draw regarding the period of especially rapid expansion in the generation after Muhammad's death?*

ARABIC CALLIGRAPHY. Muslim artists experimented with the art of calligraphy to make complex designs, sometimes abstract but often representing natural forms. This ink drawing on paper dates from the seventh century, and also represents the Muslim mastery of papermaking.

product of this rivalry in Baghdad. Not to be outdone, the caliphs at the Umayyad capital of Córdoba amassed a library of more than 400,000 volumes—at a time when a European monastery that possessed 100 books qualified as a major center of learning.

Islamic Commerce and Industry

Alongside its political and military triumphs, the transformation of tiny settlements into thriving metropolitan commercial centers was one of Islam's most remarkable achievements. Conversion to Islam actually increased the reach of this economic infrastructure, as trading contacts grew in tandem with the growth of the Islamic world. By the tenth century, Muslim merchants had penetrated into southern Russia and equatorial Africa and had become masters of the caravan routes that led eastward to India and China. Ships from the Muslim world established new trade routes across the Indian Ocean, the Persian Gulf, and the Caspian Sea, and for a time dominated the Mediterranean as well.

The growth of Muslim commerce was also sustained by a number of important new industries. Mosul, in Iraq, was a center for the manufacture of cotton cloth; Baghdad specialized in glassware, jewelry, pottery, and silks; Damascus was famous for its fine steel and for its woven-figured silk known as "damask"; Morocco and Al-Andalus were both noted for leatherworking; Toledo produced excellent swords. These and other products were carried throughout the Mediterranean world by Muslim merchants. They were also carried into central Asia, along the road to China that came to be known as the Silk Road. With them went the Islamic faith, which took root among some peoples of modern India, Pakistan, and Afghanistan.

One commodity in particular deserves special mention: paper. Muslims learned papermaking from the Chinese and became became masters of the art in their own right. Paper was cheaper to produce, easier to store, and far easier to use than papyrus or parchment. As a result, paper replaced papyrus in the Islamic world by the early eleventh century—even in Egypt, the heartland of papyrus production for almost 4,000 years.

The ready availability of paper brought about a revolution in the Islamic world. Many of the characteristic features of Islamic civilization—record keeping, high levels of literacy, even the standard form of Arabic script—would have been impossible without it. Only in the thirteenth century would western Europeans begin papermaking, and they would continue to rely on the more durable parchment for the copying of most books and documents. It was not until the advent of print that paper began to replace parchment as the reading and writing material of western Europe.

Mobility, Opportunity, and Status

As the reach of Islam extended, the preeminence of trade and ease of travel increased geographical and social mobility. Muhammad's teachings, too, stressed the equality of all Muslim men. At the courts of Baghdad and Córdoba, in consequence, careers were open to men of talent, regardless of birth or wealth. And because literacy was remarkably widespread, many could rise through education and achieve top offices through enterprise and skill.

For those men wishing instead to embrace the religious life, Islam offered two main alternatives. One was that of the *ulama*, a learned man whose studies qualified him to offer advice on aspects of religious law and practice. Complementary to *ulamas* were the Sufis, mystics who stressed individual contemplation and the cultivation of spiritual ecstasy. Sufis were usually organized into brotherhoods and eventually made many succesful efforts to convert the peoples of Africa and India to Islam. Sufism also provided a channel for the most intense religious impulses. The ability of the *ulama* and the Sufis to coexist is testimony to the cultural pluralism of the Islamic world.

The absence of comparable careers for religious women, even comparable to those available to Christian nuns (see below), is a reminder of the limits often imposed by gender. There are significant exceptions, of course. Muhammad's favored wife, Aisha (ah-EE-sha, d. 678), played an important role in the creation and circulation of *hadith* (Arabic for "narrative"): stories and sayings that shed light on the Prophet's life and teachings. But in general, women did not benefit from Muslim egalitarianism and opportunity. They were valuable mostly as indicators of a man's wealth and status. Because the Qu'ran allowed any Muslim man to marry as many as four wives, the number of women available for marriage was often far smaller than the number of men who desired to marry. This made for intense competition, and those men who had wives and daughters needed to ensure that their prized assets were safeguarded. So women were usually kept from the sight of men who were not members of the family or trusted friends, and were housed in a segregated part of the residence called the *haram* ("forbidden place"). Within these enclaves, women vied with one another for precedence and worked to advance the fortunes of their children. But this was often the only power they could exercise.

Islam's Neighbors

For the inhabitants of Byzantium, the triumph of the Abbasid caliphate in the eighth century released the Mediterranean from the pressures of Umayyad expansion. Farther west, the Franks of Gaul also benefited. Because an Umayyad dynasty still controlled Al-Andalus, the great Frankish ruler Charlemagne (SHAHR-leh-mayn, r. 768–814) could counter their power by maintaining strong relations with the Abbasid caliphate. The most famous symbol of this connection was an elephant called Abul Abbas, a gift from Harun al-Rashid to Charlemagne. More important, however, was the flow of silver that found its way from the Abbasid Empire north through Russia and the Baltic into the Rhineland, where it was exchanged for Frankish exports, especially slaves: western Europeans who were captured and sold for profit by other western Europeans. Jewels, silks, spices, and other luxury goods from India and the Far East also flowed north and west into Frankish territory. These links with the Abbasid world helped to fuel the extraordinary achievements of Charlemagne's own empire, which had a lasting effect on the culture and politics of Europe.

THE CONVERSION OF NORTHWESTERN EUROPE

At the end of the sixth century, the Frankish chronicler Gregory of Tours (c. 538–594) considered himself a Roman, living in a Roman world. Gregory took it for granted that he and his male relatives should rule, by right of birth and status, over their cities and the surrounding countryside. Like others of his senatorial class, Gregory still spoke and wrote Latin—a rather different Latin from the polished prose of Cicero, but a Latin that would certainly have been comprehensible to the Romans of the Republic. And although Gregory was aware that the western territories of the Roman Empire were now ruled by Frankish, Visigothic, and Lombard kings, he regarded at least some of these kings as Roman successors because they ruled in accordance with Roman models.

Two hundred years later, this sense of direct continuity with the earlier Roman world was no longer tenable. Instead, intellectuals at Charlemagne's court would set out to revive a Roman Empire from which they felt estranged. They sought a *renovatio Romanorum imperii*, "a renewal of the empire of the Romans." This awareness of a break with the Roman past, which developed during the seventh century, was the consequence of profound changes.

Economic and Political Instability

Even though the economy of the Roman Empire had become increasingly regionalized during the third century (Chapter 6), the Mediterranean remained an effective nexus of trade and communication. By about 650, however, this Mediterranean world disintegrated. This was partly a result of Justinian's failed efforts to reconquer the Western empire, but imperial overtaxation of Egypt and North Africa also played a role. So did the temporary disruptions caused by Muslim raiders—temporary, because the merchants and rulers of Islam would soon do much to reconstruct and encourage patterns of commerce.

The most significant causes of economic instability in northwestern Europe were therefore internal. The cities of Italy, Gaul, and Hispania could no longer maintain their walls, their public buildings, and their urban infrastructures. Although bishops and their aristocratic kinsmen still governed from these cities and continued to provide a market for certain kinds of luxury goods, barbarian kings and their nobles were moving to the countryside during the seventh century, living as much as possible from the produce of their own estates rather than purchasing their supplies in the marketplace. At the same time, much agricultural land was passing out of cultivation. This is because the slaves or servile peasants who had farmed the large plantations for hundreds of years had no state to enforce their obedience; they were able to become more independent—yet they were also less effective. Productivity declined, as did revenues.

The coinage systems of western Europe were also breaking down, which meant that wealth ceased to be portable, hindering long-distance exchange. And in any case, gold coins were now too valuable to be useful in a local market economy. By the 660s, those western European rulers who were still in a position to mint coins and guarantee their value had shifted from a gold to a silver coinage. Indeed, Europe would remain a silver-based economy for the next thousand years, until the supply of gold from European conquests in Africa and America once again made a gold standard viable (see Chapter 11).

As a result of these processes, western Europe came to rely on a two-tier economy of a kind that had not been necessary in any Western civilization since the Lydians introduced a standardized currency in the sixth century B.C.E. (Chapter 3). Gold, silver, and luxury goods circulated among the very wealthy, but most people relied on barter and various substitute currencies to facilitate transactions. Lords collected rents from their peasants in food or labor, but then found it difficult to convert these in-kind payments into the weapons, jewelry, and silks that brought prestige. This was problematic not only for social reasons but for political ones: the power of lords depended on their ability to bestow such gifts on their followers (see **Interpreting Visual Evidence**). When they could not acquire these items through trade, they had to win them through plunder and extortion. Either way, the process led to violence.

The successful chieftains of this era therefore tended to be those whose areas of influence adjoined wealthy but poorly defended territories that could be easily attacked or blackmailed. Such "soft frontiers" provided land and booty which could then be distributed to followers. So long as more conquests were made, the process of amassing power and wealth would continue. But power acquired through plunder and conquest was inherently unreliable. A few defeats might speedily reverse the fortunes of lords reliant on it, leaving their followers to seek plunder elsewhere.

Another factor contributing to the instability of power in this world was the difficulty of ensuring its peaceful transfer. Most of the rulers who established themselves during the mass migrations of the fifth and sixth centuries did not come from the traditional royal families of their peoples, and thus faced constant opposition. Moreover, the groups who took possession of territories were usually made up of many different tribes, including a sizable number of displaced Romans. Such unity as they possessed was largely the creation of the charismatic chieftain who led them, and this charisma was not easily passed on.

The Merovingian Kingdom of the Franks

Of all the groups that set up kingdoms in western Europe during the fifth and sixth centuries, only the Franks succeeded in establishing a single dynasty from which leaders would be drawn for the next 250 years. This dynasty reached back to Clovis (r. c. 481–511), a warrior-king who established an alliance with powerful bishops in Gaul by converting to Roman Christianity—emulating the example of Constantine on many levels. Clovis's family came to be known as the Merovingians, after his legendary grandfather Merovech. Clovis's own name proved even more long-lasting. As the language of the Franks merged with the Latin of Gaul to become French, the name "Clovis" lost its hard "C" and the pronunciation of the "V" was softened. It became "Louis," the name borne by kings up to the time of the French Revolution over 1,200 years later (see Chapter 18).

The power of the Merovingians was due, in part, to their capacity to transfer it from one generation to another. In medieval Europe, as in other times and places, the right of inheritance was not limited to the eldest male of a family. When it came to property or power, all the sons of a king—and frequently all his male cousins and nephews, and even his daughters—could consider themselves rightful heirs. So even when the hegemony of any family was not threatened by outsiders, the transfer of power was almost always bloody. The Merovingians managed to contain this bloodshed through various means.

Under the Merovingian kings, many elements of late Roman local administration survived. Latin literacy, fostered by a network of monasteries linked to the Frankish court, remained an important element in this administration, providing a foundation on which Charlemagne would later build. Indeed, these monasteries became the engines that made Merovingian Gaul wealthier and more stable than other regions of northwestern Europe. Approximately 550 of them were thriving by the year 700, more than 300 of which had been established in the preceding century. The cities of Frankish bishops also prospered, amassing landed possessions from which their successors would continue to profit until the French Revolution.

This redistribution of wealth reflected a fundamental shift in the economic gravity of the region. In the year 600, the wealth of Gaul was still concentrated in the south, where it had been since the Roman conquest of the area under Julius Caesar. By the year 750, however, the economic center of the kingdom lay north of the Loire, in territories that extended from the Rhineland westward to the North Sea. It was here that most of the new monastic foundations of the seventh century were established.

Behind this shift in prosperity lay a long and successful effort to bring the rich, heavy soils of northern Europe under cultivation. This effort was largely engineered by the new monasteries, which harnessed the peasant workforce and pioneered agricultural technologies adapted to the climate and terrain. The most important were heavy, wheeled plows capable of cutting and turning soils very different from those of the Mediterranean. Gradually warming weather also improved the fertility of the wet northern soils, lengthening the growing season and making possible more efficient crop-rotation systems. As food became more plentiful, the population began to expand. Although much of Frankish Gaul remained a land of scattered settlements separated by dense forests, it was far more populous by 750 than it had been in the time of Clovis. All of these developments would continue during the reign of Charlemagne and beyond.

The Power of Monasticism

As we just noted, the seventh century witnessed a rapid increase in the foundation of monastic houses all over northwestern Europe. Although monasteries had existed since the fourth century, most were located in highly Romanized areas. But beginning in the fifth century, a powerful monastic movement began in Ireland, as well, and eventually spread to the Celtic regions of Britain and from there to the Continent. Important monasteries were also established on the island of Iona, off the western coast of what is now Scotland, and at Lindisfarne, off Britain's northeastern coast. In all of these cases, close ties were forged between monks and local tribal leaders or powerful families, much to the political and economic gain of all parties.

Indeed, the material advantages of monastic innovation were a powerful incentive toward conversion. Prosperity in turn was a powerful advertisement for authority, and a chieftain who had the support of a monastery and its beneficent Christian God would be regarded as worthy of loyalty. Because monasteries played such a key role in economic development and political order, lords often granted them special privileges, freeing them from the control of local bishops and giving them jurisdiction over their own lands. Thus, monasteries became politically and economically powerful not only because they had been founded by powerful men, but because they were lordships in their own right.

Frequently, these new foundations were double monasteries that accommodated women as well as men. Some were established for women only. In either case, they were often ruled by abbesses drawn from noble or royal families. Monasticism thus became a road to political power for women. It also gave women—commoners as well as queens—freedoms they did not have elsewhere, or at any other time in history up to this point. Within the monastery, women had more control over their own minds and bodies. Outside it, they could wield enormous influence, promoting their families' diplomatic and dynastic interests without the dangers and uncertainties of pregnancy. Moreover, the prayers of holy women were regarded as particularly effective in securing divine support or retribution. This further enriched convents through donations of land and wealth, although it could not always safeguard them from violence.

THE LINDISFARNE GOSPELS. This page from one of the astonishing illuminated ("light-filled") books produced by the monastery at Lindisfarne shows the opening of the gospel of John. ▪ *Why would monastic scribes have devoted so much time, energy, and skill to the decoration of a text?* ▪ *How do these artistic motifs compare to those featured on the metalwork found at Sutton Hoo (pages 172 and 173)?* ▪ *What conclusions can you draw from these similarities?*

Interpreting Visual Evidence

The Ship Burial of Sutton Hoo

The most impressive finds in the history of British archeology have been made by amateurs. The most recent, in the summer of 2009, was the largest hoard of worked gold and silver ever found in one place (more than 5 kilograms of gold and 2.5 kilograms of silver: image A). It was discovered by a man in Staffordshire who was walking over a neighbor's farm with a metal detector. The hoard's extraordinary value—and its historical implications—can only be guessed at now; even the dating is inconclusive.

Another amateur find, made in 1939, was a royal gravesite dating from the seventh century (image B). Many scholars believe it to be the tomb of King Redwald of East Anglia, described by Bede as a baptized Christian who refused to give up the worship of his ancestral gods. The king's body was placed in a wooden structure in the middle of a 90-foot-long ship that had been dragged to the top of a bluff (a *hoo*), eleven miles from the English Channel. The ladder in the photograph of the original excavation reaches into the burial chamber.

The contents of the grave included:

- a lamp and a bronze bucket, once suspended from a chain

- a ceremonial helmet (image C), modeled on those worn by Roman cavalry

A. The Staffordshire Hoard, found in 2009.

B. The original excavation of the Burial Chamber at Sutton Hoo, 1939.

Convents and monasteries also served the interests of men, which is why kings and lords supported them. They were dynamic repositories of prayer, which could further the ambitions of their male benefactors and protect them from harm. They provided a dignified place of retirement for inconvenient but powerful women, such as the sisters and daughters of rivals or the widow of a previous ruler. And by limiting the number of powerful women who could reproduce, convents helped reduce the number of male claimants to power. Establishing aristocratic and royal women in convents was thus an important way of controlling successions and managing political disputes.

officers just before the withdrawal of the legions from Britain in 410—but decorated like helmets found in eastern Sweden

- a sword and a large, circular shield, resembling those found in Swedish burial sites

- exquisitely crafted belt buckles and shoulder clasps (image D), made of gold and garnet

- a pair of silver spoons with long handles, possibly crafted in Byzantium, inscribed in Greek with the names PAULOS and SAULOS (Paul and Saul)

- a large silver dish made in Byzantium between 491 and 518

- a bronze bowl from the eastern Mediterranean

- a six-stringed lyre in a bag made of beaver skin, similar to lyres found in Germany

- a purse containing 37 gold coins, each from a different Merovingian mint, the most recent datable to the 620s

- heaps of armor, blankets, cloaks, and other gear.

Questions for Analysis

1. What do these artifacts, and the context in which they were found, reveal about the extent of Anglo-Saxon contact with the rest of the world? Which regions are represented, and why?

2. Based on this evidence, what conclusions can you draw about Anglo-Saxon culture and values?

3. Do any of these grave-goods indicate that the occupant was a Christian king? Why or why not?

C. Sutton Hoo helmet.

D. Sutton Hoo buckles.

Monasticism played an important role in missionary activity, too. The work of Irish monks was crucial to the spread of Christianity in areas of northern Europe virtually untouched by the Roman Empire. Missionaries were also sponsored by the fledgling papacy in tandem with the Merovingian royal family—especially its women. The best example of this is the conversion of Britain's Anglo-Saxon tribes, which we glimpsed in the opening paragraph of this chapter. In 597, a group of Benedictine monks was sent by Pope Gregory I (r. 590–604) to the southeastern kingdom of Kent, where their efforts were assisted by the fact that the king, Æthelbehrt, had married a Frankish princess who was already a Christian. This pattern of influence repeated itself all over southern and eastern Britain. Writing a hundred years later in the monastery of Monkwearmouth in Northumbria, the historian Bede could claim that the tribes of England were now united in their shared allegiance to the Roman Church and its English archbishop, whose seat was the cathedral in Æthelbehrt's capital at Canterbury. Bede credited the Roman pope for initiating this remarkable feat, and the monastic rule under which he himself lived for bringing it to fruition.

The Papacy of Gregory the Great

Pope Gregory I, also known as Gregory the Great, was the first bishop of Rome to envision a new role for the papacy in northwestern Europe. We have seen that the Roman "papa" frequently asserted his superiority over other patriarchs; but in reality, he was subordinate to the emperors in Constantinople and to the greater prestige of bishops in the Christian East. As Byzantine power in Italy declined, however, Gregory sought to create a more autonomous Latin Church. An influential theologian, he is considered the successor of Jerome, Ambrose, and Augustine (Chapter 6) because he greatly extended the applicability of their teachings. Among his doctrinal contributions were an emphasis on the necessity of penance for the forgiveness of sins and the concept of Purgatory as a place where the soul could be purified before it was admitted into Heaven—instead of being sent immediately to perpetual damnation. Alongside this emphasis on penance, Gregory especially emphasized the importance of pastoral care: the proper instruction and encouragement of the laity. He even sought to increase the affective power of Christian worship by promoting the performance of music, to such a degree that the very style of singing that emerged in this period is known as "Gregorian chant."

Gregory was also a statesman and leader in the model of his Roman forebears. Within Italy, he ensured the survival of the papacy in the face of Lombard invaders by clever diplomacy and expert management of papal estates and revenues. He maintained good relations with Byzantium while asserting his authority over other bishops of the Latin Church. Yet Gregory's influence was not always benign. He was among the first to articulate the Church's official policy toward the Jews, which became increasingly negative. Building on Gregory's example, later popes would insist that the Jews' alleged role in Christ's crucifixion had deprived them of their rights in a Christian world.

THE EMPIRE OF CHARLEMAGNE

Toward the end of the seventh century, tensions among Frankish noble families were increasing. Those in the border region of Austrasia had profited from their steady push into the "soft frontier" east of the Rhine, acquiring wealth and military power in the process. In the Merovingians' heartland of Neustria, by contrast, a considerable portion of their land had been given to monasteries, which decreased their wealth and their capacity to attract followers. A succession of short-lived kings then opened the door to a series of civil wars, and finally to a decisive challenge to the Merovingian dynasty.

Kings and King-Makers

In 687, an Austrasian nobleman called Pepin (635/45–714) succeeded in forcing his way into power by making himself the king's right-hand man. He took the title *maior domus,* "big man of the house," and began to exercise royal authority while maintaining the fiction that he was merely a royal servant. He did this effectively for more than twenty-five years. After his death, his illegitimate son Charles Martel ("the Hammer," 688–741) further consolidated control over royal administration. In 733 or 734 he also repelled a Muslim force that had ventured into Frankish territory, meeting them at Tours, some 150 miles from the Merovingian capital at Paris. Although the Muslim contingent was a raiding party rather than a full-scale army, Charles' victory won him great prestige.

At the same time, Charles developed an alliance with Benedictine missionaries from England, who were attempting to convert the Low Countries and central Germany to Christianity. Charles' family had long been active in the drive to conquer and settle these areas, and he understood that missionary work and Frankish expansion could go hand in hand. Charles assisted these conversion efforts. In return, the leader of the English Benedictines, Boniface (c. 672–754), brought him into contact with the papacy.

Although Charles never sought to become king himself, he was so clearly the effective ruler of the Franks that they did not bother to choose a new king when the reigning Merovingian died in 737. But then Charles himself died in 741, and his sons Carloman and Pepin were forced to allow the election of a new king while they continued to exercise power behind the scenes. This compromise did not last long, however. In 750, Pepin decided to seize the throne for himself.

Analyzing Primary Sources

An Anglo-Saxon Slave Girl and Frankish Queen

The Anglo-Saxon Saint Balthild became the wife of the Merovingian king Clovis II (r. 639–57), but she began life as a slave. After the king's death, she was left in a precarious position at the Frankish court as regent for her son, Clothar III, and was eventually forced to enter the convent she had founded at Chelles, near Paris. The following excerpt from her Latin vita ("life") describes her rise to a position of power. It was probably written by a nun of Chelles.

[P]raise should first be sung of Him Who made the humble great and raised the pauper from the dunghill and seated him among the princes of his people. Such a one is the woman present to our minds, the venerable and great lady Balthild the queen. Divine Providence called her from across the seas. She, who came here as God's most precious and lofty pearl, was sold at a cheap price. Erchinoald, a Frankish magnate and most illustrious man, acquired her and in his service the girl behaved most honorably. . . . For she was kind-hearted and sober and prudent in all her ways, careful and plotting evil for none. . . . And since she was of the Saxon race, she was graceful in form with refined features, a most seemly woman with a smiling face and serious gait. And she so showed herself just as she ought in all things, that she pleased her master and found favor in his eyes. So he determined that she should set out the drinking cup for him in his chamber and, honored above all others as his house-keeper, stand at his side always ready to serve him. . . . She gained such happy fame that, when the said lord Erchinoald's wife died, he hoped to unite himself to Balthild, that faultless virgin, in a matronal bed. . . .

[But] when she was called to the master's chamber she hid herself secretly in a corner and threw some vile rags over herself so that no one could guess that anyone might be concealed there. . . . She hoped that she might avoid a human marriage bed and thus merit a spiritual and heavenly spouse. . . . Thereafter it happened, with God's approval, that Balthild, the maid who escaped marriage with a lord, came to be espoused to Clovis, son of the former king, Dagobert. Thus by virtue of her humility she was raised to a higher rank. . . .

Source: Excerpted from *Sainted Women of the Dark Ages*, ed. and trans. John E. Halborg, Jo Ann McNamara, and E. Gordon Whatley (Chapel Hill, NC: 1992), pp. 268–70.

Questions for Analysis

1. Based on what you have learned about the prevalence of the slave trade in early medieval Europe, what might you speculate about Balthild's actual role in Erchinoald's household?

2. Balthild would have been a contemporary of the king buried at Sutton Hoo. Is it likely that she would have been a Christian when she was sold into slavery in England? Why or why not?

3. In light of Balthild's later status as a queen and regent for her son, why would her biographer stress that she was "careful and plotting evil for none"? To what allegations or incidents might the author of this life be responding?

This turned out to be harder than he may have expected. Even though the reigning king was ineffectual, Frankish identity was bound up with loyalty to Clovis's descendants; and though tribal leaders had the power to elect a new king, they were reluctant to do so. Pepin therefore turned to the pope, trading on his father's support of the Benedictines. The pope, for his part, saw that a powerful leader of the Franks could be a potential ally in his political struggle with the Byzantine emperors over iconoclasm (which the papacy opposed) and in his military struggle against the Lombard kings for control of central Italy.

So Boniface, acting as papal emissary, anointed Pepin king of the Franks in 751. This was a new ritual, but it had a powerful biblical precedent: the ceremony by which the prophet Samuel had made Saul the first king of Israel, by anointing him with holy oil (Chapter 2). Indeed, the significance of the Old Testament association would grow under Pepin's son Charlemagne (associated with David) and his grandson Louis the Pious (associated with Solomon). To contemporary observers, however, the novelty of these proceedings underscored the uncertainty of the process by which a legitimate king had been deposed and a new king created. And as we will see, this king-making process was the first stage in the development of a principle that would ultimately limit the power of later medieval kings and modern rulers alike: the principle that kingship is an office and can be occupied, at least theoretically, by anyone. By extension, this means that if a king is ineffectual or tyrannical, he can be deposed and replaced.

The Reign of Charlemagne

Pepin's position as king was a tenuous one, and when he died it seemed likely that the Frankish kingdom would break up into mutually hostile regions: Austrasia, Neustria, and Aquitaine. That it did not was the work of Pepin's son, Charles, known to the French as Charlemagne and to the Germans as Karl der Grosse—"Charles the Great." It is from him, as well as from his grandfather Charles Martel, that this new Frankish dynasty takes the name "Carolingian" (from *Carolus*, the Latin form of "Charles").

When Charlemagne came to power in 768, he managed to unite the Franks by the tried and true method of attacking a common external enemy. In a series of campaigns, the Franks succeeded in annexing the Lombard kingdom of northern Italy, most of what is now Germany, portions of central Europe, and Catalonia. These conquests provided the victorious Franks with the spoils of war and vast new lands that enabled Charlemagne to reward his closest followers. Many of the peoples whom Charlemagne conquered were already Christians. In Saxony, however, Charlemagne's armies fought for twenty years before subduing the inhabitants and forcing their conversion. This

THE EMPIRE OF CHARLEMAGNE IN 814. When Charlemagne died in 814, he had created an empire that embraced a large portion of the lands formerly united under the Western Roman Empire. ▪ *What were the geographical limits of his power?* ▪ *How were these limits dictated by the historical forces we have been studying?* ▪ *Along what lines was Charlemagne's empire divided after his death?*

created a precedent with momentous consequences: in time, the assumption that the subjugation of a vanquished people should be accompanied by their (often unwilling) conversion would become ingrained in the ideology and practice of most Western civilizations.

To rule his vast new empire, Charlemagne enlisted the help of the Frankish warriors he had enriched. These counts (in Latin, *comites*, "followers") supervised local governance within their territories. Charlemagne also established a network of other officials who convened courts, established tolls, administered royal lands, and collected taxes. To facilitate transactions and trade, he created a new coinage system based on a division of the silver pound into units of twenty shillings, each worth twelve pennies; this system would last in parts of Europe and in Britain until the 1970s. As we noted above, much of the silver for this new coinage originated in the Abbasid caliphate and was payment for furs, cloth, and slaves captured in Charlemagne's wars.

Like Carolingian administration generally, this new monetary system depended on the regular use of written records, which means that the sources supporting historical research on Charlemagne's empire are numerous. But Charlemagne did not rely on the written word alone to make his will felt. Periodically, his court sent special messengers, known as *missi*, on tours through the countryside to relay his instructions and report back on the conduct of local administrators. This was the most thorough system of governance known in Europe since the height of the Roman Empire, reaching many parts of the Continent that the Romans had never occupied. It set the standard for royal administration in Europe for centuries.

Christianity and Kingship

Charlemagne took his responsibilities as a Christian king seriously. As his empire expanded, moreover, he came to see himself as the leader of a unified Christian society, Christendom, which he was obliged to defend. Like his contemporaries in Byzantium and Islam—as well as his Roman predecessors—he recognized no distinction between religion and politics. Religious reforms were therefore no less central to proper kingship than were justice and defense. In some ways, indeed, a king's responsibilities for his kingdom's spiritual welfare were more important than his other, secular responsibilities.

These ideas were not new in the late eighth century, but they took on a new importance because of the extraordinary power Charlemagne wielded. Like other rulers of this period, Charlemagne was able to appoint and depose bishops and abbots, just as he did his counts and other offi-

CHARLEMAGNE'S IMAGE OF AUTHORITY. A silver penny struck between 804 and 814 in Mainz (as indicated by the letter *M* at the bottom) represents Charlemagne in a highly stylized fashion, as a Roman emperor with a military cloak and laurel wreath. The inscription reads *KAROLVS IMP AVG* (Charles, Emperor, Augustus). Charlemagne's portrait is closely modeled on both Hellenistic and Roman coins.

cials. But he also changed the liturgy of Frankish churches, declared changes in basic statements of Christian belief, prohibited pagan practices, and imposed basic Christian observances on the conquered peoples of Saxony. As the dominant political power in central Italy, Charlemagne was also the protector of the papacy. Although he acknowledged the pope as spiritual leader of western Christendom, Charlemagne dealt with the bishop of Rome much as he did with other bishops in his empire. He supervised and approved papal elections, and he also protected the pope from his many enemies. To Charlemagne, such measures were clearly required if God's new chosen people, the Franks, were to avoid the fate that befell biblical Israel whenever its people turned away from their obedience to God.

The Carolingian Renaissance

Similar ideals lay behind the Carolingian Renaissance, a cultural and intellectual flowering that took place around the Carolingian court. Like their biblical exemplars David and Solomon, Charlemagne and his son Louis the Pious considered it a crucial part of their role to be patrons of learning and the arts. In so doing, they created a paradigm of the court as an intellectual and cultural center that would profoundly influence western European cultural life until the First World War (Chapter 24).

Behind the Carolingians' support for scholarship was the conviction that learning was essential to salvation.

Charlemagne therefore recruited intellectuals from all over Europe, chief among them the Anglo-Saxon monk Alcuin, whose command of classical Latin established him as the leader of the court. Under Alcuin's direction, scholars produced original Latin poetry and an impressive number of theological and pastoral tracts. But their primary efforts were devoted to recopying classical Latin texts and correcting the text of the Latin Bible, which had accumulated many generations of copyists' mistakes. Alcuin and his associates also developed a new style of handwriting with simplified letter forms and spaces inserted between words, in an effort to guard against new mistakes and making reading easier. Literacy was further facilitated by the addition of punctuation. This new style of handwriting, known as Carolingian miniscule, is the foundation for the typefaces of most modern books—including this one.

The Revival of the Western Roman Empire

On Christmas Day in the year 800, Charlemagne was crowned emperor by Pope Leo III. Centuries later, popes would cite this epochal event as precedent for the political superiority they claimed over the "Holy Roman Empire," as it came to be called (see Chapter 9). In the year 800, however, Pope Leo was entirely under Charlemagne's thumb. And Charlemagne's biographer, Einhard, would later claim that the coronation was planned without the emperor's knowledge. For one thing, it was certain to anger the true Roman emperor in Byzantium, with whom Charlemagne had strained relations. Nor did the imperial title add much to Charlemagne's position; he was already a de facto emperor in his own right. Why, then, did he accept the title and later transfer it to his son Louis?

Historians are still debating this question. What is clear, in any case, is the symbolic significance of the action. Although the Romans of Byzantium no longer influenced western Europe directly, they continued to regard it (somewhat vaguely) as an outlying province of their empire. Moreover, the emperor in Constantinople claimed to be the political successor of Caesar Augustus. Charlemagne's assumption of the imperial title was a clear slap in the face, and it deepened Byzantium's suspicion of his cordial relationship with Byzantium's enemy, Harun al-Rashid, the Abbasid caliph in Baghdad. But for Charlemagne's followers—and for all the medieval rulers who came after him—it was a declaration of independence and superiority. With only occasional interruptions, western Europeans would continue to crown Roman emperors until the nineteenth century, while territorial claims and concepts of national sovereignty continued to rest on Carolingian precedent. Whatever his own motives may have been, Charlemagne's revival of the Western Roman Empire was crucial to the developing self-consciousness of western Europe.

DISPUTED LEGACIES AND NEW ALLIANCES

When Charlemagne died in 814, his empire descended intact to his only surviving son, Louis the Pious. Under Louis, however, the empire disintegrated, and it was divided among his three sons in 840. Western Francia (the core of modern France) went to Charles the Bald; Eastern Francia (which became the principalities of Germany) went to Louis the German; and a third kingdom (stretching from the Rhineland to Rome) went to Lothair, along with the imperial title. But when Lothair's line died out in 856, this fragile compromise dissolved into open warfare, as the East and West Franks fought over Lothair's former territories and the imperial power that went with them. The heartland of this disputed domain, known to the Germans as Lotharingia and to the French as Alsace-Lorraine, would continue to be a site of bitter contention until the end of the Second World War (see Chapter 26).

The Collapse of the Carolingian Empire

Louis faced an impossible situation of a kind we have studied many times before: the task of holding together an artificial constellation of territories united by someone else. By 814, moreover, Charlemagne had pushed the borders of his empire beyond the practical limits of his administration. To the southwest, he now faced the Umayyad rulers of Al-Andalus; to the north, the pagan inhabitants of Scandinavia; and in the east, his armies were too preoccupied to secure the Slavic lands that lay beyond Saxony. Meanwhile, the pressures that had driven these conquests—the need for land and plunder—had become ever more pronounced as a result of their very success. The number of counts had tripled, from approximately 100 to 300, and each of them wanted more wealth and power.

Frustrated by their new emperor's inability to reward them, the Frankish aristocracy turned against Louis and on each other. As centralized authority broke down, the vast majority of the empire's free inhabitants found themselves increasingly dominated by local lords who treated them as if they were unfree serfs. At the same time, troubles in the Abbasid Empire caused a breakdown in the commercial system through which Scandinavian traders brought Abbasid silver into Carolingian domains. Deprived of their livelihood, these traders turned to raiding, which is what the Norse word "Viking" means. Under these combined pressures, a new map of Europe began to emerge.

The Impact of the Viking Invasions

Scandinavian traders were already familiar figures in the North Sea and Baltic ports of Europe when Charlemagne came to power. They had begun to establish strategic settlements in what is now Russia, from which they navigated down the rivers to Byzantium (through the Black Sea) and the Abbasid caliphate (through the Caspian Sea). But when the power of the Abbasids declined, they turned to plunder, ransom, tribute collection, and slaving. At first, these were small-scale operations. But soon, some Viking attacks involved organized armies numbering in the thousands. The small tribal kingdoms of the Anglo-Saxons and Celts made the British Isles easy targets, as were the kingdoms of the divided Franks.

By the tenth century, the Vikings controlled independent principalities in eastern England, Ireland, the islands of Scotland, and the region of France that is still called "Norseman-land," Normandy. A Viking people known as the Rus' established the beginnings of a kingdom that would become Russia. At the end of the tenth century, Vikings ventured farther west and colonized Iceland, Greenland, and a distant territory they called Vinland (Newfoundland, Canada). In 1016 a Viking army placed a Danish king on the English throne.

The threat of Viking attacks began to lessen with Scandinavia's conversion to Christianity, from the late tenth century onward. It was also mitigated by the fact that Viking populations quickly assimilated into the world of northwestern Europe. By 1066, when the "Norsemen" of Normandy conquered England, the English—many descended from Vikings themselves—perceived these Normans to be French.

In this era, many of the monasteries of Frankish, Anglo-Saxon, and Celtic lands were destroyed—along with countless precious books and historical artifacts. Yet the Vikings were not the only source of disorder. The local political rivalries that had replaced the centralized states of Charlemagne and the Islamic caliphates contributed mightily to the chaos and made the Vikings' successes easily won. Nor were the Vikings a source of disorder alone. In Ireland and eastern England, Vikings founded a series of new towns. As long-distance traders, Vikings transported large quantities of silver into western Europe, fueling the European economy.

In those few regions where people did succeed in fending off Viking attacks, the unifying force of victory was strong. The best example of this phenomenon is England, which had never been part of Charlemagne's empire and which had remained divided into small kingdoms at war with one other. But as a direct response to the Viking threat, a loosely consolidated kingdom emerged for the first time under Alfred the Great (r. 871–99). His success in defending his own West Saxon kingdom from Viking attacks, combined with the destruction of every other competing royal dynasty, allowed Alfred and his heirs to assemble effective armed forces, institute mechanisms of local government, found new towns, and codify English laws. In addition, Alfred established a court school

PATTERNS OF VIKING ACTIVITY AND SETTLEMENT, c. 800–1100. The Vikings were instrumental in maintaining commercial contacts among northern Europe, Byzantium, and Islam until the eighth century, when changing historical forces turned them into raiders and colonists. ▪ *What area was the original homeland of the Vikings?* ▪ *What geographic region did the Vikings first conquer, and why?* ▪ *The areas marked in green show territories that were later targeted by pillagers. Why would the Vikings have avoided settlement in these areas?*

in imitation of Charlemagne, and fostered a distinctive Anglo-Saxon literary culture. While the Anglo-Saxon vernacular had been a written language since the time of the Roman missions, it now came to rival Latin as a language of administration, history, scholarship, and spirituality. Moreover, oral traditions of poetic composition and storytelling were preserved and extended, as exemplified by the epic *Beowulf*. Until the the eleventh century, Anglo-Saxon was the only European vernacular used for regular written communication.

The Disintegration of the Islamic World

As we noted above, the declining power of the Abbasid caliphate contributed to the escalation of Viking raids. A major cause of this decline was the gradual impoverishment of the ancient Tigris-Euphrates basin, which resulted from ecological crises and a devastating revolt by the enslaved African workforce there. Tax revenues were also declining, as provincial rulers in North Africa, Egypt, and Syria retained larger and larger portions of those revenues for themselves. As their sources of income became depleted, the Abbasids were unable to support either their large civil service or the mercenary army on which they relied for defense. Massively expensive building projects, including the construction of the new Abbasid capital at Baghdad, further exacerbated the crisis.

Behind the Abbasid collapse lay two fundamental developments of great significance for the future of the Islamic world: the growing power of regional rulers and the sharpening religious divisions between Sunnis and Shi'ites, and among the Shi'ites themselves. In 909, regional and religious hostilities came together when a local Shi'ite dynasty known as the Fatimids seized control of the Abbasid province of North Africa. In 969, the Fatimids succeeded in conquering Egypt also. Meanwhile, another Shi'ite group attacked Baghdad in 927 and Mecca in 930, seizing the Kaaba. Although an Abbasid caliphate continued to exist in Baghdad until 1258 (when invading Mongol armies dispatched it), its empire had effectively disappeared by the 930s.

In Al-Andalus, disputes over succession within the Umayyad dynasty were matched by new external pressures. Beginning in the mid-ninth century, the small Christian kingdoms of northern and eastern Iberia began to encroach on Muslim territory. By the opening years of the eleventh century, the caliphate had dissolved, to be replaced by a host of smaller kingdoms, some of which paid tribute to the Christian rulers of the north.

The fractured political basis of the Islamic world deepened the divisions that had always existed among Muslim

After You Read This Chapter

Visit StudySpace for quizzes, additional review materials, and multi-media documents. **wwnorton.com/studyspace**

REVIEWING THE OBJECTIVES

- Justinian's attempted reunification of the Roman Empire proved destructive. What were its effects in the East? In the West?
- Byzantine culture was distinctive in many ways. What are some of its important features?
- The rapid expansion of Islam can be explained with reference to several historical factors. What were they?
- What accounts for the close relationship between monasticism and secular power in early medieval Europe?
- What was the Carolingian Empire, and why is it important?

groups. While Islamic rulers were extremely tolerant of religious and cultural differences when dealing with Jews and Christians, dissent within Islam itself was another matter. Under the strong rule of the caliphates, some different groups had learned to coexist; but with the disappearance of these centralized states it would be increasingly difficult to reconcile the ideal of Muslim universality with the realities of regional and ethnic differences.

CONCLUSION

The three civilizations that emerged as Rome's heirs each exhibit aspects of Roman civilization, which was itself a product of older civilizations. Which was Rome's true successor? It depends on the criteria used to make this evaluation. If imperial Rome's most fundamental characteristics were the maintenance of legal and political institutions, the answer is Byzantium. If its strength lay in combining the rich legacies of the Near East, Egypt, and the Hellenistic world, the answer is the Muslim caliphates, which also emulated Rome in promoting commerce and cultural exchange. If one associates Rome chiefly with the city itself and the Latin language of the first Romans, the answer is northwestern Europe.

There are many connections to be drawn among these three successors. All took on their defining characteristics in the sixth and seventh centuries and, by the eighth century, had developed unique strengths and weaknesses. Moreover, they had fruitful—if uneasy—relationships with one another, and many mutual dependencies. Italian traders were active in Constantinople, and Muslim traders were common in the ports of southern Italy and Gaul. Anglo-Saxon merchants were regular visitors to the Mediterranean, and Jewish merchants in the Rhineland were carrying on an active trade with the communities of Muslim Egypt, while Viking traders had opened trade routes from the Baltic through Russia to the Black Sea and were busily founding cities from Novgorod to Dublin.

But the crises of the ninth and tenth centuries disrupted these networks and created new centers of power. Western Europeans began to share a sense of common identity: within the vast territory that extended from the Baltic to the Mediterranean, and from the Pyrenees to Poland, every ruler was (or would soon be) looking to the Roman Church for spiritual guidance and to his fellow rulers for aid and alliance. At the same time, western Europe became a society mobilized for war to a degree unmatched in either Byzantium or the Islamic world. In the centuries to come, this militarization was to prove a decisive factor in the shifting relationship among Rome's heirs, not only because it led to conquest but because it spurred innovation.

PEOPLE, IDEAS, AND EVENTS IN CONTEXT

- In what ways do **JUSTINIAN'S CODE OF ROMAN LAW** and the building of **HAGIA SOPHIA** reflect his desire to revive the glories of ancient Rome?

- What were **BYZANTIUM'S** sources of stability, and of dissent? What effect did the **ICONOCLAST CONTROVERSY** have on Byzantine society?

- What factors contributed to **MUHAMMAD'S** rise to power? What are the **FIVE PILLARS** of **ISLAM** and what is the role of the **QU'RAN**?

- To what extent were the **UMAYYAD** and **ABBASID CALIPHATES** heirs of Rome? What made Islamic culture of this period distinctive?

- How did the **MEROVINGIAN** kings of the Franks acquire and hold power? How did **BENEDICTINE MONASTICISM** contribute to the economy of western Europe and how was it linked to politics?

- How did **CHARLEMAGNE** build an empire, and how did the **CAROLINGIAN RENAISSANCE** revive and extend **CLASSICAL LEARNING**?

- How did the **VIKING INVASIONS** contribute to the disorder of the ninth and tenth centuries?

CONSEQUENCES

- Arguably, each of the three civilizations that emerged in this era could claim the mantle of the Roman Empire. In your view, which one is most successful in carrying forward the legacies of the classical past?

- How do the historical circumstances in which Islam emerged compare to those that shaped early Christianity (Chapter 6)? What are some key similarities and differences?

Before You Read This Chapter

The Expansion of Europe, 950–1100

CORE OBJECTIVES

- **EXPLAIN** the reasons for the fragmentation of political power throughout most of Europe in the ninth and tenth centuries.
- **IDENTIFY** the most important outcomes of the medieval agricultural revolution.
- **DESCRIBE** the effects of the reforming movement with the Church.
- **UNDERSTAND** the motives behind the Crusades.
- **TRACE** the political, economic, social, religious, and cultural effects of the Crusades.

In the version of history popularized by medieval minstrels, Charlemagne and his knights defeat a Muslim army on Spanish soil. They then face only one remaining obstacle: the castle of a Muslim king whose stalwart courage commands the Christians' respect. So when ambassadors from the king promise his conversion in exchange for the safety of his people, Charlemagne readily agrees. One of his men must now negotiate the terms of surrender. Roland, Charlemagne's noblest knight, suggests that his stepfather Ganelon be the chosen messenger. But Ganelon is furious, certain that the mission will end in his death. Secretly, he resolves to betray his stepson and his liege lord: he convinces the Muslim king that Charlemagne only intends to trick him into converting, and thus incites the king to attack the Christian warriors as they travel homeward through the mountain pass. Because Roland is the bravest knight, Ganelon knows that he will volunteer to command the rear guard.

And so it happens. Roland's men are ambushed and his sworn companion, Olivier, urges him to call for help. But Roland refuses; he will never endanger his lord by any such dishonorable deed. Instead, he will fight to the death and, with his last ounce of strength, break his sword. For it would never do

183

to have this sacred gift of Charlemagne—made holier still by the relic in its pommel—fall into the hands of heathens. As Roland reminds Olivier, "We must not be the theme of mocking songs." The worst thing imaginable is shame; the best, to become the hero of just such an epic.

Like the *Iliad*, *The Song of Roland* is the product of an oral storytelling tradition that took shape over hundreds of years. Written down around the year 1100, it reflects the many ways in which the world had changed since the time of Charlemagne. Its very language exemplifies one such change: the language we call French. In Charlemagne's time, moreover, there was no such thing as knighthood or chivalry, there were no major castles, there was no holy war against Muslims. All of these features were added over time, to mirror a new reality.

In this chapter, we will begin to trace the processes that transformed western Europe from an economic backwater and political patchwork into the premier power among the three successor civilizations of the Roman Empire. With the increased authority and prestige of the Roman Church, European Christendom came to embrace the formerly outlying provinces of Scandinavia, Hungary, Poland, and Bohemia. Christian colonists and missionaries would also push eastward into Prussia, Lithuania, Livonia, and the Balkans. Allied Christian armies would come to dominate Muslim Spain and Constantinople. They would also establish (and eventually lose) a Latin kingdom centered on Jerusalem, and control commerce in the Mediterranean as well as trade routes to Central Asia and China. This expansion would be accompanied by a revolution in agricultural production, significant urbanization, a rising standard of living, and a growing population. It would foster the growth of territorial monarchies, create a wealthy but highly stratified new social order, and spur remarkable intellectual and cultural achievements.

WESTERN EUROPE AROUND THE YEAR 1000

In the aftermath of the Viking invasions, new political entities began to emerge in western Europe. Indeed, the Viking colony of Iceland can claim to be Europe's oldest state and the world's first parliamentary democracy. Its political institutions date back to the year 930, when settlers formed a legislative assembly called the Althing, a Norse word with the same meaning as the Latin *res publica*. In regions where Vikings settled among more established groups—the British Isles, Scandinavia, Russia, and the Low Countries—they both absorbed and affected these cultures. In Normandy, for example, the descendants of Vikings maintained marriage

alliances and ties of kinship with the rest of the Norse world, while at the same time intermarrying with the Franks and adopting their language.

The Heirs of Charlemagne

The most powerful monarchs on the Continent in this era were the Saxon kings who modeled themselves on Charlemagne. Just as the Carolingians had built their power on the conquest of Saxony in the eighth century, the Saxon kings now built theirs on the conquests of Slavic lands to the east. They also nurtured their image as guardians of Christendom. In 955, King Otto I of Saxony defeated the pagan Magyars while carrying a sacred lance that had belonged to Charlemagne. This victory established him as Charlemagne's worthy successor. In 962, accordingly, he went to Rome to be crowned emperor by Pope John XII. But Otto then turned the tables on the pope, deposing him for his scandalous lifestyle and selecting a new pope to replace him. Otto thereby laid the foundation for his successors' later claims to imperial autonomy.

Otto also advertised his inheritance of Charlemagne's power through his patronage of arts and learning. He presided over the establishment of cathedral schools and helped the bishops of his domain turn their own courts into cultural centers, too. However, Otto could not control either the papacy or the independent towns of northern Italy unless he maintained a permanent presence there. And if he remained in Italy too long, his authority in Saxony broke down. This was a dilemma that neither he nor his successors were able to solve, and the rift between local elites and the king widened when the imperial crown passed to a new dynasty, the Salians of neighboring Franconia. By the 1070s, when the Salian Henry IV attempted to assert control over Saxony, he touched off a war that was to have momentous repercussions (see below).

Aspects of Charlemagne's legacy also survived in Catalonia, where counts descended from Carolingian appointees continued to administer justice in public courts of law and to draw revenues from tolls and trade. The city of Barcelona grew rapidly as both a long-distance and a regional market under the protection of these counts. In Aquitaine also, the counts of Poitiers and Toulouse continued to rest their authority on Carolingian foundations.

In Charlemagne's own Frankish kingdom, however, Carolingian rule collapsed. In some areas, a few Carolingian institutions survived, but they were used to build up new, autonomous principalities such as Anjou and Flanders. But in the Franks' traditional heartland, Carolingian authority disappeared. The Franks still had a king, but he was no longer a descendant of Charlemagne. Moreover, his domain had been reduced to the tiny region around Paris,

EUROPE, c. 1100. This map shows the patchwork of political power in western Europe after the millennium, although it cannot accurately illustrate the degree of fragmentation within these major territories, especially those of the Holy Roman Empire. ■ *What factors account for the close relationship between Italy and the German principalities?* ■ *How are they related to the northwestern regions of the Continent and the British Isles?* ■ *Which geopolitical entities would you expect to emerge as dominant in the following centuries?*

which the local count, Hugh Capet, had managed to defend against the Vikings in 987 thus earning himself the title of king. Marooned on this Ile de France (literally, "island of France"), the Capetian kings clung to the fiction that they were the heirs of Charlemagne's greatness. Yet it would be another two hundred years before one of them made this fiction a political reality.

AN AGRICULTURAL REVOLUTION

Agricultural innovation tends to occur slowly, yet it is still appropriate to call the profound changes that took place in this period revolutionary. Indeed, it is arguable that this agricultural revolution was more important than that of the modern era (see Chapter 19).

EMPEROR OTTO THE GREAT. In this opening from a deluxe set of Gospels he commissioned for himself, Otto is shown seated on a throne and vested with the regalia of imperial and royal authority, surrounded by clerical and secular counselors, and receiving tribute from a procession of women representing the four regions of his domain: Slavinia, Germania, Gallia, and Roma. ▪ *Compare this image to that of Emperor Justinian on page 159 (Chapter 7).* ▪ *In what ways is Otto making use of similar iconography?* ▪ *What claims to power does he make thereby?*

New Technologies

The driving force behind the agricultural boom of the Middle Ages was technological: the heavy, wheeled plow developed in this era could cut and turn the rich soil of northern Europe far more effectively than traditional Mediterranean plows. Related improvements in collars and harnesses enhanced the efficiency of plow oxen and made it possible for horses to pull heavy loads without choking themselves. The development of iron horseshoes and the tandem harnessing of paired teams also made the use of horses more effective for the transport of agricultural surpluses to new markets.

Labor-saving devices further increased productivity. The wheelbarrow was a crucial invention, as was the harrow, a tool drawn over the field after plowing to level the earth and mix in the seed. Watermills represented another major innovation. The Romans had relied mainly on human- and animal-powered wheels to grind grain into flour, but the lack of such slave labor led medieval engineers—probably monks—to experiment with various ways of harnessing water power. Local lords followed suit, recognizing the mill as a source of economic and political power to which they could control access through the imposition of tolls. Mills

also drove saws for lumber, processed cloth, pressed olive oil, provided power for iron forges, and crushed pulp for manufacturing paper. They would remain the world's only source of mechanical power for manufacturing until the invention of the steam engine (see Chapter 19).

New Conditions for Growth

Climate change also played a role in this agricultural revolution. Starting in the eighth or ninth century, average temperatures in Europe gradually rose by about 1° or 2°C (3.6°F)—the same increment that has led to global warming today. Eventually, these higher temperatures made it possible to raise crops as far north as Greenland and to produce wine in southern England. Moreover, the warming climate benefited northern Europe by lengthening the growing season, while hotter summers and diminishing rainfall hurt Mediterranean agriculture in equal measure.

At the same time, the settlement of Viking and Magyar peoples decreased the disruption of planting cycles and damage to crops. Left in relative peace, monasteries could develop and implement the tools described above. Pro-

ductivity was also linked to increased population, fundamental changes in patterns of settlement, and the organization of the peasant work force.

Harnessing People

During the early Middle Ages, most farmers lived on individual plots of land worked by themselves and their families. Starting in the ninth century, however, many individual holdings were merged into large, common fields farmed collectively by entire villages. The complex resulting from such collective endeavors is sometimes called a *manor* (from the Latin verb meaning "to dwell"). Common fields increased efficiency and were more productive, allowing villagers to experiment with new crops and to support larger numbers of animals. In time, prosperous peasants might be able to establish a parish church, a communal oven, a blacksmith, a mill, and a tavern. They could also socialize and assist their neighbors. In a difficult and demanding natural environment, these were important considerations.

In many cases, the impetus for the consolidation of manors came from the peasants themselves. In other cases, a manor could be created or co-opted by a local lord. Its greater productivity meant a larger share of the peasants' surplus; it was also easier to control and exploit peasants who lived together in villages and who were bound by ties of kinship and dependence. Over time, some lords were thus able to reduce formerly free peasants to the status of serfs. Like slaves, serfs inherited their servile status; but unlike slaves, they were not supposed to be sold apart from the lands they worked. From a material perspective, there may have been little difference between a serf and and a free peasant. But as we have seen, social mobility is often tied to geographical mobility—and the inability of serfs to move freely would prevent them from achieving the liberties of those who could.

The Conquest of the Land

For centuries, farmers had known that if they sowed the same crop in the same field year after year, they would eventually exhaust the soil. The traditional solution was to divide one's land, planting half in the fall to harvest in the spring, and leaving the other half to lie fallow. In this era, however, farmers of northern Europe slowly discovered that a three-field crop-rotation system could produce a sustainable increase in overall production. One-third of the land would lie fallow or be used as pasture, one-third would be planted with winter wheat or rye to be harvested in the early summer, and one-third would be planted in the spring, with another crop to be harvested in the fall. These fields were then rotated over a three-year cycle.

This system increased the amount of land under cultivation from 50 to 67 percent, while the two separate growing seasons provided some insurance against loss due to natural disasters or inclement weather. The system also produced higher yields per acre, particularly if fodder crops like oats were a regular part of the rotation pattern, because they replaced the nitrogen that wheat and rye leach out of the soil. Both humans and animals could eat oats, and additional fodder supported more and healthier animals, increasing the efficiency of plow beasts and providing an additional source of protein through meat and milk. The new crop-rotation system also spread labor more evenly over the course of the year.

THE GROWTH OF TOWNS AND TRADE

As we observed in Chapter 7, the urban infrastructure of the Western Roman Empire was weakened in the course of the fifth and sixth centuries. In most areas, monasteries replaced cities as the nuclei of civilization in northwestern Europe. Then, under Charlemagne and his imitators, towns came to be planted by royal initiative, as centers for markets and administration. In Anglo-Saxon England, too, King Alfred and his successors established new towns in strategic locations while at the same time reviving older Roman cities.

Fostering Commerce

Although many of these towns were devastated by Viking raids, the agricultural revolution helped to revitalize them. The rapid urbanization of Europe was also fostered by the initiatives of lords who profited by providing safe havens for travelers and trade. This was especially true in the Rhineland, the Low Countries, and the independent counties of Flanders and Champagne. In southwestern Europe, towns also prospered from their status as ports or their location along overland routes connecting the Mediterranean with the Atlantic.

In Italy, which had been decimated by five centuries of warfare and invasion, the growth of towns gave rise to especially dramatic changes. Initially, the most successful cities were situated in Byzantine-controlled areas of the peninsula: Venice in the north and Amalfi, Naples, and Palermo in the south. In the eleventh century, however, Norman invasions of southern Italy disrupted this trade and opened new opportunities for the northern ports of Genoa and Pisa.

1. Cathedral
2. Alt St. Thomas
3. Alt St. Peter
4. Jung St. Peter
5. St. Nikolaus
6. St. Johann
7. St. Wilhelm
8. St. Stephen

0 50 100   200   300m

☐ Roman fortification, the 'city'
▨ Frankish settlement, called 'New City', walled at end of ninth century
▧ Extension of Frankish settlement before 1200 to include Alt St. Peter's parish
▨ Jung St. Peter's parish, walled 1202–1220
▨ St. Nikolaus parish, walled thirteenth and fourteenth centuries
▨ St. Johann Parish, walled 1374–1390
- - - St. Wilhelm parish, walled 1387–1441

THE METAMORPHOSIS OF A MEDIEVAL CITY. The city of Strasbourg, on the long-disputed border between modern Germany and France, exemplifies the multilayered dynamics of urban change throughout the Middle Ages. It began as a Roman settlement, which became the nucleus for an episcopal see—hence the cathedral (1) located in the ancient precinct. It was fortified with new walls at the end of the ninth century, as the Carolingian Empire was collapsing and the Vikings were on the move. It then responded to the renewed prosperity of the eleventh and twelfth centuries, far outgrowing its original bounds, and continued to expand for several centuries thereafter. ▪ *Note the scale of the map. What can you conclude from this about the density of settlement in a medieval city?*

From Italy, exotic goods flowed northward to the towns of Flanders and the fairs (international markets convened at certain times of the year) that enriched the county of Champagne. Flemish towns, in turn, kept up a brisk trade with England, processing English wool into the cloth which, alongside wheat and wine, was the staple commodity of medieval Europe.

It would be misleading, however, to overemphasize the role of long-distance trade. Some towns dependent on such commerce, like Venice and Genoa, attracted populations approaching 100,000 by 1300. But others that grew to be as large, including Paris and London, drew primarily on the wealth of their surrounding hinterlands. Towns large and small existed in a symbiotic relationship with the countryside, transforming raw materials into marketable goods through manufacturing.

"Town Air Makes You Free"

To modern eyes, most premodern towns would still have seemed half rural. Streets were often unpaved and animals were everywhere. Sanitary conditions were poor, and disease could spread rapidly. Fire was another omnipresent danger, because wooden and thatched buildings were clustered close together.

But these inconveniences were far outweighed by the advantages of urban life. As a German adage puts it, "Town air makes you free" (*Stadtluft macht Frei*). The citizens of most medieval towns were not subject to the arbitrary jurisdiction of a lord—or if they were, the lord realized that rewarding initiative with further freedoms fostered still more initiative and produced more wealth. Many Catalonian and Flemish towns accordingly received charters of liberty from the counts of these regions, and were given the right to govern themselves. Others seized that right: in 1127, the people of Arras, on the Franco-Flemish border, declared that they were no longer the serfs of the local monastery and banded together to form a commune, a form of representative government. The monastery was forced to free them, and then free to tax them. The arrangement was mutually beneficial: by the end of the century, Arras was the wealthiest town in northern Europe.

Urban areas further expanded through the constant immigration of free peasants and escaped serfs in search of a better life. For once a town had established its independence, newcomers could claim the status of citizens after a year and a day. For this reason, some powerful lords and rulers resisted the efforts of towns to claim independence. Almost inevitably, they paid a high price for this. In Rome, the pope's claim to secular authority over the city led to frequent uprisings. In the French city of Laon, the bishop who attempted to suppress a newly formed commune was murdered in 1112. In 1127, the count of Flanders was assassinated by a powerful family who resented his claims that they were, in fact, his serfs.

Portable Wealth: Money and Credit

The growth of towns and trade depends not only on surplus goods, initiative, and mobility. It also depends on money: it is no accident that the earliest participants in the commercial

MEDIEVAL TRADE ROUTES. ■ *What does this map reveal about the relationship between waterways and overland routes during the eleventh and twelfth centuries?* ■ *Which regions appear to be most extensively interconnected, and why?* ■ *How does the trade in certain specialized goods create particular commercial patterns?*

revolution of the Middle Ages were cities located in regions whose rulers minted and regulated a strong currency. Yet precisely because there were so many currencies in circulation, the economy also depended on moneychangers and bankers who could extend credit, thus obviating the need for merchants to travel with bags full of cash.

In western Europe, much of this crucial activity was facilitated by bankers situated within the network of close-knit Jewish communities that connected cities like Constantinople, Baghdad, and Córdoba to the burgeoning cities of the north. In many regions, Jews had a virtual monopoly on these activities, because Christians were technically forbidden to lend money at interest. This practice was called *usury* (from the Latin word for "interest"), and Christian theologians cited various passages from the Old and New Testaments which seemed to condemn it. But in practice, the Church turned a blind eye to such practices. Indeed, many prominent churchmen, including bishops, made fortunes lending money.

Still, the moral stigma attaching to this necessary practice meant that Jews were often targeted at times of crisis, just as they were the people to whom rulers would turn when they needed funds—which helps to explain why many kings, princes, and bishops protected the Jewish communities in their realms and often extended special privileges to them. The unfortunate result of this Christian hypocrisy was the circulation of conspiracy theories harmful to Jews, who were perceived as exercising control over Christians through secret channels of communication and a stranglehold on finance.

Jewish communities' reliance on the protection of powerful men also made them vulnerable when those men withdrew their support or were incapable of controlling the violence unleashed by their own policies.

VIOLENCE AND LORDSHIP

The new wealth of western Europe fostered social mobility, yet it also created a more stratified society. In the Carolingian period, the nobility had comprised a relatively small number of ancient families who counted one another as equals and married among themselves. During the tenth and eleventh centuries, however, new families began to emerge as territorial lords, rivaling and sometimes surpassing the old aristocracy in power and wealth. Some of these new families were descended from lesser officeholders in the Carolingian administration, men who had established independent powers after the empire collapsed. Others were interlopers who sustained war-bands of treasure-hungry young men.

Castles and Knights

The predatory lords who emerged in this period protected their families and followers by building strongholds: castles, from the Latin word *castellum*, "little fortress." These structures, scarcely known in Europe before the Viking invasions, came to dominate the landscape in the eleventh and twelfth centuries. The castle was both defensive and offensive. It rendered its owner more secure from arson and attack—though it was vulnerable to siege—and it enabled him to subdue the surrounding countryside. Indeed, castles often formed the nucleus of a new town by providing protection for those who clustered their dwellings close to its walls. In case of attack, these outliers could move inside.

Most early castles were modest structures built of wood, situated on earthwork mounds surrounded by a ditch or moat. But stone walls and keeps (fortified towers) soon replaced wooden palisades as the level of competitive violence increased. In Italy, rival families even built castles in the middle of towns. Eventually, some castellans ("castle-holders") acquired enough power to challenge more established authorities. These new lords didn't descend from Roman senators or Carolingian counts; instead, they boasted of lineages reaching back to successful warlords like Rollo the Viking, whom the Normans claimed to be their first duke (from the Latin *dux*, "leader").

Both the older aristocracy and these self-made lords needed the help of warriors to enforce their claims to power. Each accordingly maintained a private army of men equipped with the new weaponry and armor that the availability of iron—and new techniques for smelting it—made possible. These men fought on horseback and were therefore called "horsemen": in French, *chevaliers*, and in English, *knights*. Some were the younger sons of lords who sought to increase their chances of winning wealth by attaching themselves to the households of still greater lords. Others were youths recruited from the peasantry, mounted and armed. All that bound them together was the violent prosecution of their lord's interests. Gradually, though, knights also came to regard themselves as belonging to a special military caste with its own rules of conduct. The beginnings of this process are discernible in *The Song of Roland*, and further developments in the twelfth and thirteenth centuries would transform the meaning of chivalry from "horsemanship" to something very different (see Chapter 9).

Kings, Lords, and Vassals

Despite the emergence of self-governing cities and predatory lordships, the Capetian rulers of Paris kept alive the pretence that everyone dwelling in the lands once ruled by more powerful Frankish kings still owed allegiance to them, while the Ottonians claimed to be kings in northern Italy as well as in their own Saxon domain. In practice, however, neither the Ottonians nor the Capetians were able to control the territories they claimed to rule. Effective political and military power lay in the hands of dukes, counts, castellans, and knights. From their castles, these lords (*domini*) constructed dominions: lordships within which they exercised the rights to mint money, judge legal cases, collect taxes, impose tolls, raise troops, and wage war.

YORK CASTLE (ENGLAND). This fortification exemplifies some of the major phases of medieval castle building. The large mound is the remains of an earthwork erected on the orders of William the Conqueror in 1068, when it would have been crowned by a wooden palisade: this most basic type of construction is called a motte-and-bailey castle. York's castle remained a wooden tower until it was destroyed by fire and rebuilt in stone after 1245. It is now known as Clifford's Tower after a rebel leader called Sir Roger Clifford, who was held there prior to his execution in 1322.

The Problem of Feudalism

This highly diffused distribution of power is conventionally known as "feudalism." This is a misleading term, not least because it is a modern invention. As such, it is also confusing, because it has been used by different people to mean different things. For example, scholars influenced by the work of Karl Marx (1818–1883, see Chapter 20) once used "feudalism" to describe a "mode of production" in which wealth is entirely agricultural and cities have not yet formed; but as we have seen, this does not reflect the historical reality of the eleventh and twelfth centuries. For other scholars, "feudalism" is an aristocratic social order in which propertied men are supported by the labor of serfs attached to manors; again, this does not explain the varieties of power wielded in this period. Still others have described "feudalism" as a system in which lesser men hold land from greater men in return for military service of various kinds; but it was not always the greater man who held the most land.

Because all of these definitions are more or less anachronistic, many recent historians have abandoned the term altogether. If, however, we look for a common denominator, we can say that "feudalism" entails the abuse of official privileges for personal gain: the pattern that emerged after the Carolingian Empire had disintegrated. And although people of the time would never have heard the term "feudalism," they would have understood the word at its root: *feudum*, usually translated as "fief" (FEEF). A fief is a gift or grant that creates a kind of contractual relationship between the giver and receiver. This gift could be land, but it could also be the revenues from a toll or a mill, or an annual sum of money. In return, the recipient would owe the giver loyalty or services of some kind, and might even be subordinate to the giver, becoming the giver's *vassal* (from a Celtic word meaning "boy").

This relationship was dramatized in an act of *homage*, a powerful ceremony that made the vassal "the man" (in French, *homme*) of his lord. Typically, the vassal would kneel and place his hands together in a gesture of supplication, and the lord would cover the clasped hands with his own. He would then raise up his new "man" and exchange a kiss with him. The symbolic importance of these actions is powerfully clear: the lord (*dominus*) was literally the dominating figure, who could protect and raise up his man— but could also discipline and humiliate him.

In a violent world where no central authority existed, these personal relationships were essential to creating and maintaining order. However, these relationships were not forged or understood in the same ways all over Europe. Nor were they neatly hierarchical. "Feudalism" therefore created no "feudal pyramids," in which knights held fiefs from counts, and counts held fiefs from kings, all in an orderly fashion. Sometimes, kings would insist that the world *should* be structured this way, but they were seldom able to enforce this.

A New Feudal Monarchy: England

The first place where we can begin to observe the efforts of a particular line of kings to establish a monarchy that did operate along these lines is England. In 1066, Duke William of Normandy claimed that he was the rightful successor of the English king, Edward, who had just died. But the English elected a new king, Harold, ignoring William's claim. So William and his army crossed the English Channel to take the kingdom by force, defeating Harold's forces at the Battle of Hastings (see **Interpreting Visual Evidence** on page 192).

Now, however, William had to subjugate all of the other English chieftains who held power, many of whom also aspired to be king. He accomplished this, first, by asserting that he was king by imperial conquest as well as by succession, and that all the land of England consequently belonged to him. Then William rewarded his Norman followers with fiefs: extensive grants of land taken from their English holders, which the Norman lords were allowed to exploit and subdue; in return, William received their homage, loyalty, and a share of their revenues.

The Normans were already accustomed to holding land in return for service in Normandy. But in England, their subordination to the new king was enforced by the effective machinery of the English state and by longstanding English customs that had the force of law. In England, unlike on the Continent, only the king could coin money, collect taxes, supervise justice, and raise an army. William also retained the Anglo-Saxon officers of local government, known as sheriffs, to administer and enforce these rights. William's kingship thus represented a fusion of Carolingian-style traditions of public power with the new type of lordship that had grown up in the tenth and eleventh centuries. It was a feudal monarchy.

The Struggle for Imperial Power

We can contrast the wide-ranging powers of the new Anglo-Norman kings with those of Germany. The German king ruled only a single principality, and his imperial authority over a host of other rulers was only maintained through a close alliance with the Church. Indeed, his chief administrators were archbishops and bishops whom the emperor himself had appointed and installed in their sacred offices, just as Charlemagne had done.

The Graphic History of the Bayeux Tapestry

One of the most famous historical documents of all time is not a document at all: it is an embroidered strip of linen 231 feet long (originally much longer) and 20 inches wide. It is also not a tapestry, as its name misleadingly implies, but an elaborate exercise in needlepoint. It tells the story of the Norman Conquest of England and the events leading up to it. The circumstances of its making remain mysterious, but it was certainly commissioned by someone close to William the Conqueror (1027–1087), the Norman duke who claimed the throne of England in 1066. Indeed, its purpose was to justify William's invasion of England after Harold Godwinson (c. 1022–1066), was crowned king of England in his place (image B). One likely patron is Queen Edith of England, the widow of the late King Edward (r. 1042–66) and sister of Harold, who became a friend and advisor to William. Edith was noted for her skill in embroidery as well as for her political acumen, and she would have been able to oversee the making of this visual history by the women of her household. Two of its evocative scenes, with translations of accompanying Latin texts, are reproduced here.

A. Here Harold Sails the Sea. In this scene from the first portion of the Tapestry, Harold has been sent on an embassy by King Edward. He feasts with friends in a hall on the English coast before crossing the Channel.

B. Here Is Seated Harold, King of the English. Although Harold may have promised to relinquish his claim to the English throne, the central scene of the tapestry is his coronation. Stigant, the archbishop of Canterbury, stands on his left. Outside the cathedral, the people of London look on curiously. Some appear to be surprised or alarmed.

Questions for Analysis

1. Like a graphic novel or a comic strip, the Bayeux Tapestry tells its story through images; words (in very simple Latin) play a minor role. What do the Tapestry's artists choose to express exclusively through visualization? When do they choose to state something verbally? What might be the motivation behind these choices? What is left out of the story, or left ambiguous? What might be the reason(s) for this?

2. In addition to being a source for political and military historians, the Bayeux Tapestry provides us with fascinating glimpses into the daily life and material culture of the Middle Ages. What, for example, can you conclude about the necessary preparations for a voyage by sea, or about the history of clothing, or weaponry, or animals?

3. If Queen Edith is responsible for making the Tapestry, it would constitute one of the few surviving historical accounts by a woman prior to the twentieth century. Would the fact of the creator's gender change your perception of this artifact, or of these particular scenes? Why or why not?

R exrogat ABBAT em. MATHILDIM SupplicatAtꝗ;

MATILDA OF TUSCANY MEDIATES BETWEEN EMPEROR AND POPE. Matilda was one of the most powerful rulers in eleventh-century Europe, controlling many strategic territories in northern Italy. Fluent in German as well as Latin and Italian, she was a supporter of the reforming movement within the Church. The Latin inscription accompanying this manuscript miniature reads: "The King entreats the Abbot [i.e., the pope] and also humbles himself before Matilda." ▪ *How does this image represent the relationships among these figures?* ▪ *Which appears to be the most powerful, and why?*

acknowledge the pope's superiority. Crossing the Alps into Italy in 1077, in the depths of winter, he found Gregory at the castle of Canossa and under the protection of one of Europe's most powerful rulers, Matilda of Tuscany. Encouraged by Matilda, Henry performed an elaborate ritual of penance, standing for three successive days outside the castle, barefoot, stripped of imperial trappings, clad only in sackcloth.

This performance forestalled Henry's deposition but it did not resolve his dispute with the German nobility. And it also reversed the relationship between secular power and religious power. Since the time of Constantine, popes had been dependant on the rulers who protected them. Now an emperor had been bested by the pope.

RELIGIOUS REFORM AND PAPAL POWER

The increased power of the papacy in the eleventh century was a development that would have been hard to foresee at the time of the Charlemagne's death. But the redistribution of power within the former Carolingian Empire meant that no ruler could maintain Charlemagne's hold on the Church. Those parish churches that survived were often regarded as the personal property of some local family. Bishoprics, too, were co-opted by families who regarded Church lands and offices as their private property. Even monasteries underwent a process of privatization, becoming safe havens for aristocratic younger sons and daughters with little inclination for religious life. Meanwhile, the holders of papal office were its worst abusers. Most were incompetent or corrupt, the sons or tools of powerful Roman families. Many fathered sons who themselves succeeded to high ecclesiastical office, including that of pope. By the tenth century, the papacy's credibility had been severely compromised.

The Monastic Reform Movement

The first successful attempts to restore the spiritual authority of the Church can be traced to the founding of a new kind of monastery in Burgundy (now southeastern France). In 910, a Benedictine abbey called Cluny freed itself from any obligation to local families by placing itself under the direct protection of the papacy. Although it had a wealthy benefactor, this lord relinquished control over Cluny's property; instead, he and his family were granted special spiritual privileges, thus guaranteeing their eternal reward in Heaven.

This arrangement would set a new precedent for the relationship between monasteries and powerful families for centuries to come, as Cluny began to sponsor other

But in the latter half of the eleventh century, this close cooperation between sacred and secular authority was fractured. In 1056, the six-year-old Henry IV (1050–1106) succeeded his father as king and emperor, and the German princes of various regions tried to gain control of the royal government at the expense of Henry's regents. When Henry began to rule in his own right, in 1073, these hostilities escalated into a civil war. At the same time, the newly elected pope, Gregory VII (r. 1073–85), began to insist that no laymen—not even kings—should have any influence within the Church.

King Henry, of course, resisted any initiative that would prohibit him from selecting his own bishops, who were the key administrators of his realm. So Pope Gregory allied himself with the rebellious nobility and moved to depose Henry. In order to save his crown, Henry was thus forced to

Analyzing Primary Sources

A Miraculous Reliquary

Although pilgrimages had been a part of Christian religious practice for centuries, they became more central elements of popular piety from the tenth century on. Pilgrims brought money and spiritual prestige to the monasteries that housed miracle-working relics, and competition among monastic houses sometimes led one house to steal the relics of another. But some critics worried that these newly popular shrines were encouraging idolatry. Bernard of Angers (c. 960–1028) was one such critic. His account of a visit to the shrines of several saints, including that of Sainte Foy ("Saint Faith") at Conques in southern France, reveals the negative impression that ornate reliquaries made on him—and the power of wonder-working relics to correct that impression.

 t is an ancient custom in all of Auvergne, Rodez, Toulouse, and the neighboring regions that the local saint has a statue of gold, silver, or some other metal . . . [that] serves as a reliquary for the head of the saint or for a part of his body. The learned might see in this a superstition and a vestige of the cult of demons, and I myself . . . had the same impression the first time I saw the statue of Saint Gerard . . . resplendent with gold and stones, with an expression so human that the simple people . . . pretend that it winks at pilgrims whose prayers it answers. I admit to my shame that turning to my friend Bernerius and laughing I whispered to him in Latin, "What do you think of the idol? Wouldn't Jupiter or Mars be happy with it?" . . .

Three days later we arrived at [the shrine of] St. Faith. . . . We approached [the reliquary] but the crowd was such that we could not prostrate ourselves like so many others already lying on the floor. Unhappy, I remained standing, fixing my view on the image and murmuring this prayer, "St. Faith, you whose relics rest in this sham, come to my assistance on the day of judgment." And this time I looked at my companion . . . because I found it outrageous that all of these rational beings should be praying to a mute and inanimate object. . . .

Later I greatly regretted to have acted so stupidly toward the saint of God.

This was because among other miracles [that] Don Adalgerius, at that time dean and later . . . abbot [of Conques], told me [was] a remarkable account of a cleric named Oldaric. One day when the venerable image had to be taken to another place, . . . he restrained the crowd from bringing offerings and he insulted

The reliquary of Saint Faith, early tenth century.

and belittled the image of the saint. . . . The next night, a lady of imposing severity appeared to him: "You," she said, "how dare you insult my image?" Having said this, she flogged her enemy with a staff. . . . He survived only long enough to tell the vision in the morning.

Thus there is no place left for arguing whether the effigy of St. Faith ought to be venerated, since it is clear that he who reproached the holy martyr nevertheless retracted his reproach. Nor is it a spurious idol where nefarious rites of sacrifice or of divination are conducted, but rather a pious memorial of a holy virgin, before which great numbers of faithful people decently and eloquently implore her efficacious intercession for their sins.

Source: Bernard of Angers, "The Book of the Miracles of St. Faith," in Patrick J. Geary, ed. and trans., *Readings in Medieval History*, 3rd ed. (Peterborough, Ont., Canada: 2003), pp. 333–34 (slightly modified).

Questions for Analysis

1. Why does Bernard initially object to the display of relics in ornate reliquaries? Why would he consider this practice blasphemous? How does he become reconciled to it?

2. Can you think of present-day practices that resemble the medieval fascination with collecting, displaying, and venerating relics? What do such practices reveal about any society?

monasteries on the same model. Indeed, the foundation of daughter houses was another innovation: prior to this, all Benedictine monasteries had been independent of one another, united only by their observance of Benedict's *Rule*. Now Cluny established a network of Cluniac clones across Europe, each one performing the same elaborate round of prayer and worship for which Cluny became famous, and each one entirely free from the control of local lords.

Cluniac influence was strongest in the former Frankish territories and in Italy, where the virtual absence of effective rulers allowed monastic reforms to thrive unchecked. In Germany and Anglo-Saxon England, by contrast, monastic reform emerged as an essential responsibility of Christian kings whose role model was the pious Charlemagne. These kings, too, followed Cluniac example by insisting on the strict observance of poverty, chastity, and obedience within the monastery, and on the performance of liturgical prayer. Yet because these kings were the guarantors of the monasteries' freedom from outside interference, it was they who appointed the abbots, just as they also appointed the bishops of their kingdoms.

These parallel reforming movements made monasticism the dominant spiritual model for Latin Christianity, and monasteries' peaceful, orderly round of daily worship was regarded as mirroring the perfect harmony of Heaven. Monasteries also had an important influence on the piety of ordinary people, because many monastic communities maintained parishes that ministered to the laity. The spiritual practices that had once been unique to monks and nuns in earlier centuries therefore came to influence daily life outside the cloister.

One potent example of this new popular spirituality is the growing devotion to relics. Monasteries were often the repositories of cherished objects associated with saints, such as fragments of bone or pieces of cloth cut from the garments of some holy person. These souvenirs were believed to possess special protective and curative powers. A relic was usually buried beneath the altar of a monastery's church, and relics were also collected and displayed in elaborate reliquaries made of precious metals and studded with jewels. Indeed, the relics themselves were so valuable that monasteries competed with one another for their acquistion and even plotted the "holy theft" of a particularly prized treasure. For instance, the relics of Nicholas, a fourth-century bishop of Myra (in Turkey), were stolen from the saint's tomb during the eleventh century and brought to Bari in southeastern Italy, where Benedictine monks built a magnificent church to house them.

The possession and display of relics thus became a way for monasteries to generate revenue, since those who sought cures or favors at the shrine of a saint would often make a donation to the monastery in the saint's honor. If a saint was especially famous for a particular type of miracle, pilgrims might travel thousands of miles to visit a shrine. Saint Nicholas was famous for increasing the wealth of his suppliants, and for bestowing gifts—hence his later incarnation as Santa Claus. Those of the apostle James at Compostela (northwestern Spain) became the chief destination on a major pilgrimage route, rivaling even the holy sites of Rome and Jerusalem. Pilgrimage was another of the important ways in which the new patterns of Christian piety that developed in monasteries began to spread to the laity.

The Reform of the Papacy

By the eleventh century, the powerful movement toward spiritual renewal began to embrace the sees of bishops. This was a major change: bishops and the priests who served in their dioceses were secular clergy, living in the world (*saeculum* in Latin); it had long been expected that they would share some of the worldly preoccupations and lifestyles of their parishioners. But as their influence grew, the monasteries under the sway of Cluny began to lobby for even larger reforms, amounting to a fundamental dismantling of customs that reached back to the organization of the Church under Constantine, seven centuries earlier. They centered their attacks on simony (*SIGH-mony*), a term describing any use of ecclesiastical office for personal gain, including the purchase or sale of a bishopric or a priest's living (i.e., house, goods, and annual salary).

Even more radical was the reformers' demand that secular clergy share the lifestyles of monks, taking vows of personal poverty and celibacy. Although some early councils of the Church had attempted to regulate the marriage of bishops and priests, none had been successful. There were good reasons for this: the task of ministering to the laity was very different from the monk's task of perpetual prayer and communal life. For a thousand years, it had been conceded that the demands of priestly celibacy were not only unreasonable, they would deprive a priest's parishioners of an additional resource and ministry: that of his wife. As a result, the vast majority of parish priests all across Europe were married, and in the Eastern Orthodox Church they would remain so. Married bishops were rarer, but not unknown. In Brittany, the archbishop of Dol and his wife publicly celebrated the marriages of their daughters, endowing them with lands belonging to the bishopric; in Milan, the archbishops flatly rejected reformers' calls for celibacy, declaring that their patron saint, Ambrose (Chapter 6), had been married, too.

In Rome, the papacy remained resolutely unreformed until 1046, when the German emperor Henry III deposed three rival Roman nobles who claimed to be pope and appointed in their place his own relative, a monk who adopted the name Leo IX (r. 1049–54). Leo and his supporters began to promulgate decrees against simony and clerical marriage. They then took steps to enforce these decrees by traveling throughout the Continent, disciplining clerics deemed guilty of simony or obstinately determined not to "put away" their wives—whom the reformers insisted on calling "concubines" as a way of discrediting these respectable relationships.

Implicit in Leo's reforming efforts was a new vision of the Church as a type of feudal monarchy, with the pope at the apex of a spiritual pyramid. Not surprisingly, therefore, Leo and his successors met with considerable opposition within the Church itself, and they could only enforce their claims in regions where they had the support of secular rulers.

But when Henry III died in 1056, the regents of his child heir Henry IV (whose reign we discussed above) were neither able nor willing to stand behind the reforming movement. The Roman aristocracy seized this opportunity to install one of their own number on the papal throne. By this time, however, the reform movement had gathered momentum; a year later, a new pope had been installed who was determined to counter any interference from either the German or Italian nobility. To this end, Nicholas II (r. 1059–61) created a new legislative body, the College of Cardinals (from the Latin for "collection" of "hinges"). The College became the pivotal force for the creation of papal policy, and it also ensured the continuity of the papal office by overseeing the selection of new popes, a role it still plays today. Most fundamentally, this removed the emperor's power to oversee the process of elections himself.

The Investiture Conflict

A few years after Henry IV began to rule in his own right, the new College of Cardinals selected as pope a zealous reformer called Hildebrand, a Cluniac monk of Tuscan origins who took the name Gregory VII. Initially, pope and emperor treated one another with deference. Henry IV's position in Germany had been weakened by civil wars, and he needed papal backing to restore his authority.

Two years later, however, relations between pope and emperor were riven by a conflict that would permanently alter the relationship between spiritual and temporal rulers in western Europe. Superficially, the issue that divided Gregory and Henry was that of investiture: the right to appoint bishops and to equip them with the trappings of

office. Since the time of the Carolingians, this had been the prerogative of the emperor. But to Gregory, this practice smacked of simony, since a lay lord would obviously choose bishops who would be politically useful to him, regardless of their spiritual qualifications.

The real issue, however, was not the political power of bishops; it was control of that power. For paradoxically, the papal reform movement was predicated on liberating the Church from powerful influences in order that the Church itself might become more powerful. This was the principle that lay behind the discouraging of clerical marriage, too: Church offices and Church property had to be protected by the Church for the Church. Allowing priests to marry might encourage the handing down of offices to sons, just as allowing rulers to appoint bishops encouraged bishops to act as the rulers' agents. These practices tainted the austere authority that the pope was trying to cultivate, and it also threatened to alienate property that the papacy wanted to harness for its own purposes.

Gregory took the reform movement to a new level by insisting that adherence to these principles was not just a matter of policy but a matter of religious dogma, defined as "a truth necessary for salvation." When Henry IV defiantly proceeded to invest the new archbishop of Milan, Gregory excommunicated a number of Henry's advisors, including several bishops. Henry thereupon renounced his obedience to Gregory, calling on him to resign. Gregory responded by excommunicating Henry.

In itself, the excommunication of a king was not terribly unusual. Gregory, however, went much further by equating excommunication with deposition: since Henry was no longer a faithful son of the Church, he was no longer the king of Germany and his subjects had a sacred duty to rebel against him. It was this that occasioned Henry's humiliating stand before the castle at Canossa in January of 1077, which we discussed above. But the story does not end there, because Henry eventually used his restored powers to drive Gregory himself from Rome. In 1085, the aged pope died in exile in southern Italy. By then, however, he had established the principles on which papal governance would be based for the remainder of the Middle Ages.

In 1122, the conflict over investiture was ultimately resolved at the Concordat of Worms (VOHRMS) in Germany. Its terms declared that the emperor was forbidden to invest bishops with the *religious* symbols of their office, but was allowed to bestow their rights as *temporal* rulers, in his capacity as their overlord. In practice, then, the rulers of Europe retained a great deal of influence over ecclesiastical appointments. But they also had to acknowledge that bishops were now part of a new hierarchy headed by the pope, loyal to Rome and not to the ruler of the region in which they lived.

CRUSADING CAUSES AND OUTCOMES

Gregory VII's equation of excommunication with deposition had given the pope a powerful new weapon to use against wayward rulers. Indeed, Gregory insisted that the pope has the power to judge all men but cannot himself be judged by any earthly authority. Moreover, he asserted the pope's power to free any man from obligations to his lord, on the grounds that every Christian owes ultimate loyalty to the pope, the sole representative of Christ on earth and the arbiter of eternal life or death. These were big claims. How could they be realized? In the end, it took the appeal of a Byzantine emperor and the preaching of a crusade against Islam to unite western Christendom under the banner of the papacy.

The Expansion and Limitations of Byzantium

As western Europe expanded and grew prosperous, the Eastern Roman Empire was undergoing its own transformations. The decline of the Abbasid caliphate in Baghdad had relieved some of the pressures on the eastern frontier in the course of the ninth century. Yet at the same time, a Muslim fleet captured the Byzantine islands of Sicily and Crete; the migration of pagan Slavs into the Balkans was rapidly undermining Byzantine control of that region; and a formidable enemy had emerged in the north, as the Vikings known as the Rus' established themselves along the river systems that fed into the Black and Caspian Seas. The Rus's most important trading partner was the Abbasid caliphate, with which they exchanged slaves, honey, wax, and furs in return for silver, Indian spices, and Chinese silks. But the Rus' knew their way to Constantinople, too. In 860, while the Byzantine emperor and his army were busy elsewhere, a fleet of Russian Vikings sailed into the Black Sea and attacked the capital.

A century later, Greek-speaking missionaries began converting the Balkan Slavs to Orthodox Christianity, devising for them a written language known as Old Church Slavonic and creating the Cyrillic alphabet still used today in Bulgaria, Serbia, and Russia. Byzantine rulers also established a military and commercial alliance with the Rus' kingdom centered around Kiev. In 911, about 700 Rus' fought with the Byzantine fleet in an attack on Muslim Crete. In 957, a Kievan Christian princess named Olga was lavishly entertained on a state visit to Constantinople. And in 989, the emperor Basil II turned to Vladimir, prince of Kiev, for the troops he needed to win a civil war against an imperial rival. In return

for Vladimir's help, Basil married him to his sister Anna; and Vladimir, along with his people, accepted baptism into the Orthodox Church. Russia has remained strongly Orthodox to this day, despite Soviet efforts to dismantle the Russian Orthodox Church in the twentieth century.

At the same time, the Byzantines launched a series of successful campaigns against the Abbasids, reconquering territories that had been lost since the seventh century. Most peoples of this region had remained Christian through three centuries of benign Islamic rule, but the Armenians and the Syrians in particular had their own distinctive Christian traditions that were at odds, both doctrinally and linguistically, with the Greek-speaking church at Constantinople. Reincorporating these "heretics" into the empire thus strained the limits of Byzantine orthodoxy to a considerable degree, and it also created centers of power that lay outside the imperial capital at Constantinople. Accordingly, rivalries divided the eastern nobility and the imperial court, eventually erupting into warfare after one aristocratic family attempted a coup.

Meanwhile, these projects of reconquest and expansion were overextending the Byzantine military and its treasury. In an effort to raise cash, some emperors in the mid-eleventh century began to debase the gold coinage that had kept the empire competitive with the Muslim caliphates, thus undermining Byzantine commerce at the very moment when Venice, Genoa, and Pisa were consolidating their control in the eastern Mediterranean and taking over the lucrative trade between Muslim North Africa (including Egypt) and western Europe.

The failing economy, ongoing civil war, a divided army, and unrest in the Balkans had therefore already weakened Byzantine sovereignty when the empire was confronted with yet another threat. The Seljuqs, a powerful dynasty of Sunni Muslims who were building their own empire based in Persia, began to move westward. In 1071, they captured Armenia and moved swiftly into the Byzantine heartland of Anatolia (Turkey), where they destroyed the army sent to deflect them. In the same year, the Seljuqs captured Jerusalem, which had been part of the Shi'ite caliphate based in Egypt, ruled by the Fatimids (Chapter 7). By 1081, when the eastern nobility of Byzantium finally emerged triumphant in its ongoing bid for the imperial throne, the new emperor Alexius Comnenus (r. 1081–1118) found himself at the head of a crippled state.

The Call for a Crusade

In the first decade of his rule, Alexius managed to shore up the failing economy and to secure his hold over the Balkans. He then began to plan a campaign against the Seljuqs. But with what forces? The Byzantine army barely

THE BYZANTINE EMPIRE, c. 1025. ■ *According to this map, what political challenges faced the Byzantine Empire in the eleventh century?* ■ *How was the long-standing influence of Muslims in the Near East likely to affect the character of Byzantine culture?* ■ *How did the domain of Kievan Russia potentially create additional economic and military pressure on Byzantium, directly as well as indirectly?*

would be successful if pitted against the lightly armored Seljuqs.

It was in the hopes of recruiting a mercenary force, therefore, that Alexius approached Pope Urban II (r. 1088–99). This was a move that played into the hands of the papacy. Urban was trying hard to realize some of the powerful claims that Gregory VII had made on behalf of papal authority, and this seemed like a golden opportunity. By coming to the aid of Byzantium, he would show the restive princes of western Europe that the papacy was a force to be reckoned with. At the same time, he hoped to show that Western military and spiritual might was greater than that of the weakened East, thereby realizing a centuries-old dream of a universal Christian Church based in Rome, with the pope himself at its head. In addition, Urban would show support for another reforming effort that had gained momentum in recent years: a peace movement that was attempting to quell the endemic violence unleashed by competitive bands of knights and their rapacious lords. What better way to defuse the situation than to ship those violent energies overseas, deploying them against a common enemy?

So Alexius got far more than he had bargained for. He had needed a modest contingent of a few thousand troops, to help him reconquer Anatolia. What he got was a vast army of 100,000 men, charged by Urban II to retake the holy city of Jerusalem for Christendom. For Urban decided to interpret Alexius's request loosely. Speaking before an assembled crowd at Clermont (in France) in 1095, he announced that any knights who wished to fight, pillage, and wreak havoc could do so for a just and Christian cause by liberating the Holy Land from its Muslim captors. Here at home, he said they were riffraff and marauders, destined for hellfire and damnation; abroad, they would be crusaders, which meant that anyone fighting or dying in the service of Christ would win absolution for his sins. By taking up the cross (*crux*, hence "crusade"), a warrior stood to win glory, booty, and salvation.

The ultimate response to Urban's call exceeded all expectations. Indeed, his message was amplified by other

existed, having been decimated in Greece by a far superior cavalry of Norman knights in 1085. For by this time, the Normans had established independent principalities in southern Italy and Sicily, taking advantage of the perpetual power vacuum in those regions and showcasing the effective tactics of chivalry. This encounter between the Byzantine emperor and western Europe's best warriors was fateful: it convinced Alexius that heavily armed horsemen

ROLAND AS A CRUSADING KNIGHT. The association between knighthood and crusading helped to raise the social status of knights and contributed to the refinement of a chivalric ethos. Here, a crusading knight, dressed head to foot in expensive chain mail, is shown kneeling in homage to his lord, God.

their vows, the vast majority went home. So why did they go in the first place? The risks of dying on such a journey were high; the costs of embarking were enormous. By any rational assessment, the Crusade was a fool's errand.

Hence the importance of reckoning with the reality of the crusaders' piety. Crusading was the ultimate pilgrimage. If one could receive special blessings by traveling to Compostela, Conques, or Bari, how much more blessed would one be if one fought through to the Holy Land itself! Urban II made this point explicit at Clermont, and some preachers went even further, promising that crusaders would be entirely freed from otherworldly punishments for all sins committed up to that point in their lives, and that the souls of those who died on crusade would go straight to Heaven.

Crusade preaching also emphasized the vengeance that Christ's soldiers should exact on the Church's enemies in the East. But to some crusaders, it seemed absurd to wait until they arrived in Jerusalem to undertake this aspect of their mission. Muslims might hold Jesus's property at Jerusalem, but Christian theology held Jews responsible for the death of Jesus himself. Assaults against Jewish communities therefore began in the spring of 1096 and quickly spread eastward with the crusaders. Hundreds of Jews were killed in the German towns of Mainz, Worms, Speyer, and Cologne, and hundreds more were forcibly baptized as the price for escaping death at the hands of crusading knights. Many individual churchmen attempted to prevent these attacks, among them the bishops in whose dioceses Jews lived. But the Church's own negative propaganda thwarted these efforts, and pogroms against Europe's Jews would remain a regular and terrible feature of Christian crusading.

The Christian Conquest of Jerusalem

Surprised by the scale of the response to his appeal, Emperor Alexius did his best to move the crusaders quickly through Constantinople and into Asia Minor. But differences in outlook between the crusaders and the emperor quickly became apparent. Alexius had little interest in an expedition to Jerusalem, and insisted that the crusaders promise to restore any territory they captured to him. To the crusaders—whose view of their mission had been shaped by Urban's policies (not those of Alexius)—this seemed like treachery. The crusaders, furthermore, did not understand the Byzantine emperor's willingness to make alliances with some Muslim rulers (the Shi'ite Fatimids of Egypt and the Abbasids of Baghdad) against other Muslim rulers (the Sunni Seljuqs), and they ignorantly concluded that the Byzantines were working to undermine the crusading effort.

preachers, including a zealous priest called Peter the Hermit, who alleged that the Seljuqs had prevented him from visiting the Holy Land. Within a year, tens of thousands of warriors and a large number of women and children were on the move toward Constantinople. As with any large enterprise, the participants' motives must have varied. A few might have hoped to win principalities for themselves in the wild East. Many were the dependents of other men, and had no choice but to accompany their lords; some hoped to free themselves from dependence by fighting. Most had no idea how long the journey would be, or knew anything about the places for which they were destined.

But except for a few of the greatest lords—mostly Normans from southern Italy—the prospect of winning new lands in the East was both unlikely and undesired. Indeed, one of the greatest challenges facing the Christian kingdom established in Jerusalem after 1099 was the fact that crusaders so rarely wanted to stay there. After fulfilling

THE ROUTES OF THE CRUSADERS, 1096–1204. Compare the routes followed by participants in the first three Crusades. ▪ *What were the three main routes followed by crusaders?* ▪ *What geographical and political factors appear to be determining these trajectories?* ▪ *Why was the Fourth Crusade's route so different?*

Viewed from the perspective of Alexius, the Crusade was a disaster. But from that of the papacy, it was a triumph. In 1098, crusaders captured the old Hellenistic city of Antioch and with it most of the Syrian coast. At the end of 1099, they took Jerusalem, indiscriminately slaughtering its Muslim, Jewish, and Christian inhabitants. Their quick success stemmed mainly from the fact that their Muslim opponents were at that moment divided amongst themselves: the Fatimids had in fact recaptured Jerusalem just months before the crusaders arrived, and the defeated Seljuqs were at war with one other. Western military tactics, in particular the dominance of heavily armored knights, also played an important role in the crusaders' success. Equally critical was the naval support offered by Genoa

and Pisa, whose merchant adventurers hoped to control the Indian spice trade that passed through the Red Sea and on to Alexandria. The Crusade thereby contributed to the decline of Byzantine sovereignty and decisively altered the balance of power between Byzantium and western Europe.

The Consequences of the Crusades

For Byzantium, the consequences of the crusading movement were clearly tragic. On the Islamic world, by contrast, the impact was much more modest. The crusader kingdoms were never more than a sparsely settled cluster of colonies along the coastline of Syria and Palestine. Because the crusaders never did control the Red Sea, Muslim commerce with India and the Far East was unaffected. In any case, the crusaders did not *want* to interfere with the caravan routes that wound through their new territories. Trade between Islam and the West therefore continued despite periodic interruptions. The greatest economic gains went to the Italian maritime republics of Venice and Genoa, and to Islamic merchants who came to depend on Western markets for their goods. Both sides also gained in military terms: Westerners learned new techniques of fortification, and Muslims learned new methods of siege warfare and new respect for the uses of heavy cavalry.

But the most long-lasting consequence of the Crusades has also proved the most deadly in the long run: the development of both Christian and Islamic doctrines of holy war, the ideologies of crusade and *jihad* that continue to be so destructive in the twenty-first century. By 1144, most of the crusader principalities in Syria had been recaptured. Not long afterward, Syria and Egypt were united under the great Muslim leader Salah ad-Din (Saladin), who decisively recaptured Jerusalem in 1187. Further Crusades were launched in response, none of them successful and all of them putting renewed pressure on Byzantium. The only Latin kingdom that survived was Acre (Akko in northern Israel), and its fall in 1291 marked the end of any viable western European presence in the region—until the short-lived conquests of Napolean at the end of the eighteenth century (see Chapter 18).

Despite the movement's ultimate failure, then, crusading continued to dictate the terms of western Europeans' attitudes toward the wider world and even toward one another, as we shall see in the following chapters. It fostered a new political and religious ethos that would spur the "reconquest" of the Iberian peninsula by the Christian rulers of Spain and lead to the massacre or forced conversion of Muslims and Jews. Crusading also provided the rhetoric underlying English wars against the Welsh and the Scots, and the language that justified the massacre and dispossession of "heretics" in southern France by northern French colonists. It motivated voyages of discovery from the fifteenth century onward and the subsequent conquest of the Americas and the colonization of Asia, Africa, and Australia (Chapter 11). And it has continued to exacerbate Western relations with Islam to this day.

THE CULTURE OF THE MUSLIM WEST

It would be misleading to assert that all the consequences of the Crusades were negative. Increased intellectual and cultural contact between the Latin West and the Islamic world had an enormous impact on European learning, literature, music, and art. The study and practical applications of mathematics were revolutionized when Europeans adopted Arabic numerals and the concept of zero—first promoted in western Europe, not surprisingly, by the son of a Pisan merchant who grew up in Muslim Algeria, Leonardo Fibonacci (c. 1170–c. 1250).

Even Christian theology was transformed by contact with Islam. Muslim scholars had inherited, preserved, and developed not only Hellenistic medicine and science but the philosophy of Aristotle, which would form the basis of a new Christian philosophy in the twelfth and thirteenth centuries (see Chapter 9). Up to now, Europeans had been almost entirely ignorant of Muslim beliefs, assuming that Muslims were pagans who worshiped a god called Mahomet or Mahoun. But in 1143, a scholar called Robert of Ketton (c. 1100–c. 1160), originally from a small town in England, completed a Latin translation of the Qu'ran, working in Spain with the encouragement of the abbot of Cluny. For back in the 1130s, he and a friend, Hermann of Carinthia (in Slovenia), had traveled to the crusader kingdoms, to become students of Arabic. They exemplify the world of possibilities that had been opened up to northwestern Europeans as a result of new contacts with Islam.

Muslim Philosophy, Science, and Medicine

The scholars of Byzantium had long taken a conservative approach to Greek philosophy, in every sense of the word (Chapter 7). The dialogues of Plato and some works of Aristotle were copied and studied, but the latter's ideas were so hard to reconcile with Orthodox theology that Emperor Alexius Comnenus eventually banned the teaching of Aristotelian logic. Ironically, then, the cultures that provided the most direct access to Greek learning were Arabic-speaking, and it was through Arabic translations that western European intellectuals became acquainted with these ideas, thanks to the pioneering labors of Arabists like Robert and Hermann.

Many of these Arabic translations had been sponsored by the Abbasid court at Baghdad, which established a special school for this purpose known as the House of Wisdom. By the end of the tenth century, as a result, Arabic translations of Plato, Aristotle, Plotinus, and other Greek authors were widely available and intensively studied throughout the Muslim world. Even in the remote Persian city of Bukhara, the great Muslim philosopher and physician Avicenna (Ibn Sīnā, 980–1037) was able to read all of Aristotle's surviving works before he reached the age of eighteen.

Competing Viewpoints

Preaching the First Crusade: Two Accounts

> We owe the following account of Urban II's call for a crusade to Fulcher of Chartres, a priest who was present at the Council of Clermont in 1095 and who later served as chaplain to the first Norman king of Jerusalem, Baldwin. It forms part of Fulcher's contemporary chronicle of the First Crusade. The second account of the motives behind the crusade come from a biography of the Byzantine emperor Alexius Comnenus, written by his daughter Anna (1083–1153), who also lived through these events.

Pope Urban II's Call at Clermont, November 1195

Most beloved brethren: Urged by necessity, I, Urban, by the permission of God chief bishop and prelate over the whole world, have come into these parts as an ambassador with a divine admonition to you, the servants of God. . . .

Although, O sons of God, you have promised more firmly than ever to keep the peace among yourselves and to preserve the rights of the Church, there remains still an important work for you to do. Freshly quickened by the divine correction, you must apply the strength of your righteousness to another matter which concerns you as well as God. For your brethren who live in the East are in urgent need of your help, and you must hasten to give them the aid which has often been promised them. For, as most of you have heard, the Turks and Arabs have attacked them and have conquered the territory of Romania [the Byzantine Empire] as far west as the shore of the Mediterranean and the Hellespont. . . . They have occupied more and more of the lands of those Christians, and have overcome them in seven battles. They have killed and captured many, and have destroyed the churches and devastated the empire.

If you permit them to continue thus for a while with impunity, the faithful of God will be much more widely attacked by them. On this account I, or rather the Lord, beseech you as Christ's heralds to publish this everywhere and to persuade all people of whatever rank, footsoldiers and knights, poor and rich, to carry aid promptly to those Christians and to destroy that vile race from the lands of our friends. I say this to those who are present, but it is meant also for those who are absent. Moreover, Christ commands it.

All who die by the way, whether by land or by sea, or in battle against the pagans, shall have immediate remission of sins. This I grant them through the power of God with which I am invested. O what a disgrace, if such a despised and base race, which worships demons, should conquer a people which has the faith of omnipotent God and is made glorious with the name of Christ! With what reproaches will the Lord overwhelm us if you do not aid those who, with us, profess the Christian religion!

Let those who have been accustomed to wage unjust private warfare against the faithful now go against the infidels and end with victory this war which should have been begun long ago. Let those who for a long time have been robbers now become knights. Let those who have been fighting against their brothers and relatives now fight in a proper way against the barbarians. Let those who have been serving as mercenaries for small pay now obtain the eternal reward. Let those who have been wearing themselves out in both body

---

Like their counterparts in Byzantium, Muslim philosophers strove to reconcile Greek and Hellenistic philosophical traditions with each other and with the tenets of Islamic theology. Reconciling Aristotelianism and Neoplatonism was the easier task. Many of the translations and commentaries from which Muslim philosophers worked had already been filtered through the philosophical traditions of Alexandria and Rome. Moreover, Aristotle and the Neoplatonists shared a number of common assumptions, including the eternity of the world and the capacity of the human mind to understand the rational principles that govern the world's workings. Both traditions also stressed and soul now work for a double honor. Behold! On this side will be the sorrowful and poor, on that, the rich; on this side, the enemies of the Lord, on that, his friends. Let those who go not put off the journey, but rent their lands and collect money for their expenses; and as soon as winter is over and spring comes, let them eagerly set out on the way with God as their guide.

Source: S. J. Allen and Emilie Amt, eds., *The Crusades: A Reader* (Peterborough, Ont., Canada: 2003), pp. 39–40.

Anna Comnena Describes the Beginnings of the First Crusade

[Alexius] had no time to relax before he heard a rumour that countless Frankish armies were approaching. He dreaded their arrival, knowing as he did their uncontrollable passion, their erratic character and their irresolution, not to mention . . . their greed for money. . . . So far from despairing, however, he made every effort to prepare for war if need arose. What actually happened was more far-reaching and terrible than rumour suggested, for the whole of the West and all the barbarians who lived between the Adriatic and the Straits of Gibraltar migrated in a body to Asia, marching across Europe country by country with all their households. The reason for this mass movement is to be found more or less in the following events. A certain Kelt, called Peter [the Hermit] . . . left to worship at the Holy Sepulchre and after suffering much ill-treatment at the hands of the Turks and Saracens who were plundering the whole of Asia, he returned home with difficulty. Unable to admit defeat, . . . he worked out a clever scheme. He decided to preach in all the Latin countries. A divine voice, he said, commanded him to proclaim to all the counts in France that all should depart from their homes, set out to worship at the Holy Shrine, and . . . strive to liberate Jerusalem. . . . Surprisingly, he was successful. . . . Full of enthusiasm and ardour they thronged every highway, and with these warriors came a host of civilians, outnumbering the sand of the seashore or the stars of heaven, carrying palms and bearing crosses on their shoulders. There were women and children, too, who had left their own countries. . . .

The upheaval that ensued as men *and* women took to the road was unprecedented within living memory. The simpler folk were in very truth led on by a desire to worship at Our Lord's tomb and visit the holy places, but the more villainous characters . . . had an ulterior purpose, for they hoped on their journey to seize the capital [Jerusalem] itself, looking upon its capture as a natural consequence of the expedition. . . .

Source: Excerpted from Anna Comnena, *The Alexiad*, trans. E. R. A. Sewter (New York: 1969), pp. 308–11.

Questions for Analysis

1. Given Urban II's explanation of the problems confronting the Byzantine Empire, how do you account for the fact that the Crusades were directed toward the Holy Land, and not to the relief of Byzantium?

2. How does Anna Comnena represent the motives of Peter the Hermit and the crusaders? What distinctions does she make among the various participants?

3. Are there points of comparison between these two accounts? On what do they agree? How would you explain the differences between them?

the freedom of individual humans to choose between good and evil.

Reconciling Greek philosophy with Islamic theology was more difficult. Like Judaism and Christianity, Islam holds that a single omnipotent God created the world as an act of pure will, and that the world can exist only so long as God continues to will it. This runs counter to the Greek view of the world as eternal. Moreover, both Christian and Islamic theologies rest on the immortality of the individual human soul, another doctrine in conflict with Aristotelian and Neoplatonic thought. There were also conflicts over the concept of free will, and again Muslims and Christians had more

An Arab Aristocrat Encounters the Crusaders

Usama ibn Munqidh (1095–1188) was an Arab Muslim from Syria, whose family maintained a prominent place in the local administration even after the conquests of the Seljuqs and the Christian crusaders. He traveled widely and worked in various cities as a diplomat and scholar. He ended his life in the service of Salah ad-Din (Saladin), the great Muslim leader who reconquered Jerusalem the year before Usama's death. The following excerpt is from Usama's memoir, which he called The Book of Contemplation. *The Templars mentioned in the account are the Christian military order of the Knights of the Temple, who dedicated themselves to protecting pilgrims in Jerusalem and guarding the holy sites. Their headquarters were in the main mosque of the city, which stood on the Temple Mount.*

 nyone who is recently arrived from the Frankish lands is rougher in character than those who have become acclimated and have frequented the company of Muslims. Here is an instance of their rough character (may God abominate them!):

Whenever I went to visit the holy sites in Jerusalem, I would go in and make my way up to the al-Aqsa Mosque, beside which stood a small mosque that the Franks had converted into a church. When I went into the al-Aqsa Mosque—where the Templars, who are my friends, were—they would clear out that little mosque so that I could pray in it. One day, I went into the little mosque, recited the opening formula 'God is great!' and stood up in prayer. At this, one of the Franks rushed at me and grabbed me and turned my face towards the east, saying, 'Pray like *this!*'

A group of Templars hurried towards him, took hold of the Frank and took him away from me. I then returned to my prayers. The Frank, that very same one, took advantage of their inattention and returned, rushing upon me and turning my face to the east, saying, 'Pray like *this!*'

So the Templars came in again, grabbed him and threw him out. They apologized to me, saying, 'This man is a stranger, just arrived from the Frankish lands sometime in the past few days. He has never before seen anyone who did not pray towards the east.'

'I think I've prayed quite enough,' I said and left. I used to marvel at that devil, the change of his expression, the way he trembled and what he must have made of seeing someone praying towards Mecca.

Source: Usama ibn Munqidh, *The Book of Contemplation: Islam and the Crusades*, trans. Paul M. Cobb (New York: 2008), p. 147.

Questions for Analysis

1. What does Usama's account reveal about the variety of relationships among Christians and Muslims in the crusader kingdom of Jerusalem?

2. Who is the true outsider in this scenario? What does Usama's treatment by the Templars suggest about the policy of Christian leaders toward the city's Muslim residents?

---

in common with one another than with ancient Greek tradition. Although medieval theologians emphasized the individual responsibility of believers to choose between good and evil, virtually all Muslims—like most Christians—believed that nothing good can occur unless God actively wills it.

By adopting an array of different intellectual tactics to deal with these challenges, Islamic philosophers therefore laid the groundwork for the Christian theologians who relied on them. The most influential of these was Averroès (*ah-VER-oh-ayz*; Ibn Rushd, 1126–1198), an amazingly gifted scholar born in Córdoba and active as a judge and physician in Seville. Averroès single-handedly advanced the

study of Aristotelian logic by publishing a series of careful commentaries that sought to purge the Greek philosopher's works of all later (and confusing) Neoplatonic influences, and thus to allow for their proper analysis and interpretation. Soon translated from Arabic into Latin, these commentaries influenced the way all subsequent Christian scholars read and understood Aristotle, and they earned Averroès the admiration of poets and artists as well as scholars. His prestige was so great that Christian intellectuals called him simply "The Commentator," as if there were no others. Sadly, his learning did not impress the new Muslim dynasty that came to power in his lifetime, the Almohads,

ARISTOTLE TEACHING ARAB ASTRONOMERS. In this Arabic manuscript from the thirteenth century, Aristotle is represented as a contemporary of the astronomers he is instructing.
■ *What does this suggest about Muslims' attitude toward Greek philosophy?*

tion, diagnose cancer of the stomach, prescribe antidotes in cases of poisoning, and make notable progress in treating eye diseases. They even recognized the infectious character of bubonic plague, pointing out that it could be transmitted by clothing. Muslim physicians were also pioneers in organizing hospitals and licensing medical practitioners. At least thirty-four great hospitals were located in the principal cities of Persia, Syria, and Egypt, each with separate wards for particular illnesses, a dispensary for giving out medicine, and a library. Chief physicians and surgeons lectured to students and interns, examined them, and issued licenses to practice medicine. Even the owners of leeches (used for bloodletting, a standard medical practice) had to submit their medicinal worms for inspection at regular intervals.

Islamic scientists also made important advances in optics and chemistry, as well as mathematics. Using what Westerners know as Arabic numerals—which Muslim scholars actually adopted from the Hindus—mathematicians developed a decimal arithmetic based on place values and hinged on the concept of the zero. Their work enabled

who demanded that all philosophical inquiry be subordinated to orthodox Muslim belief. After burning several of Averroës' works, they exiled him to Morocco, where he died in 1198. Thereafter, Islamic philosophy may have had more impact on Europe than on some Islamic kingdoms.

Many Muslim philosophers were also distinguished physicians and scientists. While the study of philosophy could bring a man renown (or censure) but few tangible rewards, successful physicians and astrologers might rise to positions of wealth and power. Both astrology and medicine were applied sciences that relied on careful, accurate observation of natural phenomena. Muslim observations of the heavens were so accurate, indeed, that some astronomers corroborated the findings of Hellenistic scientists (see Chapter 4), that the earth must revolve around the sun. But because these theories conflicted with the (mistaken) assumptions of Aristotle, they were not generally accepted in the Islamic world or in Europe. Yet they may have influenced Nicolaus Copernicus (1473–1543), who is usually credited as the first to suggest that the earth orbited the sun (see Chapter 16).

Islamic accomplishments in medicine were equally remarkable. Avicenna discovered the contagious nature of tuberculosis, described pleurisy and several varieties of nervous ailments, and noted that diseases could spread through contaminated water and soil. His *Canon of Medicine* would remain an authoritative textbook in the Muslim world and in western Europe until the seventeenth century. Later Muslim physicians would learn the value of cauteriza-

IVORY PYXIS FROM AL-ANDALUS. Fashioned in the tenth century, this little round box is made from a segment of elephant tusk and would have had a matching lid (now lost). Such boxes usually held spices or incense. The decorative motifs seen here are echoed on a larger scale in contemporary architecture, reminding us that medieval Islam did not prohibit the representation of natural and fanciful figures, as is often supposed.

fundamental advances in two entirely new areas, both of which bear Arabic names: algebra and algorithms. Building on Greek geometry and their own astronomical observations, they also made great progress in spherical trigonometry. Muslim mathematicians thus brought together and pushed forward all the areas of mathematical knowledge that would later be adopted and developed in western Europe from the sixteenth century on. And they made an indispensible contribution to the burgeoning European economy, since the sophisticated accounting systems that supported commerce would have been impossible if merchants and bankers had continued to use the clumsy system of Roman numerals (try balancing your checking account this way!). Thanks to Arabic mathematics, western Europeans could now add, subtract, divide, and multiply quickly and accurately, with or without the help of another Muslim invention, the abacus.

Islamic Literature and Art

Poetry was integral to Muslim culture and identity, not least because it was the form in which Muhammad expressed the Qu'ran (Chapter 7). Not all poetry was composed in Arabic, however; particularly around the Abbasid court, poets writing in Persian enjoyed great renown. The best known of these is Umar Khayyam (d. 1123), whose *Rubaiyat* was turned into a popular English verse cycle by the Victorian poet Edward Fitzgerald (1809–1883). Although Fitzgerald's translation distorts much, the sensuality of Umar's poetic imagery ("A book of verses underneath the bough—a jug of wine, a loaf of bread—and thou") faithfully reflects themes that were common to much Muslim poetry. Jews also participated in this elite literary world, especially in Al-Andalus, where they wrote similarly sensuous, playful lyrics in both Hebrew and Arabic, praising wine, sexual intimacy, and their own songs.

Indeed, Muslim Spain saw a great flowering of Jewish intellectual life. The greatest Jewish scholar of the period was Moses Maimonides (*my-MAHN-eh-dees*, c. 1137–1204), whose systematic exposition of Jewish law in the *Mishneh Torah* earned him the title "the second Moses." Like Averroès, Maimonides may have been driven into exile by the Almohads; he traveled first to North Africa and then to Egypt, where he became famous as a teacher, jurist, and physician. Like Averroès, too, he exercised great influence on Christian theologians.

Perhaps the most distinctive of Islamic arts are those that created the spaces in which artists and intellectuals interacted with their patrons. Many characteristic elements of Muslim architecture were adapted from Byzantine models, but were then combined with the intricate tracery and ambitious scale of Persian buildings. Muslim artistry was also expressed in the magnificent gardens and fountains that adorned palaces, and in the more portable magnificence of gorgeous carpets, tooled leather, sumptuous brocaded silks and tapestries, inlaid metalwork, enameled glassware, and painted pottery. Their complex designs can

After You Read This Chapter

Visit StudySpace for quizzes, additional review materials, and multi-media documents. **wwnorton.com/studyspace**

REVIEWING THE OBJECTIVES

- The fragmentation of power in the ninth and tenth centuries created a world very different from that of Charlemagne. Describe some of the key changes. What were their causes?
- The agricultural revolution of the Middle Ages had far-reaching economic, social, and political consequences. What were they?
- The reforming movement with the Church changed the relationship between the papacy and the secular rulers of Christendom. Explain why.
- The motives behind the Crusades were political as well as religious. Why was this the case?
- The Crusades had profound effects on western Europe, Byzantium, and Islam, as well as on the relationships among different groups within these societies. In what ways were these three civilizations transformed?

often seem strikingly modern, precisely because they anticipate the abstract forms that were considered new in the twentieth century.

CONCLUSION

The new Europe that emerged in the twelfth century would rely heavily on what it had learned from the Islamic world. This is reflected in the large number of Arabic and Persian words that passed into the European languages still spoken today. Essential words for commerce and trade include *traffic*, *tariff*, *alcohol*, *muslin*, *orange*, *lemon*, *alfalfa*, *saffron*, *sugar*, *syrup*, and *musk*, to name just a few. The word *admiral* also comes from Arabic (from the title *emir*), as do words that tell the story of Europe's reliance on Islamic science and technology: *alchemy*, *algebra*, *algorithm*, *alkali*, *almanac*, *amalgam*, *cipher*, *soda*, *magazine*, *zenith*, and *zero*—not to mention the names of stars, such as Aldebaran and Betelgeuse.

In the year 1000, Europe had been the least powerful, least prosperous, and least sophisticated of the three civilizations that had emerged from the Roman world. A hundred years later, it was a force to be reckoned with. This metamorphosis rested on economic foundations: increasingly efficient agriculture, a growing population, and expanding trade. These changes produced a dynamic, expansionist, self-confident, and mobile society in which individuals cast off old roles and took on new ones with bewildering speed.

No less important, however, were the political and military changes that began to alter the map of Europe in these centuries. By 1100, the heavily armored, mounted knight had emerged as a formidable military weapon, and new conceptions of power—both spiritual and temporal—were being articulated and contested within Europe, and on crusade.

But it was not yet possible for either kings or popes to control the energies of the workers, town-dwellers, merchants, knights, and scholars whose endeavors were transforming their world. Yet a new approach to political organization was developing. Up to this point, the civilizations of the West had rested largely on two types of government: city-states and empires. City-states were more capable of mobilizing the loyalty of their citizens; as a result, they could sometimes win extraordinary victories against more-powerful imperial rivals, as the Greeks did against the Persians. But city-states were frequently divided by internal economic and social rivalries; and in the long run, they were not strong enough to defend themselves against foreign conquerors. Empires, by contrast, could win battles and maintain powerful administrative bureaucracies, but they were generally too far-flung to inspire deep loyalties among their subjects.

Where, then, do the monarchies of medieval Europe fit into this picture? How would the struggle for the control of western Europe's expanding resources be carried forward in the wake of the Crusades? And what cultural, spiritual, social, and intellectual innovations would result? These are the questions we address in Chapter 9.

PEOPLE, IDEAS, AND EVENTS IN CONTEXT

- How was Europe affected by **VIKING** raids and settlements? Which territorial rulers imitated **CAROLINGIAN** models in the wake of these upheavals?

- What new technologies drove the **AGRICULTURAL REVOLUTION** of the Middle Ages? Why did the organization of labor on **MANORS** sometimes lead to **SERFDOM**?

- What conditions led to the growth of medieval **TOWNS** and why did the formation of urban **COMMUNES** foster new types of liberty? How were **MONEY AND CREDIT** essential to medieval commerce?

- Why is **"FEUDALISM"** a problematic concept? How did the ceremony of **HOMAGE** symbolize the relationship between a **VASSAL** and his **LORD**?

- What were the causes of the **INVESTITURE CONFLICT**?

- Why did **EMPEROR ALEXIUS** ask **POPE URBAN II** for assistance? Why did the pope use this as a pretext for urging the **FIRST CRUSADE**?

- How and why did **MUSLIM LEARNING AND CULTURE** exercise a profound influence on western Europeans?

CONSEQUENCES

- In what ways does the Investiture Conflict reflect the unique historical circumstances of the late eleventh century, and in what ways can it be viewed as an extension of longer-term phenomena?

- Based on what we have learned about the relationship between political power and religious power in previous chapters, would you say that the clash between the papal and imperial powers was inevitable?

- Given the many negative aspects of the crusading movement—and its eventual failure—how might you explain the continuing appeal of crusading rhetoric down to the present day?

Before
You
Read
This
Chapter

The Consolidation of Europe, 1100–1300

CORE OBJECTIVES

- **IDENTIFY** the differences among Europe's emerging monarchies.

- **UNDERSTAND** the connections between new religious movements and the power of the papacy.

- **DEFINE** scholasticism and trace its development.

- **EXPLAIN** the changing meaning of *chivalry*.

- **DESCRIBE** the cultural trends of this era.

A t the turn of the twelfth century, the eldest son of a nobleman did something unusual: he traded lordship for scholarship. His name was Peter Abelard. In his own estimation, he was the smartest man in the world, and the best looking. He was certainly one of the most ambitious. After leaving his father's lands in Brittany and besting all the established teachers in Paris, he was appointed to the position of master in the cathedral school, one of the highest academic posts then available. There he met Heloise, the niece of a priest called Fulbert. Heloise had received an excellent education in a nearby convent, but the normal path of intellectual advancement—Abelard's school—was closed to her. So Fulbert arranged for her to become Abelard's private pupil. But she soon became more than that: his intellectual partner, his lover, and his wife.

This last step was particularly problematic, because marriage was no longer an option for clerics, and would therefore ruin Abelard's chances of a brilliant career in the Church. So it remained a secret, as did Heloise's subsequent pregnancy and the birth of their son. Yet Fulbert eventually found out and took revenge on Abelard, sending some local thugs to castrate him. Heloise and

Abelard lived out the remainder of their lives in isolation from one another, and most of what we know about their relationship comes from letters they exchanged years later, when Heloise was the leader of a new religious community and Abelard was laying the intellectual foundations of the first university.

The developments of the twelfth and thirteenth centuries altered Europe in profound and lasting ways. This period witnessed the emergence of large-scale territorial monarchies and the papacy as dominant forces, while cathedral schools and universities turned out larger and larger cohorts of the professional men needed to run the bureaucracies that supported them. In the wake of the Crusades, both ancient texts and novel ideas generated the intellectual revolution in which Abelard and Heloise participated. New artistic and technological influences were galvanizing forces, too; financed by prelates and kings, princely courts and wealthy towns engaged in an integrated and far-reaching economy. New opportunities for social advancement and new spiritual practices also transformed daily life. Moreover, new literary forms took shape as the spoken vernaculars of Europe became languages of learning, devotion, and entertainment. By 1300, the political institutions and cultural practices that still define Europe today had been formed.

THE MAKING OF MEDIEVAL MONARCHIES

As we learned in Chapter 8, the independent towns and lords of the tenth and eleventh centuries often refused to acknowledge royal authority, while kings no longer wielded the broad powers of Charlemagne. How, then, did some European rulers come to build the foundations of states that still exist today? For crucially, the *idea* of a national state, an idea forged in the twelfth and thirteenth centuries, would endure to become the basis on which the political systems of the modern world were constructed.

Not all attempts were equally successful. Some monarchies would not be consolidated until the nineteenth century (Germany is the best example) and, even then, *political unification* could not hide the continued fact of cultural and linguistic disintegration (as is evident in Italy, Belgium, and Switzerland to this day). Yet it became so vital for modern European states to trace their origins to the medieval past that those states without a medieval pedigree would eventually have to invent one.

England and the Angevin Empire of Henry II

The conquest of England in 1066 allowed the first Norman king, William, to experiment with a new type of kingship. In theory, he commanded the allegiance of every person dwelling in his kingdom. In practice, however, William needed to impose his will on his new subjects. This often took the form of violence, yet it was also expressed through the effective administrative structures of his Anglo-Saxon predecessors. This process was carried forward by his energetic son Henry I (r. 1100–35). Henry strengthened the Anglo-Norman system of local administration and instituted a method of financial accounting carried out by an office known as the Exchequer—so called because clerks moved counters around on a checkered cloth to calculate receipts and expenditures.

ABELARD AND HELOISE. This image from a thirteenth-century manuscript shows Abelard in a scholar's gown and cap and Heloise wearing a nun's habit; their gestures indicate that they are engaged in debate. The story of their passionate and doomed marriage was already famous during their lifetimes, and by the time this manuscript was copied, theirs had become the ultimate example of star-crossed love.

Henry's hands-on approach to governance was both new and unpopular. Then, as now, those opposed to "big government" could react violently, and after Henry's death a civil war lasted throughout the reign of his cousin and successor, Stephen (r. 1135–54)—until the people of England began to long for the effective royal leadership of Henry. They found it in Henry's grandson Henry of Anjou (b. 1133, r. 1154–89), who at the age of twenty-one was already the duke of Normandy and the lord of two other independent counties, Anjou and Maine. He also controlled the Aquitaine, thanks to his recent alliance with its powerful and brilliant ruler, Eleanor (1122–1204), who had annulled her first marriage to the French king Louis VII in order to marry Henry. As a result, England under Henry II found itself integrated into the political and cultural world of the Continent in unprecedented ways, as part of an Angevin empire (from Henry's position as count of Anjou).

In England, Henry II extended the reach of his grandfather's royal administration. He ordered juries (from the Latin *jus*, meaning both "law" and "right") of local men to report every major crime that occurred in their districts, and empowered them to investigate civil cases. Henry II also made it easier for common people to seek justice in royal courts. These innovations are the origin of our modern legal system, and by involving average people in the exercise of government they also generated loyalty to the king.

Yet these measures brought Henry into conflict with the Church, because the extension of royal justice impinged on that of ecclesiastical courts: tribunals overseen by bishops that claimed the exclusive right to try and sentence members of the clergy. Henry declared that clerics convicted of serious crimes should lose their clerical status and be handed over to the royal court for sentencing. Opposition to his plan came from an unexpected source: Thomas Becket, a longtime friend of Henry's who was now the archbishop of Canterbury.

Thomas was a self-made man, the son of immigrants who had benefited from the social mobility of town life (he grew up in London) to obtain an education and thereby rise through the ranks of the Church. He saw the advantages to be gained from maintaining the independence of ecclesiastical procedures, and felt bound by his episcopal office to uphold them. Henry responded to his obstinacy by exiling Thomas for several years. When Thomas returned to England in 1170, he was assassinated in his own cathedral by four of Henry's knights.

Thomas was quickly proclaimed a martyr and a saint, and his tomb at Canterbury became one of the most important pilgrimage sites of the Middle Ages. Henry, for his part, was compelled to ask the saint's forgiveness for his sins against the Church. In the long run, he did not win the

THE MURDER OF THOMAS BECKET. In this illumination from a thirteenth-century prayer book, one of the knights has struck the archbishop so violently that he has broken his sword. ▪ *How might a contemporary viewer have interpreted this?*

right to sentence clerics in royal courts, but he did retain the right to nominate clerics to high office and thereby to exercise a large measure of control over the churches in his realm.

The Meaning of Magna Carta

The most concrete proof of Henry II's success is that his government continued to work efficiently after his death, to the extent that his swashbuckling son Richard "the Lionheart" (r. 1189–99) could rule his father's empire for ten years *in absentia*, spending only about six months in England itself during all that time.

Richard was succeeded by his brother John (r. 1199–1216), an efficient administrator and far less enthusiastic warrior who lacked the means to hold the Angevin Empire

ENGLAND AND FRANCE, 1180–1223. ▪ *What areas did Henry II's Angevin Empire control in 1180?* ▪ *What would have been its effects on the political orientation of England?* ▪ *What advantages would the king of France have when challenging English control over continental territories, even though his own power was confined to the "island" (Ile) of France around Paris?*

together. By 1204, John had been forced to cede nearly all of his father's Continental possessions to the newly powerful king of France, Philip II; only the Aquitaine, the inheritance of his mother Eleanor, remained. This was politically disastrous, because the most powerful lords of England lost their ancestral lands when John lost Normandy. And when John attempted to recover these territories by raising taxes to equip an army, he only angered the barons further. In 1215 they forced John to set his seal to Magna Carta, a "great charter" that defined their own rights while limiting those of the king.

Magna Carta established some important general principles that would continue to shape the laws of England and, eventually, its colonies: the king could levy no taxes without the consent of his subjects, no free man could be punished until he had been judged guilty by a jury of his peers, no one could be arrested and imprisoned without a warrant, and no unqualified person could hold public office. The charter also provided for the establishment of a council of barons, which later came to represent the common people of England, too—Parliament (a word derived from the French "talking together"). Above all, Magna Carta expressed the extraordinary idea that a king is bound by the law of the land. By contrast, the various powerful lawgivers we have studied so far held themselves to be above the law.

In sum, Magna Carta normalized the idea that strong, centralized government was a good thing. When the barons of England revolted again in the reign of John's son, Henry III (r. 1216–72), they did so because Henry's rule was not effective enough. Henry III's son Edward (r. 1272–1307) accordingly made Parliament into a legislative body that could help run the kingdom. Since Magna Carta had demanded that no taxation be imposed without common consent, Edward convened Parliament to secure such consent. But he also used meetings of Parliament to take advice, to hear

judicial cases, to hear complaints, and to promulgate new laws. Gradually, England's feudal monarchy was becoming the constitutional monarchy it remains to this day.

Philip Augustus and the Emergence of France

Compared to the Anglo-Norman and Angevin kings of England, the king of the Franks presided over a miniscule kingdom over which he exercised little control. When the empire of Henry II was at its height, the kingdom of Louis VII (r. 1137–80)—who had lost both his wife Eleanor and her lands to that same Henry—was tiny and insignificant.

But in many ways the Capetian kings of this realm were fortunate. Against all biological odds, they managed to produce an unbroken line of able male heirs for over 300 years (from the accession of Hugh Capet in 987 to 1328). On average, each Capetian king ruled for thirty years, and this longevity also contributed greatly to political stability. And this kingdom, though small, was a rich center of agriculture and trade, and was becoming the intellectual capital of Europe, thanks to the new university that had grown around the school of Abelard in Paris.

The king who capitalized on these strengths was Philip II (r. 1180–1223), also called "Augustus" and the first to use the title "king of France"—thereby indicating that he was king of a sovereign state (rather than "king of the Franks," a loose agglomeration of people). Philip came to the throne at the age of eighteen, having witnessed the constant humiliation of his father Louis VII at the hands of Henry II. He understood that he could not win a war against either Henry or his son Richard. John, however—known to his detractors as "Soft Sword"—was another matter. So Philip declared that John owed him homage and allegiance for Normandy and its adjacent territories. When John objected, Philip declared all John's lands forfeit to the French crown and backed this declaration with armies that won decisive victories in 1204 and 1214.

With Normandy and other formerly English territories added to his domain, Philip now had the resources to build an effective system of local administration. He supplemented existing bureaucratic structures by appointing royal overseers who had judicial, administrative, and military authority. Philip drew these men from among the needy knights and lesser nobility of his own domain and rotated them frequently from region to region. This ensured their loyalty to Philip, and also prevented them from developing personal ties to the regions they governed.

Philip's administrative pattern, which recognized regional diversity while promoting centralized royal control, would continue to characterize French government down to the time of the French Revolution (see Chapter 18). Although he and his heirs experimented with representative assemblies similar to the English Parliament, the French Parlement never played a comparable role in French government. There are many reasons for this, but the most fundamental was the French nobility's exemption from taxation, something that would remain a political problem.

Other significant points of contrast between England and France would continue to mark the intertwined history of these two states. England, a far smaller country, was much more tightly unified at a much earlier date. In France, regional separatism remained (and still remains) a significant force, to the extent that ambitious insurgents have long capitalized on regional animosity toward the French government when making bids for power. While English kings could rely on local men to do much of the work of local government without pay, French kings ruled through salaried officers who had little connection to local society and, as a result, lacked effective mechanisms for mobilizing public support. In the eigtheenth century, these features would be the undoing of the French monarchy.

German Kingship and the Holy Roman Empire

The struggles between the German emperor Henry IV and the papacy ultimately led to the weakening of imperial authority (Chapter 8). But in the middle of the twelfth century, a newly elected emperor made an ambitious attempt to free himself from papal control. This was Frederick Barbarossa ("Red Beard," r. 1152–90), who coined the term "Holy Roman Empire" to describe his realm, thereby asserting that its holiness derived from the blessing of God and not from the intervention of the pope.

Frederick forged a close alliance with other German princes by supporting their efforts to control their own territories, in exchange for their support of his wars in northern Italy. Meanwhile, he attempted to bypass the power of the papacy by supporting a series of papal pretenders, or "antipopes." But this move was successfully countered by the reigning pope, Alexander III (r. 1159–81), who drove a shrewd bargain: if Frederick would concede the sovereignty of the pope's rule within Rome and its adjacent territories—lands that came to be known as the Papal States—then Alexander would concede the emperor's sovereignty within his own domains, and even his overlordship of the Church in these domains. Frederick eventually agreed.

When Frederick left for the Holy Land in 1189—joining Richard the Lionheart and Philip Augustus on the (failed)

Third Crusade to reconquer Jerusalem—he accordingly left his realm in a powerful position. Although he died soon after, his son, Henry VI, succeeded to his throne without opposition and enjoyed a huge income from the northern Italian towns; he ultimately became the king of Sicily, too. This strengthened the empire's position even further, for now the Papal States were surrounded by the lands of a single powerful ruler.

Henry VI died in 1197 at the age of thirty-two, leaving a three-year-old son as his heir apparent. This Frederick II is one of the most fascinating of all medieval rulers. Having grown up in Sicily, he spoke Arabic and Italian as well as Latin, German, and French. He was both a patron of learning and a scholar in his own right, the author of an important treatise on falconry that is still considered a model of scientific investigation. He maintained a menagerie of exotic animals, a troop of Muslim archers, and a harem of veiled and secluded women, all of whom traveled with him on his journeys.

But by the time Frederick II came of age, the German princes had become so entirely autonomous that there was little he could do except recognize their privileges in exchange for their loyalty. In Italy, meanwhile, the northern cities banded together in the Lombard League had long since ceased to pay their taxes; and the powerful administrative structure of Sicily had fallen into chaos. Frederick tackled all these problems in turn, and eventually restored control over the disparate territories of his empire.

In 1237, however, he made the mistake of asserting his rule over the northern Italian cities directly, bypassing their own independent governments. The result was a lengthy war which continued until Frederick's death in 1250. The papacy took every advantage of this situation, even excommunicating Frederick and, after his death, denying the rights of his heirs. When Frederick's last legitimate son died in 1254, the prospect of effective imperial rule died with him. For the next six hundred years, until the founding of the modern German state in 1871, political power in the Holy Roman Empire would be divided among several hundred territorial princes.

The "Reconquest" of Spain

Although the Christian kingdoms of the Iberian peninsula were even more distinct from one another than were the principalities of Germany, a unified kingdom of Spain would emerge as the most powerful monarchy in Europe and the wider Atlantic world by the end of

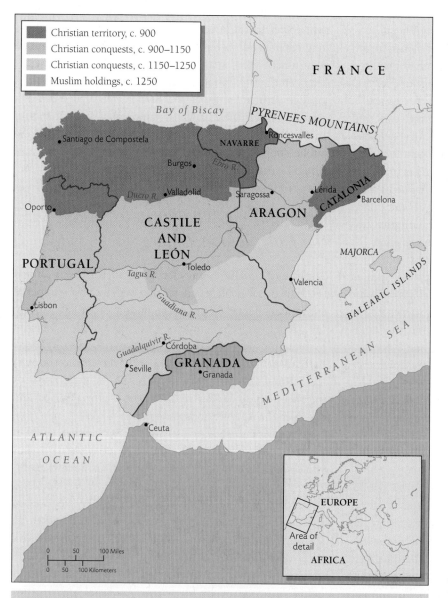

THE "RECONQUEST" OF SPAIN, 900–1250. ▪ *What were the boundaries of the Christian kingdoms in 900? 1150? 1250?* ▪ *What geographical factors might have helped to sustain these small kingdoms?* ▪ *Why might Castile have become the largest of the Christian kingdoms over time?* ▪ *How could Aragon and Catalonia have maintained important positions as wealthy and significant powers?*

the Middle Ages (a process we will continue to trace in future chapters). The key to this extraordinary development lay in the successful alliances forged among Christian rulers and their eventual defeat of Iberia's Muslim kingdoms. This process is somewhat misleadingly termed "the Reconquista," or "the reconquest" of Christian Spain. But in reality, the Roman province of Hispania had been only nominally Christian when the Visigoths settled there in the fifth century (see Chapter 6), and the Visigoths themselves had barely converted to Latin Christianity before the Muslims arrived in 711 (Chapter 7). Reality aside, conceptualizing this struggle as a holy war to "recover" Christian territory allowed Christian propagandists to cast it as another crusade.

By the middle of the twelfth century, there were four major Christian kingdoms in Iberia. In the north and northwest were the states of Navarre and León-Castile, the latter governed as a united kingdom after 1037. Beyond them to the south lay a broad swathe of Muslim territory. To the east was the Crown of Aragon, enlarged in 1137 when the count of Barcelona, who ruled the independent principality of Catalonia, married its queen. Then there was the new western kingdom of Portugal, which had been the first territory gained by Christian conquests in the ninth century and which eventually won independence from León-Castile in 1139.

Like their counterparts elsewhere in Europe, the kings of Iberia struggled to control the power of great lords. Centuries of warfare between Muslims and Christians, and among competing Christian clans, had left the landscape sown with enormous castles, and even those strongholds nominally controlled by kings were in fact the property of castellans who used them as power bases. A ruler seeking to establish sovereignty thus had to use a combination of force and effective administration. This is best exemplified by King Alfonso II of Aragon (r. 1162–96), who was also the count of Barcelona. Alfonso used documentation as the ultimate tool of power, presiding over the compilation of a richly illustrated "big book of fiefs" (*Liber feudorum maior*: see **Interpreting Visual Evidence**). This book recounted property transactions and family lineages dating back centuries, enabling Alfonso to ground his authority on his command of history.

(legal representatives) were now sent out from Rome to convey and enforce papal commands. For like the kings of England, France, and Aragon, the pope sought to establish a reputation for justice as a means of acquiring power.

The Codification of Canon Law

The growing number of cases heard in the papal court both encouraged and required the development of a systematic body of law by which such cases could be judged. Myriad papal decrees and decisions of Church councils reached back to the second century, forming a body of legal precedents known as canons (from the Greek word meaning "rules" or "supports"). The problem, though, was that these canons often contradicted one another, and so any usable compilation would have to determine which were most authoritative.

The resulting *Concordance of Discordant Canons*, first redacted around 1139 and later known as the *Decretum*, is attributed to a jurist known only as Gratian, who was presumably active in Bologna. Significantly, Gratian was influenced by the *Corpus Juris Civilis* codified under Justinian (see Chapter 7)—because another outcome of the Crusades, and of western Europe's increased contact with Byzantium, was the rediscovery of Roman law and the tradition of legal commentary associated with the great jurists of the later Roman Empire (Chapter 5).

The *Decretum* claimed ecclesiastical jurisdiction for all sorts of cases, including such matters as marriage, inheritance, and bequests. Although these cases were supposed to be heard in local ecclesiastical courts overseen by bishops, popes increasingly insisted that they alone could issue dispensations exempting certain petitioners from established precedents (such as the annulment of Eleanor's marriage to Louis VII) and moreover that the papal court should function as a final court of appeals in all cases touching the Church. Just as kings had to become more skillful administrators, so the popes of this era were almost invariably trained as canon lawyers.

The Reign of Innocent III

One examplar of this new breed of popes was Alexander III, who had dealt so skillfully with Frederick Barbarossa. Another was Innocent III (r. 1198–1216), a highly successful administrator whose chief goal was to unify all Christendom under papal hegemony. But unlike Gregory VII (Chapter 8), Innocent never questioned the right of kings and princes to rule in their own secular spheres. Instead, he saw the

THE DOMINION OF THE CHURCH

Like their secular counterparts, the popes of this era established their authority by building up bureaucratic structures that increased the visibility of papal power and its effects on daily life. Specially commissioned papal legates

Picturing Legal Transactions

Between the years 1192 and 1194, King Alfonso II of Aragon (r. 1162–1196) and his court scribes compiled a remarkable book. The codex known today as "the big book of fiefs" (*Liber feudorum maior*) may have been made to assist Alfonso and his descendants in legitimizing their authority over the many areas they controlled, but it was also a way of expressing that authority: its very existence marked a new claim to royal power. In its original form, it consisted of 888 parchment folios (1776 pages) on which 903 separate documents were copied.

This "big book" represents a new trend in Europe. In most places, claims to property were made on the basis of custom and memory, not on documentation. When property changed hands, the chief witnesses were people, and when questions arose it was these people (or their heirs) whose testimony proved ownership. But in Catalonia, the habit of documenting things had a long history, and it was not unusual for individual families to keep archives of documents. At the same time, however, documentation was never sufficient on its own: verbal exchanges of agreement and the public performance of transactions constituted legally binding ceremonies meaningful to the entire community, and the validity of these actions was not dependant on the making of a written record.

With all this in mind, it is striking that 79 of the documents copied into this book are accompanied by images that convey important messages about documentation and its limitations.

On the book's opening frontispiece (image A), King Alfonso consults with his chief archivist, Ramón de Caldes. Ramón discusses one of the charters taken from a large pile at his elbow, while a scribe makes copies behind him—perhaps to aid in the compilation of the "big book." The king is backed by men who look on approvingly.

One of the charters copied into the "big book" is accompanied by the second image (B). It records that the viscount of Nîmes betrothed his daughter, Ermengarde of Carcassone, to the count of Roussillon. Ermengarde, her flowing hair uncovered as a sign of her maidenhood, stands between her bearded father and her seated mother, Cecilia of Provence.

Questions for Analysis

1. Why would a book designed to document property transactions contain images, too? What functions could they have served?

2. Why would the artist of the "big book" have depicted the king consulting his archivist in the very first image? How does he depict the relationship between them? Which seems more powerful? Why does the artist include a group of men as witnesses to their discussion?

3. Women figure prominently in many of the book's images, including the one below. On what basis could you argue that their active presence is crucial to the transactions being described?

A. King Alfonso and Ramón de Caldes.

B. Betrothal of Ermengarde to the Count of Roussillon.

THE JEWISH BADGE. The distinctive apparel that marked Jews as different from their Christian neighbors varied from region to region. In some places it was a pointed hat, like those worn by the Old Testament Jews in this manuscript illumination from a fourteenth-century French vernacular Bible. This hat would later become associated with idiocy or witchcraft, as in the dunce's cap or the witch's peak. In other regions, Jews wore a distinctive patch on their clothing, often colored yellow to make it more visible.

assembly of the entire western church, the Fourth Lateran Council of 1215 (so called because it was held in the Roman palace and church of St. John Lateran). This council redefined the central dogmas of the Christian faith, and made one of them the acknowledgment of papal supremacy. Since a dogma is defined as "a truth necessary for salvation," this meant that all Christians had to acknowledge the pope's ultimate power; those unwilling to do so were, by definition, heretics—and as heretics, they could be prosecuted and punished.

In a further effort to achieve uniformity, the Fourth Lateran Council took an unprecedented interest in the religious education and habits of every Christian. It responded to urbanization by establishing free primary schools (for boys) in all the major cities, required bishops to recruit effective preachers, and outlawed all kinds of misbehavior on the part of the clergy. It also sought to increase the distance between Christians and their Muslim and Jewish neighbors by discouraging social relationships, economic exchanges, and intermarriage. Perhaps most disturbingly, Innocent's Council mandated that "infidels" be visibly distinguished from Christians by the wearing of distinctive clothing, the infamous "Jewish badge."

The Limits of Papal Power

Innocent's reign achieved the height of papal power, but it also sowed some seeds of future dissent. The popes of the thirteenth century continued to centralize the government of the Church, but they also became involved in protracted political struggles that compromised the papacy's credibility. For example, when one of Innocent's successors came into conflict with Frederick II, he not only excommunicated him, as Innocent might have done, he also called for a crusade against him—a cynical admission of crusading's overtly political motives. In 1300, Pope Boniface VIII (r. 1294–1303) even celebrated a papal jubilee in Rome by offering a full crusader's indulgence to every pilgrim: the promise of absolution from all sins. This implied that Rome, not Jerusalem, was henceforth the center of the Christian world.

Just nine years later, Rome had become obsolete and the new capital of Christendom was in France. King Philip IV had challenged Boniface to a political duel, and had exposed the practical limits of papal power. For when Boniface protested against the king's plan to arraign a French bishop on a charge of treason, Philip accused Boniface of heresy and sent a troop of knights to arrest him. Boniface (then in his

pope's role as regulatory and disciplinary, which meant that when rulers sinned they should be reprimanded or excommunicated by the pope—who could thereby call into question the legitimacy of their rule.

Innocent was even more insistent than his predecessors on the obligation of every Christian to obey the pope, and sought to achieve this goal in many different ways. He made the papacy financially and politically independent by expanding and consolidating papal territories in central Italy; Vatican City is now the last surviving remnant of these territories, and continues to function as an independent state within Rome and Italy. He displayed his power as kingmaker and -breaker by brokering the selection of the Holy Roman Emperor, and he also disciplined both Philip Augustus of France (for marital misconduct) and John of England, who at one point was compelled to grant England itself to the papacy, as a fief.

But the crowning achievement of Innocent's pontificate was the ratification of his agenda at a representative

seventies) was so mistreated by Philip's thugs that he died a month later. Philip then forced the new pope, Clement V, to thank him publically for his zealous defence of the faith and finally, in 1309, he moved the entire papal court to Avignon (AH-vee-nyon), a city near the southeastern border of his own realm. It would remain there until 1378 (see Chapter 10).

The papacy's capitulation to the exercise of royal force illustrates the enormous gap that had opened up between rhetoric and reality in the centuries since the Investiture Conflict (Chapter 8). Although Boniface had claimed that kings rule only through the "will and sufferance" of the Church, in fact the Church now exercised its authority only through the will and sufferance of a king. The growth of strong territorial monarchies, combined with the increasing sophistication of royal administration and propaganda, had shifted the balance of power decisively. This trend would continue into the seventeenth century, and would only be halted after a century of religious wars, when the distinction between religious and political authority would be asserted as a fundamental principle (see Chapter 14).

SPIRITUAL AWAKENINGS AND CHALLENGES

As we saw in Chapter 8, the Investiture Conflict had engaged both clergy and laity in debates over the essential meaning of Jesus Christ's life and teachings. In many regions of western Europe, the papacy's claim to jurisdictional supremacy over the whole Church was supported, but in others there was marked resistance to its encroachment on centuries-old local practices and social networks. After all, priests had been married men since the establishment of the first Christian churches, and the wives of priests were not only their husbands' companions and partners, they were also ministers to the communities in which they lived. When the papacy preached against "fornicating priests" and their "concubines," it was attacking relationships that had been socially and spiritually essential for generations.

On the one hand, therefore, the reforms of Pope Gregory VII and his successors gave common people an important role to play, by urging them to reject certain practices and sanctioning retaliation against offenders. Combined with the fervor that had been whipped up by the Crusades, the result was more widespread participation in religious life—as well as increased violence. On the other hand, however, the reforming movement severely limited the ways in which the laity were allowed to express their spirituality or to participate meaningfully in the life of the Church.

The New Monasticism

In the tenth century, the abbey of Cluny had revived the observance of Benedict's *Rule* and, at the same time, had kept Cluny and its daughter houses independent of local lords. As a result, these monasteries became lordships in their own right, acquiring extensive lands and enormous wealth. Those seeking to reject worldliness thus had to look elsewhere for a lifestyle that would foster self-denial and striving toward God. The result, beginning in the late eleventh century, was the founding of new orders such as the Carthusians, whose name derives from the Chartreuse foothills of the French Alps and whose rule requires monks to live in separate cells and to observe a life of strict asceticism.

Another new order, and one that became more widespread, was that founded at the monastery of Cîteaux in 1098. Cistercian monks followed Benedict's *Rule* in the purest and most austere way possible, and they founded new monasteries in remote areas, far from worldly temptations. They also shunned all unnecessary decoration and elaborate liturgical rites. Instead, they practiced contemplation and committed themselves to hard manual labor. Under the charismatic leadership of Bernard of Clairvaux (1090–1153), one of the most influential personalities of his age, the Cistercian order grew exponentially, from five houses in 1115 to 343 by 1153. This astonishing increase meant that many more men and women were becoming professional religious, but it also meant that still more were donating funds and lands to support monasteries and thereby participating indirectly in a life of devotion.

Another manifestation of popular piety was a new focus on the sacrament of the Mass, the liturgical reenactment of Christ's last meal with his disciples. This celebration, the Eucharist, had always been an important part of Christian religious and social practice (Chapter 6). But only in the twelfth century did it become the central act of worship in the western Church. Bernard of Clairvaux was instrumental in making it so, by developing and preaching the doctrine of transubstantiation. According to this doctrine, every Mass is a miraculous event because the priest's blessing transforms the bread and wine on the altar into the body and blood of Christ—hence the term *transubstantiation*, since earthly substances thereby become the substance of Christ's divine body.

THE MYSTERY OF THE MASS. In this manuscript illumination, the visionary Hildegard of Bingen (see below) illustrates the doctrine of transubstantiation. In the lower register, the bread and wine of the Mass have been placed on the altar and are being transformed into the body and blood of the crucified Christ, depicted in the upper register. Paired scenes from Christ's life (his birth and death, his ministry and resurrection) emphasize the fact that earthly substances—bread and wine—participate in a divine cycle of regeneration. Note that Hildegard does not imagine the mediating figure as a priest, but as the (female) Church, represented as a crowned queen and associated with the Virgin Mary. ▪ *What might be the significance of this choice?*

Not incidentally, this new theology of the Eucharist further enhanced the prestige of the priesthood by seeming to endow it with wonder-working powers. Indeed, the Latin words spoken at the consecration of the Host, *Hoc est corpus meum* ("This is my body"), were liable to be (mis)-understood as a magical formula: *Hocus pocus.*

Holy Women, Human and Divine

Popular devotion to the Eucharist was matched by another new and hugely influential religious practice: the veneration of Jesus's mother, Mary. In this development, too, Bernard of Clairvaux played an important role. Under his influence, the Church now taught that Mary had not only given birth to Jesus while still a virgin, but that she remained a virgin even after Jesus' birth—and, more radically, that she herself had been conceived without sin. This made Mary the exact opposite of Eve, the woman whose disobedience had allegedly brought sin into the world for the first time; for Mary had given birth to Christ, a second Adam, whose obedient sacrifice of himself atoned for that original sin. New doctrines also raised Mary from the position of God's humble handmaid to that of heaven's queen, with the power to intercede on behalf of all, even the worst sinners. Her soaring reputation is amply testified by the thousands of devotional images created during this period, the many stories and hymns celebrating her virtues and miracles, and the fact that practically all the magnificent new cathedrals of the age were dedicated to "Our Lady." (Hence the many churches of Notre Dame in France, the Frauenkirchen of Germany, and so on.)

The burgeoning cult of the Blessed Virgin had two contradictory effects. On the one hand, it elevated a female figure to a prominent place in the Roman Church for the first time, and it thereby celebrated virtues associated with femininity: motherhood, healing, nourishment, mercy, kindness. On the other hand, it made Mary an unobtainable model of female perfection. No real woman could begin to emulate her, and thus real women were increasingly compared to Eve and perceived as weak, deceitful, and disobediant. Moroever, the veneration of a single, idealized woman coincided exactly with the suppression of most real women's access to positions of power within the Church. As the cult of the Blessed Virgin grew, so the opportunities for aspiring holy women shrank.

This did not go unremarked at the time. The career of Heloise (c. 1090–1164) exemplifies both the avenues of advancement for women and also the successful blocking of those avenues by new constraints on women's activities. Heloise's exact contemporary, Hildegard of Bingen

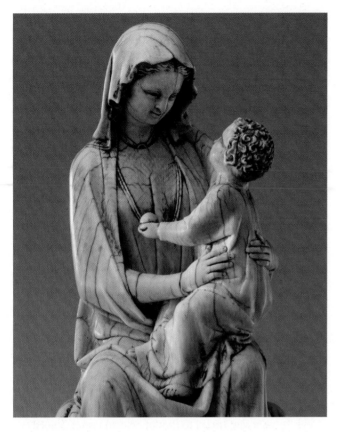

VIRGIN AND CHILD. This exquisite ivory sculpture (just over seven inches high) was carved in Paris in the mid- to late thirteenth century, as an aid to private devotion and prayer. The mother of Jesus, Mary was also regarded as the mother of all humanity, the *alma mater* ("nourishing mother") who could be relied on to protect and heal those who asked for her help.

(1098–1179), was also creative in her efforts to make a place for herself and her female followers, and more outspoken than Heloise in her criticism of attempts to thwart them. Like Heloise, she was an abbess and a highly original thinker. But she was not, like Heloise, a scholar; she was a mystic who claimed to receive regular revelations from God. She also composed hymns and ambitious musical dramas for her nuns—music now widely available on CD and MP3—and prepared treatises on subjects as diverse as cosmology, pharmacology, and medicine. Her advice was frequently sought by religious and secular authorities, including Bernard of Clairvaux and Frederick Barbarossa, and she even received a special papal dispensation that allowed her to preach publicly.

Despite all this, Hildegard had to fight constantly for her rights and those of her nuns during her lifetime, and after her death she was never officially recognized as a saint. Indeed, she was one of the first candidates for whom a new canonization process was instituted in the papal curia, as

a way of controlling the popular veneration of charismatic figures whom the Church considered threatening. So while many high-ranking clergy of her own day recognized her holiness, the papal courts of subsequent centuries would not acknowledge it. The standards of acceptable female behavior had become too narrow to contain her.

Heresy or Piety?

Christianity has been successfully transmitted to many different civilizations because it is relatively open-ended and absorbent of new influences. In this era, however, the Church began to lose its capacity to respond inclusively to new challenges, preferring instead to crack down on "heresies" that undermined its power. This trend would eventually lead to a reforming movement so intense that it could not be contained within the Church: the Protestant Reformation (see Chapter 13). For the more the Church claimed the right to control every aspect of belief and practice, the more it made itself vulnerable to those who challenged its enforcment of orthodoxy. This resulted in popular opposition to papal authority, and also to counter-initiatives aimed at harnessing popular piety to that same authority.

The best way to understand this is through Innocent III's very different responses to rather similar religious movements. On the one hand, the pope resolved to crush all disobedience of papal authority; on the other, he wanted to support idealistic groups that could be made to acknowledge papal authority. For example, Innocent labelled as "heretical" a spiritual awakening that began in southern France, that of the Cathars (from the Greek word for "purity"). He accused Cathars of beliefs that resemble Zoroastrianism (Chapter 2) and Manichaeism (Chapter 6), alleging that they held all material creation to be evil, and that they believed the power of God to be opposed by that of a malevolent deity associated with the fallen angel Lucifer. Whatever the truth of these allegations, the fact that many Cathar leaders were women made the movement "heretical" by definition.

Innocent eventually took steps to eradicate the Cathars, who were also known as Albigensians, by authorizing the violent seizure of their lands and property. But this "Albigensian Crusade" was really a war of conquest that enabled the French monarchy to expand into southern lands. Innocent also began the process of instituting inquisitorial procedures that would enable the legal prosecution, torture, and execution of convicted heretics like the Waldensians. Waldensians were lay people who followed the teachings of a merchant called Peter Waldo (or Waldes). They were active in the vernacular translation of the Gospels and

HILDEGARD OF BINGEN'S DIVINE INSPIRATION. This portrait of Hildegard and her male secretary, Volmar, appears in her book *Scivias* ("Know the Ways"). It shows Hildegard as the recipient of a divine vision (represented by tongues of heavenly fire) which she transcribes onto a wax tablet using a stylus, a common method for creating the first draft of a written work. Volmar is placed outside the frame in which her vision occurs, but he is prepared to copy it onto parchment. ▪ *What does this image tell us about medieval ideas of authorship and authority?* ▪ *What does it suggest about the relationship and status of the two figures?*

preaching and offering assistance to the poor. They also begged for a living—hence their categorization as *mendicants*, from the Latin verb *mendicare*, "to beg." But essentially the only thing that separated them from the Waldensians was their willingness to subject themselves to papal authority.

The first of these orders, formally known as the Order of Preachers, was founded by Dominic of Osma (1170–1221), a Castilian theologian. Approved in 1216, it was particularly dedicated to the prosecution of heretics and to the conversion of Jews and Muslims. At first, the Dominicans hoped to achieve these ends by preaching and public debate, and so many of its members pursued academic careers and contributed to the development of philosophy and theology; indeed, the most influential intellectual of the Middle Ages, Thomas Aquinas (1225–1274), was a Dominican (see below). But the Dominicans soon became associated with the use of other persuasive techniques through the administration of the Inquistition, which became formalized in the thirteenth century. (It is now called the Congregation for the Doctrine of the Faith, and is still staffed by members of the order.)

The Franciscans, formally known as the Order of the Friars Minor ("Little Brothers"), were quite different from the Dominicans, commited less to doctrine and discipline than to the welfare of the poor and the cultivation of personal spirituality. Whereas Dominic and his followers were ordained priests, the founder of the Franciscans was the ne'er-do-well son of an Italian merchant, Francis of Assisi (1182–1226), who eventually rebelled against the materialistic values of his father. Stripping himself (literally) of all his worldly possessions, he put on the tattered garb of a beggar and began to preach and to minister to outcasts in the darkest corners of Italian cities. Unlike Dominic, Francis did all of this without official approval, thereby risking rejection as a heretic. But when he showed himself willing to profess obedience in 1209, Innocent granted Francis and his followers permission to preach.

This was not, however, an approved religious lifestyle for women. Francis's most important female follower, Clare of Assisi (1194–1253), wanted to found an order along the same lines, but members of the Order of Poor Ladies (also known as the Poor Clares) were not allowed to work directly among the poor, as men did, but instead lived in cloistered convents supported by charitable donations. Their counterparts in northern Europe were the Beguines, communities of lay women who ministered to the poor. Their relationship with Church officials was often strained because the Beguines embraced many of the practices associated with "heretics," including the unauthorized translation and study of the Bible. The fact that they were women made them even more suspect.

dedicated to lives of poverty and preaching. For a while, the Church did not interfere with Waldensians' ministry. But when they began to preach without authorization they were condemned as heretics. Many of their leaders, too, were women.

At the same time, Innocent ratified two other popular movements and turned them into two new religious orders, the Dominicans and the Franciscans. Like the Waldensians, the friars ("brothers") of these orders imitated Jesus by

Competing Viewpoints

Two Conversion Experiences

> Peter Waldo, later branded as a heretic, and Francis of Assisi, later canonized as a saint, were both moved to take up lives of preaching and poverty after undergoing a process of conversion. These experiences exhibit some striking similarities, despite the very different fates of these two men. The first account is that of an anonymous chronicler in Peter's home town of Lyons; the second is by Francis's contemporary and hagiographer, Thomas of Celano (c. 1200–c. 1260/70).

The Conversion of Peter Waldo

At about this time, in 1173, there was a citizen of Lyons named Peter Waldo, who had made a great deal of money by the evil means of usury. One Sunday he lingered by a crowd that had gathered round a traveling storyteller, and was much struck by his words. He took him home with him, and listened carefully to his story of how St. Alexis had died a holy death in his father's house. Next morning Waldo hastened to the schools of theology to seek advice about his soul. When he had been told of the many ways of coming to God he asked the master whether any of them was more sure and reliable than the rest. The master quoted to him the words of the Lord, "If thou wilt be perfect go sell what thou hast and give it to the poor and thou shalt have treasure in heaven. And come follow me."

Waldo returned to his wife and gave her the choice between having all his movable wealth or his property in land.... She was very upset at having to do this and chose the property. From his movable wealth he returned what he had acquired wrongly, conferred a large portion on his two daughters, whom he placed in the order of Fontevrault without his wife's knowledge, and gave a still larger amount to the poor.

At this time a terrible famine was raging through Gaul and Germany.... Waldo generously distributed bread, soup and meat to anyone who came to him. On the [Feast of the] Assumption of the Virgin [August 15] he scattered money among the poor in the streets saying, "You cannot serve two masters, God and Mammon." The people around thought he had gone out of his senses. Then he stood up on a piece of high ground and said, "Friends and fellow-citizens, I am not mad as you think.... I know that many of you disapprove of my having acted so publicly. I have done so both for my own sake and for yours: for my sake, because anybody who sees me with money in future will be able to say that I am mad; for your sake, so that you may learn to place your hopes in God and not in wealth." ...

In 1177 Waldo, the citizen of Lyons whom we have already mentioned, who had vowed to God that he would possess neither gold nor silver, and take no thought for the morrow, began to make converts to his opinions. Following his example they gave all they had to the poor, and willingly devoted themselves to poverty. Gradually, both in public and in private they began to inveigh against both their own sins and those of others....

In 1178 Pope Alexander III held a council at the Lateran palace.... The council condemned heresy and all those who fostered and defended heretics. The pope embraced Waldo, and applauded the vows of voluntary poverty which he had taken, but forbade him and his companion to assume the office of preaching except at the request of the priests. They obeyed this instruction for a time, but later they disobeyed, and affronted many, bringing ruin on themselves.

Source: Excerpted from *Chronicon universale anonymi Laudunensis*, ed. and trans. Robert I. Moore, *The Birth of Popular Heresy* (London: 1975), pp. 111–13 (slightly modified).

The Conversion of Francis of Assisi

There was a man by the name of Francis, who from his earliest years was brought up by his parents proud of spirit, in accordance with the vanity of the world.... These are the wretched circumstances among which the man whom we venerate today as a saint, for he is truly a saint, lived in his youth; and almost up to the twenty-fifth year of his age, ... he outdid all his contemporaries in vanities and he came to be a promoter of evil and was

more abundantly zealous for all kinds of foolishness.... And while, not knowing how to restrain himself, he was ... worn down by a long illness, [and he] began to think of things other than he was used to thinking upon. When he had recovered somewhat and had begun to walk about the house with the support of a cane to speed the recovery of his health, he went outside one day and began to look about at the surrounding landscape with great interest. But the beauty of the fields, the pleasantness of the vineyards, and whatever else was beautiful to look upon, could stir in him no delight. He wondered therefore at the sudden change that had come over him.... From that day on, therefore, he began to despise himself....

Now since there was a certain man in the city of Assisi whom he loved more than any other because he was of the same age as the other, and since the great familiarity of their mutual affection led him to share his secrets with him, he often took him to remote places, places well suited for counsel, telling him that he had found a certain precious and great treasure. This one rejoiced and, concerned about what he heard, he willingly accompanied Francis whenever he was asked. There was a certain grotto near the city where they frequently went and talked about this treasure. The man of God, who was already holy by reason of his holy purpose, would enter the grotto, while his companion would wait for him outside; and filled with a new and singular spirit, he would pray to his Father in secret....

One day, however, when he had begged for the mercy of God most earnestly, it was shown to him by God what he was to do.... He rose up, therefore,

fortified himself with the sign of the cross, got his horse ready and mounted it, and taking with him some fine cloth to sell, he hastened to the city called Foligno. There, as usual, he sold everything he had with him ... and, free of all luggage, he started back, wondering with a religious mind what he should do with the money.... When, therefore, he neared the city of Assisi, he discovered a certain church ... built of old in honor of St. Damian but which was now threatening to collapse because it was so old.... And when he found there a certain poor priest, he kissed his sacred hands with great faith, and offered him the money he had with him, ... begging the priest to suffer him to remain with him for the sake of the Lord....

When those who knew him ... compared what he was now with what he had been ... they began to revile him miserably. Shouting out that he was mad and demented, they threw the mud of the streets and stones at him.... Now ... the report of these things finally came to his father ... [who] shut him up mercilessly in a dark place for several days.... It happened, however, when Francis's father had left home for a while on business and the man of God remained bound in the basement of the house, his mother, who was alone with him and did not approve of what her husband had done, spoke kindly to her son ... and loosening his chains, she let him go free....

He [the father] then brought his son before the bishop of the city, so that, renouncing all his possessions into his hands, he might give up everything he had.... Indeed, he [Francis] did not wait for any words nor did he speak any, but immediately putting off his clothes and

casting them aside, he gave them back to his father. Moreover, not even retaining his trousers, he stripped himself completely naked before all. The bishop, however, sensing his disposition and admiring greatly his fervor and constancy, arose and drew him within his arms and covered him with the mantle he was wearing....

Source: Excerpted from Thomas of Celano, "The First Life of Saint Francis" in *Saint Francis of Assisi: Writings and Biographies*, ed. Marion A. Habiq (Chicago: 1973), pp. 229–41.

Questions for Analysis

1. How do the conversions of Peter and Francis reflect the social and economic changes of the twelfth century? What new sources of tension and temptation are evident?

2. How do these two accounts describe these new converts' relationship(s) with their families, communities, and Church authorities? What are the similarities and differences, and why would these be important factors in determining the sanctity of either?

3. The story of Peter's conversion is written by an anonymous chronicler of Lyons, that of Francis by his follower and official biographer. How do these different perspectives shape these two accounts? Which is the more reliable, and why?

Christians against Jews

Although violence and exploitation continued to reduce the size and strength of Europe's Jewish communities, the Church's official position held that Jews posed a serious threat to Christians. It never explicitly endorsed the wilder claims made by popular rabble-rousers, but it did little to combat such attitudes either. As a result, many ordinary Christians came to believe that their Jewish neighbors were agents of evil who routinely crucified Christian children, profaned the body of Christ in the Eucharist, and spread disease in Christian communities by poisoning wells. Fanciful stories of Jewish wealth added an economic element to the development of anti-Semitism, as did the fact that the Jews' social and cultural networks facilitated rapid communication. From these, conspiracy theorists inferred the existence of organized Jewish plots to undermine Christian society, which were regularly cited as justifications for pogroms, mass executions, and other atrocities.

The precarious position of Europe's Jews worsened throughout the thirteenth century, as both secular and ecclesiastical authorities devised more systematic mechanisms for controlling and policing undesirable segments of society: not only "heretics" but the indigent poor, prostitutes, "sodomites," and lepers. The canons of the Fourth Lateran Council had mandated that Jews be exposed and marginalized through the wearing of the Jewish badge, and this made them easier targets in times of unrest. Meanwhile, the protections which Europe's rulers had once extended to their Jewish subjects were gradually withdrawn. In Iberia, the "Reconquista" had absorbed many of the Muslim kingdoms in which Jews had enjoyed a measure of tolerance, and they were not easily accommodated within the emerging monarchies of Christian Spain. Starting in the 1280s, rulers elsewhere in Europe began to expel their Jewish subjects from their kingdoms altogether, in most cases because they could no longer repay the enormous sums they had extorted from Jewish moneylenders; this was the case in the kingdoms of Sicily (1288), England (1290), and France (1306). Further expulsions followed during the fourteenth century in the Rhineland, and in 1492 from Spain. By 1500, only northern Italy and various eastern European regions (encompassed today by Poland, Belorus, and Ukraine) were home to sizable Jewish communities. They would survive there until the more efficient persecutions of the Holocaust destroyed them (see Chapter 26).

THE BURNING OF JEWS. This manuscript account, written in the German vernacular, records an incident in which Jews were accused of poisoning the wells in a Christian town—and shows the punishment meted out to them. The wooden enclosure may represent the walls of the Jewish ghetto. As in the image on page 217, the Jews are identified by their distinctive conical hats.

THE INTELLECTUAL REVOLUTION

As we noted above, the Fourth Lateran Council responded to the growing population and urbanization of Europe by mandating the education of the laity and by insisting on more rigorous training for all clergy. But even before 1215, the growth of towns had led to the growth of schools in those towns, for the most part founded by local bishops or monasteries. At the same time, the Crusades had become conduits for the transmission of Muslim learning and, through Muslim mediation, the precepts of ancient Greek philosophy. The infusion of these new ideas created an extraordinary new forum for intellectual endeavor: the university. In much the same way that ease of travel and communication had fostered a scientific revolution in the cities of the Hellenistic world (Chaper 4), so the conditions which gave rise to the university mark the beginning of a revolution in the intellectual history of Europe.

Access to Education

Around 800, Charlemagne had ordered that primary schools be established in every city and monastery of his realm. But it was not until the economic revival of the late eleventh century that such educational opportunities were widely available. By 1179, Pope Alexander III decreed that all cathedrals should set aside income for at least one schoolteacher, whose task would be to accept all comers, rich or poor, without fee. The recently martyred Thomas Becket had been an early beneficiary of such schooling.

At first, cathedral schools existed almost exclusively for the training of priests, but their curriculum was soon broadened as the growth of bureaucracies escalated the demand for men with more sophisticated skills. The most fundamental elements of this curriculum were known as the *trivium*, "the three ways": grammar, logic, and rhetoric. This meant a thorough grounding in Latin through the study of classical Roman authors, such as Cicero and Virgil (Chapter 5), and training in the formulation and expression of sound arguments. Students who mastered the trivium were fit to perform basic clerical tasks, but those who wanted to achieve the reputation and advantages of scholars had to master the remaining branches of learning. These were arithmetic, geometry, astronomy, and music: the *quadrivium* or "four ways." Together, these seven liberal arts—so called because they free the minds and bodies of those who acquire them—were the prerequisites for advanced study in philosophy, theology, law, and medicine.

Until about 1200, most students in urban schools would have belonged to the minor orders of the clergy. This means that they took vows of obedience and were immune from prosecution by secular authorities, but were not required to remain celibate—unlike priests and bishops (who were in major orders). But by the thirteenth century, most boys who entered schools were not members of the clergy and never intended to be. Some were children of wealthy families, who regarded Latin literacy as a practical necessity. Others were future notaries, estate managers, and merchants who needed to be literate and numerate in order to succeed in these careers. In many cases, Latin ceased to be the language of instruction in these schools and was replaced by the vernacular language of the region.

Formal schooling remained restricted to males. Yet many girls and women became highly educated. Heloise had an unusual degree of access to the educational milieu of Paris, but she had already received excellent preparatory training in the convent at Argentueil before she began her studies with Abelard. Most lay women were taught at home, sometimes by private tutors but more often by other women. In fact, lay women were more likely to be literate than lay men, and it is for this reason that women were often the patrons of poets and the primary readers and owners of books. Significantly, the effigy that Eleanor of Aquitaine commissioned for her own tomb shows her lying awake till Judgment Day, reading.

The Development of Scholasticism

This educational revolution led to the development of new critical methods for framing and resolving complex problems. These methods are collectively known as *scholasticism*, meaning that they had their orgins in the pedagogy of medieval schools. Scholastic methods are highly respectful of authority, but they also rely on rigorous questioning and argumentation. They therefore place great emphasis on evidence derived from reason. Indeed, scholasticism can be defined as the theory and practice of reconciling various forms of knowledge through logical debate, often called *dialectic.*

The earliest practitioner of the scholastic method is often considered to be Anselm of Canterbury (1033–1109).

THE TOMB OF ELEANOR OF AQUITAINE. Eleanor probably commissioned the effigies representing herself, her husband Henry II, and her son Richard the Lionheart (both of whom died years before she did). She was eventually buried alongside them in the vault of the convent of Fontevrault in Anjou, where she spent the last years of her life.

The central premise of Anselm's teaching was that the human mind can reconcile wisdom gained through education and experience with divine revelation—so long as one has faith in God and careful scholastic training. Building on the writings of Augustine and Boethius (Chapter 6), Anselm developed various rational proofs for the truths of Christian doctrine. The most famous of these is his proof for the existence of God, known as the ontological proof ("proof from the fact of existence") because it reasons that human beings could not have ideas of goodness or truth or justice unless some higher being had instilled these ideas in us. He further reasoned that God, as the essence of all ideals, must be "that than which nothing greater can be conceived" and as such must exist, or else God could not be the greatest thing conceivable.

Anselm's writings were influential, but the philosopher who popularized the scholastic method was Abelard. It was largely thanks to him that Paris became the intellectual capital of Europe and a magnet for ambitious young men who were attracted to Abelard's unorthodox teaching style. We can glimpse it through the audacious treatise called the *Sic et Non* ("Yes and No" or "So and Not So"). In this book, Abelard gathered a collection of seemingly contradictory statements from the Church Fathers, organized around 150 key theological problems. Like his contemporary Gratian, the codifier of canon law, his ultimate ambition was to show that these divergent authorities could be reconciled—in this case, through the skillful use of dialectic.

Yet Abelard did not propose any solutions in the *Sic et Non*, and the work therefore caused grave concern. More inflammatory still were Abelard's meditations on the doctrine of the Trinity, which circulated in a book of lectures that was denounced and burned in 1121. Twenty years later, Bernard of Clairvaux had Abelard brought up on another charge of heresy, and he was condemned a second time. But his very skills as a teacher helped to salvage his reputation, since his many pupils eventually vindicated his teachings. His student Peter Lombard would ask the same fundamental questions, but he took care to resolve the tensions which the *Sic et Non* had left open-ended. His great work, known as the *Sentences*, became the standard theological textbook of the medieval university, on which all aspirants to the doctorate were required to comment.

The Nature of the University

The emergence of the university—a unique public forum for advanced study, the questioning of received ideas, and the resolution of critical problems—was the natural exten-

sion of Abelard's teachings. His reputation and that of his students attracted many other intellectuals to Paris, and together they could offer more varied and advanced instruction than anything obtainable in the average cathedral school. By 1200, this loose association of teachers formed a *universitas* ("corporation" in Latin), and the resulting faculty began to collaborate in the higher academic study of the liberal arts, with a special emphasis on theology. At about the same time, students in Bologna came together in a *universitas* whose speciality was law.

Paris and Bologna provided the two basic models on which all medieval universities were based. In southern Europe, the universities of Montpellier, Salamanca, and Naples were patterned after Bologna, where the students themselves constituted the corporation. They hired the teachers, paid their salaries, and fined or discharged them for neglect of duty or poor instruction. The universities of northern Europe, modeled on Paris, were guilds of teachers who governed themselves and established fees for tuition and rules of conduct. By the end of the thirteenth century, the northern universities also expanded to include separate, semi-autonomous colleges, which usually provided housing for poorer students and were often endowed by a private benefactor. Over time, these colleges became centers of instruction as well as residences. The universities of Oxford and Cambridge still retain this pattern of organization.

Most of the academic degrees granted in our modern universities derive from those awarded in the Middle Ages, even though the actual courses of study are very different. Prior to the nineteenth century, no university curriculum included history or vernacular languages, or anything like the social sciences. The medieval student was assumed to know Latin grammar thoroughly before entrance into a university. On admission, he was required to spend about four years studying the basic liberal arts, which meant doing advanced work in Latin rhetoric and mastering the rules of logic. If he passed his examinations, he received the preliminary degree of bachelor of arts (the prototype of our BA). But to ensure himself a place in professional life he had to devote additional years to the pursuit of an advanced degree, the master of arts (MA) or doctor of laws, medicine, or theology. This was accomplished by reading and commenting on standard texts such as Peter Lombard's *Sentences* (theology), Gratian's *Decretum* (law), or Aristotle's *Physics* (medicine). The requirements for the degree of doctor of philosophy (PhD) included more specialized training, and those for the doctorate in theology were particularly arduous, requiring twelve or thirteen years of further study.

Student life in medieval universities was rowdy. Many students began their studies between the ages of twelve

Peter Abelard Critiques Theological Contradictions

In 1120, Abelard published the Sic et Non, *"So and Not So," a pioneering work of dialectic theology and a model for the development of later scholastic methods. In it, he arranged passages from Scripture as well as writings of the Church Fathers that had bearing on important doctrinal issues and that appeared to offer contradictory views. His eventual aim, as the prologue to this work indicates, was to reconcile these differences through the use of critical analysis.*

here are many seeming contradictions and even obscurities in the innumerable writings of the church fathers. Our respect for their authority should not stand in the way of an effort on our part to come at the truth. The obscurity and contradictions in ancient writings may be explained upon many grounds, and may be discussed without impugning the good faith and insight of the fathers. A writer may use different terms to mean the same thing, in order to avoid a monotonous repetition of the same word. Common, vague words may be employed in order that the common people may understand; and sometimes a writer sacrifices perfect accuracy in the interest of a clear general statement. Poetical, figurative language is often obscure and vague. . . .

Doubtless the fathers might err; even Peter, the prince of the apostles, fell into error; what wonder that the saints do not always show themselves inspired? The fathers did not themselves believe that they, or their companions, were always right. Augustine found himself mistaken in some cases and did not hesitate to retract his errors. He warns his admirers not to look upon his letters as they would upon the Scriptures, but to accept only those things which, upon examination, they find to be true.

All writings belonging to this class are to be read with full freedom to criticise, and with no obligation to accept unquestioningly; otherwise the way would be blocked to all discussion, and posterity be deprived of the excellent intellectual exercise of debating difficult questions of language and presentation. But an explicit exception must be made in the case of the Old and New Testaments. In the Scriptures, when anything strikes us as absurd, we may not say that the writer erred, but that the scribe made a blunder in copying the manuscripts, or that there is an error in interpretation, or that the passage is not understood. The fathers make a very careful distinction between the Scriptures and later works. They advocate a discriminating, not to say suspicious, use of the writings of their own contemporaries.

In view of these considerations, I have ventured to bring together various dicta of the holy fathers, as they came to mind, and to formulate certain questions which were suggested by the seeming contradictions in the statements. These questions ought to serve to excite tender readers to a zealous inquiry into truth and so sharpen their wits. The master key of knowledge is, indeed, a persistent and frequent questioning. Aristotle, the most clear-sighted of all the philosophers, was desirous above all things else to arouse this questioning spirit, for in his *Categories* he exhorts a student as follows: "It may well be difficult to reach a positive conclusion in these matters unless they be frequently discussed. It is by no means fruitless to be doubtful on particular points." By doubting we come to examine, and by examining we reach the truth.

Source: Peter Abelard, prologue to the *Sic et Non*, trans. James Harvey Robinson in *Readings in European History*, 2 vols. (Boston, MA: 1904), vol. 1, pp. 450–51.

Questions for Analysis

1. On what grounds can religious authorities be challenged, according to Abelard? What distinctions does he make between criticism of the Scriptures and of other authorities, and why?

2. Abelard did not attempt, in this work, to resolve the contradictions among his sources. Based on what you have learned, why would his project have seemed threatening to the authority of the Church?

THE SPREAD OF UNIVERSITIES. This map shows the geographical distribution of Europe's major universities and indicates the dates of their foundation. ▪ *Where were the first universities founded and why?* ▪ Notice the number and location of the universities founded in the fourteenth and fifteenth centuries. ▪ *What pattern do you see in these later foundations?* ▪ *What might explain this?*

and fifteen, and so were working through all the challenges of adolescence as they worked toward their degrees; this helps to explain the many injunctions against drunkenness, gambling, and other pursuits included among the canons of the Fourth Lateran Council. Moreover, university students generally believed that they constituted an independent and privileged community, apart from the local communities in which they lived. This often led to riots or even pitched battles between "town" and "gown."

That said, the time devoted to actual study was very intensive. Because books were prohibitively expensive, the primary mode of instruction was the lecture (Latin for "reading") in which a master would read an authoritative work aloud to his students and comment on it while the students took notes. As students advanced in their disciplines, they were expected to develop their own skills of analysis and interpretation in formal, public disputations. Advanced disputations could become extremely complex and abstract; sometimes they might last for days. Often they sparked public debates of great magnitude. The ninety-five theses posted by Martin Luther in 1517 were actually a set of debating points organized along these lines (see Chapter 13).

Classical Thought and Christian Theology

The intellectual revolution of the Middle Ages was further advanced by renewed access to classical philosophy and Muslim science, epitomized by the works of Avicenna and Averroès (Chapter 8). Many Greek texts were available in Latin translation after the middle of the twelfth century, and by the middle of the thirteenth nearly all of Aristotle's surviving works and much Arabic scientific knowledge was accessible to western Europeans. Scholars were now faced with the task of reconciling these "new" ideas with a thousand years of doctrinal developments. This was relatively straightforward in the case of the natural sciences, because scholasticism had already established the principles for reconciling reason and observation with faith. But many other aspects of Greek and Arabic learning were not readily compatible and therefore had to be filtered through the dialectical methods pioneered by Abelard and his pupils.

By far the greatest accomplishments in this endeavor were made by Thomas Aquinas (1225–1274), who became the leading theologian at the University of Paris. As a member of the Dominican order, Thomas was committed to the defense of faith through reason. He also believed that the study of the physical world was a legitimate way of gaining knowledge of the divine, because God had created both the world and the many ways of knowing it. Imbued with a deep confidence in the value of human reason, Thomas worked quietly and steadily on his two great summaries of theology, the *Summa contra Gentiles* (a summary of the arguments for refuting non-Christian religions) and the compendious *Summa*

Theologiae. The theology of the modern Roman Catholic Church continues to rest on Thomistic methods, doctrines, and principles.

COURTS, CITIES, AND CATHEDRALS

In the eleventh century, it was still possible to describe European society as divided among "those who worked, those who prayed, and those who fought." By 1200, such a description no longer bore much relationship to reality. New elites had emerged in the burgeoning cities of western Europe. The wealthiest members of society were merchants and bankers, and aristocrats either had to best them (by engaging in trade themselves) or join them through strategic intermarriage. The aristocracy still fought, but so did upwardly mobile knights, urban crossbowmen, longbowmen, citizen militias, and peasant levies. Meanwhile, such lines as existed between town and countryside were easily crossed. Rural people moved to towns and townspeople moved back to the countryside with regularity and ease. And the pupils of the new schools made up a growing professional class that further defied neat categorization. We have noted that careers in the Church or royal bureaucracies were particularly open to self-made, educated men. But medieval courts and cities also provided opportunities for advancement.

From Chevalerie to Chivalry

The ennoblement of chivalry and the emergence of medieval court culture were connected to the growing wealth of Europe, the competition among monarchies, and contemporary developments in military technology. In 1100, a knight could get by with a woolen tunic and leather corselet, a couple of horses, a groom, and a sword. A hundred years later, a knight needed full-body armor made of iron, a visored helmet, a broadsword, a spear, a shield, and warhorses capable of carrying all this gear. By 1250, a knight also had to keep up appearances at tournaments, which meant maintaining a string of horses, sumptuous silk clothing for himself and caparisons for his steeds, and a retinue of liveried squires and servants. As the costs of a warrior's equipment rose, the number of men who could personally afford it declined dramatically, which made knightly

display something increasingly prized by the nobility and newly rich merchants alike.

There were still other factors contributing to the prestige of knighthood. As part of a larger effort to control the violent competition for land and wealth, both secular and ecclesiastical rulers had begun to promote a new set of values that would come to redefine chivalry: bravery, loyalty, generosity, and civility. This new chivalry appealed to knights because it distinguished them from all the other "new men" who were emerging as powerful in this period, especially merchants and clerics. It also appealed to the nobility, whose status in this socially mobile world no longer depended on descent from high-born ancestors; families who *did* have such ancestors did not necessarily have the wealth to maintain a noble lifestyle, while many families who lived as "nobility" did not have prestigious ancestors.

What, then, was "nobility"? Was high status a matter of birth or was it the result of individual achievement? The amalgamation of knighthood and nobility offered something to all sides. To the older aristocracy, it was a visible sign of good breeding. To professional warriors, and to the merchants and bureaucrats who adopted its language and customs, chivalry offered a way of legitimizing social positions attained through bravery or skill. As a result, mounted combat—whether on the battlefield, in tournaments, or in the hunt—would remain the defining pastime of European gentlemen until the end of the First World War.

The Culture of the Court

Closely linked to this new ideology of chivalry was a new emphasis on *courtoisie*, "courtliness," the refined behavior appropriate to a court. This stemmed in part from practical necessity. Those great lords who could support a knightly retinue would have households full of randy young men whose appetites had to be controlled. Hence, the emerging code of chivalry encouraged a view of noblewomen as objects of veneration who could only be wooed and won by politesse, poetry, and valiant deeds; they had to be courted. Non-noble women, though, were fair game and could be taken by force if they did not yield willingly to the desires of a knight.

Whole new genres of poetry, song, and storytelling emerged in the twelfth century to celebrate the allied cultures of chivalry and courtliness. These genres stand in marked contrast to the heroic epics that are often the earliest literary artifacts of various vernacular languages: the Anglo-Saxon *Beowulf*, *The Song of Roland*, the Norse sagas, the German *Song of the Nibelungs*, and the Spanish *Poem of the Cid*. These epics portray a virile, violent society. If women are mentioned, often they are prizes to be won in battle. The courtly entertainments introduced in the twelfth century are very different. Many of them were addressed to, and commissioned by, women. In some cases, they were even composed by women, or in close collaboration with a female patron. An example of the former is the collections of *lais* (versified stories) of Marie de France, who was active during the reigns of Henry II and Eleanor of Aquitaine, and who may have been an abbess as well as a member of the Anglo-Norman aristocracy. An example of the latter is one of the Arthurian tales composed by Marie's contemporary, Chrétien de Troyes (*kray-TYAN duh TWAH*, fl. 1165–90),

MAKING A KNIGHTLY APPEARANCE. The costs of maintaining a chivalric lifestyle mounted steeply in the twelfth and thirteenth centuries, not only because a knight needed the most up-to-date equipment but because he was expected to cut a gallant figure at tournaments and to dazzle female spectators. This image is one of many sumptuous full-page illuminations in the Manesse Codex, made in Zurich in the early fourteenth century and preserving the compositions of courtly poets.

who spent some time working under the patronage of Eleanor's daughter (by her first husband, Louis VII), Marie of Champagne.

These new storytelling forms often focused on the exploits of King Arthur and his knights or some other heroic figure of the past, like Alexander the Great. But they were also attuned to the interests and concerns of women: threats to women's independence, enforced or unhappy marriages, disputed inheritances, fashion, fantasies of power. The heroine of one anonymous romance is a woman who dresses as a knight and travels the world performing valiant deeds. Other heroines accompany their husbands on quests, or defend their castles against attack, or have supernatural powers. Following in Chrétien's footsteps, the German poets Wolfram von Eschenbach and Gottfried von Strassburg vied to produce romances that retained the scope and complexity of heroic epics while featuring women in strong, central roles: Wolfram's *Parzival*, the story of the search for the Holy Grail, and Gottfried's *Tristan*, which retold the Celtic story of the adulterous love between Tristan and Isolde. Both inspired the operatic reconceptions of Richard Wagner (1813–1883).

The poetic tradition initiated by the southern French troubadours and northern French trouvères (terms deriving from the verbs *trobar/trouver*: "to discover, to invent") also contributed to the culture of chivalry. Much troubadour poetry displays sensitivity to feminine beauty and the natural world, and pays eloquent tribute to the political and sexual power of women.

But to what extent do these entertainments reflect real changes in noblewomen's status? Certainly, there were women throughout this period who wielded tremendous power, particularly in Scandinavia and parts of southern Europe, where women could inherit property, rule in their own right, and were treated as lords in fact and in name. For example, Eleanor remained sole ruler of Aquitaine throughout her long life, and she played a crucial role in the government of England at various times. The strong-willed Blanche of Castile (1188–1252), Eleanor's granddaughter, ruled France during the minority of her son Louis IX and again when he went on crusade.

Queens are not typical, of course, but their activities in this period reflect some of the opportunities open to other well-born women—and the freedoms that set most western European women apart from their counterparts in the Byzantine and Muslim worlds. A striking symbol of this is the figure of the queen in the game of chess. In the Muslim courts where the game originated, the equivalent of the queen was a male figure, the king's chief minister, who could move only diagonally, and only one square at a time. In twelfth-century Europe, this piece became the queen. Eventually, she was the only figure powerful enough to move all over the board.

Urban Opportunities and Inequalities

Towns were crucibles of activity, and as such became political powerhouses as well as economic ones. As we noted in Chapter 8, many of the towns that emerged in the twelfth century were governed by associations of citizens who undertook a wide variety of civic responsibilities. But urban governance was also apt to fall into the hands of oligarchs, a trend that became increasingly marked during the thirteenth century when the enormous wealth generated by some forms of commerce led to social inequalities. In Italy, some cities sought to control the resulting violence by turning to an outsider who would rule as a dictator for a (supposedly) limited term. Others cities adopted the model of Venice and became formal oligarchies, casting off all pretense to democracy. Some cities remained republics in principle, like Florence, but became increasingly oligarchical in practice.

But even in places where town governance was controlled by a powerful few, there were many meaningful opportunities for collective activity. Urban manufacturing was regulated by professional associations known as guilds or, in some regions, confraternities ("brotherhoods"). Guilds promoted the interests of their members by trying to preserve monopolies and limit competition. To these ends, terms of employment and membership were strictly regulated. If an apprentice or a journeyman worker (from the French *journée*, meaning "day" and, by extension, "day's work") wished to become a master, he had to produce a "masterpiece" to be judged by the masters of the guild. If the market was considered too weak to support additional master craftsmen, even a masterpiece would not secure a craftsman the coveted right to set up his own shop. Most guilds were closed to Jews and Muslims and they also restricted the opportunities available to women.

Guilds and confraternities were therefore instruments of economic control, but they were also important social, political, and cultural institutions. Most combined the functions of religious association, drinking club, and benevolent society, looking after members and their families in hard times. Guilds also empowered their members in

much the same way that unions do today, providing them with political representation and raising their social status. In Arras, there was even a guild of professional entertainers, the confraternity of jongleurs, which became the most powerful organization in the town during the thirteenth century.

The Varieties of Vernacular Entertainment

Like courts, towns fostered new kinds of vernacular entertainment in the twelfth and thirteenth centuries. Even the genres of Latin poetry, song, and drama produced in this period can be considered "vernacular" because they made use of vernacular elements (like rhyme, which had not been a feature of classical Latin poetry), dealt with current events, and were popular with a wide audience.

Perhaps the genre most representative of urban culture is the fabliau, a "fable" or short story with a salacious or satirical twist. Fabliaux drew attention to the absurdities of urban life and lampooned the different types of people who were striving to reinvent themselves in the permissive world of the town: the oafish peasant, the effete aristocrat, the corrupt priest, the sex-starved housewife, the wily student, the greedy merchant, the con man. Gender-bending and reversals of fortune are common themes. In one fabliau, a young noblewoman is forced to marry a buffoonish shopkeeper who thereby gains a knighthood. To shame him, she herself dresses as a knight and beats her husband in a jousting match. The earliest of these fabliaux come from Arras, the prosperous banking center and the entertainment capital of Europe in the thirteenth century. Thanks to Arras's close contacts with England, southern France, and Italy, many of the entertainments developed there traveled far abroad.

It was through these channels that the accomplishments of poets active in French-speaking lands came to inspire the work of Dante Alighieri (1265–1321) of Florence. Dante composed a series of semi-autobiographical songs in what he called the "sweet new style" of poetry in his native tongue, Italian, which was now so different from Latin that it had become a language in its own right. Yet Dante also strove to make his own vernacular an instrument for serious political and social critique. His great work, known in his own day as the *Comedy* (called by later admirers the *Divine Comedy*) was composed during the years he spent in exile from his beloved city, after the political party he supported was ousted from power in 1301.

The *Comedy* describes the poet's imaginary journey through Hell, Purgatory, and Paradise, a journey beginning in a "dark wood," a metaphor for the personal and political crises that threatened his faith. Dante is led out of this forest and through the first two realms by the Roman poet Virgil, who represents the best of classical culture; but Dante can only be guided toward knowledge of the divine by his deceased beloved, Beatrice, who symbolizes Christian wisdom. In the course of this visionary pilgrimage, Dante meets the souls of many historical personages and contemporaries who explain why they met their several fates: this is his ingenious way of commenting on current events and passing judgment on his enemies. In many ways, this monumental poem represents the fusion of classical and Christian cultures, Latin learning and vernacular artistry.

The Medieval Cathedral

The cathedrals constructed in Europe's major cities during this period exemplify the ways in which the cultural communities of the court, the schools, and the town came together. For although any cathedral-building campaign would have been spearheaded by a bishop looking to glorify his episcopal see, it could not be completed without the support of the nobility, the resources of the wealthy, the learning of trained theologians, and the talents of urban craftsmen. And cathedrals were not merely edifices: they were theaters for liturgy, music, drama, and preaching.

Cathedrals were not, in themselves, new: the seat of a bishop had long been known as his *cathedra*, his throne, and the church that housed it was the principal church of the diocese. But the size, splendor, and importance of cathedrals increased exponentially in the twelfth and thirteenth centuries alongside the growing power of the Church, the population of cities, and the wealth and knowledge necessary for their construction. Indeed, the cathedrals of this period are readily distinguishable from their predecessors by their architectural style, which came to be called "Gothic," while the style of earlier buildings is known as "Romanesque." As the term suggests, Romanesque buildings use the basic elements of public architecture under the

Roman Empire: the rounded arch, massive stone walls, and sturdy supporting columns. By contrast, the structural elements of Gothic architecture are the pointed arch, ribbed vaulting, and the flying buttress, an external support that strengthened the much thinner stone walls and supported enormous stained-glass windows whose light illuminated the interior.

CONCLUSION

A century ago, the American medievalist Charles Homer Haskins described the intellectual, religious, and cultural changes of this era as "the Renaissance of the twelfth cen-tury." A generation later, his student Joseph Strayer located "the medieval origins of the modern state" in this same period, and with them the modern ideas of national sovereignty and identity. In recent decades, the British medievalists R. I. Moore and Robert Bartlett have also argued that this era marks the beginning of the modern world, but not necessarily in positive ways. Moore sees the growth of strong institutions like the Church and the state as leading to "the formation of a persecuting society" in which bureaucracies are used to identify, control, and punish groups of people deemed threatening to those in power; Bartlett views this era as the key phase in a brutal process of "conquest and colonization" visible in the expansion of the Holy Roman Empire, the Norman conquest of England, the growth of papal power, and the Crusades. Most recently,

ROMANESQUE AND GOTHIC. Some distinguishing features of the Romanesque and Gothic styles are exhibited in these two churches, both dedicated to the Virgin Mary and built within a century of one another. On the left is the west front of the Church of Notre-Dame-la-Grande in Poitiers, the ancestral domain of Eleanor of Aquitaine. Constructed between 1135 and 1145, it featured rounded arches, massive supporting pillars, and small windows. On the right is the cathedral of Notre-Dame at Reims in Champagne, built between 1220 and 1299. The emphasis on stolid, horizontal registers is here replaced by soaring, vertical lines. The gabled portals, pointed arches, and bristling pinnacles all accentuate the height of this structure, while the multitude of stained-glass windows—chiefly the enormous rose window—flood the vast interior with colored light.

Thomas Bisson has argued that the twelfth century was a period of crisis, exposing the need for strong governments that can check the personal ambitions and the violence of rapacious and unscrupulous men.

Common to all of these paradigms is a recognition that European power and influence began to expand around the year 1000 and was consolidated in the twelfth and thirteenth centuries. By 1300, as a result, Europe had taken on the geographic, political, linguistic, and cultural characteristics that continue to define it today. Indeed, many European nations look to these centuries for their origins and for the monuments of their cultural heritage. Magna Carta is still cited as the foundational document of English law and English constitutional monarchy, while the territories united under the rule of Frankish kings still form the nation of France. The doctrines crystallized in

After You Read This Chapter

Visit StudySpace for quizzes, additional review materials, and multi-media documents. **wwnorton.com/studyspace**

REVIEWING THE OBJECTIVES

- The emerging monarchies of Europe shared certain features but differed from one another in significant ways. What were the major similarities and differences of kingship in England, France, and Christian Spain?
- The growth of papal power made religion an important part of daily life for all Christians in unprecedented ways, but it also limited lay spirituality and the rights of non-Christians. How?
- Scholasticism was the method of teaching and learning fostered by medieval schools but it was also a method of debating and resolving problems. How did scholasticism assist in the reconciliation of classical and Christian thought?
- The meaning of chivalry changed in the twelfth century. Why?
- New literary genres and art forms were fostered by courts, universities, and towns. What are some good examples?

medieval canon law and scholastic theology have become the core doctrines of the modern Roman Catholic Church, and devotion to the Virgin Mary is still central to the piety of millions. The religious orders that emerged to educate and govern a burgeoning medieval population continue their ministries. The daughter houses of medieval monastic orders continue to proliferate in lands unknown to medieval people: Japan, China, Australia, New Zealand, the Americas. Students still pursue the degrees first granted in medieval universities, and those who earn them wear the caps and gowns of medieval scholars. Meanwhile, poets still aspire to the eloquence of Dante, singers record the music of Hildegard, and Hollywood films are based on chivalric romances and the tragic love story of Abelard and Heloise. It is difficult to tell where the Middle Ages end and the modern world begins.

PEOPLE, IDEAS, AND EVENTS IN CONTEXT

- What was **MAGNA CARTA** and why was it made? How did **PHILIP AUGUSTUS** consolidate royal authority in France, and why were the German emperors unable to do so?
- What were the main achievements of **INNOCENT III**? Why did the imperial power of **FREDERICK II** weaken the papacy?
- How do the **CULT OF THE VIRGIN** and the careers of **HILDEGARD OF BINGEN** and **HELOISE** exemplify the ideals and realities of women's roles in the Church?
- Why were **ABELARD**'s teachings condemned by the Church? In what sense can he be considered the founder of the **UNIVERSITY OF PARIS**?
- How did noblewomen like **ELEANOR OF AQUITAINE** contribute to the emergence of a new vernacular culture? What types of entertainment are characteristic of medieval cities?

CONSEQUENCES

- The growth of towns, monarchies, and the Church increased the degree of control that those in power could exercise; but they also increased access to education and new forms of social mobility. Is this a paradox, or are these two phenomena related?
- The U.S. Constitution is based on the legal principles and institutions that emerged in medieval England, but it also drew on Roman models. Which do you consider to be more influential, and why?
- Some historians have argued that the extent and methods of persecution discernible in this era are unprecedented in the history of Western civilizations. How would you support or refute this thesis? For example, does the persecution of Jews in medieval Europe differ from their treatment under the neo-Assyrians and Chaldeans, or under the Roman Empire? Why or why not?

Before You Read This Chapter

Crisis, Unrest, and Opportunity, 1300–1500

CORE OBJECTIVES

- **EXPLAIN** the economic and social effects of the Black Death.

- **DEFINE** the concept of national monarchy and summarize its implications.

- **IDENTIFY** the factors leading to the rise of Muscovy.

- **UNDERSTAND** the significance of the conciliar movement and its defeat by the papacy.

- **DESCRIBE** the spiritual, cultural, and technological innovations of the later Middle Ages.

n June of 1381, thousands of laborers from the English countryside rose up in rebellion. Most were peasants or village craftsmen, yet the revolt was carefully coordinated. Plans were spread in coded messages circulated by word of mouth and by the followers of a renegade Oxford professor, John Wyclif, who had called for the redistribution of Church property. The rebellion's immediate cause had been a series of exorbitant taxes levied by Parliament for the support of an ongoing war with France, but its more fundamental cause was an epidemic that had occurred thirty years earlier. The Black Death had reduced the entire population of Europe by 30 to 50 percent and had drastically altered the world of the survivors. In this new world, workers were valuable and could rebel against those who paid them poorly or treated them like slaves. In that fateful summer of 1381, the laborers of England even vowed to kill all the representatives of both the Church and the government—as they put it, all the lawyers—and to destroy all the documents that had been used to keep them down. It was a revolution, and it partly succeeded. Although the leaders were eventually captured and executed, the rebellion had made the strength of the common people known to all.

237

The fourteenth and fifteenth centuries are often seen as a time of crisis. And certainly, this was an age of adversity in both Asia and Europe. Famine and plague cut fearful swaths through the population; war was a brutally recurrent fact of life; and the papacy spent seventy years in continuous exile from Italy, only to see its prestige decline further after its return to Rome. But this period was also a time of opportunity. The exhausted land of Europe recovered from centuries of overfarming while workers gained economic, social, and political power. Popular and intellectual movements sought to reform the Church; and a host of artistic and scientific innovations contributed to all of these phenomena. It was a period of intense creativity that would redefine European civilization.

THE BLACK DEATH AND ITS CONSEQUENCES

By 1300, the European economy was reaching its limits. The population had tripled since 1000, and a sea of grain fields stretched, almost unbroken, from Ireland to Ukraine. Forests were cleared, marshes drained, and still Europe was barely able to feed itself. At the same time, the warming trend that had begun in the late eighth century (Chapter 8) reversed itself. For even a reduction of one or two degrees centigrade is enough to cause substantial changes in rainfall patterns, shorten growing seasons, and so lessen productivity.

The new vulnerability of the European ecosystem was dramatically revealed in the great famine that lasted from 1315 to 1322. In these years, adverse weather conditions were nearly continuous, and the result was starvation on a very large scale. Approximately 10 to 15 percent of the population north of the Alps perished. In the decades following, cold winters and floods threatened southern Europe, and in 1343 a tsunami destroyed ports in southern Italy. Earthquakes and comets seemed like further terrifying portents of disaster.

Tracking the Black Death

The Black Death is the name given to a pandemic that spread from China to Mongolia, northern India, and the Middle East during the 1330s and 1340s. By 1346, the disease had reached the Black Sea. From there, in 1347, Genoese ships inadvertently brought it to Sicily and northern Italy. From Italy it spread westward along trade routes, moving with astonishing rapidity. By 1350 it had reached Scandinavia and northern Russia, then spread southward

THE PLAGUE CLAIMS A VICTIM. A priest gives last rites to a bedridden plague victim, as a smiling devil pierces him with a spear and Christ looks mercifully down from Heaven. ▪ *What are the possible meanings of this image?* ▪ *What does it reveal about contemporary attitudes toward death?*

again. It continued to erupt in some localities for the next 300 years. The last Europe-wide instance occurred between 1661 and 1669.

The scale of mortality is almost unimaginable: at least a third, and probably half, of Europe's people died between 1347 and 1350. By the following century, the combined effects of plague, famine, and warfare had reduced the total population further, perhaps by as much as two thirds. In Germany, more than 40,000 villages disappeared. Around Paris, more than half the farmland cultivated in 1348 had become pasture by 1450. Elsewhere, abandoned fields reverted to woodland, increasing the forested areas of Europe by as much as one third.

Immediate reactions ran the gamut from panic to resignation. Observers quickly realized that the plague was contagious, but precisely how it spread remained a mystery. Some urged people to flee from stricken areas, which caused the disease to spread even faster. Others looked for

scapegoats, and revived old conspiracy theories that implicated Jews in the poisoning of wells. Scores of Jewish communities were attacked and thousands of their inhabitants massacred in the Rhineland, southern France, and Christian Spain. (No such attacks are known to have occurred in the Muslim world.) Another response was the Flagellant movement, so called because of the whips (*flagella* in Latin) with which traveling bands of penitents lashed themselves in order to appease the wrath of God. But the unruly, hysterical mobs that gathered around the flagellants aroused concern, and the movement was suppressed by papal order.

What caused the Black Death? In 2010, scientists confirmed that it was the deadly microbe *Yersinia pestis*, which causes bubonic plague and its even deadlier cousins, pneumonic and septicemic plague. In its bubonic form, humans catch it only if they are bitten by an infected flea or rat. Bubonic

THE PROGRESS OF THE BLACK DEATH, FOURTEENTH CENTURY. ▪ *What trajectories did the Black Death follow once it was introduced into Europe?* ▪ *How might the growth of towns, trade, and travel have contributed to its spread?* ▪ *Would such a rapid advance have been likely during the early Middle Ages or even in the ancient world?*

Competing Viewpoints

Responses to the Black Death

> Many chroniclers, intellectuals, and private individuals have left accounts of the plague and its effects, and many attempted to understand why it had occurred, how it spread, and how communities should respond to it.

The Spread of the Plague According to Gabriele D'Mussis (d. 1356), a Lawyer in Piacenza (Northern Italy)

Oh God! See how the heathen Tartar races, pouring together from all sides, suddenly invested the city of Caffa [near Constantinople] and besieged the trapped Christians there for almost three years.... But behold, [in 1346] the whole army was affected by a disease which overran the Tartars and killed thousands upon thousands every day. It was as though arrows were raining down from heaven to strike and crush the Tartars' arrogance. All medical advice and attention was useless; the Tartars died as soon as the signs of disease appeared on their bodies: swellings in the armpit or groin caused by coagulating humours, followed by a putrid fever.

The dying Tartars, stunned and stupefied by the immensity of the disaster brought about by the disease, and realising that they had no hope of escape, lost interest in the siege. But they ordered corpses to be placed in catapults and lobbed into the city in the hope that the intolerable stench would kill everyone inside. What seemed like mountains of dead were thrown into the city, and the Christians could not hide or flee or escape from them, although they dumped as many of the bodies as they could in the sea. And soon the rotting corpses tainted the air and poisoned the water supply.... Moreover one infected man could carry the poison to others, and infect people and places with the disease by look alone. No one knew, or could discover, a means of defence.

Thus almost everyone who had been in the East ... fell victim ... through the bitter events of 1346 to 1348—the Chinese, Indians, Persians, Medes, Kurds, Armenians, Cilicians, Georgians, Mesopotamians, Nubians, Ethiopians, Turks, Egyptians, Arabs, Saracens and Greeks....

* * *

As it happened, among those who escaped from Caffa by boat were a few sailors who had been infected with the poisonous disease. Some boats were bound for Genoa, others went to Venice and to other Christian areas. When the sailors reached these places and mixed with the people there, it was as if they had brought evil spirits with them....

* * *

Scarcely one in seven of the Genoese survived. In Venice, where an inquiry was held into the mortality, it was found that more than 70 percent of the people had died.... The rest of Italy, Sicily, and Apulia and the neighbouring regions maintain that they have been virtually emptied of inhabitants.... The Roman Curia at Avignon, the provinces on both sides of the Rhône, Spain, France, and the Empire cry up their griefs....

* * *

Everyone has a responsibility to keep some record of the disease and the plague attacks the lymphatic system, producing enormous swellings (buboes) of the lymph nodes in the groin, neck, and armpits. Pneumonic plague results when *Y. pestis* infects the lungs, allowing the contagion to spread in the same ways as the common cold. Septicemic plague occurs when an infected flea introduces the microbe directly into the human bloodstream, causing death within hours, often before any symptoms of the disease appear. One of the things that made the Black Death so frightening, therefore, is that it manifested itself in unpredictable ways. Those afflicted by the hideous bubonic plague might actually recover, while others—seemingly untouched—might die suddenly.

deaths, and because I am myself from Piacenza I have been urged to write more about what happened there in 1348. . . .

I don't know where to begin. Cries and laments arise on all sides. Day after day one sees the Cross and the Host being carried about the city, and countless dead being buried. . . . The living made preparations for their [own] burial, and because there was not enough room for individual graves, pits had to be dug in colonnades and piazzas, where nobody had ever been buried before. It often happened that man and wife, father and son, mother and daughter, and soon the whole household and many neighbours, were buried together in one place. . . .

A Letter from the Town Council of Cologne to the Town Council of Strasbourg (Germany), 12 January 1349

Very dear friends, all sorts of rumours are now flying about against Judaism and the Jews prompted by this unexpected and unparalleled mortality of Christians. . . . Throughout our city, as in yours, many-winged Fame clamours that this mortality was initially caused, and is still being spread, by the poisoning of springs and wells, and that the Jews must have dropped poisonous substances into them. When it came to our knowledge that serious charges had been made against the Jews in several small towns and villages on the basis of this mortality, we sent numerous letters to you and to other cities and towns to uncover the truth behind these rumours, and set a thorough investigation in train. . . .

If a massacre of the Jews were to be allowed in the major cities (something which we are determined to prevent in our city, if we can, as long as the Jews are found to be innocent of these or similar actions) it could lead to the sort of outrages and disturbances which would whip up a popular revolt among the common people—and such revolts have in the past brought cities to misery and desolation. In any case we are still of the opinion that this mortality and its attendant circumstances are caused by divine vengeance and nothing else. Accordingly we intend to forbid any harassment of the Jews in our city because of these flying rumours, but to defend them faithfully and keep them safe, as our predecessors did—and we are convinced that you ought to do the same. . . .

Source: From Rosemary Horrox, ed. and trans. *The Black Death* (Manchester: 1994), pp. 16–21, 219–20.

Questions for Analysis

1. How does Gabriele d'Mussis initially explain the causes of the plague? How and why does his understanding of it change as he traces its movements from East to West?

2. Why does the Council of Cologne wish to quell violence against the Jews? How does this reasoning complement or challenge what we have learned so far about the treatment of Jews in medieval Europe?

3. In your view, do these two perspectives display a rational approach to the horrors of the Black Death? Why or why not?

The Impact on the Countryside

In the decades following the plague, a new demographic reality permanently altered established social and economic patterns. First and foremost, the drastic decrease in population meant a relative abundance of food. The price of grain fell, which made it more affordable. At the same time, the scarcity of workers made peasant labor valuable: wages rose and work became easily obtainable. With wages high and food prices low, ordinary people could now afford more bread, and could also spend their surplus cash on dairy products, meat, fish, fruits, and wine. As a result, the people of Europe in the later Middle Ages were better nourished than they have ever been—better than many are today. A recent study of fifteenth-century rubbish dumps has concluded that the people of Glasgow (Scotland) ate a healthier diet in 1405 than they did in 2005.

A healthier ecological balance was also reestablished. Forests began to recover and expand. The declining demand for grain allowed many farmers to expand their livestock herds, increasing their profits while improving the fertility of the soil through manuring. Some farmers were even able to enlarge their holdings because so much land had been abandoned.

Most of these innovations were made by small farmers, because great lords—individuals, as well as monasteries—were slower to adjust to the changing circumstances. Some landholders responded to the shortage of workers by forcing their tenants to perform additional unpaid labor. In eastern Europe, many free peasants became serfs for the first time. In Castile, Poland, and Germany, too, lords succeeded in imposing new forms of servitude. In other parts of Iberia and in Italy, actual slavery—which had nearly been eradicated during the economic boom of the twelfth and thirteenth centuries—became common for the first time in centuries.

In France, peasants remained relatively free, although many were forced to pay a variety of fees and taxes to their lords and to the king. In England, by contrast, where peasant bondage had been more common than in France, serfdom ultimately disappeared altogether. In the new world of geographical mobility and economic opportunity, English serfs were able to vote with their feet, either by moving to town or to the lands of a lord who offered more favorable terms: lower rents, fewer work requirements, and greater personal freedoms.

The Urban Impact

Many towns, overcrowded and unsanitary, were particularly vulnerable to plague. Thereafter, they were vulnerable to the effects of violence. In Florence, the population rebounded quickly after the Black Death only to be depleted again by civil unrest: by 1427, it had dropped from around 300,000 to about 100,000. In Toulouse (southern France), the population remained fairly stable until 1430, when it was reduced 75 percent by the Hundred Years' War (see below). In London and Paris, however, large-scale immigration from the countryside reversed the short-term effects of the plague. For although the overall population declined, a far larger percentage of all people were living in towns by 1500: approximately 20 percent, as opposed to 10 or 15 percent prior to the Black Death.

Fueling this urban growth was the increasing specialization of the late-medieval economy. With farmers under less pressure to produce grain in bulk, land could be devoted to livestock, dairy farming, and the production of a more diverse array of fruits and vegetables; and these could now be exchanged efficiently on the open market. Towns with links to extant trading networks benefited accordingly. In northern Germany, a group of cities even formed a coalition to build a new network, the Hanseatic League, whose members controlled commerce from Britain and Scandinavia to the Baltic. In northern Italy, the increased demand for luxury goods—which even some peasants and urban laborers could now afford—brought new wealth to the spice- and silk-trading city of Venice and to the fine-cloth manufacturers of Milan and the jewelers of Florence. Milan's armaments industry also prospered, supplying its warring neighbors and the armies of Europe.

The economic boom also stimulated the development of business practices and accounting techniques. The development of insurance contracts helped to minimize the risks associated with long-distance trading. Double-entry bookkeeping, widely used in Italy by the mid-fourteenth century, gave merchants a much clearer picture of their profits and losses than had been possible before. The Medici family of Florence established branches of their bank in each of the major cities of Europe and were careful that the failure of one would no longer bankrupt the entire firm, as previous branch-banking arrangements had done. Banks also experimented with advanced credit techniques borrowed from Muslim and Jewish financiers, allowing their clients to transfer funds between branches without any real money changing hands. Such transfers were carried out by written orders, the ancestors of the modern check.

SOCIAL MOBILITY AND SOCIAL INEQUALITY

The Black Death was ultimately beneficial for many of those who survived it. But European society did not adjust easily to the new world created by the plague. It seemed to many like a world turned upside down.

Revolts and Rebellions

Hundreds of popular rebellions challenged the status quo in many regions of Europe. In 1358, for example, peasants in northeastern France rose up violently against their lords, destroying property and even murdering targeted individuals.

This incident is known as the Jacquerie Rebellion because all French peasants were caricatured by the aristocracy as "Jacques" ("Jack"). In England, as we have already noted, a very different uprising occurred in June of 1381, much more organized and involving a much wider segment of society. Thousands of people marched on London, targeting the bureaucracies of the royal government and the Church, capturing and killing the archbishop of Canterbury, and meeting personally with the fourteen-year-old king, Richard II, to demand an end to serfdom and taxation and the redistribution of property. In Florence, workers in the cloth industry—known as the Ciompi (*chee-OM-pee*)—protested high unemployment and mistreatment by the manufacturers who also ran the Florentine government. They seized control of the city, demanding relief from taxes, full employment, and political representation. They maintained power for a remarkable six weeks before their reforms were revoked.

The local circumstances that lay behind each of these revolts are unique, but they exhibit certain common features. Those who took part in them had actually been empowered by the new economic conditions and wanted to leverage their position in order to enact even larger changes. Some rebellions, like the English Peasants' Revolt, were touched off by resistance to new and higher taxes. Others, like the Jacquerie and the revolt of the Ciompi, took place at moments when unpopular governments were weakened by factionalism. The English revolt was also fueled by widespread corruption within the Church and the royal administration.

Behind this social and political unrest, therefore, lies not poverty and hunger but the growing prosperity and self-confidence of village communities and urban workers. Although the rebels' hopes that they could fundamentally alter the conditions of their lives were frustrated, this tradition of popular rebellion would remain an important feature of Western civilizations.

Aristocratic Life in the Later Middle Ages

Despite these upheavals, the later Middle Ages was hardly a period of crisis for those in power. Quite the contrary: the great noble families of Europe were far wealthier than their ancestors had been. Nor did the plague undermine the dominant position they had established in European society. It did, however, make their world substantially more complex and uncertain.

Across Europe, most noble families continued to derive much of their revenue from vast landholdings. But many lords also tried to increase their sources of income through investment in trading ventures. In Catalonia, Italy, Germany, and England, this became common practice. In France and Castile, however, direct involvement in commerce was regarded as socially demeaning and was, therefore, avoided. Commerce could still be a route to ennoblement in these kingdoms, but once aristocratic rank was achieved one was expected to abandon these employments and adopt an appropriate way of life: maintaining a rural castle or urban palace surrounded by a lavish household, embracing the conventions of chivalry, and serving the prince at court and in war.

Nobility became, as a result, even more difficult to define than it had been during the twelfth and thirteenth centuries. In countries where nobility entailed clearly defined legal privileges—such as the right to be tried only in special courts—proven descent from noble ancestors might be required. But in most cases, nobility was expressed through display and conspicuous consumption, which meant that the lines of social distinction between noble and nonnoble families remained fuzzy. On the battlefield, too, the supremacy of the mounted knight was being threatened by the growing importance of professional soldiers, archers, and artillery experts. There were even radical critiques of

A NOBLE BANQUET. Uncle of the mad king Charles VI, the duke of Berry received enormous subsidies from the royal government, which he spent on sumptuous buildings, festivals, and artworks—including the famous Book of Hours (prayer book) that includes this image. Here, the duke (seated at right, in blue) gives a New Year's Day banquet for his household, who exchange gifts while his hunting dogs dine on scraps from the table. In the background, knights confront one another in a battle or a tournament.

aristocratic claims to innate superiority. As the English rebels put it in 1381: "When Adam dug and Eve spun, Who
then was a gentleman?" In other words, all human beings
are equal and social distinctions are entirely artificial.

Precisely because nobility was contested, those who
claimed the status took elaborate measures to assert its ex-
clusivity. This accounts, in part, for the extraordinary number, variety, and richness of the artifacts and artworks that
survive from this period. Aristocrats vied with one another
in hosting lavish banquets. They dressed in rich and ex-
travagant clothing. They maintained enormous households:
around 1400, the French duke of Berry had 400 matched
pairs of hunting dogs and 1,000 servants. They took part in
elaborately ritualized tournaments and pageants, in which
the participants pretended to be the heroes of chivalric
romances. Nobility existed only if it was recognized; and to
be recognized, noble status had to be constantly reasserted.

Rulers contributed to this process of noble self-assertion;
indeed, they were among its principal supporters. Kings
and princes across Europe competed in founding chivalric
orders such as the Knights of the Garter in England and the
Order of the Star in France. By exalting the nobility as a
class, these orders helped cement the links that bound the
aristocracy to their kings and princes. So too did the gifts,
pensions, offices, and marriage prospects that kings and
princes could bestow. Indeed, the alliance that was forged
in the fifteenth century between kings and their noble supporters would become one of the most characteristic features of "old regime" (*ancien régime*) Europe. In France,
this alliance lasted until the French Revolution of 1789.
In Germany, Austria, and Russia, it would last until the
outbreak of World War I. In England, it persisted in some
respects until World War II.

WARFARE AND NATION-BUILDING

The partnership between royalty and nobility was partly
a response to the new world created by the plague. But it
was also a product of the unprecedented scale of warfare.
Beginning in the fourteenth century and continuing into
the twentieth, Europeans were almost constantly at war.
To fight these wars, governments claimed new powers to
tax their subjects and to control their subjects' lives. Armies
became larger, military technology deadlier. Wars became
more destructive, society more militarized. As a result of
these developments, the most successful European states—
the monarchies of Portugal, Spain, and France—were ag-
gressively expansionist. By 1600, their impact would be
global (see Chapter 11).

England, France, and the Hundred Years' War

The Hundred Years' War was the largest, longest, and most
wide-ranging military conflict in the West since Rome's
wars with Carthage in the third and second centuries
B.C.E. (Chapter 5). England and France were its principal
antagonists, but almost all of Europe became involved at
some stage. Active hostilities lasted from 1337 until 1453,
interrrupted by truces of varying lengths. The roots of the
conflict, however, reached back into the 1290s, when King
Edward I of England attempted to conquer the neighboring
kingdom of Scotland, thereby provoking the Scots to ally with
France. And the threat of war continued until 1558, when
Calais, the last English toehold on the Continent, finally
passed into French hands.

The most fundamental cause of the war was the fact
that the kings of England held the duchy of Gascony as
vassals of the French king; this was part of Eleanor of
Aquitaine's former domain (Chapter 9). In the twelfth and
thirteenth centuries, when the French kings had not yet absorbed this region, this fact had seemed less of an anomaly.
But as monarchies began to claim sovereignty within the
"natural" boundaries of their domains, the English presence in "French" Gascony became more and more problematic. That England also had close commercial links with
Flanders—which consistently resisted French expansion—
added fuel to the fire. So did the French alliance with the
Scots, who had been resolutely resisting English expansion.

Complicating this situation was the disputed succession of the French crown. In 1328, the last of King
Philip IV's three sons died without leaving a son to succeed
him: the Capetian dynasty, founded by the Frankish warlord Hugh Capet in 987 (Chapter 8), had finally exhausted
itself. A new dynasty, the Valois, came to the throne—but
only by insisting that women could neither inherit royal
power nor pass it on. For otherwise, the heir to France was
Edward III of England, whose mother, Isabella, was Philip
IV's only daughter. In 1337, therefore, when the disputes
over Gascony and Scotland erupted into war, Edward raised
the stakes by claiming to be the rightful king of France.

The hostilities that make up the Hundred Years' War can
be divided into three main phases (see the map on page 245).
In the first phase, from 1337 until 1360, the English won a
series of startling military victories, most famously at Crécy
(1346), Calais (1347), and Poitiers (1356). Although France
was richer and more populous than England by a factor of
at least three to one, the English government was more effective in mobilizing the entire population, for reasons that were
discussed in Chapter 9. Moreover, the huge but poorly led

armies assembled by the French proved no match for the tactical superiority of these smaller English forces. English armies pillaged the French countryside at will, while civil wars broke out among individual French lords. Meanwhile, mercenary bands of soldiers roamed the countryside, attacking and looting peasant villages still struggling to recover from the Black Death. In 1358, popular frustration boiled over in the rebellion of the Jacquerie (discussed above).

This first phase ended in 1360, when Edward III agreed to renounce his claim to the French throne in return for full sovereignty over a greatly enlarged duchy of Gascony and the promise of a huge ransom for the king of France, whom he held captive. But the terms of the treaty were never honored. Instead, a proxy war developed in which English and French troops, organized into "Free Companies," hired themselves out in the service of warring factions in Castile and northern Italy. By 1376, when hostilities resumed between England and France, the Hundred Years' War had become a Europe-wide phenomenon.

In this second phase of the war, from 1376 to 1429, the tide quickly shifted in favor of France. The new king of France, Charles V (r. 1364–80), imposed a series of national taxes, disbanded the Free Companies, and hired the leader of one as the commander of his army. He thereby created a professional military that could match the English in discipline and tactics. His counterpart, the new king of England, Richard II (r. 1377–99), had no interest in the French war begun by his grandfather. During his minority its conduct was mismanaged by his advisors—one of the issues that had triggered the Peasants' Revolt in 1381. Yet the nobility stood to gain from the war's continuation, and Richard's failure to press his claims turned the barons against him. In 1399, Richard was deposed and eventually murdered. His cousin, Henry of Lancaster, seized the throne.

As a usurper, Henry IV (r. 1399–1413) struggled to maintain his authority in the face of repeated rebellions and was in no position to pursue the French war. When his son Henry V succeeded him in 1413, however, the new king immediately began to prepare for a renewed offensive.

THE PROGRESS OF THE HUNDRED YEARS' WAR. Here we see the changing political geography of France during the Hundred Years' War. ▪ *What areas did England control at the outbreak of war in 1337?* ▪ *How and why were the gains of 1360 (in green) reduced by 1429 (the areas in yellow)?* ▪ *What geographic and strategic advantages did the French monarchy enjoy after 1429 that might help explain its success in recapturing the French kingdom from the English?*

A brilliant diplomat, Henry sealed alliances with both the emperor in Germany and the powerful duke of Burgundy, who was in control of the French royal government. So when he invaded France in 1415, he faced only a partial army representing the anti-Burgundian faction within the royal court. Then, at Agincourt, Henry managed to win a crushing victory over a vastly larger but badly disciplined French force. By 1420, he had conquered most of northern France and had forced the aged and infirm King Charles VI (r. 1380–1422) to give him his daughter in marriage and to recognize him as heir to the throne of France—thus dispossessing the heir apparent, known as the Dauphin ("the dolphin"), the future King Charles VII.

JOAN OF ARC. A contemporary sketch of Joan was drawn in the margin of this register documenting official proceedings at the Parlement of Paris in 1429. Note that she carries a banner bearing Constantine's symbolic IHS (Chapter 6).

Henry V's astonishing success seemed to put the stamp of divine approval on his claim to be the rightful king of France. But Henry's successes also transformed the nature of the war, turning it from a profitable war of conquest into an extended and expensive military occupation. It thereby sowed the seeds of eventual English defeat.

Henry died early in 1422, at the age of 34. Charles VI of France died only a few months later. The new king of England and France, Henry VI (r. 1422–61), was an infant. Meanwhile, the Dauphin's confidence in his right to the throne had been shattered by his own mother's declaration that he was illegitimate. Then, in 1429, a peasant girl from Lorraine (a territory only nominally part of France) made her way to the Dauphin's court and announced that an angel had told her that he, Charles, was the rightful king, and that she, Joan, should drive the English out of France.

The fact that she even got a hearing underscores the hopelessness of the Dauphin's position, as does the extraordinary fact that he gave her a contingent of troops. With this force, Joan liberated the strategic city of Orléans, then under siege, after which a series of victories culminated in Charles's coronation in the cathedral of Reims, the traditional site for the crowning of French kings. But despite her victories, Joan was an embarrassment whose very charisma made her dangerous: a peasant leading aristocrats, a woman leading men, and a commoner who claimed to have been commissioned by God. When, a few months later, the Burgundians captured her in battle and handed her over to the English, King Charles VII did nothing to save her. Condemned by the theologians of Paris and tried for heresy by an English ecclesiastical court, Joan was burned to death in the market square at Rouen in 1431. She was nineteen years old.

In the war's final phase, from 1429 to 1435, the French forces whom Joan had inspired continued on the offensive. In 1435, the Duke of Burgundy withdrew from his alliance with England, and a series of French military victories brought hostilities to an end with the capture of Bordeaux. English kings would threaten to renew the war for another century, but English control over French territory would be limited to the port of Calais until it, too, fell in 1558.

The Hundred Years' War had challenged the very existence of France, but its outcome had dramatic effects on the English monarchy as well. In France, the nobility had endured the insanity of Charles VI because his government was not powerful enough to threaten them. In England, royal power was so centralized that neither the nobility nor the nation could afford the incompetent kingship of Henry VI. The result was an aristocratic rebellion that led to a full-blown civil war: the Wars of the Roses, so called—by the novelist Sir Walter Scott (1771–1832)—from the emblems of the two competing noble families, Lancaster (red) and York (white), who were both descended from Edward III. It ended only when a Lancastrian claimant, Henry Tudor (r. 1485–1509), resolved the dynastic feud by marrying Elizabeth of York, ruling as Henry VII and establishing a new dynasty whose symbol was a rose with both white and red petals. His son would be Henry VIII (see Chapter 13).

Conflict in the Holy Roman Empire and Italy

The endemic warfare that begins to characterize the history of Europe in the later Middle Ages was usually even more destructive than it proved to be in the struggle between England and France. In the lands of the Holy Roman Empire, armed conflict among territorial princes weakened all the combatants significantly. The dominant trend was toward the continuing dissolution of power, with German

princes dividing territories among their heirs while free cities and local lords strove to shake off the princes' rule.

In northern and central Italy, the last half of the fourteenth century was also marked by incessant conflict. With the papacy based in Avignon from 1309 until 1377, the Papal States collapsed and Rome itself was riven by factional violence. Warfare among northern city-states added to the chaos caused by urban rebellions. By around 1400, however, Venice, Milan, and Florence had succeeded in stabilizing their differing forms of government. Venice was now ruled by an oligarchy of merchants; Milan by a family of despots; and Florence was a nominal republic dominated by the influence of the Medici banking family. These three cities then began to expand their territories, subordinating other cities to their rule. By 1454, almost all the towns of northern Italy were allied with one of these powers. An exception was the port of Genoa, which remained an independent shipping and trading hub.

The Emergence of a United Spain

The kingdoms of the Iberian peninsula were also in constant conflict during the fourteenth and fifteenth centuries. In Castile, civil war allowed the Castilian nobility to gain independence from the crown. After 1458, Aragon was also enmeshed in a civil war over a disputed succession, a war in which both France and Castile became involved.

The solution would ultimately lie in the blending of powerful families. In 1469, Prince Ferdinand of Aragon was recognized as the undisputed heir to that throne and, in the same year, married Isabella, the heiress of Castile. Although Castile and Aragon continued to be ruled as separate kingdoms until 1714, the union of Ferdinand and Isabella enabled them to spend their extraordinary resources on the creation of Europe's most powerful army, which was initially employed to conquer Granada, the last remaining Muslim principality in Spain.

The conquest of Granada in 1492 was a turning point. Both Castile and Aragon had been shaped for centuries by their involvement in the "reconquest" of Spain, and the victory earned Ferdinand and Isabella the title of Europe's "Most Catholic" monarchs. It also meant that the crusading ethos now sought outlets elsewhere. Only a few months after the conquest of Granada, Queen Isabella granted three ships to a Genoese adventurer who promised to reach India by sailing westward across the Atlantic. He failed, of course, but he extended the crusading tradition to the New World, with enduring consequences (see Chapter 11).

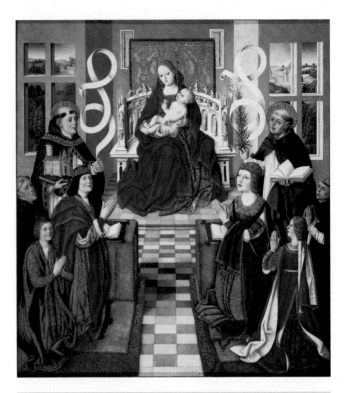

FERDINAND AND ISABELLA HONORING THE VIRGIN. In this contemporary Spanish painting, the royal couple are shown with two of their children and two household chaplains—and in the company of the Blessed Virgin, the Christ Child, and saints from the Dominican order (the Dominicans were instrumental in conducting the affairs of the Spanish Inquisition). ■ *How clear is the distinction between these holy figures and the royal family?* ■ *What message is conveyed by their proximity?*

The year 1492 also saw the expulsion of the entire Jewish community from Spain, the culmination of a process that had accelerated in the late thirteenth century (Chapter 9). The Spanish expulsion stands out, however, because of its vast scope and because of the rich cultural legacy fostered by the Jews of this region over a thousand years. The motives for ordering this expulsion are still debated. Tens of thousands of Spanish Jews had converted to Christianity between 1391 and 1420, many as a result of coercion, but for a generation or so it seemed possible that these *conversos* might successfully assimilate. Yet the conflicts that led to the union of Ferdinand and Isabella made the *conversos* targets of discriminatory legislation and fueled popular suspicions that they remained Jews in secret. The "Most Catholic" monarchs may have concluded that they needed to remove the "bad influence" posed by the continuing presence of a Jewish community in Spain. The expulsion of Jews thus enabled the creation of a new and explicitly Christian identity for the hybrid Spanish nation,

transcending the many rival regional identities there and attaching that new identity to the crown.

The Growth of National Monarchies

The later Middle Ages saw the emergence of European states more powerful and cohesive than any before. The formative twelfth and thirteenth centuries had made this possible, yet the active construction of a sense of national identity in these territories, and the fusion of that identity with kingship, were new phenomena. Forged by war and fueled by the growing cultural importance of vernacular languages, this fusion produced a new type of political organization: the national monarchy.

The advantages of these national monarchies is most clearly visible when viewed from the perspective of Italy. Until the end of the fifteenth century, the Italian city-states had appeared to be well governed and powerful, and Venice even had a maritime empire of its own. But when the armies of France and Spain invaded, neither the militias of the city-states nor the far-flung resources of Venice were a match for them. Germany and the Low Countries would suffer the same fate only a few generations later, and would remain battlegrounds for competing armies until the mid nineteenth century. But the new national monarchies brought significant disadvantages, too. They guaranteed the continued prevalence of warfare in Europe, and they eventually transported their rivalries to every corner of the globe.

THE RISE OF MUSCOVY, "THE THIRD ROME"

This era also witnessed the consolidation of a state that would become the dominant power in eastern Europe and one of the great powers of the world. Yet Russia developed very differently from the national monarchies of western Europe. It was, instead, the largest multiethnic empire in the pre-modern world. And by 1500, it claimed to be the rightful successor to the Rome of the Caesars, as well as to that of Constantine.

Kievan Rus' and the Mongol Khanate

As we saw in Chapter 8, the Viking people known as Rus' had played a key role in establishing a principality at Kiev (now in Ukraine), which maintained diplomatic and trad-

ing relations with western Europe and Byzantium. That dynamic changed with the arrival of the Mongols (whose movements will be discussed more fully in Chapter 11). Commanded by a grandson of the great Chingiz (Genghis) Khan, the Mongols overran Kiev in 1240. Two years later, they created their own state on the lower Volga River, known as the Khanate of the Golden Horde.

Initially, the Mongols ruled their Russian territories directly, even requiring Russian princes to subject themselves to the Great Khan himself, by traveling to Mongolia. Around 1300, however, the Mongols began to tolerate the existence of semi-independent principalities from which they demanded regular tribute. Kiev never recovered its dominant position, but one of the newer principalities would enable the construction of a Russian state: Muscovy, the duchy centered on Moscow.

The Rise of Muscovy and the Expansion of Poland

Moscow was the tribute-collecting center for the Mongol Khanate. Mongol support helped Moscow's dukes to absorb neighboring territories, and because Moscow was far from the Mongol base on the lower Volga, its dukes could further consolidate their strength without attracting too much attention. The location was also advantageous for forging commercial contacts with the Baltic and Black Sea regions. Yet Moscow's ties with western Europe remained undeveloped because it was loyal to the Orthodox Church of Byzantium. And Moscow's sensitivity to threats from European Christianity was further escalated by the growing strength of a Catholic kingdom on its borders.

In the thirteenth century, the small kingdom of Poland had struggled to defend itself from absorption into the Holy Roman Empire. But when the empire's strength waned after the death of Frederick II (Chapter 9), Poland's situation grew more secure. In 1386, its reigning queen, Jadwiga, married Jagiello, the duke of neighboring Lithuania, thus doubling the size of her kingdom. Lithuania had already begun to carve out an extensive territory stretching from the Baltic to modern-day Belarus and Ukraine, and this expansionist momentum increased after its union with Poland. Although many of Lithuania's aristocratic families were Orthodox Christians, the established church in Lithuania was loyal to Rome, as it was in Poland. Thus when the inhabitants of the region around Moscow began to feel threatened by Poland-Lithuania, one way of constructing a shared Muscovite identity was to direct shared hostility toward Latin Christendom.

The Russian Church and the Third Rome

As Byzantium grew weaker, the responsibility for defending Orthodox Christianity devolved onto the Russian Church. Muscovites saw themselves as the natural champions of Constantinople, which was now surrounded by the Muslim empire of the Ottoman Turks (to be discussed further in Chapter 11). But when the patriarch of Constantinople agreed to submit to the authority of Rome in 1438, in the desperate hope that the papacy would rally military support for the besieged city, Russian clergy refused to follow suit. After Constantinople fell to the Turks in 1453—predictably, without any help from Latin Christendom—the Russian Church therefore emerged as the only surviving proponent of Orthodox Christianity and the heir apparent to imperial Rome. To drive the point home, the Muscovite duke began to take the title *tsar*, "caesar." "Two Romes have fallen," said a Muscovite chonicler, "the third is still standing, and a fourth there shall not be."

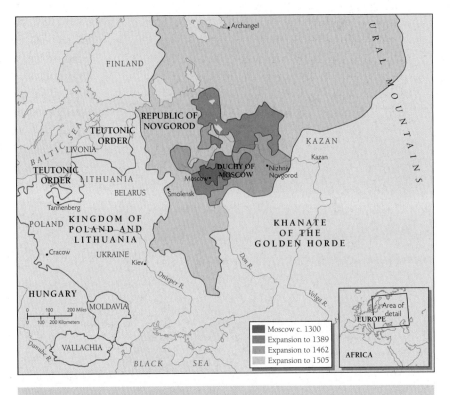

THE EXPANSION OF MUSCOVITE RUSSIA TO 1505. The grand duchy of Moscow was the heart of what would soon become the Russian Empire. ▪ *With what other empires and polities did the Muscovites have to compete during this period of expansion?* ▪ *How did the relative isolation of Moscow, compared with early Kiev, allow for the growth of Muscovite power on the one hand and Moscow's distinctive orientation on the other?* ▪ *How might the natural direction of the expansion of Muscovite power until 1505 help to encourage attitudes often at odds with those of western European civilization?*

The Reign of Ivan the Great (1462–1505)

Along with the imperial title, the Muscovite rulers borrowed the Byzantine ideology of the ruler's divine election, and this undergirded the sacred position later ascribed to the tsars. But ideology alone could not have built the Russian Empire. Behind its growth lay the steadily increasing power of Moscow's rulers, who achieved effective independence from the Mongols when a rebellious Mongol warlord named Timur the Lame (Tamburlane) destroyed the Khanate of the Golden Horde at the end of the fourteenth century. This allowed the Muscovite grand duke, Ivan III, known as Ivan the Great, to carry forward his own imperial agenda.

Ivan launched a series of conquests that annexed all the independent principalities lying between Moscow and the border of Poland-Lithuania. After invading Lithuania in 1492 and 1501, Ivan even succeeded in bringing parts of that domain under his control. Meanwhile, he married the niece of the last Byzantine emperor and rebuilt his fortified residence, known as the Kremlin, in magnificent Italianate style. He would later adopt, as his imperial insignia, a double-headed eagle representing Rome and its legions. By the time of his death in 1505, the power of the tsar was more absolute than that of any European monarch.

THE TRIALS OF THE ROMAN CHURCH

The later Middle Ages changed the Roman Church in ways that would prove definitive. The papacy endured almost seventy years of exile from Rome, followed by a debilitating forty-year schism. It then faced a protracted battle with reformers who sought to reduce the pope's role in Church governance. Though the papacy won this battle in the short term, the renewed abuse of papal power would, in the long run, bring about the permanent schism caused by the Reformation of the sixteenth century (Chapter 13).

THE PAPAL PALACE AT AVIGNON. This great palace, begun in 1339, symbolizes the apparent permanence of the papal residence in Avignon.

The "Babylonian Captivity" of the Papacy

The subjugation of papal authority to the French crown (Chapter 9) is often called the "Babylonian Captivity" of the Church, recalling the Jews' exile in Babylon during the sixth century B.C.E. (Chapter 2). From 1309 until 1378, the papal court resided at Avignon, a small city in southern France. Avignon soon proved to have a number of advantages over Rome. It was closer to the major centers of power, it was far removed from the tumultuous politics of Rome, and it was safe from the aggressive attentions of the German emperor. And as the papal bureaucracy grew in size, it became more difficult to move. In time, Avignon began to feel like home; in fact it *was* home for all of the popes elected there, who were natives of the region, as were nearly all the cardinals they appointed. This helped to cement their loyalty to the French king.

The papacy never abandoned its claims to the overlordship of Rome and the Papal States, but making good on these claims from a distance took a great deal of money. The Avignon popes accordingly imposed new taxes on the dioceses of France, England, Germany, and Spain. Judicial cases also brought large revenues into the papal coffers. Most controversially, the Avignon popes claimed the right to appoint bishops and priests to vacant offices, bypassing the electoral rights of individual dioceses and collecting huge fees from successful appointees.

By these and other measures, the Avignon popes strengthened their administrative control over the Church but weakened their moral authority. Stories of the court's unseemly luxury circulated widely, especially during the reign of the notoriously corrupt Clement VI (r. 1342–52), whose rule coincided with the Black Death. But in the subsequent decades that were transforming European society in so many other ways, calls for the papacy's return to Rome grew more insistent. The most successful of these was the letter-writing campaign of the nun and mystic Catherine of Siena (1347–1380), whose teasing but pious missives to Gregory XI (r. 1370–78) ultimately persuaded him to make the move back to Rome.

The Great Schism and the Conciliar Movement

The papacy's restoration was short-lived. A year after Gregory's return to Rome, he died. His cardinals—many of them Frenchmen—struggled to interpret the wishes of the volatile Romans and would later claim to have capitulated to the mob when they elected an Italian candidate, Urban VI. When Urban fell out with them soon afterward, the cardinals fled the city and declared his selection invalid. They then elected a new pope, a Frenchman who took the name Clement VII. Urban retaliated by naming a new, entirely Italian, College of Cardinals. The French pope and his cardinals then withdrew ignominiously to Avignon, while the Italian pope remained in Rome. The resulting rift is known as the Great Western Schism. Between 1378 and 1417, the Church was divided between two (and, ultimately, three) competing papacies, each stridently denouncing the heresy of the others.

Not surprisingly, Europe's religious allegiances fractured along the political lines drawn by the ongoing Hundred Years' War: France and her allies Scotland, Castile, Aragon, and Naples recognized the pope in Avignon; while England, Germany, northern Italy, Scandinavia, Bohemia, Poland, and Hungary recognized the Roman pope. Nor was there any obvious way to end this embarrassing state of affairs. In 1409, some cardinals from both camps met at Pisa, where they ceremoniously declared the deposition of both popes and named a new one from among their number. But neither of the popes accepted that decision, so there were now three rival popes excommunicating each other.

This debacle was ultimately addressed between 1414 and 1418 at the Council of Constance, the largest and longest ecclesiastical gathering since the Council of Nicea, over a thousand years before (Chapter 6). Its chief mission was to remove all rival claimants for papal office before agreeing on the election of a new pope: an Italian who took the name

Martin V. But many of the council's delegates had more far-reaching plans for the reform of the Church, ambitions that stemmed from the legal doctrine that gave the council power to depose and elect popes in the first place. This doctrine, known as conciliarism, holds that supreme authority within the Church rests not with the pope, but with a representative general council—and not just the council convened at Constance, but any future council. The delegates at Constance thus decreed that general councils should meet regularly to oversee the governance of the Church and to act as a check on the unbridled use of papal power.

Had conciliarism triumphed, the Reformation of the following century might not have occurred. But, perhaps predictably, Martin V and his successors did everything they could to undermine this doctrine, precisely because it limited their power. When the next general council met at Siena in 1423, Pope Martin duly sent representatives—but they then turned around and immediately went back to Rome. (The Council of Constance had specified that councils must meet frequently, but had not specified how long those meetings should last.) The following year, the delegates to a general council at Basel took steps to ensure that the pope could not dismiss their authority, after which a lengthy struggle for power ensued. Twenty-five years later, in 1449, the Council of Basel dissolved itself, bringing to an end a radical experiment in conciliar government—and dashing the hopes of those who thought it would lead to an internal reformation thorough enough to keep the Roman Church intact.

The Growth of National Churches

The papacy's victory over the conciliarists was a costly one. To win the support of Europe's kings and princes, various popes negotiated a series of treaties which granted rulers extensive authority over churches within their domains. The popes thus secured their own theoretical supremacy by surrendering their real power. For kings now received

THE GREAT SCHISM, 1378–1417. During the Great Schism, the various territories of Europe were divided in their allegiances. ▪ *What common interests would have united the supporters of the Avignon pope, or the Roman pope?* ▪ *Why would areas like Portugal and Austria waver in their support?*

many of the revenues that had previously gone to the papacy. They also acquired new powers to appoint candidates to church offices. It was a reversal of the hard-won reforms of the eleventh and twelfth centuries.

With both papal authority and spiritual prestige in decline, kings and princes became the primary figures to whom both clergy and laity looked for religious and moral guidance. The result was an increasingly close link between national monarchies and national churches, a link that would become even stronger after the Reformation (see Chapter 13). Meanwhile, the popes of the late fifteenth century became even more dependent on their own territories in central Italy, which they had to rule like other Italian princes: leading armies, jockeying for alliances, and undermining their opponents by covert operations, murder, and assassination. Judged by secular standards, these efforts paid off: the Papal States became one of the better-governed and wealthiest principalities of Italy. But such methods did nothing to increase the popes' reputation for piety, and disillusionment with the papacy became even more widespread.

Competing Viewpoints

Council or Pope?

> The Great Schism spurred a fundamental and far-reaching debate about the nature of authority within the Church. Arguments for papal supremacy rested on traditional claims that the popes were the successors of Saint Peter, to whom Jesus Christ had delegated his own authority. Arguments for the supremacy of a general council had been advanced by many intellectuals throughout the fourteenth century, but it was only in the circumstances of the schism that these arguments found a wide audience. The following documents trace the history of the controversy, from the declaration of conciliar supremacy at the Council of Constance (Haec Sancta), to the council's efforts to guarantee regular meetings of general councils thereafter (Frequens), to the papal condemnation of appeals to the authority of general councils issued in 1460 (Execrabilis).

Haec Sancta Synodus (1415)

This holy synod of Constance . . . declares that being lawfully assembled in the Holy Spirit, constituting a general council and representing the Catholic Church Militant, it has its power directly from Christ, and that all persons of whatever rank or dignity, even a Pope, are bound to obey it in matters relating to faith and the end of the Schism and the general reformation of the church of God in head and members.

Further, it declares that any person of whatever position, rank, or dignity, even a Pope, who contumaciously refuses to obey the mandates, statutes, ordinances, or regulations enacted or to be enacted by this holy synod, or by any other general council lawfully assembled, relating to the matters aforesaid or to other matters involved with them, shall, unless he repents, be . . . duly punished. . . .

Source: R. L. Loomis, ed. and trans., *The Council of Constance* (New York: 1961), p. 229

Frequens (1417)

The frequent holding of general councils is the best method of cultivating the field of the Lord, for they root out the briars, thorns, and thistles of heresies, errors, and schisms, correct abuses, make crooked things straight, and prepare the Lord's vineyard for fruitfulness and rich fertility. Neglect of general councils sows the seeds of these evils and encourages their growth. This truth is borne in upon us as we recall times past and survey the present.

Therefore by perpetual edict we . . . ordain that henceforth general councils shall be held as follows: the first within the five years immediately following the end of the present council, the second within seven years from the end of the council next after this, and subsequently every ten years forever. . . . Thus there will always be a certain continuity. Either

THE PURSUIT OF HOLINESS

Despite the travails of the institutional Church, religious devotion among the laity was more widespread and intense during the later Middle Ages than it had ever been. Some of these devotional paths led believers in directions the Church declared heretical. But for the vast majority of Christians, extreme forms of dissent held no appeal. The local parish church, and especially the sacraments performed by the parish priest, were the center of religious life.

Sacrament and Ritual

Innocent III's insistence that all Christians should have direct access to sound religious instruction (Chapter 9) ensured that nearly all of Europe was covered by a network of local parish churches by the time of the Black Death. In these churches, parish priests administered the sacraments ("holy rites") that conveyed the grace of God to individual Christians and that marked significant moments in the lifecycle of every person. There were seven sacraments:

a council will be in session or one will be expected at the end of a fixed period. . . .

Source: R. L. Loomis, ed. and trans., *The Council of Constance* (New York: 1961), pp. 246–47.

Execrabilis (1460)

An execrable abuse, unheard of in earlier times, has sprung up in our period. Some men, imbued with a spirit of rebellion and moved not by a desire for sound decisions but rather by a desire to escape the punishment for sin, suppose that they can appeal from the Pope, Vicar of Jesus Christ—from the Pope, to whom in the person of blessed Peter it was said, "Feed my sheep" and "whatever you bind on earth will be bound in heaven"—from this Pope to a future council. How harmful this is to the Christian republic, as well as how contrary to canon law, anyone who is not ignorant of the law can understand. For . . . who would not consider it ridiculous to appeal to something which does not now exist anywhere nor does anyone know when it will exist? The poor are heavily oppressed by the powerful, offenses remain unpunished, rebellion against the Holy See is encouraged, license for sin is granted, and all ecclesiastical discipline and hierarchical ranking of the Church are turned upside down.

Wishing therefore to expel this deadly poison from the Church of Christ, and concerned with the salvation of the sheep committed to us . . . with the counsel and assent of our venerable brothers, the Cardinals of the Holy Roman Church, together with the counsel and assent of all those prelates who have been trained in canon and civil law who follow our Court, and with our own certain knowledge, we condemn appeals of this kind, reject them as erroneous and abominable, and declare them to be completely null and void. And we lay down that from now on, no one should dare . . . to make such an appeal from our decisions, be they legal or theological, or from any commands at all from us or our successors. . . .

Source: Reprinted by permission of the publisher from *Defensorum Obedientiae Apostolicae Et Alia Documenta* by Gabriel Biel, edited and translated by Heiko A. Oberman, Daniel E. Zerfoss, and William J. Courtenay, pp. 224–27, Cambridge, Mass.: The Belknap Press of Harvard University Press, Copyright © 1968 by the President and Fellows of Harvard College.

Questions for Analysis

1. On what grounds does *Haec Sancta* establish the authority of a council? Why would this be considered a threat to papal power?

2. Why was it considered necessary for councils to meet regularly (*Frequens*)? What might have been the logical consequences of such regular meetings?

3. On what grounds does *Execrabilis* condemn the appeals to future councils that have no specified meeting date? Why would it not have condemned the conciliar movement altogether?

baptism, confirmation, confession (penance), marriage, extreme unction, ordination, and communion. Baptism, a ceremony of initiation administered in the early centuries of Christianity to adults (Chapter 6), became in the course of the Middle Ages a sacrament administered to infants as soon as possible after birth. Confirmation of adolescents therefore "confirmed" the promises made on a child's behalf by parents and godparents. Periodic confession of sins to a priest guaranteed forgiveness. Marriage was a relatively new sacrament, increasingly emphasized but very seldom practiced; for in order to be valid, marriage in this period required only that promises be exchanged by a man and a woman, and in many cases the fact of cohabitation was taken as proof of marriage. Extreme unction (or last rites) was administered to a dying person, and ensured the final absolution of all sins and so was essential to the assurance of salvation.

Like baptism, extreme unction could be administered in an emergency by any Christian believer. The other sacraments, however, could be administered only by a ing good works that would help the believer in his or her journey toward salvation.

But the sacrament that was most central to the lives of medieval Christians was the communion ceremony of the Mass (or the Eucharist). As we noted in Chapter 9, the ritual power of the Mass was greatly enhanced in the twelfth century, when the Church began promoting the doctrine of transubstantiation. Christians attending Mass understood that when the priest spoke the ritual words "This is my body" and "This is my blood," the substances of bread and wine held in the priest's hands were miraculously transformed into the body and blood of Jesus Christ. To consume one or both of these substances was to ingest holiness; and so powerful was this idea that many Christians only received the sacramental bread once a year, at Easter.

But in order to share in the miracle of the Eucharist one did not have to consume it: one had only to witness the elevation of the Host. So the practice of attending Mass merely to view the Host became a common form of daily devotion, as did the practice of displaying a consecrated wafer in a special reliquary called a monstrance ("showcase"). Believers sometimes attributed astonishing properties to the eucharistic Host, and rushed from church to church to see the consecrated bread as many times as possible in a day. Some of these practices were criticized as superstitious or even heretical. But by and large, these expressions of devotion were encouraged.

Spirituality and the Social Order

The spiritual and social lives of medieval Christians were inextricably intertwined; the parish church stood literally at the center of their lives. Churchyards were communal meeting places, sometimes the sites of markets, and church buildings were a refuge and a gathering place. The church's holidays marked the passage of the year, and the church's bells marked the hours of the day. The church was essential to daily life.

Yet some medieval Christians—many regarded today as saints—were not satisfied with these conventional practices and developed forms of piety that were distinctly controversial during their lifetimes. As Joan of Arc's predicament reveals, medieval women found it particularly challenging to find outlets for their piety that would not earn them the condemnation of the Church. Many therefore internalized those practices or confined them to the domestic sphere—sometimes to the inconvenience of their families and communities. For example, the young Catherine of Siena refused to help with the housework

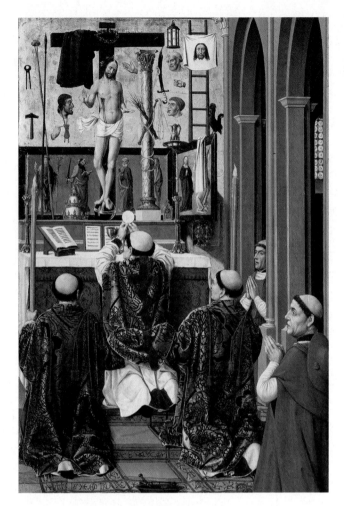

THE REAL PRESENCE OF CHRIST. This painting, executed in the mid-fifteenth century, refers to a popular legend underscoring the doctrine of transubstantiation. According to this legend, Pope Gregory the Great (c. 540–604) was celebrating Mass in his private chapel when he had a vision of the crucified Christ, whose body and blood were rendered visible when Gregory consecrated the bread and wine on the altar. Here, Christ displays his wounds to the astonished onlookers. The instruments of Christ's passion—the people and implements that tortured and killed him—are also displayed.

properly ordained priest—or, in the case of confirmation and ordination, by a bishop. Ordination was therefore the only sacrament reserved for the small percentage of those who became priests, and it conveyed to the priest his special authority to share God's grace through the sacraments: a power that could never be lost, even by a priest who led an immoral life.

This sacramental system was the foundation on which the practices of medieval popular piety rested. Pilgrimages, for example, were a form of penance. Crusading was a kind of extreme pilgrimage. Many other pious acts—saying the prayers of the rosary, for example, or giving alms to the poor—could also serve as penance for sins while constitut-

or to support her large working-class family, and instead took over one of the house's two rooms for her own private prayers. The English housewife Margery Kempe (c. 1372–c. 1439), resented the fact that she had a husband, several children, and a household to support, and in later life renounced her duties and devoted her life to performing acts of histrionic piety which alienated many of those who came into contact with her.

The extraordinary devotion of such individuals could be inspiring, but it could also threaten the Church's control and weaken the links that bound individuals to their communities. It could, therefore, be dangerous. Even less radical figures might find themselves treading on treacherous ground, especially if they published their ideas in the vernacular. The preacher Master Eckhart (c. 1260–1327), a German Dominican, taught that there was a "spark" deep within every human soul, and it was in this spark that God lived. This conveyed the message that a layperson might access divinity and attain salvation through her own efforts, without the intervention of a priest. As a result, many of Eckhart's teachings were condemned as heretical. More safely orthodox was the practical mysticism preached by Thomas à Kempis, whose *Imitation of Christ* (c. 1427) taught readers to appreciate aspects of the divine in their everyday lives. Originally written in Latin, the *Imitation* was quickly translated into many vernacular languages and is now more widely read than any other Christian book except the Bible.

Lollards and Hussites

For the most part, the threat of heretical movements was less dangerous to the Church than the corruption of the papacy. But in England and Bohemia, some popular movements did pose serious challenges. The key figure in both cases was John Wyclif (c. 1330–1384), an Oxford theologian and powerful critic of the Church. A survivor of the Black Death, Wyclif concluded that the empty sacraments of a corrupt Church could not save anyone. He therefore urged the English king to confiscate ecclesiastical wealth and to replace corrupt priests and bishops with men who would live according to apostolic standards of poverty and piety. Some of Wyclif's followers, known to their detractors as Lollards (from a word meaning "mumblers" or "beggars"), went even further, dismissing the sacraments as fraudulent attempts to extort money from the faithful. Lollard preachers also promoted an English translation of the Bible attributed to Wyclif himself.

Wyclif's teachings played an important role in the Peasants' Revolt of 1381, and Lollardy gained numerous adherents in the decades after his death. But after a failed Lollard uprising in 1414, both the movement and its supporters went underground in England.

In Bohemia and eastern Europe, however, Wyclif's ideas lived on and struck even deeper roots. They were adopted by Jan Hus (c. 1373–1415), a charismatic teacher at the royal university in Prague. Hus emphasized the centrality of the Eucharist to Christian piety and demanded that the laity be allowed to receive not only the consecrated bread but also the consecrated wine, usually reserved solely for priests. This demand became a rallying cry for the Hussite movement. Influential nobles also supported Hus,

THE TEACHINGS OF JAN HUS. An eloquent religious reformer, Jan Hus was burned at the stake in 1415 after having been found guilty of heresy at the Council of Constance. This lavishly illustrated booklet of his teachings was published over a century later in his native Bohemia, and includes texts in the Czech vernacular and in Latin. ▪ *What does this later publication suggest about the uses to which Hus's image and theology were put during the Protestant Reformation?*

partly in the hope that the reforms he demanded might restore revenues they had lost to the Church over the previous century. Accordingly, most of Bohemia was behind him when Hus traveled to the Council of Constance to publish his views and to urge the assembled delegates to undertake sweeping reforms.

But rather than giving him a hearing, the other delegates convicted Hus of heresy and had him burned at the stake. Back home, Hus's supporters raised the banner of open revolt, and the aristocracy took advantage of the situation to seize Church property. Between 1420 and 1424, armed bands of fervent Hussites defeated several armies. These victories increased popular fervor, but they also made radical reformers increasingly volatile. In 1434, accordingly, a more conservative arm of the Hussite movement was able to negotiate a settlement with the Bohemian church. By the terms of this settlement, Bohemians could receive both the bread and wine of the Mass, which thus placed them beyond the pale of Latin orthodoxy and effectively separated the Bohemian national church from the Church of Rome.

Lollardy and Hussitism exhibit a number of striking similarities. Both began in universities and then spread to the countryside. Both called for the clergy to live in simplicity and poverty, and both attracted noble support. Both movements were also strongly nationalistic, employing their own vernacular languages (English and Czech) in opposition to a "foreign" Church. They also relied on preaching and social activism. In all these respects, they established patterns that would emerge again in the stronger currents of the Protestant Reformation.

MEDIEVAL CREATIVITY AND INNOVATION

Many of the extraordinary achievements of the later Middle Ages have often been ascribed to the Renaissance, the name given to an intellectual and artistic movement that began concurrently in Italy. We will discuss this movement more fully in Chapter 12. For now, we focus on parallel developments closely tied to the trends discussed above.

Knowledge of the World and of God

In the thirteenth century, Thomas Aquinas had constructed a theological view of the world as rational, organized, and comprehensible to the inquiring human mind (Chapter 9). Confidence in this picture began to wane in the fourteenth century, even before the Black Death posed a new challenge to it. Philosophers such as the English Franciscan William of Ockham (d. 1349) denied that human reason could prove fundamental theological truths such as the existence of God. Instead, he argued that human knowledge of God depends entirely on what God himself has chosen to reveal through scripture. Humans can investigate the natural world, but there is no necessary connection between the observable regularities of nature and the unknowable essence of divinity.

This philosophical position, known as nominalism, has had an enormous impact on modern thought. The nominalists' distinction between the comprehensibility of the natural world and the incomprehensibility of God actually encourages investigation of the natural world without reference to supernatural explanations—one of the most important foundations of the scientific method (see Chapter 16). Nominalism also encourages empirical observation by positing that knowledge should rest on sensory experience rather than abstraction. Late medieval philosophy is thus fundamental to modern science.

Capturing Reality in Writing

The entertainments of the later Middle Ages also exhibit an intense interest in the world as it is. Such naturalism was not new, but authors were now able to reach a far larger and more diverse audience than their predecessors. For increasingly,

CHRISTINE DE PISAN. One of the most prolific authors of the fifteenth century, Christine used her influence to uphold the dignity of women and to celebrate their history and achievements. Here she is seen describing the prowess of an Amazon warrior who could defeat men effortlessly in armed combat.

ideas were published in the vernacular languages of Europe. Behind this phenomenon lay three interrelated developments: the growing identification between vernacular languages and national monarchies, the increasing accessibility of lay education, and the emergence of a substantial reading public for vernacular literature. We can see these influences at work in three of the major authors of this period: Giovanni Boccaccio, Geoffrey Chaucer, and Christine de Pisan.

Boccaccio (*bohk-KAHT-chee-oh*, 1313–1375) is best known for the *Decameron*, a collection of prose tales about sex, adventure, and trickery which he represents as being told over a period of ten days by a sophisticated party of ten young women and men temporarily residing in a country villa outside Florence to escape the Black Death. Boccaccio borrowed the outlines of many of these tales from earlier sources, especially the fabliaux discussed in Chapter 9, but he couched them in a freely colloquial style, in an attempt to capture the relationships and foibles of real human beings.

Similar in many ways to Boccaccio, whose influence on him was profound, is the English poet Geoffrey Chaucer (c. 1340–1400). Chaucer is among the first generation of English authors whose compositions can be understood by modern readers with relatively little effort: by the fourteenth century, the Anglo-Saxon language of England's pre-Conquest inhabitants had mixed with the French spoken by their Norman conquerors, to create the language that is the ancestor of our own. Chaucer's masterpiece is the *Canterbury Tales*. Like the *Decameron*, this is a collection of stories held together by a framing narrative. In this case, the stories are told by an array of people traveling together on a pilgrimage from London to the shrine of Saint Thomas Becket at Canterbury. But there are also significant differences between the *Decameron* and the *Canterbury Tales*. Chaucer's stories are in verse, for the most part, and they are recounted by people of all different social classes—from a high-minded knight to a poor university student to a lusty widow. Each character tells a story that is particularly illustrative of his or her own occupation and outlook, forming a kaleidoscopic human comedy.

The later Middle Ages also saw the emergence of professional authors who made their living by writing. One of the first was a woman, Christine de Pisan (c. 1365–c. 1434). Although born in northern Italy, Christine spent her adult life in France, where her husband was a member of the king's household. When he died, the widowed Christine wrote to support herself and her children. She mastered a wide variety of literary genres, including treatises on chivalry and warfare that she dedicated to her patron, Charles VI of France. She also wrote for a larger and more popular audience. Her imaginative *Book of the City of Ladies* is an extended defense of the character, capacities, and history of women, designed to refute their male detractors. Christine also took part in a vigorous pamphlet campaign that refuted misogynistic claims made by male authors like Boccaccio. This debate was ongoing for several hundred years, and became so famous that it was given a name: the *querelle des femmes*, "the debate over women." Remarkably, Christine also wrote a song in praise of Joan of Arc. Poignantly, she probably lived long enough to learn that this other extraordinary woman had been put to death for behaving in a way that was considered unwomanly.

Visualizing Reality

Just as naturalism was a dominant trait of late medieval philosophy and literature, so it was of later medieval art. The sculptors of the thirteenth century were already paying close attention to the way plants, animals, and human

THE MEETING OF JOACHIM AND ANNA BY GIOTTO. According to legend, Anna and Joachim were an aged and infertile couple who were able to conceive their only child, Mary, through divine intervention. Since Mary was supposed to have been conceived without the taint of sin, theologians taught that she had been miraculously engendered without sexual contact. Hence, this painting may portray the moment of her conception—but it also portrays the affection of husband and wife. ▪ *What values does it convey to the viewer?*

Why a Woman Can Write about Warfare

Christine de Pisan (c. 1365–c. 1434) was one of the West's first professional writers, best known today for her Book of the City of Ladies *and* The Treasure of the City of Ladies, *works which aimed to provide women with an honorable and rich history, and to combat generations of institutionalized misogyny. But in her own time, she was probably best known for the work excerpted here,* The Book of the Deeds of Arms and of Chivalry, *a manual of military strategy and conduct written at the height of the Hundred Years' War, in 1410.*

 s boldness is essential for great undertakings, and without it nothing should be risked, I think it is proper in this present work to set forth my unworthiness to treat such an exalted matter. I should not have dared even to think about it, but although boldness is blameworthy when it is foolhardy, I should state that I have not been inspired by arrogance or foolish presumption, but rather by true affection and a genuine desire for the welfare of noble men engaging in the profession of arms. I am encouraged, in the light of my other writings, to undertake to speak in this book of the most honorable office of arms and chivalry.... So to this end I have gathered together facts and subject matter from various books to produce this present volume. But inasmuch as it is fitting for this matter to be discussed factually, diligently, and sensibly ... and also in consideration of the fact that military and lay experts in the aforesaid art of chivalry are not usually clerks or writers who are expert in language, I intend to treat the matter in the plainest possible language....

As this is unusual for women, who generally are occupied in weaving, spinning, and household duties, I humbly invoke ... the wise lady Minerva [Athena], born in the land of Greece, whom the ancients esteemed highly for her great wisdom. Likewise the poet Boccaccio praises her in his *Book of Famous Women*, as do other writers praise her art and manner of making trappings of iron and steel, so let it not be held against me if I, as a woman, take it upon myself to treat of military matters....

O Minerva! goddess of arms and of chivalry, who, by understanding beyond that of other women, did find and initiate among the other noble arts and sciences the custom of forging iron and steel armaments and harness both proper and suitable for covering and protecting men's bodies against arrows slung in battle—helmets, shields, and protective covering having come first from you—you instituted and gave directions for drawing up a battle order, how to begin an assault and to engage in proper combat.... In the aforementioned country of Greece, you provided the usage of this office, and insofar as it may please you to be favorably disposed, and I in no way appear to be against the nation from which you came, the country beyond the Alps that is now called Apulia and Calabria in Italy, where you were born, let me say that like you I am an Italian woman.

Source: From *The Book of the Deeds of Arms and of Chivalry*, trans. Sumner Willard and ed. Charity Cannon Willard (University Park, PA: 1999), pp. 11–13.

Questions for Analysis

1. Christine very cleverly deflects potential criticism for her "boldness" in writing about warfare. What tactics does she use?

2. The Greco-Roman goddess Athena (Minerva) was the goddess of wisdom, weaving, and warfare. Why does Christine invoke her aid? What parallels does she draw between her own attributes and those of Minerva?

beings really looked. Carvings of leaves and flowers are clearly recognizable to modern botanists as distinct species. Statues of humans also became more realistic in their portrayals of facial expressions and bodily proportions.

In the fourteenth and fifteenth centuries, this trend toward naturalism in sculpture was extended to manuscript illumination and painting. (The latter was, to a large extent, a distinctively medieval art.) As we saw in Chapter 1, wall paintings are one of the oldest forms of artistic expression in human history, and throughout antiquity and the Middle Ages artists had decorated the walls of public and private buildings with frescoes (paintings executed on "fresh"—

wet—plaster). But in addition to frescoes, Italian artists in the thirteenth century began to adapt the techniques used by icon painters in Byzantium, making free-standing pictures on pieces of wood or canvas using tempera (pigments mixed with water and natural gums). Around 1400, painting in oils was introduced in the Low Countries, and this technique soon spread southward to Italy and beyond.

These new artistic media created new aesthetic and commercial opportunities. Artists were now able to paint and sell portable altarpieces, devotional images, and portraits. And so long as they could afford the necessary materials, they did not have to wait for a specific commission and had more freedom to put an individual stamp on their work—one of the reasons why we know the names of so many late-medieval artists. One of these, Giotto di Bondone of Florence (c. 1267–1337), painted both walls and portable wooden panels. Giotto (*gee-AHT-toh*) was preeminently an imitator of nature. Not only do his human beings and animals look lifelike, they do natural things. When Christ enters Jerusalem on Palm Sunday, boys climb trees to get a better view; when Saint Francis is laid out in death, someone checks to see whether he has really received the marks of Christ's wounds, the *stigmata*; and when the Virgin's parents, Joachim and Anna, meet after a long separation, they embrace and kiss one another tenderly. This style became the norm by 1400, and it is for this reason that Giotto is often regarded as the first painter of the Renaissance, a movement that is really an outgrowth of the Middle Ages.

In northern Europe, manuscript illumination remained the dominant artistic medium. But oil painting also caught on, especially in Flanders, where artists found a ready market for their works. Practitioners like Rogier van der Weyden (c. 1400–1464) excelled at communicating both deep piety and the minute details of everyday experience (see **Interpreting Visual Evidence**). Just as contemporary spirituality saw divinity in nature, so a Flemish painter could portray the Virgin and Child against a background of contemporary life, with people going about their business or a man urinating against a wall. This was not blasphemous; quite the contrary. It conveyed the message that the events of the Bible are constantly present, here and now.

The same immediacy is also evident in medieval drama. Plays were often devotional exercises that involved the efforts of an entire community. In the English city of York, for example, an annual series of pageants reenacted the entire history of human salvation from the Creation to the Last Judgment in a single summer day, beginning at dawn and ending late at night. Each pageant was produced by a particular craft guild and showcased that guild's special talents: "The Last Supper" was performed by the bakers,

while "The Crucifixion" was performed by the nail-makers. In Italy, confraternities competed to honor the saints with songs and processions. In Spain and Catalonia, there were elaborate dramas celebrating the life and miracles of the Virgin, one of which is still performed every year in the Basque town of Elche—the oldest European play in continuous production. Elsewhere on the Continent there were civic spectacles performed over a period of several days. But not all plays were pious. Some honored visiting kings and princes. Others celebrated the flouting of social conventions, featuring cross-dressing and the reversal of hierarchies.

Technological Advances

As in other places and times, warfare was the engine driving the development of many medieval technologies. Although explosive powder had been invented in China, it was first put to devastating use in the guns of the Hundred Years' War. The earliest cannons were as dangerous to those who fired them as to those who were targeted, but by the middle of the fifteenth century they were reliable enough to revolutionize the nature of warfare. In 1453, heavy artillery played a leading role in the outcomes of two crucial conflicts: the Ottoman Turks breached the defenses of Constantinople (see Chapter 11) and the French captured the city of Bordeaux, thereby ending the Hundred Years' War. Thereafter, cannons made it more difficult for rebellious aristocrats to hole up in their stone castles. Cannons placed aboard ships made Europe's developing navies more effective. A hand-held firearm, the pistol, was also invented, and around 1500 the musket ended forever the dominance of heavily armored cavalry, giving the advantage to foot soldiers.

A FIFTEENTH-CENTURY SIEGE WITH CANNON. Cannons were an essential element in siege warfare during the Hundred Years' War and thereafter.

Realizing Devotion

These two paintings by the Flemish artist Rogier van der Weyden (*FAN-der-VIE-den*, c. 1400–1464) capture some of the most compelling characteristics of late medieval art, particularly the trend toward realistic representations of holy figures and sacred stories. On the left (image A), the artist depicts himself as the evangelist Luke, regarded in Christian tradition as a painter of portraits; he sketches the Virgin nursing the infant Jesus in a town house overlooking a Flemish city. On the right (image B), van der Weyden imagines the entombment of the dead Christ by his followers, including the Virgin (left), Mary Magdalene (kneeling), and the disciple John (right). Here, he makes use of a motif that became increasingly prominent in the later Middle Ages: Christ as the Man of Sorrows, displaying his wounds and inviting the viewer to share in his suffering. In both paintings, van der Weyden emphasizes the humanity of his subjects rather than their iconic status (see Chapter 7), and he places them in the urban and rural landscapes of his own world.

Questions for Analysis

1. How are these paintings different from the sacred images of the earlier Middle Ages (see, for example, pages 161 and 219)? What messages does the artist convey by setting these events in his own immediate present?

2. In what ways do these paintings reflect broad changes in popular piety and medieval devotional practices? Why, for example, would the artist display the dead and wounded body of Christ—rather than depicting him as resurrected and triumphant, or as an all-seeing creator and judge?

3. In general, how would you use these images as evidence of the worldview of the fifteenth century? What do they tell us about people's attitudes, emotions, and values?

A. Saint Luke drawing the portrait of the Virgin.

B. The Deposition.

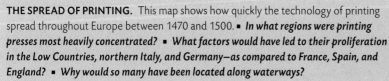

THE SPREAD OF PRINTING. This map shows how quickly the technology of printing spread throughout Europe between 1470 and 1500. ■ *In what regions were printing presses most heavily concentrated?* ■ *What factors would have led to their proliferation in the Low Countries, northern Italy, and Germany—as compared to France, Spain, and England?* ■ *Why would so many have been located along waterways?*

and expensive for private purchase, but towns vied with one another to install them in prominent public buildings. Mechanical timekeeping had two profound effects. One was the further stimulation of interest in complex machinery of all sorts. More significant was the regulation of daily life. Until the advent of clocks, time was flexible. Days had been theoretically divided into hours, minutes, and seconds since the time of the Sumerians (Chapter 1), but there had never been a way of mapping these measurements onto an actual day. Now, clocks relentlessly divided time into exact units and thus gave rise to new expectations about labor and productivity. People were expected to start and end work "on time," and many came to believe that "time is money." This emphasis on timekeeping brought new efficiencies but also created new tensions and obsessions.

The development of printing was even more momentous. A major stimulus was the more widespread availability of paper. Parchment, Europe's chief writing material since the seventh century, was extremely expensive to manufacture and even required special training on the part of scribes—one reason why writing remained a specialized skill for much of the Middle Ages, while the ability to read was common. Paper, made from rags turned into pulp by mills, was both cheaper and far easier to use. Accordingly, reading and writing also became cheaper and easier. Increased literacy led to a growing demand for books, which in turn led to experimentation with different methods of book production. A breakthrough came around 1450, when it was discovered that movable type (letter forms and punctuation marks) could be slotted into iron frames to form lines of words, and whole pages could thus be reproduced by coating those frames with ink and pressing them onto paper or parchment, after which the type could be reused. The most famous early result of this technique is the Bible completed in the workshop of Johann Gutenberg in Mainz, around 1454.

By saving labor and time, the printing press made the cost of printed books about one fifth as expensive and

Other late medieval technologies were more life enhancing. Eyeglasses, first invented in the 1280s, were perfected in the fourteenth century. The use of the magnetic compass helped ships sail farther away from land. Numerous improvements in shipbuilding, mapmaking, and navigational devices enabled Europeans to venture out into the Atlantic. We will discuss the implications of these developments in Chapter 11.

Among the many implements of modern life invented in this era, the most familiar are clocks and printed books. Mechanical clocks came into use shortly before 1300 and proliferated immediately thereafter. They were too large made book culture a more basic part of daily life. Printing thereby facilitated the rapid exchange of information and ideas, and also made it more difficult for those in power to suppress these ideas effectively. Martin Luther could create an immediate and far-flung network of support by employing this new communication technology (Chapter 13); had printing not been available, he might have died ignominiously, as Hus had a century before. The spread of books also standardized national languages. Regional dialects were often so diverse that people living within the same state could not understand each other. Now, each European country began to develop its own linguistic standards. For example, the "King's English," the dialect of London, could be promulgated throughout the realm, allowing the government to operate more efficiently.

CONCLUSION

The later Middle Ages constitute a period of tremendous creativity and revolutionary change. The effects of the Black Death were catastrophic, but the resulting labor shortages encouraged experimentation and opened up new

After You Read This Chapter

Visit StudySpace for quizzes, additional review materials, and multi-media documents. **wwnorton.com/studyspace**

REVIEWING THE OBJECTIVES

- The Black Death had short-term and long-term effects on the economy and societies of Europe. What were some of the most important changes?
- The melding of strong kingship with the promotion of national identity was a new development in the later Middle Ages. What circumstances made this possible? Why is this development significant?
- Several key factors enabled the growth of a Russian state centered on Muscovy. What were they?
- The conciliar movement sought to limit the power of the papacy. How? Why was this movement unsuccessful?
- In what ways do the spiritual, cultural, and technological innovations of the later Middle Ages reflect the political, social, and economic changes brought about by the Black Death?

opportunities. Europe's economy diversified and expanded. Increasing wealth and access to education produced new inventions, ideas, and forms of art. Medieval intellectuals came to see the natural world as operating according to its own laws, which were empirically verifiable: an essential step toward the emergence of a scientific worldview. Women were still excluded from formal schooling, but nevertheless became active—and perhaps dominant—participants in literate culture and religious life. Average men and women also became more active in cultivating their own spiritualities, at a time when the Church provided little inspiring leadership. Meanwhile, incessant warfare prompted more powerful governments to harvest a larger percentage of their subjects' wealth through taxation, which they proceeded to invest in ships, guns, and the standing armies made possible by new technologies and effective administration.

In short, the generations who survived the calamaties of famine, plague, and warfare seized the opportunities their new world presented to them. By 1500, most Europeans lived more secure lives than their ancestors had, and they stood on the verge of an extraordinary period of expansion and conquest that enabled them to dominate the globe.

PEOPLE, IDEAS, AND EVENTS IN CONTEXT

- Compare and contrast the **BLACK DEATH'S** effects on rural and urban areas.
- In what ways do the rebellions of the later fourteenth and fifteenth centuries reflect the changes brought about by the plague? How did the nobility of Europe respond to this changing world?
- What were the main causes and consequences of the **HUNDRED YEARS' WAR**? How did **FERDINAND AND ISABELLA** begin to construct a national monarchy in Spain?
- On what grounds did **MUSCOVY** claim to be "the third Rome"? What is the significance of **IVAN THE GREAT'S** use of the title **TSAR**?
- How did the **COUNCIL OF CONSTANCE** respond to the crisis of the **GREAT SCHISM**?
- How did the teachings of **JOHN WYCLIF** and **JAN HUS** critique religious trends?
- What were the major artistic and technological innovations of the later Middle Ages?

CONSEQUENCES

- In 2000, a group of historians was asked to identify the most significant historical figure of the past millennium; but rather than choosing a person (e.g., Martin Luther, Napoleon, Adolf Hitler) they chose the microbe *Yersinia pestis*. Do you agree with this assessment? Why or why not?
- In your view, which was more crucial to the formation of the modern state: the political and legal developments we surveyed in Chapter 9 or the emergence of national identities in the later Middle Ages? Why?
- Was the conciliar movement doomed to failure, given what we have learned about the history of the Roman Church? How far back in history does one need to go in order to trace the development of disputes over ecclesiastical governance?

Before You Read This Chapter

Commerce, Conquest, and Colonization, 1300–1600

CORE OBJECTIVES

- **DESCRIBE** the effects of the Mongol conquests.

- **EXPLAIN** the consequences of the Ottoman Empire's dependence on slave labor.

- **IDENTIFY** the factors that drove exploration and colonialism in the fourteenth and fifteenth centuries.

- **DEFINE** the essential difference between modern slavery and that of all previous civilizations.

- **UNDERSTAND** the far-reaching impact of the New World conquests.

When Christopher Columbus set sail from Genoa in 1492, he carried with him two influential travel narratives. One was largely factual and one was fantastic, but it is doubtful that Columbus could tell the difference between them. The first was the *Book of Marvels*, attributed to Jehan de Mandeville, an English adventurer (writing in French) who claimed to have traveled beyond the boundaries of the known world. The second was Marco Polo's account of his journeys in the Far East and of his sojourn at the court of the Great Khan in China. Both of these books shaped the Genoese mariner's expectations of what he would find during his travels, and they also shaped his descriptions of the places and peoples he encountered. As a result, it is difficult to separate fiction from reality when we read his accounts—or those of many other European explorers. What we can know for certain is that the civilizations of the New World and the Old had a profound impact on one another.

In 1352, when Mandeville's *Book of Marvels* began to circulate, Europe had become a politically coherent and culturally unified region. It had also reached its geographical limits;

there was, it seemed, no more room for expansion. With the completed conquest of Muslim territory in 1492, Ferdinand and Isabella eradicated a Muslim presence in western Europe that dated to the seventh century. Yet there was no longer any viable prospect of Latin Christendom's dominion in the Holy Land, North Africa, or any of the other Muslim territories that had been targeted by crusaders. The growing power of the Ottoman Turks was forging a new empire that would soon come to encompass all these regions, as well as the lands of the Eastern Roman Empire in Byzantium. Meanwhile, the rise of Poland-Lithuania and the emergence of Muscovy as a contender for power on

Europe's northeastern frontier arrested German princes' drive to conquer territories in eastern Europe; and their efforts would be halted altogether by the eventual absorption of these territories into the Ottoman Empire.

Europe was also reaching its ecological limits. Indeed, the pressure on its natural resources was eased only by the dramatic population losses that had resulted from the combined effects of famine, plague, and war in the fourteenth and fifteenth centuries. But despite these challenges—or because of them—Europeans did not turn inward. As land-based conquests became less viable, new maritime empires coalesced around chains of colonies that extended from the

STATES OF THE MONGOL EMPIRE. Like Alexander's, Chingiz Khan's empire was swiftly assembled and encompassed vast portions of Europe and Asia. ▪ *How many separate Mongol empires were there, and how far did they stretch geographically?* ▪ *How might the Mongol occupation of the Muslim world have aided the expansion of European trade?* ▪ *At the same time, why would it have complicated the efforts of crusader armies in the Holy Land?*

Black Sea to the Canary Islands. Trade routes were opened through the Strait of Gibraltar, resulting in greater economic integration between the Mediterranean and Atlantic economies, and increasing Europe's demand for Asian spices and African gold. By the late fifteenth century, Mediterranean mariners and colonists were reaching farther into the Atlantic and pushing down the west coast of Africa. In 1498, one such expedition would make its way to India.

The fifteenth-century expansion of the Mediterranean world into the Atlantic was the essential preliminary to Columbus's voyages, and to European colonization of the Americas. Because these later events seem so familiar, we can easily underestimate both their improbability and their significance for the Western civilizations we have been studying, as well as for the "new world" they encountered. For the indigenous peoples and empires of the Americas, the results were cataclysmic. Within a hundred years of Europeans' arrival, between 50 and 90 percent of the native population had perished from disease, massacre, and enslavement. Moreover, Europeans' capacity to further their imperial ambitions wherever ships could sail and guns could penetrate profoundly destabilized Europe and its neighbors, sharpening the divisions among competing kingdoms and empires. The effects of this process, which reached its apogee in the nineteenth century, are still being felt today.

MONGOLS, EUROPEANS, AND THE FAR EAST

Trade between the Mediterranean world and the Far East dates back to antiquity, but it was not until the late thirteenth century that Europeans were able to establish direct trading connections with India, China, and the so-called Spice Islands of the Indonesian archipelago. These connections would prove profoundly important, as much for their impact on the European imagination as for their economic significance. For the peoples of Asia, however, the appearance of European traders on the fabled Silk Road between Central Asia and China was merely a curiosity. The really consequential event in their world was the rise of the Mongol Empire that made such connections possible.

The Expansion of the Mongol Empire

The Mongols were one of many nomadic peoples inhabiting the steppes of Central Asia. Although closely connected with the Turkic populations with whom they frequently intermarried, the Mongols spoke their own distinctive language and had their own homeland, to the north of the Gobi Desert in present-day Mongolia. Sheep provided them with shelter (sheepskin tents), woolen clothing, milk, and meat. And like many nomadic peoples, the Mongols were highly accomplished horsemen and raiders. In fact, it was in part to control their raiding ventures that the Chinese had built the fortified Great Wall, many centuries before. Primarily, though, China defended itself by attempting to ensure that the Mongols remained internally divided, with their energies turned against each other.

In the late twelfth century, however, a Mongol chief named Temüjin began to unite the various tribes under his rule. He did so by incorporating the warriors of each tribe he defeated into his own army, thus building up a large military force. In 1206 his supremacy was formally acknowledged by all the Mongols, and he took the title Chingiz (Genghis) Khan, or "universal ruler." He now directed his enormous army against his neighbors, and began conquering China one region at a time. In 1279, his grandson

THE HEAD OF TIMUR THE LAME. This bust of the Mongol leader, known in the West as Tamerlane, is based on a forensic reconstruction of his exhumed skull.

Competing Viewpoints

Two Travel Accounts

Two of the books that influenced Columbus and his contemporaries were travel narratives describing the exotic worlds that lay beyond Europe: worlds that may or may not have existed as they are described. The first excerpt below is taken from the account published by Marco Polo of Venice in the early fourteenth century. The young Marco traveled overland from Constantinople to the court of Qubilai Khan in the early 1270s, together with his father and uncle. He proved to be a gifted linguist, and remained at the Mongol court until the early 1290s, when he returned to Europe after a journey through Southeast Asia, Indonesia, and the Indian Ocean. The second excerpt is from the Book of Marvels *attributed to Jehan de Mandeville, an almost entirely fictional account of wonders that also became a source for European ideas about South and East Asia. This particular passage concerns a legendary Christian figure called Prester ("Priest") John, who is alleged to have traveled to the East and become a great ruler.*

Marco Polo's Description of Java

Departing from Ziamba, and steering between south and southeast, fifteen hundred miles, you reach an island of very great size, named Java. According to the reports of some well-informed navigators, it is the greatest in the world, and has a compass above three thousand miles. It is under the dominion of one king only, nor do the inhabitants pay tribute to any other power. They are worshipers of idols.

The country abounds with rich commodities. Pepper, nutmegs, spikenard, galangal, cubebs, cloves, and all the other valuable spices and drugs, are the produce of the island; which occasion it to be visited by many ships laden with merchandise, that yields to the owners considerable profit.

The quantity of gold collected there exceeds all calculation and belief. From thence it is that . . . merchants . . . have imported, and to this day import, that metal to a great amount, and from thence also is obtained the greatest part of the spices that are distributed throughout the world. That the Great Khan [Qubilai] has not brought the island under subjection to him, must be attributed to the length of the voyage and the dangers of the navigation.

Source: *The Travels of Marco Polo*, rev. and ed. Manuel Komroff (New York: 1926), pp. 267–68.

Mandeville's Description of Prester John

This emperor Prester John has great lands and has many noble cities and good towns in his realm and many great, large islands. For all the country of India is separated into islands by the great floods that come from Paradise, that divide the land into many parts. And also in the sea he has many islands. . . .

This Prester John has under him many kings and many islands and many varied people of various conditions. And this land is full good and rich, but not so rich as is the land of the Great Khan. For the merchants do not come there so

commonly to buy merchandise as they do in the land of the Great Khan, for it is too far to travel to. . . .

[Mandeville then goes on to describe the difficulties of reaching Prester John's lands by sea.]

This emperor Prester John always takes as his wife the daughter of the Great Khan, and the Great Khan in the same way takes to wife the daughter of Prester John. For these two are the greatest lords under the heavens.

In the land of Prester John there are many diverse things, and many precious stones so great and so large that men

make them into vessels such as platters, dishes, and cups. And there are many other marvels there that it would be too cumbrous and too long to put into the writing of books. But of the principal islands and of his estate and of his law I shall tell you some part.

This emperor Prester John is Christian and a great part of his country is Christian also, although they do not hold to all the articles of our faith as we do. . . .

And he has under him 72 provinces, and in every province there is a king. And these kings have kings under them, and all are tributaries to Prester John.

And he has in his lordships many great marvels. For in his country is the sea that men call the Gravelly Sea, that is all gravel and sand without any drop of water. And it ebbs and flows in great waves as other seas do, and it is never still. . . . And a three-day journey from that sea there are great mountains out of which flows a great flood that comes out of Paradise. And it is full of precious stones without any drop of water. . . .

He dwells usually in the city of Susa [in Persia]. And there is his principal palace, which is so rich and so noble that no one will believe the report unless he has seen it. And above the chief tower of the palace there are two round pommels of gold and in each of them are two great, large rubies that shine full brightly upon the night. And the principal gates of his palace are of a precious stone that men call sardonyxes [a type of onyx], and the frames and the bars are made of ivory. And the windows of the halls and chambers are of crystal. And the tables upon which men eat, some are made of emeralds, some of amethyst, and some of gold full of precious stones. And the legs that hold up the tables are made of the same precious stones. . . .

Source: *Mandeville's Travels*, ed. M. C. Seymour (Oxford: 1967), pp. 195–99 (language modernized from Middle English by R. C. Stacey).

Questions for Analysis

1. What does Marco Polo want his readers to know about Java, and why? What does this suggest about the interests of these intended readers?

2. What does Mandeville want his readers to know about Prester John and his domains? Why are these details so important?

3. Which of these accounts seems more trustworthy, and why? Even if we cannot accept one (or both) at face value, what insight do they give us into the expectations of Columbus and the other European adventurers who relied on these accounts?

Qubilai (Kublai) Khan completed this project, thus reuniting China for the first time in centuries.

At the same time, Chingiz Khan was turning his forces westward, conquering much of Central Asia and incorporating the important commercial cities of Tashkent, Samarkand, and Bukhara into his empire. When he died in 1227, his son and successor, Ögedei (*EHRG-uh-day*), not only completed the conquest of China, he laid plans for a massive invasion of the West. Between 1237 and 1240, the Mongol horde (so called from the Turkish word *ordu*, meaning "tent" or "encampment") conquered southern Russia and then launched a two-pronged assault that pushed them farther west. The smaller of two Mongol armies swept through Poland toward eastern Germany; a larger army went southwest toward Hungary. In April of 1241, the smaller force met a hastily assembled army of Germans and Poles at the battle of Liegnitz, where the two sides fought to a bloody standstill. Two days later, the larger Mongol army annihilated the Hungarian army at the River Sajo.

It is possible that the Mongol armies could have moved even farther west after this important victory, but when the Great Khan died in December of that same year, the leaderless Mongol forces withdrew from eastern Europe. Although Mongol conquests continued in Persia, the Middle East, and China, attacks on Europe never resumed. Yet the descendants of Chingiz Khan continued to rule their enormous empire—the largest land empire in the history of the world—for another half-century. Later, under the leadership of Timur the Lame (known as Tamerlane to Europeans) it looked briefly as if the Mongol Empire might expand again. But Timur died in 1405, and thereafter the various parts of the Mongol Empire fell into the hands of local rulers, including (in Asia Minor) the Ottoman Turks. Mongol influence continued, however, in the Mughal Empire of India, whose rulers were descended from followers of Chingiz Khan.

The Mongols owed their success to the size, speed, and training of their mounted armies; to the intimidating ferocity with which they treated those who resisted them; and to their ability to adapt the traditions of their subjects to their own purposes. For example, they were highly tolerant of the religious beliefs of others—a distinct advantage in governing an empire that comprised an array of Buddhist,

VENETIAN AMBASSADORS TO THE GREAT KHAN. Around 1270, the Venetian merchants Niccolò and Matteo Polo returned to Europe after their first prolonged journey through the empire of the Great Khan, bearing with them an official letter to the Roman pope. This image shows them at the moment of their arrival at the Great Khan's court, to which they have allegedly carried a Christian cross and a Bible. It comes from a manuscript copy of Jehan de Mandeville's *Book of Marvels*, which offered readers an alternative vision of the lands and peoples described by Niccolò's famous son, Marco, who accompanied his father and uncle when they made their second journey to the Great Khan's court several years later. • *Why might many such visual references to the Polo family's adventures have been included in Mandeville's more fanciful travel narrative?*

Christian, and Muslim sects. And for the most part, Mongol governance was directed at securing the steady payment of tribute, which meant that local rulers could retain much of their power. Except in China, where a Mongol dynasty maintained an ancient and complex administrative bureaucracy, Mongol rule was highly decentralized.

A Bridge to the East

The Mongols had a keen eye for the commercial advantages of their empire. They began to control the caravan routes that led from China through Central Asia to the Black Sea. They also encouraged commercial contacts with European traders, especially through the Persian city of Tabriz, from which both land and sea routes led on to China. Until the Mongol conquests, the Silk Road had been closed to most Western merchants and travelers. But almost as soon as the Mongol Empire was established, we find Europeans venturing on its routes.

The first such travelers were Franciscan missionaries like William of Rubruck, sent by King Louis IX of France as ambassador to the Mongol court in 1253. Western merchants quickly followed. The most famous of these were three Venetians: the brothers Niccolò and Matteo Polo, and Niccolò's son, Marco. Marco Polo's account of his travels, which began when he was seventeen, includes details of his twenty-year sojourn in the service of Qubilai Khan and of his journey home through the Spice Islands, India, and Persia. The book had an enormous effect on the imagination of his contemporaries: for the next two centuries, most of what Europeans knew about the Far East they learned from Marco Polo's *Travels*. Christopher Columbus's copy of this book still survives.

European connections with the western outposts of the Silk Road would continue until the mid-fourteenth century. The Genoese were especially active in this, not least because their rivals, the Venetians, already dominated the Mediterranean trade with Alexandria and Beirut, through which the bulk of Europe's Far Eastern luxury goods continued to pass. Thereafter, however, the Mongols of Persia became more hostile to Westerners, and the Genoese finally abandoned Tabriz after attacks made their position there untenable. Then, in 1346, the Mongols of the Golden Horde besieged the Genoese colony at Caffa on the Black Sea, an event memorable because it became a conduit for the Black Death, which was passed from the Mongol army to the Genoese defenders, who transmitted it to western Europe (see Chapter 10).

The window of opportunity that made Marco Polo's travels possible was thus relatively small. By the middle of the fourteenth century, divisions among the various parts of the Mongol Empire were already making travel along the Silk Road perilous. After 1368, when the last Mongol dynasty in China was overthrown, most Westerners were excluded from the empire now ruled by the new Ming Dynasty. The overland trade routes from China to the Black Sea continued to operate, but Europeans had no easy access to them.

The integrated world that Mongol rule had briefly created continued to exercise a lasting effect on Europe, despite the relatively short time during which Europeans themselves were able to participate directly in it. European memories of the Far East would be preserved, and the dream of reestablishing close connections between Europe and China would survive to influence a new round of European commercial and imperial expansion from the late fifteenth century onward.

THE RISE OF THE OTTOMAN EMPIRE

Like the Mongols, the Turks were initially a nomadic people whose economy depended on raiding. They were already established in northwestern Anatolia when the Mongols arrived there, and were slowly converting to Islam. But unlike the established Muslim powers in the region, whom the Mongols weakened and ultimately destroyed, the Turks were the principal beneficiaries of the Mongol conquest. For when the Mongols toppled the Seljuk sultanate of Anatolia and the Abbasid caliphate of Baghdad, they eliminated the two traditional authorities that had previously kept Turkish border chieftains like the Ottomans in check. Now they were free to raid, unhindered, along the soft frontiers of Byzantium. At the same time, they remained far enough from the centers of Mongol authority to avoid being destroyed themselves.

The Conquest of Constantinople

By the end of the thirteenth century, members of the Ottoman clan had established themselves as leaders among the Turks of the Anatolian frontier. By the mid-fourteenth century, they had guaranteed their preeminence by capturing a number of important cities. These successes brought the Ottomans to the attention of the Byzantine emperor, who hired a contingent of their warriors as mercenaries in 1345. They were extraordinarily successful—so much so that the Eastern Roman Empire could not control their movements. By 1370, the Ottomans had extended their control all the way to the Danube. In 1389, an Ottoman army defeated a powerful coalition of Serbian forces at the battle of Kosovo, enabling them to extend control over Greece, Bulgaria, and the Balkans.

In 1396, the Ottoman army attacked Constantinople itself, but withdrew to repel a Western crusading force that had been sent against it. In 1402, Ottoman forces attacked Constantinople again, but were once more forced to withdraw, this time to confront a Mongolian invasion of Anatolia. Led by Timur the Lame, the Mongols captured the Ottoman sultan and destroyed his army; for the next decade it appeared that Ottoman hegemony over Anatolia might have ended. By 1413, however, Timur was dead and the Ottomans were able to resume their conquests.

Ottoman pressure on Constantinople continued during the 1420s and 1430s, producing a steady stream of Byzantine refugees bound for Italy who brought with them the surviving masterworks of classical Greek literature (see Chapter 12). But it was not until 1451 that the Ottoman sultan, Mehmet II, turned his full attention to the conquest of the imperial city. In 1453, after a brilliantly executed siege, Mehmet succeeded in breaching the walls of Constantinople. The Byzantine emperor was killed in the assault, the city was thoroughly plundered, and its remaining population was sold into slavery. The Ottomans then settled down

SULTAN MEHMET II, "THE CONQUEROR" (r. 1451–81). This portrait, executed by the Ottoman artist Siblizade Ahmed, exhibits features characteristic of both Central Asia and Europe. The sultan's pose—his aesthetic appreciation of the rose, his elegant handkerchief—are indicative of the former, as is the fact that he wears the white turban of a scholar and the thumb ring of an archer. But the subdued coloring and three-quarter profile may reflect the influence of Italian portraiture. ▪ *What did the artist achieve through this blending of styles and symbols?* ▪ *What messages does this portrait convey?*

to rule their new capital in a style reminiscent of their Byzantine predecessors.

The Ottoman conquest of Constantinople administered a cultural and psychological shock to many European rulers and intellectuals, but its economic impact was minor. Ottoman control over the former Byzantine Empire reduced Europeans' direct access to the Black Sea, but the bulk of the Far Eastern luxury trade with Europe had never passed through Black Sea ports in the first place. Europeans got most of their spices and silks through Venice, which imported them from Alexandria and Beirut, and these two cities did not fall to the Ottomans until the 1520s. So the Ottoman Empire was not necessarily the force that later motivated Portuguese efforts to locate a sea route to India and the Spice Islands. If anything, it was Portuguese access to India, and European attempts to exclude Muslims from the Indian

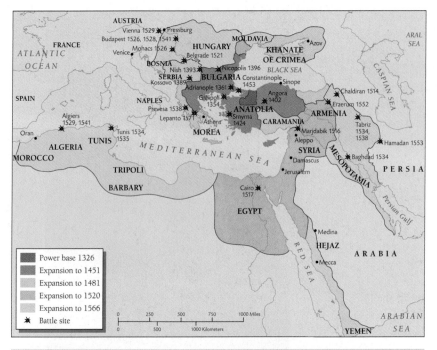

THE GROWTH OF THE OTTOMAN EMPIRE. Consider the patterns of Ottoman expansion. ■ *Where is Constantinople, and how might its capture in 1453 have facilitated further conquests?* ■ *Compare the extent of the Ottoman Empire in 1566 with that of the Byzantine Empire under Justinian (see the map on page 158). How would you account for their similarities?* ■ *How might you explain the fact that the Ottoman Empire did not continue its rapid expansion after 1566?*

spice trade, that helped spur the later Ottoman conquests of Syria, Egypt, and Hungary during the 1520s and 1530s.

But if the practical effects of the Ottoman conquest were modest where western Europe was concerned, the effects on the Turks themselves were transformative. Vast new wealth poured into Anatolia, which the Ottomans increased by carefully tending to the industrial and commercial interests of the city which they called Istanbul—the Turkish pronunciation of the Greek phrase "to/in the city." Trade routes were redirected to feed the capital, and the Ottomans became a naval power in the eastern Mediterranean and the Black Sea. As a result, Constantinople's population grew from fewer than 100,000 in 1453 to more than 500,000 in 1600, making it the largest city in the world outside of China.

War, Slavery, and Social Advancement

Despite the Ottomans' careful attention to commerce, their empire continued to rest on the spoils of conquest until the end of the sixteenth century. In order to

manage this continual expansion, the size of the Ottoman army and administration grew exponentially, drawing more and more manpower from the empire. And because the Ottoman army and administration were largely composed of slaves, the demand for more soldiers and administrators could best be met through further conquests that would capture yet more slaves. This in turn required a still larger army and even more extensive bureaucracy—and so the cycle continued. It mirrors, in many respects, the dilemma of the Roman Empire (Chapter 5). Indeed, another way in which the Ottoman Empire resembled that of Rome was in this insatiable demand for slaves.

Not only were slaves the backbone of the Ottoman army and bureaucracy, they were also critical to the lives of the Turkish upper class. One of the important measures of status in Ottoman society was the number of slaves in one's household. After 1453, new wealth permitted some elites to maintain households in the thousands. In the sixteenth century, the sultan alone possessed more than 20,000 slave attendants, not including his bodyguard and elite infantry units, both of which were also composed of slaves.

Where did all of these slaves come from? Many were captured in war. Many others were taken on raiding forays into Poland and Ukraine and shipped to the slave markets of Constantinople. But slaves were also recruited (some willingly, some by coercion) from rural areas of the Ottoman Empire itself. Because the vast majority of slaves were household servants and administrators rather than laborers, some people willingly accepted enslavement, believing that they would be better off as slaves in Constantinople than as impoverished peasants in the countryside. In the Balkans especially, many people were enslaved as children, handed over by their families to pay the "child tax" the Ottomans imposed on rural areas too poor to pay a monetary tribute. Although unquestionably a wrenching experience for families, this practice did open up opportunities for social advancement. Special academies were created at Constantinople to train the most able of the enslaved male children, and some rose to become powerful figures in the Ottoman Empire. Slavery, indeed, carried relatively little social stigma. The sultan himself was most often the son of an enslaved woman.

Analyzing Primary Sources

Ottoman Janissaries

The following account is from a memoir written by Konstantin Mihailovic, a Serbian Christian who was captured as a youth by the army of Sultan Mehmet II. For eight years, he served in the Ottoman janissary ("gate-keeper") corps. In 1463, the fortress he was defending for the Sultan was captured by the Hungarians, after which he recorded his experiences for a Christian audience.

Whenever the Turks invade foreign lands and capture their people, an imperial scribe follows immediately behind them, and whatever boys there are, he takes them all into the janissaries and gives five gold pieces for each one and sends them across the sea [to Anatolia]. There are about two thousand of these boys. If, however, the number of them from enemy peoples does not suffice, then he takes from the Christians in every village in his land who have boys, having established what is the most every village can give so that the quota will always be full. And the boys whom he takes in his own land are called *cilik*. Each one of them can leave his property to whom-ever he wants after his death. And those whom he takes among the enemies are called *pendik*. These latter after their deaths can leave nothing; rather, it goes to the emperor, except that if someone comports himself well and is so deserving that he be freed, he may leave it to whomever he wants. And on the boys who are across the sea the emperor spends nothing; rather, those to whom they are entrusted must maintain them and send them where he orders. Then they take those who are suited for it on ships and there they study and train to skirmish in battle. There the emperor already provides for them and gives them a wage. From there he chooses for his own court those who are trained and then raises their wages.

Source: Konstantin Mihailovic, *Memoirs of a Janissary* (Michigan Slavic Translations 3), trans. Benjamin Stolz (Ann Arbor, MI: 1975), pp. 157–59.

Questions for Analysis

1. Why might the Ottoman emperor have established this system for "recruiting" and training janissaries? What are its strengths and weaknesses?

2. Based on your knowledge of Western civilizations, how unusual would you deem this method of raising troops? How does it compare to the strategies of other rulers we have studied?

Because Muslims were not permitted to enslave other Muslims, the vast majority of Ottoman slaves were Christian—although many eventually converted to Islam. And because so many of the elite positions within Ottoman government were held by these slaves, the paradoxical result was that Muslims, including the Turks themselves, were effectively excluded from the main avenues of social and political influence in the Ottoman Empire. Nor was this power limited to the government and the army. Commerce and business also remained largely in the hands of non-Muslims, most frequently Greeks, Syrians, and Jews. Jews in particular found in the Ottoman Empire a welcome refuge from the persecutions and expulsions that had characterized Jewish life in late-medieval Europe. After their expulsion from Spain in 1492, more than 100,000 Spanish (Sephardic) Jews ultimately immigrated to the territories of the Ottoman Empire.

Religious Conflicts

The Ottoman sultans were Sunni Muslims who lent staunch support to the religious and legal pronouncements of the Islamic schools in their realm. When Ottomans captured the cities of Medina and Mecca in 1516, they also became the defenders of the two principal holy sites of Islam. Soon after, they captured Jerusalem and Cairo, too, putting an end to the Mamluk sultanate of Egypt and becoming the keepers of the Holy Land. In 1538, accordingly, the Ottoman ruler formally adopted the title of caliph, thereby declaring himself to be the legitimate successor of Muhammad.

In keeping with Sunni traditions, the Ottomans were tolerant of non-Muslims, especially during the fifteenth and sixteenth centuries. They organized the major religious groups of their empire into legally recognized units

OTTOMAN ORTHODOXY. This genealogical chart is designed to show the descent of Sultan Mehmet III (r. 1595–1603) from his own illustrious ancestors—both warriors and scholars—as well as from Muhammad, whose central image is piously veiled. ▪ *Why was it desirable for the Ottoman sultans to proclaim themselves caliphs, too, and therefore heirs to Muhammad?* ▪ *How might this have increased the hostility between the Sunni Turks and the Shi'ite Muslims of neighboring Persia?*

support from their Orthodox Christian subjects, even during their wars with the Christians of western Europe. The Ottomans' principal religious conflicts were therefore not with their own subjects, but with the Shi'ite Muslim dynasty that ruled neighboring Persia. Time and again during the sixteenth century, Ottoman expeditions into western Europe had to be abandoned when hostilities erupted with the Persians.

The Ottomans and Europe

For a variety of reasons, the contest between the Ottoman Empire and the rulers of western Europe never lived up to the rhetoric of holy war that both sides employed in their propaganda. In Europe, especially, there were internal divisions that frustrated any attempts to mount a unified campaign. By the sixteenth century, as we shall see (Chapters 13 and 14), Catholic and Protestant sects were turning that same crusading rhetoric against one another. But even before that, Christian military initiatives were ineffectual. In 1396, a Western crusader army was annihilated by the Ottomans at the battle of Nicopolis, and Ottoman armies besieged Vienna several times during the following two centuries.

But apart from these few dramatic events, conflicts between the Ottomans and the rulers of western Europe were fought out mainly through pirate raids and naval battles in the Mediterranean. The result was a steady escalation in the scale and cost of navies. In 1571, when a combined Habsburg and Venetian force defeated the Ottoman fleet at Lepanto, more than 400 ships took part, with both sides deploying naval forces ten times larger than they had possessed half a century before. Although undeniably a victory for the Habsburgs and their Venetian allies, the battle of Lepanto was far less decisive than is often suggested. The Ottoman navy was speedily rebuilt; and by no means did Lepanto put an end to Ottoman influence over the eastern Mediterranean Sea.

Moreover, both Ottoman and Habsburg interests soon shifted away from their conflict with each other. The Ottomans embarked on a long and costly war with Persia, while the Spanish Habsburgs turned their attention toward their new empire across the Atlantic. By the mid-seventeenth century, when a new round of conflicts began, the strength of the Ottoman Empire had been sapped by the tensions that arose within the empire itself as it ceased to expand. Although it would last until 1918 (see Chapter 24), it was in no position to rival the global hegemony that European powers were beginning to achieve.

and permitted them considerable rights of self-government. After 1453, when they gained control of Constantinople, the Ottomans were particularly careful to protect and promote the authority of the Greek Orthodox patriarch of Constantinople. As a result, the Ottomans enjoyed staunch

EUROPEAN EXPLORATION AND COLONIALISM

During the fifteenth century, Europeans focused their commercial ambitions more and more on the western Mediterranean and Atlantic. As we noted above, this reorientation can be attributed only partially to the rising power of the Ottoman Empire. It was more significantly the product of two related developments: the growing importance of the African gold trade and the growth of European colonial empires in the western Mediterranean.

The Search for African Gold

The European trade in African gold was not new. It had been going on for centuries, facilitated by Muslim middlemen whose caravans brought it from the Niger River to the North African ports of Algiers and Tunis. In the thirteenth century, Catalan and Genoese merchants established trading colonies in Tunis to expedite this process, exchanging woolen cloth from northern Europe for North African grain and sub-Saharan gold.

But the demand for gold was greatly accelerated during the fourteenth century, when a silver shortage began to affect the entire European economy. Silver production—which enabled the circulation of coinage in Europe—fell markedly as Europeans reached the limits of their technological capacity to extract ore from deep mines. This shortfall was compounded during the fifteenth century by a serious cash-flow problem: more European silver was moving east in the spice trade than could now be replenished from extant sources. Gold therefore represented an obvious alternative currency for large transactions, and in the thirteenth century some European rulers began minting gold coins. But Europe itself had few natural gold reserves. To maintain and expand gold coinages, therefore, new and larger supplies of gold were needed. The most obvious source was Africa.

The Mediterranean Empires of Catalonia, Venice, and Genoa

European interest in the African gold trade coincided with the creation of entrepreneurial empires in the Mediterranean. During the thirteenth century, the Catalans had conquered and colonized a series of western Mediterranean islands, including Majorca, Ibiza, Minorca, Sicily, and Sardinia. Except in Sicily, the pattern of Catalan exploitation was largely the same on all these islands: expulsion or extermination of the existing population, usually Muslim; the extension of economic concessions to attract new settlers; and a heavy reliance on slave labor to produce foodstuffs and raw materials for export.

These new colonial efforts were mainly carried out by private individuals operating under royal charters. They therefore contrast strongly with older patterns of Venetian colonization, which had long been controlled directly by the city's rulers, and which focused mainly on the eastern Mediterranean where the Venetians dominated the trade in spices and silks. The Genoese, to take yet another case, had extensive interests in the western Mediterranean, where they traded bulk goods such as cloth, hides, grain, timber, and sugar. But Genoese colonies tended to be more informal than either Venetian or Catalan colonies, constituting family networks rather than an extension of state sovereignty. The Genoese were also more closely integrated with the societies of North Africa, Spain, and the Black Sea than were their Venetian or Catalan counterparts.

Genoese colonists pioneered the production of sugar and sweet wines in the western Mediterranean and later in the Atlantic islands off the west coast of Africa, particularly

SPANISH GALLEON. The larger, full-bottomed ships that came into use during the fifteenth century would become engines of imperial conquest—and the vessels that brought the riches of those conquests back to Europe. This wooden model was made for the Museo Storico Navale di Venezia (Naval History Museum) in Venice.

Madeira. Meanwhile, they moved away from reliance on the oared galleys favored by the Venetians and began to use larger, fuller-bodied sailing ships that could carry greater volumes of cargo. With further modifications to accommodate the rougher sailing conditions of the Atlantic Ocean, these were the ships that would carry sixteenth-century Europeans around the globe.

From the Mediterranean to the Atlantic

For centuries, European maritime commerce had been divided between a Mediterranean and a northeastern Atlantic world. Starting around 1270, however, Italian merchants began to sail through the Strait of Gibraltar and on up to the wool-producing regions of England and the Netherlands. This was a step toward the extension of Mediterranean patterns of commerce into the Atlantic Ocean. Another step was the discovery (or possibly the rediscovery) of the Atlantic island chains known as the Canaries and the Azores, which Genoese sailors reached in the fourteenth century. Efforts to colonize the Canary Islands, and to convert and enslave their inhabitants, began almost immediately. But an effective conquest of these islands did not really begin until the fifteenth century, when it was undertaken by Portugal and completed by Castile. The Canaries, thereafter, became the base from which further Portuguese voyages down the west coast of Africa proceeded. They were also the jumping-off point from which Christopher Columbus would sail westward across the Atlantic Ocean in the hope of reaching Asia.

Naval Technology and Navigation

These new European empires of the fifteenth and sixteenth centuries rested on a mastery of the oceans and demanded new naval technologies. The Portuguese caravel—the workhorse ship of the fifteenth-century voyages to Africa—was based on designs that had been in use among Portuguese fishermen since the thirteenth century. Starting in the 1440s, however, Portuguese shipwrights began building larger caravels of about 50 tons displacement with two masts, each carrying a triangular (lateen) sail. Columbus's *Niña* was of this design, although it was refitted with two square sails to enable it to sail more efficiently before the wind during an Atlantic crossing. Such ships required much smaller crews than did the multi-oared galleys that were still commonly used in the Mediterranean. By the end of the fifteenth century, even larger

caravels of around 200 tons were being constructed, with a third mast and a combination of square and lateen sails.

Europeans were also making significant advances in navigation during the fifteenth and sixteenth centuries. Quadrants, which could calculate latitude in the Northern Hemisphere by the height of the North Star above the horizon, were in widespread use by the 1450s. As sailors approached the equator, however, the quadrant became less and less useful, and navigators instead made use of astrolabes, which reckoned latitude by the height of the sun. Like quadrants, astrolabes had been known in western Europe for centuries. But it was not until the 1480s that the astrolabe became a really useful instrument for seaborne navigation, with the preparation of standard tables sponsored by the Portuguese crown. Compasses, too, were coming into more widespread use during the fifteenth century. Longitude, however, remained impossible to calculate accurately until the eighteenth century, when the invention of the marine chronometer finally made it possible to keep accurate time at sea. In this earlier era, Europeans sailing east or west across the oceans generally had to rely on their skill at dead reckoning to determine where they were on the globe.

European sailors also benefited from a new interest in maps and navigational charts. Especially important to Atlantic sailors were books known as *rutters* or *routiers*. These contained detailed sailing instructions and descriptions of the coastal landmarks a pilot could expect to encounter en route to a variety of destinations. Mediterranean sailors had used similar books since at least the fourteenth century: known as *portolani*, or portolan charts, they mapped the ports along the coastlines, tracked prevailing winds and tides, and warned

PORTOLAN CHART. Maritime maps like this one were crucial navigational aids, and came to be widely used outside the Mediterranean in the fifteenth century. This chart, made by Vesconte Maggiolo in 1541, plainly shows the Mediterranean and Atlantic coastlines of Europe and North Africa.

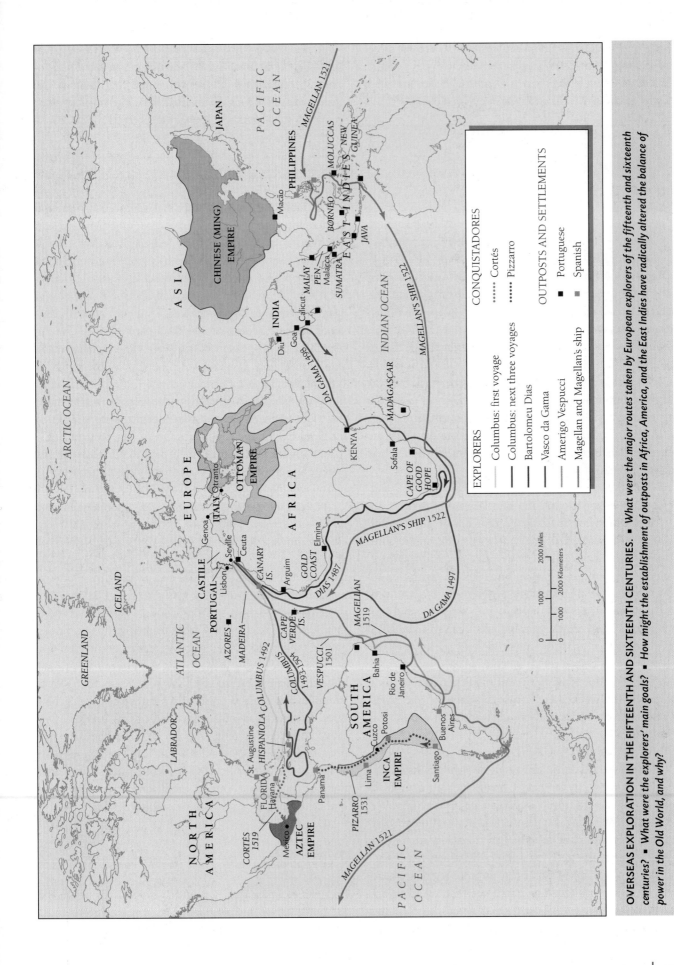

OVERSEAS EXPLORATION IN THE FIFTEENTH AND SIXTEENTH CENTURIES. ▪ *What were the major routes taken by European explorers of the fifteenth and sixteenth centuries?* ▪ *What were the explorers' main goals?* ▪ *How might the establishment of outposts in Africa, America, and the East Indies have radically altered the balance of power in the Old World, and why?*

of reefs and shallow harbors. In the fifteenth century, these map-making techniques were extended to the Atlantic Ocean; by the end of the sixteenth century, the accumulated knowledge contained in rutters spanned the globe.

Portugal, Africa, and the Sea Route to India

As we have seen, it was among the Portuguese that two critical interests—the African gold trade and Atlantic colonization—first came together. Their successes were rapid. In 1415, a Portuguese expedition captured the North African port of Ceuta. During the 1420s, the Portuguese colonized both the island of Madeira and the Canary Islands. During the 1430s, they extended these colonization efforts to the Azores. By the 1440s, they had reached the Cape Verde Islands off Africa's west coast. In 1444, Portuguese explorers first landed on the West African mainland, in the area between the Senegal and the Gambia river mouths, where they began to collect cargoes of gold and slaves for export back to Portugal. By the 1470s, Portuguese sailors had rounded the West African "bulge" and were exploring the Gulf of Guinea. In 1483, they reached the mouth of the Congo River.

In 1488, the Portuguese captain Bartolomeu Dias was accidentally blown around the southern tip of Africa by a gale, after which he named the point "Cape of Storms." But the king of Portugal, João II (r. 1481–95), took a more optimistic view of Dias's achievement: he renamed it the Cape of Good Hope and began planning a naval expedition to India. In 1497–98, accordingly, Vasco da Gama rounded the cape and then, with the help of a Muslim navigator named Ibn Majid, crossed the Indian Ocean to Calicut on the southwestern coast of India, opening up for the first time a sea route between Europe and the Far Eastern spice trade. Although da Gama lost half his fleet and one-third of his men on this two-year voyage, his cargo of spices was so valuable that his losses were deemed insignificant. His heroism became legendary, and his story became the basis for the Portuguese national epic, the *Lusiads*.

Now masters of the quickest route to riches in the world, the Portuguese swiftly capitalized on da Gama's accomplishment. Portuguese trading fleets sailed regularly to India after 1500. In 1509, the Portuguese defeated an Ottoman fleet and then blockaded the mouth of the Red Sea, attempting to cut off one of the traditional routes by which spices had traveled to Alexandria and Beirut, in order to monopolize trade. By 1510, Portuguese military forces had established a series of forts along the western Indian coastline, including their headquarters at Goa. In 1511, Portuguese ships seized

Malacca, a center of the spice trade on the Malay peninsula. By 1515, they had reached the Spice Islands and the coast of China. So completely did the Portuguese now dominate the spice trade that even the Venetians were forced to buy their pepper in the Portuguese capital of Lisbon by the 1520s.

Artillery and Empire

Larger, more maneuverable ships and improved navigational aids made it possible for the Portuguese and other European mariners to reach Africa, Asia, and the Americas by sea. But fundamentally, these sixteenth-century European commercial empires were a military achievement. As such, they reflected what Europeans had learned in their wars against each other during the fourteenth and fifteenth centuries. Perhaps the most critical military advance was the increasing sophistication of artillery, a development made possible not only by gunpowder but by improved metallurgical techniques for casting cannon barrels. By the middle of the fifteenth century, as we observed in Chapter 10, the use of artillery pieces had rendered the stone walls of medieval castles and towns obsolete, a fact brought home in 1453 by the successful French siege of Bordeaux (which ended the Hundred Years' War), and by the Ottoman siege of Constantinople (which ended the Byzantine Empire).

Indeed, the new ship designs were important in part because their larger size made it possible to mount more effective guns on them. European vessels were now conceived as floating artillery platforms, with scores of guns mounted in fixed positions along their sides and swivel guns mounted fore and aft. These guns were vastly expensive, as were the ships that carried them; but for those rulers who could afford them, such ships made it possible to project military power around the world. Just being able to reach a destination was not enough; although Vasco da Gama had been able to sail into the Indian Ocean in 1498, the Portuguese did not gain control of that ocean until 1509, when they defeated a combined Ottoman and Indian naval force at the battle of Div. Thus, Portuguese trading outposts in Africa and Asia also became fortifications, built not so much to guard against the attacks of native peoples as to ward off assaults from other Europeans. Without this essential military component, European maritime empires could not have existed.

Prince Henry the Navigator

Because we know that Portuguese expeditions down the African coast ultimately opened up a sea route to India and the Far East, it is tempting to presume that this was

their goal from the beginning. Hence the traditional narrative of these events presents exploration as their mission, India as their goal, and Prince Henry the Navigator (1394–1460) as the guiding genius behind them. But it was only a generation after Henry's death, in the 1480s, that India became the target toward which these voyages were directed. Before this time, Portuguese involvement in Africa was driven instead by much more traditional goals: crusading ambitions against the Muslims of North Africa; the desire to establish direct links with the sources of African gold production south of the Sahara Desert; the desire to colonize the Atlantic islands; the burgeoning market for slaves in Europe and in the Ottoman Empire; and the hope that they might find the kingdom of the legendary Prester John.

Still, Prince Henry remains a central figure in the history of Portuguese exploration. He personally directed eight of the thirty-five Portuguese voyages to Africa that occurred during his lifetime, and he played an important part in organizing the Portuguese colonization of Madeira, the Canary Islands, and the Azores. He also pioneered the Portuguese slave trade, first on the Canaries (whose population was almost entirely eradicated) and then along the Senegambian coast of western Africa. His main motivation was to outflank the cross-Saharan African gold trade by intercepting this trade at its source. This was also his reason for colonizing the Canary Islands, which he saw as a staging ground for expeditions into the African interior. He was therefore a man of his time rather than one ahead of his time: a crusader against Islam, a lord seeking resources to support his followers, and an aspiring merchant who hoped to make a killing in the gold trade but instead found his main profits in slaving.

Atlantic Colonization and Slave Networks

Although slavery had effectively disappeared in much of northwestern Europe by the early twelfth century, slavery continued in Iberia, Italy, and elsewhere in the Mediterranean world. It existed, however, on a small scale; there were no slave-powered factories or large-scale agricultural systems in this period. The major slave markets and slave economies, as we have noted, were in the Ottoman Empire. And, as had been the case since antiquity, no aspect of this slave trade was racially based. Most slaves of this era were European Christians, predominantly Poles, Ukrainians, Greeks, and Bulgarians; in previous eras, they had been Germanic and Celtic peoples.

What was new about slavery in the fifteenth century, then, was its racialization—an aspect of modern slavery that has made an indelible impact on our own society. To Europeans, African slaves were visibly distinctive in ways that other slaves were not, and it became convenient for those who dealt in them to justify the mass deportation of entire populations by alleging their racial inferiority and their "natural" fitness for a life of bondage. This nefarious practice has had long-lasting and tragic consequences.

From as early as the mid-fifteenth century, Lisbon began to emerge as a significant market for enslaved Africans. Something on the order of 15,000 to 20,000 men and women were sold there within a twenty-year period during Prince Henry's lifetime. In the following half century, the numbers amounted to perhaps 150,000. For the most part, the purchasers of these slaves regarded them as status symbols; it became fashionable to have African footmen, page boys, and ladies' maids. In the Atlantic colonies—Madeira, the Canaries, and the Azores—land was worked mainly by European settlers and sharecroppers. Slave labor, if employed at all, was generally used only in sugar mills. On Madeira and the Canaries, where sugar became the predominant cash crop during the last quarter of the fifteenth century, some slaves were therefore introduced. But even sugar production did not lead to the widespread introduction of slavery on these islands.

However, a new kind of slave-based sugar plantation began to emerge in Portugal's Atlantic colonies in the 1460s, starting on the Cape Verde Islands and then extending southward into the Gulf of Guinea. These islands were not populated when the Portuguese began to settle them, and their climate generally discouraged most Europeans from living there. They were ideally located, however, along the routes of slave traders venturing outward from the nearby West African coast. It was this plantation model that would be exported to Brazil by the Portuguese and to the Caribbean islands of the Americas by their Spanish conquerors, with devastating consequences.

NEW WORLD ENCOUNTERS

When King Ferdinand and Queen Isabella of Spain decided to underwrite a voyage of exploration, they were hoping to steal some thunder from the successful Portuguese ventures of the past half century. For it was clear that tiny Portugal would soon dominate the sea-lanes if rival entrepreneurs did not attempt to find alternate routes. Hence the bold—and ill-informed—decision to reach Asia by sailing west. Like his contemporaries, the sailor called Christoffa Corombo (in his own Genoese dialect) understood that the world

THE AZTEC CITY OF TENOCHTITLÁN. The Spanish conquistador Bernal Díaz del Castillo (1492–1585) took part in the conquest of the Aztec Empire and later wrote an account of his adventures. His admiring description of the Aztec capital at Tenochtitlán records that the Spaniards were amazed to see a huge city built in the midst of a vast lake, with gigantic buildings arranged in a meticulous urban plan around a central square, and broad causeways linking the city to the mainland. This hand-colored woodcut was included in an early edition of Hernando Cortés's letters to Emperor Charles V, printed at Nuremberg (Germany) in 1524.

was a sphere. But like them, he also thought it was much smaller than it actually is. (As we saw in Chapter 4, the accurate calculation of the globe's circumference, made in ancient Alexandria, had been suppressed centuries later by the Roman geographer Ptolemy.) Furthermore, it had been accepted since antiquity that there were only three continents: Europe, Asia, and Africa.

What made the scheme seem plausible to Ferdinand and Isabella was, first, the discovery and colonization of the Canary Islands and the Azores, which had reinforced the hypothesis that the Atlantic was dotted with islands all the way to Japan; and second, the Genoese mariner's egregious miscalculation of the earth's size, which convinced him that he could reach Japan and China in about a month's clear sailing after leaving the Canary Islands. The man we know as Christopher Columbus (1451–1506) never realized his mistake. When he reached the Bahamas and the island of Hispaniola in 1492, after only a month's sailing, he returned to Spain and reported that he had reached the outer islands of Asia.

Discoveries

Of course, Columbus was not the first European to set foot on the American continents. As we noted in Chapter 7, Viking sailors briefly settled present-day Newfoundland, Labrador, and perhaps even portions of New England around the year 1000. But knowledge of these Viking landings had been forgotten or ignored outside of Iceland for hundreds of years. Moreover, the tiny Scandinavian colonies on Greenland had been abandoned by the fifteenth century, when the cooling of the climate (Chapter 10) destroyed the fragile ecosystems that had barely sustained the lives of Norse settlers there.

Although Columbus brought back no Asian spices to prove that he had found an alternate route on his voyages, he did return with some small samples of gold and a few indigenous people—whose existence gave promise of entire tribes that might be "saved" (by conversion to Christianity) and enslaved by Europeans. This provided sufficient incentive for the Spanish monarchs to finance three more expeditions by Columbus, and many more by others. Soon the mainlands of two hitherto unknown continents were identified, as were clusters of new islands. Gradually, Europeans reached the conclusion that what they had encountered was an entirely "New World," and one that had—shockingly—never been foretold either by the teachings of Christianity or the wisdom of the ancients. Awareness of this fact was most widely publicized by the Italian explorer and geographer Amerigo Vespucci (1454–1512), whose name was soon adapted as a descriptor for the new continents (see **Interpreting Visual Evidence** on page 281).

At first, the realization that this world was not, in fact, an outpost of Asia came as a disappointment to the Spanish: two major land masses and two vast oceans disrupted their plans to beat the Portuguese to the Spice Islands. But this sense of frustration began to lift in 1513, when Vasco Núñez de Balboa first viewed the Pacific Ocean from the Isthmus of Panama. Thereafter, Ferdinand and Isabella's grandson, the Holy Roman Emperor Charles V, renewed their dream: he accepted Ferdinand Magellan's proposal to see whether a route to Asia could be found by sailing around South America.

But Magellan's voyage of 1519 demonstrated beyond question that the globe was simply too large for any such plan to be feasible. Of the five ships that left Spain under his command, only one returned, three years later, having been forced to circumnavigate the globe. Out of a crew of 265 sailors, only eighteen survived. Most had died of scurvy or starvation; Magellan himself had been killed in a skirmish with native peoples in the Philippines.

This fiasco ended all hope of discovering an easy southwest passage to Asia—although the deadly dream of a

Interpreting Visual Evidence

America as an Object of Desire

Under the influence of Mandeville's *Book of Marvels* and a host of other popular narratives, Columbus and his fellow voyagers were prepared to find the New World full of cannibals. They also assumed that the indigenous peoples' custom of wearing little or no clothing—not to mention their "savagery"—would render their women sexually available. In the letters he sent back to Europe, Columbus recounts one notable encounter with a "cannibal girl" whom he had taken captive in his tent. Her wantonly naked body aroused his desire, yet she resisted his advances so fiercely that he had to tie her up—which of course made it easier for him to "subdue" her. In the end, he cheerfully reports, the girl's sexual performance was so satisfying that she might have been trained, as he put it, in a "school for whores."

The Flemish artist Jan van der Straet (1523–1605) would have heard many such reports of the encounters between (mostly male) Europeans and the peoples of the New World. This engraving, based on one of his drawings, is among the thousands of mass-produced images that circulated widely in Europe, thanks to the invention of printing. It imagines the first encounter between a male "Americus" (like Columbus, or Amerigo Vespucci himself) and the New World, "America," depicted as a voluptuous, available woman. The Latin caption reads: "America rises to meet Americus; and whenever he calls her, she will always be aroused."

Questions for Analysis

1. The New World itself—America—is imagined as female in this image. Why is this? What messages might this—and the suggestive caption—have conveyed to a European viewer?

2. Study the details of this image carefully. What does each symbolize, and how do they work together as an allegory of conquest and colonization?

3. On what stereotypes of indigenous peoples does this image draw? Notice, for example, the cannibalistic campfire of the group in the background, or the enticing posture of "America."

Americen Americus retexit, & *Semel vocauit inde semper excitam*.

Ioan: Stradanus invent.
Theodor: Galle sculp.
AMERICA.

---

northwest passage survived, and motivated many European explorers of North America into the twentieth century. It has been revived today: in our age of global warming, the retreat of Arctic pack ice has led to the opening of new shipping lanes, and in 2008 the first commercial voyage successfully traversed the Arctic Ocean.

The Spanish Conquest of America

Although the discovery of two continents was initially construed as a setback, it quickly became clear that this New World had great wealth of its own. From the start, Columbus's gold samples, in themselves rather paltry, had nurtured

A Spanish Critique of New World Conquest

Not all Europeans approved of European imperialism or its "civilizing" effects on the peoples of the New World. One of the most influential contemporary critics was Bartolomé de las Casas (1474–1566), who left his home city of Seville at the age of eighteen, joined the Dominican order, and eventually became bishop of Chiapas (in Mexico). Although he was a product of his times—he owned many slaves—he was also prescient in discerning the devastating effects of European settlement in the West Indies and Central America, and he particularly deplored the exploitation and extermination of indigenous populations. The following excerpt is from one of the many eloquent manifestos he published in an attempt to gain the sympathies of the Spanish crown and to reach a wide readership. It was printed in 1542.

 od made all the peoples of this area, many and varied as they are, as open and as innocent as can be imagined. The simplest people in the world—unassuming, long-suffering, unassertive, and submissive—they are without malice or guile, and are utterly faithful and obedient both to their own native lords and to the Spaniards in whose service they now find themselves.... They are innocent and pure in mind and have a lively intelligence, all of which makes them particularly receptive to learning and understanding the truths of our Catholic faith and to being instructed in virtue; indeed, God has invested them with fewer impediments in this regard than any other people on earth....

It was upon these gentle lambs . . . that from the very first day they clapped eyes on them the Spanish fell like ravening wolves upon the fold, or like tigers and savage lions who have not eaten meat for days. The pattern established at the outset has remained unchanged to this day, and the Spaniards still do nothing save tear the natives to shreds, murder them, and inflict upon them untold misery, suffering, and distress, tormenting, harrying, and persecuting them mercilessly....

When the Spanish first journeyed there, the indigenous population of the island of Hispaniola stood at some three million; today only two hundred survive. The island of Cuba, which extends for a distance almost as great as that separating Valladolid from Rome, is now to all intents and purposes uninhabited; and two other large, beautiful, and fertile islands, Puerto Rico and Jamaica, have been similarly devastated. Not a living soul remains today on any of the islands

hopes that gold might lie piled in ingots somewhere in these vast new lands, ready to enrich any European adventurer who discovered them. Rumor fed rumor, until a few free-lance Spanish soldiers really did strike it rich beyond their most avaricious imaginings. Between 1519 and 1521, the *conquistador* (Spanish for "conqueror") Hernándo Cortés, accompanied by a force of only 600 men, unwittingly contributed to the destruction of the Aztec Empire of Mexico and was accordingly on hand to plunder its rulers' fabulous wealth. Then in 1533, another conquistador, Francisco Pizarro, spearheaded efforts that toppled the highly centralized South American empire of the Incas and seized its great stores of gold and silver. His force numbered only 180. Despite the sophistication and enormous resources of these two extra-

SPANISH CONQUISTADORS IN MEXICO. This sixteenth-century drawing of conquistadors slaughtering the Aztec aristocracy emphasizes the advantages that plate armor and steel weaponry gave to European soldiers.

of the Bahamas . . . even though every single one of the sixty or so islands in the group . . . is more fertile and more beautiful than the Royal Gardens in Seville and the climate is as healthy as anywhere on earth. The native population, which once numbered some five hundred thousand, was wiped out by forcible expatriation to the island of Hispaniola, a policy adopted by the Spaniards in an endeavour to make up losses among the indigenous population of that island. . . .

At a conservative estimate, the despotic and diabolical behaviour of the Christians has, over the last forty years, led to the unjust and totally unwarranted deaths of more than twelve million souls, women and children among them. . . .

The reason the Christians have murdered on such a vast scale and killed anyone and everyone in their way is purely and simply greed. . . . The Spaniards have shown not the slightest consideration for these people, treating them (and I speak from first-hand experience, having been there from the outset) not as brute animals—indeed, I would to God they had done and had shown them the consideration they afford their animals—so much as piles of dung in the middle of the road. They have had as little concern for their souls as for their bodies, all the millions that have perished having gone to their deaths with no knowledge of God and without the benefit of the Sacraments. One fact in all this is widely known and beyond dispute, for even the tyrannical murderers themselves acknowledge the truth of it: the indigenous peoples never did the Europeans any harm whatever. . . .

Source: Bartolomé de la Casas, *A Short Account of the Destruction of the Indies*, trans. Nigel Griffin (Harmondsworth: 1992), pp. 9–12.

Questions for Analysis

1. Given his perspective on the behavior of his countrymen, how might Bartolomé de las Casas have justified his own presence in New Spain (Mexico)? What do you think he may have hoped to achieve by publishing this account?

2. What comparisons does the author make between the New Spain and the Old, and between indigenous peoples and Europeans? What is he trying to convey?

3. Compare this account with the contemporary engraving on page 281. What new light does this excerpt throw on that visual allegory? How might a reader-viewer of the time have reconciled these two very different pictures of European imperialism?

ordinary civilizations—the Aztec capital of Tenochtitlán (*ten-och-tit-LAN*, now Mexico City) rivaled any European city in size and amazed its conquerors by the height and grandeur of its buildings—Cortés and Pizarro had the advantage. They had cannons, firearms, steel swords, armor, and horses: all unknown to the native peoples of the Americas. But a more potent weapon turned out to be their own germs and the indigenous peo-ples' extreme susceptibility to infectious European diseases, which had already weakened these populations as a result of their earlier contacts with explorers and settlers following in the wake of Columbus. Those peoples who survived were promised liberation from the oppressive regimes of the Aztecs and Incas—little knowing how much worse their new oppressors would be.

The Profits of Empire

Cortés and Pizarro captured hoards of gold and silver that had been accumulated for centuries by the indigenous peoples of Mexico and Peru. Almost immediately, however, a search for the sources of these precious metals was launched. The first gold deposits were discovered on Hispaniola, where surface mines were speedily established using native laborers, who died in appalling numbers from disease, brutality, and overwork. Of the approximately 1 million native inhabitants who had welcomed Columbus in 1492, only 100,000 survived by 1510: 90 percent of the population had died within a generation. By 1538, there were fewer than 500 left alive.

With the loss of so many workers, the mines of Hispaniola became uneconomical to operate, and the European colonists turned instead to cattle raising and sugar production. Modeling their sugarcane plantations on those of the Cape Verde Islands and St. Thomas (São Tomé) in the Gulf of Guinea, colonists began to import thousands of African slaves to labor in the new industry. Sugar production was, by its nature, a capital-intensive undertaking. The need to import slave labor added further to its costs, guaranteeing that control over the new industry would fall into the hands of a few extremely wealthy planters and financiers. Meanwhile, cattle ranching on the Mexican mainland had a devastating effect on the fragile ecosystem of Central America.

Yet mining continued to shape the Spanish colonies of Central and South America in fundamental ways. Gold was the lure that had initially drawn the Spanish to the New World, but silver became their most lucrative export. Even before the discovery of vast silver deposits north of Mexico City and at Potosí in Bolivia, between 1543 and 1548, the Spanish crown had taken steps to assume direct control over its new colonies' wealth. It was therefore to the Spanish crown that the profits from these astonishingly productive mines accrued. Potosí quickly became the most important mining town in the world. By 1570, it numbered 120,000 inhabitants, despite being located at an altitude of 15,000 feet, where the temperature never climbs above 59°F. As on Hispaniola, enslaved native laborers died by the tens of thousands in these mines and in the disease-infested boomtowns that surrounded them.

Thereafter, new mining techniques made it possible to produce even greater quantities of silver, though at the cost of still greater mortality among the native laborers. Between 1571 and 1586, silver production at Potosí quadrupled, reaching a peak in the 1590s, when 10 million ounces of silver per year were arriving in Spain from the Americas. (In the 1540s, the corresponding figure was only 1.5 million ounces.) By contrast, the peak years of domestic European silver production yielded only about 3 million ounces of silver per year between 1525 and 1535, and this figure dropped steadily from about 1550 on.

Europe's silver shortage therefore came to an end during the sixteenth century, but the silver that now circulated there came almost entirely from the New World. And this massive infusion of silver into the European economy accelerated an inflation that had already begun in the late fifteenth century. Initially, it had been driven by the renewed growth of the European population, an expanding economy, and a relatively fixed supply of food. From the 1540s on, however, inflation was largely the product of the greatly increased supply of coinage that was now entering the

After You Read
This Chapter

REVIEWING THE OBJECTIVES

- The conquests of the Mongols made a significant impact on Europe. What were some key effects?
- The Ottomans' dependence on slavery had a number of notable consequences. What were they?
- Colonialism and overseas exploration were driven by an array of factors. Identify some of the main economic and technological changes that occurred during the fourteenth and fifteenth centuries.
- In what ways did the practice of slavery and its justification change in the fifteenth century?
- The "discovery" of the New World had profound effects on the Old World, as well as on the indigenous peoples of the Americas. Describe some of these effects.

European economy. The result was a rapid rise in prices. Although the effects of this were felt throughout Europe, Spain was particularly hard hit. Prices doubled between 1500 and 1560, and they doubled again between 1560 and 1600. These price spikes in turn undermined the competitiveness of Spanish industries. Then, when the flow of New World silver slowed dramatically during the 1620s and 1630s, the Spanish economy collapsed.

After 1600, when smaller quantities of New World silver were entering the European economy, prices rose more slowly. But the price of grain still ballooned to five or six times the level of the previous century by 1650, producing social dislocation and widespread misery for many of Europe's poorest inhabitants (see Chapter 14). In England, for example, the period between about 1590 and 1610 was the most desperate the country had experienced since the Great Famine, nearly three hundred years before. As the population rose and wages fell, living standards declined dramatically. Indeed, if we compute living standards by dividing the price of an average basket of food by the average daily wage of a common laborer, then standards of living were lower in England at the beginning of the modern era than they had been at any time during the Middle Ages. It is no wonder, then, that so many Europeans found emigration to the Americas a tempting prospect.

CONCLUSION

By 1600, commerce, colonization, and overseas conquest had profoundly changed both Europe and the wider world. Even though Europeans had little direct contact with China after the fall of the Mongol Empire, the economy of Europe was still closely tied to that of Asia through the trade routes maintained by the Ottoman Empire. At the same time, the emergence of Portugal and Spain as Europe's leading long-distance traders was moving the center of economic gravity away from the Mediterranean toward the Atlantic. Displaced by Ottoman Constantinople from its role as the principal conduit for the spice trade, Venice gradually declined, while the Genoese moved increasingly into the world of finance, backing the commercial ventures of other powers, particularly Spain, whose Atlantic ports bustled with vessels and shone with wealth. By the mid-seventeenth century, however, both Spain and Portugal had become the victims of their own success. They would retain their American colonies until the nineteenth century, but it would be the Dutch, the French, and especially the English who would establish the most successful European empires in North America, Asia, Africa, and Australia. Meanwhile, these and other developments were moving Italy to the center of European affairs for the first time since the fragmentation of the Roman Empire. How this happened is the subject of Chapter 12.

PEOPLE, IDEAS, AND EVENTS IN CONTEXT

- What circumstances enabled **MARCO POLO**'s travels in the East? Why was the period of commercial contact between the **MONGOL EMPIRE** and Europe so brief?

- What forces drove the **OTTOMAN EMPIRE** to expand its reach? Why was the Ottoman caliph more tolerant of Jews and Christians than of dissent within Islam?

- What set the **GENOESE** entrepreneurs apart from other colonial powers in the Mediterranean?

- How does **PRINCE HENRY THE NAVIGATOR** exemplify the motives for pursuing overseas expansion, as well as the mythology that has grown up around these early efforts?

- What were the expectations that launched **COLUMBUS**'s voyage? Why were **FERDINAND AND ISABELLA** of Spain motivated to finance it?

- What advantages did the Spanish **CONQUISTADORS** have over the native peoples of the **AMERICAS**? What were the immediate effects of European conquest?

CONSEQUENCES

- How do the patterns of conquest and colonization discussed in this chapter compare to those of earlier periods, particularly those of antiquity? Which developments seem new? Which are familiar?

- In what ways did the slave trade of the Atlantic world differ from the slave economies of antiquity? How might Europeans have used Greek and Roman justifications of slavery in defense of these new ventures? (See Chapters 4 and 5.)

- How important a role does technology play in the developments we have surveyed in this chapter? In your view, which technological innovation was of the greatest historical significance, and why?

Before You Read This Chapter

STORY LINES

- The intellectual and artistic phenomenon known as the Renaissance is contemporaneous with both the later Middle Ages (Chapter 10) and the beginnings of Europe's colonial expansion into the Atlantic (Chapter 11).

- The Renaissance began in Italy, where the absence of centralized political power created nostalgia for an era when Rome and its empire had ruled the world. At the same time, the competition among small city-states suggested that models for their governance might be found in ancient Greece.

- Knowledge of the classics and of the Greek language was facilitated at this time by the flight of Greek-speaking intellectuals from Constantinople to Italy, as the Ottoman Turks absorbed the lands of the Byzantine Empire.

- In time, the literary, artistic, and philosophical achievements of Renaissance Italy came to influence all of Europe.

CHRONOLOGY

1304–1374	Lifetime of Petrarch
1377	The papacy returns to Rome
1378–1417	The Great Schism
1434	The Medici family comes to rule Florence
1440	Lorenzo Valla debunks the "Donation of Constantine"
1453	The fall of Constantinople prompts a diaspora of Greek scholars
1455	Invention of the printing press
1492	Columbus's first voyage
1498	Leonardo da Vinci's *The Last Supper*
1511	Raphael's *The School of Athens*
1512	Michelangelo completes the Sistine ceiling
1513	Niccolò Machiavelli's *The Prince*
1514	Albrecht Dürer's *Saint Jerome*
1516	Thomas More publishes *Utopia* Erasmus completes his new translation of the New Testament
1528	Castiglione's *Book of the Courtier*

Renaissance Ideals and Realities, c. 1350–1550

CORE OBJECTIVES

- **DEFINE** the movement known as the Renaissance.
- **EXPLAIN** why the Renaissance began in Italy.
- **IDENTIFY** the principle characteristics of Renaissance art.
- **UNDERSTAND** the relationship between Renaissance ideals and political realities.
- **DESCRIBE** the ways in which the Renaissance of northern Europe differed from that of Italy.

Rummaging through some old books in a cathedral library, an Italian bureaucrat attached to the papal curia at Avignon was surprised to find a manuscript of Cicero's letters—letters that no living person had known to exist. They had probably been copied in the time of Charlemagne, and had then been forgotten for hundreds of years. How many other works of this great Roman orator had met the same fate? he wondered. And how many more books might still remain to be discovered? Clearly, thought Francesco Petrarca (1304–1374), he was living in an age of ignorance. A great gulf seemed to open up between his own time and that of the ancients: a middle age that separated him from those well-loved models.

For centuries, Christian intellectuals had regarded "the middle ages" as the time between Adam's expulsion from Eden and the birth of Christ. But now, Petrarca redefined that concept and applied it to his own era. According to him, this "dark age" was not the pagan past but the time that separated him from direct communion with the classics. Yet this did not stop him from trying to bridge the gap. "I would have written to you long ago," he wrote in a Latin letter to the Greek poet Homer (dead for over two thousand years), "had it not been for the fact that we lack a common language."

Petrarca (known to English-speakers as Petrarch) would become famous in his own day as an Italian poet, a Latin stylist, and a tireless advocate for the resuscitation of classical antiquity. The values that he and his contemporaries began to espouse would give rise to a new intellectual and artistic movement in Italy, a movement strongly critical of the present and admiring of a past that had disappeared with the fragmentation of Rome's empire and the end of Italy's greatness. We know this movement as the Renaissance, the French word for "rebirth" that was applied to it in the nineteenth century. It has since become shorthand for the epoch following the Middle Ages, but it is really a parallel phenomenon—as the overlapping chronologies of this chapter and the two previous chapters show. Talking about the Renaissance is therefore a way of talking about some significant changes in education and outlook that transformed the culture of Italy from the late fourteenth to the early sixteenth centuries, and which eventually influenced the rest of Europe in important ways.

MEDIEVAL OR RENAISSANCE?

The term *renaissance* has usually been taken literally, as though the cultural accomplishments of antiquity had ceased to be appreciated and imitated, and therefore needed to be "reborn." Yet we have been tracing the enduring influence of classical civilization throughout the Middle Ages for many chapters, and we have noted the reverence accorded to Aristotle, Virgil, Cicero, and a host of other figures, as well as the persistence of Roman law and Roman institutions. It is also misleading to characterize the Renaissance as rejecting the fervent Christianity of the Middle Ages, and as a return to the pagan past: however much the scholars and artists of this age loved the pagan classics, none saw them as superseding Christianity. Indeed, all discussions of "the Renaissance" must be qualified by the fact that there was no single set of Renaissance ideals, and must recognize that these ideals were constantly reshaped and determined by political, social, and economic realities.

Renaissance Classicism

Renaissance thinkers and artists were enormously diverse in their attitudes, achievements, and approaches. That said, one can certainly find distinguishing traits that make the concept of a "Renaissance" meaningful. With respect to knowledge of the classics, for example, there was a significant quantitative difference between the learning of the Middle Ages and that of the Renaissance. Medieval scholars knew many Roman authors—especially Virgil, Ovid, and Cicero—but the discovery of "new" works by Livy, Tacitus, and Lucretius expanded the classical canon considerably. Equally important was the recovery of Greek literature. In the twelfth and thirteenth centuries, as we have seen (Chapters 8 and 9), Greek scientific and philosophical works became available to western Europeans thanks to increased contact with Islam; but no Greek poems or plays were available in Latin translations, and neither were the major dialogues of Plato. Nor could more than a handful of western Europeans read the language of ancient Greece. But as the Ottoman Turks put increasing pressure on the shrinking borders of the Byzantine Empire (Chapter 11), more and more Greek-speaking intellectuals fled to Italy, bringing their books and their knowledge with them.

Renaissance thinkers not only knew many more classical texts, they used them in new ways. Medieval intellectuals had long regarded ancient sources as complementing and confirming their own assumptions. By contrast, the new reading methods of the Renaissance fostered an increased awareness of the conceptual gap that separated their contemporary world from that of antiquity. At the same time, the structural similarities between ancient Greek poleis and the city-states of Italy encouraged political theorists to use these ancient forms of government as models. This firm determination to learn from antiquity was even more pronounced in the realms of architecture and art, areas in which classical models contributed most strikingly to the creation of a distinctive Renaissance style.

Finally, although Renaissance culture was by no means pagan, it was more overtly materialistic and more commercialized. For one thing, the competition among and within Italian city-states fostered a culture of display and conspicuous consumption. The relative weakness of the Church in Italy also contributed to the growth of secular power and a more worldly outlook. Italian bishoprics were small and relatively powerless compared to those north of the Alps, and Italian universities were much more independent of ecclesiastical supervision than those elsewhere. Even the papacy—restored to Rome after Petrarch's death—was severely limited, not the least because the papacy's role as a political rival in central Italy compromised its moral authority. All these factors fostered the emergence of new aesthetics and aspirations.

Renaissance Humanism

The most basic of Renaissance intellectual ideals is summarized in the term *humanism*. This was a program of study that aimed to replace the scholastic emphasis on logic and metaphysics with the study of language, literature, rhetoric, history, and ethics. The humanists also preferred ancient literature to the writings of more recent authors. Although some wrote in both Latin and the vernacular, most humanists regarded contemporary vernacular literature as a lesser diversion for the uneducated; serious scholarship and praiseworthy poetry could be written only in Latin or Greek. Latin, moreover, had to be the classical Latin of Cicero and Virgil, not the evolving, changing Latin of the universities and the Church.

Renaissance humanists therefore condemned the living Latin of their scholastic contemporaries as a barbarous departure from ancient (and therefore "correct") standards of Latin style. Despite their belief that they were thereby reviving the study of the classics, the humanists actually contributed to Latin's demise. By insisting on ancient standards of grammar, syntax, and diction, they turned Latin into a fossilized language that ceased to have any direct relevance to daily life. They thus hastened, ironically and unwittingly, the ultimate triumph of the various European vernaculars as languages of intellectual and cultural life, while bringing about the death of Latin as a common European language.

Humanists were convinced that their own educational program was the best way to produce virtuous citizens and able public officials. And because women were excluded from Italian political life, the education of women was therefore of little concern to most humanists, although some aristocratic women did acquire humanist training. Here again there are paradoxes: for as more and more Italian city-states fell into the hands of autocratic rulers, the humanist educational curriculum lost its immediate connection to the republican ideals of Italian political life. Nevertheless, humanists never lost their conviction that the study of the "humanities" (as the humanist curriculum came to be known) was the best way to produce political leaders.

THE RENAISSANCE OF ITALY

Although the Renaissance eventually became a Europe-wide intellectual and artistic movement, it developed first and most distinctively in Italy. Understanding why this happened is important not only to explaining the origins of this movement, but also to understanding its essential characteristics.

The most fundamental reason was that, after the Black Death, northern Italy became the most urbanized region of Europe. Moreover, Italian aristocrats customarily lived in urban centers rather than in rural castles, and consequently became more fully involved in urban public affairs than their counterparts north of the Alps. Elsewhere in Europe, moreover, most aristocrats lived on the income from their landed estates, while rich town dwellers gained their living from trade; but in Italy, many town-dwelling aristocrats engaged in banking or mercantile enterprises while many rich mercantile families imitated the manners of the aristocracy. The noted Florentine family the Medici, for example, originally came from the rustic region north of Florence. But they eventually made a fortune in banking and commerce, and were able to assimilate into the aristocracy.

The results of these developments are tied to the history of the new humanist education mentioned above. Not only was there great demand for the skills of reading and accounting necessary to become a successful merchant in Italy, but the richest and most prominent families sought to find teachers who would impart to their sons the knowledge

POPE JULIUS II (r. 1503–13). This portrait of one of the most powerful popes of the Renaissance—it was he who commissioned Michelangelo's paintings in the Sistine Chapel—was executed by Raffaello Sanzio da Urbino, known as Raphael (1483–1520). The acorns atop the posts of the throne are visual puns on the pope's family name, della Rovere ("of the oak"). ■ *What impression of the pope's personality does this portrait convey?*

Competing Viewpoints

The Humanists' Educational Program

> These three selections illustrate the confidence placed by humanists in their elite educational program, and their conviction that it would be of supreme value to the state as well as to the individual students who pursued it. Not everyone agreed with the humanists' claims, however, and a good deal of self-promotion lies behind them.

Vergerius on Liberal Studies

We call those studies *liberal* which are worthy of a free man; those studies by which we attain and practice virtue and wisdom; that education which calls forth, trains, and develops those highest gifts of body and of mind which ennoble men, and which are rightly judged to rank next in dignity to virtue only. . . . It is, then, of the highest importance that even from infancy this aim, this effort, should constantly be kept alive in growing minds. For . . . we shall not have attained wisdom in our later years unless in our earliest we have sincerely entered on its search. [P. P. Vergerius (1370–1444), "Concerning Excellent Traits."]

Alberti on the Importance of Literature

Letters are indeed so important that without them one would be considered nothing but a rustic, no matter how much a gentlemen [he may be by birth]. I'd much rather see a young nobleman with a book than with a falcon in his hand. . . .

Be diligent, then, you young people, in your studies. Do all you can to learn about the events of the past that are worthy of memory. Try to understand all the useful things that have been passed on to you. Feed your minds on good maxims. Learn the delights of embellishing your souls with good morals. Strive to be kind and considerate [of others] when conducting civil business. Get to know those things human and divine that have been put at your disposal in books for good reason. Nowhere [else] will you find . . . the elegance of a verse of Homer, or Virgil, or of some other excellent poet. You will find no field so delightful or flowering as in one of the orations of Demosthenes, Cicero, Livy, Xenophon, and other such pleasant and perfect orators. No effort is more fully compensated . . . as the constant reading and rereading of good things. From such reading you will rise rich in good maxims and good arguments, strong in your ability to persuade others and get them to listen to you; among the citizens you will willingly be heard, admired, praised, and loved. [Leon Battista Alberti (1404–1472), "On the Family."]

and skills necessary to cutting a figure in society and speaking with authority in public affairs. Consequently, Italy produced a large number of lay educators, many of whom also demonstrated their learning by producing political and ethical treatises and works of literature. Italian schools and tutors accordingly turned out the best-educated urban elites in all of Europe, men who became wealthy, knowledgeable patrons ready to invest in the cultivation of new ideas and new forms of literary and artistic expression.

A second reason why late-medieval Italy was the birthplace of an intellectual and artistic movement has to do with its vexed political situation. Unlike France, England, Spain, and the kingdoms of Scandinavia and eastern Europe, Italy had many competing political institutions, the most important of which—the papacy and the Holy Roman Empire—based their claims on different sources of authority. Italians therefore looked to the classical past for their time of unity and glory, dreaming of a day when Rome

Bruni on the Humanist Curriculum

The foundations of all true learning must be laid in the sound and thorough knowledge of Latin: which implies study marked by a broad spirit, accurate scholarship, and careful attention to details. Unless this solid basis be secured it is useless to attempt to rear an enduring edifice. Without it the great monuments of literature are unintelligible, and the art of composition impossible. To attain this essential knowledge we must never relax our careful attention to the grammar of the language, but perpetually confirm and extend our acquaintance with it until it is thoroughly our own. . . .

But the wider question now confronts us, that of the subject matter of our studies, that which I have already called the realities of fact and principle, as distinct from literary form. . . . First among such studies I place History: a subject which must not on any account be neglected by one who aspires to true cultivation. . . . For the careful study of the past enlarges our foresight in contemporary affairs and affords to citizens and to monarchs lessons . . . in the or-

dering of public policy. From History, also, we draw our store of examples of moral precepts. . . .

The great Orators of antiquity must by all means be included. Nowhere do we find the virtues more warmly extolled, the vices so fiercely decried. From them we may learn, also, how to express consolation, encouragement, dissuasion, or advice. . . .

Familiarity with the great poets of antiquity is essential to any claim to true education. For in their writings we find deep speculations upon Nature, and upon the Causes and Origins of things, which must carry weight with us both from their antiquity and from their authorship. . . .

Proficiency in literary form, not accompanied by broad acquaintance with facts and truths, is a barren attainment; whilst information, however vast, which lacks all grace of expression would seem to be put under a bushel or partly thrown away. . . . Where, however, this double capacity exists—breadth of learning and grace of style—we allow the highest title to distinction and to abiding

fame. . . . [Leonardo Bruni (1369–1444), *"Concerning the Study of Literature."*]

Sources: Vergerius and Bruni: William Harrison Woodward, ed., *Vittorino da Feltre and Other Humanist Educators* (London: 1897), pp. 96–110, 124–29, 132–33. Alberti: Eric Cochrane and Julius Kirshner, eds., *University of Chicago Readings in Western Civilization*. Vol. 5: *The Renaissance* (Chicago: 1986), pp. 81–82.

Questions for Analysis

1. What is the purpose of education, according to these authorities? What elements do their programs share? What are their potential areas of contention?

2. Why did humanists such as Leonardo Bruni consider the study of history essential to education?

would be, again, the center of the world. They boasted that ancient Roman monuments were omnipresent in their landscape, and that classical Latin literature referred to cities and sites they recognized as their own.

Italians were particularly intent on reappropriating their classical heritage because they were seeking to establish an independent cultural identity that could help them oppose the intellectual and political supremacy of France. The removal of the papacy to Avignon for most of the fourteenth

century and the subsequent Great Schism (Chapter 10) had heightened antagonism between the city-states of Italy and the burgeoning nation-states and empires of the Continent. This coincided with a rejection of the scholasticism taught in northern Europe's universities, and the embrace of the intellectual alternatives offered by new readings of classical sources. As Roman literature and learning took hold in the imaginations of Italy's intellectuals, so too did Roman art and architecture, for Roman models could help Italians create an artistic alternative to French Gothic, just as Roman learning offered an intellectual alternative to the scholasticism of Paris.

Finally, the Italian Renaissance could not have occurred without the underpinning of Italian wealth gained through the increasing commercial ventures described in Chapter 11. This meant that talented men seeking employment and patronage were more likely to stay at home than to seek opportunities abroad. Investment in art and learning also arose from an intensification of urban pride and the growing concentration of individual and family wealth in urban areas. Cities themselves became primary patrons of artists and scholars in the fourteenth century. During the fifteenth century, however, when most city-states succumbed to the hereditary rule of powerful dynasties, patronage was monopolized by the princely aristocracy. Among these great princes were the popes in Rome, who controlled the Papal States and for a few decades made Rome the artistic capital of Europe.

LITERARY AND INTELLECTUAL ACTIVITY

We have already encountered the man who strove to leave behind "the middle age" of his own time, and who is therefore considered the founder of the Renaissance movement: Francesco Petrarca (1304–1374). Petrarch was a trained cleric, but he believed that the scholastic theology taught in universities was misguided, because it concentrated on abstract speculation rather than the achievement of virtue and ethical conduct. Instead, he felt that the truly Christian writer must cultivate literary eloquence, and so inspire others to do good through the pursuit of beauty and truth. For him, the best models of eloquence were to be found in the classical texts of Latin literature, which were doubly valuable because they were also filled with ethical wisdom. Petrarch dedicated himself, therefore, to rediscovering such texts and to writing his own poems and moral treatises in a Latin style modeled on that of classical authors. But Petrarch was also a prolific vernacular poet. His Italian sonnets—which spawned a new literary genre—were written in praise of his semi-fictional beloved, Laura, in the chivalrous style of the troubadours. They were widely admired and imitated, inspiring poets in other European vernaculars. William Shakespeare (1564–1616) would later adopt the form.

Petrarch's ultimate ideal for human conduct was a solitary life of contemplation. But subsequent Italian thinkers and scholars, located mainly in Florence, developed a different vision of life's true purpose. For them, the goal of classical education was civic. Humanists such as Leonardo Bruni (c. 1370–1444) and Leon Battista Alberti (1404–1472) agreed with Petrarch on the importance of eloquence and the value of classical literature, but they also taught that man's nature equipped him for action, for usefulness to his family and society, and for serving the state: ideally, a city-state after the Florentine model. In their view, ambition and the quest for glory were noble impulses that ought to be encouraged and channeled toward these political and social ends. They also refused to condemn the accumulation of material possessions, arguing that the history of human progress is inseparable from the human dominion of the earth and its resources.

Many of the humanists' civic ideals are expressed in Alberti's treatise *On the Family* (1443), in which he argued that the nuclear family is the fundamental unit of the city-state and should be governed in such a way as to further the city-state's political, social, and economic goals. Alberti accordingly argued that the family should mirror the city-state's own organization, and he thus consigned women—who, in reality, governed the household—to child-bearing, child-rearing, and subservience to men. He asserted, furthermore, that women should play no role whatsoever in the public sphere. Although such dismissals of women's abilities were fiercely resisted by actual women, the humanism of the Renaissance was characterized by a pervasive denigration of them—a denigration often mirrored in the works of the classical literature these humanists so much admired.

The Emergence of Textual Scholarship

The humanists of Florence also went far beyond Petrarch in their knowledge of classical (especially Greek) literature and philosophy. In this they were aided by a number of Byzantine scholars who had migrated to Italy in the first half of the fifteenth century and who gave instruction in the language. There were also attempts on the part of Italians to acquire Greek masterpieces for themselves, which often involved journeys back to Constantinople. In 1423, for example, one adventurous scholar managed to bring back 238 manuscript books, among them rare works of Sophocles, Euripides, and Thucydides, all of which were quickly paraphrased in Latin and thus made accessible to western Europeans for the first time. By 1500, most of the Greek classics, including the writings of Plato, the dramatists, and the historians, had been translated and were more widely available than they had ever been, even in their own day.

Analyzing Primary Sources

Machiavelli's Patriotism

These passages are from the concluding chapter of Machiavelli's treatise The Prince. *Like the book itself, they are addressed to Lorenzo de' Medici, head of Florence's most powerful family. Here, Machiavelli laments Italy's "barbarian occupation" by foreign powers, by which he means the invading armies of France, Spain, and the Holy Roman Empire. He may also be alluding to the many companies of foreign mercenaries that fought for Italy's various city-states.*

 eflecting on the matters set forth above and considering within myself whether the times were propitious in Italy at present to honor a new prince and whether there is at hand the matter suitable for a prudent and virtuous leader to mold in a new form, giving honor to himself and benefit to the citizens of the country, I have arrived at the opinion that all circumstances now favor such a prince, and I cannot think of a time more propitious for him than the present. If, as I said, it was necessary in order to make apparent the virtue of Moses, that the people of Israel should be enslaved in Egypt, and that the Persians should be oppressed by the Medes to provide an opportunity to illustrate the greatness and the spirit of Cyrus, and that the Athenians should be scattered in order to show the excellence of Theseus, thus at the present time, in order to reveal the valor of an Italian spirit, it was essential that Italy should fall to her present low estate, more enslaved than the Hebrews, more servile than the Persians, more disunited than the Athenians,

leaderless and lawless, beaten, despoiled, lacerated, overrun and crushed under every kind of misfortune. . . . So Italy now, left almost lifeless, awaits the coming of one who will heal her wounds, putting an end to the sacking and looting in Lombardy and the spoliation and extortions in the Realm of Naples and Tuscany, and cleanse her sores that have been so long festering. Behold how she prays God to send her someone to redeem her from the cruelty and insolence of the barbarians. See how she is ready and willing to follow any banner so long as there be someone to take it up. Nor has she at present any hope of finding her redeemer save only in your illustrious house [the Medici] which has been so highly exalted both by its own merits and by fortune and which has been favored by God and the church, of which it is now ruler. . . .

This opportunity, therefore, should not be allowed to pass, and Italy, after such a long wait, must be allowed to behold her redeemer. I cannot describe the joy with which he will be received in all these provinces which have suffered so much from the foreign deluge, nor with

what thirst for vengeance, nor with what firm devotion, what solemn delight, what tears! What gates could be closed to him, what people could deny him obedience, what envy could withstand him, what Italian could withhold allegiance from him? THIS BARBARIAN OCCUPATION STINKS IN THE NOSTRILS OF ALL OF US. Let your illustrious house then take up this cause with the spirit and the hope with which one undertakes a truly just enterprise. . . .

Source: Niccolò Machiavelli, *The Prince,* trans. and ed. Thomas G. Bergin (Arlington Heights, IL: 1947), pp. 75–76, 78.

Questions for Analysis

1. Why does Machiavelli argue that Italy needed the type of ruler he described in *The Prince*?

2. According to Machiavelli, what was wrong with the Italy of his own day? What does "patriotism" mean for him?

3. How does Machiavelli use historical precedents and parallels to make his argument?

This influx of new texts spurred a new interest in textual criticism. A pioneer in this activity was Lorenzo Valla (1407–1457). Born in Rome and active primarily as a secretary to the king of Naples and Sicily, Valla had no allegiance to the republican ideals of the Florentine humanists. Instead, he turned his skills to the painstaking analysis of Greek and Latin texts in order to show how the thorough study of language could discredit old assumptions about these texts' meanings, and even unmask some texts as forgeries. For example, papal propagandists argued that the papacy's claim to secular power in Europe derived from rights granted to the bishop of Rome by the emperor Constantine in the fourth century, enshrined in the so-called Donation of Constantine. By analyzing the language

The Blending of Classical and Christian

he paintings known today as *The Birth of Venus* (image A) and *The Madonna of the Pomegranate* (image B) were both executed by Sandro Botticelli in Florence in the years 1485–87. Separately and together, they exhibit the artist's signature devotion to blending classical and Christian motifs. For example, Neoplatonic philosophers like Ficino taught that all pagan myths prefigure Christian truths—including the story that Aphrodite, goddess of love, was miraculously engendered from the foam of the sea by the god of Time. This helps to explain the visual reference to a pomegranate in the painting of the Virgin

A. *The Birth of Venus.*

of this spurious document, Valla proved that it could not have been written in the time of Constantine because it contained more recent Latin usages and vocabulary. He concluded that it had in fact been the work of a papal supporter active many centuries after Constantine's death. This demonstration not only discredited the more traditional methods of scholasticism, it introduced the concept of anachronism into all subsequent textual study and historical thought. Indeed, Valla also applied his expert knowledge of Greek to elucidating the meaning of Saint Paul's

holding the infant Jesus. In Greek mythology, the pomegranate was the fruit whose seeds were eaten by Persephone, daughter of the goddess of fertility, when she was sent to the Underworld to become the bride of Hades. Because she had eaten six of these seeds, Persephone was allowed to return to her mother Demeter for only part of the year; in the winter months, consequently, the Earth becomes less fertile, because Demeter is in mourning for her child.

Questions for Analysis

1. Some scholars have argued that *The Birth of Venus* can be read as an allegory of Christian love that also prefigures the Blessed Virgin's immaculate conception and sinless nature. How would you go about proving this? What elements in this painting and in the myth of Aphrodite's birth lend themselves to that interpretation?

2. In what ways can the cyclical story of Jesus's death and resurrection, which Christians celebrate each year, be linked to the Greek myth invoked by *The Madonna of the Pomegranate*?

3. Like many artists, Botticelli used the same models for an array of different pictures. Do you recognize the resemblance between the Virgin and Venus? How does the depiction of the same young woman in these two different contexts underscore the relationship between pagan mythology and Christian sacred history?

B. *The Madonna of the Pomegranate.*

letters, which he believed had been obscured by Jerome's Latin translation (Chapter 6). This work was to prove an important link between Italian Renaissance scholarship and the subsequent Christian humanism of the north, which in turn fed into the Reformation (see Chapter 13).

Renaissance Neoplatonism

In the wake of these discoveries, Italian thought became dominated by a new interest in the philosophy of Plato (Chapter 4) and the Neoplatonism of Plotinus (Chapter 6). So many

intellectuals were engaged in the study of Plato that scholars used to believe that there was even a "Platonic Academy" in Florence; but in reality, the work of intellectuals like Marsilio Ficino (1433–1499) and Giovanni Pico della Mirandola (1463–1494) was informally fostered by the patronage of the wealthy Cosimo de' Medici.

From the standpoint of posterity, Ficino's greatest achievement was his translation of Plato's works into Latin, which made them widely available to Europeans. Ficino's Platonic philosophy moved away from the ethics of civic humanism. He taught that the individual should look primarily to the salvation of the immortal soul from its "always miserable" mortal body: a very Platonic idea. His disciple

Pico likewise rejected the mundanity of public affairs, arguing that man has the capacity to achieve union with God through the exercise of his unique individual talents, a glory that can be attained in life as well as in death.

The Influence of Machiavelli

The greatness of these humanist scholars lay not in their originality but in their efforts to popularize aspects of ancient thought. And none of them was so influential in this regard as the era's greatest philosophical pragmatist, the Florentine Niccolò Machiavelli (1469–1527). Machiavelli's political writings both reflect the unstable condition of Italy and strive to address it. By the end of the fifteenth century, Italy had become the arena of bloody international struggles. Both France and Spain had invaded the peninsula and were competing for the allegiance of the Italian city-states, which in turn were torn by internal dissension.

In 1498, Machiavelli became a prominent official in the government of the new Florentine Republic, set up four years earlier when the French invasion had led to the expulsion of the Medici. His duties largely involved diplomatic missions to other Italian city-states. While in Rome, he became fascinated with the attempt of Cesare Borgia, son of Pope Alexander VI, to create his own principality in central Italy. He noted with approval Cesare's ruthlessness and his complete subordination of personal ethics to political ends. In 1512, when the Medici returned to overthrow the fledgling republic of Florence, Machiavelli was stripped of his position. Disappointed and embittered, he retired to the country and devoted his energies to the articulation of a new political philosophy that he hoped would earn him a powerful job.

On the surface, Machiavelli's two great works of political analysis appear to contradict each other. In his *Discourses on Livy*, which drew on the works of that Roman historian, he praised the ancient Roman Republic as a model for his own contemporaries, lauding constitutional government, equality among citizens,

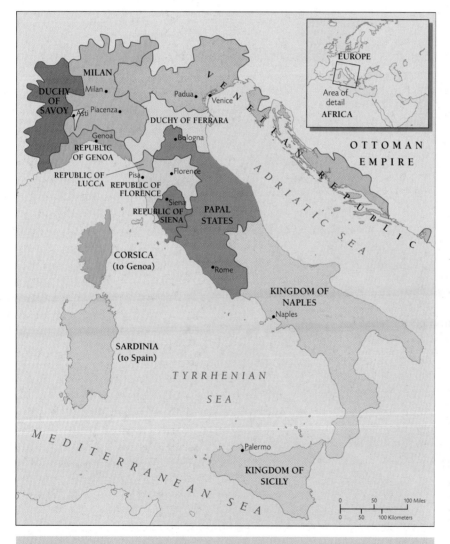

THE STATES OF ITALY, c. 1494. This map shows the divisions of Italy on the eve of the French invasion in 1494. Contemporary observers often described Italy as being divided among five great powers: Milan, Venice, Florence, the Papal States, and the Kingdom of the Two Sicilies (based in Naples). ▪ *Which of these powers would have been most capable of expanding their territories?* ▪ *Which neighboring states would have been most threatened by such attempts at expansion?* ▪ *Why would Florence and the Papal States so often find themselves in conflict with each other?*

and the subordination of religion to the service of the state. There is little doubt, in fact, that Machiavelli was a committed believer in the free city-state as the ideal form of human government. But Machiavelli also wrote *The Prince*, "a handbook for tyrants" in the eyes of his critics, and he dedicated this work to Lorenzo, son of Piero de' Medici, whose family had overthrown the Florentine republic that Machiavelli himself had served.

Because *The Prince* has been so much more widely read than the *Discourses*, interpretations of Machiavelli's political thought have often mistaken the former as an endorsement of power for its own sake. Machiavelli's real position was quite different. In the political chaos of early-sixteenth-century Italy, Machiavelli saw the likes of Cesare Borgia as the only hope for revitalizing the spirit of independence among his contemporaries, and so making Italy fit, eventually, for self-governance. However dark his vision of human nature, Machiavelli never ceased to hope that his Italian contemporaries would rise up, expel their French and Spanish conquerors, and restore ancient traditions of liberty and equality. He regarded a period of despotism as a necessary step toward that end, not as a permanent and desirable form of government.

Machiavelli remains a controversial figure. Some modern scholars, like many of his own contemporary readers, see him as disdainful of conventional morality, interested solely in the acquisition and exercise of power as an end in itself. Others see him as an Italian patriot, who viewed princely tyranny as the only way to liberate Italy from its foreign conquerors. Still others see him as influenced by Saint Augustine, who understood that in a fallen world populated by sinful people, a ruler's good intentions do not guarantee that his policies will have good results. Accordingly, Machiavelli insisted that a prince's actions must be judged by their consequences and not by their intrinsic moral quality. He argued that "the necessity of preserving the state will often compel a prince to take actions which are opposed to loyalty, charity, humanity, and religion. . . . So far as he is able, a prince should stick to the path of good. But, if the necessity arises, he should know how to follow evil."

The Ideal of the Courtier

Far more congenial to contemporary tastes than the shockingly frank political theories of Machiavelli were the guidelines for proper aristocratic conduct offered in *The Book of the Courtier* (1528), by the diplomat and nobleman Baldassare Castiglione. This forerunner of modern handbooks of etiquette stands in sharp contrast to earlier treatises on civic humanism. Whereas Bruni and Alberti taught the sober virtues of strenuous service on behalf of the city-state, Castiglione taught how to attain the elegant and seemingly effortless skills necessary for advancement in Italy's princely courts. More than anyone else, Castiglione developed and popularized a set of talents now associated with the "Renaissance man": one accomplished in many different pursuits, witty, canny, and stylish. Castiglione also eschewed the misogyny of the humanists by stressing the ways in which court ladies could rise to influence and prominence through the graceful exercise of their womanly powers. Widely read throughout Europe, Castiglione's *Courtier* set the standard for polite behavior into the nineteenth century.

RENAISSANCE ARTS

Without question, the most enduring legacy of the Italian Renaissance has been the contributions of its artists, particularly those who embraced new techniques and approaches to painting. We have already noted (Chapter 10) the creative and economic opportunities afforded by this medium, which freed artists from having to work on site and on commission: paintings executed on wooden panels are portable—unlike wall paintings—and can be displayed in different settings, reach different markets, and be more widely distributed. To these benefits, the artists of Italy added an important technical ingredient: mastery of a vanishing (one-point) perspective that gave to painting an illusion of three-dimensional space. Fifteenth-century artists also experimented with effects of light and shade, and studied intently the anatomy and proportions of the human body.

Meanwhile, increasing private wealth and the growth of lay patronage opened up new markets and created a huge demand for a diverse array of visual narratives: not only religious images, which were as important as ever, but the depiction of classical subjects. Portraiture also came into its own, as princes and merchants alike sought to glorify themselves and their families. The use of oil paints, a medium that had been pioneered in Flanders, further revolutionized fifteenth-century painting styles. Because oil does not dry as quickly as water-based pigments, a painter can work more carefully, taking time with the more difficult parts of a picture and making corrections as he or she goes along.

Painting in Florence

In the fifteenth century, the majority of the great painters were Florentines. First among them was the precocious Masaccio (1401–1428) who, although he died at the age of twenty-seven, inspired the work of artists for the next

THE IMPACT OF PERSPECTIVE. Masaccio's painting *The Trinity with the Virgin* illustrates the startling sense of depth made possible by observing the rules of perspective.

century. Masaccio's greatness rested on his successful employment of one-point perspective and his use of dramatic lighting effects. Both are evident in his painting of the Trinity, where the body of the crucified Christ appears to be thrust forward by the impassive figure of God the Father, while the Virgin's gaze directly engages the viewer.

Masaccio's best-known successor was Sandro Botticelli (1445–1510), who was equally drawn to classical and Christian subjects. Botticelli excels in depicting graceful motion and the sensuous pleasures of nature. He is most famous today for paintings that evoke classical mythology without any overtly Christian frame of reference. For centuries, indeed, these were taken to be expressions of Renaissance "paganism," but many can be understood as Christian allegories (see *Interpreting Visual Evidence*).

The most technically adventurous and versatile artist of this period was Leonardo da Vinci (1452–1519). Leonardo personifies our ideal of the Renaissance man: he was a painter, architect, musician, mathematician, engineer, and inventor. The illegitimate son of a notary, Leonardo set up an artist's shop in Florence by the time he was twenty-five and gained the patronage of the Medici ruler, Lorenzo the Magnificent. But Leonardo had a weakness: he worked

slowly, and he had difficulty finishing anything. This naturally displeased Lorenzo and other Florentine patrons, who regarded artists as craftsmen who worked on commission, and on their patrons' time—not their own. Leonardo, however, strongly objected to this view; he considered himself to be an inspired, independent innovator. He therefore left Florence in 1482 and went to work for the court of the Sforza dictators in Milan, where he was given freer rein in structuring his time and work (see page 302). He remained there until the French invasion of 1499; he then wandered about, finally accepting the patronage of the French king, Francis I, under whose auspices he lived and worked until his death.

Leonardo's approach to painting was that it should be the most accurate possible imitation of nature. He based his work on his own detailed observations: a blade of grass, the wing of a bird, a waterfall. He obtained human corpses for dissection and reconstructed in drawing the minutest features of anatomy, carrying this knowledge over to his paintings. Indeed, Leonardo was convinced of the essential divinity in all living things. It is not surprising, therefore, that he was a vegetarian and that he went to the marketplace to buy caged birds, which he released to their native habitat. *The Virgin of the Rocks* typifies not only his marvelous technical skill but also his passion for science and his belief in the universe as a well-ordered place. The figures are arranged geometrically, with every stone and plant depicted in accurate detail.

Leonardo's *The Last Supper*, painted on the refectory walls of a monastery in Milan (and now in an advanced state of decay) is a study of human psychology. A serene Christ,

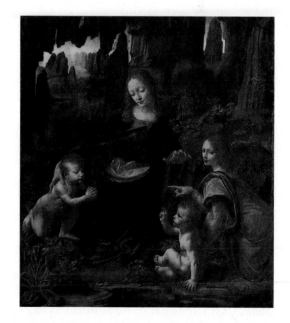

THE VIRGIN OF THE ROCKS. This painting reveals Leonardo's interest in the variety of human faces and facial expressions, and in natural settings.

resigned to his terrible fate, has just announced to his disciples that one of them will betray him. The artist succeeds in portraying the mingled emotions of surprise, horror, and guilt on the faces of the disciples as they gradually perceive the meaning of their master's statement. He also implicated the painting's original viewers in this dramatic scene, since they too dined alongside Christ, in the very same room.

The Venetian and Roman Schools

The innovations of Florentine artists were widely imitated. By the end of the fifteenth century, they had influenced a group of painters active in the wealthy city of Venice, among them Tiziano Vecelli, better known as Titian (c. 1490–1576). Many of Titian's paintings evoke the luxurious, pleasure-loving life of this thriving commercial center. For although they copied Florentine techniques, most Venetian painters showed little of that city's concerns for philosophical issues and religious allegory. Their aim was to appeal to the senses by painting idyllic landscapes and sumptuous portraits of the rich and powerful. In this subordination of form and meaning to color and elegance they may have mirrored the tastes of the men for whom they worked.

Rome, too, became a major artistic center in this era, and a place where the Florentine school exerted a more potent influence. Among its eminent painters was Raffaello Sanzio (1483–1520) or Raphael, a native of Urbino. Although Raphael was influenced by Leonardo, he cultivated a more spiritual and philosophical approach to his subjects, suggestive of Botticelli. As we noted in Chapter 4, his fresco *The School of Athens* depicts both the harmony and the differences of Platonic and Aristotelian thought (see page 86). It also includes a number of Raphael's contemporaries as models. The image of Plato is actually a portrait of Leonardo, while the architect Donato Bramante (c. 1444–1514) stands in for the geometer Euclid, and Michelangelo for the philosopher Heraclitus.

Michelangelo Buonarroti (1475–1564), who spent many decades in Rome, was actually a native of Florence. If Leonardo was a naturalist, Michelangelo was an idealist, despite the harsh political and material realities of the conditions in which he worked. He was also a polymath: painter, sculptor, architect, poet—and he expressed himself in all these forms with a similar power.

Michelangelo's greatest achievements in painting appear in a single location, the Sistine Chapel of the Vatican palace, yet they are products of two different periods in the artist's life and consequently exemplify two different artistic styles and outlooks on the human condition. More famous are the extraordinary frescoes painted on the ceiling from 1508 to 1512, depicting scenes from the book of Genesis. All the panels in this series, including *The Creation of Adam*, exemplify the young artist's commitment to classical artistic principles. Correspondingly, all affirm the sublimity of the Creation and the heroic qualities of humankind. But a quarter of a century later, when Michelangelo returned to work in the Sistine Chapel, both his style and mood had changed dramatically. In the enormous *Last Judgment*, a fresco done for the Chapel's altar wall in 1536, Michelangelo repudiated classical restraint and substituted a style that communicated the older man's pessimistic conception of humanity. He included himself in it: but unlike Raphael's, his self-portrait is a doomed soul whose flayed skin is all that remains of worldly ambition.

Renaissance Sculpture

Sculpture was not a new medium for artists, the way that oil painting was, but it too was an important area of Renaissance innovation. Statues were not only incorporated into columns or doorways or as effigies on tombs; for the first

THE LAST SUPPER. This fresco on the refectory wall of the monastery of Santa Maria delle Grazie in Milan is a testament to both the powers and limitations of Leonardo's artistry. It skillfully employs the techniques of one-point perspective to create the illusion that Jesus and his disciples are actually dining at the monastery's head table; but because Leonardo had not mastered the techniques of fresco painting, he applied tempera pigments to a dry wall which had been coated with a sealing agent. As a result, the painting's colors began to fade just years after its completion. By the middle of the sixteenth century, it had seriously deteriorated. Large portions of it are now invisible.

that of Michelangelo—whose *David*, executed in 1501, was a public expression of Florentine ideals, not merely graceful but heroic. Michelangelo regarded sculpture as the most exalted of the arts because it allowed the artist to imitate God most fully in recreating human forms. Furthermore, in Michelangelo's view, the most divinely inspired sculptor disdained slavish naturalism: anyone can make a plaster cast of a human figure, but only an inspired creative genius can endow his sculpted figures with a sense of life. Accordingly, Michelangelo's sculpture subordinated reality to the force of his imagination and sought to express his ideals in ever more astonishing forms. He also insisted on working in marble (the "noblest" sculptural material) and created a figure twice as large as life. By sculpting a serenely confident young man at the peak of physical fitness, Michelangelo celebrated the Florentine republic's own efforts to resist tyrants and uphold ideals of civic justice.

Yet the serenity seen in *David* is no longer prominent in the works of Michelangelo's later life, when (as in his painting) he began to explore the use of anatomical distortion to create effects of emotional intensity. While his statues remained awesome in scale, they also communicate rage, depression, and sorrow. The culmination of this trend is his unfinished but intensely moving *Descent from the Cross*, a depiction of an old man (the sculptor himself) grieving over the distorted, slumping body of the dead Christ.

Renaissance Architecture

time since late antiquity they became figures "in the round." By freeing sculpture from its reliance on architecture, the Renaissance reestablished it as a separate, secular art form.

The first great master of Renaissance sculpture was Donatello (c. 1386–1466). His bronze statue of David, triumphant over the head of the slain Goliath, is the first free-standing nude of the period. Yet this David is clearly an agile adolescent rather than a muscular Greek athlete like

To a much greater extent than either sculpture or painting, Renaissance architecture had its roots in the past. The Gothic style pioneered in northern France (Chapter 9) had seldom found a friendly reception in Italy; most of the buildings constructed there during the Middle Ages were Romanesque in style, and the great architects of the Renaissance generally adopted their building plans from these structures—some of which they believed (mistakenly)

THE POWER AND VULNERABILITY OF THE MALE BODY. Donatello's *David* (left) was the first free-standing nude executed since antiquity. It shows the Hebrew leader as an adolescent youth, and is a little over 5 feet tall. The *David* by Michelangelo (center) stands thirteen feet high, and was placed prominently in front of Florence's city hall to proclaim the city's power and humanistic values. Michelangelo's *Descent from the Cross* (right), which shows Christ's broken body in the arms of the elderly Nicodemus, was made by the sculptor for his own tomb. (The gospels describe Nicodemus as a Pharisee who became a follower of Jesus and who was present at his death.) ▪ *Why would Michelangelo choose this figure to represent himself?* ▪ *How does his representation of David—and the context in which this figure was displayed—compare to that of Donatello?*

to be ancient rather than medieval. They also copied decorative devices from the authentic ruins of ancient Rome.

Renaissance buildings emphasize geometrical proportion. Italian architects of this era, under the influence of Neoplatonism, concluded that certain mathematical ratios reflect the harmony of the universe. For example, the proportions of the human body serve as the basis for the proportions of the quintessential Renaissance building: St. Peter's Basilica in Rome. Designed by some of the most celebrated architects of the time, including Bramante and Michelangelo, it is still one of the largest buildings in the world. Yet it seems smaller than a Gothic cathedral because it is built to human scale. The same artful proportions are evident in smaller-scale buildings, too, as in the aristocratic country houses designed by the northern Italian architect Andrea Palladio (1508–1580), who created secular

miniatures of ancient temples (such as the Roman Pantheon) to glorify the aristocrats who dwelled within them.

The Waning of the Renaissance in Italy

The intensive intellectual and artistic activity that characterizes the Renaissance began to wane toward the end of the fifteenth century. The causes of this decline are varied. The French invasion of 1494 and the incessant warfare that ensued were among the major factors. A second invasion created uninterrupted warfare from 1499 until 1529. Alliances and counteralliances followed each other in bewildering succession, but they managed only to prolong the hostilities. The worst blow came in 1527, when rampaging troops sacked the city of Rome, causing enormous destruction. Only in 1529

Analyzing Primary Sources

Leonardo da Vinci Applies for a Job

Few sources illuminate the tensions between Renaissance ideals and realities better than the résumé of accomplishments submitted by Leonardo da Vinci to a prospective employer, Ludovico Sforza of Milan. In the following letter, Leonardo explains why he deserves to be appointed chief architect and military engineer in the duke's household administration. He got the job, and moved to Milan in 1481.

1. I have the kind of bridges that are extremely light and strong, made to be carried with great ease, and with them you may pursue, and, at any time, flee from the enemy; . . . and also methods of burning and destroying those of the enemy.

2. I know how, when a place is under attack, to eliminate the water from the trenches, and make endless variety of bridges . . . and other machines. . . .

3. . . . I have methods for destroying every rock or other fortress, even if it were built on rock, etc.

4. I also have other kinds of mortars [bombs] that are most convenient and easy to carry. . . .

5. And if it should be a sea battle, I have many kinds of machines that are most efficient for offense and defense. . . .

6. I also have means that are noiseless to reach a designated area by secret and tortuous mines. . . .

7. I will make covered chariots, safe and unattackable, which can penetrate the enemy with their artillery. . . .

8. In case of need I will make big guns, mortars, and light ordnance of fine and useful forms that are out of the ordinary.

9. If the operation of bombardment should fail, I would contrive catapults, mangonels, trabocchi [trebuchets], and other machines of marvelous efficacy and unusualness. In short, I can, according to each case in question, contrive various and endless means of offense and defense.

10. In time of peace I believe I can give perfect satisfaction that is equal to any other in the field of architecture and the construction of buildings. . . . I can execute sculpture in marble, bronze, or clay, and also in painting I do the best that can be done, and as well as any other, whoever he may be.

Having now, most illustrious Lord, sufficiently seen the specimens of all those who consider themselves master craftsmen of instruments of war, and that the invention and operation of such instruments are no different from those in common use, I shall now endeavor . . . to explain myself to your Excellency by revealing to your Lordship my secrets. . . .

Source: Excerpted from Leonardo da Vinci, *The Notebooks*, in *The Italian Renaissance Reader*, eds. Julia Conaway and Mark Mosa (Harmondsworth: 1987), pp. 195–96.

Questions for Analysis

1. Based on the qualifications highlighted by Leonardo in this letter, what can you conclude about the political situation in Milan and the priorities of its duke? What can you conclude about the state of military technologies in this period and the conduct of warfare?

2. What do you make of the fact that Leonardo mentions his artistic endeavors only at the end of the letter? Does this fact alter your opinion or impression of him? Why or why not?

did the papacy's champion, Emperor Charles V, manage to gain control over most of the Italian peninsula, putting an end to the fighting for a time (see Chapter 15).

To these political disasters was added a waning of Italian prosperity. A virtual monopoly of trade with Asia in the fifteenth century had been one of the chief economic underpinnings for Renaissance patronage, but the gradual shifting of trade routes from the Mediterranean to the Atlantic region (Chapter 11), slowly eroded Italy's supremacy as the center of European trade. Warfare also contributed to Italy's economic hardships. As Italian wealth diminished, there was less and less of a surplus to support artistic endeavors. But by this time, Renaissance ideas and techniques were spreading from Italy to the rest of Europe;

ST. PETER'S BASILICA, ROME. This eighteenth-century painting shows the massive interior of the Renaissance building. But were it not for the perspective provided by the tiny human figures, the human eye would be fooled into thinking this a much smaller space.

so even as Italy's political and economic power waned, its cultural and intellectual cachet lent it more prominence than it had enjoyed for centuries.

THE RENAISSANCE NORTH OF THE ALPS

Contacts between Italy and northern Europe ensured that primacy: Italian merchants and financiers were familiar figures at northern courts; students from all over Europe studied at Italian universities such as Bologna or Padua; poets (including Geoffrey Chaucer, Chapter 10) and their works traveled to and from Italy; and northern soldiers were frequent participants in Italian wars. Only at the end of the fifteenth century, however, were the new currents of Italian Renaissance learning exported to Spain and northern Europe.

A variety of explanations have been offered for this delay. Northern European intellectual life in the later Middle Ages was dominated by universities such as Paris, Oxford, and Charles University in Prague, whose curricula focused on the study of philosophical logic and Christian theology. This approach left little room for the study of classical literature. In Italy, by contrast, universities were more often professional schools for law and medicine, and universities themselves exercised much less influence over intellectual life. As a result, a more secular, urban-oriented educational tradition took shape in Italy, within which

Renaissance humanism was able to develop. Even in the sixteenth century, northern scholars influenced by Italian Renaissance ideals usually worked outside the university system, under the patronage of kings and princes.

Before the sixteenth century, northern rulers were less interested in patronizing artists and intellectuals than were the city-states and princes of Italy. In Italy, as we have seen, such patronage was an important arena for competition among political rivals. In northern Europe, however, political units were larger and political rivals were fewer. It was therefore less necessary to use art for political purposes in a kingdom than it was in a city-state. In Florence, a statue erected in a central square would be seen by nearly all the city's residents. In Paris, such a statue would be seen by only a tiny minority of the French king's subjects. But in the sixteenth century, as northern nobles began to spend more time in residence at the royal court, kings could be reasonably certain that their patronage of artists and intellectuals would be noticed by those whom they were trying to impress.

Christian Humanism and the Career of Erasmus

The northern Renaissance was the product of the grafting of certain Italian Renaissance ideals onto preexisting northern traditions. This can be seen very clearly in the case of the most prominent northern Renaissance intellectual movement: Christian humanism. Although they shared the Italian humanists' rejection of scholasticism, northern Christian humanists more often sought ethical guidance from biblical and religious precepts than from Cicero or Virgil. Like their Italian counterparts, then, they sought wisdom from antiquity; but the antiquity they had in mind was Christian rather than classical—the antiquity, that is, of the New Testament and the early Church. Similarly, northern Renaissance artists were inspired by the accomplishments of Italian masters to learn classical techniques. But northern artists depicted classical subject matter far less frequently than did Italians, and almost never portrayed completely nude human figures.

Any discussion of the northern Renaissance must begin with the career of Desiderius Erasmus (c. 1469–1536). The illegitimate son of a priest, Erasmus was born near Rotterdam in the Netherlands. Forced into a monastery against his will when he was a teenager, the young Erasmus found little formal instruction there but plenty of freedom to read what he liked. He devoured all the classics he could get his hands on and the writings of the Church Fathers (Chapter 6). When he was about thirty years old, he obtained permission to leave the monastery and enroll in the University of Paris, where he completed the requirements for the degree of bachelor of divinity.

But Erasmus subsequently rebelled against what he considered the arid learning of Parisian scholasticism. Nor did he ever serve actively as a priest. Instead, he made his living from teaching, writing, and the proceeds of various ecclesiastical offices that required no pastoral duties. Ever on the lookout for new patrons, he traveled often to England, stayed once for three years in Italy, and resided in several different cities in Germany and the Netherlands before settling finally, toward the end of his life, in Basel (Switzerland). By means of a voluminous correspondence that he kept up with learned friends, Erasmus became the leader of a humanist circle. And through the popularity of his numerous publications, he became the arbiter of northern European cultural tastes during his lifetime.

Erasmus's urbane Latin style and humor earned him a wide audience on those grounds alone, yet he intended everything he wrote to promote what he called the "philosophy of Christ." Erasmus believed that the society of his day was caught up in corruption and immorality because people had lost sight of the simple teachings of the Gospels. Accordingly, he offered his contemporaries three different kinds of publication: clever satires meant to show people the error of their ways, serious moral treatises meant to offer guidance toward proper Christian behavior, and scholarly editions of basic Christian texts.

In the first category belong the works of Erasmus that are still widely read today: *The Praise of Folly* (1509), in which he ridiculed hypocrisy and dogmatism as well as ignorance and gullibility; and the *Colloquies* (from the Latin for "discussions," 1518), in which he held up contemporary religious practices for examination in a more serious but still pervasively ironic tone. In such works, Erasmus let fictional characters do the talking; hence his own views can be determined only by inference from their points of view. But in his second mode, Erasmus did not hesitate to speak clearly in his own voice. The most prominent treatises in this genre are the quietly eloquent *Handbook of the Christian Knight* (1503), which urged the laity to pursue lives of serene inward piety, and the *Complaint of Peace* (1517), which pleaded movingly for Christian pacifism. Erasmus's pacifism was one of his most deeply held values, and he returned to it again and again in his published works.

Despite the success of these varied writings, Erasmus considered textual scholarship his greatest achievement. Revering the authority of Augustine, Jerome, and Ambrose, he brought out reliable editions of all their works. He also used his extraordinary command of Latin and Greek to produce a more accurate edition of the New Testament. After reading Lorenzo Valla's *Notes on the New Testament* in 1504, Erasmus became convinced that nothing was more imperative than divesting these biblical books of the myriad errors in transcription and translation that had piled up in the course of preceding centuries—for no one could be a good Christian without being certain of what Christ's message really was. Hence he spent ten years studying and comparing all the early Greek biblical manuscripts he could find, in order to establish an authoritative text. Erasmus's Greek New Testament, published in 1516 with explanatory notes and his own new Latin translation, became one of the most important scholarly landmarks of all time. In the hands of Martin Luther, it would play a critical role in the early stages of the Reformation (see Chapter 13).

ERASMUS **BY HANS HOLBEIN THE YOUNGER.** This is generally regarded as the most evocative portrait of the preeminent Christian humanist.

The Influence of Erasmus

One of Erasmus's closest friends, and a close second to him in distinction among Christian humanists, was the Englishman Sir Thomas More (1478–1535). Following a

SIR THOMAS MORE BY HANS HOLBEIN THE YOUNGER. Holbein's skill in rendering the gravity and interiority of his subject is matched by his masterful representation of the sumptuous chain of office, furred mantle, and velvet sleeves that indicate the political and professional status of Henry VIII's chancellor.

it is useful," war and monasticism do not exist, and toleration is granted to all who recognize the existence of God and the immortality of the soul. Although More advanced no explicit arguments in favor of Christianity, he probably meant to imply that if the Utopians could manage their society so well without the benefit of Christian revelation, Europeans who knew the Gospels ought to be able to do even better.

Erasmus and More head a long list of energetic and eloquent Christian humanists who made signal contributions to the collective enterprise of revolutionizing the study of early Christianity, and their achievements had a direct influence on Martin Luther and other Protestant reformers. Yet very few of them were willing to join Luther in rejecting the fundamental principles on which the power of the Church was based. Most tried to remain within its fold while still espousing an ideal of inward piety and scholarly inquiry. But as the leaders of the Church grew less and less tolerant of dissent, even mild criticism came to seem like heresy. Erasmus himself died

successful career as a lawyer and as speaker of the House of Commons, More was appointed lord chancellor of England in 1529. He was not long in this position, however, before he opposed the king's design to establish a national church under royal control, thus denying the supremacy of the pope (see Chapter 13). In 1534, when More refused to take an oath acknowledging Henry as head of the Church of England, he was imprisoned in the Tower of London and executed a year later. He is now revered as a Catholic martyr.

Much earlier, however, in 1516, More published the work for which he is best remembered, *Utopia* ("No-place" in Greek). Purporting to describe an ideal community on an imaginary island, the book is really an Erasmian critique of the glaring abuses of the era—poverty undeserved and wealth unearned, drastic punishments, and the senseless slaughter of war. The inhabitants of Utopia hold all their goods in common, work only six hours a day so that all may have leisure for intellectual pursuits, and practice the natural virtues of wisdom, moderation, fortitude, and justice. Iron is the precious metal "because

SAINT JEROME IN HIS STUDY BY DÜRER. Jerome, the biblical translator of the fourth century (Chapter 6), was a hero to both Dürer and Erasmus: the paragon of inspired Christian scholarship. Note how the scene exudes contentment, even down to the sleeping lion, which seems more like an overgrown tabby cat than a symbol of Christ.

The Renaissance North of the Alps | 305

early enough to escape persecution, but several of his less fortunate followers lived on to suffer as victims of the Inquisition.

The Literature of the Northern Renaissance

Although Christian humanism would be severely challenged by the Reformation, the northern artistic Renaissance continued throughout the sixteenth century. Poets in France and England vied with one another to adapt the elegant lyric forms pioneered by Petrarch, particularly the sonnet. Meanwhile, the more satirical side of Renaissance humanism was embraced by the French writer François Rabelais (*RA-beh-lay*, c. 1494–1553). Like Erasmus, whom he greatly admired, Rabelais began his career in the Church, but soon left the cloister to study medicine. A practicing physician, Rabelais interspersed his professional activities with literary endeavors, the most enduring of which is *Gargantua and Pantagruel*, fictional chronicles of the lives and times of giants whose gross appetites serve as vehicles for much lusty humor. Like Erasmus, Rabelais satirized religious ceremonialism, scholasticism, superstition, and bigotry. But unlike Erasmus, who wrote in a highly cultivated Latin style comprehensible only to learned readers, Rabelais chose to address a far wider audience by writing in extremely crude French, and by glorifying every human impulse as natural and healthy.

Northern Architecture and Art

Although many architects in northern Europe continued to build in the flamboyant Gothic style of the later Middle Ages, the classical values of Italian architects can be seen in some of the splendid new castles constructed in France's Loire valley—châteaux too elegant to be defensible—and in the royal palace (now museum) of the Louvre in Paris, which replaced an old twelfth-century fortress. The influence of Renaissance ideals is also visible in the work of the foremost artist of this era, the German Albrecht Dürer (1471–1528). Dürer (*DIRR-er*) who mastered the techniques of proportion and perspective, and who also shared with contemporary Italians a fascination with nature and the human body. But Dürer never really embraced classical allegory, drawing inspiration instead from Christian legends and the Christian humanism of Erasmus. Thus Dürer's serenely radiant engraving of Saint Jerome expresses the scholarly absorption that Erasmus may have enjoyed while working quietly in his study.

Indeed, Dürer aspired to immortalize Erasmus himself in a major portrait, but circumstances prevented him from doing this because the paths of the two men crossed only once. Instead, the accomplishment of capturing Erasmus's spirit in oils was left to another great northern artist, the German Hans Holbein the Younger (1497–1543, see page 304). During a stay in England, Holbein also painted an acute portrait of Erasmus's kindred spirit Sir Thomas More, whom a contemporary called "a man of . . . sad gravity; a

After You Read This Chapter

REVIEWING THE OBJECTIVES

- The Renaissance was an intellectual and cultural movement that coincided with the later Middle Ages but fostered a new outlook on the world. Explain the ways in which this outlook differed from its medieval counterpart.
- The Renaissance began in Italy. Why?
- What was the relationship between Renaissance ideals and Italy's political realities?
- What were the principal features of Renaissance art?
- How were Renaissance ideas adapted in northern Europe?

man for all seasons" (see page 305). These two portraits in and of themselves point to a major difference between medieval and Renaissance culture. Whereas the Middle Ages produced no convincing naturalistic likenesses of any leading intellectual figures, Renaissance culture's glorification of human individuality created the environment in which Holbein was able to make Erasmus and More come to life.

CONCLUSION

The ideals of the Renaissance stand in sharp contrast to the harsh realities alongside which they coexisted, and in which they were rooted. They arose from the devastating events of the fourteenth century, which had a particularly drastic effect on Italy. Ravaged by the Black Death, abandoned by the papacy, reduced to the status of pawn in other powers' rivalries, Italy was exposed as a mere shadow of what it had been under the Roman Empire. It was therefore to the precedents and glories of the past that Italian intellectuals, artists, and statesmen looked for inspirations.

But to which aspects of the past? Some humanists may have wanted to revive the principles of the Roman Republic, but many of them worked for ambitious despots who modeled themselves on Rome's dictators or on the tyrants of ancient Greece. Artists could thrive in the atmosphere of competition and one-upmanship that characterized Italy's warring principalities and city-states, but they could also find themselves reduced to the status of servants in the households of the wealthy and powerful—or forced to subordinate their artistry to the demands of warfare and espionage. Access to a widening array of classical texts, in Greek as well as Latin, broadened the horizons of Renaissance readers; yet women were largely barred from the humanist education that led men to boast of their proximity to God. New critical tools enabled the study of classical texts, but the insistence on a return to the "pure" language of the Roman Empire eventually succeeded in bringing about the death of Latin as a living medium of communication.

Although the Renaissance began in northern Italy, where it filled a cultural and political vacuum, it did not remain confined there. By the end of the fifteenth century, humanist approaches to education and textual criticism had begun to influence intellectual endeavors all over Europe. The techniques of Renaissance artists melded with the artistry of the later Middle Ages in striking ways, while opportunities for patronage expanded along with the demand for artworks and the prestige they lent to their owners. Eventually, the theories that undergirded Renaissance politics—civic and princely—were being used to legitimize many different kinds of power, including that of the papacy. All of these trends would be carried forward into the sixteenth century, and would have a role to play in the upheaval that shattered Europe's fragile religious unity and tenuous balance of power. It is to this upheaval, the Reformation, that we turn in Chapter 13.

PEOPLE, IDEAS, AND EVENTS IN CONTEXT

- Why was the ancient past so important to the intellectuals and artists of the **RENAISSANCE**? What was **HUMANISM**, and how did it influence education during this era?
- What were the political and economic underpinnings of the Renaissance? How do the **MEDICI** of Florence and the papacy exemplify new trends in patronage?
- What were some major scholarly achievements of the Renaissance? How did **LORENZO VALLA** and **NICCOLÒ MACHIAVELLI** advance new intellectual and political ideas?
- How do the works of **BOTTICELLI**, **LEONARDO**, **RAPHAEL**, and **MICHELANGELO** capture Renaissance ideals? Which is the most paradigmatic Renaissance artist, in your opinion, and why?
- How did Christian humanists like **DESIDERIUS ERASMUS** and **THOMAS MORE** apply Renaissance ideas in new ways? How were these ideas expressed in art?

CONSEQUENCES

- The Renaissance is often described as being the antithesis of the Middle Ages, yet it was actually a simultaneous movement. Can you think of other eras when two or more divergent trends have coexisted?
- To what extent do the ideals of the Renaissance anticipate those we associate with modernity? To what extent are they more faithful to either the Christian or the classical past?
- Phrases like "Renaissance man" and "a Renaissance education" are still part of our common vocabulary. Given what you have learned in this chapter, how has your understanding of such phrases changed? How would you explain their true meaning to others?

STORY LINES

- The movement catalyzed by Martin Luther's challenge to the Church grew out of many earlier attempts at reform, but it was also a response to more recent religious and political developments.

- Within a decade after Luther's break with Rome, religious dissent was widespread and a number of different Protestant faiths were taking root in various regions of Europe.

- Protestantism not only transformed the political landscape of Europe, it changed the basic structures of the family and attitudes toward marriage and sexuality—in ways which still shape our lives today.

- These changes also affected the structures and doctrine of the Roman Catholic ("universal") Church, which reemerged as an institution different in many ways from the medieval Church.

Before You Read This Chapter

CHRONOLOGY

1517	Luther posts ninety-five theses
1520s	Lutheranism becomes the official religion of Scandinavian countries
1521	Luther is excommunicated at the Diet of Worms
1525	Swabian peasants' revolt
1529	Luther breaks with Zwingli
1534	Henry VIII establishes the Church of England
1534	Ignatius Loyola founds the Society of Jesus (the Jesuits)
1541	Geneva adopts a theocratic government based on Calvinism
1545–1563	Council of Trent is convened
1553–1558	Mary Tudor attempts to restore the Catholic faith in England
1559	Elizabeth reestablishes Protestantism in England
1564	Index of prohibited books is published for the first time

The Age of Dissent and Division, 1500–1600

n the year 1500, Europe's future seemed bright. After two centuries of economic, social, and political turmoil, its economy was expanding, its cities were growing, and the monarchs of many states were securely established on their thrones. The population was increasing, and governments at every level were extending and deepening their control over people's lives. Europeans had also embarked on a new period of colonial expansion. And although the papacy pursued its territorial wars in Italy, the Church itself had weathered the storms of the Avignon captivity and the Great Schism. Heresies had been suppressed or contained. In the struggle over conciliarism, the papacy had won the support of all major European rulers, which effectively relegated the conciliarists to academic isolation at the University of Paris. Meanwhile, at the local level, the devotion of ordinary Christians was strong and the parish was a crucial site of community identity. To be sure, there were some problems. The educational standards of parish clergy were higher than they had ever been, but reformers noted that too many priests were ignorant or neglectful of their spiritual duties. Monasticism, by and large, seemed to have lost

its spiritual fire. Religious enthusiasm sometimes led to superstition. Yet on the whole, the Church's problems were manageable.

No one could have predicted that Europe's religious and political coherence would be irreparably shattered in the course of a generation, or that the next century would witness an appallingly destructive series of wars. Nor could anyone have foreseen that the catalyst for these extraordinary events would be a university professor. For it was Martin Luther (1483–1546), a German monk and teacher of theology, who set off the chain reaction we know as the Reformation. Initially intended as a call for another phase in the Church's long history of internal reforms, Luther's teachings would instead launch a religious revolution that would splinter western Christendom into a variety of Protestant ("dissenting") faiths, while prompting the Church of Rome to re-affirm its status as the only true Catholic ("universal") faith, through a parallel revolution. These movements deepened existing divisions among peoples, rulers, and states, while opening up new divisions and points of contention. The result was a profound transformation of the religious, social, and political landscape that affected the lives of everyone in Europe—and everyone in the new European colonies, then and now.

MARTIN LUTHER'S CHALLENGE

To explain the impact of Martin Luther's ideas, we must answer three central questions:

1. Why did Luther's theology lead him to break with Rome?
2. Why did large numbers of people rally to his cause?
3. Why did so many German princes and towns impose the new religion within their territories?

As we shall see, those who followed Luther found his message appealing for different reasons. Many peasants hoped that the new religion would free them from the oppression of their lords; towns and princes thought it would allow them to consolidate their political independence; political leaders thought it would liberate Germany from the demands of foreign popes bent on feathering their own nest in central Italy.

Despite these differences, what Luther's followers shared was a conviction that their new understanding of Christianity would lead them to Heaven, whereas the traditional religion of Rome would not. For this reason, *reformation* is a misleading term for the movement they initiated. Although Luther himself began as a reformer seeking to change the Church

from within, he quickly developed into an uncompromising opponent of its principles and practices. Many of his followers were even more radical. The movement that began with Luther therefore went beyond "reformation." It was a definitive assault on institutions that had been in place for over a thousand years.

Luther's Quest for Justice

Although Martin Luther would become an inspiration to millions, he was a terrible disappointment to his father. The elder Luther was a Thuringian peasant who had prospered by leasing some mines. Eager to see his clever son rise further, he sent young Luther to the University of Erfurt to study law. In 1505, however, Martin shattered his father's hopes by becoming a monk of the Augustinian order. In some sense, though, Luther remained true to his roots: throughout his life, he lived simply and preferred to express himself in the vigorous, earthy vernacular of the German peasantry. He was, indeed, famous for his coarse (often obscene) language.

Luther arrived at his new understanding of religious truth by a dramatic conversion experience. As a monk, he zealously pursued all the traditional means for achieving his own salvation. Yet, try as he might, Luther could find no spiritual peace because he feared that he could never perform enough good deeds to deserve so great a gift as salvation. Then, in 1513, he hit upon an insight that changed the course of his life.

Luther's insight was a new understanding of God's justice. For years, he had worried that it seemed unfair for God to issue commandments that he knew human beings could not observe, and then to punish them with eternal

MARTIN LUTHER. This late portrait is by Lucas Cranach the Elder (1472–1553), court painter to the electors of Brandenburg and a friend of Luther.

damnation. But Luther's further study of the Bible revealed to him that God's justice has nothing to do with his power to punish, but rather with his mercy in saving sinful mortals through faith. As Luther later wrote, "At last, by the mercy of God, I began to understand the justice of God as that by which God makes *us* just, in his mercy and through faith . . . and at this I felt as though I had been born again, and had gone through open gates into paradise."

After that, everything seemed to fall into place. Lecturing at the University of Wittenberg in the years immediately following, Luther pondered a passage in Saint Paul's Letter to the Romans—"[T]he just shall live by faith" (1:17)—until he reached his central doctrine of "justification by faith alone." Luther concluded that God's justice does not demand endless good works and religious rituals for salvation, because humans can never be saved by their own efforts. Rather, humans are saved by God's grace alone, which God offers as an utterly undeserved gift. Men and women are therefore "justified" (i.e., made worthy of salvation) by faith alone. Those whom God has justified through faith will manifest that fact by performing works of piety and charity, but such works are not what saves them. Piety and charity are merely visible signs of each believer's invisible spiritual state, which is known to God alone.

The essence of this doctrine was not original to Luther. It had been central to the thought of Augustine (see Chapter 6), the patron saint of Luther's own monastic order. During the twelfth and thirteenth centuries, however, theologians such as Peter Lombard and Thomas Aquinas (Chapter 9) had developed a very different understanding of salvation. They emphasized the role that the Church itself (through its sacraments) and the individual believer (through acts of piety and charity) could play in the process of salvation. None of these theologians claimed that a human being could earn his or her way to Heaven by good works alone, but the late medieval Church unwittingly encouraged this misunderstanding by presenting the process of salvation in increasingly quantitative terms—declaring, for example, that by performing a specific action (such as a pilgrimage or a pious donation), a believer could reduce the penance she or he owed to God by a specific number of days.

By the late fifteenth century, popes began to proclaim that the dead could speed their way through Purgatory by means of indulgences: special remissions of penitential obligations. When indulgences were first conceived, in the eleventh and twelfth centuries, they could be earned only through difficult spiritual exercises, such as joining a crusade (see Chapter 8). By the end of the fifteenth century, however, indulgences were for sale.

To many, this looked like simony: the sin of exchanging God's grace for cash. It had been a practice loudly condemned by Wyclif and his followers (Chapter 10), and it was even more widely criticized by reformers like Erasmus (Chapter 12). But Luther's objections to indulgences had much more radical consequences, because they rested on a set of theological presuppositions that, taken to their logical conclusion, resulted in dismantling much of contemporary religious practice, not to mention the authority and sanctity of the Church. Surprisingly, Luther himself does not appear to have realized this at first.

LUTHER'S TRANSLATION OF THE BIBLE. The printing press was instrumental to the rapid dissemination of Luther's messages, as well as those of his supporters and challengers. Also essential was the fact that Luther addressed his audience in plain language, in their native German, and that pamphlets and vernacular Bibles like this one could be rapidly and cheaply mass-produced.

The Scandal of Indulgences

Luther developed his ideas as a university professor in the relative privacy of the classroom. But in 1517 he was provoked into attacking indulgences more publicly. The worldly

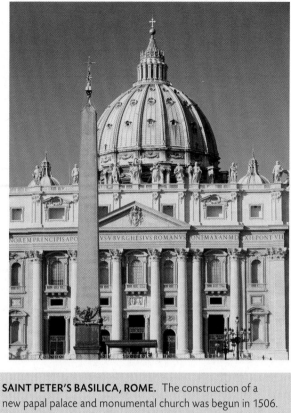

SAINT PETER'S BASILICA, ROME. The construction of a new papal palace and monumental church was begun in 1506. This enormous complex replaced a modest basilica built by Constantine on the site of the apostle Peter's tomb. ■ *How might this building project have been interpreted in different ways, depending on one's attitude toward the papacy?*

longer needed to confess their sins to a priest but could instead purchase grace with money. Tetzel was thus putting innocent souls at risk. So on the eve of the feast of All Souls (Halloween night) in 1517, Luther published a list of ninety-five theses that he was prepared to debate, all aimed at dismantling the doctrine of indulgences. According to tradition, he nailed this document to the door of the church—and whether or not he did so in fact, the metaphor is clear.

Luther wrote up these points for debate in Latin, not German, and meant them for academic discussion within the University of Wittenberg. But when some unknown person translated and published them, the hitherto obscure academic suddenly gained widespread notoriety. Tetzel and his allies now demanded that Luther withdraw his theses. Rather than backing down, however, Luther became even bolder in his attacks. In 1519, at a public disputation held before throngs in Leipzig, Luther defiantly maintained that the pope and all clerics were merely fallible men, and that the highest authority for an individual's conscience was the truth of Scripture. Pope Leo X responded by charging Luther with heresy; after that, Luther had no alternative but to break with the Church.

Luther's year of greatest activity came in 1520 when, in the midst of the crisis caused by his defiance, he composed a series of pamphlets setting forth his three primary premises: justification by faith, the authority of Scripture, and "the priesthood of all believers." We have already examined the meaning of the first premise. By the second, Luther meant that the reading of Scripture took precedence over Church traditions—including the teachings of all theologians—and that beliefs (such as Purgatory) or practices (such as prayers to the saints) not explicitly grounded in Scripture could be rejected as human inventions. Luther also declared that Christian believers were spiritually equal before God, which meant denying that priests, monks, and nuns had any special qualities by virtue of their vocations: hence "the priesthood of all believers."

From these premises a host of practical consequences followed. Because works could not lead to salvation, Luther declared fasts, pilgrimages, and the veneration of relics to be spiritually valueless. He also called for the dissolution of all monasteries and convents. He advocated a demystification of religious rites, proposing the substitution of German and other vernacular languages for Latin, and calling for a reduction in the number of sacraments from seven to two. In his view, the only true sacraments were baptism and the Eucharist, both of which had been instituted by Christ. (Initially, he included penance, too.) But although Luther continued to teach that Christ was physically and spiritually present in the consecrated bread and wine of the Eucharist, he insisted that it was only through the faith

prince Albert of Hohenzollern had paid a large sum for papal permission to hold the bishoprics of Magdeburg and Halberstadt concurrently—even though, at twenty-three, he was not old enough to be a bishop at all. Moreover, when the prestigious and lucrative archbishopric of Mainz fell vacant in the next year, Albert bought that, too. Obtaining the necessary funds by taking out loans from a German banking firm, he then struck a bargain with Pope Leo X (r. 1513–21): Leo would authorize the sale of indulgences in Albert's ecclesiastical territories, with the understanding that half of the income would go to Rome for the building of St. Peter's Basilica, the other half going to Albert.

Luther did not know the sordid details of Albert's bargain, but he did know that a Dominican friar named Tetzel was soon hawking indulgences throughout much of the region, and that Tetzel was deliberately giving people the impression that an indulgence was an automatic ticket to Heaven for oneself or one's loved ones in Purgatory. For Luther, this was doubly offensive: not only was Tetzel violating Luther's conviction that people are saved by faith, he was also misleading people into thinking that they no

of each individual believer that this sacrament could lead anyone to God. To further emphasize that clergy had no supernatural authority, he insisted on calling them "ministers" or "pastors" rather than priests, and he proposed to abolish the entire ecclesiastical hierarchy, from popes to bishops on down. Finally, on the principle that no spiritual distinction existed between clergy and laity, Luther argued that ministers could and should marry. In 1525 he himself took a wife, Katharina von Bora, one of a dozen nuns whom he had helped to escape from a Cistercian convent.

The Challenge to Rome

As word of Luther's defiance spread, his pamphlets became a publishing sensation. Whereas the average press run of a printed book before 1520 had been 1,000 copies, the first run of *To the Christian Nobility* (1520) was 4,000—and it sold out in a few days. Many thousands of copies quickly followed. Even more popular were woodcut illustrations mocking the papacy and exalting Luther. These sold in the tens of thousands and could be readily understood even by the illiterate. (See *Interpreting Visual Evidence.*)

Luther's denunciations reflected widespread public dissatisfaction with the conduct and corruption of recent popes. Pope Alexander VI (r. 1492–1503) had bribed cardinals to gain his office, and had then used the money raised from the papal jubilee of 1500 to support the military campaigns of his illegitimate son. He was also suspected of incest with his own daughter, Lucrezia Borgia. Julius II (r. 1503–13) devoted his reign to enlarging the Papal States in a series of wars; a contemporary remarked of him that he would have gained great glory—if only he had been a secular prince. Leo X (r. 1513–21), Luther's opponent, was a member of the Medici family of Florence and held a very different view of the Church and its earthly mission.

In Germany, resentment of the papacy ran especially high because there were no special agreements (concordats) limiting papal authority in its principalities, as there were in Spain, France, and England (see Chapter 10). As a result, German princes complained that papal taxes were so exorbitant that the country was drained of its wealth. Meanwhile, Germans felt that they had almost no influence over papal policy. Frenchmen, Spaniards, and Italians dominated the College of Cardinals and the papal bureaucracy, and the popes were almost always Italian (as they would continue to be until 1978 and the election of John Paul II). As a result, graduates from the rapidly growing German universities almost never found employment in Rome. Instead, many joined the throngs of Luther's supporters to become leaders of the new religious movement.

THE EMPEROR CHARLES V. This portrait by the Venetian painter Titian depicts Europe's most powerful ruler sitting quietly in a chair, dressed in simple clothing of the kind worn by judges or bureaucrats. ▪ *Why might Charles have chosen to represent himself in this way—rather than in the regalia of his many royal, imperial, and princely offices?*

The Condemnation at Worms

In the year 1520, Pope Leo X issued a papal edict condemning Luther's publications, and threatening him with excommunication if he did not recant. This edict was of the most solemn kind, known as a *bulla* or "bull," from the lead seal it bore. Luther's reponse was flagrant: rather than acquiescing to the pope's demand, he staged a public burning of the document. Thereafter, his heresy confirmed, he was formally consigned to punishment by his lay overlord, the elector Frederick "the Wise" of Saxony. Frederick, however, proved a supporter of Luther and a critic of the papacy. Rather than burning Luther at the stake for heresy, Frederick declared that Luther had not yet received a fair hearing. Early in 1521, he brought Luther to the city of Worms to be examined by a select representative assembly known as a "diet."

At Worms, the diet's presiding officer was the newly elected Holy Roman emperor, Charles V. As a member of the Habsburg family, he had been born and bred in his ancestral holding of Flanders, part of the Netherlands. By 1521, through the unpredictable workings of dynastic inheritance, marriage, election, and luck, he had become not only the ruler of the Netherlands, but also king of Bohemia and Hungary, Holy Roman Emperor, duke of Austria, duke of Milan, and ruler of the Franche-Comté. And as the grandson of Ferdinand and Isabella on his mother's side, he was

Decoding Printed Propaganda

The printing press has been credited with helping to spread the teachings of Martin Luther and so with securing the success of the Protestant Reformation. But even before Luther's critiques were published, reformers were using this new technology to disseminate images that attacked the corruption of the Church. After Luther rose to prominence, both his supporters and detractors vied with one another in disseminating propaganda that appealed, visually, to a lay audience and that could be understood even by those who were unable to read.

The first pair of images below is really a single printed artifact datable to around 1500: an early example of a "pop-up" card. It shows Pope Alexander VI (r. 1492–1503) as stately pontiff (image A) whose true identity is concealed by a flap. When the flap is raised (image B), he is revealed as a devil. The Latin texts read: "Alexander VI, *pontifex maximus*" (image A) and "I am the pope" (image B).

The other two images represent two sides of the debate over Luther's new theology as it had developed by 1530, and both do so with reference to the same image: the seven-headed beast mentioned in the Bible's Book of

A. Alexander as pontiff.

B. Alexander as a devil.

also king of Spain; king of Naples, Sicily, and Sardinia; and ruler of all the Spanish possessions in the New World. Governing such an extraordinary combination of territories posed enormous challenges. Charles's empire had no capital and no centralized administrative institutions; it shared no common language, no common culture, and no geographically contiguous borders. It thus stood completely apart from the growing nationalism of late medieval political life.

Charles recognized the diversity of his enormous empire and tried wherever possible to rule it through local

Revelation. On the left below (image C), a Lutheran engraving shows the papacy as the beast, with seven heads representing seven orders of Catholic clergy. The sign on the cross (referring to the sign hung over the head of the crucified Christ) reads, in German: "For money, a sack full of indulgences." (The Latin words on either side say "Kingdom of the Devil.") On the right (image D), a Catholic engraving produced in Germany shows Luther as Revelation's beast, with seven heads labeled: "Doctor–Martin–Luther–Heretic–Hypocrite–Fanatic–Barabbas," the last alluding to the thief who should have been executed instead of Jesus, according to the Gospels.

Questions for Analysis

1. Given that this attack on Pope Alexander VI precedes Martin Luther's critique of the Church by nearly two decades, what can you conclude about its intended audience? To what extent can it be read as a barometer of popular disapproval? What might have been the reason(s) for the use of the concealing flap?

2. What do you make of the fact that both Catholic and Protestant propagandists were using the same imagery? What do you make of the key differences? For example, note that the seven-headed beast representing the papacy sprouts out of an altar on which a Eucharistic chalice is displayed, while the seven-headed Martin Luther is reading a book.

3. All of these printed images also make use of words. What are some of the different relationships between these two media (words and images)? Would the message of each image be clear without the use of texts? Why or why not?

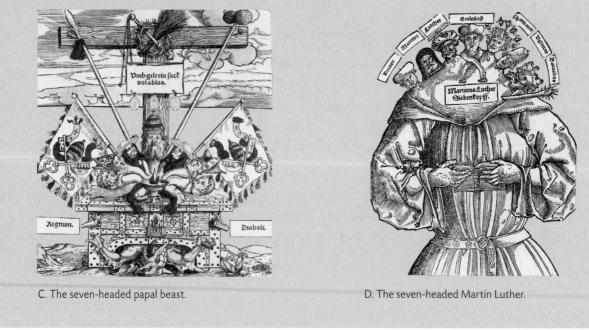

C. The seven-headed papal beast.

D. The seven-headed Martin Luther.

officials and institutions. But he could not tolerate threats to the two fundamental forces that held his empire together: himself, in his role as emperor, and Catholicism, as the religion of Rome was coming to be called. There was therefore little doubt that the Diet of Worms would condemn Martin Luther for heresy. But when Luther refused to back down, thereby endangering his life, his lord Frederick the Wise once again intervened, this time arranging for Luther to be "kidnapped" and hidden for a year at the elector's castle of the Wartburg, where he was kept out of harm's way.

The following regions are labeled on the map:

NORWAY, SWEDEN, RUSSIA, TEUTONIC ORDER, NORTH SEA, DENMARK, BALTIC SEA, PRUSSIA, IRELAND, ENGLAND, London, BRANDENBURG, Warsaw, LITHUANIA, ATLANTIC OCEAN, Aachen, Cologne, SAXONY, POLAND, HOLY ROMAN EMPIRE, Paris, Verdun, Prague, BOHEMIA, Augsburg, Vienna, AUSTRIA, FRANCE, FRANCHE-COMTÉ, HUNGARY, Milan, Venice, VENETIAN REPUBLIC, Genoa, OTTOMAN EMPIRE, Valladolid, SPAIN, Marseille, Florence, Danube R., PORTUGAL, Madrid, ARAGON, REPUBLIC OF GENOA, PAPAL STATES, CORSICA, Toledo, CASTILE, Rome, Constantinople, Seville, BALEARIC ISLANDS, Naples, NAPLES, SARDINIA, MEDITERRANEAN SEA, Palermo, SICILY, OTTOMAN EMPIRE

Legend:
— Boundary of the Holy Roman Empire
▨ Possessions of Charles V (Spanish Habsburgs)

Inset: EUROPE, AFRICA, Area of detail

THE EUROPEAN EMPIRE OF CHARLES V, c. 1550. Charles V ruled a vast variety of widely dispersed territories in Europe and the New World, and as Holy Roman Emperor he was also the titular ruler of Germany. ▪ *What were the main countries and kingdoms under his control?* ▪ *Which regions would have been most threatened by Charles's extraordinary power, and where might the rulers of these regions turn for allies?* ▪ *How might the expansion of the Ottoman Empire have complicated the political and religious struggles within Christian Europe?*

practices within their territories? This is a crucial development, because popular support for Luther would not have been enough to ensure the success of his teachings. Indeed, it was only in those territories where rulers formally established Lutheranism that the new religion prevailed. Elsewhere in Germany, Luther's sympathizers were forced to flee, face death, or conform to Catholicism.

The power of individual rulers to determine the religion of their territories reflects developments we noted in Chapter 10. Kings and great lords had long sought to control appointments to Church offices in their own realms, to restrict the flow of money to Rome, and to limit the independence of ecclesiastical courts. In the fifteenth century, the most powerful rulers in western Europe—primarily the kings of France and Spain—had therefore taken advantage of the continuing struggles between the papacy and the conciliarists to extract such concessions from the embattled popes. But in Germany, as noted above, neither the emperor nor individual princes were strong enough to secure special treatment.

This changed as a result of Luther's initiatives. As early as 1520, Luther recognized that he could never hope to institute new religious practices without the strong arms of princes, so he explicitly encouraged them to confiscate the wealth of the Church as an incentive. At first the princes bided their time. But when they realized that Luther had enormous public support, several moved to introduce Lutheranism into their territories. Personal piety surely played a role in individual cases, but political and economic considerations were generally more decisive. Protestant princes could consolidate authority by naming their own pastors, collecting taxes usually sent to Rome, and curtailing the jurisdiction of Church courts. They could also guarantee that the political and religious boundaries of their territories would now coincide. No longer would a rival ecclesiastical prince (such as a bishop or archbishop) be able to use his spiritual position to undermine a secular prince's sovereignty.

Similar considerations also moved a number of free German cities (independent of territorial princes) to adopt Lutheranism. Town councils and guild masters could thus establish themselves as the supreme governing authorities

Thereafter, Luther was never again in mortal danger. Although the Diet of Worms proclaimed him an outlaw, this edict was never enforced. Instead, Charles V left Germany in order to conduct a war with France. In 1522, Luther returned in triumph to Wittenberg, to find that the changes he had called for had already been put into practice by his university supporters. When several German princes formally converted to Lutheranism, they brought their territories with them. In a little over a decade, a new form of Christianity had been established.

The German Princes and the Lutheran Church

At this point, the last of our three major questions must be addressed: Why did some German princes, secure in their own powers, nonetheless establish Lutheran religious

within their towns, cutting out local bishops or powerful monasteries. Given the added fact that monasteries and convents could be shut down and their lands appropriated, the practical advantages of the new faith were overwhelming—quite apart from any considerations of religious zeal.

Once safely ensconced in Wittenberg under princely protection, Luther began to express his own political and social views ever more vehemently. In a treatise of 1523, *On Temporal Authority*, he insisted that "godly" (Protestant) rulers must be obeyed in all things and that even "ungodly" ones should never be actively resisted since tyranny "is not to be resisted but endured." In 1525, when peasants throughout Germany rebelled against their landlords, Luther therefore responded with intense hostility. In his vituperative pamphlet of 1525, *Against the Thievish, Murderous Hordes of Peasants*, he urged readers to hunt down the rebels as though they were mad dogs. After the ruthless suppression of this revolt, which may have cost as many as 100,000 lives, the firm alliance of Lutheranism with state power helped preserve and sanction the existing social order.

As for Luther himself, he concentrated in his last years on debating with younger, more radical religious reformers. Never tiring in his prolific literary activity, he wrote an average of one treatise every two weeks for twenty-five years. Many of these are colored by extreme anti-Semitism, one of Luther's less positive legacies.

THE SPREAD OF PROTESTANTISM

Originating as a term applied to Lutherans who "protested" against an imperial diet convened in 1529, the word *Protestant* was soon applied to a much wider range of dissenting Christianities. Lutheranism itself struck lasting roots only in northern Germany and Scandinavia, where it became the state religion of Denmark, Norway, and Sweden as early as the 1520s. Early Lutheran successes in southern Germany, Poland, and Hungary were eventually rolled back. Elsewhere in Europe, meanwhile, competing forms of Protestantism soon emerged from the seeds that Luther had sown. By the 1550s, Protestantism had become an increasingly diverse and divisive movement.

Protestantism in Switzerland

In the early sixteenth century, Switzerland was ruled neither by kings nor by territorial princes; instead, prosperous Swiss cities were either independent or on the verge of becoming so. Hence, when the leading citizens of a Swiss municipality decided to adopt Protestant reforms, no one could stop them. Although religious arrangements varied from city to city, three main forms of Protestantism emerged in Switzerland between 1520 to 1550: Zwinglianism, Anabaptism, and Calvinism.

Zwinglianism, founded by Ulrich Zwingli (*TSVING-lee,* 1484–1531) in Zürich, was the most theologically moderate form of the three. Zwingli began his career as a Catholic priest, but his humanist inspired study of the Bible convinced him that Catholic theology conflicted with the Gospels. His biblical

CONFESSIONAL DIFFERENCES, c. 1560. The religious affiliations (confessions) of Europe's territories had become very complicated by the year 1560, roughly a generation after the adoption of Lutheranism in some areas. ■ *What major countries and kingdoms had embraced Protestantism by 1560?* ■ *To what extent do these divisions conform to political boundaries, and to what extent would they have complicated the political situation?* ■ *Why might Lutheranism have spread north, into Scandinavia, rather than south?*

THE ANABAPTISTS' CAGES, THEN AND NOW. After the three Anabaptist leaders of Münster were executed in 1535, their corpses were prominently displayed in cages hung from a tower of the marketplace church. As can be seen from the photo on the right, the bones are gone but the iron cages remain. ▪ *What would be the purpose of keeping these cages on display?*

studies eventually led him to condemn religious images and hierarchical authority, yet he did not speak out publicly until Luther set the precedent. In 1522, Zwingli began attacking the authority of the Church openly. Soon much of northern Switzerland had accepted his religious leadership.

Zwingli's reforms closely resembled those of the Lutherans in Germany. Zwingli differed from Luther, however, as to the theology of the Eucharist: whereas Luther believed in the real presence of Christ's body in the sacrament, for Zwingli the Eucharist conferred no grace at all; it was simply a reminder and communal celebration of Christ's historical sacrifice. This fundamental disagreement prevented Lutherans and Zwinglians from uniting in a common Protestant front. Fighting independently, Zwingli fell in battle against Catholic forces in 1531. Soon thereafter, his movement was absorbed by the more systematic Protestantism of John Calvin (see below).

Before Calvinism prevailed, however, a far more radical form of Protestantism arose in Switzerland and Germany: Anabaptism. The first Anabaptists were members of Zwingli's circle in Zürich, but they broke with him around 1525 on the issue of infant baptism. Anabaptists were convinced that the sacrament of baptism was only effective if administered to willing adults who understood its significance, and they required followers who had been baptized as infants to be baptized again as adults (the term *Anabaptism* means "rebaptism"). This doctrine reflected the Anabaptists' fundamental belief that the true church of Christ was a small community of believers whose members had to make a deliberate, inspired

decision to join it. No other Protestant groups were prepared to go so far in rejecting the traditional view of the Church as a single vast body to which all members of Christian society belonged from birth. Yet in its first few years the movement did gain numerous adherents, above all because it appealed to sincere spiritual values in calling for pacifism, strict personal morality, and extreme simplicity of worship.

This changed when a group of Anabaptist extremists managed to gain control of the German city of Münster in 1534. These zealots combined sectarianism with millenarianism: the belief that God intends to institute a completely new order of justice and spirituality throughout the world before the end of time. Determined to help bring about this goal, the extremists attempted to turn Münster into a new Jerusalem. A former tailor named John of Leyden assumed the title "King of the New Temple" and proclaimed himself the successor of the Hebrew king David. Under his leadership, Anabaptist religious practices were made obligatory, private property was abolished, and even polygamy was permitted on the grounds of Old Testament precedents. Such practices were deeply shocking to Protestants and Catholics alike. Accordingly, Münster was besieged and captured by Catholic forces little more than a year after the Anabaptist takeover; the new "David," together with two of his lieutenants, was put to death by torture and their decaying bodies displayed in cages hung from a church in the marketplace.

Thereafter, Anabaptists throughout Europe were ruthlessly persecuted on all sides. The few who survived banded together in the Mennonite sect, named for its founder, the Dutchman Menno Simons (c. 1496–1561). This sect, dedicated to pacifism and a simple "religion of the heart," has continued to exist to the present day and is particularly strong in the central United States.

John Calvin's Reformed Theology

A year after the events in Münster, a twenty-six-year-old Frenchman named John Calvin (1509–1564), published the first version of his *Institutes of the Christian Religion*, the most influential formulation of Protestant theology ever written. Born in Noyon in northern France, Calvin had originally trained for the law. By 1533 he was studying the Greek and Latin classics while living off the income from a priestly benefice. As he later wrote, although he was "obstinately devoted to the superstitions of popery," at this time in his life he experienced a miraculous conversion. He became a Protestant theologian and propagandist, and evenually fled to the Swiss city of Basel to escape persecution.

Although some aspects of Calvin's early career resemble those of Luther, the two men were very different. Luther

was emotionally volatile and a lover of controversy. He responded to theological problems piecemeal as they arose or as the impulse struck him; he never attempted to systematize his beliefs. Calvin, however, was coolly analytical and resolved to set forth all the principles of Protestantism comprehensively, logically, and systematically. As a result, Calvin's *Institutes* became the Protestant equivalent of Thomas Aquinas's *Summa Theologiae* (Chapter 9).

Calvin's austere theology started with the omnipotence of God. For Calvin, the entire universe depends utterly on the will of the Almighty, who created all things for his greater glory. Because of man's original fall from grace, all human beings are sinners by nature, bound to an evil inheritance they cannot escape. Nevertheless, God (for reasons of his own) has predestined some for eternal salvation and damned all the rest to the torments of Hell. Nothing that human beings may do can alter this fate: all souls are stamped with God's blessing or curse before they are born. Nevertheless, Christians cannot be indifferent to their conduct on earth. If they are among the elect, God will implant in them the desire to live according to his laws. Upright conduct is thus a sign, though not an infallible one, that an individual has been chosen to sit at the throne of glory. Membership in the reformed church (as Calvinist churches are more properly known) is another presumptive sign of election to salvation. But most of all, Calvin urged Christians to conceive of themselves as chosen instruments of God, charged to work actively to fulfill God's purposes on earth. Because sin offends God, Christians should do all they can to prevent it, not because their actions will lead to anyone's salvation, but simply because God's glory is diminished if sin is allowed to flourish unchecked.

Calvin always acknowledged a great theological debt to Luther, but his religious teachings diverged in several essentials. First of all, Luther's attitude toward proper Christian conduct in the world was much more passive than Calvin's. For Luther, a Christian should endure the trials of this life through suffering, whereas for Calvin the world was to be actively mastered through unceasing labor for God's sake. Calvin's religion was also more legalistic than Luther's. Luther, for example, insisted that his followers attend church on Sunday, but he did not demand that during the remainder of the day they refrain from all pleasure. Calvin, however, issued stern strictures against worldliness of any sort on the Sabbath and forbade all sorts of minor self-indulgences on other days.

The two men also differed on fundamental matters of church governance and worship. Although Luther broke with the Catholic system of hierarchical church government, Lutheran district superintendents exercised some of the same powers as bishops, including supervision of parish clergy. Luther also retained many features of traditional worship, including altars, music, and ritual. Calvin, however, rejected everything that smacked of "popery." He argued for the elimination of all traces of hierarchy within the church. Instead, each congregation should elect its own ministers, and assemblies of ministers and "elders" (laymen responsible for maintaining proper religious conduct) were to govern the reformed church as a whole. Calvin also insisted on the utmost simplicity in worship, prohibiting (among much else) vestments, processions, instrumental music, and religious images of any sort. He also dispensed with all remaining vestiges of Catholic sacramental theology by making the sermon, rather than the Eucharist, the centerpiece of worship.

Calvinism in Geneva

Calvin was intent on putting his religious teachings into practice. Sensing an opportunity in the French-speaking Swiss city of Geneva—then in the throes of political and religious upheaval—he moved there late in 1536 and immediately began preaching and organizing. In 1538, his activities caused him to be expelled by the city council, but in 1541 he returned and brought the city under his sway.

Under Calvin's guidance, Geneva's government became a theocracy. Supreme authority was vested in a "Consistory" composed of lay elders and pastors, whose weekly meetings Calvin dominated. Aside from passing legislation, the Consistory's main function was to supervise morality, both public and private. To this end, Geneva was divided into districts, and a committee of the Consistory visited every household, without prior warning, to check on the behavior of its members. Dancing, card playing, attending the theater, and working or playing on the Sabbath—all were outlawed as works of the devil. Murder, treason, adultery, witchcraft, blasphemy, and heresy were all capital crimes. Even penalties for lesser crimes were severe. During the first four years after Calvin gained control in Geneva, there were fifty-eight executions in this city with a total population of only 16,000.

As objectionable as this may seem today, Calvin's Geneva was a beacon of light to thousands of Protestants throughout Europe in the mid-sixteenth century. Calvin's disciple John Knox, who brought the reformed church to Scotland, declared Geneva "the most perfect school of Christ that ever was on earth since the days of the Apostles." Converts such as Knox flocked to Geneva for refuge or instruction and then returned home to become ardent proselytizers for the new religion. Geneva thus became the center of an international movement dedicated to spreading reformed religion to the rest of Europe through organized missionary activity and propaganda.

These efforts were remarkably successful. By the end of the sixteenth century, Calvinists were a majority in Scotland (where they were known as Presbyterians) and Holland (where they founded the Dutch Reformed Church). They were also influential in England. Although the Church of England adopted reformed theology but not reformed worship, Calvinists there who sought further reforms in worship were known as Puritans. There were also substantial Calvinist minorities in France (where they were called Huguenots), Germany, Hungary, Lithuania, and Poland.

THE DOMESTICATION OF REFORM

Protestantism was a movement whose radical claims for the spiritual equality of all Christian believers had the potential to undermine the political, social, and even gender hierarchies on which European society rested. Luther himself did not anticipate that his ideas might have such implications, and he was genuinely shocked when the rebellious German peasants and the radical Anabaptists at Münster interpreted his teachings in this way. And Luther was by no means the only staunchly conservative Protestant. Most Protestant reformers depended on the support of existing social and political leaders: territorial princes, but also the ruling elites of towns. As a result, the Reformation movement was speedily "domesticated," in two senses. Its revolutionary potential was muffled, and there was an increasing emphasis on the patriarchal family as the central institution of Protestant life.

Reform and Discipline

As we have seen (Chapter 10), injunctions to lead a more disciplined and godly life had been a frequent message of fifteenth-century religious reform movements. Many of these efforts were actively promoted by princes and town councils, most famously perhaps in Florence, where the Dominican preacher Girolamo Savonarola led the city on an extraordinary but short-lived campaign of puritanism and moral reform between 1494 and 1498. But there are many other examples of rulers legislating against immoral behavior. When Desiderius Erasmus called on secular authorities to think of themselves as abbots and of their territories as giant monasteries, he was sounding an already-familiar theme.

Protestant rulers, however, took the need to enforce godly discipline with particular seriousness, because the depravity of human nature was a fundamental tenet of Protestant belief. Following Saint Augustine (Chapter 6), Protestants believed that people would inevitably turn out

bad unless they were compelled to be good. It was, therefore, the responsibility of secular and religious leaders to control and punish the behavior of their people, because otherwise their evil deeds would anger God and destroy human society.

Protestant godliness began with the discipline of children. Luther himself wrote two catechisms (instructional tracts) designed to teach children the tenets of their faith and the obligations—toward parents, masters, and rulers—that God imposed on them. Luther also insisted that all children, boys and girls alike, should be taught to read the Bible in their own languages. Schooling thus became a characteristically Protestant preoccupation. Even the Protestant family was designated a "school of godliness" in which fathers were expected to instruct and discipline their wives, their children, and their household servants.

Family life in the early sixteenth century left much to be desired in the eyes of Protestant reformers. Drunkenness, domestic violence, illicit sexual relations, lewd dancing, and the blasphemous swearing of oaths were frequent topics of reforming discourse. Various methods of discipline were attempted, including public confessions of wrongdoing, public penances and shamings, exclusion from church services, and even imprisonment. All these efforts met with varying, but generally modest, success. To create godly Protestant families, and to enforce godly discipline on entire communities, was going to require the active cooperation of godly authorities.

Protestantism, Government, and the Family

The domestication of the Reformation in this sense—its embeddedness in daily life—in the free towns of Germany and Switzerland began and from there spread westward to the New World. Protestant attacks on monasticism and clerical celibacy had found a receptive audience among townsmen who resented the immunity of monastic houses from taxation and regarded clerical celibacy as a subterfuge for the seduction of their own wives and daughters. Protestant emphasis on the depravity of the human will and the consequent need for that will to be disciplined by authority also resonated powerfully with guilds and town governments, which were anxious to maintain and increase their control. By eliminating the competing jurisdictional authority of the Catholic Church, Protestantism allowed town governments to consolidate all authority into their own hands.

Meanwhile, Protestantism reinforced the control of individual men over their own households by emphasizing the family as the basic unit of religious education. An

all-powerful father figure was now expected to assume responsibility for instructing and disciplining his household. At the same time, Protestantism introduced a new religious ideal for women. No longer was the celibate nun the exemplar of female holiness; in her place now stood the married and obedient "goodwife." To some extent, then, Protestantism resolved the tensions between piety and sexuality that had long characterized Christian teachings, by declaring the holiness of marital sex.

But this did not promote a new view of women's spiritual potential, nor did it elevate their social and political status; quite the contrary. Luther regarded women as more sexually driven than men and less capable of controlling their sexual desires—despite the fact that Luther confessed himself to be utterly incapable of celibacy. His opposition to women's monasteries allegedly rested on his belief that it was impossible for women to remain chaste, so that sequestering them simply made illicit behavior inevitable. To prevent sin, it was therefore necessary that all women should be married, preferably at a young age, and so placed under the governance of a godly husband.

For the most part, Protestant town governments were happy to cooperate in shutting down monasteries for women. The convent's property went to the town, after all. But conflicts still arose between Protestant reformers and town fathers over marriage and sexuality, especially over the reformers' insistence that both men and women should marry young as a restraint on lust. In many German towns, men were traditionally expected to delay marriage until they had achieved the status of a master craftsman. Accordingly, apprentices and journeymen were not supposed to marry. Instead, they were expected to frequent brothels and taverns, a legally sanctioned outlet for extramarital sexuality long viewed as necessary to men's physical well-being—but a practice that Protestant reformers now deemed morally abhorrent.

Towns responded in a variety of ways to these opposing pressures. Some instituted special committees to police public morals, of the sort we have noted in Calvin's Geneva. Some abandoned Protestantism altogether. Others, like Augsburg, alternated back and forth between Protestantism and Catholicism for several decades. Yet regardless of a town's final choice of religious allegiance, a revolution was taking place with respect to attitudes toward public morality. In their competition with each other, neither Catholics nor Protestants wished to be seen as soft on sin. The result, by 1600, was the widespread abolition of publicly licensed brothels, the outlawing of prostitution, and far stricter governmental supervision of many other aspects of private life than had ever been the case in any Western civilization up to this point in time.

The Control of Marriage

Protestantism also increased parents' control over their children's choice of marital partners. Although the medieval Church had defined marriage as a sacrament, it did not require the involvement of a priest: the mutual free consent of two individuals, even if exchanged without witnesses or parental approval, was enough to constitute a legally valid marriage. Opposition to this doctrine came from many quarters, however. Because marriage involved rights of inheritance to property, it was regarded as too important a matter to be left to the choice of adolescents. Instead, parents wanted the power to prevent unsuitable matches and, in some cases, to force their children to accept the marriage arrangements their families might negotiate on their behalf.

Protestantism offered an opportunity to achieve such control. Luther had declared marriage to be a purely secular matter, not a sacrament at all, and one that could be regulated as governing authorities thought best. Calvin largely followed suit, although Calvinist theocracy drew less of a distinction than did Lutheranism between the powers of church and state. Even the Catholic Church was eventually forced to give way; although it never abandoned its insistence that both members of a couple must freely consent, it eventually required formal public notice of intent to marry and insisted on the presence of a priest at the actual wedding ceremony. Both of these measures were supposed to prevent elopements, allowing families time to intervene before an unsuitable marriage was concluded. In somewhat different ways, then, both Protestantism and Catholicism moved to strengthen the control that parents could exercise over their children—and, in the case of Protestantism, that husbands could exercise over their wives.

THE REFORMATION OF ENGLAND

In England, the Reformation took a rather different course than it did in continental Europe. Although a tradition of popular reform had long flourished there, the number of dissidents was usually small and their influence limited. Nor was England particularly oppressed by the papal exactions and abuses that roiled Germany. When the sixteenth century began, English monarchs already exercised close control over Church appointments within their kingdom; they also received the lion's share of the papal taxation collected from England. Why, then, did sixteenth-century England become a Protestant country at all?

Marriage and Celibacy: Two Views

These two selections illustrate strongly contrasting views on the spiritual value of marriage versus celibacy. The first selection is part of Martin Luther's more general attack on monasticism, which emphasizes his contention that marriage is the natural and divinely intended state for all human beings. The second selection, from the decrees of the Council of Trent (1545–63), restates traditional Catholic teaching on the holiness of marriage but also emphasizes the spiritual superiority of virginity and the necessity of clerical celibacy.

Luther's Views on Celibacy

Listen! In all my days I have not heard the confession of a nun, but in the light of Scripture I shall hit upon how matters fare with her and know I shall not be lying. If a girl is not sustained by great and exceptional grace, she can live without a man as little as she can without eating, drinking, sleeping, and other natural necessities.

Nor, on the other hand, can a man dispense with a wife. The reason for this is that procreating children is an urge planted as deeply in human nature as eating and drinking. That is why God has given and put into the body the organs, arteries, fluxes, and everything that serves it. Therefore what is he doing who would check this process and keep nature from running its desired and intended course? He is attempting to keep nature from being nature, fire from burning, water from wetting, and a man from eating, drinking, and sleeping.

Source: E. M. Plass, ed., *What Luther Says,* vol. 2 (St. Louis, MO: 1959), pp. 888–89.

Canons on the Sacrament of Matrimony (1563)

Canon 1. If anyone says that matrimony is not truly and properly one of the seven sacraments . . . instituted by Christ the Lord, but has been devised by men in the Church and does not confer grace, let him be anathema [cursed].

Canon 9. If anyone says that clerics constituted in sacred orders or regulars [monks and nuns] who have made solemn profession of chastity can contract marriage . . . and that all who feel that they have not the gift of chastity, even though they have made such a vow, can contract marriage, let him be anathema, since God does not refuse that gift to those who ask for it rightly, neither does *he suffer us to be tempted above that which we are able.*

Canon 10: If anyone says that the married state excels the state of virginity or celibacy, and that it is better and happier to be united in matrimony than to remain in virginity or celibacy, let him be anathema.

Source: H. J. Schroeder, trans., *Canons and Decrees of the Council of Trent* (St. Louis, MO: 1941), pp. 181–82.

Questions for Analysis

1. On what grounds does Luther attack the practice of celibacy? Do you agree with his basic premise?

2. How do the later canons of the Catholic Church respond to Protestant views like Luther's? What appears to be at stake in this defense of marriage and celibacy?

"The King's Great Matter"

By 1527, King Henry VIII of England had been married for eighteen years to Ferdinand and Isabella's daughter, Catherine of Aragon. Yet all the offspring of this union had been stillborn or died in infancy, with the exception of a daughter, Mary. Because Henry needed a male heir to preserve the peaceful succession to the throne, and because Catherine was now past childbearing age—and had shown no signs of pregnancy for over a decade—Henry had politi-

cal reasons to propose a change of wife. He also had more personal motives, having become infatuated with a lady-in-waiting named Anne Boleyn.

Henry therefore appealed to Rome to annul his marriage to Catherine, arguing that because she had previously been married to his older brother Arthur (who had died in adolescence), Henry's marriage to Catherine had been invalid from the beginning. As Henry's representatives pointed out, the Bible pronounced it "an unclean thing" for a man to take his brother's wife and cursed such a marriage with childlessness (Leviticus 20:21). Even a papal dispensation—which Henry and Catherine had long before obtained for their marriage—could not exempt them from such a clear prohibition, as the marriage's childlessness appeared to prove.

Henry's suit put Pope Clement VII (r. 1523–34) in an awkward position. Popes in the past had granted annulments to reigning monarchs on far weaker grounds than the ones Henry was alleging. If, however, the pope granted Henry's annulment, he would cast doubt on the validity of all papal dispensations because he would be repealing a previous papal decree. More seriously, he would provoke the wrath of the emperor Charles V, Catherine of Aragon's nephew, whose armies were in firm command of Rome and who at that moment held the pope himself in captivity. Clement was trapped; all he could do was procrastinate and hope that the matter would resolve itself.

Exasperated by the delay, Henry began to increase pressure on the pope. In 1531, he compelled an assembly of English clergy to declare him "protector and only supreme head" of the Church in England. In 1532, he encouraged Parliament to produce an inflammatory list of grievances against the English clergy and used this to force them to concede his right to approve or disapprove all Church legislation. In January of 1533, Henry preemptively married Anne Boleyn (already pregnant) even though his marriage to Queen Catherine had still not been annulled. The new archbishop of Canterbury, Thomas Cranmer, provided the required annulment, acting on his own authority.

In September, Princess Elizabeth was born; her father, disappointed again in his hopes for a son, refused to attend her christening. Nevertheless, Parliament settled the succession to the throne on the children of Henry and Anne, redirected all papal revenues from England into the king's hands, prohibited appeals to the papal court, and formally declared "the King's highness to be Supreme Head of the Church of England." In 1536, Henry executed his former tutor and chancellor Sir Thomas More (Chapter 12) for his refusal to accept the marriage or endorse this declaration of supremacy. He also took the first steps toward dissolving England's monasteries. By the end of 1539, their lands and wealth were confiscated by the king, who distributed them to his supporters.

These measures broke the bonds that linked the English Church to Rome, but they did not make England a truly Protestant country. Although certain traditional practices (such as pilgrimages and the veneration of relics) were prohibited, the English Church remained overwhelmingly Catholic in organization, doctrine, ritual, and language. Oral confession to priests, masses for the dead, and clerical celibacy were all confirmed; the Latin Mass continued; and Catholic Eucharistic doctrine was not only confirmed but its denial made punishable by death. To most English people, only the disappearance of the monasteries and the king's own continuing matrimonial adventures were evidence that their Church was no longer in communion with Rome.

The Reign of Edward VI

For truly committed Protestants, and especially those who had visited Calvin's Geneva, the changes Henry VIII enforced on the English Church did not go nearly far enough. In 1547, the accession of the nine-year-old king Edward VI (Henry's son by his third wife, Jane Seymour) gave them their opportunity to finish the task of reform. Encouraged by the apparent sympathies of the young king, Edward's government moved quickly to reform the creeds and ceremonies of the English Church. Priests were permitted to marry; English services replaced Latin ones; the veneration of images was discouraged, and the images themselves defaced or destroyed; formal prayers for the dead were forbidden, and endowments for such prayers were confiscated; and new articles of belief were drawn up,

HENRY VIII OF ENGLAND. Hans Holbein the Younger executed several portraits of the English king. This one represents him in middle age, confident of his powers.

repuditating all sacraments except baptism and communion and affirming the Protestant doctrine of justification by faith alone. Most radically, a new prayer book was published to define precisely how the new English-language services of the Church were to be conducted. By 1553, when the youthful Edward died, the English Church appeared to have become a distinctly Protestant institution.

Mary Tudor and the Restoration of Catholicism

Edward's successor, however, was his pious and much older half-sister Mary (r. 1553–58), granddaughter of "the most Catholic monarchs" of Spain, Ferdinand and Isabella (see Chapter 11). Mary speedily reversed her brother's religious policies, restoring the Latin Mass and requiring married priests to give up their wives. She even prevailed on Parliament to vote a return to papal allegiance. Hundreds of Protestant leaders fled abroad, many to Geneva; others, including Archbishop Thomas Cranmer, were burned at the stake. News of these martyrdoms spread like wildfire through Protestant Europe. In England, however, Mary's policies sparked relatively little resistance. After two decades of religious upheaval, most English men and women were probably hoping that Mary's reign would bring some stability to their lives.

This, however, Mary could not do. The executions she ordered were insufficient to wipe out religious resistance—instead, Protestant propaganda about "Bloody Mary" caused widespread unease. Nor could Mary do anything to restore monasticism: too many leading families had profited from

Henry VIII's dissolution for this to be reversed. Mary's marriage to her cousin Philip, Charles V's son and heir to the Spanish throne, was another miscalculation. Although the marriage treaty stipulated that Philip could not succeed Mary in the event of her death, some of her English subjects never trusted him. When the queen allowed herself to be drawn into a war with France on Spain's behalf—in which England lost Calais, its last foothold on the European continent—many English people became highly disaffected. Ultimately, however, what doomed Mary's policies was simply the accident of biology: Mary was unable to conceive an heir and, when she died after only five years of rule, her throne passed to her Protestant half-sister.

The Elizabethan Compromise

The daughter of Henry VIII and Anne Boleyn, Elizabeth (r. 1558–1603) was predisposed in favor of Protestantism by the circumstances of her parents' marriage as well as by her upbringing. But Elizabeth was no zealot, and wisely recognized that supporting radical Protestantism in England might provoke bitter sectarian strife. Accordingly, she presided over what is often known as "the Elizabethan settlement." Under Elizabeth, Parliament repealed Mary's Catholic legislation, prohibited foreign religious powers (i.e., the pope) from exercising any authority within England, and declared the queen "supreme governor" of the English church—a more seemly title than Henry VIII's "supreme head," since most Protestants believed that Christ alone was the head of the Church. She also adopted many of the Protestant liturgical reforms instituted under her brother Edward, including a revised version of the prayer book. But she retained vestiges of Catholic practice too, including bishops, church courts, elaborate liturgy, and vestments for the clergy.

On most doctrinal matters, including predestination and free will, Elizabeth's Thirty-Nine Articles of Faith (approved in 1562) struck a decidedly Protestant, even Calvinist, tone. But the prayer book was more moderate, and on the critical issue of the Eucharist was deliberately ambiguous. Indeed, by combining Catholic and Protestant interpretations of the last supper and its commemoration, the prayer book permitted an enormous latitude for competing interpretations of the service by priests and parishioners alike.

Yet religious tensions persisted in Elizabethan England, not only between Protestants and Catholics but also between moderate and more extreme Protestants. The queen's artful fudging of these competing Christianities was by no means a recipe for success. Rather, what preserved "the Elizabethan settlement," and ultimately made England a Protestant country, was the extraordinary length of Queen

QUEEN MARY AND QUEEN ELIZABETH. The two daughters of Henry VIII were the first two queens regnant of England: the first women to rule there in their own right. Despite the similar challenges they faced, they had strikingly different fates and have been treated very differently in popular histories. ■ *How do these two portraits suggest differences in their personalities and their self-representation as rulers?*

Elizabeth's reign combined with the fact that for much of that time Protestant England was at war with Catholic Spain. Under Elizabeth, Protestantism and English nationalism gradually fused together into a potent conviction that God himself had chosen England for greatness. After 1588, when English naval forces won an improbable victory over Spain's "Invincible Armada" (Chapter 11), Protestantism and Englishness became nearly indistinguishable to most of Queen Elizabeth's subjects. Laws against Catholic practices became increasingly severe, and although an English Catholic tradition did survive, its adherents were a persecuted minority. Significant, too, was the situation in Ireland, where the vast majority of the population remained Catholic despite the government's efforts to impose Protestantism on them. By 1603, Irishness was as firmly identified with Catholicism as was Englishness with Protestantism; but it was the Protestants who were in power.

THE REBIRTH OF THE CATHOLIC CHURCH

So far, our emphasis on the spread of Protestantism has cast the spotlight on dissident reformers such as Luther and Calvin. But there was also a powerful internal reform movement within the Church during the sixteenth century, which resulted in the birth (or rebirth) of a Catholic ("universal") faith. For some, this movement is the "Catholic Reformation"; for others, it is the "Counter-Reformation." Those who prefer the former term emphasize that the Church carried forward significant reforming movements that can be traced back to the eleventh century (Chapter 8) and which gained new momentum in the wake of the Great Schism (Chapter 10). Others, however, insist that most Catholic reformers of this period were inspired primarily by the urgent need to resist Protestantism and to strengthen the Church's power to oppose it.

Catholic Reforms

Even before Luther's challenge to the Church, as we have seen, there was a movement for moral and institutional reform within some religious orders. But while these efforts received strong support from several secular rulers, the papacy showed little interest in them. In northern Europe, Christian humanists such as Erasmus and Thomas More played an especially central role, not only by criticizing abuses and editing sacred texts but also by encouraging the laity to lead lives of sincere religious piety (Chapter 12).

As a response to the challenges posed by Protestantism, however, these internal reforms proved entirely inadequate. Starting in the 1530s, therefore, a more aggressive phase of reform began to gather momentum. The leading Counter-Reformation popes—Paul III (r. 1534–49), Paul IV (r. 1555–59), Pius V (r. 1566–72), and Sixtus V (r. 1585–90)—were the most zealous leaders of the Church since the twelfth century. All led upright lives; some, indeed, were so grimly ascetic that contemporaries longed for the bad old days. Yet in confronting Protestantism, an excessively holy pope was vastly preferable to a self-indulgent one. And these Counter-Reformation popes were not merely holy men. They were also accomplished administrators who reorganized papal finances and filled ecclesiastical offices with bishops and abbots no less renowned for austerity and holiness than themselves.

Papal reform efforts intensified at the Council of Trent, a General Catholic Council convoked by Paul III in 1545, which met at intervals thereafter until 1563. The decisions taken at Trent (a provincial capital of the Holy Roman Empire, located in modern-day Italy) provided the foundations on which a new Catholic Church would be erected. Although the council began by debating some form of compromise with Protestantism, it ended by reaffirming all of the traditional tenets challenged by Protestant critics. "Good works" were affirmed as necessary for salvation, and all seven sacraments were declared indispensable means of grace. Transubstantiation, Purgatory, the invocation of saints, and the rule of celibacy for the clergy were all confirmed as dogmas—essential elements—of the Catholic faith. The Bible (even in its imperfect Vulgate form) and the teachings of the Catholic fathers and medieval theologians were held to be of equal authority. Papal supremacy over every bishop and priest was expressly maintained, and the supremacy of the pope over any Church council was taken for granted outright, signalling a final defeat of the conciliar movement (Chapter 10). The Council of Trent even reaffirmed the doctrine of indulgences that had touched off the Lutheran revolt, although it condemned the worst abuses connected with their sale.

The legislation of Trent was not confined to matters of doctrine. To improve pastoral care of the laity, bishops and priests were forbidden to hold more than one spiritual office. To address the problem of an ignorant priesthood, a theological seminary was to be established in every diocese. The council also suppressed a variety of local religious practices and saints' cults, replacing them with new cults authorized and approved by Rome. To prevent heretical ideas from corrupting the faithful, the council further decided to censor or suppress dangerous books. In 1564, a specially appointed commission published the first *Index of Prohibited Books*, an official list of forbidden writings. All of Erasmus's works were immediately placed on the *Index*,

THE INSPIRATION OF SAINT JEROME BY GUIDO RENI. The Council of Trent declared Saint Jerome's Latin translation of the Bible, the Vulgate, to be the official version of the Catholic Church. Since biblical scholars had long known that Saint Jerome's translation contained numerous errors, Catholic defenders of the Vulgate insisted that even his mistakes had been divinely inspired. ▪ *How does Guido Reni's painting of 1635 attempt to make this point?*

even though he had been a chosen champion of the Church only forty years before. It was to become symbolic of the doctrinal intolerance that characterized sixteenth-century Christianity, both in its Catholic and Protestant varieties. It was maintained until 1966, when it was abolished after the Second Vatican Council.

Ignatius Loyola and the Society of Jesus

In addition to the independent activities of popes and the legislation of the Council of Trent, a third main force propelling the Counter-Reformation was the foundation of the Society of Jesus (commonly known as the Jesuits) by Ignatius Loyola (1491–1556). In the midst of a career as a mercenary, this young Spanish nobleman had been wounded in battle in 1521, the same year in which Luther defied authority at the Diet of Worms. While recuperating, Ignatius turned from the reading of chivalric romances to a romantic vernacular retelling of the life of Jesus—and on the strength of this, decided to become a spiritual soldier of Christ. For ten months he lived as a hermit in a cave near the town of Manresa, where he experienced ecstatic visions and worked out the principles of his subsequent guidebook, the *Spiritual Exercises*. This manual, completed in 1535 and first published in 1541, offered practical advice on how to master one's will and serve God through a systematic

program of meditations. It eventually became a basic handbook for all Jesuits and has been widely studied by Catholic laypeople as well. Indeed, Loyola's *Spiritual Exercises* ranks alongside Calvin's *Institutes* as the most influential religious text of the sixteenth century.

The Jesuit order originated as a small group of six disciples who gathered around Loyola during his belated career as a student in Paris. They vowed to serve God in poverty, chastity, and missionary work, and were formally constituted by Pope Paul III in 1540. By the time of Loyola's death, the Society of Jesus already numbered some 1,500 members. It was by far the most militant of the religious orders fostered by the Catholic reform movements of the sixteenth century: not merely a monastic society, but a company of soldiers sworn to defend the faith with weapons of eloquence, persuasion, and instruction in correct doctrines. Yet the Society also became accomplished in more worldly methods of exerting influence; its organization was patterned after that of a military unit, whose commander in chief enforced iron discipline on all members. Individuality was suppressed, and a soldierlike obedience was required from the rank and file. Indeed, the Jesuit general, sometimes known as the "black pope" (from the color of the order's habit), was elected for life and answered only to the pope in Rome, to whom all senior Jesuits took a special vow of strict obedience. As a result of this vow, all Jesuits were held to be at the pope's disposal at all times.

As missionaries, the early Jesuits preached to non-Christians in India, China, and Spanish America. One of Loyola's closest associates, Francis Xavier (1506–1552), baptized thousands of native people and traveled thousands of miles in South and East Asia. For although Loyola had not at first conceived of his society as a batallion of "shock troops" in the fight against Protestantism, that is what it primarily became. Through preaching and diplomacy—sometimes at the risk of their lives—Jesuits in the second half of the sixteenth century fanned out across the globe. In many places, they were instrumental in keeping rulers and their subjects loyal to Catholicism; in others they met martyrdom; and in some others, notably Poland and parts of Germany and France, they succeeded in regaining territory previously lost to Protestantism. Wherever they were allowed to settle, they set up schools and colleges, based on the conviction that only a vigorous Catholicism nurtured by widespread literacy and education could combat Protestantism.

A New Catholic Christianity

The greatest achievement of these reform movements was the revitalization of the Roman Church. Had it not been for such determined efforts, Catholicism would not have swept

Analyzing Primary Sources

The Demands of Obedience

The necessity of obedience in the spiritual formation of monks and nuns can be traced back to the Rule of Saint Benedict *in the early sixth century (Chapter 6). In keeping with the mission of its founder, Ignatius of Loyola (1491–1556), the Society of Jesus brought a new militancy to this old ideal.*

Rules for Thinking with the Church

1. Always to be ready to obey with mind and heart, setting aside all judgment of one's own, the true spouse of Jesus Christ, our holy mother, our infallible and orthodox mistress, the Catholic Church, whose authority is exercised over us by the hierarchy.

2. To commend the confession of sins to a priest as it is practised in the Church; the reception of the Holy Eucharist once a year, or better still every week, or at least every month, with the necessary preparation. . . .

4. To have a great esteem for the religious orders, and to give the preference to celibacy or virginity over the married state. . . .

6. To praise relics, the veneration and invocation of Saints: also the stations, and pious pilgrimages, indulgences, jubilees, the custom of lighting candles in the churches, and other such aids to piety and devotion. . . .

9. To uphold especially all the precepts of the Church, and not censure them in any manner; but, on the contrary, to defend them promptly, with reasons drawn from all sources, against those who criticize them.

10. To be eager to commend the decrees, mandates, traditions, rites, and customs of the Fathers in the Faith or our superiors. . . .

11. That we may be altogether of the same mind and in conformity with the Church herself, if she shall have defined anything to be black which to our eyes appears to be white, we ought in like manner to pronounce it to be black. For we must undoubtingly believe, that the Spirit of our Lord Jesus Christ, and the Spirit of the Orthodox Church His Spouse, by which Spirit we are governed and directed to salvation, is the same. . . .

From the *Constitutions of the Jesuit Order*

Let us with the utmost pains strain every nerve of our strength to exhibit this virtue of obedience, firstly to the Highest Pontiff, then to the Superiors of the Society; so that in all things . . . we may be most ready to obey his voice, just as if it issued from Christ our Lord . . . leaving any work, even a letter, that we have begun and have not yet finished; by directing to this goal all our strength and intention in the Lord, that holy obedience may be made perfect in us in every respect, in performance, in will, in intellect; by submitting to whatever may be enjoined on us with great readiness, with spiritual joy and perseverance; by persuading ourselves that all things [commanded] are just; by rejecting with a kind of blind obedience all opposing opinion or judgment of our own. . . .

Source: Henry Bettenson, ed., *Documents of the Christian Church,* 2nd ed. (Oxford: 1967), pp. 259–61.

Questions for Analysis

1. How might Loyola's career as a soldier have inspired the language used in his "Rules for Thinking with the Church"?

2. In what ways do these Jesuit principles respond directly to the challenges of Protestant reformers?

over the globe during the seventeenth and eighteenth centuries or reemerged in Europe as a vigorous spiritual force. There were some other consequences, as well. One was the advancement of lay literacy in Catholic countries. Another was the growth of intense concern for acts of charity: because Catholicism continued to emphasize good works as well as faith, charitable activities took on an extremely important role.

There was also a renewed emphasis on the role of religious women. Reformed Catholicism did not exalt marriage as a route to holiness to the same degree as did Protestantism, but it did encourage the piety of a female religious elite. For example, it embraced the mysticism of Saint Teresa of Avila (1515–1582) and established new orders of nuns, such as the Ursulines and the Sisters of Charity. Both Protestants and Catholics continued to exclude women from the priest-hood or ministry, but Catholic women could pursue religious lives with at least some degree of independence, and the convent continued to be a route toward spiritual and even political advancement in Catholic countries.

The new Catholic Church did not, however, perpetuate the tolerant Christianity of Erasmus. Instead, Christian humanists lost favor with the papacy, and even Catholic scientists such as Galileo were regarded with suspicion (see Chapter 16). Yet contemporary Protestantism was just as intolerant, and even more hostile to the cause of rational thought. Indeed, because Catholic theologians turned for guidance to the scholasticism of Thomas Aquinas (Chapter 9), they tended to be much more committed to the dignity of human reason than were their Protestant counterparts, who emphasized the literal interpretation of the Bible and the importance of unquestioning faith. It is no coincidence that René Descartes, one of the pioneers of rational philosophy ("I think, therefore I am"), was educated by Jesuits.

It would be wrong, therefore, to claim that the Protestantism of this era was more forward-looking or progressive than Catholicism. Both were, in fact, products of their times. Each variety of Protestantism responded to specific historical conditions and the needs of specific peoples in specific places, while carrying forward certain aspects of the Christian tradition considered valuable by those communities. The Catholic Church also responded to new spiri-tual, political, and social realities—to such an extent that it must be regarded as distinct from either the early Church of the later Roman Empire or even the oft-reformed Church of the Middle Ages. That is why the phrase "Roman Catholic Church" has not been used in this book prior to this chapter, because the Roman Catholic Church as we know it emerged for the first time in the sixteenth century. Like Protestantism, it is a modern phenomenon.

CONCLUSION

The Reformation grew out of the complex historical processes that we have been tracing through the last few chapters. Foremost among these was the increasing power of Europe's sovereign states (Chapter 10). As we have seen, those German princes who embraced Protestantism were moved to do so by the desire for sovereignty. The kings of Denmark, Sweden, and England followed suit for many of the same reasons. Since Protestant leaders preached absolute obedience to godly rulers, and since the state in Protestant countries assumed direct control of its churches, Protestantism bolstered state power. Yet the power of the state had been growing for a long time prior to this, especially in such countries as France and Spain, where Catholic kings already exercised most of the same rights that were seized by Lutheran German princes and by

After You Read This Chapter

Visit StudySpace for quizzes, additional review materials, and multi-media documents. **wwnorton.com/studyspace**

REVIEWING THE OBJECTIVES

- The main premises of Luther's theology had political and social implications, too. What were they?
- A number of different Protestant movements rose in the sixteenth century. What were they, and how did they differ from one another?
- The Reformation had a profound effect on the basic structures of family life and on attitudes toward marriage and morality. Describe these changes.
- The Church of England was established in response to a specific political situation. What was this?
- How did the Catholic Church respond to the challenge of Protestantism?

Henry VIII of England. Those rulers who aligned themselves with Catholicism, then, had the same need to bolster their sovereignty and authority.

Ideas of national identity, too, were already influential and thus available for manipulation by Protestants and Catholics alike. These new religions, in turn, became sources of identity and disunity. Until the sixteenth century, for example, the peoples in the different regions of Germany spoke such different dialects that they had difficulty understanding each other. But Luther's German Bible gained such currency that it eventually became the linguistic standard for all these disparate regions, which eventually began to conceive of themselves as part of a single community. Yet religion alone could not achieve the political unification of Germany, which did not occur for another three hundred years (see Chapter 21); indeed, religion contributed to existing divisions by cementing the opposition of Catholic princes and peoples. Elsewhere in Europe—as in the Netherlands, where Protestants fought successfully against a foreign, Catholic overlord—religion created a shared identity where politics could not. In England, where it is arguable that a sense of nationalism had already been fostered before the Reformation, membership in the Church of England became a new, but not uncontested, attribute of "Englishness."

Ideals characteristic of the Renaissance (Chapter 12) also contributed something to the Reformation and the Catholic responses to it. The criticisms of Christian humanists helped to prepare Europe for the challenges of Lutheranism, and close textual study of the Bible led to the publication of the newer, more accurate editions used by Protestant reformers. For example, Erasmus's improved edition of the Latin New Testament enabled Luther to reach some crucial conclusions and became the foundation for Luther's own translation of the Bible. Yet Erasmus was no supporter of Lutheran principles and most other Christian humanists followed suit, shunning Protestantism as soon as it became clear to them what Luther was actually teaching. Indeed, in certain basic respects, Protestant principles were completely at odds with the principles, politics, and beliefs of most Renaissance humanists, who were staunch supporters of the Catholic Church.

In the New World and Asia, both Protestantism and Catholicism became forces of imperialism and new catalysts for competition. The race to secure colonies and resources now became a race for converts, too. In the process, the confessional divisions of Europe were mapped onto these far-flung territories, often with violent results. And over the course of the ensuing century, newly sovereign nation-states would continue to struggle for hegemony at home and abroad, setting off a series of religious wars that would cause as much destruction as any plague. We will discuss these upheavals and their long-term consequences in Chapter 14.

PEOPLE, IDEAS, AND EVENTS IN CONTEXT

- How did **MARTIN LUTHER**'s attack on **INDULGENCES** tap into more widespread criticism of the papacy? What role did the printing press and the German vernacular play in the dissemination of Luther's ideas?

- Why did many German principalities and cities rally to Luther's cause? Why did his condemnation at the **DIET OF WORMS** not lead to his execution on charges of heresy?

- How did the Protestant teachings of **ULRICH ZWINGLI**, **JOHN CALVIN**, and the **ANABAPTISTS** differ from one another and from those of Luther?

- What factors made some of Europe's territories more receptive to **PROTESTANTISM** than others? Why, for example, did Switzerland, the Netherlands, and the countries of Scandinavia embrace it?

- How did the **REFORMATION** alter the status and lives of women in Europe? Why did it strengthen male authority in the family?

- Why did **HENRY VIII** break with Rome? How did the **CHURCH OF ENGLAND** differ from Protestant churches elsewhere in Europe?

- What decisions were made at the **COUNCIL OF TRENT**? What were the founding principles of **IGNATIUS LOYOLA**'s **SOCIETY OF JESUS**, and what was its role in the **COUNTER-REFORMATION** of the **ROMAN CATHOLIC CHURCH**?

CONSEQUENCES

- Our study of Western civilizations has shown that reforming movements are nothing new: Christianity has been continuously reformed throughout its long history. What made this Reformation so different?

- Was a Protestant break with the Catholic Church inevitable? Why or why not?

- The political, social, and religious structures put in place during the Reformation continue to shape our lives in such profound ways that we scarcely notice them—or we assume them to be inevitable and natural. In your view, what is the most far-reaching consequence of this age of dissent and division, and why? In what ways has it formed your own values and assumptions?

STORY LINES

- The religious differences that divided Europe during Martin Luther's lifetime soon erupted into prolonged, widespread warfare. At the same time, deeply entrenched political convictions contributed to the length, ferocity, and extent of these wars.

- Social and economic tensions also played a role in the violence of this period, manifested in new forms of intolerance and persecution. For the first time, accusations of witchcraft were supported by intellectual arguments and sanctioned by the state.

- States themselves were becoming more powerful, as other sources of authority seemed less secure. Political philosophers and politicians worked to bolster this power and to define the sovereignty of the state.

- For all Its violence—or perhaps, because of it this period was an extremely fertile one for the arts, fostering the genius of French intellectuals, English poets and playwrights, and artists in Spain, Italy, and the Netherlands.

CHRONOLOGY

1540–1555	Regional wars in Germany
1547–1616	Lifetime of Miguel de Cervantes
1562–1598	French wars of religion
1564–1616	Lifetime of William Shakespeare
1566–1609	Dutch wars with Spain
1572–1580	Montaigne composes his *Essays*
1576	Jean Bodin publishes *Six Books of the Commonwealth*
1603	Reign of King James VI of Scotland begins in England
1618–1648	Thirty Years' War
1625–1649	Reign of King Charles I of England
1642–1649	English Civil War
1643–1715	Reign of Louis XIV of France
1649	Charles I of England is executed by act of Parliament
1651	Hobbes publishes *Leviathan*
1660	Restoration of the monarchy in England
1670	Publication of Pascal's *Pensées*

Before You Read This Chapter

Religion, Warfare, and Sovereignty: 1540–1660

CORE OBJECTIVES

- **UNDERSTAND** the ways in which early modern religious and political conflicts were intertwined.

- **TRACE** the main phases of religious warfare on the Continent.

- **IDENTIFY** the causes for Spain's decline and France's rise to power.

- **EXPLAIN** the origins and significance of the English Civil War.

- **DESCRIBE** some of the ways that intellectuals and artists responded to the challenges of this era.

n the early spring of 1592, a new play was mounted at the Rose Theatre, one of the enclosed places of entertainment recently constructed in London's suburbs. It was the prequel to two vastly popular plays that chronicled the dynastic wars that had divided England in the fifteenth century, when English losses in the Hundred Years' War gave way to civil wars at home. The play, *The First Part of Henry VI*, was intended to explore the origins of those wars during the reign of the child-king who had suceeded the heroic Henry V, and it completed a trilogy that launched an ambitious young playwright called Will Shakespeare.

Civil strife was a hot topic in the sixteenth century. Shakespeare's England was much more peaceful and unified than almost any other country in Europe, but that unity was fragile. It had been shattered numerous times because of ongoing religious divisions, and it was only being maintained by a growing sense of national identity. Shakespeare's early plays promoted that identity by celebrating the superiority of the average Englishman over his European neighbors, who were often represented as either ridiculous or villainous. So in this new play, the most interesting and ultimately dangerous character is the French heroine Joan of Arc, whose fervent Catholic faith turns out to be

331

a mask for witchcraft. In Shakespeare's version of her legend, Joan attempts to be released from the tortures of the stake by claiming to be pregnant, and dies calling on her demon familiars to rescue her from the flames.

Shakespeare's plays, like many other products of contemporary popular culture, reveal the profound tensions that fractured the kingdoms and communities of Europe in the century after the Reformation. Martin Luther's call for universal access to the Bible had not resulted in a unified interpretation of the Christian faith; nor did his dream of a "priesthood of all believers" topple the clerical hierarchy of the Roman Church. Instead, Europe's religious divisions multiplied, often crystallizing along political lines. By the time of Luther's death in 1546, a clear pattern had already emerged. With only rare exceptions, Protestantism triumphed in areas where those in power stood to gain by rejecting the Church's hold over them; meanwhile, Catholicism prevailed in territories whose rulers had forged close political alliances with Rome. In both cases, Protestants and Catholics clung to the same belief in the mutual interdependence of religion and politics, an old certainty that had also undergirded the civilization of ancient Rome (Chapter 5) and most other Western civilizations before it.

Ironically, then, Catholics and Protestants were united in one conviction: western Europe had to return to a single religious faith enforced by properly constituted political authorities. What they could not agree on was *which* faith—and which authorities. The result was a brutal series of wars whose reverberations continue to be felt in many regions of Europe and in her former colonies. Vastly expensive and destructive, these wars affected everyone from peasants to princes. Yet it would be misleading to suggest that they were caused by religious differences alone. Regional tensions, dynastic politics, and nascent nationalist tendencies were also potent contributors to the violence. Together, these forces brought into question the very survival of the political institutions that had emerged in the twelfth and thirteenth centuries (Chapter 9). Faced with the prospect of annihilation, those who still held power a century later were forced to embrace, gradually and grudgingly, a notion that had long seemed impossible: religious tolerance as the only way to preserve political, social, and economic order.

SOURCES OF TENSION AND UNREST

The troubles that engulfed Europe during the long, traumatic century between 1540 and 1660 caught contemporaries unaware. Most of Europe had enjoyed steady economic growth since the middle of the fifteenth century, and the colonization of the Americas seemed certain to be the basis of greater prosperity to come. Political trends too seemed auspicious, because most western European governments were becoming more efficient and effective. By the middle of the sixteenth century, however, there were warning signs.

The Price Revolution

The first of these warning signs was economic: an unprecedented inflation in prices that began in the latter half of the sixteenth century. In Flanders, the cost of wheat tripled between 1550 and 1600; grain prices in Paris quadrupled; and the overall cost of living in England more than doubled. The twentieth century would see much more dizzying inflations than this, but in the sixteenth century the skyrocketing of prices was a terrifying novelty, what many historians describe as the "price revolution."

Two developments in particular underlay the soaring prices. The first was demographic. Starting in the later fifteenth century, Europe's population began to grow again after the plague-induced decline of the fourteenth century (Chapter 10); roughly estimated, Europe had about 50 million people around 1450, and 90 million around 1600. Because Europe's food supply remained more or less constant, owing to the lack of any noteworthy breakthroughs in agricultural technology analogous to those of the eleventh century (Chapter 8), food prices were driven sharply higher by greater demand. At the same time, wages stagnated or even declined. As a result, workers around 1600 were paying a higher percentage of their wages to buy food.

Population trends explain much, but other explanations for the great inflation are also necessary. Foremost among these is the enormous influx of bullion from Spanish America. In just four years, from 1556 to 1560, roughly 10 million ducats' worth of silver passed through the Spanish port of Seville. That figure doubled between 1576 and 1580, and between 1591 and 1595 it more than quadrupled. Most of this silver was used by the Spanish crown to pay its foreign creditors and its armies abroad; as a result, this bullion quickly circulated throughout Europe, where much of it was minted into coins. This dramatic increase in the volume of money in circulation fueled the spiral of rising prices. "I learned a proverb here," said a French traveler to Spain in 1603: "everything costs a lot, except silver."

Aggressive entrepreneurs and large-scale farmers profited most from the changed economic circumstances, while the masses of laboring people were hurt the most because wages rose far more slowly than prices. Moreover, because the cost of food staples rose at a sharper rate than the cost of most other items, poor people had to spend an ever-greater percentage of their paltry incomes on necessities. The picture that emerges is one of the rich getting richer and the poor getting poorer.

The price revolution also placed new pressures on the sovereign states of Europe. Since inflation depressed the real value of money, fixed incomes from taxes and tolls yielded less and less income. So governments were forced to raise taxes merely to keep their revenues constant. But to compound this problem, most states needed more real income because they were engaging in more wars; and warfare was becoming increasingly expensive. The only recourse, then, was to raise taxes precipitously. Hence governments faced continuous threats of defiance and even armed resistance from their subjects. A few areas—notably the Netherlands—bucked the trend, and the wealthy were usually able to hold their own, but the lives of the poor in many places deteriorated further as the mid-seventeenth century saw particularly destructive wars in which helpless civilians were plundered by rapacious tax collectors or looting soldiers, sometimes both. The Black Death also returned, wreaking havoc in London and elsewhere during the 1660s.

Political and Religious Instability

Compounding these problems were the disunities inherent within major European monarchies. Most states had grown during the later Middle Ages by absorbing or colonizing smaller, autonomous territories—sometimes by conquest, but more often through marriage alliances or inheritance arrangements among ruling families. At first, some degree of provincial autonomy was usually preserved. But in the period we are now examining, governments began making ever-greater financial claims on all their subjects while trying to enforce religious uniformity. As a result, rulers often rode roughshod over the rights of these traditionally independent provinces.

At the same time, claims to sovereignty—that is, to the unity, autonomy, and authority of a state—were increasingly made on the basis of religious uniformity. Both Catholic and Protestant rulers felt that religious minorities, if allowed to flourish in their realms, would inevitably engage in sedition; nor were they always wrong, since militant Calvinists and Jesuits were indeed dedicated to subverting constituted powers in areas where their parties had not yet triumphed. Thus states tried to extirpate all poten-

tial religious resistance and, in the process, sometimes provoked civil wars in which each side tended to assume there could be no victory until the other was exterminated. And of course, civil wars could become international in scope if foreign powers chose to aid their embattled religious allies.

Regionalism, economic grievances, and religious animosities were thus compounded into a volatile and destructive mixture. Nor was that all, since most governments seeking money and/or religious uniformity tried to rule with a firmer hand than before and thus increasingly provoked armed resistance from subjects seeking to preserve traditional liberties. As a result, the long century between 1540 and 1660 was one of the most turbulent in all of European history.

A CENTURY OF RELIGIOUS WARS

The greatest single cause of warfare during this period was religious conflict. These "wars of religion" are usually divided into four phases:

    I. a series of regional wars in Germany from the 1540s to 1555
    II. the French wars of religion from 1562 until 1598
    III. the simultaneous revolts of the (Protestant) Dutch against the (Catholic) Spanish Habsburg Empire between 1566 and 1609
    IV. the Thirty Years' War that devasted German-speaking lands again, between 1618 and 1648.

In addition, as we shall see, the English Civil War resulted in part from religious differences, even though it is not usually considered a war of religion (see below).

Regional Warfare in Germany

Wars between Catholics and Protestant rulers in Germany began in the 1540s, less than a generation after Lutheranism first took hold there. As we have seen, the Holy Roman emperor, Charles V, was also king of Spain and a devout supporter of the Church (Chapter 13). His goal was to reestablish Catholic unity in Germany by launching a military campaign against several German princes who had instituted Lutheran worship in their territories. But despite several notable victories, Charles's efforts failed. In part, this was because he was simultaneously involved in wars against France, but primarily it was because the Catholic princes of Germany also worked against him, fearing that any suppression of Protestant princes might suppress their own independence, too. As a result, the Catholic princes' support for the foreign-born Charles was only lukewarm; at times, they even joined with Protestants in battle against the emperor.

This regional warfare sputtered on and off until a compromise was reached via the Peace of Augsburg in 1555. Its governing principle was *cuius regio, eius religio*: "as the ruler, so the religion." This meant that in those principalities where Lutherans ruled, Lutheranism would be the sole state religion; but where Catholic princes ruled, the people of their territories would also be Catholic. For better and for worse, the Peace of Augsburg was a historical milestone. For the first time since Luther had been excommunicated, Catholic rulers were forced to acknowledge the legality of Protestantism. But the peace set a dangerous precedent because it legitimated the principle that no sovereign state could tolerate religious diversity. Moreover, it excluded Calvinism entirely, and thus spurred German Calvinists to become aggressive opponents of the status quo.

The French Wars of Religion

From the 1560s on, Europe's religious wars became far more brutal, partly because the combatants had become more intransigent and partly because they were aggravated by regional and dynastic animosities. For example, Calvin's Geneva bordered on France; and because Calvin himself was a Frenchman, Calvinist missionaries made considerable headway. But their concentration in the southern part of France reflected long-standing hostilities that reached back to the ravages of northern French "crusaders" against Albigensian "heretics" during the thirteenth century (Chapter 9). Also assisting the Calvinist cause was the conversion of many aristocratic Frenchwomen, who in turn won over their husbands, many of whom maintained large private armies. The foremost example of these was Jeanne d'Albret, queen of Navarre, who converted her husband, the prominent aristocrat Antoine de Bourbon, and her brother-in-law, the prince of Condé.

Within two decades, French Calvinists—known as Huguenots (*YOO-guh-nohs*) for reasons that remain obscure—made up between 10 and 20 percent of the population. Although they lived uneasily alongside their Catholic neighbors, there was no open warfare until 1562, when the reigning king died unexpectedly, leaving a young child

as his heir. This spurred a struggle between two factions which formed along religious lines: the Huguenots, led by the prince of Condé, and the Catholics, led by the duke of Guise. And since both Catholics and Protestants believed that a kingdom could have only one *roi, foi,* and *loi* ("king," "faith," and "law"), this political struggle turned into a religious war. Although the Huguenots were not numerous enough to gain a victory, they were too strong to be defeated entirely, especially in their stronghold of southern France. Hence warfare dragged on for a decade until a truce was arranged in 1572. This truce required the young Huguenot leader, Prince Henry of Navarre, to marry the Catholic sister of the reigning French king.

Yet this compromise was placed in jeopardy by the powerful dowager queen of France, Catherine de' Medici, scion of the Florentine family that was closely aligned with the papacy (Chapter 13). Instead of honoring the truce, she plotted with members of the Catholic faction at court to kill all the Huguenot leaders while they were assembled in Paris for her daugher's wedding. In the early morning of St. Bartholomew's Day in 1572 (August 24), most of these leaders were murdered in their beds, while thousands of other Protestants were slaughtered in the streets or drowned in the Seine by Catholic mobs. When word of the Parisian massacre spread to the provinces, some 10,000 more Huguenots were killed. Henry of Navarre escaped, along with his new bride; but now the conflict entered an even more bitter phase.

Catherine's death in 1589 enabled Henry of Navarre to be crowned king as Henry IV, but peace was not restored until he renounced his Protestant faith in order to placate France's Catholic majority. In 1598, however, he offered limited religious freedom to the Huguenots by issuing the Edict of Nantes, which recognized Catholicism as the official religion of the kingdom but allowed Huguenot aristocrats to hold Protestant services privately in their homes, while other Huguenots were allowed to worship in certain specified places at certain times. The Huguenot party was also permitted to fortify some towns, especially in the south and west, for their own military defense. Huguenots were further guaranteed the right to hold public office and to enter universities and hospitals.

The Edict of Nantes did not guarantee absolute freedom of worship, but it was still a major stride in the direction of tolerance. Unfortunately, however, the effect was to divide the kingdom into separate religious enclaves. In southern and western France, Huguenots established their own law courts, staffed by their own judges. They also received substantial powers of self-government. The edict thus represented a concession to the long-standing traditions of

The Devastation of the Thirty Years' War

The author of the following excerpt, Hans Jakob Christoph von Grimmelshausen (1621–1676), barely survived the horrors of the Thirty Years' War. His parents were killed, probably when he was thirteen years old, and he himself was kidnapped the following year and forced into the army. By age fifteen, he was a soldier. His darkly satiric masterpiece, Simplicissimus (The Simpleton), *drew heavily on these experiences. Although technically a fictional memoir, it portrays with brutal accuracy the terrible realities of this era.*

Although it was not my intention to take the peaceloving reader with these troopers to my dad's house and farm, seeing that matters will go ill therein, yet the course of my history demands that I should leave to kind posterity an account of what manner of cruelties were now and again practised in this our German war: yes, and moreover testify by my own example that such evils must often have been sent to us by the goodness of Almighty God for our profit. For, gentle reader, who would ever have taught me that there was a God in Heaven if these soldiers had not destroyed my dad's house, and by such a deed driven me out among folk who gave me all fitting instruction thereupon? . . .

The first thing these troopers did was, that they stabled their horses: thereafter each fell to his appointed task: which task was neither more nor less than ruin and destruction. For though some began to slaughter and to boil and to roast so that it looked as if there should be a merry banquet forward, yet others there were who did but storm through the house above and below stairs. Others stowed together great parcels of cloth and apparel and all manner of household stuff, as if they would set up a frippery market. All that they had no mind to take with them they cut in pieces. Some thrust their swords through the hay and straw as if they had not enough sheep and swine to slaughter: and some shook the feathers out of the beds and in their stead stuffed in bacon and other dried meat and provisions as if such were better and softer to sleep upon. Others broke the stove and the windows as if they had a never-ending summer to promise. Houseware of copper and tin they beat flat, and packed such vessels, all bent and spoiled, in with the rest. Bedsteads, tables, chairs, and benches they burned, though there lay many cords of dry wood in the yard. Pots and pipkins must all go to pieces, either because they would eat none but roast flesh, or because their purpose was to make there but a single meal.

Our maid was so handled in the stable that she could not come out, which is a shame to tell of. Our man they laid bound upon the ground, thrust a gag into his mouth, and poured a pailful of filthy water into his body: and by this, which they called a Swedish draught, they forced him to lead a party of them to another place where they captured men and beasts, and brought them back to our farm, in which company were my dad, my mother, and our Ursula.

And now they began: first to take the flints out of their pistols and in place of them to jam the peasants' thumbs in and so to torture the poor rogues as if they had been about the burning of witches: for one of them they had taken they thrust into the baking oven and there lit a fire under him, although he had as yet confessed no crime: as for another, they put a cord round his head and so twisted it tight with a piece of wood that the blood gushed from his mouth and nose and ears. In a word each had his own device to torture the peasants, and each peasant his several tortures.

Source: Hans Jakob Christoph von Grimmelshausen, *Simplicissimus*, trans. S. Goodrich (New York: 1995), pp. 1–3, 8–10, 32–35.

Questions for Analysis

1. The first-person narrator here recounts the atrocities committed "in this our German war," in which both perpetrators and victims are German. How believable is this description? Why does he emphasize this? What lends it credibility?

2. Why might Grimmelshausen have chosen to publish his account as a satirical fiction, rather than as a straightforward historical narrative or autobiography? How would this choice affect a reader's response to scenes such as this?

provincial autonomy within the various regions of France, raising the fear that the kingdom might once again crumble into its constituent parts, as it had during the Hundred Years' War. On its own terms, however, the Edict of Nantes was a success. France began to recover from decades of devastation, and peace was maintained even after Henry IV was assassinated by a Catholic in 1610.

The Revolt of the Netherlands

Bitter warfare also broke out between Catholics and Protestants in the Low Countries. For almost a century, the territories comprising much of the modern-day Netherlands and Belgium had been ruled by the Habsburg family of Holy Roman emperors, who also ruled Spain. The southern Netherlands in particular had prospered greatly from this. Through trade and manufacture, their inhabitants generated the greatest per capita wealth of all Europe, and their metropolis of Antwerp was northern Europe's leading commercial and financial center. Moreover, the half-century rule of Charles V had been successful here. Charles had been born in the Flemish city of Ghent, and had a strong rapport with his Flemish subjects, whom he allowed a large measure of self-government.

But a year after the Peace of Augsburg in 1555, Charles V retired to a monastery and ceded all of his vast territories outside of the Holy Roman Empire and Hungary to his son Philip II (r. 1556–98). Unlike Charles, Philip had been born in Spain and made Spain his residence and the focus of his policy. He viewed the Netherlands primarily as a source of income. So the better to exploit the region's wealth, Philip tried to tighten his control over it, which aroused the resentment of the region's fiercely independent cities. A religious storm was also brewing. French Calvinists were beginning to stream into the southern Netherlands, intent on making converts. Within decades, there were more Calvinists in Antwerp than in Geneva. To Philip, an ardent supporter of the Roman Catholic Church, this was intolerable.

Worried by the growing tensions, a group of Catholic aristocrats petitioned Philip to allow toleration for Calvinists within the Netherlands. They were led by William of Orange, known as "William the Silent" because he was so successful at hiding his religious and political leanings. But before Philip could respond, radical Protestant mobs began ransacking Catholic churches, desecrating altars, smashing statuary, and shattering stained-glass windows. Local troops brought the situation under control, but Philip nonetheless decided to dispatch an army of 10,000 Spanish soliders, led by the duke of Alva, to wipe out Protestantism in the Netherlands. Alva's rule quickly became a reign of terror. Operating under martial law, his "Council of Blood" examined some 12,000 people on charges of heresy or sedition, of whom 9,000 were convicted and thousands executed. William fled the country, and all hope for peace in the Netherlands seemed lost.

Yet the tide turned quickly. The exiled William converted openly to Protestantism and sought help from religious allies in France, Germany, and England; meanwhile, organized bands of Protestant privateers harassed Spanish shipping. In 1572, William was able to seize the northern Netherlands, even though the north had been predominantly Catholic. Thereafter, geography played a major role in determining the outcome of the conflict. Spanish armies were stopped by a combination of impassable rivers and dikes that could be opened to flood out the invaders. Although William was assassinated by a Catholic in 1584, his son continued to lead the resistance until the Spanish crown agreed to recognize the independence of a northern Dutch Republic in 1609. For ironically, the pressures of war and persecution had made the whole north Calvinist, whereas the south—which remained under Spanish control—returned to Catholicism.

England and the Spanish Armada

Religious strife could spark civil war, as in France, or political rebellion, as in the Netherlands. But it could also provoke warfare between sovereign states, as in the struggle between England and Spain. As we noted in Chapter 13, the Catholic queen Mary of England (r. 1553–58), herself the granddaughter of Ferdinand and Isabella, had married her cousin Philip II of Spain in 1554. After her death, Philip appears to have extended a marriage proposal to her half-sister, the Protestant queen Elizabeth (r. 1558–1603)— and to have been rejected. Adding to the animosity created by religious differences and dynastic politics was the fact that English economic interests were directly opposed to those of Spain: English seafarers and traders were steadily making inroads into Spanish naval and commercial networks. The greatest source of antagonism lay in the Atlantic, where English privateers, with the tacit consent of Queen Elizabeth, began attacking Spanish treasure ships. Taking as an excuse the Spanish oppression of Protestants in the Netherlands, English sea captains such as Sir Francis Drake and Sir John Hawkins plundered Spanish vessels on the high seas. In a particularly dramatic exploit lasting from 1577 to 1580, prevailing winds and lust for gold propelled Drake all the way around the world, to return

THE "ARMADA PORTRAIT" OF ELIZABETH. This is one of several portraits that commemorated the defeat of the Spanish Armada in 1588. Through the window on the left (the queen's right hand), an English flotilla sails serenely on sunny seas; on the right, Spanish ships are wrecked by a "Protestant wind." Elizabeth's right hand rests protectively—and commandingly—on the globe. ■ *How would you "read" this image?*

with stolen Spanish treasure worth twice as much as Queen Elizabeth's annual revenue.

All this might have been sufficient provocation, but Philip resolved to invade the island only after the English openly allied with Dutch rebels in 1585. Even then, Philip moved slowly. Finally, in 1588 he dispatched an enormous fleet, confidently called the "Invincible Armada." However, the smaller English warships, more agile and armed with longer-range guns, outmaneuvered the Spanish fleet, while English fireships set some Spanish galleons ablaze and forced the rest to break formation. A fierce "Protestant wind" did the rest. After a disastrous circumnavigation of the British Isles and Ireland, the shattered Spanish flotilla limped home with almost half its ships lost. Elizabeth quickly took credit for her country's miraculous escape.

The Thirty Years' War

After the Peace of Augsburg in 1555, the balance of powers between Protestant and Catholic territories within the Holy Roman Empire had remained largely undisturbed. In 1618, however, the Catholic Habsburg prince who ruled Poland, Austria, and Hungary was elected king of Protestant Bohemia, prompting a rebellion among the Bohemian aristocracy. When this same prince, Ferdinand, became Holy Roman Emperor a year later, German Catholic forces were

sent to crush the rebellion against him. But this military intervention threatened the political autonomy of all German princes, Catholic and Protestant alike. So when the Lutheran king of Sweden, Gustavus Adolphus, championed the Protestant cause in 1630, he was welcomed by several German Catholic princes, too.

To make matters still more complicated, the Swedish king's Protestant army was secretly subsidized by Catholic France, whose policy was then dictated by Cardinal Richelieu (*RIH-shlyuh*, 1585–1642). Richelieu was determined to prevent France from being surrounded by a strong Habsburg alliance on the north, east, and south. But when Gustavus died in battle in 1632, Cardinal Richelieu found himself having to conduct the war on his own. In 1635, France openly declared itself for Sweden, against Austria and Spain. In the middle lay Germany, a helpless battleground.

Germany suffered more from warfare in the terrible years between 1618 and 1648 than than at any time until the twentieth century. Several German cities were besieged and sacked nine or ten times over, and soldiers from all nations, who had to sustain themselves by plunder, gave no quarter to defenseless civilians. With plague and disease adding to the toll of outright butchery, some parts of Germany lost more than half their populations.

The eventual adoption of the Peace of Westphalia in 1648 was a watershed in European history. It marked the emergence of France as the predominant power on the Continent, a position it would hold for the next two centuries. The greatest losers in the conflict (aside from the millions of German victims) were the Austrian Habsburgs, who were forced to surrender all the territory they had gained and to abandon their hopes of using the office of Holy Roman Emperor to dominate central Europe. Spain became increasingly relegated to the margins of Europe, and Germany remained a volatile checkerboard of Protestant and Catholic principalities.

DIVERGENT POLITICAL PATHS: SPAIN AND FRANCE

The long century of war between 1540 and 1648 decisively altered the balance of power among the major kingdoms of western Europe. Germany emerged from the Thirty Years' War a devastated and exhausted land. Spain, too, was crippled by its unremitting military exertions. The French monarchy, by contrast, steadily increased its power. By 1660, France had become the most powerful country on the European mainland. In England, meanwhile, a bloody

Portugal, which had been annexed by Phillip II in 1580), half of Italy, half of the Netherlands, all of Central and South America, and the Philippine Islands in the Pacific Ocean—was the mightiest power not just in Europe but in the world. Yet only a half century later, this empire was beginning to fall apart.

Spain's greatest underlying weakness was economic. At first this may seem odd, considering that in 1600—as in the three or four previous decades—huge amounts of American silver were being unloaded at the port of Seville. Yet as contemporaries themselves recognized, the New World that Spain had conquered was now conquering Spain. Lacking both agricultural and mineral resources of its own, Spain desperately needed to develop industries and a balanced trading pattern, as some of its Atlantic rivals were doing. But the Spanish nobility prized honor and chivalric ideals over practical business affairs. They used imperial silver to buy manufactured goods from other parts of Europe and, as a result, had no incentive to develop industries and exports of their own. When the river of silver began to abate, Spain was plunged into debt.

Meanwhile, the crown's commitment to supporting the Roman Catholic Church and maintaining Spain's international dominance meant the continuance of costly wars. Even in the relatively peaceful year of 1608, about 4 million ducats—out of a total revenue of 7 million—were spent on military ventures. Spain's involvement in the Thirty Years' War was the last straw. In 1643, French troops inflicted a stunning defeat on the famed Spanish infantry at Rocroi in nothern France, the first time that a Spanish army had been overcome in battle since the end of the "Reconquista" (Chapter 11).

By then, two of Spain's Iberian territories were in open revolt. The governing power of Spain lay entirely in Castile, which had emerged as the dominant power after the marriage of Queen Isabella to Ferdinand of Aragon in 1469. In the absence of any great hardships, semi-autonomous Catalonia had endured Castilian hegemony. But in 1640, when the

EUROPE AT THE END OF THE THIRTY YEARS' WAR. This map shows the fragile political checkerboard that resulted from the Peace of Westphalia in 1648. ▪ *When you compare this map to the map on page 316 in Chapter 13, what are the most significant territorial changes between 1550 and 1648?* ▪ *Which regions would have been weakened or endangered by this arrangement?* ▪ *Which would be in a strong position to dominate Europe?*

civil war had broken out between the king and his critics in Parliament, culminating in an unprecedented event: the legal execution of a reigning monarch by his own parliamentary government.

The Decline of Spain

The story of Spain's fall from grandeur unfolds almost as relentlessly as a Greek tragedy. In 1600, the Spanish Empire—comprising all of the Iberian Peninsula (including

strains of warfare induced Castile to limit Catalan liberties and to raise more money and men for combat, Catalonia revolted. When the Portuguese learned of the Catalan uprising, they revolted as well, followed by southern Italians who rose up against Castilian viceroys in Naples and Sicily in 1647. It was only by chance that Spain's greatest external enemies, France and England, could not act in time to take advantage of its plight. This gave the Castilian government time to put down the Italian revolts; by 1652 it had also brought Catalonia to heel. But Portugal retained its independence, while Spain's isolation after the Peace of Westphalia further increased.

The Growth of France

A comparison of the fortunes of Spain and France in the first half of the seventeenth century shows some striking similarities. Both countries were of almost identical size, and both had been created by the same process of accretion and conquest over the course of the previous centuries (Chapters 9 and 10). Just as the Castilian crown had gained Aragon, Catalonia, Granada, and then Portugal, so the kingdom of France had grown by adding such diverse territories as Languedoc, Provence, Burgundy, and Brittany. Since the inhabitants of all these territories cherished traditions of local independence and their own distinct languages and cultures, and since French and Spanish monarchs were determined to govern their provinces ever more firmly—especially when the costs of the Thirty Years' War made ruthless tax collecting an urgent necessity—a direct confrontation between both central governments and their provinces became inevitable in both cases.

The fact that France emerged powerfully from this while Spain did not can be attributed in part to France's greater natural resources and the greater prestige of the French monarchy. Most subjects of the French king, including those from the outlying provinces, were loyal to him. Certainly they had excellent reason to be so during the reign of Henry IV. Having established religious peace by the Edict of Nantes, the affable Henry declared that there should be a chicken in every family's pot each Sunday, and therefore set out to restore the prosperity of a country devastated by civil war. And France had enormous economic resiliency, owing primarily to its extremely rich and varied agricultural productivity. Unlike Spain, which had to import food, France was able to feed itself well; and Henry's finance minister, the duke of Sully, quickly ensured that it did just that. Among other things, Sully distributed free

copies of a guide to recommended farming techniques and financed the building or rebuilding of roads, bridges, and canals to facilitate the flow of goods. Henry IV, meanwhile, ordered the construction of royal factories to manufacture luxury goods such as crystal, glass, and tapestries while supporting the growth of silk, linen, and woolen cloth industries in many different parts of the country. Henry's patronage also allowed the explorer Samuel de Champlain to claim parts of Canada as France's first foothold in the New World.

The Reign of Cardinal Richelieu

Henry IV's reign can be counted as one of the most benevolent and effective in France's history. Far less benevolent was that of Henry's de facto successor, Cardinal Richelieu. The real king of France, Henry's son Louis XIII (r. 1610–43), came to the throne at the age of nine. But his reign was dominated by his chief minister of state. It was Richelieu who centralized royal power at home and expanded French influence abroad. For example, when Huguenots rebelled against certain restrictions that had been placed on them by the Edict of Nantes, Richelieu amended the edict to revoke their political and military rights altogether. He then moved to gain more income for the crown by ending the semi-autonomy of Burgundy, the Dauphiné, and Provence so that he could introduce direct royal taxation in all three areas. Later, to make sure taxes were efficiently collected, Richelieu instituted a new system of local government by royal officials who were expressly commissioned to put down provincial resistance. By these and other methods, Richelieu made the French monarchy more powerful and far-reaching than any in Europe and managed to double the crown's income during his rule. He also engaged in ambitious foreign wars against the Habsburgs of Austria and Spain, as we have seen. Yet increased centralization and France's costly involvement in the Thirty Years' War would lead to increased internal pressures in the years after Richelieu's death.

The Fronde

An immediate reaction to French governmental control was the series of uncoordinated revolts known collectively as the *Fronde* (from the French word for "slingshot"), which occured in 1643, a year after Richelieu's death. Louis XIII had just been succeeded by the five-year-old Louis XIV,

whose regents were his mother, Anne of Austria, and Cardinal Mazarin, who was rumored to be her lover. Both were foreigners—Anne was a Habsburg and Mazarin was an Italian adventurer named Giulio Mazarini—and many of their subjects, including some extremely powerful nobles, hated them. Popular resentments were greater still because the costs of the ongoing Thirty Years' War were now combined with several consecutive years of bad harvests.

Neither the aristocratic leaders of the Fronde nor the commoners who joined them in revolt claimed to be resisting the young king; their targets were the alleged corruption and mismanagement of Mazarin. Some of the rebels, indeed, insisted that part of Mazarin's fault lay in his pursuit of Richelieu's centralizing, antiprovincial policy. But most aristocrats wanted to become part of this centralizing process. So when Louis XIV began to rule in his own right in 1651, and pretexts for revolt against corrupt ministers no longer existed, the opposition was soon silenced. Yet Louis XIV remembered the turbulence of the Fronde for the rest of his life, and resolved never to let his aristocracy or his provinces get out of hand. Pursuing this policy, he became the most effective absolute monarch in Europe (see Chapter 15).

MONARCHY AND CIVIL WAR IN ENGLAND

The power of Louis XIV in France stands in stark contrast to the challenges faced by his older contemporary, King Charles I of England. Of all the revolts that shook mid-seventeenth-century Europe, the most radical in its consequences was the English Civil War. The causes of this conflict were similar to those that sparked rebellions in Spain and France: hostilities between the component parts of a composite kingdom; religious animosities between Catholics and Protestants and within the ruling camp; struggles for power among competing factions of aristocrats at court; and a fiscal system that could not keep pace with the increasing costs of government, much less those of war. But in England, these conflicts led to the deposition and execution of the king (1649), an eleven-year "interregnum" during which England was ruled as a parliamentary republic (1649–60), and ultimately to the restoration of the monarchy under conditions designed to safeguard Parliament's place in government, an arrangement that has endured up to the present day.

The Origins of the English Civil War

The chain of events leading to war between royalist and Parliamentary forces in 1642 can be traced to the last decades of Queen Elizabeth's reign. During the 1590s, the expenses of war with Spain, together with a rebellion in Ireland, widespread crop failures, and the inadequacies of the antiquated English taxation system, drove the queen's government deeply into debt. Factional disputes around the court also became more bitter as courtiers, anticipating the aging queen's death, jockeyed for position under her presumed successor, the Scottish king James Stuart (James VI). Only on her deathbed, however, did the queen finally confirm that her throne should go to her Scottish cousin. As a result, neither James nor his new English subjects knew very much about each other when he took the throne at the end of 1603, ruling England as James I.

The relationship did not begin well. James's English subjects looked down on the Scots whom he brought with him to London. Although English courtiers were pleased to accept their new king's generosity to themselves, they resented the grants he made to his Scottish supporters. James, meanwhile, saw that to resolve his debts he had to have more revenue. But rather than bargain with parliamentary representatives for increased taxation, he chose to lecture them on the prerogatives of kingship. When this approach failed, James raised what revenues he could without Parliament's approval, by imposing new tolls on trade and selling trading monopolies to favored courtiers. These measures aroused further resentments and so made voluntary grants of taxation from Parliament even less likely.

James was more adept with respect to religious policy. Scotland had been a firmly Calvinist country since the 1560s. England, too, was a Protestant country, but of a very different kind, since the Church of England retained many of the rituals, hierarchies, and doctrines of the medieval Catholic Church (Chapter 13). Although a significant number of English Protestants wanted to bring their church more firmly into line with Calvinist principles, others resisted such efforts and labeled their Calvinist opponents "Puritans." As king, James was compelled to mediate these conflicts. By and large, he did so successfully. In Scotland, he convinced the reformed (Calvinist) church to retain bishops as leaders; in England, he encouraged Calvinist doctrine while resisting any alterations to the religious tenets articulated in the English Prayer Book and the Thirty-Nine Articles of the Faith. Only in Ireland, which remained overwhelmingly Catholic, did James stir up future trouble. By encouraging the "plantation" of more than 8,000 Scottish

Calvinists in the northern province of Ulster, he undermined the property rights of Irish Catholics and created religious animosities that still continues today.

The Reign of Charles Stuart

In 1625, James was succeeded by his surviving son, Charles. Charles almost immediately launched a new war with Spain, exacerbating his financial problems. He then alarmed his Protestant subjects by marrying Henrietta Maria, the Catholic daughter of France's Louis XIII. The situation became truly dangerous, however, when Charles and his archbishop of Canterbury, William Laud, began to favor the most anti-Calvinist elements in the English church, thus threatening the allegiance of the forthrightly Calvinist church in Scotland. The Scots rebelled, and in 1640 a Scottish army marched south into England to demand the withdrawal of Charles's "Catholicizing" reforms.

To meet the Scottish threat, Charles was forced to summon the English Parliament, something he (like his father) had avoided doing. Relations between the king and Parliament had broken down severely in the late 1620s, when Charles responded to Parliament's denial of additional funds by demanding loans from his subjects—and punishing those who refused by forcing them to lodge soldiers in their homes, or throwing them into prison without trial. In response, Parliament compelled the king to accept the Petition of Right in 1628, which declared all taxes not voted by Parliament illegal, condemned the quartering of soldiers in private houses, and prohibited arbitrary imprisonment and martial law in time of peace. Angered rather than chastened by the Petition of Right, Charles resolved to rule England without Parliament, funding his government during the 1630s with a variety of levies and fines imposed without parliamentary consent.

When the Scottish invasion of 1640 finally forced Charles to summon a new Parliament, therefore, its representatives were determined to impose a series of radical reforms on the king's government before they would even consider granting him money to raise an army. Charles initially cooperated with these reforms, even allowing Parliament to execute his chief minister. But it soon became clear that parliamentary leaders had no intention of fighting the Scots, and actually shared with them a common Calvinist outlook. In 1642, Charles attempted to break this stalemate by marching his own guards into the House of Commons and attempting to arrest its leaders. When he failed in this, he withdrew from London to raise an army

CHARLES I. King Charles of England was a connoisseur of the arts and a patron of artists. He was adept at using portraiture to convey the magnificence of his tastes and the grandeur of his conception of kingship. ■ *How does this portrait by Anthony Van Dyck compare to the engravings of the "martyred" king on page 344 in* Interpreting Visual Evidence?

of Royalist supporters. Parliament responded by levying its own armed force and voting the taxation to pay for it. By the end of 1642, open warfare had erupted between the English king and the English government—something inconceivable in France, where the king and the government were inseparable.

Arrayed on the king's side were most of England's aristocrats and largest landowners, who were almost all loyal to the established Church of England, despite their opposition to some of Charles's own religious innovations. The parliamentary forces, by contrast, were made up of smaller landholders, tradesmen, and artisans, many of whom were Puritan sympathizers. The king's royalist supporters were commonly known by the aristocratic name of Cavaliers. Their opponents, who cut their hair short in contempt for the fashionable custom of wearing long curls, were derisively called Roundheads. At first the Cavaliers, having obvious advantages of military experience, won most of the victories.

Debating the English Civil War

The English Civil War raised fundamental questions about political rights and responsibilities. Many of these are addressed in the two excerpts below. The first comes from a lengthy debate held within the General Council of Cromwell's army in October of 1647. The second is taken from the speech given by King Charles, moments before his execution in 1649.

The Army Debates, 1647

Colonel Rainsborough: Really, I think that the poorest man that is in England has a life to live as the greatest man, and therefore truly, sir, I think it's clear, that every man that is to live under a government ought first by his own consent to put himself under that government, and I do think that the poorest man in England is not at all bound in a strict sense to that government that he has not had a voice to put himself under . . . insomuch that I should doubt whether I was an Englishman or not, that should doubt of these things.

General Ireton: Give me leave to tell you, that if you make this the rule, I think you must fly for refuge to an absolute natural right, and you must deny all civil right, and I am sure it will come to that in the consequence. . . . For my part, I think it is no right at all. I think that no person has a right to an interest or share in the disposing of the affairs of the kingdom, and in determining or choosing those that shall determine what laws we shall be ruled by here, no person has a right to this that has not a permanent fixed interest in this kingdom, and those persons together are properly the represented of this kingdom who, taken together, and consequently are to make up the representers of this kingdom. . . .

We talk of birthright. Truly, birthright there is. . . . [M]en may justly have by birthright, by their very being born in England, that we should not seclude them out of England. That we should not refuse to give them air and place and ground, and the freedom of the highways and other things, to live amongst us, not any man that is born here, though he in birth or by his birth there come nothing at all that is part of the permanent interest of this kingdom to him. That I think is due to a man by birth. But that by a man's being born here he shall have a share in that power that shall dispose of the lands here, and of all things here, I do not think it is a sufficient ground.

Source: *Divine Right and Democracy: An Anthology of Political Writing in Stuart England*, ed. David Wootton (New York: 1986), pp. 286–87 (language modernized).

In 1644, however, the parliamentary army was effectively reorganized, and afterward the fortunes of battle shifted. The royalist forces were badly beaten, and in 1646 the king was compelled to surrender. Soon thereafter, the episcopal hierarchy of the Church of England was abolished and a Calvinist-style reformed church was mandated throughout England and Wales.

The struggle might have ended here had not a quarrel developed within the parliamentary party. The majority of its members were ready to restore Charles to the throne as a limited monarch, under an arrangement whereby a uniformly Calvinist faith would be imposed on both Scotland and England as the state religion. But a radical minority of Puritans distrusted Charles and insisted on religious tolera-

tion for themselves and all other Protestants. Their leader was Oliver Cromwell (1599–1658), who had risen to command the Roundhead army, which he had reconstituted as "the New Model Army." Ultimately, he became the new leader of Parliament, too.

The Fall of Charles Stuart and the Commonwealth

Taking advantage of the dissension within the ranks of his opponents, Charles renewed the war in 1648 but, after a brief campaign, was forced again to surrender. Cromwell

Charles I on the Scaffold, 1649

I think it is my duty, to God first, and to my country, for to clear myself both as an honest man, a good king, and a good Christian.

I shall begin first with my innocence. In truth I think it not very needful for me to insist long upon this, for all the world knows that I never did begin a war with the two Houses of Parliament, and I call God to witness, to whom I must shortly make an account, that I never did intend to incroach upon their privileges. . . .

As for the people—truly I desire their liberty and freedom as much as anybody whatsoever. But I must tell you that their liberty and freedom consists in having of government those laws by which their lives and goods may be most their own. It is not for having share in government. That is nothing pertaining to them.

A subject and a sovereign are clean different things, and therefore, until they do that—I mean that you do put the people in that liberty as I say—certainly they will never enjoy themselves.

Sirs, it was for this that now I am come here. If I would have given way to an arbitrary way, for to have all laws changed according to the power of the sword, I needed not to have come here. And therefore I tell you (and I pray God it be not laid to your charge) that I am the martyr of the people.

Source: Brian Tierney, Donald Kagan, and L. Pearce Williams, eds., *Great Issues in Western Civilization* (New York: 1967), pp. 46–47.

Questions for Analysis

1. What fundamental issues are at stake in both of these excerpts? How do the debaters within the parliamentary army (first excerpt) define "natural" and "civil" rights?

2. How does Charles defend his position? What is his theory of kingship? How does it conflict with the ideas expressed in the army's debate?

3. It is interesting that none of the participants in these debates seem to have recognized the implications of their arguments for the political rights of women. Why would that have been the case?

was now resolved to end the life of "that man of blood" and, ejecting all the moderates from Parliament by force, he obliged this "Rump" (remaining) Parliament to put the king on trial and eventually to condemn him to death for treason against his own subjects. Charles Stuart was publicly beheaded on January 30, 1649: the first time in history that a reigning king had been legally deposed and executed by his own government. Europeans reacted to his death with horror, astonishment, or rejoicing, depending on their own political convictions (see **Interpreting Visual Evidence** on page 344).

A short time later, Parliament's hereditary House of Lords was abolished and England was declared a Commonwealth, an English translation of the Latin *res publica*. But

founding a republic was far easier than maintaining one. Technically, the Rump Parliament continued as the legislative body; but Cromwell, with the army at his command, possessed the real power. In 1653, he marched a detachment of troops into the Rump Parliament, which he dissolved in his own favor. The Commonwealth ceased to exist and was replaced by the "Protectorate," a thinly disguised autocracy established under a constitution drafted by officers of the army. Called the Instrument of Government, this text is the nearest approximation to a written constitution England has ever had. Extensive powers were given to Cromwell as Lord Protector, and his office was made hereditary. At first, a new Parliament exercised limited authority to make laws and levy taxes, but in 1655

Interpreting Visual Evidence

The Execution of a King

This allegorical engraving (image A) accompanied a pamphlet called *Eikon Basilike* ("The Kingly Image"), which began to circulate in Britain just weeks after the execution of King Charles I. It purported to be an autobiographical account of the king's last days and a justification of his royal policies. It was intended to arouse widespread sympathy for the king and his exiled heir, Charles II, and it succeeded admirably: the cult of Charles "King and Martyr" became increasingly popular. Here, the Latin inscription on the shaft of light suggests that Charles's piety will beam "brighter through the shadows," while the scrolls at the left proclaim that "virtue grows beneath weight" and "unmoved, triumphant." Charles's earthly crown (on the floor at his side) is "splendid and heavy," while the crown of thorns he grasps is "bitter and light" and the heavenly crown is "blessed and eternal." Even people who could not read these and other Latin mottoes would have known that Charles's last words were: "I shall go from a corruptible to an incorruptible Crown, where no disturbance can be."

A. King Charles I as a kingly martyr.

At the same time, broadsides showing the moment of execution (image B) circulated in various European countries with explanatory captions. This one was

Cromwell abruptly dismissed its members. Thereafter the government became a virtual dictatorship, with Cromwell wielding a sovereignty more absolute than any previous English monarch had ever dreamed of claiming. Indeed, many contemporary intellectuals noted the similarities between these events and those that had given rise to the Principate of Augustus after the death of Julius Caesar (Chapter 5).

The Restoration of the Monarchy

Given the choice between a Puritan military dictatorship and the old royalist regime, most of England opted for the latter. Years of unpopular Calvinist austerities—such as the prohibition of any public recreation on Sundays and the closing of London's theaters—had made people long for the milder Church of England, and for monarchy. So not long after

printed in Germany, and there are almost identical versions surviving from the Netherlands. It shows members of the crowd fainting and turning away at the sight of blood spurting from the king's neck, while the executioner holds up the severed head.

B. The execution of Charles I.

Questions for Analysis

1. How would you interpret the message of the first image? How might it have been read differently by Catholics and by Protestants, within Britain and in Europe?

2. What would have been the political motives underlying the publication and display of these images? For example, would you expect the depiction of the king's execution to be intended as supportive of monarchy, or as antiroyalist? Why?

3. Given what you have learned about political and religious divisions in Europe at the time of the king's execution, where do you think the first image would have found the most sympathetic audiences? Why might it be significant that the second image circulated more in Germany and the Netherlands, rather than in France or Spain?

Cromwell's death in 1658, one of his generals seized power and called for the election of a new Parliament, which met in the spring of 1660. Almost overnight, England was a monarchy again and Charles I's exiled son, Charles II, was proclaimed its king and recalled from the court of his cousin, Louis XIV.

Charles II (r. 1660–85) restored bishops to the Church of England but he did not return to the provocative religious policies of his father. Quipping that he did not wish to "resume his travels," Charles agreed to respect Parliament and to observe the Petition of Right that had so enraged his father. He also accepted all the legislation passed by Parliament immediately before the outbreak of civil war in 1642, including the requirement that Parliament be summoned at least once every three years. England thus emerged from its civil war as a limited monarchy, in which power was exercised by "the king in Parliament." It remains a constitutional monarchy to this day.

THE PROBLEM OF DOUBT AND THE QUEST FOR CERTAINTY

Between 1540 and 1660, Europeans were forced to confront a world in which all that they had once taken for granted was suddenly cast into doubt. Vast new continents had been discovered in the Americas, populated by millions of people whose very existence compelled Europeans to rethink some of their most basic ideas about humanity and human nature. Equally disorienting, the religious uniformity of medieval Europe, although never absolute, had been shattered to an unprecedented extent by the Reformation and the religious wars that arose from it. In 1540, it was still possible to imagine that these religious divisions might be temporary. By 1660, it was clear they would be permanent. No longer could Europeans regard revealed religious faith as an adequate foundation for universal philosophical conclusions, for even Christians now disagreed about the fundamental truths of faith. Political allegiances were similarly under threat, as intellectuals and common people alike began to assert a right to resist princes with whom they disagreed. Even morality and custom were beginning to seem arbitrary, detached from the natural ordering of the world.

Europeans responded to this pervasive climate of doubt in a variety of ways, ranging from radical skepticism to authoritarian assertions of ecclesiastical control and political absolutism. What united their responses, however, was a sometimes desperate search for new foundations on which to construct some measure of certainty in the face of enormous change.

Witchcraft and the Power of the State

Adding to Europeans' fears was the conviction of many that witchcraft was a new and increasing threat to their world. Although the belief that certain individuals could heal or harm through the practice of magic had always been widespread, it was not until the late fifteenth century that authorities began to insist that such powers could derive only from some kind of satanic bargain. Once this belief became widely accepted, judicial officers became much more active in seeking out suspected witches for prosecution. In 1484, Pope Innocent VIII had ordered papal inquisitors to use all means at their disposal to detect and eliminate witchcraft, even condoning the torture of suspected witches. Predictably, torture increased the number of accused witches who "confessed" to their alleged crimes;

and as more accused witches "confessed," more and more witches were "discovered," tried, and executed—even in Protestant realms like England and Scotland where torture was not legal and where the Inquisition of the Roman Catholic Church did not operate.

In considering the rash of witchcraft persecutions that swept early modern Europe, then, we need to keep two facts in mind. First of all, witchcraft trials were by no means limited to Catholic countries: Protestant reformers believed in the insidious powers of Satan just as much as Catholics did, if not more so. Second, it was only when religious authorities' efforts to detect witchcraft were backed by the coercive powers of secular governments that the fear of witches could translate into imprisonment, torture, and execution. It was therefore through this fundamental agreement between Catholics and Protestants, and with the complicity of secular states, that a witch craze could claim tens of thousands of victims, of whom the vast majority were women.

The final death toll will never be known, but in the 1620s there were, on average, 100 burnings a year in the German cities of Würzburg and Bamberg; around the same time, it was said that the town square of Wolfenbüttel "looked like a little forest, so crowded were the stakes." When accusations of witchcraft diminished in Europe, they became endemic in some European colonies, such as the English settlement of Salem, Massachusetts.

This witch mania reflects the fears that early modern Europeans held about the adequacy of traditional remedies (such as prayers, relics, and holy water) to combat the evils of their world, another consequence of religious dissent and uncertainty. It also reflects their growing conviction that only the state had the power to protect them. Even in Catholic countries, where witchcraft prosecutions were sometimes begun in ecclesiastical courts, these cases would be transferred to the state's courts for final judgment and punishment, because Church courts were forbidden to impose capital penalties. In most Protestant countries, where ecclesiastical courts had been abolished (only England retained them), the entire process of detecting, prosecuting, and punishing suspected witches was carried out under the supervision of the state. In both Catholic and Protestant countries, the result of these witchcraft trials was thus a considerable increase in the scope of the state's powers to regulate the lives of its subjects.

The Search for a Source of Authority

The crisis of Europe's "iron century"—the name given to this era by some contemporary intellectuals—was fundamentally a crisis of authority, with far-reaching implications.

Attempts to reestablish some foundation for a new authority therefore took many forms. For the French nobleman Michel de Montaigne (1533–1592), who wrote during the height of the French wars of religion, the result was a searching skepticism about the possibilities of any certain knowledge whatsoever. The son of a Catholic father and a Huguenot mother of Jewish ancestry, the well-to-do Montaigne retired from a legal career at the age of thirty-eight to devote himself to a life of reflection. The *Essays* that resulted were a new literary form originally conceived as "experiments" (the French *essai* means "attempt").

Although the range of subjects covered by the *Essays* is wide, two main themes are dominant. One is constant questioning. Making his motto *Que sais-je?* ("What do I know?"), Montaigne decided that he knew very little for certain. According to him, "it is folly to measure truth and error by our own capacities," because our capacities are severely limited. As he maintained in one of his most famous essays, "On Cannibals," what may seem indisputably true and moral to one nation may seem absolutely false to another, because "everyone gives the title of barbarism to everything that is not of his usage." From this, Montaigne's second main principle followed: the need for moderation. Because all people think they know the perfect religion and the perfect government, yet few agree on what that perfection might be, Montaigne concluded that no religion or government is really perfect, and consequently no belief is worth fighting or dying for. Instead, people should accept the teachings of religion on faith, and obey the governments constituted to rule over them, without resorting to fanaticism in either sphere.

Although Montaigne's writings seem modern in many ways—that is, familiar to us today—he was very much a man of his time, and also the product of a long philosophical tradition reaching back to antiquity (Chapters 3 and 4). At heart, he was a Stoic: in a world governed by unpredictable fortune, he believed that the best human strategy was to face the good and the bad with steadfastness and dignity.

Another attempt to resolve the problem of doubt was offered by the French philosopher Blaise Pascal (1623–1662). Pascal began his career as a mathematician and scientist. But at age thirty he abandoned science after a profound conversion experience. This led him to embrace an extreme form of puritanical Catholicism known as Jansenism (after its Flemish founder, Cornelius Jansen). From then until his death, he worked on a highly ambitious philosophical-religious project meant to establish the truth of Christianity by appealing simultaneously to intellect and emotion.

After his premature death, the results of this effort were published as a series of "Thoughts" (*Pensées*). In this collection of intellectual fragments, Pascal argues that faith alone can resolve the contradictions of the world and that "the heart has its reasons of which reason itself knows nothing." Pascal's *Pensées* express the author's own terror, anguish, and awe in the face of evil and uncertainty, but present that awe as evidence for the existence of God. Pascal's hope was that, on this foundation, some measure of confidence in humanity and its capacity for self-knowledge could be rediscovered, thus avoiding both the dogmatism and the extreme skepticism that were so prominent in seventeenth-century society.

Theories of Absolute Government

Montaigne's contemporary, the French lawyer Jean Bodin (1530–1596), took a more active approach to the problem of uncertain authority. He wanted to resolve the disorders of the day by reestablishing the powers of the state on new and more secure foundations. Like Montaigne, Bodin was particularly troubled by the upheavals caused by the religious wars in France; he had witnessed the St. Bartholomew's Day Massacre of 1572. But he was resolved to offer a practical, political solution to such turbulence. In his monumental *Six Books of the Commonwealth* (1576), he developed a theory of absolute state sovereignty.

According to Bodin, the state arises from the needs of collections of families and, once constituted, should brook no opposition to its authority because maintaining order is its paramount duty. For Bodin, sovereignty was "the most high, absolute, and perpetual power over all subjects," which could make and enforce laws without the consent of those governed by the state—precisely what Charles I of England would have argued, and precisely what his rebellious subjects disputed. Although Bodin acknowledged the possibility of government by the aristocracy or even by a democracy, he assumed that the powerful nation-states of his day would have to be ruled by monarchs, and insisted that such monarchs should in no way be limited—whether by legislative and judicial bodies, or even by the laws of their own predecessors. Even if the ruler proved a tyrant, Bodin insisted that his subjects had no right to resist, for any resistance would open the door "to a licentious anarchy which is worse than the harshest tyranny in the world."

Bodin's younger contemporary, Thomas Hobbes (1588–1679) was moved by the turmoil of the English Civil War to advance a new political theory in his treatise *Leviathan* (1651). Yet Hobbes's formulation differs from that of Bodin in several respects. Whereas Bodin assumed that absolute sovereign power should be vested in a monarch, Hobbes argued that any form of government capable of protecting

its subjects' lives and property might act as sovereign and hence all-powerful. And whereas Bodin defined his state as "the lawful government of families" and did not believe that the state could abridge private property rights, Hobbes's state exists to rule over individuals, and is thus licensed to trample over both liberty and property if the government's own survival is at stake.

But the most fundamental difference between Bodin and Hobbes lay in the latter's uncompromisingly pessimistic view of human nature. Hobbes posited that the "state of nature" that existed before government was "war of all against all." Because man naturally behaves as "a wolf" toward other men, human life without government is necessarily "solitary, poor, nasty, brutish, and short." To escape such consequences, people must therefore surrender their liberties to a sovereign ruler in exchange for his obligation to keep the peace. Having traded away their liberties, subjects have no right to win them back, and the sovereign may rule as he likes—free to oppress his subjects in any way other than to kill them, an act that would negate the very purpose of his rule, which is to preserve his people's lives.

THE ART OF BEING HUMAN

Doubt and uncertainty were also primary themes in the profusion of literature and art produced in this era. Moved by the ambiguities and ironies of existence and the horrors of war and persecution, writers and artists sought to find redemptive qualities in human suffering and hardship.

The Adventures of Don Quixote

A timeless example of this artistic response is the satirical novel *Don Quixote*, which its author, Miguel de Cervantes (1547–1616), composed largely in prison. It recounts the adventures of an idealistic Spanish gentleman, Don Quixote of La Mancha, who becomes deranged by his constant reading of chivalric romances. His mind filled with all kinds of fantastic adventures, he sets out at the age of fifty on the slippery road of knight-errantry, imagining windmills to be glowering giants and flocks of sheep to be armies of infidels. His distorted worldview also mistakes inns for castles and serving girls for courtly ladies. His sidekick, Sancho Panza, is his exact opposite: a plain, practical man with his feet on the ground, content with modest bodily plea-

sures. Yet Cervantes does not suggest that realism is categorically preferable to "quixotic" idealism. Rather, these two men represent different facets of human nature. On the one hand, *Don Quixote* is a devastating satire of the anachronistic chivalric mentality that was already hastening Spain's decline. On the other, it is a sincere celebration of the human capacity for optimism and goodness.

English Playwrights and Poets

In the late sixteenth century, the emergence of public playhouses made drama an especially effective mass medium for the expression of opinions, the dissemination of ideas, and the articulation of national identies. This was especially so in England during the last two decades of Elizabeth's reign and that of her successor, James. Among the large number of playwrights at work in London during this era, the most noteworthy are Christopher Marlowe (1564–1593), Ben Jonson (c. 1572–1637), and William Shakespeare (1564–1616). Marlowe, who may have been a spy for Elizabeth's government and who was mysteriously murdered in a tavern brawl before he reached the age of thirty, was extremely popular in his own day. In plays such as *Tamburlaine* (1587/8)—about the life of the Mongolian emperor Timur the Lame (Chapter 11)—and *Doctor Faustus* (c. 1589), Marlowe created vibrant heroes who pursue larger-than-life ambitions only to be felled by their own human limitations. In contrast to the heroic tragedies of Marlowe, Ben Jonson wrote dark comedies that expose human vices and foibles. In the particularly bleak *Volpone* (1606), Jonson shows people behaving like deceitful and lustful animals. In the later *Alchemist* (1610), he balances an attack on pseudo-scientific quackery with admiration for resourceful lower-class characters who cleverly take advantage of their supposed betters.

William Shakespeare was born into the family of a tradesman in the provincial town of Stratford-upon-Avon, where he attained a modest education before moving to London around the age of twenty. There he found employment in the theater as an actor and playwright, a "maker of plays." He eventually earned a reputation as a poet, too, but it was his success at the box office that enabled him to retire, rich, to his native Stratford about twenty-five years later. Shakespeare composed or collaborated in the writing of an unknown number of plays, of which some forty survive in whole or in part. They have since become a kind of secular English Bible, and owe their longevity to the author's unrivaled gifts of verbal expression, humor, and psychological insight.

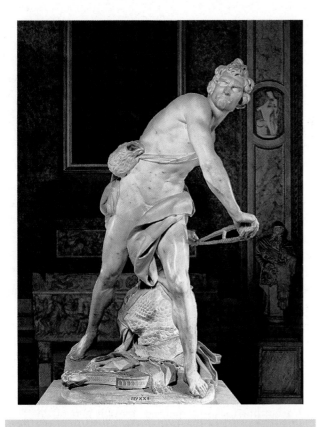

DAVID BY BERNINI (1598–1680). Whereas the earlier conceptions of David by the Renaissance sculptors Donatello and Michelangelo were serene and dignified (see page 301), the Baroque sculptor Bernini chose to portray his young hero at the peak of physical exertion. ▪ *Can you discern the influence of Hellenistic sculpture (Chapter 4, pages 102–3) in this work?* ▪ *What are some shared characteristics?*

Shakespeare's dramas fall thematically into three groups. Those written during the playwright's early years reflect the political, religious, and social upheavals of the late sixteenth century. As we have already seen, these include many history plays which recount episodes from England's medieval past and the struggles that established the Tudor dynasty of Elizabeth's grandfather, Henry VII. They also include the lyrical tragedy *Romeo and Juliet* (1595/6) and a number of comedies, including *A Midsummer Night's Dream* (1595/6), *Much Ado about Nothing* (1598/9), *As You Like It* (1599), and *Twelfth Night* (1601/2). Most explore fundamental problems of identity, honor and ambition, love and friendship.

The plays from Shakespeare's second period are, like other contemporary artworks, characterized by a troubled searching into the mysteries and meaning of human existence. They showcase the perils of indecisive idealism (*Hamlet,*

1600/1) and the abuse of power (*Measure for Measure,* 1604), culminating in the searing tragedies of *King Lear* (1605) and *Macbeth* (1606). Finally, those plays composed at the end of his career emphasize the possibilities of reconciliation and peace, even after years of misunderstanding and sorrow: *Cymbeline* (1609/10), *A Winter's Tale* (1610/11), and *The Tempest* (1611), which is an extended reflection on the paradoxical relationship between the weakness of human nature and the power of the human artist.

Though less versatile than Shakespeare, the Puritan poet John Milton (1608–1674) is considered to be his equal in the grandeur of his artistic vision. The leading publicist of Oliver Cromwell's regime, Milton wrote the official defense of the beheading of Charles I as well as a number of treatises justifying Puritan ideologies. But he loved the Greek and Latin classics at least as much as the Bible. When forced into retirement by the accession of Charles II, Milton (now blind) embarked on a classical epic based on Genesis, *Paradise Lost* (1667). Setting out to "justify the ways of God to man," Milton first plays "devil's advocate" by creating the compelling character of Satan, who defies God with boldness and subtlety. Indeed, the eloquence of his Satan is never quite counterbalanced by the supposed hero, Adam, who learns to accept the human lot of moral responsibility.

The Artistry of Southern Europe

The ironies and tensions inherent in human existence were also explored in the visual arts. In Italy and Spain, many painters of the sixteenth century cultivated a highly dramatic and emotionally compelling style sometimes known as "Mannerism." The most unusual of these artists was El Greco ("the Greek," c. 1541–1614), a pupil of the Venetian master Tintoretto (1518–1594). Born Domenikos Theotokopoulos on the Greek island of Crete, El Greco absorbed some of the stylized elongation characteristic of Byzantine icon painting (Chapter 7) before traveling to Italy. He eventually settled in Spain. Many of his paintings were too strange to be greatly appreciated in his own day and even now appear so *avant garde* as to be almost surreal. His *View of Toledo* (c. 1596–1600), for example, is a transfigured landcape, mysteriously lit from within. Equally amazing are his swirling Biblical scenes and the stunning portraits of gaunt, dignified saints who radiate austerity and spiritual insight.

The dominant artistic style of southern Europe in the seventeenth century was that of the Baroque, a school

VIEW OF TOLEDO BY EL GRECO. This is one of many landscape portraits representing the hilltop city that became the artist's home in later life. Its supple "Mannerist" style almost defies historical periodization.

of self-referentiality. It shows the artist himself at work on a double portrait of the Spanish king and queen, but the scene is dominated by the children and servants of the royal family.

Dutch Painting in the Golden Age

Southern Europe's main rival for artistic laurels was the Netherlands, where many painters explored the theme of man's greatness and wretchedness to the fullest. Pieter Bruegel the Elder (*BROY-ghul*, c. 1525–1569) exulted in portraying the busy, elemental life of the peasantry. Most famous in this respect are his rollicking *Peasant Wedding* and *Peasant Dance* (1568) and his spacious *Harvesters* (1565), whose vistas celebrate the natural rhythms of life. But late in his career, Bruegel became appalled by the intolerance and bloodshed of religious warfare, expressing his criticism in an understated yet searing manner. From a distance, *The Massacre of the Innocents* (c. 1567) looks like a snug scene of Flemish village life; but in fact, soldiers are methodically slaughtering helpless infants, just as Herod's soldiers once did, according to the Gospel account of Jesus's birth.

whose name has become a synonym for elaborate, highly wrought sculpture and architectural details. The Baroque style originated in Rome during the Counter-Reformation and promoted a glorified Catholic worldview. Its most imaginative and influential figure was the architect and sculptor Gianlorenzo Bernini (1598–1680), a frequent employee of the papacy who created the sweeping colonnades leading up to St. Peter's Basilica. Bernini's architecture retained such classical elements as columns and domes but combined them in ways meant to express aggressiveness and power. This was also the aim of Bernini's sculpture, which drew inspiration from the restless motion and artistic bravado of Hellenistic statuary (Chapter 4).

Although the Baroque movement began in Rome and was originally expressed in three dimensions, characteristics of this style can also be found in painting. Many consider its greatest master to be the Spanish artist Diego Velázquez (1599–1660). Unlike Bernini, Velázquez was a court painter in Madrid, not a servant of the Church. And although many of his canvases display a Baroque attention to motion and drama, his most characteristic work is more restrained and conceptually thoughtful. An example is *The Maids of Honor*, completed around 1656 and a masterpiece

THE MAIDS OF HONOR (LAS MENINAS) BY DIEGO VELÁZQUEZ. The artist himself (at left) is shown working at his easel and gazing out at the viewer—or at the subjects of his double portrait, the Spanish king and queen, visible in a distant mirror. But the real focus of the painting is the delicate, impish princess in the center, flanked by two young ladies-in-waiting, a dwarf, and another royal child. Courtiers in the background look on.

THE MASSACRE OF THE INNOCENTS BY BRUEGEL (c. 1525–1569).
This painting shows how effectively art can be used as a means
of political and social commentary. Here, Bruegel depicts the
suffering of the Netherlands at the hands of the Spanish in his own
day, with reference to the Biblical story of Herod's slaughter of Jewish
children after the birth of Jesus—thereby conflating these two historical
incidents.

THE HORRORS OF WAR BY RUBENS (1577–1640). In his old age,
Rubens took a far more critical view of war than he had done for most of
his earlier career. Here, the war-god Mars casts aside his mistress Venus,
goddess of love, and threatens humanity with death and destruction.

SELF-PORTRAITS. Self-portraits became common during the sixteenth and seventeenth centuries, reflecting the intense
introspection of the period. Left: Rembrandt painted more than sixty self-portraits; this one, dating from around 1660, captures
the artist's creativity, theatricality (note the costume), and honesty of self-examination. Right: Judith Leyster (1609–1660) was
a contemporary of Rembrandt who pursued a successful career during her early twenties, before she married. Respected in her
own day, she was all but forgotten for centuries—but is once again the object of much attention.

Vastly different from Bruegel was the Netherlandish painter Peter Paul Rubens (1577–1640) of Antwerp. Since the Baroque was an international movement closely linked to the spread of the Counter-Reformation, it should offer no surprise that Baroque style was extremely well represented in just that part of the Netherlands which, after long warfare, had been retained by Spain and reintroduced to the Catholic faith. Rubens painted literally thousands of robust canvases that glorified resurgent Catholicism or exalted second-rate aristocrats by portraying them as epic heroes. But Rubens was not lacking in subtlety or depth. Although he celebrated martial valor for most of his career, his late *The Horrors of War* (1657/8) movingly portrays what he himself called "the grief of unfortunate Europe."

Living across the border from the Spanish Netherlands in the staunchly Calvinist Dutch Republic, Rembrandt van Rijn (*vahn-REEN*, 1606–1669) belonged to a society that was too austere to tolerate the unbuckled realism of Bruegel or the fleshy excess of Rubens. Yet Rembrandt managed to put both realistic and Baroque traits to new uses. In his early career, he gained fame and fortune as a painter of biblical scenes and as a portrait painter who knew how to flatter his subjects. But his later portraits, including several self-portraits, are highly introspective and suggest that only part of the story is being told. Equally compelling is the frank gaze of Rembrandt's slightly younger contemporary, Judith Leyster (1609–1660), who looks out of her own self-portrait with a refreshingly optimistic and good-humored expression.

After You Read This Chapter

(S) Visit StudySpace for quizzes, additional review materials, and multi-media documents. **wwnorton.com/studyspace**

REVIEWING THE OBJECTIVES

- Religious and political conflicts have always been intertwined, but the combination was especially deadly in the era between 1540 and 1660. Why was this?
- Although the religious warfare of this period seems almost continuous, it took distinctive forms in France, the Netherlands, and Germany. Explain why.
- What factors led to the decline of Spain as Europe's dominant power, and to the rise of France?
- The main causes of the English Civil War can be traced back to the reign of Elizabeth I and her successor, James Stuart of Scotland. What were the main sources of disagreement between the Stuart monarchy and Parliament?
- Intellectuals and artists responded to the challenges of this era in creative ways. Identify some of the major figures and ideas that emerged from this period of crisis.

CONCLUSION

Between 1540 and 1660, Europe was racked by a combination of religious warfare, political rebellion, and economic crisis that undermined confidence in traditional structures of authority. The result was disillusionment, skepticism, and a search for new foundations on which to rebuild strong political and social institutions. For artists and intellectuals, the period proved to be one of the most creative epochs in the history of Western civilizations. But for most common people, the century was one of extraordinary suffering.

By 1660, after a hundred years of destructive efforts to restore the religious unity of Europe through war, a de facto religious toleration among states was beginning to emerge as the only way to preserve political order. But within states, toleration was still very limited. In territories where religious rivalries ran too deep to be overcome, rulers began to discover that loyalty to the state could override even religious divisions among their subjects. The end result of this century of crises was a strengthening of Europeans' reliance on the state's capacity to heal their wounds and right their wrongs, with religion relegated more and more to the private sphere of individual conscience. In the following centuries, this new confidence in the state as an autonomous moral agent acting in accordance with its own "reasons of state" and for its own purposes, would prove a powerful challenge to the traditions of limited consensual government that had emerged from the Middle Ages.

PEOPLE, IDEAS, AND EVENTS IN CONTEXT

- What were the main sources of instability in Europe during the sixteenth century? How did the **PRICE REVOLUTION** exacerbate these?
- How did the **EDICT OF NANTES** challenge the doctrine *CUIUS REGIO, EIUS RELIGIO* ("as the ruler, so the religion") established by the **PEACE OF AUGSBURG**?
- What were the initial causes of the **THIRTY YEARS' WAR**? Why did Sweden and France become involved in it?
- Describe the political configuration of Europe after the **PEACE OF WESTPHALIA**. Why did Spain's power decline while France emerged as dominant? How did the policies of **CARDINAL RICHELIEU** strengthen the power of the French monarchy?
- What factors led to the **ENGLISH CIVIL WAR** and the execution of **CHARLES I**?
- In what ways did the **WITCH CRAZE** of early modern Europe reveal the religious and social tensions of the sixteenth and seventeenth centuries?
- How did **MONTAIGNE** and **PASCAL** respond to the problem of authority? What were the differences between **JEAN BODIN**'s theory of absolute sovereignty and that of **THOMAS HOBBES**?

CONSEQUENCES

- The period between 1540 and 1660 is considered to be one of the most turbulent in Europe's history, but it also has deep roots in the more distant past of Western civilizations. How far back would you trace the origins of this "perfect storm"?
- The execution of King Charles I of England was a watershed event, and yet the English monarchy itself survived this crisis. How would you account for this remarkable fact? In what ways did the concept of English kingship have to change in order for monarchy itself to survive?
- In your view, do the various artistic movements of this era seem especially modern? Or are they better understood as comparable to the movements responding to the crisis of the Black Death (Chapter 10), or to the artistic innovations characteristic of the Renaissance (Chapter 12)? What elements make a work of art seem "modern"?

Before You Read This Chapter

Absolutism and Empire, 1660–1789

In the mountainous region of south-central France known as the Auvergne in the 1660s, the marquis of Canillac had a notorious reputation. His noble title gave him the right to collect minor taxes on special occasions, but he insisted that these small privileges be converted into annual tributes. To collect these payments, he housed in his castle twelve accomplices whom he called his apostles. Their other nicknames—one was known as Break Everything—gave a more accurate sense of their activities in the local villages. The marquis imprisoned those who resisted and forced their families to buy their freedom. In an earlier age, the marquis might have gotten away with this profitable arrangement. In 1662, however, he ran up against the authority of a king, Louis XIV, who was determined to demonstrate that the power of the central monarch was absolute. The marquis was brought up on charges before a special court of judges from Paris. He was found guilty and forced to pay a large fine. The king confiscated his property and had the marquis's castle destroyed.

Louis XIV's special court in the Auvergne heard nearly a thousand civil cases over four months in 1662. It convicted

692 people, and many of them, like the marquis of Canillac, were noble. The verdicts were an extraordinary example of Louis XIV's ability to project his authority into the remote corners of his realm and to do so in a way that diminished the power of other elites. During his long reign (1643–1715), Louis XIV systematically pursued such a policy on many fronts, asserting his power over the nobility, the clergy, and the provincial courts. Increasingly, these elites were forced to look to the crown to guarantee their interests, and their own power became more closely connected with the sacred aura of the monarchy itself. Louis XIV's model of kingship was so successful that it became known as absolute monarchy. In recognition of the success and influence of Louis XIV's political system, the period from around 1660 (when the English monarchy was restored and Louis XIV began his personal rule in France) to 1789 (when the French Revolution erupted) is traditionally known as the age of absolutism. This is a crucial period in the development of the modern, centralized, bureaucratic state.

Absolutism was a political theory that encouraged rulers to claim complete sovereignty within their territories. An absolute monarch could make law, dispense justice, create and direct a bureaucracy, declare war, and levy taxes, without the approval of any other governing body. Assertions of absolute authority were buttressed by claims that rulers governed by divine right with power granted by God. Absolutist theorists frequently compared this authority to the power of fathers in the household. After the chaos of the previous century, many Europeans came to believe that it was only by exalting the sovereignty of absolute rulers that order could be restored to European life.

European monarchs also successfully projected their power abroad during this period. By 1660, the French, Spanish, Portuguese, English, and Dutch had all established important colonies in the Americas and in Asia. These colonies created important trading networks that brought profitable new consumer goods such as sugar, tobacco, and coffee to a wide public in Europe, while also encouraging the spread of slavery to produce these goods. Rivalry among colonial powers to control the trade in slaves and consumer goods was intense. In the eighteenth century, Europe's wars were driven by colonial considerations and imperial conflicts, as global commerce assumed a growing role in the European economy.

Absolutism was not the only political theory used by European governments during this period. England, Scotland, the Dutch Republic, Switzerland, Venice, Sweden, and Poland-Lithuania were all either limited monarchies, or republics. In Russia, an extreme autocracy emerged that gave the tsar a degree of control over his subjects' lives and property far beyond anything imagined by western European absolutists. Even in Russia, however, absolutism was never unlimited in practice. Even the most absolute monarchs could rule effectively only with the consent of their subjects (particularly the nobility). When serious opposition erupted, even absolutists were forced to back down. In 1789, when an outright political revolution occurred, the entire structure of absolutism came crashing to the ground.

THE APPEAL AND JUSTIFICATION OF ABSOLUTISM

Absolutism's promise of stability was an appealing alternative to the disorder of the "iron century" that preceded it. Louis XIV was profoundly disturbed by an aristocratic revolt that occurred while he was still a child. Louis saw the revolt as a horrid affront not only to his own person but to the majesty of the French state he personified. Such experiences convinced him that he must rule assertively and without limitation if France was to survive as a great European state.

Absolutist monarchs sought control of the state's armed forces and its legal system and demanded the right to collect and spend the state's financial resources at will. To achieve these goals, they also needed to create an efficient, centralized bureaucracy that owed its allegiance directly to the monarch. Creating and sustaining such a bureaucracy was expensive but essential to the larger absolutist goal of weakening the special interests that hindered the free exercise of royal power. The nobility and the clergy, with their traditional legal privileges; the political authority of semi-autonomous regions; and representative assemblies such as parliaments, diets, or estates general were all obstacles—in the eyes of absolutists—to strong, centralized monarchical government. The history of abolutism is a history of attempts by aspiring absolutists to bring such institutions to heel.

In most Protestant countries, the power of the church had already been subordinated to the state when the age of absolutism began. In France, Spain, and Austria, however, where Roman Catholicism remained the state religion, absolutist monarchs now devoted considerable attention to bringing the church and its clergy under royal control.

The most important potential opponents of royal absolutism were not churchmen, however, but nobles. Monarchs dealt with this threat in various ways. Louis XIV deprived the French nobility of political power in the provinces but increased their social prestige by making them live at his lavish court at Versailles. Peter the Great of Russia (r. 1689–1725) forced his nobles into lifelong government service. Later in the century, Catherine II of Russia (r. 1762–96) struck a bargain whereby, in return for vast estates and a variety of privileges (including exemption from taxation), the Russian nobility virtually surrendered the administrative and political power of the state into the empress's hands. In Prussia, the army was staffed by nobles, as was generally the case in Spain, France, and England.

The most effective absolutist monarchies of the eighteenth century continued to trade privileges for allegiance, so that nobles came to see their own interests as tied to those of the crown. For this reason, cooperation and negotiation more often characterized the relations between kings and nobles during the eighteenth-century *ancien régime* ("old regime") than did open conflict.

THE ABSOLUTISM OF LOUIS XIV

In Louis XIV's state portrait, it is almost impossible to discern the human being behind the facade of the absolute monarch, dressed in his coronation robes and surrounded by the symbols of his authority. That facade was artfully constructed by Louis, who recognized more fully than any other early modern ruler the importance of theater to effective kingship. Previous monarchs realized the importance of displays of power and majesty, but Louis and his successors took this to unprecedented levels, staging theatrical demonstrations of their sovereignty to enhance their position as rulers endowed with godlike powers.

Performing Royalty at Versailles

Louis's most elaborate exhibitions of his sovereignty took place at his palace at Versailles (vair-SY), the town outside of Paris to which he moved his court. The palace and its grounds became a stage for Louis's performance of his daily rituals and demonstrations of royal power. Inside, tapestries and paintings celebrated French military victories and royal triumphs; mirrors reflected shimmering light throughout the building. In the vast gardens outside, statues of the Greek god Apollo, god of the sun, recalled Louis's claim to be the "Sun King" of France. Noblemen vied to attend him when he arose from bed, ate his meals, strolled in his gardens, or rode to the hunt. France's leading nobles were required to reside with him at Versailles for a portion of the year; the splendor of Louis's court was deliberately calculated to blind them to the possibility of

disobedience while raising their prestige by associating them with himself. At the same time, the almost impossibly detailed rules of etiquette at court left these privileged nobles in constant suspense, forever fearful of offending the king by committing some trivial violation of proper manners.

Of course, the nobility did not surrender their social and political power entirely under the absolutist system. The social order defended by the monarchy was still a hierarchical one, and the nobility retained enormous privileges and rights over local peasants within their jurisdiction. The absolutist system may have forced the nobility to depend on the crown to defend their privileges, but it did not seek to undermine their superior place in society. In this sense, the relationship between Louis XIV and the nobility was more of a negotiated settlement than a complete victory of the king over other powerful elites. In their own way, absolutists depended on the consent of those they ruled.

Administration and Centralization

Louis defined his responsibilities in absolutist terms: to concentrate royal power so as to produce domestic tranquility. While coopting the nobility into his own theater of royalty, he also recruited the upper bourgeoisie as royal administrators and especially as intendants, responsible for administering the thirty-six *généralités* into which France was divided. Louis's administrators devoted much of their time and energy to collecting the taxes necessary to finance the large standing army on which his aggressive foreign policy depended. Absolutism was fundamentally an approach to government by which ambitious monarchs could increase their own power through conquest and display. As such, it was enormously expensive. In addition to the *taille*, or land tax, which increased throughout the seventeenth century, Louis's government introduced a *capitation* (a head tax) and pressed successfully for the collection of indirect taxes on salt (the *gabelle*), wine, tobacco, and other goods. Because the nobility was exempt from the *taille*, its burden fell most heavily on the peasantry, whose local revolts Louis easily crushed.

Regional opposition was curtailed, but not eliminated, during Louis's reign. By removing the provincial nobility to Versailles, Louis cut them off from their local sources of power and influence. To restrict the powers of regional *parlements*, Louis decreed that members of any *parlement* that refused to approve and enforce his laws would be summarily exiled. The Estates-General, the national French representative assembly last summoned in 1614, did not meet at all during Louis's reign. It would not meet again until 1789.

Competing Viewpoints

Absolutism and Patriarchy

> These selections show how two political theorists justified royal absolutism by deriving it from the absolute authority of a father over his household. Bishop Jacques-Benigne Bossuet (1627–1704) was a famous French preacher who served as tutor to the son of King Louis XIV of France before becoming bishop of Meaux. Sir Robert Filmer (1588–1653) was an English political theorist. Filmer's works attracted particular attention in the 1680s, when John Locke directed the first of his Two Treatises of Government to refuting Filmer's views on the patriarchal nature of royal authority.

Bossuet on the Nature of Monarchical Authority

There are four characteristics or qualities essential to royal authority. First, royal authority is sacred; Secondly, it is paternal; Thirdly, it is absolute; Fourthly, it is subject to reason.... All power comes from God.... Thus princes act as ministers of God and his lieutenants on earth. It is through them that he exercises his empire.... In this way ... the royal throne is not the throne of a man, but the throne of God himself....

We have seen that kings hold the place of God, who is the true Father of the human race. We have also seen that the first idea of power that there was among men, is that of paternal power; and that kings were fashioned on the model of fathers. Moreover, all the world agrees that obedience, which is due to public power, is only found . . . in the precept which obliges one to honor his parents. From all this it appears that the name "king" is a father's name, and that goodness is the most natural quality in kings....

Royal authority is absolute. In order to make this term odious and insupportable, many pretend to confuse absolute government and arbitrary government. But nothing is more distinct, as we shall make clear when we speak of justice.... The prince need account to no one for what he ordains.... Without this absolute authority, he can neither do good nor suppress evil: his power must be such that no one can hope to escape him.... [T]he sole defense of individuals against the public power must be their innocence....

One must, then, obey princes as if they were justice itself, without which there is neither order nor justice in affairs. They are gods, and share in some way in divine independence.... It follows from this that he who does not want to obey the prince ... is condemned irremissibly to death as an enemy of public peace and of human society.... The prince can correct himself when he knows that he has done badly; but against his authority there can be no remedy....

Source: Jacques-Benigne Bossuet, *Politics Drawn from the Very Words of Holy Scripture*, trans. Patrick Riley (Cambridge: 1990), pp. 46–69, 81–83.

Louis XIV's Religious Policies

Both for reasons of state and of personal conscience, Louis was determined to impose religious unity on France, regardless of the economic and social costs. Although the vast majority of the French population was Roman Catholic, French Catholics were divided among different groups. Louis supported the Jesuits in their efforts to create a Counter-Reformation Catholic Church in France. Louis's support for the Jesuits upset the traditional Gallican Catholics of France, however, who desired a French church independent of papal, Jesuit, and Spanish influence. As a result of this dissension among Catholics, the religious aura of Louis's kingship diminished during the course of his reign.

Against the Protestant Huguenots, however, Louis waged unrelenting war. Protestant churches and schools were destroyed, and Protestants were banned from many professions, including medicine and printing. In 1685, Louis revoked the Edict of Nantes, the legal foundation of the toleration Huguenots had enjoyed since 1598. Many families converted,

Filmer on the Patriarchal Origins of Royal Authority

The first government in the world was monarchical, in the father of all flesh, Adam, being commanded to multiply, and people the earth, and to subdue it, and having dominion given him over all creatures, was thereby the monarch of the whole world; none of his posterity had any right to possess anything, but by his grant or permission, or by succession from him. . . . Adam was the father, king, and lord over his family: a son, a subject, and a servant or a slave were one and the same thing at first. . . .

I cannot find any one place or text in the Bible where any power . . . is given to a people either to govern themselves, or to choose themselves governors, or to alter the manner of government at their pleasure. The power of government is settled and fixed by the commandment of "honour thy father"; if there were a higher power than the fatherly, then this commandment could not stand and be observed. . . .

All power on earth is either derived or usurped from the fatherly power, there being no other original to be found of any power whatsoever. For if there should be granted two sorts of power without any subordination of one to the other, they would be in perpetual strife which should be the supreme, for two supremes cannot agree. If the fatherly power be supreme, then the power of the people must be subordinate and depend on it. If the power of the people be supreme, then the fatherly power must submit to it, and cannot be exercised without the licence of the people, which must quite destroy the frame and course of nature. Even the power which God himself exercises over mankind is by right of fatherhood: he is both the king and father of us all. As God has exalted the dignity of earthly kings . . . by saying they are gods, so . . . he has been pleased . . . [t]o humble himself by assuming the title of a king to express his power, and not the title of any popular government.

Source: Robert Filmer, "Observations upon Aristotle's Politiques" (1652), in *Divine Right and Democracy: An Anthology of Political Writing in Stuart England,* ed. David Wootton (Harmondsworth: 1986), pp. 110–18.

Questions for Analysis

1. Bossuet's definition of *absolutism* connected the sacred power of kings with the paternal authority of fathers within the household. What consequences does he draw from defining the relationship between king and subjects in this way?

2. What does Filmer mean when he says, "All power on earth is either derived or usurped from the fatherly power"? How many examples does he give of paternal or monarchical power?

3. Bossuet and Filmer make obedience the basis for order and justice in the world. What alternative political systems did they most fear?

but 200,000 Protestant refugees fled to England, Holland, Germany, and America, bringing with them their professional and artisanal skills. This was an enormous loss to France.

Colbert and Royal Finance

Louis's drive to unify and centralize France depended on a vast increase in royal revenues engineered by Jean Baptiste Colbert, the king's finance minister from 1664 until his death in 1683. Colbert tightened the process of tax collection and eliminated wherever possible the practice of tax farming (which permitted collection agents to retain for themselves a percentage of the taxes they gathered for the king). When Colbert assumed office, only about 25 percent of the taxes collected throughout the kingdom reached the treasury. By the time he died, that figure had risen to 80 percent. Colbert also tried to increase the nation's income by controlling and regulating foreign trade. As a confirmed mercantilist, Colbert believed that France's wealth

The Performance and Display of Absolute Power at the Court of Louis XIV

Historians studying the history of absolutism and the court of Louis XIV in particular have emphasized the Sun King's (image B) brilliant use of symbols and display to demonstrate his personal embodiment of sovereignty. Royal portraits, such as that painted by Hyacinthe Rigaud in 1701 (image A), vividly illustrate the degree to which Louis's power was based on a studied performance. His pose, with his exposed and shapely calf, was an important indication of power and virility, necessary elements of legitimacy for a hereditary monarch. In the elaborate rituals of court life at Versailles, Louis often placed his own body at the center of attention, performing in one instance as the god Apollo in a ballet before his assembled courtiers. His movements through the countryside (image C), accompanied by a retinue of soldiers, servants, and aristocrats, were another occasion for highly stylized ritual demonstrations of his quasi-divine status. Finally, of course, the construction of his palace at Versailles (image D), with its symmetrical architecture and its sculpted gardens, was a demonstration that his power extended over the natural world as easily as it did over the lives of his subjects.

Questions for Analysis

1. Who was the intended audience for the king's performance of absolute sovereignty?

2. Who were Louis's primary competitors in this contest for eminence through the performance of power?

3. What possible political dangers might lay in wait for a regime that invested so heavily in the sumptuous display of semi-divine authority?

A. Hyacinthe Rigaud's 1701 portrait of Louis XIV.

B. Louis XIV as the Sun King.

C. *The Royal Procession of Louis XIV* by Adam Franz van der Meulen.

D. *Louis XIV arrives at the Palace of Versailles* by Pierre Patel.

would increase if its imports were reduced and its exports increased. He therefore imposed tariffs on foreign goods imported into France while using state money to promote the domestic manufacture of formerly imported goods, such as silk, lace, tapestries, and glass. He was especially anxious to create domestic industries capable of producing the goods France would need for war.

Despite Colbert's efforts to increase crown revenues, his policies ultimately foundered on the insatiable demands of Louis XIV's wars (see page 364). Colbert himself foresaw this result when he lectured the king in 1680: "Trade is the source of public finance and public finance is the vital nerve of war. . . . I beg your Majesty to permit me only to say to him that in war as in peace he has never consulted the amount of money available in determining his expenditures." Louis, however, paid him no heed. By the end of Louis's reign, his aggressive foreign policy lay in ruins and his country's finances had been shattered by the unsustainable costs of war.

ALTERNATIVES TO ABSOLUTISM

Although absolutism was the dominant model for seventeenth- and eighteenth-century European monarchs, it was by no means the only system by which Europeans governed themselves. A republican oligarchy continued to rule in Venice. In the Netherlands, the territories that had won their independence from Spain during the early seventeenth century combined to form the United Provinces, also a republic. The most significant exception to the trend toward absolutism, however, was the English monarchy.

Limited Monarchy: The Case of England

While the powers of representative assemblies were being undermined across much of Europe, the English Parliament was the longest-surviving such body in Europe. English political theorists had long seen their government as a mixed monarchy, composed of monarchical, noble, and nonnoble elements. During the seventeenth century, these traditions came under threat, first through Charles I's attempts to rule without Parliament and then during Oliver Cromwell's dictatorial Protectorate. The restoration of the monarchy in 1660 resolved the question of whether England would in future be a republic or a monarchy, but the sort of monarchy England would become remained an open question.

THE REIGN OF CHARLES II

Despite the fact that he was the son of the beheaded and much-hated Charles I, Charles II (r. 1660–85) was initially welcomed by most English men and women. He declared limited religious toleration for Protestant "dissenters" (Protestants who were not members of the Church of England). He promised to observe the Magna Carta and the Petition of Right, declaring, with characteristic good humor, that he did not wish to "resume his travels." The unbuttoned moral atmosphere of his court, with its risqué plays, dancing, and sexual licentiousness, reflected a public desire to forget the restraints of the Puritan past.

During the 1670s Charles began openly to model his kingship on the absolutism of Louis XIV. As a result, the great men of England soon came to be publicly divided between Charles's supporters (called "Tories," a popular nick-

CHARLES II OF ENGLAND (r. 1660–85) IN HIS CORONATION ROBES. This full frontal portrait of the monarch, holding the symbols of his rule, seems to confront the viewer personally with the overwhelming authority of the sovereign's gaze. Compare this classic image of the absolutist monarch with the very different portraits of William and Mary, who ruled after the Glorious Revolution of 1688 (page 363). ▪ *What had changed between 1660, when Charles II came to the throne, and 1688, when the more popular William and Mary became the rulers of England?*

name for Irish Catholic bandits) and his opponents (known as "Whigs," a nickname for Scottish Presbyterian rebels).

Religion also remained a divisive issue. Charles was sympathetic to Roman Catholicism, even to the point of a deathbed conversion in 1685. During the 1670s, he briefly suspended civil penalties against Catholics and Protestant dissenters by asserting his right as king to ignore Parliamentary legislation. The resulting public outcry compelled him to retreat, but this controversy, together with rising opposition to Charles's ardently Catholic brother James as the heir to the throne, led to a series of Whig electoral victories between 1679 and 1681. Charles died in 1685 with his power enhanced, but he left behind a political and religious legacy that was to be the undoing of his less able successor.

THE REIGN OF JAMES II

James II was the very opposite of his worldly brother. A zealous Catholic convert, he alienated his Tory supporters, who were close to the established Church of England, by suspending the laws preventing Catholics and Protestant dissenters from holding political office. James flaunted his own Roman Catholicism, openly declaring his wish that his subjects convert and publicly parading papal legates through the streets of London. In June 1688, he ordered all Church of England clergymen to read his decree of religious toleration from their pulpits. Seven bishops refused and were promptly imprisoned. At their trial, however, they were declared not guilty of sedition, to the enormous satisfaction of the Protestant English populace.

When James declared in 1688 that his newborn son and heir was to be raised a Catholic, a delegation of Whigs and Tories crossed the channel to Holland to invite Mary Stuart and her Protestant husband, William of Orange, to cross to England with an invading army to preserve Protestantism and English liberties by summoning a new Parliament.

THE GLORIOUS REVOLUTION

James fled the country, and Parliament declared the throne vacant, clearing the way for William and Mary to succeed him. William III and Mary II ruled as joint sovereigns until Mary's death in 1694, and William ruled alone until 1702. The Bill of Rights, passed by Parliament and accepted by the new king and queen in 1689, reaffirmed English civil liberties such as trial by jury, habeas corpus (a guarantee that no one could be imprisoned unless charged with a crime), and the right to petition the monarch through Parliament. The Bill of Rights further declared that the monarchy was sub-

WILLIAM AND MARY. In 1688, William of Orange and his wife, Mary Stuart, became joint Protestant rulers of England in a bloodless coup that took power from her father, the Catholic James II. Compare this contemporary print with the portraits of Louis XIV (page 360) and Charles II (page 362). ▪ *What relationship does it seem to depict between the royal couple and their subjects?* ▪ *What is the significance of the gathered crowd in the public square in the background?* ▪ *How is this different from the spectacle of divine authority projected by Louis XIV or the image of Charles II looking straight at the viewer?*

ject to the law of the land. The Act of Toleration, also passed in 1689, granted Protestant dissenters the right to worship freely, though not to hold political office. And in 1701, the Act of Succession ordained that every future English monarch must be a member of the Church of England.

The English soon referred to the events of 1688 and 1689 as the "Glorious Revolution" because it firmly established England as a mixed monarchy governed by the "king in Parliament." Although William and Mary and their successors continued to exercise a large measure of executive power, after 1688 no English monarch attempted to govern without Parliament, which has met annually from that time on. Parliament, and especially the House of Commons, also strengthened its control over taxation and expenditure.

Yet 1688 was not all glory. It was a revolution that consolidated the position of large property holders, whose control over local government had been threatened by Charles II and James II. It thus restored the status quo on behalf of a wealthy class of magnates that would soon become even wealthier from government patronage and the profits of war. It also brought misery to the Catholic minority in Scotland and to the Catholic majority in Ireland. After 1690, power in Ireland would lie firmly in the hands of a "Protestant Ascendancy," whose dominance over Irish society would last until modern times.

JOHN LOCKE AND THE CONTRACT THEORY OF GOVERNMENT

The Glorious Revolution was the product of unique circumstances, but it also reflected antiabsolutist theories of politics that were taking shape in the late seventeenth century. Chief among these opponents of absolutism was the Englishman John Locke (1632–1704), whose *Two Treatises of Government* were written before the revolution but published for the first time in 1690.

Locke maintained that humans had originally lived in a state of nature characterized by absolute freedom and equality, with no government of any kind. The only law was the law of nature (which Locke equated with the law of reason), by which individuals enforced for themselves their natural rights to life, liberty, and property. Soon, however, humans began to perceive that the inconveniences of the state of nature outweighed its advantages. Accordingly, they agreed first to establish a civil society based on absolute equality and then to set up a government to arbitrate the disputes that might arise within this civil society. But they did not make government's powers absolute. All powers not expressly surrendered to the government were reserved to the people themselves; as a result, governmental authority was both contractual and conditional. If a government exceeded or abused the authority granted to it, society had the right to dissolve it and create another.

Locke condemned absolutism in every form. He denounced absolute monarchy, but he was also critical of claims for the sovereignty of parliaments. Government, he argued, had been instituted to protect life, liberty, and property; no political authority could infringe these natural rights. The law of nature was therefore an automatic and absolute limitation on every branch of government. In the late eighteenth century, Locke's ideas would resurface as part of the intellectual background of both the American and French revolutions.

During the beginning of the eighteenth century, then, both France and Britain had solved the problem of political dissent and social disorder in their own way. The emergence of a stable constitutional monarchy in England after 1688 contrasted vividly with the absolutist system developed by Louis XIV, but both systems worked well enough to contain the immediate threat to royal authority posed by a powerful class of landed nobles. Domestic stability was no guarantee of international peace, however, and the period from 1661, when Louis XIV assumed personal rule, to his death in 1715, was marked by almost constant warfare.

WAR AND THE BALANCE OF POWER, 1661–1715

Louis XIV's foreign policy reflected his belief that military victories abroad were necessary to reinforce the glory of his realm and the power that he wielded at home. Louis's wars also sought to meet the threat posed by the Habsburg powers in Spain, the Spanish Netherlands, and the Holy Roman Empire. Through a series of conquests in the Low Countries, Louis expanded his territory. In response, William of Orange (r. 1672–1702) organized the League of Augsburg, which over time included Holland, England, Spain, Sweden, several German states, and the Austrian Habsburgs. The resulting Nine Years' War extended from Ireland to India to North America (where it was known as King William's War).

The League of Augsburg reflected the emergence of a new diplomatic goal in western and central Europe: the preservation of a balance of power. This goal would animate European diplomacy for the next two hundred years, until the balance-of-power system collapsed with the outbreak of the First World War. The main proponents of balance of power diplomacy were England, the United Provinces (Holland), Prussia, and Austria. By 1697, the league forced Louis XIV to make peace, because France was exhausted by war and famine. Louis gave back much of his recent gains but kept Strasbourg and the surrounding territory of Alsace. He was nevertheless looking at the real prize: a French claim to succeed to the throne of Spain and so control the Spanish Empire in the Americas, Italy, the Netherlands, and the Philippines.

The War of the Spanish Succession

In the 1690s it became clear that King Charles II of Spain (r. 1665–1700) would soon die without a clear heir, and both Louis XIV of France and Leopold I of Austria (r. 1658–1705) were interested in promoting their own relatives to succeed him. Either solution would have upset the balance of power in Europe, and several schemes to divide the Spanish realm between French and Austrian candidates were discussed. Meanwhile, King Charles II's advisers sought to avoid partition by passing the entire Spanish Empire to a single heir: Louis XIV's grandson, Philip of Anjou. When Charles II died, Philip V (1700–1746) was proclaimed king of Spain, and the War of the Spanish Succession began, with England, the United Provinces, Austria, and Prussia arrayed against France, Bavaria, and Spain. Although William of Orange died in 1702, just as the war was beginning, his generals led an extraordinary march deep into the European Continent, inflicting a devastating defeat on the French and their Bavarian allies at Blenheim (1704). Soon after, the English captured Gibraltar, establishing a commercial foothold in the Mediterranean. By 1709, France was on the verge of defeat, but when they met the British at the battle of Malplaquet in present-day Belgium they inflicted twenty-four thousand casualties before retreating from the field. Meanwhile, the costs of the campaign created a chorus of complaints from English and Dutch merchants, who feared the damage that was being done to trade and commerce. Queen Anne of England (Mary's sister and William's successor) gradually grew disillusioned with the war, and her government sent out peace feelers to France.

The Treaty of Utrecht

In 1713, the war finally came to an end with the Treaty of Utrecht. Its terms were reasonably fair to all sides. Philip V, Louis XIV's grandson, remained on the throne of Spain and retained Spain's colonial empire intact. In return, Louis agreed that France and Spain would never be united under the same ruler. Austria gained territories in the Spanish Netherlands and Italy, including Milan and Naples. The biggest winner by far was Great Britain, as the combined kingdoms of England and Scotland were known after 1707. The British kept Gibraltar and Minorca in the Mediterranean and also acquired substantial French territory in North America and the Caribbean. Even more valuable, however, Britain also extracted from Spain the right to transport and sell African slaves in Spanish America. As a result, the British were now poised to become the principal slave merchants and the dominant colonial and commercial power of the eighteenth-century world.

The Treaty of Utrecht reshaped the balance of power in western Europe in fundamental ways. Spain's collapse was already precipitous; by 1713 it was complete. Holland's decline was more gradual, but by 1713, its greatest days were also over. In the Atlantic world, Britain and France were now the dominant powers. Although they would duel for another half century for control of North America, the balance of colonial power tilted decisively in Britain's favor after Utrecht. Within Europe, the myth of French military

supremacy had been shattered. Britain's navy, not France's army, would rule the new imperial and commercial world of the eighteenth century.

THE REMAKING OF CENTRAL AND EASTERN EUROPE

The decades between 1680 and 1720 were also decisive in reshaping the balance of power in central and eastern Europe. As Ottoman power waned, the Austro-Hungarian Empire of the Habsburgs emerged as the dominant power in central and southeastern Europe. To the north, Brandenburg-Prussia was also a rising power. The most dramatic changes, however, occurred in Russia, which emerged from a long war with Sweden as the dominant power in the Baltic Sea and would soon threaten the combined kingdom of Poland-Lithuania.

The Habsburg Empire

In 1683, the Ottoman Turks launched their last assault on Vienna. Only the arrival of seventy thousand Polish troops saved the Austrian capital from capture. Thereafter, Ottoman power in southeastern Europe declined rapidly. By 1718, Austria had reconquered all of Hungary from the Ottomans, and also Transylvania and Serbia. With Hungary now a buffer state between Austria and the Ottomans, Vienna emerged as one of the great cultural and political capitals of eighteenth-century Europe, and Austria became one of the arbiters of the European balance of power.

Although the Austrian Habsburgs retained their title as Holy Roman Emperors and after 1713 also held lands in the Netherlands and Italy, their real power lay in Austria, Bohemia, Moravia, Galicia, and Hungary. These territories were geographically contiguous, but they were deeply divided by ethnicity, religion, and language. Despite the centralizing efforts of a series of Habsburg rulers, their empire would remain a rather loose confederation of distinct territories.

In Bohemia and Moravia, the Habsburgs encouraged landlords to produce crops for export by forcing peasants to provide three days of unpaid work per week to their lords. In return, the landed elites of these territories permitted the emperors to reduce the political independence of their traditional legislative estates. In Hungary, however, the powerful and independent nobility resisted such compromises, and Hungary remained a semi-autonomous region within the empire whose support the Austrians could never take for granted.

MARIA THERESA OF AUSTRIA AND HER FAMILY. A formidable and capable ruler who fought to maintain Austria's dominance in central Europe against the claims of Frederick the Great of Prussia, Maria Theresa had sixteen children, including Marie Antoinette, later queen of France as wife of Louis XVI. ▪ *Why did she emphasize her role as mother in a royal portrait such as this one, rather than her undeniable political skills?* ▪ *How does this compare to the portraits of William and Mary or of Louis XIV elsewhere in this chapter?*

After 1740, the empress Maria Theresa (r. 1740–80) and her son Joseph II (r. 1765–90; from 1765 until 1780 the two were co-rulers) pioneered a new style of "enlightened absolutism" within their empire: centralizing the administration in Vienna, increasing taxation, creating a professional standing army, and tightening their control over the church while creating a statewide system of primary education, relaxing censorship, and instituting a new, more liberal criminal code. But in practice, Habsburg absolutism, whether enlightened or not, was always limited by the diversity of its imperial territories and by the weakness of its local governmental institutions.

The Rise of Brandenburg-Prussia

After the Ottoman collapse, the main threat to Austria came from the rising power of Brandenburg-Prussia. Like Austria, Prussia was a composite state made up of several geographically divided territories acquired through inheritance by the Hohenzollern family. Their two main holdings were Brandenburg, centered on its capital city, Berlin, and

the duchy of East Prussia. Between these two territories lay Swedish Pomerania and a substantial part of the kingdom of Poland. The Hohenzollerns' aim was to unite their state by acquiring these intervening territories. Over the course of more than a century of steady state building, they finally succeeded in doing so. In the process, Brandenburg-Prussia became a dominant military power and a key player in the balance-of-power diplomacy of the mid-eighteenth century.

The foundations for Prussian expansion were laid by Frederick William, the "Great Elector" (r. 1640–88). He obtained East Prussia from Poland in exchange for help in a war against Sweden. Behind the Elector's diplomatic triumphs lay his success in building an army and mobilizing the resources to pay for it. He gave the powerful nobles of his territories (known as *Junkers*) the right to enserf their peasants, and he guaranteed them immunity from taxation. In exchange, they staffed the officer corps of his army and supported his highly autocratic taxation system. Secure in their estates and made increasingly wealthy in the grain trade, the Junkers surrendered management of the Prussian state to the Elector's newly reformed bureaucracy, which set about its main task: increasing the size and strength of the Prussian army.

The Great Elector's son, Frederick I (r. 1688–1713) earned the right to call himself "king in Prussia" from the Austrian emperor and devoted his attention to developing the cultural life of his new royal capital, Berlin. His son, Frederick William I (r. 1713–40) focused, like his grandfather, on building the army. During his reign, the Prussian army became the fourth largest in Europe, after those of France, Austria, and Russia. To support his army, Frederick William I increased taxes and shunned the luxuries of court life.

Frederick William I had made Prussia a strong state. His son Frederick II the Great (r. 1740–86) raised his country to the status of a major power. As soon as he became king in 1740, Frederick mobilized the army his father had never taken into battle and occupied the Austrian province of Silesia. The new Habsburg empress, Maria Theresa, counterattacked; but despite the support of both Britain and Hungary, she was unable to recover Silesia. Emboldened, Frederick spent the rest of his reign consolidating his gains in Silesia and extending his control over the Polish territories that lay between Prussia and Brandenburg. Through relentless diplomacy and frequent war, by 1786 Frederick transformed Prussia into a powerful, contiguous territorial kingdom with the most professional and efficient bureaucracy in Europe, staffed with nobles from the powerful Junker class.

Frederick was an enlightened absolutist. He supervised a series of social reforms, prohibited the judicial torture of accused criminals, abolished the bribing of judges,

THE CITY OF STETTIN UNDER SIEGE BY THE GREAT ELECTOR, FREDERICK WILLIAM, IN THE WINTER OF 1677–78 (c. 1680). This painting depicts the growing sophistication and organization of military operations under the Prussian monarchy. Improvements in artillery and siege tactics forced cities to adopt new defensive strategies, especially the zone of battlements and protective walls that became ubiquitous in central Europe during this period. ▪ *How might these developments have shaped the layout of Europe's growing towns and cities?* ▪ *How might this emphasis on the military and its attendant bureaucracy have affected the relationship between the monarchy and the nobility or between the king and his subjects?*

and established a system of elementary schools. Although strongly anti-Semitic, he encouraged religious toleration and declared that he would happily build a mosque in Berlin if he could find enough Muslims to fill it. On his own royal estates he abolished capital punishment, curtailed the forced labor services of his peasantry, and granted them long leases on the land they worked. He encouraged scientific forestry and the cultivation of new crops. He cleared new lands in Silesia and brought in thousands of immigrants to cultivate them. When wars ruined their farms, he supplied his peasants with new livestock and tools. But he never attempted to extend these reforms to the estates of the Prussian nobility. To have done so would have alienated the very group on whom Frederick's rule depended.

AUTOCRACY IN RUSSIA

An even more dramatic transformation took place in Russia under Tsar Peter I (1672–1725). Peter's accomplishments alone would have earned him his title of "Great." But his imposing height—he was six feet eight inches tall—as well as his mercurial personality—jesting one moment, raging

the next—certainly added to the outsize impression he made on his contemporaries. Peter was not the first tsar to bring his country into contact with western Europe, but his policies were decisive in making Russia a great European power.

The Early Years of Peter's Reign

Since 1613 Russia had been ruled by members of the Romanov Dynasty, who had attempted to restore political stability after the chaotic "time of troubles" that followed the death of Ivan the Terrible in 1584. Like Louis XIV of France, Peter came to the throne as a young boy, and his minority was marked by political dissension and court intrigue. In 1689, however, at the age of seventeen, he overthrew the regency of his half-sister Sophia and assumed personal control of the state. Determined to make Russia into a great military power, the young tsar traveled to Holland and England during the 1690s to study shipbuilding and to recruit skilled foreign workers to help him build a navy. While he was abroad, however, his elite palace guard (the *streltsy*) rebelled, attempting to restore Sophia to the throne. Peter quickly returned home and crushed the rebellion with striking savagery.

The Transformation of the Tsarist State

Peter is most famous as the tsar who attempted to westernize Russia by imposing a series of social and cultural reforms on the traditional Russian nobility: ordering noblemen to cut off their long beards and flowing sleeves; publishing a book of manners that forbade spitting on the floor and eating with one's fingers; encouraging polite conversation between the sexes; and requiring noblewomen to appear, together with men, in Western garb at weddings, banquets, and other public occasions. Thousands of western European experts were brought to Russia to staff the new schools and academies Peter built; to design the new buildings he constructed; and to serve in the tsar's army, navy, and administration.

These measures were important, but the tsar was not primarily motivated by a desire to modernize or westernize Russia. Peter's policies transformed Russian life in fundamental ways, but his real goal was to make Russia a great military power, not to remake Russian society. His new taxation system (1724), for example, which assessed taxes on individuals rather than on households, rendered many of the traditional divisions of Russian peasant society obsolete. It was created, however, to raise more money for war. His Table of Ranks, imposed in 1722, had a similar

PETER THE GREAT CUTS THE BEARD OF AN OLD BELIEVER.
This woodcut depicts the Russian emperor's enthusiastic policy of westernization, as he pushed everybody in Russia who was not a peasant to adopt Western styles of clothes and grooming. The Old Believer (a member of a religious sect in Russia) protests that he has paid the beard tax and should therefore be exempt.
▪ *Why would an individual's choices about personal appearance be so politically significant in Peter's Russia?* ▪ *What customs were the target of Peter's reforms?*

impact on the nobility. By insisting that all nobles must work their way up from the (lower) landlord class to the (higher) administrative class and to the (highest) military class, Peter reversed the traditional hierarchy of Russian noble society, which had valued landlords by birth above administrators and soldiers who had risen by merit. But he also created a powerful new incentive to lure his nobility into administrative and military service to the tsar.

Peter the Great was the absolute master of his empire to a degree unmatched elsewhere in Europe. After 1649, Russian peasants were legally the property of their landlords; by 1750, half were serfs and the other half were state peasants who lived on lands owned by the tsar himself. State peasants could be conscripted to serve as soldiers in the tsar's army, as workers in his factories (whose productive capacity increased enormously during Peter's reign), or

as forced laborers in his building projects. Serfs could also be taxed by the tsar and summoned for military service, as could their lords. All Russians, of whatever rank, were expected to serve the tsar, and all Russia was considered in some sense to belong to him.

To further consolidate his power, Peter replaced the Duma—the nation's rudimentary national assembly—with a hand-picked senate, a group of nine administrators who supervised military and civilian affairs. In religious matters, he took direct control over the Russian Orthodox Church by appointing an imperial official to manage its affairs. To cope with the demands of war, he also fashioned a new, larger, and more efficient administration, for which he recruited both nobles and nonnobles. One of his principal advisers, Alexander Menshikov, began his career as a cook and finished as a prince. This degree of social mobility would have been impossible in any contemporary western European country. Instead, noble status depended on governmental service, with all nobles expected to participate in Peter's army or administration. The administrative machinery Peter devised furnished Russia with its ruling class for the next two hundred years.

Peter's Foreign Policy

The goal of Peter's foreign policy was to secure year-round ports for Russia on the Black Sea and the Baltic Sea. In the Black Sea, his enemy was the Ottomans, and he had little success. In the north, however, Peter achieved much more. In 1700, he began what would become a twenty-one-year war with Sweden, then the dominant power in the Baltic Sea. By 1703, Peter had secured a foothold on the Gulf of Finland and immediately began to build a new capital city there, which he named St. Petersburg. The centerpiece of the new city was a royal palace designed to imitate and rival Louis XIV's Versailles.

The Great Northern War with Sweden ended in 1721 with the Peace of Nystad. This treaty marks a realignment of power in eastern Europe comparable to that effected by the Treaty of Utrecht in the West. Sweden lost substantial territories to Hanover, Prussia, and Russia, and was now a second-rank power. Poland-Lithuania was also a declining power; by the end of the eighteenth century, the kingdom would disappear altogether, its territories swallowed up by Russia, Austria, and Prussia. The victors at Nystad were the Prussians and the Russians. These two powers secured their position along the Baltic coast, positioning themselves to take advantage of the lucrative eastern European grain trade with western Europe.

Peter's victory came at enormous cost. Direct taxation increased 500 percent during his reign, and his army in the 1720s numbered more than three hundred thousand men. Nevertheless, Peter made Russia a force to be reckoned with on the European scene. A series of ineffective tsars followed, mostly creatures of the palace guard, under whom the resentful nobles reversed many of Peter the Great's reforms. In 1762, however, the crown passed to Catherine the Great, a ruler whose ambitions and determination were equal to those of her great predecessor.

Catherine the Great and the Partition of Poland

Catherine was a German who came to the throne in 1762 on the death of her husband, the weak (and possibly mad) Tsar Peter III, who was deposed and executed in a palace coup that Catherine herself may have helped arrange. Although she cultivated an image of herself as an enlightened ruler, Catherine was determined not to lose the support of the nobility who had placed her on the throne. As a result, her efforts at social reform did not extend much beyond the founding of hospitals and orphanages and the creation of an elementary school system for the children of the provincial nobility. Like her contemporary enlightened absolutists Joseph of Austria and Frederick the Great of Prussia, she too summoned a commission, in 1767, to codify and revise Russian law. But few of its radical proposals (which included the abolition of capital punishment, an end to judicial torture, and prohibitions on the selling of serfs) were ever implemented. When a peasant revolt led by a Cossack named Emelyan Pugachev briefly threatened Moscow in 1773–75, Catherine responded by further centralizing her own government and by tightening aristocratic control over the peasantry.

Catherine's greatest achievements were gained through war and diplomacy. In 1769, she renewed Peter the Great's push to secure a warm-water port on the Black Sea. In the resulting war with the Ottoman Turks (which ended in 1774), Russia won control over the northern coast of the Black Sea, secured the independence of Crimea (which Russia would annex in 1783), and obtained safe passage for Russian ships through the Bosporus and into the Mediterranean Sea. In the course of this campaign, Russia also won control over several Ottoman provinces in the Balkans.

Russia's gains alarmed Austria, however, which now found itself with the powerful Russian Empire on its southern doorstep. Prussia too was threatening to become in-

CATHERINE THE GREAT.

volved in the war as an ally of the Ottomans. Frederick the Great's real interests, however, lay much closer to home. To preserve the peace among Russia, Prussia, and Austria, he proposed instead a partition of Poland. Russia would abandon its Balkan conquests and, in return, would acquire the grain fields of eastern Poland, along with a population of 1 to 2 million Poles. Austria would take Galicia (divided between Poland and Ukraine today), acquiring 2.5 million Poles. Prussia, meanwhile, would take the coastal regions of Poland, including the port of Gdansk (Danzig). As a result of this agreement, finalized in 1772, Poland lost about 30 percent of its territory and about half of its population.

Poland was now paying the price for its political conservatism. Alone among the major central European powers, the Polish nobility had successfully opposed any move toward monarchical centralization as a threat to its liberties, among which was the right of any individual noble to veto any measure proposed in the Polish representative assembly, the Diet. In 1772, King Stanislaus reluctantly accepted the partition of his country because he was too weak to resist it. In 1793 the Russians and Prussians took two more enormous bites out of Poland, and a final swallow by Russia, Austria, and Prussia in 1795 left nothing of Poland at all.

COMMERCE AND CONSUMPTION

Despite the increased military power of Russia, Prussia, and Austria, the balance of power within Europe was shifting steadily toward the West during the eighteenth century. The North Atlantic economies in particular were growing more rapidly than those anywhere else in Europe. As a result, France and Britain were becoming preponderant powers both in Europe and the wider world.

Economic Growth in Eighteenth-Century Europe

The reasons for this rapid economic and demographic growth in northwestern Europe are complex. In Britain and Holland, new, more intensive agricultural systems produced more food per acre. New crops, especially maize and potatoes (both introduced to Europe from the Americas),

POPULATION GROWTH c. 1600. ▪ *Where did the population grow more rapidly?* ▪ *Why were the largest gains in population on the coasts?* ▪ *How did urbanization affect patterns of life and trade?*

also helped increase the supply of food. Infectious disease continued to kill half of all Europeans before the age of twenty, but plague was ceasing to be a major killer, as a degree of immunity began to emerge within the European population.

Northwestern Europe was also becoming increasingly urbanized. Across Europe as a whole the total number of urban dwellers did not change markedly between 1600 and 1800. What did change was, first, the fact that larger cities were increasingly concentrated in northern and western Europe and, second, the extraordinary growth of the very largest cities. Amsterdam, the hub of early modern international commerce, increased from 30,000 in 1530 to 200,000 by 1800. Naples, the busy Mediterranean port, went from a population of 300,000 in 1600 to nearly half a million by the late eighteenth century. Even more spectacular population growth occurred in the administrative capitals of Europe. London grew from 674,000 in 1700 to 860,000 a century later. Paris went from 180,000 people in 1600 to more than 500,000 in 1800.

The rising prosperity of northwestern Europe depended on developments in trade and manufacturing as well as agriculture. Spurred by improvements in transportation, entrepreneurs began to promote the production of textiles in the countryside. They distributed ("put out") wool and flax to rural workers who would card, spin, and weave it into cloth on a piece-rate basis. The entrepreneur then collected and sold the finished cloth in a market that extended from local towns to international exporters. For country dwellers, this system (sometimes called *protoindustrialization*) provided welcome employment during otherwise slack seasons of the agricultural year. For the merchant-entrepreneurs who administered it, the system allowed them to avoid expensive guild restrictions in the towns and to reduce the overall costs of production. The putting-out system led to increased employment and higher levels of industrial production, not only for textiles but also for iron, metalworking, and even toy and clock making.

The role of cities as manufacturing centers also continued to grow during the eighteenth century. In northern France, a million men and women were employed in the textile trade in Amiens, Lille, and Rheims. The rulers of Prussia made it their policy to develop Berlin as a manufacturing center, taking advantage of an influx of French Protestants to establish a silk-weaving industry there. Most urban manufacturing took place in small shops employing from five to twenty journeymen working under a master. But the scale of such enterprise was growing and becoming more specialized, as workshops began to group together to form a single manufacturing district in which several thousand workers might be employed to produce the same product.

Techniques in some crafts remained much as they had been for centuries. In others, however, inventions changed the pattern of work as well as the nature of the product. Knitting frames, simple devices to speed the manufacture of textile goods, made their appearance in Britain and Holland. Wire-drawing machines and slitting mills, the latter enabling nail makers to convert iron bars into rods, spread from Germany into Britain. Techniques for printing colored designs directly on calico cloth were imported from Asia. New and more efficient printing presses appeared, first in Holland and then elsewhere.

Workers did not readily accept innovations of this kind. Labor-saving machines threw people out of work. Artisans, especially those organized into guilds, were by nature conservative, anxious to protect not only their rights but also the secrets of their trade. Often, therefore, governments would intervene to block the widespread use of machines if they threatened to increase unemployment or in some other way to create unrest. States might also intervene to protect the interests of their powerful commercial and financial backers. Mercantilist doctrines could also impede innovation. In both Paris and Lyons, for example, the use of indigo dyes was banned because they were manufactured abroad. But the pressures for economic innovation were irresistible, because behind them lay an insatiable eighteenth-century appetite for goods.

A World of Goods

In the eighteenth century, for the first time, a mass market for consumer goods emerged in Europe, and especially in northwestern Europe. Houses were now stocked with hitherto uncommon luxuries such as sugar, tobacco, tea, coffee, chocolate, newspapers, books, pictures, clocks, toys, china, glassware, pewter, silver plate, soap, razors, furniture (including beds with mattresses, chairs, and chests of drawers), shoes, cotton cloth, and spare clothing. Demand for such products consistently outstripped the supply, causing prices for these items to rise faster than the price of foodstuffs throughout the century. But the demand for them continued unabated.

The exploding consumer economy of the eighteenth century spurred demand for manufactured goods of all sorts. But it also encouraged the provision of services. In eighteenth-century Britain, the service sector was the fastest-growing part of the economy, outstripping both agriculture and manufacturing. Almost everywhere in urban Europe, the eighteenth century was the golden age of the small shopkeeper. People bought more prepared foods and more ready-made (as opposed to personally tailored) clothing. Advertising became an important part of doing

TOPSY-TURVY WORLD BY JAN STEEN. This Dutch painting depicts a household in the throes of the exploding consumer economy that hit Europe in the eighteenth century. Consumer goods ranging from silver and china to clothing and furniture cluttered the houses of ordinary people as never before.

business, helping create demand for new products and shaping popular taste for changing fashions. Even political allegiances could be expressed through consumption when people purchased plates and glasses commemorating favorite rulers or causes.

The result of all these developments was a European economy vastly more complex, more specialized, more integrated, more commercialized, and more productive than anything the world had seen before.

COLONIZATION AND TRADE IN THE SEVENTEENTH CENTURY

Many of the new consumer goods that propelled the economy of eighteenth-century Europe, including such staples as sugar, tobacco, tea, coffee, chocolate, china, and cotton cloth, were the products of Europe's growing colonial empires in Asia, Africa, and the Americas. The economic history of these empires is part of a broader pattern of accelerating global connection beginning in the late fifteenth century that witnessed an extraordinary exchange of peoples, plants, animals, diseases, goods, and culture between the African and Eurasian land mass on the one hand, and the Americas, Australia, and the Pacific Islands on the other. Historians refer to this as the "Columbian exchange"—a reference to Columbus's voyage in 1492—and many see it as a fundamental turning point in

human history and in the history of the earth's ecology. The exchange brought new agricultural products to Europe—such as cane sugar, tobacco, corn, and the potato—and new domesticated animals to the Americas and Australia, transforming agriculture on both sides of the Atlantic and the Pacific Oceans, and reshaping the landscape itself. The transfer of human populations in the form of settlers, merchants, and slaves accelerated the process of cultural change for many peoples, even as other groups saw their cultures wiped out through violence or forced resettlement. The accompanying transfer of disease agents, meanwhile, had devastating effects—some historians suggest that between 50 and 90 percent of the pre-Columbian population of the Americas died from communicable diseases brought from Europe such as smallpox, cholera, influenza, typhoid, and measles.

Europe's growing colonial empires between the fifteenth and eighteenth centuries were thus a part of a series of fundamental changes that transformed people's lives, and their relation to their environment over the long term in many parts of the world. Europe's growing wealth during this period had complex causes, but it is impossible to imagine the prosperity of the eighteenth century without understanding this history of colonialism.

Spanish Colonialism

After the exploits of the conquistadors, the Spanish established colonial governments in Peru and in Mexico, which they controlled from Madrid. In keeping with the doctrines of mercantilism, the Spanish government allowed only Spanish merchants to trade with their American colonies, requiring all colonial exports and imports to pass through a single Spanish port (first Seville, then later the more navigable port of Cadíz). During the sixteenth century, this system worked reasonably well. The Spanish colonial economy was dominated by mining; the lucrative market for silver in East Asia even made it profitable to establish an outpost in Manila, where Spanish merchants exchanged Asian silk for South American bullion. But Spain also took steps to promote farming and ranching in Central and South America and established settlements in Florida and California.

Throughout this empire, a relatively small number of Spaniards had conquered complex and highly populous Native American societies. To rule these new territories, the Spanish replaced existing elites with Spanish administrators and churchmen. By and large, they did not attempt to uproot or eliminate existing native cultures but focused on controlling and exploiting native labor for their own profit, above all in extracting mineral resources. The native peoples of Spanish America already lived, for the most part, in large, well-organized villages and towns. The Spanish collected tribute from these communities and attempted to convert them to Catholicism but did not attempt to change their basic patterns of life.

The result was widespread cultural assimilation between the Spanish colonizers and the native populations, combined with a relatively high degree of intermarriage between them. Out of this reality emerged a complex and distinctive system of racial and social castes, with Spaniards at the top, peoples of mixed descent (combinations of Spanish, African, and Native American) in the middle, and nontribal American Indians at the bottom. In theory, these racial categories corresponded with class distinctions, but in practice race and class did not always coincide, and race itself was often a social fiction. Individuals of mixed descent who prospered economically often found ways to establish their "pure" Spanish ancestry by adopting the social practices that characterized elite (that is, Spanish) status. Spaniards always remained at the top of the social hierarchy, however, even when they fell into poverty.

The wealth of Spain's colonial trade tempted the merchants of other countries to win a share of the treasure for themselves. Probably the boldest challengers were the English, whose leading buccaneer was Sir Francis Drake. Three times Drake raided the east and west coasts of Spanish America. His career illustrates the mixture of piracy and patriotism that characterized England's early efforts to break into the colonial trade. Until the 1650s, however, the English could only dent the lucrative Spanish trade in bullion, hides, silks, and slaves.

French Colonialism

French colonial policy matured under Louis XIV's mercantilist finance minister, Jean Baptiste Colbert. Realizing the profits to be made in responding to Europe's growing demand for sugar, he encouraged the development of sugar-producing colonies in the West Indies, the largest of which was Saint-Domingue (present-day Haiti). Sugar, virtually unknown in Christian Europe during the Middle Ages, became a popular luxury item in the late fifteenth century. It took the slave plantations of the Caribbean to turn sugar into a mass-market product. By 1750, slaves in Saint-Domingue produced 40 percent of the world's sugar and 50 percent of its coffee, exporting more sugar than Jamaica, Cuba, and Brazil combined. France also dominated the interior of the North American continent, where French traders brought furs to the American Indians and missionaries preached Christianity in a vast territory that stretched from Quebec to Louisiana. The financial returns from North America were never large, however, and never matched the profits from the Caribbean sugar colonies or from the trading posts that the French maintained in India.

Like the Spanish colonies, the French colonies were established and administered as direct crown enterprises. The elite of French colonial society were military officers and administrators sent from Paris. Below their ranks were fishermen, fur traders, small farmers, and common soldiers who constituted the bulk of French settlers in North America. Because the fishing and the fur trades relied on cooperative relationships with native peoples, a mutual economic interdependence grew up between the French colonies and the peoples of the surrounding region. Intermarriage, especially between French traders and native women, was common. These North American colonies remained dependent on the wages and supplies sent to them from the mother country. Only rarely did they become truly self-sustaining economic enterprises.

The phenomenally successful sugar plantations of the Caribbean had their own social structure, with slaves at the bottom, people of mixed African and European descent forming a middle layer, and wealthy European plantation

ILLINOIS INDIANS TRADING WITH FRENCH SETTLERS. This engraving from Nicholas De Fer's 1705 map of the Western Hemisphere illustrates the economic interdependence that developed between early French colonies and the native peoples of the surrounding region. ■ *How did this differ from relations between Native Americans and English agricultural communities on the Atlantic coast?*

owners at the top, controlling the lucrative trade with the outside world. Because the monarchy controlled the prices that colonial plantation owners could charge French merchants for their goods, traders in Europe who bought the goods for resale abroad could also make vast fortunes. Historians estimate that as many as a million of the twenty-five million inhabitants of France in the eighteenth century lived off the money flowing through this colonial trade, making the slave colonies of the Caribbean a powerful force for economic change in France.

English Colonialism

Unlike those of Spain, England's American colonies had no significant mineral wealth. As a result, English colonists sought profits by establishing agricultural settlements in North America and the Caribbean basin. Their first permanent, though ultimately unsuccessful, colony was founded in 1607 at Jamestown, Virginia. Over the next forty years, eighty thousand English emigrants would sail to more than twenty autonomous settlements in the New World. Many of these early settlers were driven by religious motives. The Pilgrims who landed at Plymouth, Massachusetts, in 1620 were one of many dissident groups, both Protestant and Catholic, that sought to escape the English government's religious intolerance by emigrating to North America. Strikingly, however, English colonists showed little interest in trying to convert Native American peoples to Christianity. Missionaries played a much larger role in Spanish efforts to colonize Central and South America and French efforts to penetrate the North American hinterlands.

These English colonies did not begin as crown enterprises as in the Spanish or French empires. Instead they were private ventures, either proprietary (as in Maryland and Pennsylvania) or joint-stock companies (as in Virginia and the Massachusetts Bay colony). Building on their experience in Ireland, English colonists established planned settlements known as plantations, in which they attempted to replicate as many features of English life as possible. Geography also contributed to the English settlement patterns, as the rivers and bays of the northeast Atlantic coast provided the first locations for colonists. Aside from the Hudson, however, there were no great rivers to lead colonists very far inland, and the English colonies clung to the coast and to each other.

Once they realized the profits to be made in colonial trade, however, the governments of both Oliver Cromwell and Charles II began to intervene in their management. Mercantilist-inspired navigation acts, passed in 1651 and 1660, decreed that exports from English colonies to the mother country be carried in English ships and forbade the direct exporting of "enumerated" products, such as sugar and tobacco, directly from the colonies to foreign ports. The English sugar-producing colonies competed directly with the French, and during the eighteenth century, profits from the tiny islands of Jamaica and Barbados were worth more than all British imports from China and India combined. Tobacco, which was first brought to Europe by the Spaniards, became profitable as smoking caught on in Europe in the seventeenth century, popularized by English explorers who learned about it from Native Americans in Virginia. Governments at first joined the church in condemning it, but eventually encouraged its production and consumption, realizing the profits to be made from the trade.

The early English colonies in North America soon grew into agricultural communities populated by small- and medium-scale landholders. In part this reflected the kinds of people recruited by the private colonial enterprises for settlement in North America. But the focus on agriculture also resulted from the demographic catastrophe that struck the native populations of the Atlantic seaboard during the second half of the sixteenth century. European diseases—brought by Spanish armies and by the French, British, and Portuguese fisherman who frequented the rich fishing banks off the New England coast—had already decimated the native peoples of eastern North America even before the first European colonists set foot there. By the early seventeenth century, a great deal of rich agricultural land had been abandoned simply because there were no longer enough native farmers to till it.

Unlike the Spanish, English colonists along the Atlantic seaboard had neither the need nor the opportunity to control a large native labor force. What they wanted, rather, was complete and exclusive control over native lands. To this end, the English colonists soon set out to eliminate, through expulsion and massacre, the indigenous peoples of their colonies. There were exceptions—in the Quaker colony of Pennsylvania, colonists and Native Americans maintained friendly relations for more than half a century. In the Carolinas, on the other hand, there was widespread enslavement of native peoples, either for sale to the West Indies or, from the 1690s, to work on the rice plantations along the coast. Elsewhere, however, attempts to enslave the native peoples of North American failed. When English planters looked for bond laborers, they either recruited indentured servants from England (most of whom would be freed after a specified period of service) or purchased African captives (who would usually be enslaved for life).

In contrast to the Spanish and French colonies, intermarriage between English colonists and native populations was rare. Instead, a rigid racial division emerged that distinguished all Europeans from all Native Americans and

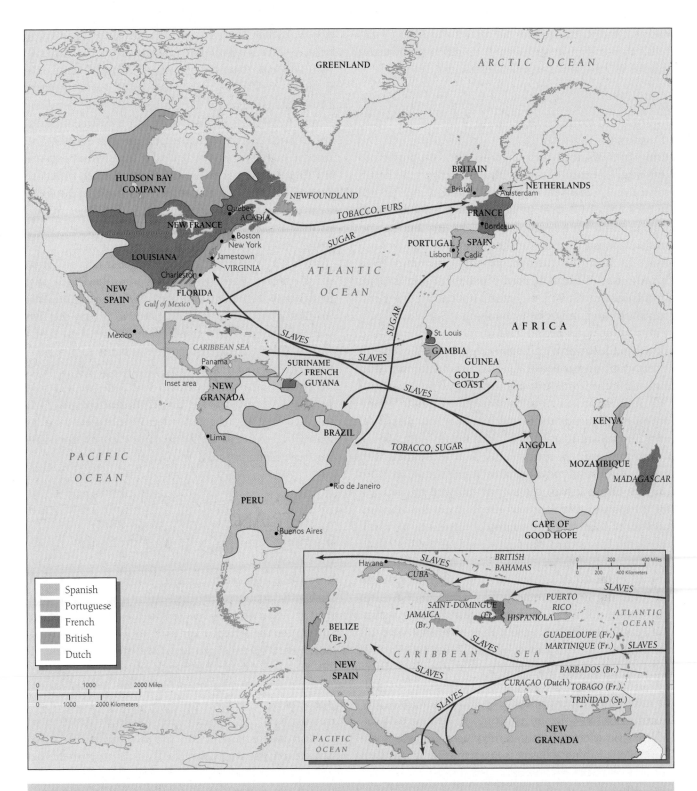

THE ATLANTIC WORLD c. 1700. ▪ *Why were European governments so concerned with closely controlling the means by which certain products traveled from the colonies to European ports?* ▪ *What products did French and British colonies in North America provide to the European market in the eighteenth century?* ▪ *Which colonies were most dependent on slave labor?* ▪ *What products did they produce?*

Africans. Intermarriage between natives and Africans was relatively common, but between the English and the native peoples of the colonies an unbridgeable gulf developed.

Dutch Colonialism

Until the 1670s, the Dutch controlled the most prosperous commercial empire of the seventeenth century. Although some Dutch settlements were established, including one at the Cape of Good Hope in modern-day South Africa, Dutch colonialism generally followed the "fort and factory" model established by the Portuguese in Asia. In Southeast Asia, the Dutch East India Company, founded in 1602, seized control of Sumatra, Borneo, and the Moluccas (Spice Islands), driving Portuguese traders from an area they had previously dominated and establishing a Dutch monopoly within Europe over pepper, cinnamon, nutmeg, mace, and cloves. In the Western Hemisphere, however, their achievements were less spectacular. After a series of trade wars with England, in 1667 they formally surrendered their colony of New Amsterdam (subsequently renamed New York), retaining only Surinam (off the northern coast of South America) and Curaçao and Tobago (in the West Indies). Although the Dutch dominated the seventeenth-century slave trade with Africa, they lost this position to the British after 1713.

The Dutch also pioneered new financial mechanisms for investing in colonial enterprises. One of the most important of these was the joint-stock company, of which the Dutch East India Company was among the first. Such companies raised cash by selling shares in their enterprise to investors. Even though the investors might not take any role in managing the company, they were joint owners of the business and therefore entitled to a share in the profits. Initially, the Dutch East India Company intended to pay off its investors ten years after its founding, but the directors soon recognized the impossibility of this plan. The directors therefore urged investors anxious to realize their profits to sell their shares on the Amsterdam stock exchange to other investors, thereby ensuring the continued operation of their enterprise and, in the process, establishing a method of continuous business financing that would soon spread to elsewhere in Europe.

Colonial Rivalries

The fortunes of these colonial empires changed dramatically in the course of the seventeenth and early eighteenth centuries. Spain proved unable to defend its early monopoly over colonial trade, and in 1650 the Spanish suffered a crippling blow when they were forced to surrender Jamaica and several treasure ships lying off of the Spanish harbor of Cadíz. By 1700, although Spain still possessed a colonial empire, it lay at the mercy of its more dynamic rivals. Portugal, too, found it impossible to prevent foreign penetration of its colonial empire. In 1703, the English signed a treaty with Portugal allowing English merchants to export woolens duty-free into Portugal and allowing Portugal to ship its wines duty-free into England. Access to Portugal also led British merchants to trade with the Portuguese colony of Brazil, an important sugar producer and the largest of all the American markets for African slaves. In the eighteenth century, English merchants would dominate these Brazilian trade routes.

The 1713 Treaty of Utrecht opened a new era of colonial rivalries. The biggest losers were the Dutch, who gained only a guarantee of their own borders, and the Spanish, who were forced to concede to Britain the right to market slaves in the Spanish colonies. The winners were the British (who acquired large chunks of territory in North America) and to a lesser extent, the French, who retained Quebec and other territories in North America, as well as their foothold in India. The eighteenth century would witness a continuing struggle between Britain and France for control over the expanding commerce that now bound the European economy to the Americas and to Asia.

THE TRIANGULAR TRADE IN SUGAR AND SLAVES

During the eighteenth century, European colonial trade came to be dominated by trans-Atlantic routes that developed in response to the increased demand for sugar and tobacco and the corresponding market for slaves to produce these goods on American and Caribbean plantations. In this "triangular" trade, naval superiority gave Britain a decisive advantage over its French, Spanish, Portuguese, and Dutch rivals. Typically, a British ship might begin its voyage from New England with a consignment of rum and sail to Africa, where the rum would be exchanged for a cargo of slaves. From the west coast of Africa the ship would then cross the South Atlantic to the sugar colonies of Jamaica or Barbados, where slaves would be traded for molasses. It would then make the final leg of the journey back to New England, where the molasses would be made into rum. A variant triangle might see cheap manufactured goods move from England to Africa, where they would be traded for slaves. Those slaves would then be shipped to Virginia and exchanged for tobacco, which would be shipped to England and processed there for sale throughout Europe.

The cultivation of New World sugar and tobacco depended on slave labor. As European demand for these products increased, so too did the traffic in enslaved Africans. At the height of the Atlantic slave trade in the eighteenth century, seventy-five to ninety thousand Africans were shipped across the Atlantic yearly: at least six million in the eighteenth century, out of a total of over eleven million for the entire history of the trade. About 35 percent went to English and French Caribbean plantations, 5 percent (roughly five hundred thousand) to North America, and the rest to the Portuguese colony of Brazil and to the Spanish colonies in Central and South America. By the 1780s, there were more than five hundred thousand slaves on the largest French plantation island, Saint-Domingue, and at least two hundred thousand on its English counterpart, Jamaica.

Although run as a monopoly by various governments in the sixteenth and early seventeenth centuries, the slave trade in the eighteenth century was open to private entrepreneurs who operated ports on the West African coast. These traders exchanged Indian cloth, metal goods, rum, and firearms with African slave merchants in return for their human cargo, who would then be packed by the hundreds into the holds of slave ships for the gruesome Middle Passage across the Atlantic (so called to distinguish it from the slave ship's voyage from Europe to Africa, and then from the colonies back to Europe). Shackled belowdecks without sanitary facilities, the captive men, women, and children suffered horribly. The mortality rate, however, remained at about 10 or 11 percent, not much higher than the rate for a normal sea voyage of a hundred days or more. Since traders had to invest as much as £10 per slave in their enterprise, they were generally anxious to ensure that their consignment would reach its destination in good enough condition to be sold for a profit.

The Commercial Rivalry between Britain and France

British dominance of the slave trade gave it decisive advantages in its colonial struggles with France. As one Englishman wrote in 1749, the slave trade had provided

HOW SLAVES WERE STOWED ABOARD SHIP DURING THE MIDDLE PASSAGE. Men were "housed" on the right; women on the left; children in the middle. The human cargo was jammed onto platforms six feet wide without sufficient headroom to permit an adult to sit up. This diagram is from evidence gathered by English abolitionists and depicts conditions on the Liverpool slave ship *Brookes*.

"an unexhastible fund of wealth to this nation." But even apart from the slave trade, the value of colonial commerce was increasing dramatically during the eighteenth century. French colonial trade, valued at 25 million livres in 1716, rose to 263 million livres in 1789. In England, during roughly the same period, foreign trade increased in value from £10 million to £40 million, the latter amount more than twice that for France.

The growing value of colonial commerce tied the interests of governments and transoceanic merchants together in an increasingly tight embrace. Merchants engaged in the colonial trade depended on their governments to protect and defend their overseas investments; but governments depended in turn on merchants and their financial backers to build the ships and sustain the trade on which national power depended. In the eighteenth century, even the ability to wage war rested largely (and increasingly) on a government's ability to borrow the necessary funds from wealthy investors and then to pay back those debts, with interest, over time. As it did in commerce, so too in finance, Britain came to enjoy a decisive advantage in this respect over France. The Bank of England, founded in the 1690s, managed the English national debt with great success, providing the funds required for war by selling shares to investors, then repaying those investors at moderate rates of interest. In contrast, chronic governmental indebtedness forced the French crown to borrow at ruinously high rates of interest, provoking a series of fiscal crises that in 1789 finally led to the collapse of the French monarchy.

Analyzing Primary Sources

The American Declaration of Independence

The Declaration of Independence, issued from Philadelphia on July 4, 1776, is perhaps the most famous single document of American history. But its familiarity does not lessen its interest as a statement of political philosophy. The indebtedness of the document's authors to the ideas of John Locke will be obvious from the selections here. But Locke, in turn, drew many of his ideas about the contractual and conditional nature of human government from the conciliarist thinkers of the fifteenth and early sixteenth centuries. The appeal of absolutism notwithstanding, the declaration shows how vigorous the medieval tradition of contractual, limited government remained at the end of the eighteenth century.

 hen in the course of human events, it becomes necessary for one people to dissolve the political bonds which have connected them with another, and to assume among the powers of the earth the separate and equal station to which the Laws of Nature and of Nature's God entitle them, a decent respect to the opinions of mankind requires that they should declare the causes which impel them to the separation. . . . We hold these truths to be self-evident, that all men are created equal, that they are endowed by their Creator with certain unalienable rights, that among these are Life, Liberty and the pursuit of Happiness. . . . That to secure these rights, Governments are instituted among men, deriving their just powers from the consent of the governed. . . . That whenever any form of Government becomes destructive of these ends, it is the Right of the People to alter or to abolish it, and to institute new Government, laying its foundation upon such principles and organizing its power in such form, as to them shall seem most likely to effect their Safety and Happiness. Prudence, indeed, will dictate that Governments long established should not be changed for light and transient causes; and accordingly all experience has shown, that mankind are more disposed to suffer, while evils are sufferable, than to right themselves by abolishing the forms to which they are accustomed. But when a long train of abuses and usurpations, pursuing invariably the same Object, evinces a design to reduce them under absolute despotism, it is their right, it is their duty, to throw off such Government, and to provide new Guards for their future security. . . . Such has been the patient sufferance of these Colonies; and such is now the necessity which constrains them to alter their former Systems of Government. . . .

Questions for Analysis

1. Who are "the people" mentioned in the first sentence of this selection? Are the rights of "the people" the same as individual rights? How did the authors of this declaration come to think of themselves as the representatives of such a body?

2. What is the purpose of government, according to this document? Who gets to decide if the government is doing its job?

3. How would Robert Filmer or Bossuet have viewed such a declaration? How might John Locke have defended it?

War and Empire in the Eighteenth-Century World

After 1713, western Europe remained largely at peace for a generation. In 1740, however, that peace was shattered when Frederick the Great of Prussia took advantage of the accession of a woman, the empress Maria Theresa, to the throne of Austria to seize the Austrian province of Silesia (discussed earlier in this chapter). In the resulting War of the Austrian Succession (1740–48), France and Spain sided with Prussia, against Britain, the Dutch Republic, and Austria. This war quickly spread beyond the frontiers of Europe, as the French and the British continued to struggle for dominance in India and North America.

These colonial conflicts reignited when Prussia once again attacked Austria in 1756. This time, however, Prussia allied itself with Great Britain. Austria found support from both France and Russia. In Europe, the Seven Years' War (1756–63) ended in stalemate. In India and North America, however, the war had decisive consequences. In India, mercenary troops employed by the British East India Company joined with native allies to eliminate their French competitors. In North America (where the conflict was known as the French and Indian War), British troops captured both Louisbourg and Quebec and also drove French forces from the Ohio River Valley and the Great Lakes. By the Treaty of Paris in 1763, which brought the Seven Years' War to an end, France formally surrendered both Canada and India to the British. Six years later, the French East India Company was dissolved.

The American Revolution

Along the Atlantic seaboard, however, the rapidly growing British colonies were beginning to chafe at rule from London. To recover some of the costs of the Seven Years' War and to pay for the continuing costs of protecting its colonial subjects, the British Parliament imposed a series of new taxes on its American colonies. These taxes were immediately unpopular. Colonists complained that because they had no representatives in Parliament, they were being taxed without their consent—a fundamental violation of their rights as British subjects. They also complained that British restrictions on

colonial trade, particularly the requirement that certain goods pass first through British ports before being shipped to the Continent, were strangling American livelihoods and making it impossible to pay even the king's legitimate taxes.

The British government, led since 1760 by the young and inexperienced George III, responded to these complaints with a badly calculated mixture of vacillation and force. Various taxes were imposed and then withdrawn in the face of colonial resistance. In 1773, however, when East India Company tea was dumped in Boston Harbor by rebellious colonials objecting to the customs duties that had been imposed on it, the British government closed the port of Boston and curtailed the colony's representative institutions. These "Coercive Acts" galvanized the support of the other American colonies for Massachusetts. In 1774, representatives from all the American colonies met at Philadelphia to form the Continental Congress to negotiate with the crown over their grievances. In April 1775, however, local militiamen at Lexington and Concord clashed with regular British troops sent to disarm them. Soon thereafter, the Continental Congress began raising an army, and an outright rebellion erupted against the British government.

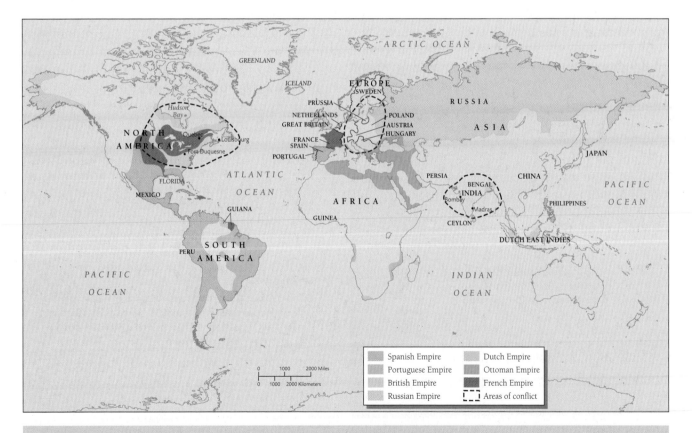

THE SEVEN YEARS' WAR, 1756–63. ▪ *What continents were involved in the Seven Years' War?* ▪ *What was the impact of naval power on the outcome of the war?* ▪ *What were the consequences for the colonies involved in the conflict?*

On July 4, 1776, the thirteen colonies formally declared their independence from Great Britain. During the first two years of the war, it seemed unlikely that such independence would ever become a reality. In 1778, however, France, anxious to undermine the colonial hegemony Great Britain had established since 1713, joined the war on the side of the Americans. Spain entered the war in support of France, hoping to recover Gibraltar and Florida (the latter lost in 1763 to Britain). In 1780, Britain also declared war on the Dutch Republic for continuing to trade with the rebellious colonies. Now facing a coalition of its colonial rivals, Great Britain saw the war turn against it. In 1781, combined land and sea operations by French and American troops forced the surrender of the main British army at Yorktown in Virginia. As the defeated British soldiers surrendered their weapons, their band played a song entitled "The World Turned Upside Down."

Negotiations for peace began soon after the defeat at Yorktown but were not concluded until September 1783. The Treaty of Paris left Great Britain in control of Canada and Gibraltar. Spain retained its possessions west of the Mississippi River and recovered Florida. The United States gained its independence; its western border was fixed on the Mississippi River, and it secured valuable fishing rights off the eastern coast of Canada. France gained only the satisfaction of defeating its colonial rival; but even that satisfaction was short lived. Six years later, the massive debts France had incurred in supporting the American Revolution helped bring about another, very different kind of revolution in France that would permanently alter the history of Europe.

CONCLUSION

Seen in this light, the American War of Independence was the final military conflict in a century-long struggle between Great Britain and France for colonial dominance. But the consequences of Britain's defeat in 1783 were far less significant than might have been expected. Even after American independence, Great Britain would remain the most important trading partner for its former American colonies, while elsewhere around the globe, the commercial dominance Britain had already established would continue to grow. The profits of slavery certainly helped fuel the eighteenth-century British economy; by the end of the century, however, British trade and manufacturing had reached such high levels of productivity that even the abolition of the slave trade (in 1808) and of slavery itself (in 1833) did not impede its continuing growth.

The economic prosperity of late-eighteenth-century Britain was mirrored to some degree throughout northwestern Europe. Improved transportation systems, more-reliable

After You Read
This Chapter

Ⓢ Visit StudySpace for quizzes, additional review materials, and multi-media documents. **wwnorton.com/studyspace**

REVIEWING THE OBJECTIVES

- Absolutist rulers claimed a monopoly of power and authority within their realms. What did they do to achieve this goal?
- Monarchies in both western and eastern Europe adopted the absolutist system, but they faced different challenges. How did the absolutist monarchies in eastern Europe differ from their counterparts in western Europe?
- England developed an alternative to absolutism by the end of the seventeenth century. What was it?
- The commercial revolution of the eighteenth century resulted in major changes in the European economy. What were they?
- Colonial expansion in the Atlantic world and the African slave trade connected Africa and the Americas with Europe in new ways. Who profited most from the Atlantic's new political and economic relationships?

WARS BETWEEN EUROPEAN POWERS, 1688–1789	
Glorious Revolution	1688–89
War of the League of Augsburg	1689–97
War of the Spanish Succession	1702–13
Seven Years' War	1756–63
The Russo-Turkish War	1768–74
American Revolution	1775–83

food supplies, and growing quantities of consumer goods brought improved standards of living to large numbers of Europeans, even as the overall population of Europe was rising faster after 1750 than it had ever done before. Population growth was especially rapid in the cities, where a new urban middle class was emerging whose tastes drove the market for goods and whose opinions were reshaping the world of ideas.

But the prosperity of late-eighteenth-century Europe remained very unevenly distributed. In the cities, rich and poor lived separate lives in separate neighborhoods. In the countryside, regions bypassed by the developing commercial economy of the period continued to suffer from hunger and famine, just as they had done in the sixteenth and seventeenth centuries. In eastern Europe the contrasts between rich and poor were even more extreme, as many peasants fell into a new style of serfdom that would last until the end of the nineteenth century. War, too, remained a fact of European life, bringing death and destruction to hundreds of thousands of people across the continent and around the world—yet another consequence of the world-wide reach of these European colonial empires.

Political change was more gradual. Throughout Europe, the powers of governments steadily increased. Administrators became more numerous, more efficient, and more demanding, partly to meet the mounting costs of war but also because governments were starting to take on a much wider range of responsibilities for the welfare of their subjects. Despite the increasing scope of government, however, the structure and principles of government changed relatively little. Apart from Great Britain and the Dutch Republic, the great powers of eighteenth-century Europe were still governed by rulers who styled themselves as absolutist monarchs in the mold of Louis XIV. By 1789, however, the European world was a vastly different place than it had been a century before, when the Sun King had dominated European politics. The full extent of those differences was about to be revealed.

PEOPLE, IDEAS, AND EVENTS IN CONTEXT

- What did **LOUIS XIV** of France, **PETER THE GREAT** of Russia, **FREDERICK THE GREAT** of Prussia, and **MARIA THERESA** of Austria have in common? How did they deal with those who resisted their attempts to impose absolutist rule?
- What limits to royal power were recognized in Great Britain as a result of the **GLORIOUS REVOLUTION**?
- What does the **TREATY OF UTRECHT** (1713) tell us about the diminished influence of Spain and the corresponding rise of Britain as a European power?
- How did European monarchies use the economic theory known as **MERCANTILISM** to strengthen the power and wealth of their kingdoms?
- What was the **COLUMBIAN EXCHANGE**? What combination of demographic, cultural, and ecological transformations are contained within this idea?
- How did the **COMMERCIAL REVOLUTION** change social life in Europe?
- What was the **TRIANGULAR TRADE** and how was it related to the growth of commerce in the Atlantic world during this period?
- What debt does the American **DECLARATION OF INDEPENDENCE** owe to the ideas of the English political thinker **JOHN LOCKE**?

CONSEQUENCES

- Was any European monarch's power ever really *absolute*?
- What do you suppose had more effect on the lives of ordinary Europeans: the rise of absolutist regimes or the commercial revolution of the eighteenth century?
- In a world in which a British merchant's fortune depended on the price of molasses in Boston, the demand for African slaves in Jamaica, and the price of rum in Senegal, could one already speak of *globalization*?

Rulers of Principal States

THE CAROLINGIAN DYNASTY

Pepin of Heristal, Mayor of the Palace, 687–714
Charles Martel, Mayor of the Palace, 715–741
Pepin III, Mayor of the Palace, 741–751; King, 751–768
Charlemagne, King, 768–814; Emperor, 800–814
Louis the Pious, Emperor, 814–840

West Francia

Charles the Bald, King, 840–877; Emperor, 875–877
Louis II, King, 877–879
Louis III, King, 879–882
Carloman, King, 879–884

Middle Kingdoms

Lothair, Emperor, 840–855
Louis (Italy), Emperor, 855–875
Charles (Provence), King, 855–863
Lothair II (Lorraine), King, 855–869

East Francia

Ludwig, King, 840–876
Carloman, King, 876–880
Ludwig, King, 876–882
Charles the Fat, Emperor, 876–887

HOLY ROMAN EMPERORS

Saxon Dynasty

Otto I, 962–973
Otto II, 973–983
Otto III, 983–1002
Henry II, 1002–1024

Franconian Dynasty

Conrad II, 1024–1039
Henry III, 1039–1056
Henry IV, 1056–1106
Henry V, 1106–1125
Lothair II (Saxony), 1125–1137

Hohenstaufen Dynasty

Conrad III, 1138–1152
Frederick I (Barbarossa), 1152–1190
Henry VI, 1190–1197
Philip of Swabia, 1198–1208 } Rivals
Otto IV (Welf), 1198–1215

Frederick II, 1220–1250
Conrad IV, 1250–1254

Interregnum, 1254–1273

Emperors from Various Dynasties

Rudolf I (Habsburg), 1273–1291
Adolf (Nassau), 1292–1298
Albert I (Habsburg), 1298–1308
Henry VII (Luxemburg), 1308–1313
Ludwig IV (Wittelsbach), 1314–1347
Charles IV (Luxemburg), 1347–1378
Wenceslas (Luxemburg), 1378–1400
Rupert (Wittelsbach), 1400–1410
Sigismund (Luxemburg), 1410–1437

Habsburg Dynasty

Albert II, 1438–1439
Frederick III, 1440–1493

Maximilian I, 1493–1519
Charles V, 1519–1556
Ferdinand I, 1556–1564
Maximilian II, 1564–1576
Rudolf II, 1576–1612
Matthias, 1612–1619
Ferdinand II, 1619–1637
Ferdinand III, 1637–1657

Leopold I, 1658–1705
Joseph I, 1705–1711
Charles VI, 1711–1740
Charles VII (not a Habsburg), 1742–1745
Francis I, 1745–1765
Joseph II, 1765–1790
Leopold II, 1790–1792
Francis II, 1792–1806

RULERS OF FRANCE FROM HUGH CAPET

Capetian Dynasty

Hugh Capet, 987–996
Robert II, 996–1031
Henry I, 1031–1060
Philip I, 1060–1108
Louis VI, 1108–1137
Louis VII, 1137–1180
Philip II (Augustus), 1180–1223
Louis VIII, 1223–1226
Louis IX (St. Louis), 1226–1270
Philip III, 1270–1285
Philip IV, 1285–1314
Louis X, 1314–1316
Philip V, 1316–1322
Charles lV, 1322–1328

Valois Dynasty

Philip VI, 1328–1350
John, 1350–1364
Charles V, 1364–1380
Charles VI, 1380–1422
Charles VII, 1422–1461
Louis XI, 1461–1483
Charles VIII, 1483–1498
Louis XII, 1498–1515
Francis I, 1515–1547

Henry II, 1547–1559
Francis II, 1559–1560
Charles IX, 1560–1574
Henry III, 1574–1589

Bourbon Dynasty

Henry IV, 1589–1610
Louis XIII, 1610–1643
Louis XIV, 1643–1715
Louis XV, 1715–1774
Louis XVI, 1774–1792

After 1792

First Republic, 1792–1799
Napoleon Bonaparte, First Consul, 1799–1804
Napoleon I, Emperor, 1804–1814
Louis XVIII (Bourbon dynasty), 1814–1824
Charles X (Bourbon dynasty), 1824–1830
Louis Philippe, 1830–1848
Second Republic, 1848–1852
Napoleon III, Emperor, 1852–1870
Third Republic, 1870–1940
Pétain regime, 1940–1944
Provisional government, 1944–1946
Fourth Republic, 1946–1958
Fifth Republic, 1958–

RULERS OF ENGLAND

Anglo-Saxon Dynasty

Alfred the Great, 871–899
Edward the Elder, 899–924
Ethelstan, 924–939
Edmund I, 939–946
Edred, 946–955
Edwy, 955–959
Edgar, 959–975

Edward the Martyr, 975–978
Ethelred the Unready, 978–1016
Canute, 1016–1035 (Danish Nationality)
Harold I, 1035–1040
Hardicanute, 1040–1042
Edward the Confessor, 1042–1066
Harold II, 1066

House of Normandy

William I (the Conqueror), 1066–1087
William II, 1087–1100
Henry I, 1100–1135
Stephen, 1135–1154

House of Plantagenet

Henry II, 1154–1189
Richard I, 1189–1199
John, 1199–1216
Henry III, 1216–1272
Edward I, 1272–1307
Edward II, 1307–1327
Edward III, 1327–1377
Richard II, 1377–1399

House of Lancaster

Henry IV, 1399–1413
Henry V, 1413–1422
Henry VI, 1422–1461

House of York

Edward IV, 1461–1483
Edward V, 1483
Richard III, 1483–1485

House of Tudor

Henry VII, 1485–1509
Henry VIII, 1509–1547
Edward VI, 1547–1553
Mary, 1553–1558
Elizabeth I, 1558–1603

House of Stuart

James I, 1603–1625
Charles I, 1625–1649

Commonwealth and Protectorate, 1649–1659

House of Stuart Restored

Charles II, 1660–1685
James II, 1685–1688
William III and Mary II, 1689–1694
William III alone, 1694–1702
Anne, 1702–1714

House of Hanover

George I, 1714–1727
George II, 1727–1760
George III, 1760–1820
George IV, 1820–1830
William IV, 1830–1837
Victoria, 1837–1901

House of Saxe-Coburg-Gotha

Edward VII, 1901–1910
George V, 1910–1917

House of Windsor

George V, 1917–1936
Edward VIII, 1936
George VI, 1936–1952
Elizabeth II, 1952–

RULERS OF AUSTRIA AND AUSTRIA-HUNGARY

*Maximilian I (Archduke), 1493–1519
*Charles V, 1519–1556
*Ferdinand I, 1556–1564
*Maximilian II, 1564–1576
*Rudolf II, 1576–1612
*Matthias, 1612–1619
*Ferdinand II, 1619–1637
*Ferdinand III, 1637–1657
*Leopold I, 1658–1705
*Joseph I, 1705–1711
*Charles VI, 1711–1740
Maria Theresa, 1740–1780

*Joseph II, 1780–1790
*Leopold II, 1790–1792
*Francis II, 1792–1835 (Emperor of Austria as Francis I after 1804)
Ferdinand I, 1835–1848
Francis Joseph, 1848–1916 (after 1867 Emperor of Austria and King of Hungary)
Charles I, 1916–1918 (Emperor of Austria and King of Hungary)
Republic of Austria, 1918–1938 (dictatorship after 1934)
Republic restored, under Allied occupation, 1945–1956
Free Republic, 1956–

*also bore title of Holy Roman Emperor

RULERS OF PRUSSIA AND GERMANY

*Frederick I, 1701–1713
*Frederick William I, 1713–1740
*Frederick II (the Great), 1740–1786
*Frederick William II, 1786–1797
*Frederick William III,1797–1840
*Frederick William IV, 1840–1861
*William I, 1861–1888 (German Emperor after 1871)
Frederick III, 1888

*Kings of Prussia

*William II, 1888–1918
Weimar Republic, 1918–1933
Third Reich (Nazi Dictatorship), 1933–1945
Allied occupation, 1945–1952
Division into Federal Republic of Germany in west and German Democratic Republic in east, 1949–1991
Federal Republic of Germany (united), 1991–

RULERS OF RUSSIA

Ivan III, 1462–1505
Vasily III, 1505–1533
Ivan IV, 1533–1584
Theodore I, 1534–1598
Boris Godunov, 1598–1605
Theodore II,1605
Vasily IV, 1606–1610
Michael, 1613–1645
Alexius, 1645–1676
Theodore III, 1676–1682
Ivan V and Peter I, 1682–1689
Peter I (the Great), 1689–1725
Catherine I, 1725–1727
Peter II, 1727–1730

Anna, 1730–1740
Ivan VI, 1740–1741
Elizabeth, 1741–1762
Peter III, 1762
Catherine II (the Great), 1762–1796
Paul, 1796–1801
Alexander I,1801–1825
Nicholas I, 1825–1855
Alexander II,1855–1881
Alexander III, 1881–1894
Nicholas II, 1894–1917
Soviet Republic, 1917–1991
Russian Federation, 1991–

RULERS OF UNIFIED SPAIN

Ferdinand { and Isabella, 1479–1504
and Philip I, 1504–1506
and Charles I, 1506–1516
Charles I (Holy Roman Emperor Charles V), 1516–1556
Philip II, 1556–1598
Philip III, 1598–1621
Philip IV, 1621–1665
Charles II, 1665–1700
Philip V, 1700–1746
Ferdinand VI, 1746–1759
Charles III, 1759–1788
Charles IV, 1788–1808

Ferdinand VII, 1808
Joseph Bonaparte, 1808–1813
Ferdinand VII (restored), 1814–1833
Isabella II, 1833–1868
Republic, 1868–1870
Amadeo, 1870–1873
Republic, 1873–1874
Alfonso XII, 1874–1885
Alfonso XIII, 1886–1931
Republic, 1931–1939
Fascist Dictatorship, 1939–1975
Juan Carlos I, 1975–

RULERS OF ITALY

Victor Emmanuel II, 1861–1878
Humbert I, 1878–1900
Victor Emmanuel III, 1900–1946

Fascist Dictatorship, 1922-1943 (maintained in northern
   Italy until 1945)
Humbert II, May 9–June 13, 1946
Republic, 1946–

PROMINENT POPES

Silvester I, 314–335
Leo I, 440–461
Gelasius I, 492–496
Gregory I, 590–604
Nicholas I, 858–867
Silvester II, 999–1003
Leo IX, 1049–1054
Nicholas II, 1058–1061
Gregory VII, 1073–1085
Urban II, 1088–1099
Paschal II, 1099–1118
Alexander III, 1159–1181
Innocent III, 1198–1216
Gregory IX, 1227–1241
Innocent IV, 1243–1254
Boniface VIII, 1294–1303
John XXII, 1316–1334
Nicholas V, 1447–1455
Pius II, 1458–1464

Alexander VI, 1492–1503
Julius II, 1503–1513
Leo X, 1513–1521
Paul III, 1534–1549
Paul IV, 1555–1559
Sixtus V, 1585–1590
Urban VIII, 1623–1644
Gregory XVI, 1831–1846
Pius IX, 1846–1878
Leo XIII, 1878–1903
Pius X, 1903–1914
Benedict XV, 1914–1922
Pius XI, 1922–1939
Pius XII, 1939–1958
John XXIII, 1958–1963
Paul VI, 1963–1978
John Paul I, 1978
John Paul II, 1978–2005
Benedict XVI 2005–

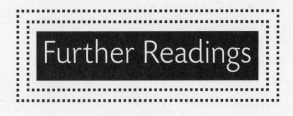
Further Readings

CHAPTER 1

Aldred, Cyril. *The Egyptians*. 3d ed. London, 1998. An indispensable, lively overview of Egyptian culture and history by one of the great masters of Egyptology.

Baines, J., and J. Málek. *Atlas of Ancient Egypt*. Rev. ed. New York, 2000. A reliable, well-illustrated survey, with excellent maps.

Bottéro, Jean. *Everyday Life in Ancient Mesopotamia*. Trans. Antonia Nevill. Baltimore, MD, 2001. A wide-ranging, interdisciplinary account.

Bottéro, Jean. *Religion in Ancient Mesopotamia*. Chicago, 2001. An accessible, engaging survey.

George, Andrew, trans. *The Epic of Gilgamesh: A New Translation. The Babylonian Epic Poem and Other Texts in Akkadian and Sumerian*. New York and London, 1999. The newest and most reliable translation, which carefully distinguishes the chronological "layers" of this famous text; also includes many related texts.

Hodder, Ian. *The Leopard's Tale:Revealing the Mysteries of Çatalhöyük*. London and New York, 2006. The most up-to-date account of this fascinating archaeological site, written for general readers by the director of the excavation.

Hornung, Erik. *History of Ancient Egypt: An Introduction*. Ithaca, NY, 1999. Concise and authoritative.

Kemp, Barry J. *Ancient Egypt: Anatomy of a Civilization*. London, 1989. An imaginative examination of Egyptian social and intellectual history.

Leick, Gwendolyn. *The Babylonians: An Introduction*. London and New York, 2002. A wide-ranging survey of Babylonian civilization across the centuries.

Lichteim, Miriam. *Ancient Egyptian Literature: A Book of Readings*. 3 vols. Berkeley, CA, 1973–1980. A compilation used by students and scholars alike.

McDowell, A. G. *Village Life in Ancient Egypt: Laundry Lists and Love Songs*. Oxford, 1999. A fascinating collection of translated texts recovered from an Egyptian peasant village, dating from 1539 to 1075 B.C.E.

Mertz, Barbara. *Red Land, Black Land: Daily Life in Ancient Egypt*. Rev. ed. New York, 1990. Emphasizes the role of the Nile and the forbidding natural environment of Egypt.

Pollock, Susan. *Ancient Mesopotamia*. Cambridge, 1999. An advanced textbook that draws on theoretical anthropology to interpret Mesopotamian civilization up to 2100 B.C.E.

Redford, Donald B., ed. *The Oxford Encyclopedia of Ancient Egypt*. 3 vols. New York, 2001. An indispensible reference work, intended for both specialists and beginners.

Roaf, Michael. *Cultural Atlas of Mesopotamia and the Ancient Near East*. New York, 1990. An informative, authoritative, and lavishly illustrated guide, with excellent maps.

Robins, Gay. *The Art of Ancient Egypt*. London, 1997. An excellent survey, now the standard account.

Shafer, Byron E., ed. *Religion in Ancient Egypt: Gods, Myths, and Personal Practice*. London, 1991. A scholarly examination of Egyptian belief and ritual, with contributions from leading authorities.

Shaw, Ian, ed. *The Oxford History of Ancient Egypt*. Oxford, 2000. An outstanding collaborative survey of Egyptian history from the Stone Age to c. 300 C.E., with excellent bibliographical essays.

Smail, Daniel Lord. *On Deep History and the Brain*. Berkeley, 2008. A pioneering introduction to the historical uses of neuroscience and evolutionary biology.

Snell, Daniel C., ed. *A Companion to the Ancient Near East*. Oxford, 2005. A topical survey of recent scholarly work, particularly strong on society, economy, and culture.

Wengrow, David. *The Archaeology of Early Egypt: Social Transformations in North-East Africa, 10,000 to 2650 B.C.* Cambridge, 2006. An authoritative account of archeological evidence and its interpretation.

CHAPTER 2

Aubet, Maria Eugenia. *Phoenicia and the West: Politics, Colonies, and Trade*. Trans. Mary Turton. Cambridge, 1993. An intelligent and thought-provoking examination of Phoenician civilization and its influence.

Boardman, John. *Assyrian and Babylonian Empires and Other States of the Near East from the Eighth to the Sixth Centuries B.C.* New York, 1991. Scholarly and authoritative.

Boardman, John. *Persia and the West*. London, 2000. A great book by a distinguished scholar, with a particular focus on art and architecture as projections of Persian imperial ideologies.

Boyce, Mary. *Textual Sources for the Study of Zoroastrianism*. Totowa, NJ, 1984. An invaluable collection of documents.

Bryce, Trevor. *The Kingdom of the Hittites*. Oxford, 1998. And *Life and Society in the Hittite World*. Oxford, 2002. An extraordinary synthesis, now the standard account of Hittite political, military, and daily life.

Curtis, John. *Ancient Persia*. Cambridge, MA, 1990. Concise, solid, reliable.

Dever, William. *Who Were the Early Israelites and Where Did They Come From?* Grand Rapids, MI, 2003. A balanced, fair-minded account with excellent bibliographical guidance to recent work.

Dickinson, O. T. P. K. *The Aegean Bronze Age.* Cambridge, 1994. An excellent summary of archaeological evidence and scholarly argument concerning Minoan, Mycenaean, and other cultures of the Bronze Age Aegean basin.

Dothan, Trude, and Moshe Dothan. *Peoples of the Sea: The Search for the Philistines.* New York, 1992. The essential starting point for understanding Philistine culture and its links to the Aegean basin.

Drews, Robert. *The End of the Bronze Age: Changes in Warfare and the Catastrophe ca. 1200 B.C.* Princeton, NJ, 1993. A stimulating analysis and survey, with excellent bibliographies.

Finkelstein, Israel, and Nadav Na'aman, eds. *From Nomadism to Monarchy: Archaeological and Historical Aspects of Early Israel.* Jerusalem, 1994. Scholarly articles on the Hebrews' transformation from pastoralists to a sedentary society focused on the worship of Yahweh.

Fitton, J. Lesley. *Minoans: Peoples of the Past* (British Museum Publications). London, 2002. A careful, reliable debunking of myths about the Minoans, written for nonspecialists.

Kamm, Antony. *The Israelites: An Introduction.* New York, 1999. A short, accessible history of the land and people of Israel up to 135 C.E., aimed at students and general readers.

Kuhrt, Amélie. *The Ancient Near East, c. 3000–330 B.C.* 2 vols. London and New York, 1995. An outstanding survey, written for students, that includes Egypt and Israel as well as Mesopotamia, Babylonia, Assyria, and Persia.

Luckenbill, Daniel David, ed. and trans. *Ancient Records of Assyria and Babylonia.* 2 vols. Chicago, 1926–27. Still one of the best and most readily accessible collections of primary sources on Assyrian attitudes and policies in war, religion, and politics.

Metzger, Bruce M., and Michael D. Coogan, eds. *The Oxford Companion to the Bible.* New York, 1993. An outstanding reference work, with contributions by leading authorities.

Niditch, Susan. *Ancient Israelite Religion.* New York, 1997. A short introduction designed for students, emphasizing the diversity of Hebrew religious practices.

Redford, Donald B. *Egypt, Canaan, and Israel in Ancient Times.* Princeton, NJ, 1992. An overview of the interactions between these peoples from about 1200 B.C.E. to the beginning of the Common Era.

Renfrew, Colin. *Archaeology and Language: The Puzzle of Indo-European Origins.* Cambridge, 1987. A masterful but controversial work by one of the most creative archaeologists of the twentieth century.

Saggs, H. W. F. *The Might That Was Assyria.* London, 1984. A lively narrative history of the Assyrian Empire, with analysis of the institutions that underlay its strength.

Sandars, Nancy K. *The Sea Peoples: Warriors of the Ancient Mediterranean.* Rev. ed. London, 1985. An introductory account for students and scholars.

Tubb, Jonathan N., and Rupert L. Chapman. *Archaeology and the Bible.* London, 1990. A good starting point for students that clearly illustrates the difficulties in linking archeological evidence to biblical accounts of early Hebrew history and society.

Wood, Michael. *In Search of the Trojan War.* New York, 1985. Aimed at a general audience, this carefully researched and engagingly written book is an excellent introduction to the late–Bronze Age context of the Trojan War.

CHAPTER 3

Penguin Classics and the Loeb Classical Library both offer reliable translations of Greek literary, philosophical, and historical texts.

Beard, Mary. *The Parthenon.* Cambridge, MA, 2003. A book that traces the successive stages of this monument's construction, deconstruction, reconstruction, and restoration.

Boardman, John, Jaspar Griffin, and Oswyn Murray, eds. *Greece and the Hellenistic World.* Oxford, 1988. A reprint of the Greek and Hellenistic chapters from *The Oxford History of the Classical World,* originally published in 1986. Excellent, stimulating surveys, accessible to a general audience.

Brunschwig, Jacques, and Geoffrey E. R. Lloyd. *Greek Thought: A Guide to Classical Knowledge.* Translated by Catherine Porter. Cambridge, MA, 2000. An outstanding work of reference.

Buckley, Terry, ed. *Aspects of Greek History, 750–323 B.C.: A Source-Based Approach.* London, 1999. An outstanding collection of source materials.

Cartledge, Paul A. *The Spartans: An Epic History.* New York, 2003. A lively and authoritative history of Sparta from its origins to the Roman conquest.

Dover, Kenneth J. *Greek Homosexuality.* Cambridge, MA, 1978. The standard account of an important subject.

Fantham, Elaine, Helene Foley, Natalie Kampen, Sarah B. Pomeroy, and H. A. Shapiro. *Women in the Classical World: Image and Text.* Oxford, 1994. Wide-ranging analysis drawing on both visual and written sources, covering both the Greek and the Roman periods.

Fornara, Charles W., and Loren J. Samons II. *Athens from Cleisthenes to Pericles.* Berkeley, 1991. An excellent narrative history of Athenian politics during the first half of the fifth century B.C.E.

Freeman, Charles. *The Greek Achievement: The Foundation of the Western World.* New York, 1999. An admiring survey written for a general audience.

Garlan, Yvon. *Slavery in Ancient Greece.* Ithaca, NY, 1988. Now the standard account.

Hanson, Victor Davis. *The Other Greeks: The Family Farm and the Agrarian Roots of Western Civilization.* New York, 1995. Polemical and idiosyncratic, but convincing in its emphasis on smallholding farmers as the backbone of Greek urban society.

Havelock, Eric A. *The Literate Revolution in Greece and Its Cultural Consequences.* Princeton, 1982. A now-classic account of the wide-ranging effects of writing on Greek society.

Jones, Nicholas F. *Ancient Greece: State and Society.* Upper Saddle River, NJ, 1997. A concise survey from the Minoans up to the end of the Classical Period that emphasizes the connections between the social order and politics.

Lefkowitz, Mary, and Maureen Fant. *Women's Life in Greece and Rome: A Source Book in Translation.* 3rd ed. Baltimore, MD, 2005. A remarkably wide-ranging collection, topically arranged, invaluable to students.

Levi, Peter. *Atlas of the Greek World*. New York, 1984. Excellent maps and illustrations supplement an outstanding text.

Morris, Ian, and Barry Powell, eds. *A New Companion to Homer*. Leiden, 1997. A collection of thirty specialized but accessible scholarly articles, encompassing the most recent research on Homer and Dark Age Greece.

Pomeroy, Sarah B., Stanley M. Burstein, Walter Donlan, and Jennifer Tolbert Roberts. *Ancient Greece: A Political, Social, and Cultural History*. Oxford, 1999. An outstanding textbook; clear and lively.

Price, Simon. *Religions of the Ancient Greeks*. Cambridge, 1999. Concise and authoritative, this survey extends from the Archaic Period up to the fifth century C.E.

Seaford, Richard. *Money and the Greek Mind: Homer, Philosophy, Tragedy*. Cambridge, 2004. A provocative study of portable wealth and its far-reaching effects.

Strassler, Robert B., ed. *The Landmark Thucydides*. New York, 1996. Reprints the classic Richard Crawley translation with maps, commentary, notes, and appendices by leading scholars.

Thomas, Carol G., and Craig Conant. *Citadel to City-State: The Transformation of Greece, 1200–700 B.C.E.* Bloomington, IN, 1999. A lucid and accessible study that examines developments at a number of different Dark Age sites.

Thomas, Rosalind. *Oral Tradition and Written Record in Classical Athens*. Cambridge, 1989. A fascinating look at how oral epic, lyric, and drama were transmitted over time.

CHAPTER 4

Penguin Classics and the Loeb Classical Library both offer reliable translations of scores of literary and historical texts from this period. Particularly important are historical works by Arrian (*Anabasis of Alexander*), Plutarch (*Life of Alexander*), and Polybius (*The Histories*).

Adcock, F. E. *The Greek and Macedonian Art of War*. Berkeley, 1957. Still a valuable introduction to the guiding principles and assumptions of warfare in the fourth century.

Austin, M. M. *The Hellenistic World from Alexander to the Roman Conquest: A Selection of Ancient Sources in Translation*. Cambridge, 1981. A good collection of primary documents.

Bagnall, R. S., and P. Derow. *Greek Historical Documents: The Hellenistic Period*. Chico, CA, 1981. Another useful collection.

Borza, Eugene N. *In the Shadow of Olympus: The Emergence of Macedon*. Princeton, NJ, 1990. The standard account of the rise of Macedon up to the accession of Philip II.

Bosworth, A. B. *Conquest and Empire: The Reign of Alexander the Great*. Cambridge, 1988. A political and military analysis of Alexander's career that strips away the romance, maintaining a clear vision of the ruthlessness and human cost of his conquests.

Bosworth, A. B. *The Legacy of Alexander: Politics, Warfare, and Propaganda under the Successors*. Oxford, 2002. The most recent survey of the half century following Alexander's death and of the people who created the Hellenistic kingdoms of Egypt, Persia, and Macedon.

Burstein, Stanley M., ed. and trans. *The Hellenistic Age from the Battle of Ipsos to the Death of Kleopatra VII*. Cambridge, 1985. An excellent collection, with sources not found elsewhere.

Cartledge, Paul. *Agesilaus and the Crisis of Sparta*. Baltimore, MD, 1987. A thorough but readable analysis of the social and political challenges besetting Sparta in the fourth century B.C.E.

Cartledge, Paul. *Alexander the Great: The Hunt for a New Past*. Woodstock, NY, 2004. A compelling account of Alexander's life, times, and influences.

Green, Peter. *Alexander to Actium: The Historical Evolution of the Hellenistic Age*. Berkeley, CA. 1990. An outstanding, comprehensive, and wide-ranging history of the period.

Green, Peter. *Alexander of Macedon, 356–323 B.C.* Berkeley, CA, 1991. Revised edition of the author's earlier biography; entertainingly written, rich in detail and insight.

———. *The Hellenistic Age: A Short History*. New York, 2007. An authoritative synthesis that carries the history of Greek influence into the fourth century C.E.

Nicholas, G. L. *The Genius of Alexander the Great*. Chapel Hill, NC, 1998. A clear, authoritative, admiring account, distilling a lifetime of research on the subject.

Hansen, Mogens H. *The Athenian Democracy in the Age of Demosthenes*. Oxford, 1991. An examination of the political institutions of Athens in the fourth century B.C.E.

Lloyd, Geoffrey, and Nathan Sivin. *The Way and the Word: Science and Medicine in Early China and Greece*. New Haven, CT, 2002. An extraordinary comparative study.

Ober, Josiah. *Mass and Elite in Democratic Athens: Rhetoric, Ideology, and the Power of the People*. Princeton, NJ, 1989. An excellent study of the ideology of democracy in Athens that borrows from the insights of modern social science.

Pollitt, Jerome J. *Art in the Hellenistic Age*. New York, 1986. The standard account, blending cultural history with art history.

Sherwin-White, Susan, and Amélie Kuhrt. *From Samarkhand to Sardis: A New Approach to the Seleucid Empire*. London, 1993. A stimulating examination of the relationship between rulers and ruled in the vast expanses of the Seleucid Empire.

Shipley, Graham. *The Greek World after Alexander, 323–30 B.C.* New York and London, 2000. A study of the social, intellectual, and artistic changes in the Hellenistic era.

Thomas, Carol G. *Alexander the Great in His World*. Oxford and Malden, MA, 2007. A study of the contexts—familial, political, and social—that shaped Alexander's career.

Tripolitis, Antonia. *Religions of the Hellenistic-Roman Age*. Grand Rapids, MI, 2002. Survey of the variety of religious experience, ritual, and belief in the centuries before the emergence of Christianity.

Tritle, Lawrence A., ed. *The Greek World in the Fourth Century: From the Fall of the Athenian Empire to the Successors of Alexander*. New York, 1997. A wide-ranging collection of scholarly essays.

Worthington, Ian. *Alexander the Great: A Reader*. London and New York, 2002. A collection of influential interpretations of Alexander by modern historians.

CHAPTER 5

Translations of Roman authors are available in both the Penguin Classics series and in the Loeb Classical Library.

Barker, Graeme, and Tom Rasmussen. *The Etruscans*. Oxford and Malden, MA, 1998. A fine survey, from the Blackwell *Peoples of Europe* series.

Beard, Mary. *Pompeii: The Life of a Roman Town*. A fascinating, cutting-edge study of daily life.

Boardman, John, Jasper Griffin, and Oswyn Murray. *The Oxford History of the Roman World*. Oxford, 1990. Reprint of relevant portions of the excellent *Oxford History of the Classical World* (1986). Stimulating, accessible topical chapters by British specialists.

Cornell, T. J. *The Beginnings of Rome: Italy and Rome from the Bronze Age to the Punic Wars (c. 1000–264 B.C.)*. London, 1995. An ambitious survey of the archaeological and historical evidence for early Rome.

Crawford, Michael. *The Roman Republic,* 2d ed. Cambridge, MA, 1993. A lively, fast-paced survey of republican Rome. An excellent place to start.

Fantham, Elaine, Helene Peet Foley, Natalie Boymel Kampen, Sarah B. Pomeroy, and H. Alan Shapiro. *Women in the Classical World*. Oxford, 1994. An expert survey of both Greece and Rome.

Garnsey, Peter, and Richard Saller. *The Roman Empire: Economy, Society, and Culture*. Berkeley, CA, 1987. A straightforward short survey.

Gruen, Erich S. *The Hellenistic World and the Coming of Rome*. 2 vols. Berkeley, CA, 1984. A massive survey, focused on the unpredictable rise of Rome to a position of dominance within the Mediterranean world.

Harris, William V. *War and Imperialism in Republican Rome, 327–70 B.C.* Oxford, 1979. A challenging study arguing that Rome's need for military conquest and expansion was deeply embedded in the fabric of Roman life.

Lancel, Serge. *Carthage: A History*. Trans. Antonia Nevill. Oxford, 1995. An account of Rome's great rival for control of the Mediterranean world.

Lewis, Naphtali, and M. Reinhold. *Roman Civilization: Selected Readings*. 2 vols. New York, 1951–55. The standard collection, especially for political and economic subjects. Vol. 1 covers the republic; vol. 2, the empire.

Millar, Fergus G. B. *The Emperor in the Roman World, 31 B.C.–A.D. 337*. London, 1977. A classic work that showed (among much else) the importance of emperor worship to the religious outlook of the Roman Empire.

———. *The Crowd in Rome in the Late Republic*. Ann Arbor, MI, 1999. A revisionist account that emphasizes the reality of Roman democracy in the late republic, against those who would see the period's politics as entirely under the control of aristocratic families.

Ward, Allen M., Fritz Heichelheim, and Cedric A. Yeo. *A History of the Roman People*, 3d ed. Upper Saddle River, NJ, 1999. An informative, well-organized textbook covering Roman history from its beginnings to the end of the sixth century C.E.

Watkin, David. *The Roman Forum*. London, 2009. A history of the successive buildings and archeological excavations of this central Roman space.

Wells, Colin. *The Roman Empire,* 2d ed. Cambridge, MA, 1992. An easily readable survey from the reign of Augustus to the midthird century C.E., particularly useful for its treatment of the relationship between the Roman central government and its Italian provinces.

Wiseman, T. P. *Remembering the Roman People*. Oxford, 2009. A collection of studies devoted to popular politics in the late republic.

Woolf, Greg. *Becoming Roman: The Origins of Provincial Civilization in Gaul*. Cambridge, 1998. An exemplary study of how provincial elites made themselves "Roman."

CHAPTER 6

Augustine. *The City of God*. Trans. Henry Bettenson. Baltimore, MD, 1972.

———. *Confessions*. Trans. Henry M. Chadwick. Oxford, 1991.

———. *On Christian Doctrine*. Trans. D. W. Robertson Jr. New York, 1958.

Boethius. *The Consolation of Philosophy*. Trans. R. Green. Indianapolis, IN, 1962.

Bowersock, G. W., Peter Brown, and Oleg Grabar. *Late Antiquity: A Guide to the Postclassical World*. Cambridge, MA, 1999. An authoritative compilation. The first half is devoted to essays on the cultural features of the period; the second half is organized as an encyclopedia.

Brown, Peter. *Augustine of Hippo*. Berkeley, CA, 1967. A great biography by the great scholar of late antiquity.

———. *The Body and Society: Men, Women and Sexual Renunciation in Early Christianity*. New York, 1988. A revealing study of the fundamental transformations wrought by Christianity in the late antique world.

———. *Power and Persuasion in Late Antiquity: Toward a Christian Empire*. Madison, WI, 1992. An important account of Christianity's effects on the political culture of the later Roman Empire.

———. *The Rise of Western Christendom: Triumph and Diversity, 200–1000,* 2d ed. Oxford, 2002. An evocative picture of Christianity's spread eastward and northward from the Mediterranean world.

Brown, Peter. *The World of Late Antiquity*. New York, 1971. Still the best short survey of the period, with excellent illustrations.

Cameron, Averil. *The Later Roman Empire, A.D. 284–430*. London, 1993. Now the standard account of its period, with an emphasis on imperial politics.

———. *The Mediterranean World in Late Antiquity, A.D. 395–600*. London, 1993. Masterful, with excellent, succinct bibliographical essays.

Cassiodorus. *An Introduction to Divine and Human Readings*. Trans. L. W. Jones. New York, 1946.

Chadwick, Henry M. *Augustine*. Oxford, 1986. A short introduction to Augustine's thought.

———. *Boethius*. Oxford, 1981. An intellectual biography of this important thinker.

Clark, Gillian. *Christianity and Roman Society*. Cambridge, 2004. A short, stimulating survey that places early Christianity firmly in its Roman social context.

Clark, Gillian. *Women in Late Antiquity*. Oxford, 1993. A clear, compact account of an important subject.

Coogan, Michael, ed. *The Oxford History of the Biblical World*. Oxford, 1998. A reliable but rather traditional account of the historical events recounted in the Hebrew Bible and the New Testament.

Ehrman, Bart D. *The New Testament: A Historical Introduction to the Early Christian Writings*, 4th ed. Oxford, 2008. The standard textbook by a leading authority.

Eusebius. *The History of the Church*. Trans. G. A. Williamson. Baltimore, MD, 1965. A contemporary account of Constantine's reign, written by one of his courtier-bishops.

———. *Eusebius' Life of Constantine*. Trans. Averil Cameron and Stuart Hall. Oxford, 1999. An admiring biography that reflects Constantine's own vision of his religious authority.

Hopkins, Keith. *A World Full of Gods: The Strange Triumph of Christianity*. Penguin, 1999. An imaginative study of religious pluralism in the Roman world and the context in which Christianity emerged.

Kulikowski, Michael. *Rome's Gothic Wars: From the Third Century to Alaric*. Cambridge, 2007. An authoritative and critical account.

Lane Fox, Robin. *Pagans and Christians*. New York, 1987. A subtle, perceptive, and highly readable exploration of the pagan world within which Christianity grew up.

Lawrence, Clifford Hugh. *Medieval Monasticism*, 3d ed. London, 2000. Concise, perceptive survey of monasticism from its beginnings to the end of the Middle Ages.

Markus, R. A. *The End of Ancient Christianity*. New York, 1990. An expert synthetic study of Christianity in the western Roman Empire between 350 and 600 C.E.

Pagels, Elaine. *The Gnostic Gospels*. New York, 1979. A pathbreaking study of the noncanonical gospels and the history of their exclusion from the Bible.

Pelikan, Jaroslav. *The Christian Tradition*. Vol. 1, *The Emergence of the Catholic Tradition*. Chicago, 1971. A history of Christian doctrine that is one of the tours-de-force of twentieth-century scholarship.

Potter, David. *The Roman Empire at Bay*, A.D. *180–395*. London and New York, 2004. The most up-to-date account of the empire's reorganization and transformation in this era.

Sanders, E. P. *The Historical Figure of Jesus*. London and New York, 1993. A fine study of Jesus in his first-century Jewish context.

Shanks, Hershel, ed. *Christianity and Rabbinic Judaism: A Parallel History of Their Origins and Early Development*. Washington, DC, 1992. Accessible chapters written by top authorities, describing both Jewish and Christian developments from the first to the sixth centuries C.E.

Sherwin-White, A. N. *Roman Society and Roman Law in the New Testament*. Oxford, 1963. A fascinating reading of the New Testament in its historical context.

Wallace-Hadrill, John Michael. *The Barbarian West*, 3d ed. London, 1966. A classic analysis of the hybrid culture of the late Roman West.

Whittaker, C. R. *Frontiers of the Roman Empire: A Social and Economic Study*. Baltimore, MD, 1994. A convincing picture of the frontiers of the Roman Empire as zones of intensive cultural interaction.

Williams, Stephen. *Diocletian and the Roman Recovery*. New York, 1997. Thorough and authoritative.

CHAPTER 7

Bede. *A History of the English Church and People*. Trans. Leo Sherley-Price. Baltimore, MD, 1955. The fundamental source for early Anglo-Saxon history.

Bloom, Jonathan M. *Paper Before Print: The Impact and History of Paper in the Islamic World*. New Haven, CT, 2001. A fascinating account, with beautiful illustrations.

Boniface. *Letters of Saint Boniface*. Trans. Ephraim Emerton. New York, 1972.

Campbell, James, ed. *The Anglo-Saxons*. Oxford, 1982. An authoritative and splendidly illustrated volume.

Collins, Roger. *Early Medieval Europe, 300–1000*. 2d ed. New York, 1999. Dry and detailed, but a useful textbook nonetheless.

Donner, Fred. *The Early Islamic Conquests*. Princeton, NJ, 1981. A scholarly but readable narrative and analysis.

Einhard and Notker the Stammerer. *Two Lives of Charlemagne*. Trans. Lewis Thorpe. Baltimore, MD, 1969. Lively and entertaining works of contemporary biography.

Fletcher, Richard A. *The Barbarian Conversion: From Paganism to Christianity*. Berkeley, CA, 1999. Slow paced but informative and perceptive.

———. *Moorish Spain*. Berkeley, CA, 1993. The best short survey in English.

Geanakoplos, Deno John, ed. *Byzantium: Church, Society and Civilization Seen through Contemporary Eyes*. Chicago, 1984. An outstanding source book.

Gregory, Timothy E. *A History of Byzantium*. Malden, MA, and Oxford, 2005. The most accessible of the recent textbooks on Byzantium. An excellent place to start.

Herrin, Judith. *The Formation of Christendom*. Princeton, NJ, 1987. A synthetic history of the Christian civilizations of Byzantium and western Europe from 500 to 800, written by a prominent historian.

Hodges, Richard, and David Whitehouse. *Mohammed, Charlemagne and the Origins of Europe*. London, 1983. A critical analysis of the "Pirenne thesis," reexaming the relationship between the Mediterranean world and northern Europe.

Hourani, Albert. *A History of the Arab Peoples*. New York, 1992. A sympathetic and clear survey written for nonspecialists.

Kazhdan, Alexander P., ed. *The Oxford Dictionary of Byzantium*. 3 vols. Oxford, 1991. An authoritative reference work.

Kennedy, Hugh. *The Prophet and the Age of the Caliphates*. 2d ed. Harlow, UK, 2004. A lucid introduction to the political history of the Islamic world from the sixth through the eleventh centuries.

Krautheimer, Richard. *Early Christian and Byzantine Architecture*. 4th ed. New York, 1986. A classic work by one of the greatest Byzantine art historians of the twentieth century.

Mango, Cyril, ed. *The Oxford History of Byzantium.* Oxford and New York, 2002. Full of sharp judgments and attractively illustrated.

McCormick, Michael. *The Origins of the European Economy: Communications and Commerce A.D. 300–900.* Cambridge, 2002. An astonishing reinterpretation of the evidence for the myriad contacts between Christian Europe and Islam.

McKitterick, Rosamond. *Charlemagne: The Formation of a European Identity.* Cambridge, 2008. A history of Charlemagne's career and its lasting impact by an eminent scholar of the Carolingian world.

———, ed. *The Uses of Literacy in Early Medieval Europe.* New York, 1990. A superb collection of essays.

McNamara, Jo Ann, and John E. Halborg, eds. *Sainted Women of the Dark Ages.* Durham, NC, 1992. Translated saints' lives from Merovingian and Carolingian Europe.

Murray, A. C., ed. *From Roman to Merovingian Gaul: A Reader.* Toronto, 2000. An excellent collection of sources.

Pelikan, Jaroslav. *The Christian Tradition.* Vol. II, *The Spirit of Eastern Christendom.* Chicago, 1974. An outstanding synthetic treatment of the doctrines of Byzantine Christianity.

Procopius. *The Secret History.* Trans. G. A. Williamson. Baltimore, MD, 1966. An "unauthorized" account of Justinian's reign, written by the emperor's offical historian.

Reuter, Timothy. *Germany in the Early Middle Ages, 800–1056.* New York, 1991. The best survey in English.

Sawyer, Peter, ed. *The Oxford Illustrated History of the Vikings.* Oxford, 1997. The best one-volume account, lavishly illustrated.

Todd, Malcolm. *The Early Germans.* Oxford, 1992. A reliable survey, particularly strong in its use of archaeological evidence.

Treadgold, Warren. *A History of the Byzantine State and Society.* Stanford, CA, 1997. A massive, encyclopedic narrative of the political, economic, and military history of Byzantium from 284 until 1461.

Wallace-Hadrill, John Michael. *Early Germanic Kingship in England and on the Continent.* Oxford, 1971. A classic analysis of changing ideas about kingship in early medieval Europe, emphasizing the links between Anglo-Saxon and Carolingian cultures.

———. *The Frankish Church.* Oxford, 1983. A masterful account that links the Merovingian and Carolingian churches.

Watt, W. Montgomery. *Islamic Philosophy and Theology,* 2d ed. Edinburgh, UK, 1985. The standard English account.

Wemple, Suzanne Fonay. *Women in Frankish Society: Marriage and the Cloister, 500–900.* Philadelphia, PA, 1981. An influential account of changing attitudes toward marriage among the early Franks.

Whittow, Mark. *The Making of Orthodox Byzantium, 600–1025.* London, 1996. Emphasizes the centrality of orthodoxy in shaping Byzantine history. Particularly good on Byzantine relations with the peoples outside the empire.

Wickham, Chris. *Framing the Middle Ages: Europe and the Mediterranean, 400–800.* Oxford, 2007. An eye-opening history that spans the transitional periods of late antiquity and the early Middle Ages, paying careful attention to regional differences.

Wood, Ian. *The Merovingian Kingdoms, 450–751.* New York, 1994. A detailed study, but difficult for beginners.

CHAPTER 8

Amt, Emily, ed. *Women's Lives in Medieval Europe: A Sourcebook.* New York, 1993. An excellent collection of primary texts.

The Song of Roland. Trans. Robert Harrison. Penguin, 1970. A lively translation.

Arnold, Benjamin. *Princes and Territories in Medieval Germany.* Cambridge and New York, 1991. The best such survey in English.

Blumenthal, Uta-Renate. *The Investiture Controversy.* Philadelphia, 1988. A clear review of a complicated subject.

Burman, Thomas E. *Reading the Qur'ān in Latin Christendom, 1140–1560.* Philadelphia, 2007. A fascinating account of the Qu'ran's reception in medieval Europe.

Dunbabin, Jean. *France in the Making, 843–1180,* 2d ed. Oxford and New York, 2000. An authoritative survey of the disparate territories that came to make up the medieval French kingdom.

Dyer, Christopher. *Making a Living in the Middle Ages: The People of Britain 850–1520.* New Haven, 2002. A splendid new synthesis that combines social, economic, and archaeological evidence.

Fuhrmann, Horst. *Germany in the High Middle Ages, c. 1050–1200.* Cambridge, 1986. A useful, short history of twelfth-century Germany.

Hicks, Carola. *The Bayeux Tapestry: The Life Story of Masterpiece.* London, 2006. An art historian's engrossing account of the making, reception, and interpretation of this amazing artifact.

Jones, P. J. *The Italian City-State: From Commune to Signoria.* Oxford and New York, 1997. A fundamental reinterpretation of the evidence.

Kaeuper, Richard W. *Chivalry and Violence in Medieval Europe.* Oxford and New York, 1999. A darker view of chivalry than Keen's.

Keen, Maurice. *Chivalry.* New Haven, CT, 1984. A comprehensive treatment of chivalry from its origins to the sixteenth century.

Leyser, Henrietta. *Medieval Women: A Social History of Women in England, 440–1500.* New York, 1995. Although limited to one country, this is the best of the recent surveys treating medieval women.

Leyser, Karl. *Rule and Conflict in an Early Medieval Society: Ottonian Saxony.* Oxford, 1979. A concise, challenging account of the dynamics of rule in tenth-century Saxony, paying special attention to the importance of royal women.

Lopez, Robert S., and Irving W. Raymond, eds. *Medieval Trade in the Mediterranean World.* New York, 1990. A pathbreaking collection of source material.

Miller, Maureen C. *Power and the Holy in the Age of the Investiture Conflict. A Brief History with Documents.* Boston, 2005. A stimulating approach to the eleventh-century conflicts over temporal and spiritual power, with many newly translated sources.

Moore, Robert I. *The First European Revolution, c. 970–1215.* Oxford and Cambridge, MA, 2000. A remarkable description of the ways in which European society was fundamentally reshaped during the eleventh and twelfth centuries.

Peters, F. E. *Aristotle and the Arabs.* New York, 1968. Well written and engaging.

Reilly, Bernard F. *The Medieval Spains*. New York, 1993. A succinct account that covers the entire Iberian peninsula from 500 to 1500.

Reynolds, Susan. *Fiefs and Vassals: The Medieval Evidence Reinterpreted*. Oxford and New York, 1994. A detailed revisionist history of "feudalism."

Sheingorn, Pamela, trans. *The Book of Sainte Foy*. Philadelphia, 1995.

Southern, Richard W. *The Making of the Middle Ages*. New Haven, CT, 1992. A classic work, first published in 1951 but still fresh and exciting.

Stillman, Norman A. *The Jews of Arab Lands: A History and Source Book*. Philadelphia, PA, 1979. An essential resource.

Stow, Kenneth R. *Alienated Minority: The Jews of Medieval Latin Europe*. Cambridge, MA, 1992. An excellent survey.

Tierney, Brian. *The Crisis of Church and State, 1050–1300*. Toronto, 1988. An indispensable collection for both teachers and students.

CHAPTER 9

Abelard and Heloise. *The Letters and Other Writings*. Trans. William Levitan. Indianapolis, 2007. A beautiful and accurate translation of the correspondence and related documents, with a full introduction and notes.

Abulafia, David. *Frederick II: A Medieval Emperor*. London and New York, 1988. A reliable biography that strips away much of the legend that has hitherto surrounded this monarch.

Abulafia, David, ed. *The New Cambridge Medieval History. Volume 5: c. 1198–c. 1300*. Cambridge, 1999. Contributions by more than thirty specialists. Excellent bibliographies.

Baldwin, John W. *The Government of Philip Augustus*. Berkeley and Los Angeles, CA, 1986. A landmark scholarly account.

Bartlett, Robert. *The Making of Europe: Conquest, Colonization and Cultural Change, 950–1350*. Princeton, NJ, 1993. A wide-ranging examination of the economic, social, and religious expansion of Europe, full of stimulating insights.

Bisson, Thomas N. *The Crisis of the Twelfth Century: Power, Lordship, and the Origins of European Government*. Princeton, NJ, 2009. A new interpretation of the evidence.

Boswell, John E. *Christianity, Social Tolerance, and Homosexuality: Gay People in Western Europe from the Beginning of the Christian Era to the Fourteenth Century*. Chicago, 1980. A pioneering account, hotly debated but highly respected.

Camille, Michael. *Gothic Art: Glorious Visions*. New York, 1996. A succinct and beautifully illustrated introduction.

Chrétien de Troyes. *Arthurian Romances*. Trans. W. W. Kibler. New York, 1991.

Clanchy, Michael T. *Abelard: A Medieval Life*. Oxford and Cambridge, MA, 1997. A great biography.

———. *From Memory to Written Record: England, 1066–1307*. Oxford, 1992. A fascinating and hugely influential account of this revolutionary shift.

Cobban, Alan B. *The Medieval Universities*. London, 1975. The best short treatment in English.

Colish, Marcia. *Medieval Foundations of the Western Intellectual Tradition, 400–1400*. New Haven, CT, 1997. An encyclopedic work, best used as a reference.

Dante Alighieri. *The Divine Comedy*. Trans. Mark Musa. 3 vols. Baltimore, MD, 1984–86.

Dronke, Peter. *Women Writers of the Middle Ages*. New York, 1984. A rich literary study.

Fassler, Margot. *Gothic Song: Victorine Seqeunces and Augustinian Reform in Twelfth-Century Paris*. Cambridge, UK, 1993. The emergence of new musical genres and their cultural context.

Gillingham, John. *The Angevin Empire*, 2d ed. Oxford and New York, 2001. The best treatment by far of its subject, brief but full of ideas.

Gottfried von Strassburg. *Tristan*. Trans. A. T. Hatto. Baltimore, MD, 1960.

Hallam, Elizabeth, and Judith Everard. *Capetian France, 987–1328*, 2d ed. New York, 2001. A clear and well-organized account.

Haskins, Charles Homer. *The Renaissance of the Twelfth Century*. Cambridge, MA, 1927. A classic and influential study.

Jordan, William C. *Europe in the High Middle Ages: The Penguin History of Europe*. Vol. III. New York and London, 2003. An outstanding new survey.

Knowles, David. *The Evolution of Medieval Thought*, 2d ed. London, 1988. An authoritative survey, thoroughly revised in the second edition.

Lambert, Malcolm. *Medieval Heresy*, 3d ed. Oxford and Cambridge, 2002. The standard synthesis; deeply learned and fully annotated.

Lawrence, Clifford Hugh. *The Friars: The Impact of the Early Mendicant Movement on Western Society*. London and New York, 1994. The best short introduction to the early history of the Franciscans and the Dominicans.

Leclerq, Jean. *The Love of Learning and the Desire for God*, 3d ed. New York, 1982. A beautiful interpretation of twelfth-century monastic culture and the influence of Bernard of Clairvaux.

Little, Lester. *Religious Poverty and Profit Economy in Medieval Europe*. Ithaca, 1978. A fascinating study of the relationship between religious practice and economic reality.

Marie de France. *Lais*. Trans. Glyn S. Burgess and Keith Busby. Harmondsworth, UK, 1999. A compelling and entertaining prose translation.

Moore, R. I. *The Formation of a Persecuting Society: Authority and Deviance in Western Europe, 950–1250*. 2d ed. Malden, MA, 2007. This new edition responds to some of the debates generated by the publication of the first in 1987.

Morris, Colin. *The Papal Monarchy: The Western Church from 1050 to 1250*. Oxford, 1989. An excellent scholarly survey; part of the Oxford History of the Christian Church series.

Newman, Barbara, ed. *Voice of the Living Light: Hildegard of Bingen and Her World*. Berkeley and Los Angeles, CA, 1998. An introduction to Hildegard's life and work.

Otto, Bishop of Freising. *The Deeds of Frederick Barbarossa*. Trans. C. C. Mierow. New York, 1953. A contemporary chronicle interesting enough to read from start to finish.

Smalley, Beryl. *The Study of the Bible in the Middle Ages*, 3d ed. Oxford, 1983. The standard work, gracefully written and illuminating.

Southern, Richard W. *Western Society and the Church in the Middle Ages*. Baltimore, MD, 1970. An insightful interpretation of the interplay between society and religion by one of the greatest historians of the twentieth century.

Strayer, Joseph R. *On the Medieval Origins of the Modern State*. With new forewords by Charles Tilly and William Chester Jordan. Princeton, 2005. This new edition of Strayer's series of lectures places them in their scholarly context.

Swanson, R. N. *The Twelfth-Century Renaissance*. Manchester, UK, 1999. An updated survey of the intellectual developments of the twelfth century.

Symes, Carol. *A Common Stage: Theater and Public Life in Medieval Arras*. Ithaca, NY, 2007. A study of a vibrant cultural hub.

Wakefield, Walter, and Austin P. Evans, eds. and trans. *Heresies of the High Middle Ages*. New York, 1969, 1991. A comprehensive collection of sources.

Wilhelm, James J., ed. and trans. *Medieval Song: An Anthology of Hymns and Lyrics*. New York, 1971. An excellent collection of sacred and secular poetry that illustrates the connections between them.

Wolfram von Eschenbach. *Parzival*. Trans. H. M. Mustard and C. E. Passage. New York, 1961.

CHAPTER 10

Allmand, Christopher T., ed. *Society at War: The Experience of England and France During the Hundred Years' War*. Edinburgh, 1973. An outstanding collection of documents.

———. *The Hundred Years' War: England and France at War, c. 1300–c. 1450*. Cambridge and New York, 1988. Still the best analytic account of the war; after a short narrative, the book is organized topically.

Boccaccio, Giovanni. *The Decameron*. Trans. Mark Musa and P. E. Bondanella. New York, 1977.

Bynum, Caroline Walker. *Holy Feast and Holy Fast: The Religious Significance of Food to Medieval Women*. Berkeley and Los Angeles, 1988. One of the most influential and important works of scholarship published in the late twentieth century.

Chaucer, Geoffrey. *The Canterbury Tales*. Trans. Nevill Coghill. New York, 1951. A modern English verse translation, lightly annotated.

Cohn, Samuel K., Jr. *Lust for Liberty: The Politics of Social Revolt in Medieval Europe, 1200–1425. Italy, France, and Flanders*. Cambridge, MA, 2006. An important new study.

Cole, Bruce. *Giotto and Florentine Painting, 1280–1375*. New York, 1976. A clear and stimulating introduction.

Crummey, Robert O. *The Formation of Muscovy, 1304–1613*. New York, 1987. The standard account.

Dobson, R. Barrie. *The Peasants' Revolt of 1381*, 2d ed. London, 1983. A comprehensive source collection, with excellent introductions to the documents.

Dyer, Christopher. *Standards of Living in the Later Middle Ages: Social Change in England, c. 1200–1520*. Cambridge and New York, 1989. Detailed but highly rewarding.

Froissart, Jean. *Chronicles*. Trans. Geoffrey Brereton. Baltimore, MD, 1968. A selection from the most famous contemporary account of the Hundred Years' War to about 1400.

Hobbins, Daniel, ed. and trans. *The Trial of Joan of Arc*. Cambridge, MA, 2007. A new and excellent translation of the transcripts of Joan's trial.

Horrox, Rosemary, ed. *The Black Death*. New York, 1994. A fine collection of documents reflecting the impact of the Black Death, especially in England.

John Hus at the Council of Constance. Trans. M. Spinka, New York, 1965. The translation of a Czech chronicle with an expert introduction and appended documents.

Jordan, William Chester. *The Great Famine: Northern Europe in the Early Fourteenth Century*. Princeton, NJ, 1996. An outstanding social and economic study.

Keen, Maurice, ed. *Medieval Warfare: A History*. Oxford and New York, 1999. The most attractive introduction to this important subject. Lively and well illustrated.

Kempe, Margery. *The Book of Margery Kempe*. Trans. Barry Windeatt. New York, 1985. A fascinating personal narrative by an early-fifteenth-century Englishwoman who hoped she might be a saint.

Lerner, Robert E. *The Heresy of the Free Spirit in the Later Middle Ages*, 2d ed. Notre Dame, IN, 1991. A revealing study of a heretical movement that hardly existed at all.

Lewis, Peter S. *Later Medieval France: The Polity*. London, 1968. Still fresh and suggestive after forty years. A masterwork.

Memoirs of a Renaissance Pope: The Commentaries of Pius II. Abridged ed. Trans. F. A. Gragg, New York, 1959. Remarkable insights into the mind of a particularly well-educated mid-fifteenth-century pope.

Nicholas, David. *The Transformation of Europe, 1300–1600*. Oxford and New York, 1999. The best textbook presently available.

Oakley, Francis C. *The Western Church in the Later Middle Ages*. Ithaca, NY, 1979. The best book by far on the history of conciliarism, the late medieval papacy, Hussitism, and the efforts at institutional reform during this period. On popular piety, see Swanson.

Shirley, Janet, trans. *A Parisian Journal, 1405–1449*. Oxford, 1968. A marvelous panorama of Parisian life recorded by an eyewitness.

Sumption, Jonathan. *The Hundred Years' War*. Vol. 1: *Trial by Battle*. Vol. 2: *Trial by Fire*. Philadelphia, 1999. The first two volumes of a massive narrative history of the war, carrying the story up to 1369.

Swanson, R. N. *Religion and Devotion in Europe, c. 1215–c. 1515*. Cambridge and New York, 1995. An excellent study of late-medieval popular piety; an excellent complement to Oakley.

Vaughan, Richard. *Valois Burgundy*. London, 1975. A summation of the author's four-volume study of the Burgundian dukes.

Ziegler, Philip. *The Black Death*. New York, 1969. A popular account, but reliable and engrossing.

CHAPTER 11

Abu-Lughod, Janet L. *Before European Hegemony: The World System A.D. 1250–1350*. Oxford and New York, 1989. A study of the trading links among Europe, the Middle East, India, and China, with special attention to the role of the Mongol Empire; extensive bibliography.

Allsen, Thomas T. *Culture and Conquest in Mongol Eurasia*. Cambridge and New York, 2001. A synthesis of the author's earlier studies, emphasizing Mongol involvement in the cultural and commercial exchanges that linked China, Central Asia, and Europe.

Amitai-Preiss, Reuven, and David O. Morgan, eds. *The Mongol Empire and Its Legacy*. Leiden, 1999. A collection of essays that represents some of the new trends in Mongol studies.

Christian, David. *A History of Russia, Central Asia and Mongolia*. Vol. 1, *Inner Eurasia from Prehistory to the Mongol Empire*. Oxford, 1998. The authoritative English-language work on the subject.

Coles, Paul. *The Ottoman Impact on Europe*. London, 1968. An excellent introductory text, still valuable despite its age.

Fernández-Armesto, Felipe. *Before Columbus: Exploration and Colonisation from the Mediterranean to the Atlantic, 1229–1492*. London, 1987. An indispensible study of the medieval background to the sixteenth-century European colonial empires.

———. *Columbus*. Oxford and New York, 1991. An excellent biography that stresses the millenarian ideas that underlay Columbus's thinking.

Flint, Valerie I. J. *The Imaginative Landscape of Christopher Columbus*. Princeton, NJ, 1992. A short, suggestive analysis of the intellectual influences that shaped Columbus's geographical ideas.

Goffman, Daniel. *The Ottoman Empire and Early Modern Europe*. Cambridge and New York, 2002. A revisionist account that presents the Ottoman Empire as a European state.

The History and the Life of Chinggis Khan: The Secret History of the Mongols. Trans. Urgunge Onon. Leiden, 1997. A newer version of *The Secret History*, now the standard English version of this important Mongol source.

Inalcik, Halil. *The Ottoman Empire: The Classical Age, 1300–1600*. London, 1973. The standard history by the dean of Turkish historians.

———, ed. *An Economic and Social History of the Ottoman Empire, 1300–1914*. Cambridge, 1994. An important collection of essays, spanning the full range of Ottoman history.

Jackson, Peter. *The Mongols and the West, 1221–1410*. Harlow, UK, 2005. A well-written survey that emphasizes the interactions among the Mongol, Latin Christian, and Muslim worlds.

Kafadar, Cemal. *Between Two Worlds: The Construction of the Ottoman State*. Berkeley and Los Angeles, 1995. An important study of Ottoman origins in the border regions between Byzantium, the Seljuk Turks, and the Mongols.

Larner, John. *Marco Polo and the Discovery of the World*. New Haven, CT, 1999. A study of the influence of Marco Polo's *Travels* on Europeans.

Morgan, David. *The Mongols*. 2d ed. Oxford, 2007. An accessible introduction to Mongol history and its sources, written by a noted expert on medieval Persia.

Parker, Geoffrey. *The Military Revolution: Military Innovation and the Rise of the West (1500–1800)*. 2d ed. Cambridge and New York, 1996. A work of fundamental importance for understanding the global dominance achieved by early modern Europeans.

Phillips, J. R. S. *The Medieval Expansion of Europe*. 2d ed. Oxford, 1998. An outstanding study of the thirteenth- and fourteenth-century background to the fifteenth-century expansion of Europe. Important synthetic treatment of European relations with the Mongols, China, Africa, and North America. The second edition includes a new introduction and a bibliographical essay; the text is the same as in the first edition (1988).

Phillips, William D., Jr., and Carla R. Phillips. *The Worlds of Christopher Columbus*. Cambridge and New York, 1991. The first book to read on Columbus: accessible, engaging, and scholarly. Then read Fernández-Armesto's biography.

Ratchnevsky, Paul. *Genghis Khan: His Life and Legacy*. Trans. Thomas Nivison Haining. Oxford, 1991. An English translation and abridgment of a book first published in German in 1983. The author was one of the greatest Mongol historians of his generation.

Rossabi, M. *Khubilai Khan: His Life and Times*. Berkeley, CA, 1988. The standard English biography.

Russell, Peter. *Prince Henry "The Navigator": A Life*. New Haven, CT, 2000. A masterly biography by a great historian who has spent a lifetime on the subject. The only book one now needs to read on Prince Henry.

Saunders, J. J. *The History of the Mongol Conquests*. London, 1971. Still the standard English-language introduction; somewhat more positive about the Mongols' accomplishments than is Morgan.

Scammell, Geoffrey V. *The First Imperial Age: European Overseas Expansion, 1400–1715*. London, 1989. A useful introductory survey, with a particular focus on English and French colonization.

The Book of Prophecies, Edited by Christopher Columbus. Trans. Blair Sullivan, ed. Roberto Rusconi. Berkeley and Los Angeles, 1996. After his third voyage, from which Columbus was returned to Spain in chains, he compiled a book of quotations from various sources selected to emphasize the millenarian implications of his discoveries; a fascinating insight into the mind of the explorer.

The Four Voyages: Christopher Columbus. Trans. J. M. Cohen. New York, 1992. Columbus's own self-serving account of his four voyages to the Indies.

Mandeville's Travels. Ed. M. C. Seymour. Oxford, 1968. An edition of the *Book of Marvels* based on the Middle English version popular in the fifteenth century.

The Secret History of the Mongols. Trans. F. W. Cleaves. Cambridge, MA, 1982.

The Secret History of the Mongols and Other Pieces. Trans. Arthur Waley. London, 1963. The later Chinese abridgment of the Mongol original.

The Travels of Marco Polo, trans. R. E. Latham. Baltimore, MD, 1958. The most accessible edition of this remarkably interesting work.

CHAPTER 12

Alberti, Leon Battista. *The Family in Renaissance Florence (Della Famiglia)*. Trans. Renée Neu Watkins. Columbia, SC, 1969.

Baxandall, Michael. *Painting and Experience in Fifteenth-Century Italy*. Oxford, 1972. A classic study of the perceptual world of the Renaissance.

Brucker, Gene. *Florence, the Golden Age, 1138–1737*. Berkeley and Los Angeles, CA, 1998. The standard account.

Bruni, Leonardo. *The Humanism of Leonardo Bruni: Selected Texts.* Trans. Gordon Griffiths, James Hankins, and David Thompson. Binghamton, NY, 1987. Excellent translations, with introductions, to the Latin works of a key Renaissance humanist.

Burke, Peter. *The Renaissance.* New York, 1997. A brief introduction by an influential modern historian.

Burkhardt, Jacob. *The Civilization of the Renaissance in Italy.* Many editions. The nineteenth-century work that first crystallized an image of the Italian Renaissance, and with which scholars have been wrestling ever since.

Cassirer, Ernst, et al., eds. *The Renaissance Philosophy of Man.* Chicago, 1948. Important original works by Petrarch, Ficino, and Pico della Mirandola, among others.

Castiglione, Baldassare. *The Book of the Courtier.* Many editions. The translations by C. S. Singleton (New York, 1959) and by George Bull (New York, 1967) are both excellent.

Cellini, Benvenuto. *Autobiography.* Trans. George Bull. Baltimore, MD, 1956. This Florentine goldsmith (1500–1571) is the source for many of the most famous stories about the artists of the Florentine Renaissance.

Cochrane, Eric, and Julius Kirshner, eds. *The Renaissance.* Chicago, 1986. An outstanding collection, from the University of Chicago Readings in Western Civilization series.

Erasmus, Desiderius. *The Praise of Folly.* Trans. J. Wilson. Ann Arbor, MI, 1958.

Fox, Alistair. *Thomas More: History and Providence.* Oxford, 1982. A balanced account of a man too easily idealized.

Grafton, Anthony, and Lisa Jardine. *From Humanism to the Humanities: Education and the Liberal Arts in Fifteenth- and Sixteenth-Century Europe.* London, 1986. An account that presents Renaissance humanism as the elitist cultural program of a self-interested group of pedagogues.

Grendler, Paul, ed. *Encyclopedia of the Renaissance.* New York, 1999. A valuable reference work.

Hale, John R. *The Civilization of Europe in the Renaissance.* New York, 1993. A synthetic volume summarizing the life's work of a major Renaissance historian.

Hankins, James. *Plato in the Italian Renaissance.* Leiden and New York, 1990. A definitive study of the reception and influence of Plato on Renaissance intellectuals.

————, ed. *Renaissance Civic Humanism: Reappraisals and Reflections.* Cambridge and New York, 2000. An excellent collection of scholarly essays reassessing republicanism in the Renaissance.

Jardine, Lisa. *Worldly Goods.* London, 1996. A revisionist account that emphasizes the acquisitive materialism of Italian Renaissance society and culture.

Kanter, Laurence, Hilliard T. Goldfarb, and James Hankins. *Botticelli's Witness: Changing Style in a Changing Florence.* Boston, 1997. This catalog for an exhibition of Botticelli's works, at the Gardner Museum in Boston, offers an excellent introduction to the painter and his world.

King, Margaret L. *Women of the Renaissance.* Chicago, 1991. Deals with women in all walks of life and in a variety of roles.

Kristeller, Paul O. *Eight Philosophers of the Italian Renaissance.* Stanford, 1964. An admirably clear and accurate account that fully appreciates the connections between medieval and Renaissance thought.

————. *Renaissance Thought: The Classic, Scholastic, and Humanistic Strains.* New York, 1961. Very helpful in defining the main trends of Renaissance thought.

Lane, Frederic C. *Venice: A Maritime Republic.* Baltimore, MD, 1973. An authoritative account.

Machiavelli, Niccolò. *The Discourses* and *The Prince.* Many editions. These two books must be read together if one is to understand Machiavelli's political ideas properly.

Martines, Lauro. *Power and Imagination: City-States in Renaissance Italy.* New York, 1979. Insightful account of the connections among politics, society, culture, and art.

More, Thomas. *Utopia.* Many editions.

Murray, Linda. *High Renaissance and Mannerism.* London, 1985. The place to begin a study of fifteenth- and sixteenth-century Italian art.

Olson, Roberta, *Italian Renaissance Sculpture.* New York, 1992. The most accessible introduction to the subject.

Perkins, Leeman L. *Music in the Age of the Renaissance.* New York, 1999. A massive new study that needs to be read in conjunction with Reese.

Rabelais, François. *Gargantua and Pantagruel.* Trans. J. M. Cohen. Baltimore, MD, 1955. A robust modern translation.

Reese, Gustave. *Music in the Renaissance,* rev. ed. New York, 1959. A great book; still authoritative, despite the more recent work by Perkins, which supplements but does not replace it.

Rice, Eugene F., Jr., and Anthony Grafton. *The Foundations of Early Modern Europe, 1460–1559,* 2d ed. New York, 1994. The best textbook account of its period.

Rowland, Ingrid D. *The Culture of the High Renaissance: Ancients and Moderns in Sixteenth-Century Rome.* Cambridge and New York, 2000. Beautifully written examination of the social, intellectual, and economic foundations of the Renaissance in Rome.

CHAPTER 13

Bainton, Roland. *Erasmus of Christendom.* New York, 1969. Still the best biography in English of the Dutch reformer and intellectual.

————. *Here I Stand: A Life of Martin Luther.* Nashville, TN, 1950. Although old and obviously biased in Luther's favor, this remains an absorbing and dramatic introduction to Luther's life and thought.

Benedict, Philip. *Christ's Churches Purely Reformed: A Social History of Calvinism.* New Haven, CT, 2002. A wide-ranging recent survey of Calvinism in both western and eastern Europe.

Bossy, John. *Christianity in the West, 1400–1700.* Oxford and New York, 1985. A brilliant, challenging picture of the changes that took place in Christian piety and practice as a result of the sixteenth-century reformations.

Bouwsma, William J. *John Calvin: A Sixteenth-Century Portrait.* Oxford and New York, 1988. The best biography of the magisterial reformer.

Collinson, Patrick. *The Religion of Protestants: The Church in English Society, 1559–1625.* Oxford, 1982. A great book by a noted historian of early English Protestantism.

Dixon, C. Scott, ed. *The German Reformation: The Essential Readings.* Oxford, 1999. A collection of important recent articles.

Duffy, Eamon. *The Stripping of the Altars: Traditional Religion in England, c. 1400–c. 1550.* A brilliant study of religious exchange at the parish level.

Hillerbrand, Hans J., ed. *The Protestant Reformation.* New York, 1967. Source selections are particularly good for illuminating the political consequences of Reformation theological ideas.

John Calvin: Selections from His Writings, ed. John Dillenberger. Garden City, NY, 1971. A judicious selection, drawn mainly from Calvin's *Institutes.*

Loyola, Ignatius. *Personal Writings.* Trans. by Joseph A. Munitiz and Philip Endean. London and New York, 1996. An excellent collection that includes Loyola's autobiography, his spiritual diary, and some of his letters, as well as his *Spiritual Exercises.*

Luebke, David, ed. *The Counter-Reformation: The Essential Readings.* Oxford, 1999. A collection of nine important recent essays.

MacCulloch, Diarmaid. *Reformation: Europe's House Divided, 1490–1700.* London and New York, 2003. A definitive new survey; the best single-volume history of its subject in a generation.

Martin Luther: Selections from His Writings, ed. John Dillenberger. Garden City, NY, 1961. The standard selection, especially good on Luther's theological ideas.

McGrath, Alister E. *Reformation Thought: An Introduction.* Oxford, 1993. A useful explanation, accessible to non-Christians, of the theological ideas of the major Protestant reformers.

Mullett, Michael A. *The Catholic Reformation.* London, 2000. A sympathetic survey of Catholicism from the mid-sixteenth to the eighteenth century that presents the mid-sixteenth-century Council of Trent as a continuation of earlier reform efforts.

Oberman, Heiko A. *Luther: Man between God and the Devil.* Trans. by Eileen Walliser-Schwarzbart. New Haven, CT, 1989. A biography stressing Luther's preoccupation with sin, death, and the devil.

O'Malley, John W. *The First Jesuits.* Cambridge, MA, 1993. A scholarly account of the origins and early years of the Society of Jesus.

———. *Trent and All That: Renaming Catholicism in the Early Modern Era.* Cambridge, MA, 2000. Short, lively, and with a full bibliography.

Pettegree, Andrew, ed. *The Reformation World.* New York, 2000. An exhaustive multi-author work representing the most recent thinking about the Reformation.

Pelikan, Jaroslav. *Reformation of Church and Dogma, 1300–1700.* Vol. 4 of *A History of Christian Dogma.* Chicago, 1984. A masterful synthesis of Reformation theology in its late-medieval context.

Roper, Lyndal. *The Holy Household: Women and Morals in Reformation Augsburg.* Oxford, 1989. A pathbreaking study of Protestantism's effects on a single town, with special attention to its impact on attitudes toward women, the family, and marriage.

Shagan, Ethan H. *Popular Politics and the English Reformation.* Cambridge, 2002. Argues that the English Reformation reflects an ongoing process of negotiation, resistance, and response.

Tracy, James D. *Europe's Reformations, 1450–1650.* 2d ed. Lanham, MD, 2006. An outstanding survey, especially strong on Dutch and Swiss developments, but excellent throughout.

Williams, George H. *The Radical Reformation.* 3d ed. Kirksville, MO, 1992. Originally published in 1962, this is still the best book on Anabaptism and its offshoots.

CHAPTER 14

Bonney, Richard. *The European Dynastic States, 1494–1660.* Oxford and New York, 1991. An excellent survey of continental Europe during the "long" sixteenth century.

Briggs, Robin. *Early Modern France, 1560–1715,* 2d ed. Oxford and New York, 1997. Updated and authoritative, with new bibliographies.

———. *Witches and Neighbors: The Social and Cultural Context of European Witchcraft.* New York, 1996. An influential recent account of Continental witchcraft.

Cervantes, Miguel de. *Don Quixote.* Trans. Edith Grossman. New York, 2003. A splendid new translation.

Clarke, Stuart. *Thinking with Demons: The Idea of Witchcraft in Early Modern Europe.* Oxford and New York, 1999. By placing demonology into the context of sixteenth- and seventeenth-century intellectual history, Clarke makes sense of it in new and exciting ways.

Cochrane, Eric, Charles M. Gray, and Mark A. Kishlansky. *Early Modern Europe: Crisis of Authority.* Chicago, 1987. An outstanding source collection from the University of Chicago Readings in Western Civilization series.

Held, Julius S., and Donald Posner. *Seventeenth- and Eighteenth-Century Art: Baroque Painting, Sculpture, Architecture.* New York, 1971. The most complete and best-organized introductory review of the subject in English.

Hibbard, Howard. *Bernini.* Baltimore, MD, 1965. The basic study in English of this central figure of Baroque artistic activity.

Hirst, Derek. *England in Conflict, 1603–1660: Kingdom, Community, Commonwealth.* Oxford and New York, 1999. A complete revision of the author's *Authority and Conflict* (1986), this is an up-to-date and balanced account of a period that has been a historical battleground over the past twenty years.

Hobbes, Thomas. *Leviathan.* Ed. Richard Tuck. 2d ed. Cambridge and New York, 1996. The most recent edition, containing the entirety of *Leviathan,* not just the first two parts.

Holt, Mack P. *The French Wars of Religion, 1562–1629.* Cambridge and New York, 1995. A clear account of a confusing time.

Kors, Alan Charles, and Edward Peters. *Witchcraft in Europe, 400–1700: A Documentary History,* 2d ed. Philadelphia, 2000. A superb collection of documents, significantly expanded in the second edition, with up-to-date commentary.

Kingdon, Robert. *Myths about the St. Bartholomew's Day Massacres, 1572–1576.* Cambridge, MA, 1988. A detailed account of this pivotal moment in the history of France.

Levack, Brian P. *The Witch-Hunt in Early Modern Europe,* 2d ed. London and New York, 1995. The best account of the persecution of suspected witches; coverage extends from Europe in 1450 to America in 1750.

Levin, Carole. *The Heart and Stomach of a King: Elizabeth I and the Politics of Sex and Power.* Philadelphia, 1994. A provocative argument for the importance of Elizabeth's gender for understanding her reign.

Limm, Peter, ed. *The Thirty Years' War*. London, 1984. An outstanding short survey, followed by a selection of primary-source documents.

Lynch, John. *Spain, 1516–1598: From Nation-State to World Empire*. Oxford and Cambridge, MA, 1991. The best book in English on Spain at the pinnacle of its sixteenth-century power.

MacCaffrey, Wallace. *Elizabeth I*. New York, 1993. An outstanding traditional biography by an excellent scholar.

Martin, Colin, and Geoffrey Parker. *The Spanish Armada*. London, 1988. Incorporates recent discoveries from undersea archaeology with more traditional historical sources.

Martin, John Rupert. *Baroque*. New York, 1977. A thought-provoking, thematic treatment, less a survey than an essay on the painting, sculpture, and architecture of the period.

Mattingly, Garrett. *The Armada*. Boston, 1959. A great narrative history that reads like a novel; for more recent work, however, see Martin and Parker.

Parker, Geoffrey. *The Dutch Revolt*, 2d ed. Ithaca, NY, 1989. The standard survey in English on the revolt of the Netherlands.

———. *Philip II*. Boston, 1978. A fine biography by an expert in both the Spanish and the Dutch sources.

———, ed. *The Thirty Years' War*, rev. ed. London and New York, 1987. A wide-ranging collection of essays by scholarly experts.

Pascal, Blaise. *Pensées* (French-English edition). Ed. H. F. Stewart. London, 1950.

Quint, David. *Montaigne and the Quality of Mercy: Ethical and Political Themes in the "Essais."* Princeton, NJ, 1999. A fine treatment that presents Montaigne's thought as a response to the French wars of religion.

Roberts, Michael. *Gustavus Adolphus and the Rise of Sweden*. London, 1973. Still the authoritative English-language account.

Russell, Conrad. *The Causes of the English Civil War*. Oxford, 1990. A penetrating and provocative analysis by one of the leading "revisionist" historians of the period.

Tracy, James D. *Holland under Habsburg Rule, 1506–1566: The Formation of a Body Politic*. Berkeley and Los Angeles, CA, 1990. A political history and analysis of the formative years of the Dutch state.

Van Gelderen, Martin. *Political Theory of the Dutch Revolt*. Cambridge, 1995. A fine book on a subject whose importance is too easily overlooked.

CHAPTER 15

Beik, William. *Louis XIV and Absolutism*. New York, 2000. A helpful short examination of the French king, the theory of absolutism, and the social consequences of absolutist rule. Supplemented by translated documents from the period.

Jones, Colin. *The Great Nation: France From Louis XV to Napoleon*. New York, 2002. An excellent and readable scholarly account that argues that the France of Louis XV in the eighteenth century was even more dominant than the kingdom of Louis XIV in the preceding century.

Kishlansky, Mark A. *A Monarchy Transformed: Britain, 1603–1714*. London, 1996. An excellent survey that takes seriously its claims to be a "British" rather than merely an "English" history.

Klein, Herbert S. *The Atlantic Slave Trade*. Cambridge and New York, 1999. An accessible survey by a leading quantitative historian.

Koch, H. W. *A History of Prussia*. London, 1978. Still the best account of its subject.

Lewis, William Roger, gen. ed. *The Oxford History of the British Empire*. Vol. I: *The Origins of Empire: British Overseas Enterprise to the Close of the Seventeenth Century*, ed. Nicholas Canny. Vol. II: *The Eighteenth Century*, ed. Peter J. Marshall. Oxford and New York, 1998. A definitive, multiauthor account.

Locke, John. *Two Treatises of Government*. Ed. Peter Laslett. Rev. ed. Cambridge and New York, 1963. Laslett has revolutionized our understanding of the historical and ideological context of Locke's political writings.

Miller, John, ed. *Absolutism in Seventeenth-Century Europe*. London, 1990. An excellent, multiauthor survey, organized by country.

Monod, Paul K. *The Power of Kings: Monarchy and Religion in Europe, 1589–1715*. New Haven, Conn. 1999. A study of the seventeenth century's declining confidence in the divinity of kings.

Quataert, Donald. *The Ottoman Empire, 1700–1822*. Cambridge and New York, 2000. Well balanced and intended to be read by students.

Riasanovsky, Nicholas V., and Steinberg, Mark D. *A History of Russia*. 7th ed. Oxford and New York, 2005. Far and away the best single-volume textbook on Russian history: balanced, comprehensive, intelligent, and with full bibliographies.

Saint-Simon, Louis. *Historical Memoirs*. Many editions. The classic source for life at Louis XIV's Versailles.

Thomas, Hugh. *The Slave Trade: The History of the Atlantic Slave Trade, 1440–1870*. London and New York, 1997. A survey notable for its breadth and depth of coverage and for its attractive prose style.

Tracy, James D. *The Rise of Merchant Empires: Long-Distance Trade in the Early Modern World, 1350–1750*. Cambridge and New York, 1990. Important collection of essays by leading authorities.

White, Richard. *It's Your Misfortune and None of My Own: A History of the American West*. Norman, Okla., 1991. An outstanding textbook with excellent introductory chapters on European colonialism in the Americas.

Glossary

1973 OPEC oil embargo Some leaders in the Arab-dominated Organization of the Petroleum Exporting Countries (OPEC) wanted to use oil as a weapon against the West in the Arab-Israeli conflict. After the 1972 Arab-Israeli war, OPEC instituted an oil embargo against Western powers. The embargo increased the price of oil and sparked spiraling inflation and economic troubles in Western nations, triggering in turn a cycle of dangerous recession that lasted nearly a decade. In response, Western governments began viewing the Middle Eastern oil regions as areas of strategic importance.

Abbasid Caliphate (750–930) The Abbasid family claimed to be descendants of Muhammad, and in 750 they successfully led a rebellion against the Umayyads, seizing control of Muslim territories in Arabia, Persia, North Africa, and the Near East. The Abbasids modeled their behavior and administration on that of the Persian princes and their rule on that of the Persian Empire, establishing a new capital at Baghdad.

Peter Abelard (1079–1142) Highly influential philosopher, theologian, and teacher, often considered the founder of the University of Paris.

absolutism Form of government in which one body, usually the monarch, controls the right to make war, tax, judge, and coin money. The term was often used to refer to the state monarchies in seventeenth- and eighteenth-century Europe. In other countries the end of feudalism is often associated with the legal abolition of serfdom, as in Russia in 1861.

abstract expressionism The mid-twentieth-century school of art based in New York that included Jackson Pollock, Willem de Kooning, and Franz Kline. It emphasized form, color, gesture, and feeling instead of figurative subjects.

Academy of Sciences This French institute of scientific inquiry was founded in 1666 by Louis XIV. France's statesmen exerted control over the academy and sought to share in the rewards of any discoveries its members made.

Aeneas Mythical founder of Rome, Aeneas was a refugee from the city of Troy whose adventures were described by the poet Virgil in the *Aeneid*, which mimicked the oral epics of Homer.

Aetolian and Achaean Leagues These two alliances among Greek poleis formed during the Hellenistic period in opposition to the Antigonids of Macedonia. Unlike the earlier defensive alliances of the classic period, each league represented a real attempt to form a political federation.

African National Congress (ANC) Multiracial organization founded in 1912 whose goal was to end racial discrimination in South Africa.

Afrikaners Descendants of the original Dutch settlers of South Africa; formerly referred to as Boers.

agricultural revolution Numerous agricultural revolutions have occurred in the history of western civilizations. One of the most significant began in the tenth century C.E., and increased the amount of land under cultivation as well as the productivity of the land. This revolution was made possible through the use of new technology, an increase in global temperatures, and more efficient methods of cultivation.

AIDS Acquired Immunodeficiency Syndrome. AIDS first appeared in the 1970s and has developed into a global health catastrophe; it is spreading most quickly in developing nations in Africa and Asia.

Akhenaten (r. 1352–1336) Pharaoh whose attempt to promote the worship of the sun god, Aten, ultimately weakened his dynasty's position in Egypt.

Alexander the Great (356–323 B.C.E.) The Macedonian king whose conquests of the Persian Empire and Egypt created a new Hellenistic world.

Tsar Alexander II (1818–1881) After the Crimean War, Tsar Alexander embarked on a program of reform and modernization, which included the emancipation of the serfs. A radical assassin killed him in 1881.

Alexius Comnenus (1057–1118) This Byzantine emperor requested Pope Urban II's help in raising an army to recapture Anatolia from the Seljuq Turks. Instead, Pope Urban II called for knights to go to the Holy Land and liberate it from its Muslim captors, which launched the First Crusade.

Algerian War (1954–1962) The war between France and Algerians seeking independence. Led by the National Liberation Front (FLN), guerrillas fought the French army in the mountains and desert of Algeria. The FLN also initiated a campaign of bombing and terrorism in Algerian cities that led French soldiers to torture many Algerians, attracting world attention and international scandal.

Allied Powers The First World War coalition of Great Britain, Ireland, Belgium, France, Italy, Russia, Portugal, Greece, Serbia, Montenegro, Albania, and Romania.

al Qaeda The radical Islamic organization founded in the late 1980s by former *mujahidin* who had fought against the Soviet Union in Afghanistan. Al Qaeda carried out the 9/11 terrorist attacks and is responsible as well for attacks in Africa, southeast Asia, Europe, and the Middle East.

Americanization The fear of many Europeans, since the 1920s, that U.S. cultural products, such as film, television, and music,

exerted too much influence. Many of the criticisms centered on America's emphasis on mass production and organization. The fears about Americanization were not limited to culture. They extended to corporations, business techniques, global trade, and marketing.

Americas The name given to the two great land masses of the New World, derived from the name of the Italian geographer Amerigo Vespucci. In 1492, Christopher Columbus reached the Bahamas and the island of Hispaniola, which began an era of Spanish conquest in North and South America. Originally, the Spanish sought a route to Asia. Instead they discovered two continents whose wealth they decided to exploit. They were especially interested in gold and silver, which they either stole from indigenous peoples or mined using indigenous peoples as labor. Silver became Spain's most lucrative export from the New World.

Ambrose (c. 340–397) One of the early "fathers" of the Church, he helped to define the relationship between the sacred authority of bishops and other Church leaders and the secular authority of worldly rulers. He believed that secular rulers were a part of the Church, and therefore subject to it.

Amnesty International Nongovernmental organization formed in 1961 to defend "prisoners of conscience"—those detained for their beliefs, color, sex, ethnic origin, language, or religion.

Anabaptists Protestant movement that emerged in Switzerland in 1521; its adherents insisted that only adults could be baptized Christians.

anarchists In the nineteenth century, they were a political movement with the aim of establishing small-scale, localized, and self-sufficient democratic communities that could guarantee a maximum of individual sovereignty. Renouncing parties, unions and any form of modern mass organization, the anarchists fell back on the tradition of conspiratorial violence.

Anti–Corn Law League This organization successfully lobbied Parliament to repeal Britain's Corn Laws in 1846. The Corn Laws of 1815 had protected British landowners and farmers from foreign competition by establishing high tariffs, which kept bread prices artificially high for British consumers. The League saw these laws as unfair protection of the aristocracy and pushed for their repeal in the name of free trade.

anti-Semitism Anti-Semitism refers to hostility toward Jewish people. Religious forms of anti-Semitism have a long history in Europe, but in the nineteenth century anti-Semitism emerged as a potent ideology for mobilizing new constituencies in the era of mass politics. Playing on popular conspiracy theories about alleged Jewish influence in society, anti-Semites effectively rallied large bodies of supporters in France during the Dreyfus Affair, and then again during the rise of National Socialism in Germany after the First World War. The Holocaust would not have been possible without the acquiescence or cooperation of many thousands of people who shared anti-Semitic views.

apartheid The racial segregation policy of the Afrikaner-dominated South African government. Legislated in 1948 by the Afrikaner National Party, it existed in South Africa for many years.

appeasement The policy pursued by Western governments in the face of German, Italian, and Japanese aggression leading up to the Second World War. The policy, which attempted to accommodate and negotiate peace with the aggressive nations, was based on the belief that another global war like the First World War was unimaginable, a belief that Germany and its allies had been mistreated by the terms of the Treaty of Versailles, and a fear that fascist Germany and its allies protected the West from the spread of Soviet communism.

Thomas Aquinas (1225–1274) Dominican friar and theologian whose systematic approach to Christian doctrine was influenced by Aristotle.

Arab-Israeli conflict Between the founding of the state of Israel in 1948 and the present, a series of wars has been fought between Israel and neighboring Arab nations: the war of 1948 when Israel defeated attempts by Egypt, Jordon, Iraq, Syria, and Lebanon to prevent the creation of the new state; the 1956 war between Israel and Egypt over the Sinai peninsula; the 1967 war, when Israel gained control of additional land in the Golan Heights, the West Bank, the Gaza strip, and in the Sinai; and the Yom Kippur War of 1973, when Israel once again fought with forces from Egypt and Syria. A particularly difficult issue in all of these conflicts has been the situation of the 950,000 Palestinian refugees made homeless by the first war in 1948, and the movement of Israeli settlers into the occupied territories (outside of Israel's original borders). In the late 1970s, peace talks between Israel and Egypt inspired some hope of peace, but an on-going cycle of violence between Palestinians and the Israeli military have made a final settlement elusive.

Arab nationalism During the period of decolonization, secular forms of Arab nationalism, or pan-Arabism, found a wide following in many countries of the Middle East, especially in Egypt, Syria, and Iraq.

Arianism A variety of Christianity condemned as a heresy by the Roman Church, it derives from the teaching of a fourth-century priest called Arius, who rejected the idea that Jesus could be the divine equal of God.

aristocracy From the Greek word meaning "rule of the best." By 1000 B.C.E., the accumulated wealth of successful traders in Greece had created a new type of social class, which was based on wealth rather than warfare or birth. These men saw their wealth as a reflection of their superior qualities and aspired to emulate the heroes of old.

Aristotle (384–322 B.C.E.) A student of Plato, his philosophy was based on the rational analysis of the material world. In contrast to his teacher, he stressed the rigorous investigation of real phenomena, rather than the development of universal ethics. He was, in turn, the teacher of Alexander the Great.

Asiatic Society A cultural organization founded in 1784 by British Orientalists who lauded native culture but believed in colonial rule.

Assyrians A Semitic-speaking people that moved into northern Mesopotamia around 2400 B.C.E.

Athens Athens emerged as the Greek polis with the most markedly democratic form of government through a series of political struggles during the sixth century B.C.E. After its key role in the defeat of two invading Persian forces, Athens became the preeminent naval power of ancient Greece and the exemplar

of Greek culture. But it antagonized many other poleis, and became embroiled in a war with Sparta and her allies in 431 B.C.E. Called the Peloponnesian War, this bloody conflict lasted until Athens was defeated in 404 B.C.E.

atomic bomb In 1945, the United States dropped atomic bombs on Hiroshima and Nagasaki in Japan, ending the Second World War. In 1949, the Soviet Union tested their first atomic bomb, and in 1953 both superpowers demonstrated their new hydrogen bombs. Strategically, the nuclearization of warfare polarized the world. Countries without nuclear weapons found it difficult to avoid joining either the Soviet or American military pacts. Over time countries split into two groups: the superpowers with enormous military budgets and those countries that relied on agreements and international law. The nuclearization of warfare also encouraged "proxy wars" between clients of superpowers. Culturally, the hydrogen bomb came to symbolize the age and both humanity's power and vulnerability.

Augustine of Hippo (c. 354–397) One of the most influential theologians of all time, Augustine described his conversion to Christianity in his autobiographical *Confessions* and articulated a new Christian worldview in *The City of God*, among other works.

Augustus (63 B.C.E.–14 C.E.) Born Gaius Octavius, this grandnephew and adopted son of Julius Caesar came to power in 27 B.C.E. His reign signals the end of the Roman Republic and the beginning of the Principate, the period when Rome was dominated by autocratic emperors.

Auschwitz-Birkenau The Nazi concentration camp in Poland that was designed to systematically murder Jews and gypsies. Between 1942 and 1944 over one million people were killed in Auschwitz-Birkenau.

Austro-Hungarian Empire The dual monarchy established by the Habsburg family in 1867; it collapsed at the end of the First World War.

authoritarianism A centralized and dictatorial form of government, proclaimed by its adherents to be superior to parliamentary democracy. Authoritarian governments claim to be above the law, do not respect individual rights, and do not tolerate political opposition. Authoritarian regimes that have developed a central ideology such as fascism or communism are sometimes termed "totalitarian."

Avignon A city in southeastern France that became the seat of the papacy between 1305 and 1377, a period known as the "Babylonian Captivity" of the Roman Church.

Aztecs An indigenous people of central Mexico; their empire was conquered by Spanish conquistadors in the sixteenth century.

baby boom (1950s) The post–Second World War upswing in U.S. birth rates; it reversed a century of decline.

Babylon An ancient city between the Tigris and Euphrates rivers, which became the capital of Hammurabi's empire in the eighteenth century B.C.E. and continued to be an important administrative and commercial capital under many subsequent imperial powers, including the Neo-Assyrians, Chaldeans, Persians, and Romans. It was here that Alexander the Great died in 323 B.C.E.

Francis Bacon (1561–1626) British philosopher and scientist who pioneered the scientific method and inductive reasoning. In other words, he argued that thinkers should amass many observations and then draw general conclusions or propose theories on the basis of this data.

Balfour Declaration A letter dated November 2, 1917, by Lord Arthur J. Balfour, British Foreign Secretary, that promised a homeland for the Jews in Palestine.

Laura Bassi (1711–1778) She was accepted into the Academy of Science in Bologna for her work in mathematics, which made her one of the few women to be accepted into a scientific academy in the seventeenth century.

Bastille The Bastille was a royal fortress and prison in Paris. In June of 1789, a revolutionary crowd attacked the Bastille to show support for the newly created National Assembly. The fall of the Bastille was the first instance of the people's role in revolutionary change in France.

Bay of Pigs (1961) The unsuccessful invasion of Cuba by Cuban exiles, supported by the U.S. government. The rebels intended to incite an insurrection in Cuba and overthrow the communist regime of Fidel Castro.

Cesare Beccaria (1738–1794) An influential writer during the Enlightenment who advocated for legal reforms. He believed that the only legitimate rationale for punishments was to maintain social order and to prevent other crimes. He argued for the greatest possible leniency compatible with deterrence and opposed torture and the death penalty.

Beer Hall Putsch (1923) An early attempt by the Nazi party to seize power in Munich; Adolf Hitler was imprisoned for a year after the incident.

Benedict of Nursia (c. 480–c. 547) Benedict's rule for monks formed the basis of western monasticism and is still observed in monasteries all over the world.

Benedictine Monasticism This form of monasticism was developed by Benedict of Nursia. Its followers adhere to a defined cycle of daily prayers, lessons, communal worship, and manual labor.

Berlin airlift (1948) The transport of vital supplies to West Berlin by air, primarily under U.S. auspices, in response to a blockade of the city that had been instituted by the Soviet Union to force the Allies to abandon West Berlin.

Berlin Conference (1884) At this conference, the leading colonial powers met and established ground rules for the partition of Africa by European nations. By 1914, 90 percent of African territory was under European control. The Berlin Conference ceded control of the Congo region to a private company run by King Leopold II of Belgium. They agreed to make the Congo valleys open to free trade and commerce, to end the slave trade in the region, and to establish a Congo Free State. In reality, King Leopold II's company established a regime that was so brutal in its treatment of local populations that an international scandal forced the Belgian state to take over the colony in 1908.

Berlin wall The wall built in 1961 by East German Communists to prevent citizens of East Germany from fleeing to West Germany; it was torn down in 1989.

birth control pill This oral contraceptive became widely available in the mid-1960s. For the first time, women had a simple method of birth control that they could take themselves.

Otto von Bismarck (1815–1898) The prime minister of Prussia and later the first chancellor of a unified Germany, Bismarck was the architect of German unification and helped to consolidate the new nation's economic and military power.

Black Death The epidemic of bubonic plague that ravaged Europe, Asia, and North Africa in the fourteenth century, killing one third to one half of the population.

Black Jacobins A nickname for the rebels in Saint Domingue, including Toussaint L'Ouverture, a former slave who in 1791 led the slaves of this French colony in the largest and most successful slave insurrection.

Black Panthers A radical African American group that came together in the 1960s; the Black Panthers advocated black separatism and pan-Africanism.

Blackshirts The troops of Mussolini's fascist regime; the squads received money from Italian landowners to attack socialist leaders.

Black Tuesday (October 29, 1929) The day on which the U.S. stock market crashed, plunging U.S. and international trading systems into crisis and leading the world into the "Great Depression."

William Blake (1757–1827) Romantic writer who criticized industrial society and factories. He championed the imagination and poetic vision, seeing both as transcending the limits of the material world.

Blitzkrieg The German "lightning war" strategy used during the Second World War; the Germans invaded Poland, France, Russia, and other countries with fast-moving and well-coordinated attacks using aircraft, tanks and other armored vehicles, followed by infantry.

Bloody Sunday On January 22, 1905, the Russian tsar's guards killed 130 demonstrators who were protesting the tsar's mistreatment of workers and the middle class.

Jean Bodin (1530–1596) A French political philosopher whose *Six Books of the Commonwealth* advanced a theory of absolute sovereignty, on the grounds that the state's paramount duty is to maintain order and that monarchs should therefore exercise unlimited power.

Boer War (1898–1902) Conflict between British and ethnically European Afrikaners in South Africa, with terrible casualties on both sides.

Boethius (c. 480–524) Member of a prominent Roman family, he sought to preserve aspects of ancient learning by compiling a series of handbooks and anthologies appropriate for Christian readers. His translations of Greek philosophy provided a crucial link between classical Greek thought and the early intellectual culture of Christianity.

Simon de Bolivar (1783–1830) Venezuelan-born general called "The Liberator" for his assistance in helping Bolivia, Panama, Colombia, Ecuador, Peru, and Venezuela win independence from Spain.

Bolsheviks Former members of the Russian Social Democratic Party who advocated the destruction of capitalist political and economic institutions and started the Russian Revolution. In 1918 the Bolsheviks changed their name to the Russian Communist Party. Prominent Bolsheviks included Vladimir Lenin and Josef Stalin. Leon Trotsky joined the Bolsheviks late but became a prominent leader in the early years of the Russian Revolution.

Napoleon Bonaparte (1769–1821) Corsican-born French general who seized power and ruled as dictator from 1799 to 1814. After the successful conquest of much of Europe, he was defeated by Russian and Prussian forces and died in exile.

Sandro Botticelli (1445–1510) An Italian painter devoted to the blending of classical and Christian motifs by using ideas associated with the pagan past to illuminate sacred stories.

bourgeoisie Term for the middle class, derived from the French word for a town-dweller, *bourgeois*.

Boxer Rebellion (1899–1900) Chinese peasant movement that opposed foreign influence, especially that of Christian missionaries; it was finally put down after the Boxers were defeated by a foreign army composed mostly of Japanese, Russian, British, French, and American soldiers.

Tycho Brahe (1546–1601) Danish astronomer who believed that the careful study of the heavens would unlock the secrets of the universe. For over twenty years, he charted the movements of significant objects in the night sky, compiling the finest set of astronomical data in Europe.

British Commonwealth of Nations Formed in 1926, the Commonwealth conferred "dominion status" on Britain's white settler colonies in Canada, Australia, and New Zealand.

Bronze Age (3200–1200 B.C.E.) The name given to the era characterized by the discovery of techniques for smelting bronze (an alloy of copper and tin), which was then the strongest known metal.

Brownshirts Troops of young German men who dedicated themselves to the Nazi cause in the early 1930s by holding street marches, mass rallies, and confrontations. They engaged in beatings of Jews and anyone who opposed the Nazis.

Lord Byron (1788–1824) Writer and poet whose life helped give the Romantics their reputation as rebels against conformity. He was known for his love affairs, his defense of working-class movements, and his passionate engagement in politics, which led to his death in the war for Greek independence.

Byzantium The name of a small settlement located at the mouth of the Black Sea and at the crossroads between Europe and Asia, it was chosen by Constantine as the site for his new imperial capital of Constantinople in 324 C.E. Modern historians use this name to refer to the eastern Roman Empire that persisted in this region until 1453, but the inhabitants of that empire referred to themselves as Romans.

Julius Caesar (100–44 B.C.E.) The Roman general who conquered the Gauls, invaded Britain, and expanded Rome's territory in Asia Minor. He became the dictator of Rome in 46 B.C.E. His assassination led to the rise of his grandnephew and adopted son, Gaius Octavius Caesar, who ruled the Roman Empire as Caesar Augustus.

caliphs Islamic rulers who claim descent from the prophet Muhammad.

John Calvin (1509–1564) French-born theologian and reformer whose radical form of Protestantism was adopted in many Swiss cities, notably Geneva.

Canary Islands Islands off the western coast of Africa that were colonized by Portugal and Spain in the mid-fifteenth century, after which they became bases for further expeditions around the African coast and across the Atlantic.

Carbonari An underground organization that opposed the Concert of Europe's restoration of monarchies. They held influence in southern Europe during the 1820s, especially in Italy.

Carolingian Derived from the Latin name Carolus (Charles), this term refers to the Frankish dynasty that began with the rise to power of Charlemagne's grandfather, Charles Martel (688–741). At its height under Charlemagne (Charles the Great), the dynasty controlled what is now France, Germany, northern Italy, Catalonia and portions of central Europe. The Carolingian Empire collapsed under the combined weight of Viking raids, economic disintegration, and the growing power of local lords.

Carolingian Renaissance A cultural and intellectual flowering that took place around the court of Charlemagne in the late eighth and early ninth centuries.

Carthage The great maritime empire that grew out of Phoenician trading colonies in North Africa and rivaled the power of Rome. Its wars with Rome, collectively known as the Punic Wars, ended in its destruction in 146 B.C.E.

Cassidorus (c. 490–c. 583) Member of an old senatorial family, he was largely responsible for introducing classical learning into the monastic curriculum and for turning monasteries into centers for the collection, preservation, and transmission of knowledge. His *Institutes*, an influential handbook of classical literature for Christian readers, was intended as a preface to more intensive study of theology and the Bible.

Catholic Church The "universal" (catholic) church based in Rome, which was redefined in the sixteenth century, when the Counter-Reformation resulted in the rebirth of the Catholic faith at the Council of Trent.

Margaret Cavendish (1623–1673) English natural philosopher who developed her own speculative natural philosophy. She used this philosophy to critique those who excluded her from scientific debate.

Camillo Benso di Cavour (1810–1861) Prime minister of Piedmont-Sardinia and founder of the Italian Liberal Party; he played a key role in the movement for Italian unification under the Piedmontese king, Victor Emmanuel II.

Central Powers The First World War alliance between Germany, Austria-Hungary, Bulgaria, and Turkey.

Charlemagne (742–814) As king of the Franks (767–813), Charles "the Great" consolidated much of western Europe under his rule. In 800 he was crowned emperor by the pope in Rome, establishing a problematic precedent that would have wide-ranging consequences for western Europe's relationship with the eastern Roman Empire in Byzantium and for the relationship between the papacy and secular rulers.

Charles I (1625–1649) The second Stuart king of England, Charles attempted to rule without the support of Parliament, sparking a controversy that erupted into civil war in 1642. The king's forces were ultimately defeated and Charles himself was executed by act of Parliament, the first time in history that a reigning king was legally deposed and executed by his own government.

Chartists A working-class movement in Britain which called for reform of the political system in Britain during the 1840s. They were supporters of the "People's Charter," which had six demands: universal white male suffrage, secret ballots, an end to property qualifications as a condition of public office, annual parliamentary elections, salaries for members of the House of Commons, and equal electoral districts.

Chernobyl (1986) Site of the world's worst nuclear power accident; in Ukraine, formerly part of the Soviet Union.

Christine de Pisan (c. 1364–c. 1431) Born in Italy, Christine spent her adult life attached to the French court and, after her husband's death, became the first lay woman to earn her living by writing. She is the author of treatises in warfare and chivalry, as well as of books and pamphlets that challenge longstanding misogynistic claims.

Church of England Founded by Henry VIII in the 1530s, as a consequence of his break with the authority of the Roman pope.

Winston Churchill (1874–1965) British prime minister who led the country during the Second World War. He also coined the phrase "Iron Curtain" in a speech at Westminster College in 1946.

Cicero (106–43 B.C.E.) Influential Roman senator, orator, Stoic philosopher, and prose stylist. His published writings still form the basis of the instruction in classical Latin grammar and usage.

Cincinnatus (519–c. 430 B.C.E.) A legendary citizen-farmer of Rome who reluctantly accepted an appointment as dictator. After defeating Rome's enemies, he allegedly left his political office and returned to his farm.

Civil Constitution of the Clergy Issued by the French National Assembly in 1790, the Civil Constitution of the Clergy decreed that all bishops and priests should be subject to the authority of the state. Their salaries were to be paid out of the public treasury, and they were required to swear allegiance to the new state, making it clear they served France rather than Rome. The Assembly's aim was to make the Catholic Church of France a truly national and civil institution.

civilizing mission An argument made by Europeans to justify colonial expansion in the nineteenth century. Supporters of this idea believed that Europeans had a duty to impose western ideas of economic and political progress on the indigenous peoples they ruled over in their colonies. In practice, the colonial powers often found that ambitious plans to impose European practices on colonial subjects led to unrest that threatened the stability of colonial rule, and by the early twentieth century most colonial powers were more cautious in their plans for political or cultural transformation.

Civil Rights Movement The Second World War increased African American migration from the American South to northern cities, intensifying a drive for rights, dignity, and independence. By 1960, civil rights groups had started organizing boycotts and demonstrations directed at discrimination against blacks in the South. During the 1960s, civil rights laws passed under President Lyndon B. Johnson did bring African Americans some equality with regard to voting rights and, to a much lesser degree, school desegregation. However, racism continued in

areas such as housing, job opportunities, and the economic development of African American communities.

Civil War (1861–1865) Conflict between the northern and southern states of America that cost over 600,000 lives; this struggle led to the abolition of slavery in the United States.

Classical learning The study of ancient Greek and Latin texts. After Christianity became the only legal religion of the Roman Empire, scholars needed to find a way to make classical learning applicable to a Christian way of life. Christian monks played a significant role in resolving this problem by reinterpreting the classics for a Christian audience.

Cluny A powerful Benedictine monastery founded in 910 whose enormous wealth and prestige would derive from its independence from secular authorities, as well as from its wide network of daughter houses (priories).

Cold War (1945–1991) Ideological, political, and economic conflict in which the USSR and Eastern Europe opposed the United States and Western Europe in the decades after the Second World War. The Cold War's origins lay in the breakup of the wartime alliance between the United States and the Soviet Union in 1945, and resulted in a division of Europe into two spheres: the West, commited to market capitalism, and the East, which sought to build Socialist republics in areas under Soviet Control. The Cold War ended with the collapse of the Soviet Union in 1991.

collectivization Stalin's plan for nationalizing agricultural production, begun in 1929. 25 million peasants were forced to give up their land and join 250,000 large collective farms. Many who resisted were deported to labor camps in the Far East, and Stalin's government cut off food rations to those areas most marked by resistance to collectivization. In the ensuing man-made famines, millions of people starved to death.

Christopher Columbus (1451–1506) A Genoese sailor who persuaded King Ferdinand and Queen Isabella of Spain to fund his expedition across the Atlantic, with the purpose of discovering a new trade route to Asia. His miscalculations landed him in the Bahamas and the island of Hispaniola in 1492.

Committee of Public Safety Political body during the French Revolution that was controlled by the Jacobins, who defended the revolution by executing thousands during the Reign of Terror (September 1793–July 1794).

commune A community of individuals who have banded together in a sworn association, with the aim of establishing their independence and setting up their own form of representative government. Many medieval towns originally founded by lords or monasteries gained their independence through such methods.

The Communist Manifesto Radical pamphlet by Karl Marx (1818–1883) that predicted the downfall of the capitalist system and its replacement by a classless egalitarian society. Marx believed that this revolution would be accomplished by workers (the proletariat).

Compromise of 1867 Agreement between the Habsburgs and the peoples living in Hungarian parts of the empire that the Habsburg state would be officially known as the Austro-Hungarian Empire.

Concert of Europe (1814–1815) The body of diplomatic agreements designed primarily by Austrian minister Klemens von Metternich between 1814 and 1848, and supported by other European powers until 1914. Its goal was to maintain a balance of power on the Continent and to prevent destabilizing social and political change in Europe.

Congress of Vienna (1814–1815) **and Restoration** International conference to reorganize Europe after the downfall of Napoleon and the French Revolution. European monarchies restored the Bourbon family to the French throne, agreed to respect each other's borders and to cooperate in guarding against future revolutions and war.

conquistador Spanish term for "conqueror," applied to the mercenaries and adventurers who campaigned against indigenous peoples in central and southern America.

Conservatism In the nineteenth century, conservatives aimed to legitimize and solidify the monarchy's authority and the hierarchical social order. They believed that change had to be slow, incremental, and managed so that the structures of authority were strengthened and not weakened.

Constantine (275–337) The first emperor of Rome to convert to Christianity, Constantine came to power in 312. In 324, he founded a new imperial capital, Constantinople, on the site of a maritime settlement known as Byzantium.

Constantinople Founded by the emperor Constantine on the site of a village called Byzantium, Constantinople became the new capital of the Roman Empire in 324 and continued to be the seat of imperial power after its capture by the Ottoman Turks in 1453. It is now known as Istanbul.

Nicholas Copernicus (1473–1543) Polish astronomer who advanced the idea that the earth moved around the sun.

cosmopolitanism Stemming from the Greek word meaning "universal city," the culture characteristic of the Hellenistic world challenged and transformed the more narrow worldview of the Greek polis.

cotton gin Invented by Eli Whitney in 1793, this device mechanized the process of separating cotton seeds from the cotton fiber, which sped up the production of cotton and reduced its price. This change made slavery profitable in the United States.

Council of Constance (1417–1420) A meeting of clergy and theologians in an effort to resolve the Great Schism within the Roman Church. The council deposed all rival papal candidates and elected a new pope, Martin V, but it also adopted the doctrine of conciliarism, which holds that the supreme authority within the Church rests with a representative general council and not with the pope. However, Martin V himself was an opponent of this doctrine, and refused to be bound by it.

Council of Trent The name given to a series of meetings held in the Italian city of Trent (Trento) between 1545 and 1563, when leaders of the Roman Church reaffirmed Catholic doctrine and instituted internal reforms.

Counter-Reformation The movement to counter the Protestant Reformation, initiated by the Catholic Church at the Council of Trent in 1545.

coup d'état French term for the overthrow of an established government by a group of conspirators, usually with military support.

Crimean War (1854–1856) War waged by Russia against Great Britain and France. Spurred by Russia's encroachment on Ottoman territories, the conflict revealed Russia's military weakness when Russian forces fell to British and French troops.

Cuban missile crisis (1962) Diplomatic standoff between the United States and the Soviet Union that was provoked by the Soviet Union's attempt to base nuclear missiles in Cuba; it brought the world closer to nuclear war than ever before or since.

Cuius regio, eius religio A Latin phrase meaning "as the ruler, so the religion." Adopted as a part of the settlement of the Peace of Augsburg in 1555, it meant that those principalities ruled by Lutherans would have Lutheranism as their official religion and those ruled by Catholics must practice Catholicism.

cult of domesticity Concept associated with Victorian England that idealized women as nurturing wives and mothers.

cult of the Virgin The beliefs and practices associated with the veneration of Mary the mother of Jesus, which became increasingly popular in the twelfth century.

cuneiform An early writing system that began to develop in Mesopotamia in the fourth millennium B.C.E. By 3100 B.C.E., its distinctive markings were impressed on clay tablets using a wedge-shaped stylus.

Cyrus the Great (c. 585–529 B.C.E.) As architect of the Persian Empire, Cyrus extended his dominion over a vast territory stretching from the Persian Gulf to the Mediterranean and incorporating the ancient civilizations of Mesopotamia. His successors ruled this Persian Empire as "Great Kings."

Darius (521–486 B.C.E.) The Persian emperor whose conflict with Aristagoras, the Greek ruler of Miletus, ignited the Persian Wars. In 490 B.C.E., Darius sent a large army to punish the Athenians for their intervention in Persian imperial affairs, but this force was defeated by Athenian hoplites on the plain of Marathon.

Charles Darwin (1809–1882) British naturalist who wrote *On the Origin of Species* and developed the theory of natural selection to explain the evolution of organisms.

D-Day (June 6, 1944) Date of the Allied invasion of Normandy, under General Dwight Eisenhower, to liberate Western Europe from German occupation.

Decembrists Russian army officers who were influenced by events in France and formed secret societies that espoused liberal governance. They were put down by Nicholas I in December 1825.

Declaration of Independence (1776) Historic document stating the principles of government on which the United States was founded.

Declaration of the Rights of Man and of the Citizen (1789) French charter of liberties formulated by the National Assembly during the French Revolution. The seventeen articles later became the preamble to the new constitution, which the Assembly finished in 1791.

democracy In ancient Greece, this form of government allowed a class of propertied male citizens to participate in the governance of their polis; but excluded women, slaves, and citizens without property from the political process. As a result, the ruling class amounted to only a small percentage of the entire population.

René Descartes (1596–1650) French philosopher and mathematician who emphasized the use of deductive reasoning.

Denis Diderot (1713–1784) French *philosophe* and author who was the guiding force behind the publication of the first encyclopedia. The encyclopedia showed how reason could be applied to nearly all realms of thought, and aimed to be a compendium of all human knowledge.

Dien Bien Phu (1954) Defining battle in the war between French colonialists and the Viet Minh that secured North Vietnam for Ho Chi Minh and his army and left the south to form its own government, to be supported by France and the United States.

Diet of Worms The select council of the Church that convened in the German city of Worms and condemned Martin Luther on a charge of heresy in 1521.

Diocletian (245–316) As emperor of Rome from 284 to 305, Diocletian recognized that the empire could not be governed by one man in one place. His solution was to divide the empire into four parts, each with its own imperial ruler, but he himself remained the dominant ruler of the resulting tetrarchy (rule of four). He also initiated the Great Persecution, a time when many Christians became martyrs to their faith.

Directory (1795–1799) Executive committee that governed after the fall of Robespierre and held control until the coup of Napoleon Bonaparte.

Discourse on Method Philosophical treatise by René Descartes (1596–1650) proposing that the path to knowledge was through logical deduction, beginning with one's own self: "I think, therefore I am."

Dominican Order Also called the Order of Preachers, it was founded by Dominic of Osma (1170–1221), a Castilian preacher and theologian, and approved by Innocent III in 1216. The order was dedicated to the rooting out of heresy and the conversion of Jews and Muslims. Many of its members held teaching positions in European universities and contributed to the development of medieval philosophy and theology. Others became the leading administrators of the Inquisition.

Dominion in the British Commonwealth Canadian promise to maintain their fealty to the British crown, even after their independence in 1867. Later applied to Australia and New Zealand.

Dreyfus Affair The 1894 French scandal surrounding accusations that a Jewish captain, Alfred Dreyfus, sold military secrets to the Germans. Convicted, Dreyfus was sentenced to solitary confinement for life. However, after public outcry, it was revealed that the trial documents were forgeries, and Dreyfus was pardoned after a second trial in 1899. In 1906 he was fully exonerated and reinstated in the army. The affair revealed the depths of popular anti-Semitism in France.

Alexander Dubček (1921–1992) Communist leader of the Czechoslovakian government who advocated for "socialism with a human face." He encouraged debate within the party, academic and artistic freedom, and less censorship, which led to the "Prague spring" of 1968. People in other parts of Eastern Europe began to demonstrate in support of Dubček and demand their own reforms. When Dubček tried to democratize the Communist party and did not attend a meeting of the

Warsaw Pact, the Soviets sent tanks and troops into Prague and ousted Dubček and his allies.

Duma The Russian parliament, created in response to the revolution of 1905.

Dunkirk The French port on the English Channel where the British and French forces retreated after sustaining heavy losses against the German military. Between May 27 and June 4, 1940, the Royal Navy evacuated over three hundred thousand troops using commercial and pleasure boats.

Earth Summit (1992) Meeting in Rio de Janeiro between many of the world's governments in an effort to address international environmental problems.

Eastern Front Battlefront between Berlin and Moscow during the First and Second World Wars..

East India Company (1600–1858) British charter company created to outperform Portuguese and Spanish traders in the Far East; in the eighteenth century the company became, in effect, the ruler of a large part of India. There was also a Dutch East India Company.

Edict of Nantes (1598) Issued by Henry IV of France in an effort to end religious violence. The edict declared France to be a Catholic country, but tolerated some forms of Protestant worship.

Eleanor of Aquitaine (1122–1204) Ruler of the wealthy province of Aquitaine and wife of Louis VII of France, Eleanor had her marriage annulled in order to marry the young count of Anjou, Henry Plantagenet, who became King Henry of England a year later. Mother of two future kings of England, she was an important patron of the arts.

Elizabeth I (1533–1603) Protestant daughter of Henry VIII and his second wife, Anne Boleyn, Elizabeth succeeded her sister Mary as the second queen regnant of England (1558–1603).

emancipation of the serfs (1861) The abolition of serfdom was central to Tsar Alexander II's program of modernization and reform, but it produced a limited amount of change. Former serfs now had legal rights. However, farm land was granted to the village communes instead of to individuals. The land was of poor quality and the former serfs had to pay for it in installments to the village commune.

emperor Originally the term for any conquering commander of the Roman army whose victories merited celebration in an official triumph. After Augustus seized power in 27 B.C.E., it was the title born by the sole ruler of the Roman Empire.

empire A centralized political entity consolidated through the conquest and colonization of other nations or peoples in order to benefit the ruler and/or his homeland.

Enabling Act (1933) Emergency act passed by the Reichstag (German parliament) that helped transform Hitler from Germany's chancellor, or prime minister, into a dictator, following the suspicious burning of the Reichstag building and a suspension of civil liberties.

enclosure Long process of privatizing what had been public agricultural land in eighteenth-century Britain; it helped to stimulate the development of commercial agriculture and forced many people in rural areas to seek work in cities during the early stages of industrialization.

The Encyclopedia Joint venture of French *philosophe* writers, led by Denis Diderot (1713–1784), which proposed to summarize all modern knowledge in a multivolume illustrated work with over 70,000 articles.

Friedrich Engels (1820–1895) German social and political philosopher who collaborated with Karl Marx on many publications.

English Civil War (1642–1649) Conflicts between the English Parliament and King Charles I erupted into civil war, which ended in the defeat of the royalists and the execution of Charles on charges of treason against the crown. A short time later, Parliament's hereditary House of Lords was abolished and England was declared a Commonwealth.

English Navigation Act of 1651 Act stipulating that only English ships could carry goods between the mother country and its colonies.

Enlightenment Intellectual movement in eighteenth-century Europe, that believed in human betterment through the application of reason to solve social, economic, and political problems.

Epicureanism A philosophical position articulated by Epicurus of Athens (c. 342–270 B.C.E.), who rejected the idea of an ordered universe governed by divine forces; instead, he emphasized individual agency and proposed that the highest good is the pursuit of pleasure.

Desiderius Erasmus (c. 1469–1536) Dutch-born scholar, social commentator, and Catholic humanist whose new translation of the Bible influenced the theology of Martin Luther.

Estates-General The representative body of the three estates in France. In 1789, King Louis XVI summoned the Estates-General to meet for the first time since 1614 because it seemed to be the only solution to France's worsening economic crisis and financial chaos.

Etruscans Settlers of the Italian peninsula who dominated the region from the late Bronze Age until the rise of the Roman Republic in the sixth century B.C.E.

Euclid Hellenistic mathematician whose *Elements of Geometry* forms the basis of modern geometry.

eugenics A Greek term, meaning "good birth," referring to the project of "breeding" a superior human race. It was popularly championed by scientists, politicians, and social critics in the late nineteenth and early twentieth centuries.

European Common Market (1957) The Treaty of Rome created the European Economic Community (EEC) or Common Market. The original members were France, West Germany, Italy, Belgium, Holland, and Luxembourg. The EEC sought to abolish trade barriers between its members and it pledged itself to common external tariffs, the free movement of labor and capital among the member nations, and uniform wage structures and social security systems to create similar working conditions in all member countries.

European Union (EU) Successor organization to the European Economic Community or European Common Market, formed by the Maastricht Treaty, which took effect in 1993. Currently 27 member states compose the EU, which has a governing council, an international court, and a parliament. Over time, member states of the EU have relinquished some of their sovereignty, and cooperation has evolved into a community with a single currency, the euro.

Exclusion Act of 1882 U.S. congressional act prohibiting nearly all immigration from China to the United States; fueled by animosity toward Chinese workers in the American West.

existentialism Philosophical movement that arose out of the Second World War and emphasized the absurdity of human condition. Led by Jean-Paul Sartre and Albert Camus, existentialists encouraged humans to take responsibility for their own decisions and dilemmas.

fascism The doctrine founded by Benito Mussolini, which emphasized three main ideas: statism ("nothing above the state, nothing outside the state, nothing against the state"), nationalism, and militarism. Its name derives from the Latin *fasces*, a symbol of Roman imperial power adopted by Mussolini.

Fashoda Incident (1898) Disagreements between the French and the British over land claims in North Africa led to a standoff between armies of the two nations at the Sudanese town of Fashoda. The crisis was solved diplomatically. France ceded southern Sudan to Britain in exchange for a stop to further expansion by the British.

The Feminine Mystique Groundbreaking book by feminist Betty Friedan (b. 1921), which tried to define "femininity" and explored how women internalized those definitions.

Franz Ferdinand (1863–1914) Archduke of Austria and heir to the Austro-Hungarian Empire; his assassination led to the beginning of the First World War.

Ferdinand (1452–1516) **and Isabella** (1451–1504) In 1469, Ferdinand of Aragon married the heiress to Castile, Isabella. Their union allowed them to pursue several ambitious policies, including the conquest of Granada, the last Muslim principality in Spain, and the expulsion of Spain's large Jewish community. In 1492, Isabella granted three ships to Christopher Columbus of Genoa (Italy), who went on to claim portions of the New World for Spain.

Fertile Crescent An area of fertile land in what is now Syria, Israel, Turkey, eastern Iraq, and western Iran that was able to sustain settlements due to its wetter climate and abundant natural food resources. Some of the earliest known civilizations emerged there between 9000 and 4500 B.C.E.

feudalism A problematic modern term that attempts to explain the diffusion of power in medieval Europe, and the many different kinds of political, social, and economic relationships that were forged through the giving and receiving of fiefs (*feoda*). But because it is anachronistic and inadequate, this term has been rejected by most historians of the medieval period.

First Crusade (1095–1099) Launched by Pope Urban II in response to a request from the Byzantine emperor Alexius Comnenus, who had asked for a small contingent of knights to assist him in fighting Turkish forces in Anatolia; Urban instead directed the crusaders' energies toward the Holy Land and the recapture of Jerusalem, promising those who took the cross (*crux*) that they would merit eternal salvation if they died in the attempt. This crusade prompted attacks against Jews throughout Europe

and resulted in six subsequent—and unsuccessful—military campaigns.

First World War A total war from August 1914 to November 1918, involving the armies of Britain, France, and Russia (the Allies) against Germany, Austria-Hungary, and the Ottoman Empire (the Central Powers). Italy joined the Allies in 1915, and the United States joined them in 1917, helping to tip the balance in favor of the Allies, who also drew upon the populations and raw materials of their colonial possessions. Also known as the Great War.

Five Pillars of Islam The Muslim teaching that salvation is only assured through observance of five basic precepts: submission to God's will as described in the teachings of Muhammad, frequent prayer, ritual fasting, the giving of alms, and an annual pilgrimage to Mecca (the Hajj).

Five-Year Plan Soviet effort launched under Stalin in 1928 to replace the market with a state-owned and state-managed economy in order to promote rapid economic development over a five-year period and thereby "catch and overtake" the leading capitalist countries. The First Five-Year Plan was followed by the Second Five-Year Plan (1933–1937) and so on, until the collapse of the Soviet Union in 1991.

fly shuttle Invented by John Kay in 1733, this device sped up the process of weaving.

Fourteen Points President Woodrow Wilson proposed these points as the foundation on which to build peace in the world after the First World War. They called for an end to secret treaties, "open covenants, openly arrived at," freedom of the seas, the removal of international tariffs, the reduction of arms, the "self-determination of peoples," and the establishment of a League of Nations to settle international conflicts.

Franciscan Order Also known as the Order of the Friars Minor. The earliest Franciscans were followers of Francis of Assisi (1182–1226) and strove, like him, to imitate the life and example of Jesus. The order was formally established by Pope Innocent III in 1209. Its special mission was the care and instruction of the urban poor.

Frankfurt Parliament (1848–1849) Failed attempt to create a unified Germany under constitutional principles. In 1849, the assembly offered the crown of the new German nation to Frederick William IV of Prussia, but he refused the offer and suppressed a brief protest. The delegates went home disillusioned.

Frederick the Great (1712–1786) Prussian ruler (1740–1786) who engaged the nobility in maintaining a strong military and bureaucracy, and led Prussian armies to notable military victories. He also encouraged Enlightenment rationalism and artistic endeavors.

French Revolution of 1789 In 1788, a severe financial crisis forced the French monarchy to convene an assembly known as the Estates General, representing the three estates of the realm: the clergy, the nobility, and the commons (known as the Third Estate). When the Estates General met in 1789, representatives of the Third Estate demanded major constitutional changes, and when the King and his government proved uncooperative, the Third Estate broke with the other two estates and renamed themselves the National Assembly, demanding a written constitution. The position of the National Assembly was confirmed by a popular uprising in Paris and the King was forced to accept the transformation of France into a constitutional monarchy. This constitutional phase of the revolution lasted until 1972, when the pressures of foreign invasion and the emergence of a more radical revolutionary movement caused the collapse of the monarchy and the establishment of a Republic in France.

French Revolution of 1830 The French popular revolt against Charles X's July Ordinances of 1830, which dissolved the French Chamber of Deputies and restricted suffrage to exclude almost everyone except the nobility. After several days of violence, Charles abdicated the throne and was replaced by a constitutional monarch, Louis Philippe.

French Revolution of 1848 Revolution overthrowing Louis Philippe in February, 1848, leading to the formation of the Second Republic (1848–1852). Initially enjoying broad support from both the middle classes and laborers in Paris, the new government became more conservative after elections in which the French peasantry participated for the first time. A workers' revolt was violently repressed in June, 1848, and in December 1848, Napoleon Bonaparte's nephew, Louis-Napoleon Bonaparte, was elected president. In 1852, Louis-Napoleon declared himself emperor and abolished the republic.

Sigmund Freud (1856–1939) The Austrian physician who founded the discipline of psychoanalysis and suggested that human behavior was largely motivated by unconscious and irrational forces.

Galileo Galilei (1564–1642) Italian physicist and inventor; the implications of his ideas raised the ire of the Catholic Church, and he was forced to retract most of his findings.

Gallipoli (1915) In the First World War, a combined force of French, British, Australian and New Zealand troops tried to invade the Gallipoli peninsula, in the first large-scale amphibious attack in history, and seize it from the Turks. After seven months of fighting, the Allies had lost 200,000 soldiers. Defeated, they withdrew.

Mohandas K. (Mahatma) Gandhi (1869–1948) The Indian leader who advocated nonviolent noncooperation to protest colonial rule and helped win home rule for India in 1947.

Giuseppe Garibaldi (1807–1882) Italian revolutionary leader who led the fight to free Sicily and Naples from the Habsburg Empire; the lands were then peaceably annexed by Sardinia to produce a unified Italy.

Gaul The region of the Roman Empire that was home to the Celtic people of that name, comprising modern France, Belgium, and western Germany.

Geneva Peace Conference (1954) International conference to restore peace in Korea and Indochina. The chief participants were the United States, the Soviet Union, Great Britain, France, the People's Republic of China, North Korea, South Korea, Vietnam, the Viet Minh party, Laos, and Cambodia. The conference resulted in the division of North and South Vietnam.

Genoese Inhabitants of the maritime city on Italy's northwestern coast, the Genoese were active in trading ventures along the Silk Road and in the establishment of trading colonies in the Mediterranean. They were also involved in the world of finance and backed the commercial ventures of other powers, especially Spain's.

German Democratic Republic Nation founded from the Soviet zone of occupation of Germany after the Second World War; also known as East Germany.

German Social Democratic Party Founded in 1875, it was the most powerful socialist party in Europe before 1917.

Gilgamesh Sumerian ruler of the city of Uruk around 2700 B.C.E., Gilgamesh became the hero of one of the world's oldest epics, which circulated orally for nearly a millennium before being written down.

globalization The term used to describe political, social, and economic networks that span the globe. These global exchanges are not limited by nation-states and in recent decades are associated with new technologies, such as the Internet. Globalization is not new, however, as human cultures and economies have been in contact with one another for centuries.

Gold Coast Name that European mariners and merchants gave to that part of West Equatorial Africa from which gold and slaves were exported. Originally controlled by the Portuguese, this area later became the British colony of the Gold Coast.

Mikhail Gorbachev (1931–) Soviet leader who attempted to reform the Soviet Union through his programs of *glasnost* and *perestroika* in the late 1980s. He encouraged open discussions in other countries in the Soviet bloc, which helped inspire the velvet revolutions throughout Eastern Europe. Eventually the political, social, and economic upheaval he had unleashed would lead to the breakup of the Soviet Union.

Gothic style A type of graceful architecture emerging in twelfth- and thirteenth-century England and France. The style is characterized by pointed arches, delicate decoration, and large windows.

Olympe de Gouges (1748–1793) French political radical and feminist whose *Declaration of the Rights of Woman* demanded an equal place for women in France.

Great Depression Global economic crisis following the U.S. stock market crash on October 29, 1929, and ending with the onset of the Second World War.

Great Fear (1789) Following the outbreak of revolution in Paris, fear spread throughout the French countryside, as rumors circulated that armies of brigands or royal troops were coming. The peasants and villagers organized into militias, while others attacked and burned the manor houses in order to destroy the records of manorial dues.

Great Schism (1378–1417) Also known as the Great Western Schism, to distinguish it from the longstanding rupture between the Greek East and Latin West. During the schism, the Roman Church was divided between two (and, ultimately, three) competing popes. Each pope claimed to be legitimate and each denounced the heresy of the others.

Great Terror (1936–1938) The systematic murder of nearly a million people and the deportation of another million and a half to labor camps by Stalin's regime in an attempt to consolidate power and remove perceived enemies.

Greek East After the founding of Constantinople, the eastern Greek-speaking half of the Roman Empire grew more populous, prosperous and central to imperial policy. Its inhabitants considered themselves to be the true heirs of Rome, and their own Orthodox Church to be the true manifestation of Jesus' ministry.

Greek Independence Nationalists in Greece revolted against the Ottoman Empire and fought a war that ended in Greek independence in 1827. They received crucial help from British, French, and Russian troops as well as widespread sympathy throughout Europe.

Pope Gregory I (r. 590–604) Also known as Gregory the Great, he was the first bishop of Rome to successfully negotiate a more universal role for the papacy. His political and theological agenda widened the rift between the western Latin (Catholic) Church and the eastern Greek (Orthodox) Church in Byzantium. He also articulated the Church's official position on the status of Jews, promoted affective approaches to religious worship, encouraged the Benedictine monastic movement, and sponsored missionary expeditions.

Guernica The Basque town bombed by German planes in April 1937 during the Spanish Civil War. It is also the subject of Pablo Picasso's famous painting from the same year.

guilds Professional organizations in commercial towns that regulated business and safeguarded the privileges of those practicing a particular craft. Often identical to confraternities ("brotherhoods").

Gulag The vast system of forced labor camps under the Soviet regime; it originated in 1919 in a small monastery near the Arctic Circle and spread throughout the Soviet Union. Penal labor was required of both ordinary criminals and those accused of political crimes. Tens of millions of people were sent to the camps between 1928 and 1953; the exact figure is unknown.

Gulf War (1991) Armed conflict between Iraq and a coalition of thirty-two nations, including the United States, Britain, Egypt, France, and Saudi Arabia. The seeds of the war were planted with Iraq's invasion of Kuwait on August 2, 1990.

Habsburg Empire Ruling house of Austria, which once ruled the Netherlands, Spain, and central Europe but came to settle in lands along the Danube River. It played a prominent role in European affairs for many centuries. In 1867, the Habsburg Empire was reorganized into the Austro-Hungarian Dual Monarchy, and in 1918 it collapsed.

Hagia Sophia The enormous church dedicated to "Holy Wisdom," built in Constantinople at the behest of the emperor Justinian in the sixth century C.E. When Constantinople fell to Ottoman forces in 1453, it became an important mosque.

Haitian Revolution (1802–1804) In 1802, Napoleon sought to reassert French control of Saint-Domingue, but stiff resistance and yellow fever crushed the French army. In 1804, Jean-Jacques Dessalines, a general in the army of former slaves, declared the independent state of Haiti. (See **slave revolt in Saint-Domingue**)

Hajj The annual pilgrimage to Mecca; an obligation for Muslims.

Hammurabi Ruler of Babylon from 1792 to 1750 B.C.E., Hammurabi issued a collection of laws that were greatly influential in the Near East and which constitute the world's oldest surviving law code.

Harlem Renaissance Cultural movement in the 1920s that was based in Harlem, a part of New York City with a large African American population. The movement gave voice to black novelists, poets, painters, and musicians, many of whom used their art to protest racial subordination.

Hatshepsut (1479–1458 C.E.) As a pharaoh during the New Kingdom, she launched several successful military campaigns and extended trade and diplomacy. She was an ambitious builder who probably constructed the first tomb in the Valley of the Kings. Though she never pretended to be a man, she was routinely portrayed with a masculine figure and a ceremonial beard.

Hebrews Originally a pastoral people divided among several tribes, they were briefly united under the rule of David and his son, Solomon, who promoted the worship of a single god, Yahweh, and constructed the first temple at the new capital city of Jerusalem. After Solomon's death, the Hebrew tribes were divided between the two kingdoms of Israel and Judah, which were eventually conquered by the Neo-Assyrian and Chaldean empires. It was in captivity that the Hebrews came to define themselves through worship of Yahweh, and to develop a religion, Judaism, that could exist outside of Judea. They were liberated by the Persian king Cyrus the Great in 539 B.C.E.

Hellenistic art The art of the Hellenistic period bridged the tastes, ideals, and customs of classical Greece and those that would be more characteristic of Rome. The Romans strove to emulate Hellenistic city planning and civic culture, and thereby exported Hellenistic culture to their own far-flung colonies in western Europe.

Hellenistic culture The "Greek-like" culture that dominated the ancient world in the wake of Alexander's conquests.

Hellenistic kingdoms Following the death of Alexander the Great, his vast empire was divided into three separate states: Ptolemaic Egypt (under the rule of the general Ptolemy and his successors), Seleucid Asia (ruled by the general Seleucus and his heirs) and Antigonid Greece (governed by Antigonus of Macedonia). Each state maintained its independence, but the shared characteristics of Greco-Macedonian rule and a shared Greek culture and heritage bound them together in a united cosmopolitan world.

Hellenistic world The various western civilizations of antiquity that were loosely united by shared Greek language and culture, especially around the eastern Mediterranean.

Heloise (c. 1090–1164) One of the foremost scholars of her time, she became the pupil and the wife of the philosopher and teacher Peter Abelard. In later life, she was the founder of a new religious order for women.

Henry VIII (1491–1547) King of England from 1509 until his death, Henry rejected the authority of the Roman Church in 1534 when the pope refused to annul his marriage to his queen, Catherine of Aragon; he became the founder of the Church of England.

Henry of Navarre (1553–1610) Crowned King Henry IV of France, he renounced his Protestantism but granted limited toleration for Huguenots (French Protestants) by the Edict of Nantes in 1598.

Prince Henry the Navigator (1394–1460) A member of the Portuguese royal family, Henry encouraged the exploration and conquest of western Africa and the trade in gold and slaves.

hieroglyphs The writing system of ancient Egypt, based on a complicated series of pictorial symbols. It fell out of use when Egypt was absorbed into the Roman Empire, and was only deciphered after the discovery of the Rosetta Stone in the early nineteenth century.

Hildegard of Bingen (1098–1179) A powerful abbess, theologian, scientist, musician, and visionary who claimed to receive regular revelations from God. Although highly influential in her own day, she was never officially canonized by the Church, in part because her strong personality no longer matched the changing ideal of female piety.

Hiroshima Japanese port devastated by an atomic bomb on August 6, 1945.

Adolf Hitler (1889–1945) The author of *Mein Kampf* and leader of the Nazis who became chancellor of Germany in 1933. Hitler and his Nazi regime started the Second World War and orchestrated the systematic murder of over five million Jews.

Hitler-Stalin Pact (1939) Treaty between Stalin and Hitler, which promised Stalin a share of Poland, Finland, the Baltic States, and Bessarabia in the event of a German invasion of Poland, which began shortly thereafter, on September 1, 1939.

HIV epidemic The first cases of HIV-AIDS appeared in the late 1970s. As HIV-AIDS became a global crisis, international organizations recognized the need for an early, swift, and comprehensive response to future outbreaks of disease.

Thomas Hobbes (1588–1679) English political philosopher whose *Leviathan* argued that any form of government capable of protecting its subjects' lives and property might act as an all-powerful sovereign. This government should be allowed to trample over both liberty and property for the sake of its own survival and that of his subjects. For in his natural state, Hobbes argued, man was like "a wolf" toward other men.

Holy Roman Empire The loosely allied collection of lands in central and western Europe ruled by the kings of Germany (and later Austria) from the twelfth century until 1806. Its origins are usually identified with the empire of Charlemagne, the Frankish king who was crowned emperor of Rome by the pope in 800.

homage A ceremony in which an individual becomes the "man" (French: *homme*) of a lord.

Homer (fl. 8ᵗʰ c. B.C.E.) A Greek rhapsode ("weaver" of stories) credited with merging centuries of poetic tradition in the epics known as the *Iliad* and the *Odyssey*.

hoplite A Greek foot-soldier armed with a spear or short sword and protected by a large round shield (*hoplon*). In battle, hoplites stood shoulder to shoulder in a close formation called a phalanx.

Huguenots French Protestants who endured severe persecution in the sixteenth and seventeenth centuries.

humanism A program of study associated with the movement known as the Renaissance, humanism aimed to replace the scholastic emphasis on logic and philosophy with the study of ancient languages, literature, history, and ethics.

human rights The belief that all people have the right to legal equality, freedom of religion and speech, and the right to participate in government. Human rights laws prohibit torture, cruel punishment, and slavery.

David Hume (1711–1776) Scottish writer who applied Newton's method of scientific inquiry and skepticism to the study of morality, the mind, and government.

Hundred Years' War (1337–1453) A series of wars between England and France, fought mostly on French soil and prompted by the territorial and political claims of English monarchs.

Jan Hus (c. 1373–1415) A Czech reformer who adopted many of the teachings of the English theolojan John Wyclif, and who also demanded that the laity be allowed to receive both the consecrated bread and wine of the Eucharist. The Council of Constance burned him at the stake for heresy. In response, his supporters, the Hussites, revolted against the Church.

Saddam Hussein (1937–2006) The former dictator of Iraq who invaded Iran in 1980 and started the eight-year-long Iran-Iraq War; invaded Kuwait in 1990, which led to the Gulf War of 1991; and was overthrown when the United States invaded Iraq in 2003. Involved in Iraqi politics since the mid-1960s, Hussein became the official head of state in 1979.

Iconoclast Controversy (717–787) A serious and often violent theological debate that raged in Byzantium after Emperor Leo III ordered the destruction of religious art on the grounds that any image representing a divine or holy personage is prone to promote idol worship and blasphemy. Iconoclast means "breaker of icons." Those who supported the veneration of icons were called "iconodules," "adherents of icons."

Il-khanate Mongol-founded dynasty in thirteenth-century Persia.

Indian National Congress Formed in 1885, this Indian political party worked to achieve Indian independence from British colonial control. The Congress was led by Ghandi in the 1920s and 1930s.

Indian Rebellion of 1857 The uprising began near Delhi, when the military disciplined a regiment of Indian soldiers employed by the British for refusing to use rifle cartridges greased with pork fat—unacceptable to either Hindus or Muslims. Rebels attacked law courts and burned tax rolls, protesting debt and corruption. The mutiny spread through large areas of northwest India before being violently suppressed by British troops.

Indo-Europeans A group of people speaking variations of the same language who moved into the Near East and Mediterranean region shortly after 2000 B.C.E.

indulgences Grants exempting Catholic Christians from the performance of penance, either in life or after death. The abusive trade in indulgences was a major catalyst of the Protestant Reformation.

Inkas The highly centralized South American empire that was toppled by the Spanish conquistador Francisco Pizarro in 1533.

Innocent III (1160/61–1216) As pope, he wanted to unify all of Christendom under papal hegemony. He furthered this goal at the Fourth Lateran Council of 1215, which defined one of the Church's dogmas as the acknowledgement of papal supremacy. The council also took an unprecedented interest in the religious education and habits of every Christian.

Inquisition Tribunal of the Roman Church that aims to enforce religious orthodoxy and conformity.

International Monetary Fund (IMF) Established in 1945 to ensure international cooperation regarding currency exchange and monetary policy, the IMF is a specialized agency of the United Nations.

Investiture Conflict The name given to a series of debates over the limitations of spiritual and secular power in Europe during the eleventh and early twelfth century, it came to a head when Pope Gregory VII and Emperor Henry IV of Germany both claimed the right to appoint and invest bishops with the regalia of office. After years of diplomatic and military hostility, it was partially settled by the Concordat of Worms in 1122.

Irish potato famine Period of agricultural blight from 1845 to 1849 whose devastating results produced widespread starvation and led to mass emigration to America.

Iron Curtain Term coined by Winston Churchill in 1946 to refer to the borders of Eastern European nations that lay within the zone of Soviet control.

Italian invasion of Ethiopia (1896) Italy invaded Ethiopia, which was the last major independent African kingdom. Menelik II, the Ethiopian emperor, soundly defeated them.

Ivan the Great (1440–1505) Russian ruler who annexed neighboring territories and consolidated his empire's position as a European power.

Jacobins Radical French political group during the French Revolution that took power after 1792, executed the French king, and sought to remake French culture.

Jacquerie Violent 1358 peasant uprising in northern France, incited by disease, war, and taxes.

James I (1566–1625) Monarch who ruled Scotland as James VI, and who succeeded Elizabeth I as king of England in 1603. He oversaw the English vernacular translation of the Bible known by his name.

Janissaries Corps of enslaved soldiers recruited as children from the Christian provinces of the Ottoman Empire and brought up to display intense personal loyalty to the Ottoman sultan, who used these forces to curb local autonomy and as his personal bodyguards.

Jerome (c. 340–420) One of the early "fathers" of the Church, he translated the Bible from Hebrew and Greek into a popular form of Latin—hence the name by which this translation is known: the Vulgate, or "vulgar" (popular), Bible.

Jesuits The religious order formally known as the Society of Jesus, founded in 1540 by Ignatius Loyola to combat the spread of Protestantism. The Jesuits would become active in politics, education, and missionary work.

Jesus (c. 4 B.C.E.–c. 30 C.E.) A Jewish preacher and teacher in the rural areas of Galilee and Judea who was arrested for seditious political activity, tried, and crucified by the Romans. After his execution, his followers claimed that he had been resurrected from the dead and taken up into heaven. They began to teach that Jesus had been the divine representative of God, the Messiah foretold by ancient Hebrew prophets, and that he had suffered for the sins of humanity and would return to judge all the world's inhabitants at the end of time.

Joan of Arc (c. 1412–1431) A peasant girl from the province of Lorraine who claimed to have been commanded by God to lead French forces against the English occupying army during the Hundred Years' War. Successful in her efforts, she was betrayed by the French king and handed over to the English, who condemned her to death for heresy. Her reputation underwent a process of rehabilitation, but she was not officially canonized as a saint until 1920.

Judaism The religion of the Hebrews as it developed in the centuries after the establishment of the Hebrew kingdoms under David and Solomon, especially during the period of Babylonian Captivity.

Justinian (527–565) Emperor of Rome who unsuccessfully attempted to reunite the eastern and western portions of the empire. Also known for his important codification of Roman law, in the *Corpus Juris Civilis*.

Justinian's Code of Roman Law Formally known as the *Corpus Juris Civilis* or "body of civil law," this compendium consisted of a systematic compilation of imperial statutes, the writings of Rome's great legal authorities, a textbook of legal principles, and the legislation of Justinian and his immediate successors. As the most authoritative collection of Roman law, it formed the basis of canon law (the legal system of the Roman Church) and became essential to the developing legal traditions of every European state, as well as of many countries around the world.

Das Kapital (Capital) The 1867 book by Karl Marx that outlined the theory behind historical materialism and attacked the socioeconomic inequities of capitalism.

Johannes Kepler (1571–1630) Mathematician and astronomer who elaborated on and corrected Copernicus's theory and is chiefly remembered for his discovery of the three laws of planetary motion that bear his name.

Keynesian Revolution Post-depression economic ideas developed by the British economist John Maynard Keynes, wherein the state took a greater role in managing the economy, stimulating it by increasing the money supply and creating jobs.

KGB Soviet political police and spy agency, first formed as the Cheka not long after the Bolshevik coup in October 1917. It grew to more than 750,000 operatives with military rank by the 1980s.

Chingiz Khan (c. 1167–1227) "Oceanic Ruler," the title adopted by the Mongol chieftain Temujin, founder of a dynasty that conquered much of southern Asia.

Khanate The major political unit of the vast Mongol Empire. There were four Khanates, including the Yuan Empire in China, forged by Chingiz Khan's grandson Kubilai in the thirteenth century.

Ruhollah Khomeini (1902–1989) Iranian Shi'ite religious leader who led the revolution in Iran after the abdication of the Shah in 1979. His government allowed some limited economic and political populism combined with strict constructions of Islamic law, restrictions on women's public life, and the prohibition of ideas or activities linked to Western influence.

Nikita Khrushchev (1894–1971) Leader of the Soviet Union during the Cuban missile crisis, Khrushchev came to power after Stalin's death in 1953. His reforms and criticisms of the excesses of the Stalin regime led to his fall from power in 1964.

Kremlin Once synonymous with the Soviet government, it refers to Moscow's walled city center and the palace originally built by Ivan the Great.

Kristallnacht Organized attack by Nazis and their supporters on the Jews of Germany following the assassination of a German embassy official by a Jewish man in Paris. Throughout Germany, thousands of stores, schools, cemeteries and synagogues were attacked on November 9, 1938. Dozens of people were killed, and tens of thousands of Jews were arrested and held in camps, where many were tortured and killed in the ensuing months.

Labour party Founded in Britain in 1900, this party represented workers and was based on socialist principles.

Latin West After the founding of Constantinople, the western Latin-speaking half of the Roman Empire became poorer and more peripheral, but it also fostered the emergence of new barbarian kingdoms. At the same time, the Roman pope claimed to have inherited both the authority of Jesus and the essential elements of Roman imperial authority.

League of Nations International organization founded after the First World War to solve international disputes through arbitration; it was dissolved in 1946 and its assets were transferred to the United Nations.

Vladimir Lenin (1870–1924) Leader of the Bolshevik Revolution in Russia (1917) and the first leader of the Soviet Union.

Leviathan A book by Thomas Hobbes (1588–1679) that recommended a ruler have unrestricted power.

liberalism Political and social theory that judges the effectiveness of a government in terms of its ability to protect individual rights. Liberals support representative forms of government, free trade, and freedom of speech and religion. In the economic realm, liberals believe that individuals should be free to engage in commercial or business activities without interference from the state or their community.

lithograph Art form that involves putting writing or design on stone and producing printed impressions.

John Locke (1632–1704) English philosopher and political theorist known for his contributions to liberalism. Locke had great faith in human reason, and believed that just societies were those which infringed the least on the natural rights and freedoms of individuals. This led him to assert that a government's legitimacy depended on the consent of the governed, a view that had a profound effect on the authors of the United States' Declaration of Independence.

Louis XIV (1638–1715) Called the "Sun King," he was known for his success at strengthening the institutions of the French absolutist state.

Louis XVI (1754–1793) Well-meaning but ineffectual king of France, finally deposed and executed during the French Revolution.

Ignatius Loyola (1491–1556) Founder of the Society of Jesus (commonly known as the Jesuits), whose members vowed to serve God through poverty, chastity, and missionary work. He abandoned his first career as a mercenary after reading an account of Christ's life written in his native Spanish.

Lucretia According to Roman legend, Lucretia was a virtuous Roman wife who was raped by the son of Rome's last king and who virtuously committed suicide in order to avoid bringing shame on her family.

Luftwaffe Literally "air weapon," this is the name of the German air force, which was founded during the First World War, disbanded in 1945, and reestablished when West Germany joined NATO in 1950.

Lusitania The British passenger liner that was sunk by a German U-boat (submarine) on May 7, 1915. Public outrage over the sinking contibuted to the U.S. decision to enter the First World War.

Martin Luther (1483–1546) A German monk and professor of theology whose critique of the papacy launched the Protestant Reformation.

ma'at The Egyptian term for the serene order of the universe, with which the individual soul (*ka*) must remain in harmony. The power of the pharaoh was linked to ma'at, insofar as it ensured the prosperity of the kingdom. After the upheavals of the First Intermediate Period, the perception of the pharaoh's relationship with ma'at was revealed to be conditional, something that had to be earned.

Niccolo Machiavelli (1469–1527) As the author of *The Prince* and the *Discourses on Livy*, he looked to the Roman past for paradigms of greatness, while at the same time hoping to win the patronage of contemporary rulers who would restore Italy's political independence.

Magna Carta The "Great Charter" of 1215, enacted during the reign of King John of England and designed to limit his powers. Regarded now as a landmark in the development of constitutional government. In its own time, its purpose was to restore the power of great lords.

Magyar nationalism Lajos Kossuth led this national movement in the Hungarian region of the Habsburg Empire, calling for national independence for Hungary in 1848. With the support of Russia, the Habsburg army crushed the movement and all other revolutionary activities in the empire. Kossuth fled into exile.

Moses Maimonides (c. 1137–1204) Jewish scholar, physician, and scriptural commentator whose *Mishneh Torah* is a fundamental exposition of Jewish law.

Thomas Malthus (1766–1834) British political economist who believed that populations inevitably grew faster than the available food supply. Societies that could not control their population growth would be checked only by famine, disease, poverty, and infant malnutrition. He argued that governments could not alleviate poverty. Instead, the poor had to exercise "moral restraint," postpone marriage, and have fewer children.

Nelson Mandela (b. 1918) The South African opponent of apartheid who led the African National Congress and was imprisoned from 1962 until 1990. After his release from prison, he worked with Prime Minister Frederik Willem De Klerk to establish majority rule. Mandela became the first black president of South Africa in 1994.

Manhattan Project The secret U.S. government research project to develop the first nuclear bomb. The vast project involved dozens of sites across the United States, including New Mexico, Tennessee, Illinois, California, Utah, and Washington. The first test of a nuclear bomb was near Alamogordo, New Mexico on July 16, 1945.

manors Common farmland worked collectively by the inhabitants of entire villages, sometimes on their own initiative, sometimes at the behest of a lord.

Mao Zedong (1893–1976) The leader of the Chinese Revolution who defeated the Nationalists in 1949 and established the Communist regime in China.

Marne A major battle of the First World War in September 1914, which halted the German invasion of France and led to protracted trench warfare on the Western Front.

Marshall Plan Economic aid package given to Europe by the United States after the Second World War to promote reconstruction and economic development and to secure the countries from a feared communist takeover.

Karl Marx (1818–1883) German philosopher and economist who believed that a revolution of the working classes would overthrow the capitalist order and create a classless society. Author of *Das Kapital* and *The Communist Manifesto*.

Marxists Followers of the socialist political economist Karl Marx who called for workers everywhere to unite and create an independent political force. Marxists believed that industrialization produced an inevitable struggle between laborers and the class of capitalist property owners, and that this struggle would culminate in a revolution that would abolish private property and establish a society committed to social equality.

Mary; see cult of the Virgin.

Mary I (1516–1558) Catholic daughter of Henry VIII and his first wife, Catherine of Aragon, Mary Tudor was the first queen regnant of England. Her attempts to reinstitute Catholicism in England met with limited success, and after her early death she was labeled "Bloody Mary" by the Protestant supporters of her half sister and successor, Elizabeth I.

mass culture The spread of literacy and public education in the nineteenth century created a new audience for print entertainment and a new class of entrepreneurs in the media to cater to this audience. The invention of radio, film, and television in the twentieth century carried this development to another level, as millions of consumers were now accessible to the producers of news, information, and entertainment. The rise of this "mass culture" has been celebrated as an expression of popular tastes but also criticized as a vehicle for the manipulation of populations through clever and seductive propaganda.

Mayans Native American peoples whose culturally and politically sophisticated empire encompassed lands in present-day Mexico and Guatemala.

Giuseppe Mazzini (1805–1872) Founder of Young Italy and an ideological leader of the Italian nationalist movement.

Mecca Center of an important commercial network of the Arabian Peninsula and birthplace of the prophet Muhammad. It is now considered the holiest site in the Islamic world.

Medici A powerful dynasty of Florentine bankers and politicians whose ancestors were originally apothecaries ("medics").

Meiji Empire Empire created under the leadership of Mutsuhito, emperor of Japan from 1868 until 1912. During the Meiji period Japan became a world industrial and naval power.

Mensheviks Within the Russian Social Democratic Party, the Mensheviks advocated slow changes and a gradual move toward socialism, in contrast with the Bolsheviks, who wanted to push for a proletarian revolution. Mensheviks believed that a proletarian revolution in Russia was premature and that the country needed to complete its capitalist development first.

mercantilism A theory and policy for directing the economy of monarchical states between 1600 and 1800 based on the assumption that wealth and power depended on a favorable balance of trade (more exports and fewer imports) and the accumulation of precious metals. Mercantilists advocated forms of economic protectionism to promote domestic production.

Maria Sybilla Merian (1647–1717) A scientific illustrator and an important early entomologist. She conducted research on two continents and published the well-received *Metamorphosis of the Insects of Surinam*.

Merovingian A Frankish dynasty that claimed descent from a legendary ancestor called Merovic, the Merovingians were the only powerful family to establish a lasting kingdom in western Europe during the fifth and sixth centuries.

Mesopotamia The "land between the Tigris and the Euphrates rivers," Tigris and Euphrates where the civilization of Sumer, the first urban society, flourished.

Klemens von Metternich (1773–1859) Austrian foreign minister whose primary goals were to bolster the legitimacy of monarchies and, after the defeat of Napoleon, to prevent another large-scale war in Europe. At the Congress of Vienna, he opposed social and political change and wanted to check Russian and French expansion.

Michelangelo Buonarroti (1475–1564) A virtuoso Florentine sculptor, painter, and poet who spent much of his career in the service of the papacy. He is best known for the decoration of the Sistine Chapel and for his monumental sculptures.

Middle Kingdom of Egypt (2055–1650 B.C.E.) The period following the First Intermediate Period of dynastic warfare, which ended with the reassertion of pharonic rule under Mentuhotep II.

Miletus A Greek polis and Persian colony on the Ionian coast of Asia Minor. Influenced by the cultures of Mesopotamia, Egypt, and Lydia, it produced several of the ancient world's first scientists and sophists. Thereafter, a political conflict between the ruler of Miletus, Aristagoras, and the Persian Emperor, Darius, sparked the Persian Wars with Greece.

John Stuart Mill (1806–1873) English liberal philosopher whose faith in human reason led him to support a broad variety of civic and political freedoms for men and women, including the right to vote and the right to free speech.

Slobodan Milosevic (1941–2006) The Serbian nationalist politician who became president of Serbia and whose policies during the Balkan wars of the early 1990s led to the deaths of thousands of Croatians, Bosnian Muslims, Albanians, and Kosovars. After leaving office in 2000 he was arrested and tried for war crimes at the International Court in The Hague. The trial ended before a verdict with his death in 2006.

Minoan Crete A sea empire based at Knossos on the Greek island of Crete and named for the legendary King Minos. The Minoans dominated the Aegean for much of the second millennium B.C.E.

Modernism There were several different modernist movements in art and literature, but they shared three key characteristics. First, they had a sense that the world had radically changed and that this change should be embraced. Second, they believed that traditional aesthetic values and assumptions about creativity were ill-suited to the present. Third, they developed a new conception of what art could do that emphasized expression over representation and insisted on the value of novelty, experimentation, and creative freedom.

Mongols A nomadic people from the steppes of Central Asia who were united under the ruler Chingiz Khan. His conquest of China was continued by his grandson Kubilai and his great-grandson son Ogedei, whose army also seized southern Russia and then moved through Hungary and through Poland toward eastern Germany. The Mongol armies withdrew from Eastern Europe after the death of Ogedei, but his descendents continued to rule his vast empire for another half century.

Michel de Montaigne (1533–1592) French philosopher and social commentator, best known for his *Essays*.

Montesquieu (1689–1755) An Enlightenment *philosophe* whose most influential work was *The Spirit of Laws*. In this work he analyzed the structures that shaped law and categorized governments into three types: republics, monarchies, and despotisms. His ideas about the separation of powers between the executive, the legislative, and the judicial branches of government influenced the authors of the United States Constitution.

Thomas More (1478–1535) Christian humanist, English statesman, and author of *Utopia*. In 1529, he was appointed Lord Chancellor of England but resigned because he opposed King Henry VIII's plans to establish a national church under royal control. He was eventually executed for refusing to take an oath acknowledging Henry to be the head of the Church of England, and has since been canonized by the Catholic Church.

mos maiorum Literally translated as "the code of the elders" or "the custom of ancestors." This unwritten code governed the lives of Romans under the Republic and stressed the importance of showing reverence to ancestral tradition. It was sacrosanct and essential to Roman identity, and an important influence on Roman culture, law, and religion.

Wolfgang Amadeus Mozart (1756–1791) Austrian composer, famous at a young age as a concert musician and later celebrated as a prolific composer of instrumental music and operas that are seen as the apogee of the Classical style in music.

Muhammad (570–632 C.E.) The founder of Islam, regarded as God's last and greatest prophet by his followers.

Munich Conference (1938) Hitler met with the leaders of Britain, France, and Italy and negotiated an agreement that gave Germany a major slice of Czechoslovakia. British prime minister Chamberlain believed that the agreement would bring peace to Europe. Instead, Germany invaded and seized the rest of Czechoslovakia.

Muscovy The duchy centered on Moscow whose dukes saw themselves as heirs to the Roman Empire. In the early fourteenth century, Moscow was under the control of the Mongol Khanate. After the collapse of the Khanate, the Muscovite grand duke, Ivan III, conquered all the Russian principalities between Moscow and the border of Poland-Lithuania, and then Lithuania itself. By the time of his death, Ivan had established Muscovy as a dominant power.

Muslim learning and culture The Crusades brought the Latin West in contact with the Islamic world, which impacted European culture in myriad ways. Europeans adapted Arabic numerals and mathematical concepts as well as Arabic and Persian words. Through Arabic translations, western scholars gained access to Greek learning, which had a profound influence on Christian theology. European scholars also learned from the Islamic world's accomplishments in medicine and science.

Benito Mussolini (1883–1945) The Italian founder of the Fascist party who came to power in Italy in 1922 and allied himself with Hitler and the Nazis during the Second World War.

Mycenaean Greece (1600–1200 B.C.E.) The term used to describe the civilization of Greece in the late Bronze Age, when territorial kingdoms like Mycenae formed around a king, a warrior caste, and a palace bureaucracy.

Nagasaki Second Japanese city on which the United States dropped an atomic bomb. The attack took place on August 9, 1945; the Japanese surrendered shortly thereafter, ending the Second World War.

Napoleon III (1808–1873) Nephew of Napoleon Bonaparte, Napoleon III was elected president of the French Second Republic in 1848 and made himself emperor of France in 1852. During his reign (1852–70), he rebuilt the French capital of Paris. Defeated in the France-Prussian War of 1870, he went into exile.

Napoleonic Code Legal code drafted by Napoleon in 1804 and based on Justinian's *Corpus Iuris Civilis*. It distilled different legal traditions to create one uniform law. The code confirmed the abolition of feudal privileges of all kinds and set the conditions for exercising property rights.

Napoleon's military campaigns In 1805, the Russians, Prussians, Austrians, Swedes, and British attempted to contain Napoleon, but he defeated them. Out of his victories, Napoleon created a new empire and affiliated states. In 1808, he invaded Spain, but fierce resistance prevented Napoleon from achieving a complete victory. In 1812, Napoleon invaded Russia, and his army was decimated as it retreated from Moscow during the winter. After the Russian campaign, the united European powers defeated Napoleon and forced him into exile. He escaped and reassumed command of his army, but the European powers defeated him for the final time at the Battle of Waterloo.

Gamal Abdel Nasser (1918–1970) Former president of Egypt and the most prominent spokesman for secular pan-Arabism. He became a target for Islamist critics, such as Sayyid Qutb and the Muslim Brotherhood, angered by the Western-influenced policies of his regime.

National Assembly of France Governing body of France that succeeded the Estates-General in 1789 during the French Revolution. It was composed of, and defined by, the delegates of the Third Estate.

National Association for the Advancement of Colored People (NAACP) Founded in 1910, this U.S. civil rights organization was dedicated to ending inequality and segregation for black Americans.

National Convention The governing body of France from September 1792 to October 1795. It declared France a republic and then tried and executed the French king. The Convention also confiscated the property of the enemies of the revolution, instituted a policy of de-Christianization, changed marriage and inheritance laws, abolished slavery in its colonies, placed a cap on the price of necessities, and ended the compensation of nobles for their lost privileges.

nationalism Movement to unify a country under one government based on perceptions of the population's common history, customs, and social traditions.

nationalism in Yugoslavia In the 1990s, Slobodan Milosevic and his allies reignited Serbian nationalism in the former Yugoslavia, which led non-Serb republics in Croatia and Slovenia to seek independence. The country erupted into war, with the worst violence taking place in Bosnia, a multi-ethnic region with Serb, Croatian and Bosnian Muslim populations. European diplomats proved powerless to stop attempts by Croatian and Serbian military and paramilitary forces to claim territory through ethnic cleansing and violent intimidation. Atrocities were committed on all sides, but pro-Serb forces were responsible for the most deaths.

NATO The North Atlantic Treaty Organization, a 1949 military agreement between the United States, Canada, Great Britain, and eight Western European nations, which declared that an armed attack against any one of the members would be regarded as an attack against all. Created during the Cold War in the face of the Soviet Union's control of Eastern Europe, NATO continues to exist today and the membership of twenty-eight states includes former members of the Warsaw Pact as well as Albania and Turkey.

Nazi party Founded in the early 1920s, the National Socialist German Workers' Party (NSDAP) gained control over Germany under the leadership of Adolf Hitler in 1933 and continued in power until Germany was defeated in 1945.

Nazism The political movement in Germany led by Adolf Hitler, which advocated a violent anti-Semitic, anti-Marxist, pan-German ideology.

Neo-Assyrian Empire (883–859 B.C.E.–612–605 B.C.E.) Assurnasirpal II laid the foundations of the Neo-Assyrian Empire through military campaigns against neighboring peoples. Eventually, the empire stretched from the Mediterranean Sea to Western Iran. A military dictatorship governed the empire through its army, which it used to frighten and oppress both its subjects and its enemies. The empire's ideology was based on waging holy war in the name of its principal god, Assur, and the exaction of tribute through terror.

Neoliberalism Neoliberals believe that free markets, profit incentives, and restraints on both budget deficits and social welfare programs are the best guarantee of individual liberties. Beginning in the 1980s, neoliberal theory was used to structure the policy of financial institutions like the International Monetary Fund and the World Bank, which turned away from interventionist policies in favor of market-driven models of economic development.

Neolithic Revolution The "New" Stone Age, which began around 11,000 B.C.E., saw new technological and social developments, including managed food production, the beginnings of permanent settlements, and the rapid intensification of trade.

Neoplatonism A school of thought based on the teachings of Plato and prevalent in the Roman Empire, which had a profound effect on the formation of Christian theology. Neoplatonists argued that nature is a book written by its creator to reveal the ways of God to humanity. Convinced that God's perfection must be reflected in nature, neoplatonists searched for the ideal and perfect structures that they believed must lie behind the "shadows" of the everyday world.

New Deal President Franklin Delano Roosevelt's package of government reforms that were enacted during the depression of the 1930s to provide jobs for the unemployed, social welfare programs for the poor, and security to the financial markets.

New Economic Policy In 1921, the Bolsheviks abandoned war communism in favor of the New Economic Policy (NEP). Under NEP, the state still controlled all major industry and financial concerns, while individuals could own private property, trade freely within limits, and farm their own land for their own benefit. Fixed taxes replaced grain requisition. The policy successfully helped Soviet agriculture recover from the civil war, but was later abandoned in favor of collectivization.

Isaac Newton (1642–1727) One of the foremost scientists of all time, Newton was an English mathematician and physicist; he is noted for his development of calculus, work on the properties of light, and theory of gravitation.

Tsar Nicholas II (1868–1918) The last Russian tsar, who abdicated the throne in 1917. He and his family were executed by the Bolsheviks on July 17, 1918.

Friedrich Nietzsche (1844–1900) The German philosopher who denied the possibility of knowing absolute "truth" or "reality," since all knowledge comes filtered through linguistic, scientific, or artistic systems of representation. He also criticized Judeo-Christian morality for instilling a repressive conformity that drained civilization of its vitality.

nongovernmental organizations (NGOs) Private organizations like the Red Cross that play a large role in international affairs.

North American Free Trade Agreement (NAFTA) Treaty negotiated in the early 1990s to promote free trade among Canada, the United States, and Mexico.

Novum Organum Work by English statesman and scientist Francis Bacon (1561–1626) that advanced a philosophy of study through observation.

October Days (1789) The high price of bread and the rumor that the king was unwilling to cooperate with the assembly caused the women who worked in Paris's large central market to march to Versailles along with their supporters to address the king. Not satisfied with their initial reception, they broke through the palace gates and called for the king to return to Paris from Versailles, which he did the following day.

Old Kingdom of Egypt (c. 2686–2160 B.C.E.) During this time, the pharaohs controlled a powerful and centralized bureaucratic state whose vast human and material resources are exemplified by the pyramids of Giza. This period came to an end as the pharaoh's authority collapsed, leading to a period of dynastic warfare and localized rule.

OPEC (Organization of the Petroleum Exporting Countries) Organization created in 1960 by oil-producing countries in the Middle East, South America, and Africa to regulate the production and pricing of crude oil.

Operation Barbarossa The codename for Hitler's invasion of the Soviet Union in 1941.

Opium Wars (1839–1842) War fought between the British and Qing China to protect British trade in opium; resulted in the ceding of Hong Kong to the British.

Oracle at Delphi The most important shrine in ancient Greece. The priestess of Apollo who attended the shrine was believed to have the power to predict the future.

Ottoman Empire (c.1300–1923) During the thirteenth century, the Ottoman dynasty established itself as leader of the Turks. From the fourteenth to sixteenth centuries, they conquered Anatolia, Armenia, Syria, and North Africa as well as parts of southeastern Europe, the Crimea, and areas along the Red Sea. Portions of the Ottoman Empire persisted up to the time of the First World War, but it was dismantled in the years following it.

Reza Pahlavi (1919–1980) The Western-friendly Shah of Iran who was installed during a 1953 coup supported by Britain and the United States. After a lengthy economic downturn, public unrest, and personal illness, he retired from public life under popular pressure in 1979.

Pan-African Conference 1900 assembly in London that sought to draw attention to the sovereignty of African people and their mistreatment by colonial powers.

Panhellenism The "all Greek" culture that allowed ancient Greek colonies to maintain a connection to their homeland and to each other through their shared language and heritage. These colonies also exported their culture into new areas and created new Greek-speaking enclaves, which permanently changed the cultural geography of the Mediterranean world.

pan-Slavism Cultural movement that sought to unite native Slavic peoples within the Russian and Habsburg empires under Russian leadership.

Partition of India (1947) At independence, British India was partitioned into the nations of India and Pakistan. The majority of the population in India was Hindu and the majority of the population in Pakistan was Muslim. The process of partition brought brutal religious and ethnic warfare. More than one million Hindus and Muslims died and twelve million became refugees.

Blaise Pascal (1623–1662) A Catholic philosopher who wanted to establish the truth of Christianity by appealing simultaneously to intellect and emotion. In his *Pensées*, he argued that faith alone can resolve the world's contradictions and that his own awe in the face of evil and uncertainty must be evidence of God's existence.

Paul of Tarsus Originally known as Saul, Paul was a Greek-speaking Jew and Roman citizen who underwent a miraculous conversion experience and became the most important proponent of Christianity in the 50s and 60s C.E.

Pax Romana (27 B.C.E.–180 C.E.) Literally translated as "the Roman Peace." During this time, the Roman world enjoyed an unprecedented period of peace and political stability.

Peace of Augsburg A settlement negotiated in 1555 among factions within the Holy Roman Empire, it formulated the principle *cuius regio, eius religio*, "he who rules, his religion": meaning that the inhabitants of any given territory should follow the religion of its ruler, whether Catholic or Protestant.

Peace of Paris The 1919 Paris Peace Conference established the terms to end the First World War. Great Britain, France, Italy, and the United States signed five treaties with each of the defeated nations: Germany, Austria, Hungary, Turkey, and Bulgaria. The settlement is notable for the territory that Germany had to give up, including large parts of Prussia to the new state of Poland, and Alsace and Lorraine to France; the disarming of Germany; and the "war guilt" provision, which required Germany and its allies to pay massive reparations to the victors.

Peace of Westphalia (1648) An agreement reached at the end of the Thirty Years' War that altered the political map of Europe. France emerged as the predominant power on the Continent, while the Austrian Habsburgs had to surrender all the territories they had gained and could no longer use the office of the Holy Roman Emperor to dominate central Europe. Spain was marginalized and Germany became a volatile combination of Protestant and Catholic principalities.

Pearl Harbor The American naval base in Hawaii that was bombed by the Japanese on December 7, 1941, bringing the United States into the Second World War.

peasantry Term used in continental Europe to refer to rural populations that lived from agriculture. Some peasants were free, and could own land. Serfs were peasants who were legally bound to the land, and subject to the authority of the local lord.

Peloponnesian War The name given to the series of wars fought between Sparta (on the Greek Peloponnesus) and Athens from 431 B.C.E. to 404 B.C.E., and which ended in the defeat of Athens and the loss of her imperial power.

perestroika Introduced by Soviet leader Mikhail Gorbachev in June 1987, perestroika was the name given to economic and political reforms begun earlier in his tenure. It restructured the state bureaucracy, reduced the privileges of the political elite, and instituted a shift from the centrally planned economy to a mixed economy, combining planning with the operation of market forces.

Periclean Athens Following his election as *strategos* in 461 B.C.E., Pericles pushed through political reforms in Athens, which gave poorer citizens greater influence in politics. He promoted Athenians' sense of superiority through ambitious public works projects and lavish festivals to honor the gods, thus ensuring his continual reelection. But eventually, Athens' growing arrogance and aggression alienated it from the rest of the Greek world.

Pericles (c. 495–429) Athenian politician who occupied the office of strategos for thirty years and who presided over a series of civic reforms, building campaigns, and imperialist initiatives.

Persian Empire Consolidated by Cyrus the Great in 559, this empire eventually stretched from the Persian Gulf to the Mediterranean, and also encompassed Egypt. Persian rulers were able to hold this empire together through a policy of tolerance and a mixture of local and centralized governance. This imperial model of government would be adopted by many future empires.

Persian Wars (490–479 B.C.E.) In 501 B.C.E., a political conflict between the Greek ruler of Miletus, Aristagoras, and the Persian Emperor, Darius, sparked the first of the Persian Wars when Darius sent an army to punish Athens for its intervention on the side of the Greeks. Despite being heavily outnumbered, Athenian hoplites defeated the Persian army at the plain of Marathon. In 480 B.C.E., Darius' son Xerxes invaded Greece but was defeated at sea and on land by combined Greek forces under the leadership of Athens and Sparta.

Peter the Great (1672–1725) Energetic tsar who transformed Russia into a leading European country by centralizing government, modernizing the army, creating a navy, and reforming education and the economy.

Francesco Petrarca (Petrarch) (1304–1374) Italian scholar who revived interest in classical writing styles and was famed for his vernacular love sonnets.

pharaoh A term meaning "household" which became the title borne by the rulers of ancient Egypt. The pharaoh was regarded as the divine representative of the gods and the embodiment of Egypt itself. The powerful and centralized bureaucratic state ruled by the pharaohs was more stable and long-lived than any another civilization in world history, lasting (with few interruptions) for approximately three thousand years.

Pharisees A group of Jewish teachers and preachers that emerged in the third century B.C.E. They insisted that all of Yahweh's (God's) commandments were binding on all Jews.

Philip II (382–336 B.C.E.) King of Macedonia and father of Alexander, he consolidated the southern Balkans and the Greek city-states under Macedonian domination.

Philip II Augustus (1165–1223) The first French ruler to use the title "king of France" rather than "king of the French." After he captured Normandy and its adjacent territories from the English, he built an effective system of local administration, which recognized regional diversity while promoting centralized royal control. This administrative pattern would characterize French government until the French Revolution.

Philistines Descendants of the Sea Peoples who fled to the region that now bears their name, Palestine, after their defeat at the hands of the pharaoh Ramses III. They dominated their neighbors, the Hebrews, who used writing as an effective means of discrediting them (the Philistines themselves did not leave a written record to contest the Hebrews' views).

philosophe During the Enlightenment, this word referred to a person whose reflections were unhampered by the constraints of religion or dogma.

Phoenicians A Semitic people known for their trade in exotic purple dyes and other luxury goods, they originally settled in present-day Lebanon around 1200 B.C.E. and from there established commercial colonies throughout the Mediterranean, notably Carthage.

Plato (429–349 B.C.E.) A student of Socrates, Plato dedicated his life to transmitting his teacher's legacy through the writing of dialogues on philosophical subjects, in which Socrates himself plays the major role. The longest and most famous of these, known as the *Republic*, describes an idealized polis governed by a superior group of individuals chosen for their natural attributes of intelligence and character, who rule as "philosopher-kings."

Plotinus (204–270 C.E.) A Neoplatonist philosopher who taught that everything in existence has its ultimate source in the divine, and that the highest goal of life should be the mystic reunion of the soul with this divine source, something that can be achieved through contemplation and asceticism. This outlook blended with that of early Christianity and was instrumental in the spread of that religion within the Roman Empire.

poleis One of the major political innovations of the ancient Greeks was the *polis*, or city-state (plural *poleis*). These independent social and political entities began to emerge in the ninth century B.C.E., organized around an urban center and fostering markets, meeting places, and religious worship; frequently, poleis also controlled some surrounding territory.

Marco Polo (1254–1324) Venetian merchant who traveled through Asia for twenty years and published his observations in a widely read memoir.

population growth In the nineteenth century, Europe experienced a dramatic population growth. During this period, the spread of rural manufacturing allowed men and women to begin marrying younger and raising families earlier, which increased the size of the average family. As the population grew, the portion of young and fertile people also increased, which reinforced the population growth. By 1900, population growth was strongest in Britain and Germany, and slower in France.

Potsdam (1945) At this conference, Truman, Churchill and Stalin met to discuss their options at the conclusion of the Second World War, including making territorial changes to Germany and its allies and the question of war reparations.

Prague spring A period of political liberalization in Czechoslovakia between January and August 1968 that was initiated by Alexander Dubček, the Czech leader. This period of expanding freedom and openness in this Eastern bloc nation ended on August 20, when the USSR and Warsaw Pact countries invaded with 200,000 troops and 5,000 tanks.

pre-Socratics A group of philosophers in the Greek city of Miletus, who raised questions about humans' relationship with the natural world and the gods, and who formulated rational theories to explain the physical universe they observed. Their name reflects the fact that they flourished prior to the lifetime of Socrates.

Price Revolution An unprecedented inflation in prices in the latter half of the sixteenth century, resulting in part from the enormous influx of silver bullion from Spanish America.

Principate Modern term for the centuries of autocratic rule by the successors of Augustus, who seized power in 27 B.C.E. and styled himself *princeps* or Rome's "first man." See **Roman Republic**.

Protestantism The name given to the many dissenting varieties of Christianity that emerged during the Reformation in sixteenth-century western Europe. While Protestant beliefs and practices differed widely, all were united in their rejection of papal authority and the dogmas of the Roman Catholic Church.

Provisional Government After the collapse of the Russian monarchy, leaders in the Duma organized this government and hoped to establish a democratic system under constitutional rule. They also refused to concede military defeat, and it was impossible to institute domestic reforms and fight a war at the same time. As conditions worsened, the Bolsheviks gained support. In October 1917, they attacked the provisional government and seized control.

Claudius Ptolomeus, called Ptolemy (c. 85–165 C.E.) A Greek-speaking geographer and astronomer active in Roman Alexandria, he rejected the findings of previous Hellenistic scientists in favor of the erroneous theories of Aristotle, publishing highly influential treatises that promulgated these errors and suppressed (for example) the accurate findings of Aristarchus (who had discovered the Heliocentric universe) and Erathosthenes (who had calculated the circumference of the earth).

Ptolemaic system Ptolemy of Alexandria promoted Aristotle's understanding of cosmology. In this system, the heavens orbit the earth in an organized hierarchy of spheres, and the earth and the heavens are made of different matter and subject to different laws of motion. A prime mover produces the motion of the celestial bodies.

Ptolemy (c. 367–c. 284 B.C.E.) One of Alexander the Great's trusted generals (and possibly his half brother), he became pharaoh of Egypt and founded a new dynasty that lasted until that kingdom's absorption into the Roman Empire in 30 B.C.E.

Punic Wars (264–146 B.C.E.) Three periods of warfare between Rome and Carthage, two maritime empires who struggled for dominance of the Mediterranean. Rome emerged as the victor, destroyed the city of Carthage and took control of Sicily, North Africa and Hispania (Spain).

pyramid Constructed during the third millennium B.C.E., these structures were monuments to the power and divinity of the pharaohs entombed inside them.

Qu'ran (often Koran) Islam's holy scriptures, comprised of the prophecies revealed to Muhammad and redacted during and after his death.

Raphael (Raffaelo Sarazio) (1483–1520) Italian painter active in Rome, his works include *The School of Athens*.

realism Artistic and literary style which sought to portray common situations as they would appear in reality.

Realpolitik Political strategy based on advancing power for its own sake.

reason The human capacity to solve problems and discover truth in ways that can be verified intellectually. Philosophers distinguish the knowledge gained from reason from the teachings of instinct, imagination, and faith, which are verified according to different criteria.

Reformation Religious and political movement in sixteenth-century Europe that led to a break between dissenting forms of Christianity and the Roman Catholic Church; notable figures include Martin Luther and John Calvin.

Reich A term for the German state. The First Reich corresponded to the Holy Roman Empire (9th c.–1806), the Second Reich was from 1871 to 1919, and the Third Reich lasted from 1933 through May 1945.

Renaissance From the French word "rebirth," this term came to be used in the nineteenth century to describe the artistic, intellectual, and cultural movement that emerged in Italy after 1300, and which sought to recover and emulate the heritage of the classical past.

Restoration period (1815–1848) European movement after the defeat of Napoleon to restore Europe to its pre–French Revolution status and to prevent the spread of revolutionary or liberal political movements.

Cardinal Richelieu (1585–1642) First minister to King Louis XIII, he is considered by many to have ruled France in all but name, centralizing political power and suppressing dissent.

Roman army Under the Republic, the Roman army was made up of citizen-soldiers who were required to serve in wartime. As Rome's empire grew, the need for more fighting men led to the extension of citizenship rights and, eventually, to the development of a vast, professional, standing army that numbered as many as 300,000 by the middle of the third century B.C.E. By that time, however, citizens were not themselves required to serve, and many legions were made up of paid conscripts and foreign mercenaries.

Roman citizenship The rights and responsibilities of Rome's citizens were gradually extended to the free (male) inhabitants of other Italian provinces and later to most provinces in the Roman world. In contrast to slaves and non-Romans, Romans had the right to be tried in an imperial court and could not be legally subjected to torture.

Roman Republic The Romans traced the founding of their republic to the overthrow of their last king and the establishment of a unique form of constitutional government, in which the power of the aristocracy (embodied by the Senate) was checked by the executive rule of two elected consuls and the collective will of the people. For hundreds of years, this balance of power provided the Republic with a measure of political stability and prevented any single individual or clique from gaining too much power.

Romanticism Beginning in Germany and England in the late eighteenth century and continuing up to the end of the nineteenth century, Romanticism was a movement in art, music, and literature that countered the rationalism of the Enlightenment by placing greater value on human emotions and the power of nature to stimulate creativity.

Jean-Jacques Rousseau (1712–1778) Philosopher and radical political theorist whose *Social Contract* attacked privilege and inequality. One of the primary principles of Rousseau's political philosophy is that politics and morality should not be separated.

Royal Society This British society's goal was to pursue collective research. Members would conduct experiments, record the results, and share them with their peers, who would study the methods, reproduce the experiment, and assess the results.

The arrangement gave English scientists a sense of common purpose as well as a system to reach a consensus on facts.

Russian Revolution of 1905 After Russia's defeat in the Russo-Japanese War, Russians began clamoring for political reforms. Protests grew over the course of 1905, and the autocracy lost control of entire towns and regions as workers went on strike, soldiers mutinied, and peasants revolted. Forced to yield, Tsar Nicholas II issued the October Manifesto, which pledged individual liberties and provided for the election of a parliament (called the Duma). The most radical of the revolutionary groups were put down with force, and the pace of political change remained very slow in the aftermath of the revolution.

Russo-Japanese War (1904–1905) Japanese and Russian expansion collided in Mongolia and Manchuria. Russia was humiliated after the Japanese navy sunk its fleet, which helped provoke a revolt in Russia and led to an American-brokered peace treaty.

Saint Bartholomew's Day Massacre The mass murder of French Protestants (Huguenots) instigated by Queen Catherine de' Medici of France and carried out by Catholics. It began in Paris on 24 August 1572 and spread to other parts of France, continuing into October of that year. More than 70,000 people were killed.

salons Informal gatherings of intellectuals and aristocrats that allowed discourse about Enlightenment ideas.

Sappho (c. 620–c. 550 B.C.E.) One of the most celebrated Greek poets, she was revered as "the Tenth Muse" and emulated by many male poets. Ironically, though, only two of her poems survive intact, and the rest must be pieced together from fragments quoted by later poets.

Sargon the Great (r. 2334–2279 B.C.E.) The Akkadian ruler who consolidated power in Mesopotamia.

SARS epidemic (2003) The successful containment of severe acute respiratory syndrome (SARS) is an example of how international health organizations can effectively work together to recognize and respond to a disease outbreak. The disease itself, however, is a reminder of the dangers that exist in a globalized economy with a high degree of mobility in both populations and goods.

Schlieffen Plan Devised by German general Alfred von Schlieffen in 1905 to avoid the dilemma of a two-front war against France and Russia. The Schlieffen Plan required that Germany attack France first through Belgium and secure a quick victory before wheeling to the east to meet the slower armies of the Russians on the Eastern Front. The Schlieffen Plan was put into operation on August 2, 1914, at the outset of the First World War.

Scientific Revolution of Antiquity The Hellenistic period was the most brilliant age in the history of science before the seventeenth century C.E. Aristarchus of Samos posited the existence of a heliocentric universe. Eratosthenes of Alexandria accurately calculated the circumference of the earth. Archimedes turned physics into its own branch of experimental science. Hellenistic anatomists became the first to practice human dissection, which improved their understanding of human physiology. Ironically, most of these discoveries were suppressed by pseudo-scientists who flourished under the Roman Empire during the second century C.E., notably Claudus Ptolomeus Ptolemy) and Aelius Galenus (Galen).

second industrial revolution The technological developments in the last third of the nineteenth century, which included new techniques for refining and producing steel; increased availability of electricity for industrial, commercial, and domestic use; advances in chemical manufacturing; and the creation of the internal combustion engine.

Second World War Worldwide war that began in September 1939 in Europe, and even earlier in Asia (the Japanese invasion of Manchuria began in 1931), pitting Britain, the United States, and the Soviet Union (the Allies) against Nazi Germany, Italy, and Japan (the Axis). The war ended in 1945 with Germany and Japan's defeat.

Seleucus (d. 280 B.C.E.) The Macedonian general who ruled the Persian heartland of Alexander the Great's empire.

Semitic The Semitic language family has the longest recorded history of any linguistic group and is the root for most languages of the Middle and Near East. Ancient Semitic languages include those of the ancient Babylonians and Assyrians, Phoenician, the classical form of Hebrew, early dialects of Aramaic, and the classical Arabic of the Qu'ran.

Sepoy Mutiny of 1857 See **Indian Rebellion of 1857**.

serf An unfree peasant laborer. Unlike slaves, serfs are "attached" to the land they work, and are not supposed to be sold apart from that land.

William Shakespeare (1564–1616) An English playwright who flourished during the reigns of Elizabeth I and James I, Shakespeare received a basic education in his hometown of Stratford-upon-Avon and worked in London as an actor before achieving success as a dramatist and poet.

Shi'ites An often-persecuted minority within Islam, Shi'ites believe that only descendants of Muhammad's successor Ali and his wife Fatimah (Muhammad's daughter) can have any authority over the Muslim community. Today, Shi'ites constitute the ruling party in Iran and are numerous in Iraq, but otherwise comprise only 10 percent of Muslims worldwide.

Abbé Sieyès (1748–1836) In 1789, he wrote the pamphlet "What is the Third Estate?" in which he posed fundamental questions about the rights of the Third Estate and helped provoke its secession from the Estates-General. He was a leader at the Tennis Court Oath, but he later helped Napoleon seize power.

Sinn Féin The Irish revolutionary organization that formed in 1900 to fight for Irish independence.

Sino-Japanese War (1894–1895) Conflict over the control of Korea in which China was forced to cede the province of Taiwan to Japan.

slave revolt in Saint-Domingue (1791–1804) In September of 1791, the largest slave rebellion in history broke out in Saint-Domingue, an important French colony in the Caribbean. In 1794, the revolutionary government in France abolished slavery in the colonies, though this act was essentially only recognizing the liberty that the slaves had seized by their own actions. Napoleon reestablished slavery in the French Caribbean in 1802, but failed in his attempt to reconquer Saint-Domingue. Armies commanded by former slaves succeeded in winning independence for a new nation, Haiti, in 1804, making the revolt in Saint-Domingue the first successful slave revolt in history.

slavery The practice of subjugating people to a life of bondage, and of selling or trading these unfree people. For most of human history, slavery had no racial or ethnic basis, and was widely practiced by all cultures and civilizations. Anyone could become a slave, for example, by being captured in war or by being sold for the payment of a debt. It was only in the fifteenth century, with the growth of the African slave trade, that slavery came to be associated with particular races and peoples.

Adam Smith (1723–1790) Scottish economist and liberal philosopher who proposed that competition between self-interested individuals led naturally to a healthy economy. He became famous for his influential book, *The Wealth of Nations* (1776).

Social Darwinism Belief that Charles Darwin's theory of natural selection (evolution) was applicable to human societies and justified the right of the ruling classes or countries to dominate the weak.

social democracy The belief that democracy and social welfare go hand in hand, and that diminishing the sharp inequalities of class society is crucial to fortifying democratic culture.

socialism Political ideology that calls for a classless society with collective ownership of all property.

Society of Jesus; see **Jesuits**.

Socrates (469–399 B.C.E.) The Athenian philosopher and teacher who promoted the careful examination of all inherited opinions and assumptions on the grounds that "the unexamined life is not worth living." A veteran of the Peloponnesian War, he was tried and condemned by his fellow citizens for engaging in allegedly seditious activities, and was executed in 399 B.C.E. His most influential pupils were the philosopher Plato and the historian and social commentator Xenophon.

Solon (d. 559 B.C.E.) Elected archon in 594 B.C.E., this Athenian aristocrat enacted a series of political and economic reforms that formed the basis of Athenian democracy.

Somme (1916) During this battle of the First World War, Allied forces attempted to take entrenched German positions from July to mid-November of 1916. Neither side was able to make any real gains despite massive casualties: 500,000 Germans, 400,000 British, and 200,000 French.

Soviet bloc International alliance that included the East European countries of the Warsaw Pact as well as the Soviet Union; it also came to include Cuba.

soviets Local councils elected by workers and soldiers in Russia. Socialists started organizing these councils in 1905, and the Petrograd soviet in the capital emerged as one of the centers of power after the Russian monarchy collapsed in 1917 in the midst of World War I. The soviets became increasingly powerful and pressed for social reform, the redistribution of land, and called for Russian withdrawal from the war effort.

Spanish-American War (1898) War between the United States and Spain in Cuba, Puerto Rico, and the Philippines. It ended with a treaty in which the United States took over the Philippines, Guam, and Puerto Rico; Cuba won partial independence.

Spanish Armada Supposedly invincible fleet of warships sent against England by Philip II of Spain in 1588 but vanquished by the English fleet and bad weather in the English Channel.

Sparta Around 650 B.C.E., after the suppression of a slave revolt, Spartan rulers militarized their society in order to prevent future rebellions and to protect Sparta's superior position in Greece, orienting their society toward the maintenance of their army. Sparta briefly joined forces with Athens and other poleis in the second war with Persia in 480–479 B.C.E., but these two rivals ultimately fell out again in 431 B.C.E., when Sparta and her Peloponnesian allies went to war against Athens and her allies. This bloody conflict lasted until Athens was defeated in 404 B.C.E., after Sparta received military aid from the Persians.

Spartiate A full citizen of Sparta, hence a professional soldier of the hoplite phalanx.

spinning jenny Invention of James Hargreaves (c. 1720–1774) that revolutionized the British textile industry by allowing a worker to spin much more thread than was possible on a hand spinner.

SS (Schutzstaffel) Formed in 1925 to serve as Hitler's personal security force and to guard Nazi party (NSDAP) meetings, the SS grew into a large militarized organization that became notorious for their participation in carrying out Nazi policies.

Joseph Stalin (1879–1953) The Bolshevik leader who succeeded Lenin as the leader of the Soviet Union and ruled until his death in 1953.

Stalingrad (1942–1943) The turning point on the Eastern Front during the Second World War came when the German army tried to take the city of Stalingrad in an effort to break the back of Soviet industry. The German and Soviet armies fought a bitter battle, in which more than half a million German, Italian, and Romanian soldiers were killed and the Soviets suffered over a million casualties. The German army surrendered after over five months of fighting. After Stalingrad, the Soviet army launched a series of attacks that pushed the Germans back.

Stoicism An ancient philosophy derived from the teachings of Zeno of Athens (fl. c. 300) and widely influential within the Roman Empire; it also impacted the development of Christianity. Stoics believe in the essential orderliness of the cosmos, and that everything that occurs happens for the best. Since everything is determined in accordance with rational purpose, no individual is master of his or her fate, and the only agency that human beings have consists in their responses to good fortune or adversity.

Sumerians The ancient inhabitants of southern Mesopotamia (modern Iraq and Kuwait) whose sophisticated civilization emerged around 4000 B.C.E.

Sunnis Proponents of Islam's customary religious practices (*sunna*) as they developed under the first two caliphs to succeed Muhammad, his father-in-law Abu-Bakr and his disciple Umar. Sunni orthodoxy is dominant within Islam, but is opposed by the Shi'ites (from the Arabic word *shi'a*, "faction").

Syndicalists A nineteenth century political movement that embraced a strategy of strikes and sabotage by workers. Their hope was that a general strike of all workers would bring down the capitalist state and replace it with workers' syndicates or trade associations. Their refusal to participate in politics limited their ability to command a wide influence.

tabula rasa Term used by John Locke (1632–1704) to describe man's mind before he acquired ideas as a result of experience; Latin for "clean slate."

Tennis Court Oath (1789) Oath taken by representatives of the Third Estate in June, 1789, in which they pledged to form a National Assembly and write a constitution limiting the powers of the king.

Reign of Terror (1793–1794) Campaign at the height of the French Revolution in which violence, including systematic executions of opponents of the revolution, was used to purge France of its "enemies" and to extend the revolution beyond its borders; radicals executed as many as 40,000 persons who were judged enemies of the state.

Tetrarchy The result of Diocletian's political reforms of the late third century C.E., which divided the Roman Empire into four quadrants.

Theban Hegemony The term describing the period when the polis of Thebes dominated the Greek mainland, which reached its height after 371 B.C.E., under leadership of the Theban general Epaminondas. It was in Thebes that the future King Philip II of Macedon spent his youth, and it was the defeat of Thebes and Athens at the hands of Philip and Alexander—at the Battle of Chaeronea in 338—that Macedonian hegemony was forcefully asserted.

theory of evolution Darwin's theory that linked biology to history. Darwin believed that competition between different organisms and struggle with the environment were fundamental and unavoidable facts of life. In this struggle, those individuals who were better adapted to their environment survived, while the weak perished. This produced a "natural selection," or favoring of certain adaptive traits over time, leading to a gradual evolution of different species.

Third Estate The population of France under the Old Regime was divided into three estates, corporate bodies that determined an individual's rights or obligations under royal law. The nobility constituted the First Estate, the clergy the Second, and the commoners (the vast bulk of the population) made up the Third Estate.

Third Reich The German state from 1933 to 1945 under Adolf Hitler and the Nazi party.

Third World Nations—mostly in Asia, Latin America, and Africa—that are not highly industrialized.

Thirty Years' War (1618–1648) Beginning as a conflict between Protestants and Catholics in Germany, this series of skirmishes escalated into a general European war fought on German soil by armies from Sweden, France, and the Holy Roman Empire.

Timur the Lame (1336–1405) Also known as Tamerlane, he was the last ruler of the Mongol Khans' Asian empire.

Marshal Tito (1892–1980) The Yugoslavian communist and resistance leader who became the leader of Yugoslavia and fought to keep his government independent of the Soviet Union. In response, the Soviet Union expelled Yugoslavia from the communist countries' economic and military pacts.

towns Centers for markets and administration. Towns existed in a symbiotic relationship with the countryside. They provided markets for surplus food from outlying farms as well as producing manufactured goods. In the Middle Ages, towns tended to grow up around a castle or monastery which afforded protection.

Treaty of Brest-Litovsk (1918) Separate peace between imperial Germany and the new Bolshevik regime in Russia. The treaty acknowledged the German victory on the Eastern Front and withdrew Russia from the war.

Treaty of Utrecht (1713) Resolution to the War of Spanish Succession that reestablished a balance of power in Europe, to the benefit of Britain and in ways that disadvantaged Spain, Holland, and France.

Treaty of Versailles Signed on June 28, 1919, this peace settlement ended the First World War and required Germany to surrender a large part of its most valuable territories and to pay huge reparations to the Allies.

trench warfare Weapons such as barbed wire and the machine gun gave tremendous advantage to defensive positions in World War I, leading to prolonged battles between entrenched armies in fixed positions. The trenches eventually consisted of twenty-five thousand miles of holes and ditches that stretched across the Western Front in northern France, from the Atlantic cost to the Swiss border during the First World War, On the eastern front, the large expanse of territories made trench warfare less significant.

triangular trade The eighteenth-century commercial Atlantic shipping pattern that took rum from New England to Africa, traded it for slaves taken to the West Indies, and brought sugar back to New England to be processed into rum.

Triple Entente Alliance developed before the First World War that eventually included Britain, France, and Russia.

Truman Doctrine (1947) Declaration promising U.S. economic and military intervention to counter any attempt by the Soviet Union to expand its influence. Often cited as a key moment in the origins of the Cold War.

tsar Russian word for "emperor," derived from the Latin *caesar* and similar to the German *kaiser,* it was the title claimed by the rulers of medieval Muscovy and of the later Russian Empire.

Ubaid culture An early civilization that flourished in Mesopotamia between 5500 and 4000 B.C.E., it was characterized by large village settlements and temple complexes: a precursor to the more urban civilization of the Sumerians.

Umayyad Caliphate (661–930) The Umayyad family resisted the authority of the first two caliphs who succeeded Muhammad, but eventually placed a member of their own family in that position of power. The Umayyad Caliphate ruled the Islamic world from 661 to 750, modeling their administration on that of the Roman Empire. But after a rebellion led by the rival Abbasid family, the power of the Umayyad Caliphate was confined to their territories in al-Andalus (Spain).

Universal Declaration of Human Rights (1948) United Nations declaration that laid out the rights to which all human beings were entitled.

University of Paris The reputation of Peter Abelard and his students attracted many intellectuals to Paris in the twelfth century, some of whom began offering instruction to aspiring scholars. By 1200, this loose association of teachers had formed themselves into a UNIVERSITAS, or corporation. They began collaborating in the higher academic study of the liberal arts with a special emphasis on theology.

Pope Urban II (1042?–1099) Instigator of the First Crusade (1096–1099), who promised that anyone who fought or died in the service of the Church would receive absolution from sin.

urban populations During the nineteenth century, urban populations in Europe increased six fold. For the most part, urban areas had medieval infrastructures, which new populations and industries overwhelmed. As a result, many European cities became overcrowded and unhealthy.

Utopia Title of a semi-satirical social critique by the English statesman Sir Thomas More (1478–1535); the word derives from the Greek "best place" or "no place."

Lorenzo Valla (1407–1457) One of the first practitioners of scientific philology (the historical study of language), Valla's analysis of the so-called Donation of Constantine showed that the document could not possibly have been written in the fourth century C.E., but must have been forged centuries later.

vassal A person who pledges to be loyal and subservient to a lord in exchange for land, income, or protection.

velvet revolutions The peaceful political revolutions throughout Eastern Europe in 1989.

Verdun (1916) This battle between German and French forces lasted for ten months during the First World War. The Germans saw the battle as a chance to break French morale through a war of attrition, and the French believed the battle to be a symbol of France's strength. In the end, over 400,000 lives were lost and the German offensive failed.

Versailles Conference (1919) Peace conference between the victors of the First World War; resulted in the Treaty of Versailles, which forced Germany to pay reparations and to give up its colonies to the victors.

Queen Victoria (1819–1901) Influential monarch who reigned from 1837 until her death; she presided over the expansion of the British Empire as well as the evolution of English politics and social and economic reforms.

Viet Cong Vietnamese communist group formed in 1954; committed to overthrowing the government of South Vietnam and reunifying North and South Vietnam.

Vikings (800–1000) The collapse of the Abbasid Caliphate disrupted Scandinavian commercial networks and turned traders into raiders (the word "viking" describes the activity of raiding). These raids often escalated into invasions that contributed to the collapse of the Carolingian Empire, resulted in the devastation of settled territories, and ended with the establishment of Viking colonies. By the tenth century, Vikings controlled areas of eastern England, Scotland, the islands of Ireland, Iceland, Greenland, and parts of northern France. They had also established the beginnings of the kingdom that became Russia and made exploratory voyages to North America, founding a settlement at Newfoundland (Canada).

Leonardo da Vinci (1452–1519) Florentine inventor, sculptor, architect, and painter whose breadth of interests typifies the ideal of "the Renaissance man."

A Vindication of the Rights of Woman Noted work of Mary Wollstonecraft (1759–1797), English republican who applied Enlightenment political ideas to issues of gender.

Virgil (70–19 B.C.E.) An influential Roman poet who wrote under the patronage of the emperor Augustus. His *Aeneid* mimicked the ancient Greek epics of Homer, and told the mythical tale of Rome's founding by the Trojan refugee Aeneas.

Visigoths The tribes of "west" Goths who sacked Rome in 410 C.E. and later established a kingdom in the Roman province of Hispania (Spain).

Voltaire Pseudonym of French philosopher and satirist Francois Marie Arouet (1694–1778), who championed the cause of human dignity against state and church oppression. Noted deist and author of *Candide*.

Lech Walsea (1943–) Leader of the Polish labor movement Solidarity, which organized a series of strikes across Poland in 1980. They protested working conditions, shortages, and high prices. Above all, they demanded an independent labor union. Solidarity's leaders were imprisoned and the union banned, but they launched a new series of strikes in 1988, which led to the legalization of Solidarity and open elections.

war communism The Russian civil war forced the Bolsheviks to take a more radical economic stance. They requisitioned grain from the peasantry and outlawed private trade in consumer goods as "speculation." They also militarized production facilities and abolished money.

Wars of the Roses Fifteenth-century civil conflict between the English dynastic houses of Lancaster and York, each of which was symbolized by the heraldic device of a rose (red and white, respectively). It was ultimately resolved by the accession of the Lancastrian king Henry VII, who married Elizabeth of York.

Warsaw Pact (1955–1991) Military alliance between the USSR and other communist states that was established as a response to the creation of the NATO alliance.

The Wealth of Nations 1776 treatise by Adam Smith, whose laissez-faire ideas predicted the economic boom of the Industrial Revolution.

Weimar Republic The government of Germany between 1919 and the rise of Hitler and the Nazi party.

Western Front Military front that stretched from the English Channel through Belgium and France to the Alps during the First World War.

Whites Refers to the "counterrevolutionaries" of the Bolshevik Revolution (1918–1921) who fought the Bolsheviks (the "Reds"); included former supporters of the tsar, Social Democrats, and large independent peasant armies.

William the Conqueror (1027–1087) Duke of Normandy who laid claim to the throne of England in 1066, defeating the Anglo-Saxon King Harold at the Battle of Hastings. He and his Norman followers imposed imperial rule in England through a brutal campaign of military conquest, surveillance, and the suppression of the indigenous Anglo-Saxon language.

William of Ockham (d. 1349) An English philosopher and Franciscan friar, he denied that human reason could prove fundamental theological truths, such as the existence of God: he argued that there is no necessary connection between the observable laws of nature and the unknowable essence of divinity. His theories, derived from the work of earlier scholastics, form the basis of the scientific method.

Woodrow Wilson (1856–1924) U.S. president who requested and received a declaration of war from Congress so that America could enter the First World War. After the war, his prominent role in the Paris Peace Conference signaled the rise of the United States as a world power. He also proposed the Fourteen Points, which influenced the peace negotiations.

Maria Winkelmann (1670–1720) German astronomer who worked with her husband in his observatory. Despite discovering a comet and preparing calendars for the Berlin Academy of Sciences, the academy would not let her take her husband's place within the body after he died.

Witch craze The rash of persecutions that took place in both Catholic and Protestant countries of early modern Europe and her colonies, facilitated by secular governments and religious authorities.

women's associations Because European women were excluded from the workings of parliamentary and mass politics, some women formed organizations to press for political and civil rights. Some groups focused on establishing educational opportunities for women, while others campaigned energetically for the vote.

William Wordsworth (1770–1850) Romantic writer whose central themes were nature, simplicity, and feeling. He considered nature to be man's most trustworthy teacher and source of sublime power that nourished the human soul.

World Bank International agency established in 1944 to provide economic assistance to war-torn nations and countries in need of economic development.

John Wyclif (c. 1330–1384) A professor of theology at the University of Oxford, Wyclif urged the English king to confiscate ecclesiastical wealth and to replace corrupt priests and bishops with men who would live according to the apostolic standards of poverty and piety. He advocated direct access to the Scriptures and promoted an English translation of the Bible. His teachings played an important role in the Peasants' Revolt of 1381 and inspired the still more radical initiatives of a group known as Lollards.

Xerxes (519?–465 B.C.E.) Xerxes succeeded his father, Darius, as Great King of Persia. Seeking to avenge his father's shame and eradicate any future threats to Persian hegemony, he launched his own invasion of Greece in 480 B.C.E. An allied Greek army defeated his forces in 479 B.C.E.

Yalta Accords Meeting between President Franklin D. Roosevelt, Prime Minister Winston Churchill, and Premier Joseph Stalin that occurred in the Crimea in 1945 shortly before the end of the Second World War to plan for the postwar order.

Young Turks The 1908 Turkish reformist movement that aimed to modernize the Ottoman Empire, restore parliamentary rule, and depose Sultan Abdul Hamid II.

ziggurats Temples constructed under the Dynasty of Ur in what is now Iraq, beginning around 2100 B.C.E.

Zionism A political movement dating to the end of the nineteenth century holding that the Jewish people constitute a nation and are entitled to a national homeland. Zionists rejected a policy of Jewish assimilation, and advocated the reestablishment of a Jewish homeland in Palestine.

Zollverein In 1834, Prussia started a customs union, which established free trade among the German states and a uniform tariff against the rest of the world. By the 1840s, the union included almost all of the German states except German Austria. It is considered an important precedent for the political unification of Germany, which was completed in 1870 under Prussian leadership.

Zoroastrianism One of the three major universal faiths of the ancient world, alongside Judaism and Christianity, it was derived from the teachings of the Persian Zoroaster around 600 B.C.E. Zoroaster redefined religion as an ethical practice common to all, rather than as a set of rituals and superstitions that cause divisions among people. Zoroastrianism teaches that there is one supreme god in the universe, Ahura-Mazda (Wise Lord), but that his goodness will be constantly assailed by the forces of evil until the arrival of a final "judgment day." Proponents of this faith should therefore help good to triumph over evil by leading a good life, and by performing acts of compassion and charity. Zoroastrianism exercised a profound influence over many early Christians, including Augustine.

Ulrich Zwingli (1484–1531) A former priest from the Swiss city of Zurich, Zwingli joined Luther and Calvin in attacking the authority of the Roman Catholic Church.

Resource, NY; **p. 257**: Cameraphoto Arte, Venice/Art Resource, NY; **p. 259**: Bibliothèque Royale Albert I, Brussels; **p. 260 left**: Bildarchiv Preussischer Kulturbesitz/Art Resource, NY; **p. 260 right**: Scala/Art Resource, NY

Chapter 11: p. 264–265: The Art Archive/Topkapi Museum Istanbul/Gianni Dagli Orti; **p. 267**: John Massey Stewart Picture Library; **p. 270**: Bibliotheque Nationale, Paris, France/The Bridgeman Art Library; **p. 271**: Werner Forman Archive/Topkapi Palace Library, Istanbul/Art Resource, NY; **p. 274**: Mansell/TimePix; **p. 275**: Myriam Thyes/Wikimedia commons; **p. 276**: Wikimedia Commons; **p. 280**: AKG-images; **p. 281**: Bibliotheque Nationale, Paris, France/Giraudon/The Bridgeman Art Library; **p. 282**: Wikimedia Commons

Chapter 12: p. 286–287: Erich Lessing/Art Resource, NY; **p. 289**: Erich Lessing/Art Resource, NY; **p. 294**: Erich Lessing/Art Resource, NY; **p. 295**: Galleria degli Uffizi, Florence, Italy/The Bridgeman Art Library; **p. 298 top**: Erich Lessing/Art Resource, NY; **p. 298 bottom**: Réunion des Musées Nationaux/Art Resource, NY; **p. 299**: Scala/Art Resource, NY; **p. 300 top**: Vatican Museums and Galleries, Vatican City, Italy/Alinari/The Bridgeman Art Library; **p. 300 bottom**: Scala/Art Resource, NY; **p. 301 left**: Nimatallah/Art Resource, NY; **p. 301 center**: Scala/Art Resource, NY; **p. 301 right**: Erich Lessing/Art Resource, NY; **p. 303**: Bildarchiv Preussischer Kulturbesitz/Art Resource, NY; **p. 304**: Louvre, Paris, France/Giraudon/The Bridgeman Art Library; **p. 305 top**: National Portrait Gallery, London, UK/The Bridgeman Art Library; **p. 305 bottom**: Bildarchiv Preussischer Kulturbesitz/Art Resource, NY

Chapter 13: p. 308–309: The Art Archive/Nationalmuseet Copenhagen Denmark/Alfredo Dagli Orti; **p. 310**: Scala/Art Resource, NY; **p. 311**: Bildarchiv Preussischer Kulturbesitz/Art Resource, NY;

p. 312: Sandro Vannini/Corbis; **p. 313**: Bayerische taatsgemäldesammlungen/Alte Pinakothek, Munich; **p. 314 left**: Staatsbibliothek, Bern; **p. 314 right**: Staatsbibliothek, Bern; **p. 315 left**: By permission of the British Library/Art Resource, NY; **p. 315 right**: Staatliche Museen zu Berlin-Preußischer Kulturbesitz, Kupferstichkabinett; **p. 323**: National Trust/Art Resource, NY; **p. 324 left**: Scala/Art Resource, NY; **p. 324 right**: Scala/Art Resource, NY; **p. 326**: Kunsthistorisches Museum, Vienna

Chapter 14: p. 330–331: Woburn Abbey, Bedfordshire, UK/The Bridgeman Art Library International; **p. 337**: Wikimedia Commons; **p. 341**: Wikimedia Commons; **p. 344**: Wikimedia Commons; **p. 345**: Interfoto/Alamy; **p. 349**: Scala/Art Resource, NY; **p. 350 top**: Image copyright © The Metropolitan Museum of Art/Art Resource, NY; **p. 350 bottom**: Museo del Prado, Madrid; **p. 351 top L**: Erich Lessing/Art Resource, NY; **p. 351 top R**: Nimatallah/Art Resrouce, NY; **p. 351 bottom L**: © English Heritage Photo Library; **p. 351 bottom R**: Gift of Mr. and Mrs. Robert Woods Bliss, © 1997 Board of Trustees, National Gallery of Art, Washington, D.C.

Chapter 15: p. 354–355: The Royal Collection © 2010 Her Majesty Queen Elizabeth II; **p. 360 left**: Erich Lessing/Art Resource, NY; **p.360 right**: Réunion des Musées Nationaux/Art Resource, NY; **p.361 bottom**: Giraudon/Art Resource, NY; **p.361 top**: With kind permission of the University of Edinburgh/The Bridgeman Art Library International; **p. 362**: The Royal Collection © 2010 Her Majesty Queen Elizabeth II; **p. 363**: Snark/Art Resource, NY; **p. 366**: Scala/Art Resource, NY; **p.367**: Bildarchiv Preussischer Kulturbesitz/Art Resource, NY; **p. 368**: Courtesy Dr. Alexander Boguslawski, Professor of Russian Studies, Rollins College; **p. 369**: Giraudon/Art Resource, NY; **p. 372**: Ali Meyer/Corbis; **p. 373**: Corbis; **p. 377**: Wikimedia Commons